The
**Definitive Guide**
TO

in Central California
# FISHING

by CHRIS SHAFFER

## Extremely Important! You must read this.

While all of us love and cherish the great outdoors, at all times we must remember that many vast dangers are found in our precious rural lands. Many sites in this book require hiking on trails, places where there is no trail or the trail is no longer maintained. Many of these trails require stream crossings that are both simple and very complex, as well as treks through snow, climbs over mountains, both with stable and loose structures. Although we have strived to our greatest ability to point out the dangers you'll encounter, both the author and publisher of the book urge you to use the highest respect of carefulness while being in the outdoors, and does not assume liability or responsibility for any loss due to injury and or death that occur in the outdoors or while traveling to, or visiting any site in the book. Keep in mind that rivers, creeks and lakes fluctuate in an instant. Unstable and unsafe weather, water and road conditions can create harmful and deadly hazards. Hikers and anglers drown or are seriously injured due to the use of poor judgment and because they over estimate their human capabilities. Jumping, diving, sliding off rocks and walking the streambed can be dangerous. You are responsible for checking the depth of the water and locating submerged structures. Please use extreme caution at all times. In certain locations in this book the line between public and private property can be very vague. Do your best to respect all private property and obey all no trespassing signs.

With all this in mind, please have a great time, be safe and remember to practice catch and release.

This book could not have been done without the help and support of several people. A special thank you goes out to Blake, Dan and Cheryl Lezak for their tremendous support, both personally and financially. Without them, this book would be just an idea. Also, a thanks to Christian Perez, Tony Abel, Blake Lezak, Scott Wiessner, Stephen Wiessner and Brett Ross for assisting me on many of the long and extensive trips. To the California Department of Fish and Game employees who gathered information to help make this book a success, specifically, Biologists Jim Houk, Randy Kelly, Curtis Milliron and Roger Ellis, your help and thoughts are priceless. David Del Bourgo, you did a fantastic job editing this book.

Printed in Canada
Edited by **David Del Bourgo**
Book Design and Production by **Erika Loseman**
Book Distributed by American West Books, Western Hoegee and Sunbelt Publications

Send all questions and comments to Shafdog Publications:
23548 Calabasas Road #202
Calabasas, Ca. 91302
cshaffer@fishingcalifornia.net
8182242145 ex 46
Or visit us on the web @ **www.fishingcalifornia.net**
**www.californiawaterfalls.com**

All photos Copyright Chris Shaffer except:
**P. vi** Courtesy of Rojer George **P. 2, 245** Dan Lezak **P. 8** Skyler Teitelbaum **P. iii, 15** Brett Ross **P. 19, 59, 119, 157** Tony Abel **P. 39** Courtesy of Sierra Catfish Farm **P. v, 54-55, 255, 268, 283** Courtesy of California Department of Fish and Game **P. 111** Courtesy of Captain Jack **P. 138** Blake Lezak **P. 141, 145** Courtesy of Lee Haskin **P. v, 150-151** Courtesy of Jerome Clayton **P. 155-156** Courtesy of San Antonio Lake **P. 194** Courtesy of Phil Johnson **P. 207** Courtesy of McSwain Marina **P. 209** (Left) Courtesy of Lefty's Lure Company **P. 233** Courtesy of Springfield Trout Farm **P. 249** Courtesy of Bridgeport Guide Service **P. 277** Courtesy of Kayvon Kadjar **P. 372** (Right), **373** Courtesy of Sierra Drifters Guide Service **P. 390, 481** Christian Perez **P. 451** Stephen Wiessner

It had been too long. Todd, Chris, Scott, Stephen, Christian, Brett, Tom and I hadn't all been together since our high school days, I refused to let these friendships fade like distant memories.

It had been too long: too long since we all sat around a table and played cards; too long since we talked about the women who were and weren't in our lives; too long since we sang karaoke, too long since we all met at the park to kick a soccer ball.

I was always the ringleader of the group. I organized the trips, provided the food, drinks, hospitality and anything else that was necessary for an unforgettable night.

Every few weeks I talked to at least one of my old high school buddies. They all sounded well, but unfortunately stressed. The change of lifestyle and accepting the responsibility of becoming an adult was beginning to cause most of my pals to tense up. Life's smallest daily stresses were beginning to get to them. Being the old leader of the pack I took it upon myself to try to ease those tensions.

And I had the perfect remedy.

*Ice fishing at Lake Sabrina*

Luckily, we all still lived in the Los Angeles area. So, after I worked out the glitches and helped everybody figure out how to shuffle their weekend plan to allow everyone to sneak away from their families, girlfriends and jobs, we all met in front of my house at six sharp on a cloudy September Friday night.

I'd spent all day getting ready. Part of the deal was nobody else had to bring anything. I'd have it all ready for them when they arrived. First, I made our typically Costco run. Then I went to the local tackle shop and had new line put on the reels, threw into the boat at least a dozen sleeping bags, three tents, two dozen blankets, six lanterns, two stoves, all the toilet paper I could find and what I thought would be the rest of the camping gear we'd need.

By the time we were done giving hugs, high-fives and telling stories, it was no surprise we didn't leave till eight. Most of them were tired from a long week at work, anyway, and a few arrived late. Personally, I was exhausted. I'd just returned from a backpacking trip, and I'd only slept 20 hours in the last four days.

Of course, I promised I'd do all the driving too. That is as long as I could pick the music. There would be no hard core rap, country or heavy metal. Sorry guys.

Sure I was sleepy, but a combination of Styx, James Taylor, Reo Speedwagon, a Burger King chicken sandwich, Dr. Peppers and an aware Tom in the front seat next to me kept me awake for the duration of the ride. After we left Mojave, my six other friends had fallen asleep.

Tom and I smiled with the passing of each town.

Olancha..... Lone Pine.... Independence ...

In the mountains above Bishop and on the Eastern Slope of the Sierra Nevada Mountains, Lake Sabrina got closer with each minute. It was now 30 minutes past midnight and a lightening storm had awakened all the snoozers.

When we reached Big Pine, Todd yelled from the way-back, "What are you doing? Don't you want to get there tonight?" Obviously he was asleep when we passed the 25 mph sign and was wondering why I was driving 20 mph. Todd had never been on Highway 395 before and didn't believe me when I told him Inyo County relies on tickets for a lot of their income. Driving over the speed limit would get you a ticket. I found that out the hard way the year before.

*Electrofishing at Millerton Lake*

Everyone was now awake. Bishop was getting closer.

It was 51 degrees in Bishop, which is at 4,175 feet. I'd studied meteorology in college and remembered that the dry adiabatic rate was 5.5 degrees for each 1,000 feet. Theoretically, that meant because Lake Sabrina was at 9,128 feet, it was supposed to be 27.5 degrees cooler. Brrrr....

Scott figured it was a good idea for us to begin to acclimate ourselves to our new, unfamiliar environment. He was the first to roll his window down. And also, the first to get hit with a punch. Trying to get him to roll up his window, Christian, who'd yet to put on his jacket, gave him a few dead arms.

We pulled into Sabrina Campground on the Middle Fork of Bishop Creek. Fortunately, the skies had cleared and the lightening had ceased. By the time we set up camp it was 3 a.m. There were no objections to sleep.

Three hours of sleep proved to be enough for me. However, the rest of the group struggled to unzip their warm sleeping bags. It was 6 a.m. The sun had risen, but there was a big problem. It was raining, and I'd left the rain gear at home. We waited until the store at Lake Sabrina opened and purchased trash bags for $1 each. Cutting a hole in the bags, we wore them over our upper bodies.

*A bass caught in a pond near Bishop.*

With eight of us on my 19-foot aluminum boat, we rode across the lake to where Bishop Creek entered. This was my usual hot spot. Too bad the rain had shut off the bite. We'd been fishing for four hours. Not a bite, a nibble, nor any snags.

I'd been fishing since I was able to flush the toilet by myself, but it didn't hit me until now why I loved to fish so much.

Fishing wasn't just about catching fish. Among many other things, it was about camaraderie. The instant I passed out the fishing poles and watched a few of my friends dip their hands into jars of Power Bait, while others guided night crawlers onto their hooks and Chris and I cast lures, everything became apparent.

"Smalls, you get a bite yet," I heard. "Pecker, how about you?" "Mamma's boy, you seen any fish over there?" "Hey Bigbird, are their any fish on the fish finder?"

Although many years ago I'd made these names up, I hadn't heard them since we played AYSO and club soccer together.

Fishing brought back our teenage years.

The conditions were miserable. Six inches of water sloshed on the bottom of the boat, soaking our shoes, numbing our toes and sending shivers from our knees to our arms, but the joy of fishing had removed the stress from our souls. Happiness had returned. The good old days seemed like they were yesterday. My friends appeared to be rejuvenated.

*Crappie from Santa Margarita Lake*

INTRODUCTION

For a change it didn't matter what college either of us went to, how much our job paid, if we were married, had kids, or how our stocks were doing. We were transported back to our childhood. Back where there were no worries. Where we didn't have to worry about the car payment, pay the cell phone bill or make this month's rent.

We were fishing. We were happy. The weekend getaway had proved to be the perfect solution.

We were a diverse group, Todd was still trying to get into the fire department, Brett and Scott were teachers, Chris was an accountant, Christian was coaching soccer, Tom was repairing engines for the Postal Service and Stephen was working at a car dealership. The fish didn't care who we were. They couldn't see the color of our skin or tell that most of us practiced different religions. They didn't put us in social classes or tax brackets.

Looking onto the lake's glassy surface and admiring the golden, yellow and orange leaves of the alder trees that lined the rocky shore, while we watched our bobbers bounce up and down on the surface, we were in one of the places where humans are truly created equal. There was no prejudice, no favorites, just a group of old buddies who although hadn't all been together in years, it seemed like we'd never been apart.

*Fishing the Kern River*

Fishing is not just a sport, a hobby, a challenge, game or a national pastime. Fishing is a tonic for the soul. It has the magical power to make good bad, to turn a frown into a smile and to wipe tears away.

It's an inexpensive getaway for millions of Americans to have fun. Living in California, we have the resources the rest of the country can only dream about. And Central California is one of the most diverse and finest fisheries in the US.

From 14,494 feet at Mt. Whitney, the tallest point in the continental US, to 282 feet below sea level at Badwater, the lowest point, fishing opportunities are endless. There are thousands of miles of streams, hundreds of lakes, rivers, canals and man-made park lakes that offer anglers a chance at catching more than two-dozen species of fish.

Being able to share my experiences with the rest of the fishing community, as well as relaying those told to me by others, has been a dream of mine. This book, the second in the series of the Definitive Guides, aims at providing you with the most accurate, up-to-date and easy-to-read information on many of Central California's fishing holes.

As your author I have personally visited, fished and learned about every spot in the book, but I didn't stop there. I quizzed California Department of Fish and Game biologists, wardens, fishing guides, locals, park rangers and anyone else who has had contact with these waters, to provide you with the information you'll need to catch more fish and enjoy yourself while doing so.

It tells anglers how to target world-record spotted bass in Pine Flat Reservoir, state-record brown trout in Bridgeport's Twin Lakes, pure golden trout in Golden Trout Creek, giant striped bass in San Luis Reservoir, pure steelhead in Whale Rock Reservoir, a possible state record largemouth bass at Lake Success, stocked trout in Dinkey Creek, self-sustaining populations of brook trout in Sequoia National Park's Twin Lakes and much, much more.

But this book is not just for anglers. By describing wildlife found in various areas, detailed trail directions to hike-to lakes it caters to hikers, backpackers, nature lovers and anyone who enjoys the outdoors.

I've had the time of my life compiling this book. I hope you have as much fun reading it and fishing these new lakes and streams that I enjoyed discovering.

## Chris Shaffer
Author

*next page Panfish from Hensley Lake*

INTRODUCTION

# HOW TO USE THIS BOOK

This book has been carefully designed to make finding your ideal fishing spot easy. First, it helps you to figure out how to plan the proper destination to fit your particular tastes and life-style, and to provide you, your family and friends with the most enjoyable fishing experience possible.

When you flip the pages to the graph located after this section, you'll see a listing of all the fishing spots written about in this book, along with eight categories to help you choose your destination. These categories ("easy access," "camping," "good for kids," "backpacking option," "family friendly," "beginners welcome," "hard-core anglers" and "scenery") provide an overview of what each fishing spot has to offer. By cross-indexing your requirements and desires, you'll be able to quickly locate those few fishing holes that you might want to visit.

For those who want to choose their desired fishing location by geography, the book has been broken into 25 geographical regions, all located in Central California. After selecting your desired region, go to the map preceding the section about that particular region. It will list all of the lakes, rivers and streams in that area. Then, it's as simple as choosing your ideal fishing spot and flipping to the corresponding page to learn more about it.

If you already know which body of water you want to fish, open to the table of contents and turn to the page with your favorite fishing hole.

Once you've chosen a location, the rest is easy. Each article is written and structured in a user-friendly format that provides you with quick, fun and easy reading.

The book is set up with 10 different categories containing all the information you could ever want to know about each lake, river or stream. The structure is as follows. ...

### NAME OF FISHING HOLE
Rating
Species present
Fish Stocked
Facilities
Contact Information
Directions
Lake Information
Tips For Making the Trip
Nearby Attractions

### Rating:
The ratings are based upon a comparison of all fishing spots in California, not just in Central California. A "ten" is the best possible score and "one" is the worst. A "one" means there are no fish present at all and a "ten" qualifies it as one of the top 20 fisheries in the state.

All of the ratings are based on ideal weather and fishing conditions. Remember, fishing conditions can change in an instant: skies can darken, bites can shut off, fish can die when water becomes too warm or cold, or due to a lack of oxygen.

The ratings are based on a number of factors, including, but not limited to, catch rates, the amount of fish in the body of water and the number of trophy size fish.

### Species:
Just below the rating is a list of all the species of catchable fish inhabiting the waters. Species include: golden, cutthroat, rainbow, brown and brook trout; channel and white catfish; largemouth, smallmouth, striped and spotted bass; green and red ear sunfish; carp; bluegill; warmouths; crappie; black and brown bullhead; steelhead; goldfish; sturgeon; kokanee and chinook salmon. Non-game fish such as shad and minnows are not listed, but may be present.

## Stocks:

Both trout and catfish are stocked in most Central California lakes, rivers and streams. Stocking numbers are provided in pounds, which usually differs greatly from the actual number of fish planted. For example, in most places in Central California, the California Department of Fish and Game stocks half-pound trout; for every pound, typically, two fish are stocked. Fish are also planted as three- to four-inch fingerlings and five- to six-inch sub-catchables. To find the actual number of fish stocked in any particular place, consult the "Lake Information" section of its write-up.

Stocking information totals are from 2000. Each year the amount of fish stocked can change. Places can be added to, or deleted from the stocking list. Also, poor water quality, low water levels and high water levels can affect the number of fish planted. Check the "Lake Information" section for the times of the year that plants take place.

Trout are planted by any of five different companies and/or agencies, including the CA DFG, Mt. Lassen Trout Farms, Calaveras Trout Farm and the American Trout and Salmon Company and Alpers Trout Farm.

Fish stocked by the CA DFG in the Eastern Sierra come from either the Mt. Whitney Fish Hatchery and the Fish Springs Hatchery in Inyo County or the Hot Creek Fish Hatchery located near Mammoth in Mono County. The Kern River Fish Hatchery in Kernville, the San Joaquin Fish Hatchery near Fresno and the Moccasin Fish Hatchery near Don Pedro Reservoir handle waters to be planted in the Western Sierra and Central Valley. The Silverado Planting Base in Yountville is responsible for the Central Coast waters. The Fillmore Fish Hatchery in Ventura County plants waters in San Luis Obispo County. The fish that come from the DFG,

are rainbow trout, brown trout, brook trout, cutthroat trout, kokanee salmon, chinook salmon and golden trout. Mt. Lassen Trout Farm stocks rainbows. Calaveras plants brown, rainbow and brook trout. Alpers plants only rainbows, while the American Trout and Salmon Company stocks browns, only in South Lake.

As for catfish, the CA DFG does stock them but they don't raise them. To decide where the CA DFG purchases the cats a closed bidding is held. The breeder with the lowest bid gets to stock the fish. Bidders are located across the state. The number of pounds of catfish planted is listed, however a total number of fish is not tallied. Almost all catfish planted are channel cats. The catfish generally range from one to three pounds.

## Facilities:

Listed in the "Facilities" section are the services provided at the various lakes and streams. Services in the surrounding communities are not discussed in that section, however they are sometimes mentioned elsewhere. Services listed are as follows: Fish Cleaning Stations, Ranger Stations, Restrooms, Launch Ramps, Gas, General Stores, Campgrounds, RV Hookups, Snack Bars, Restaurants, Boats, Canoes, Kayaks, Paddleboat and Sailboat Rentals, Lodging, Picnic Areas, Recreation Areas, Fishing Piers, Playgrounds, Horseshoe Pits, Visitor Centers, Boat Tours, Marinas and Bait and Tackle Shops.

### Contact Information:

The "Contact" section is dedicated to providing phone numbers to help you plan your trip. This section includes numbers to check on the latest weather and fishing conditions, and to find lodging, tourist information and the best fishing guides at your destination.

All of the fishing guides written about in this book have been thoroughly checked to ensure they are qualified, well mannered, certified, courteous, knowledgeable, fair and will provide you with an enjoyable fishing experience.

### Directions:

To make accessing some of these remote locations easy, all of the directions tell you how to get to your desired destination from a major city.

### Lake Information:

The "Lake Information" section can be found in the body of each write-up. It tells you everything you need to know about fishing your favorite lake, river or stream. It includes information about how to catch the fish, where to find the fish and which baits and lures are best to use. In addition, the surrounding area and its wildlife are often described. In an attempt to help bring these exciting destinations to life, I sometimes tell about interesting and humorous personal experiences.

### Tips For Making the Trip:

One of the most helpful sections is called "If You Plan to Make the Trip." This covers the "plan ahead" stage where you are warned of obstacles and/or hazards you might want to prepare for prior to visiting these various destinations. For example, in the winter some destinations may require chains; fishing and day-use fees may be charged; some streams dry-up by summer; and roads to certain locations are often closed by heavy rains, snow or torrential flows. Other questions that might arise are also answered. Is night fishing allowed? Are there special regulations? Are only electric boat motors allowed? Where can you buy supplies? Do you need to keep an eye out for rattlesnakes? If four-wheel drive is required, or if the roads are poorly maintained, that information will also be discussed in this section. Is this destination sometimes closed to fishing? All this and more is covered in this section.

### Nearby Attractions:

Perhaps you want to spend a whole day at your destination instead of just a few hours, and you want to bring the family along. No problem. Listed in the "Also Nearby" section are ideas for places to take your family, including amusement parks, other fishing sites, waterfalls, hiking trails, historic sites, shopping and more.

# ICON LEGEND

*Descriptions for the iconic representations within the following graph*

**E**    Easy Access

    Camping

    Good For Kids

    Backpacking Option

    Family Friendly

**B**    Beginners Welcome

    Hardcore Fisherman

    Great Scenery

| | E | ⛺ | 👫 | 🥾 | 👪 | B | 🎣 | 🌲 |
|---|---|---|---|---|---|---|---|---|
| **1 Bakersfield/Lake Isabella** | | | | | | | | |
| Buena Vista Lakes | X | X | X | | X | X | X | |
| Hart Park Lake | X | | X | | X | X | | |
| Ming Lake | X | | | | X | X | | |
| Kern River (Lower) | | | | | | | | |
| Erskine Creek | X | X | | | X | | X | |
| Lake Isabella | X | X | X | | X | X | | X |
| Alder Creek | X | X | X | | X | X | | X |
| Cedar Creek | X | | X | | X | X | | |
| Woollomes Lake | | | | | | | | |
| **2 Southern Western Sierra/Kern River Drainage** | | | | | | | | |
| Kern River (North Fork) | X | X | | | X | X | X | X |
| South Creek | X | X | | | | | X | X |
| Bone Creek | X | X | X | | X | X | | X |
| Nobe Young Creek | X | X | X | | X | X | | X |
| Dry Meadow Creek | X | X | X | | X | X | | X |
| Peppermint Creek (Lower) | X | X | X | | X | X | | X |
| Freeman Creek | | | | | | X | | |
| Peppermint Creek (Upper) | X | X | X | | X | X | | X |
| Deer Creek | X | X | X | | X | X | | |
| Poso Creek | X | | X | | X | X | | X |
| **3 Tule/Kaweah River Drainages** | | | | | | | | |
| MF/SF of the Tule River (Cedar Slope) | X | X | X | | X | X | X | X |
| MF/SF of the Tule River (Camp Nelson) | X | X | X | | X | X | X | X |
| NF/MF of the Tule River (Wishon Camp) | X | X | X | X | X | X | X | |
| MF of the Tule River | X | X | X | | | X | | |
| Lake Success | X | X | | | | X | | |
| Bear Creek | | | | | | | | |
| Balch Park Lakes | X | X | X | | X | X | | X |
| Redwood Lake (Hedrick Pond) | X | X | X | | X | X | | X |
| Sierra Callish Farm | X | | | | X | X | | |
| Lake Kaweah | X | X | | | | X | | |
| North Fork Kaweah River | X | | | | X | X | | |
| Kaweah River (Lower) | X | | | | X | X | | |
| Stoney Creek | X | X | X | | X | X | | |
| Big Meadows Creek | X | X | X | | X | X | | |
| Weaver Lake | | X | | X | | X | | X |
| **4 Golden Trout Wilderness** | | | | | | | | |
| Kern River | | X | | X | | | X | X |
| Little Kern River | | X | | X | | | X | X |
| Little Kern Lake | | X | | X | | X | | |
| Kern Lake | | X | | X | | X | X | |
| Golden Trout Creek | | X | | X | | | | X |
| Chicken Springs Lake | | X | | X | | | | X |
| Twin Lakes | | X | | X | | | X | X |
| Maggie Lakes (Lower, Middle, Upper) | | X | X | X | | X | X | X |
| NF of the MF of the Tule River | X | | | X | | | X | X |
| **5 Oakhurst/San Joaquin River Drainage** | | | | | | | | |
| Bass Lake | X | X | X | | X | X | X | X |
| North Fork Willow Creek | X | X | X | | X | X | | |
| Nelder Creek | X | X | X | | X | X | | X |
| Lewis Creek | X | | X | | X | | | X |
| Big Creek (Upper) | X | X | X | | X | X | | |
| Big Creek (Fish Camp) | X | X | X | | X | X | | |
| Manzanita Lake | X | | X | | X | X | | |
| Corrine Lake | X | | X | | X | X | | |
| Kerckoff Reservoir | X | X | | | | | X | |
| Redinger Lake | X | | | | | | X | |
| Fish Creek | X | X | X | | X | X | | X |
| Rock Creek | X | X | X | | X | X | | X |
| Chiquito Creek (West Fork) | X | X | X | | X | X | | X |
| Chiquito Creek | X | X | X | | X | X | X | X |
| Mammoth Pool Reservoir | X | X | | | X | X | X | X |
| Granite Creek | X | X | | | X | | X | X |

## 6 Sierra National Forest (North)

| | E | ⛺ | 👫 | 🥾 | 👨‍👩‍👧‍👦 | B | 🎣 | 🌲 |
|---|---|---|---|---|---|---|---|---|
| Edison Lake | X | X | X | X | X | X | X | X |
| Mono Creek | X | X | | | X | X | | X |
| Florence Lake | X | X | | X | | | X | X |
| San Joaquin River (Jackass Meadow) | X | X | X | | X | X | X | X |
| Ward Lake | X | X | X | | X | X | | X |
| San Joaquin River (Mono Hot Springs) | X | X | X | | X | X | | X |
| Portal Forebay | X | X | X | | X | X | | X |
| College Lake | | | | X | | X | | X |
| George Lake | | X | | X | | X | | X |
| Twin Lakes (Kaiser Wilderness) | | X | | X | | X | | X |
| Rancheria Creek | X | | X | | | X | | X |
| Big Creek (Huntington) | X | | X | | | X | | X |
| Tamarack Creek | X | | X | | | X | | X |
| Huntington Lake | X | X | X | | X | X | X | X |
| Shaver Lake | X | X | X | | X | X | X | X |
| Dinkey Creek | X | X | X | | X | X | | X |
| Courtright Reservoir | X | X | X | | | X | X | X |
| Wishon Reservoir | X | | X | | | X | X | X |

## 7 Kings River Drainage/Fresno Region

| | E | ⛺ | 👫 | 🥾 | 👨‍👩‍👧‍👦 | B | 🎣 | 🌲 |
|---|---|---|---|---|---|---|---|---|
| Kings River (South Fork) | X | X | | X | X | | X | X |
| Hume Lake | X | X | X | | X | X | | X |
| Tenmile Creek | X | X | X | | X | X | | X |
| Bearskin Creek | X | X | X | | X | X | | X |
| Big Creek (Kings) | X | X | X | | X | X | | |
| Pine Flat Reservoir | X | X | | | | X | | |
| Kings River (Below Pine Flat) | X | X | | | | | | |
| Avocado Lake | X | | X | | X | X | | |
| Kings River (Reedley) | X | | | | | | | |
| Whispering Lakes | X | | X | | X | X | | |
| Millerton Lake | X | X | | | | X | | |
| San Joaquin River (Below Friant Dam) | X | | | | | | | |
| Lost Lake | X | | X | | X | X | | |
| Fresno Slough | X | X | | | | X | | |

## 8 Los Banos Region

| | E | ⛺ | 👫 | 🥾 | 👨‍👩‍👧‍👦 | B | 🎣 | 🌲 |
|---|---|---|---|---|---|---|---|---|
| Los Banos Reservoir | X | X | X | | | X | X | |
| O'Neill Forebay | X | X | | | | X | | |
| San Luis Reservoir | X | X | | | | X | | |
| San Justo Reservoir | X | | X | | | X | X | |

## 9 Central Coast Region

| | E | ⛺ | 👫 | 🥾 | 👨‍👩‍👧‍👦 | B | 🎣 | 🌲 |
|---|---|---|---|---|---|---|---|---|
| Lopez Lake | X | X | X | | X | X | X | |
| Laguna Lake | X | | | | X | | X | X |
| Santa Margarita Lake | X | X | X | | X | X | X | X |
| Whale Rock Reservoir | | | | | | X | | |
| Atascadero Lake | X | | X | | X | X | | |
| San Antonio Lake | X | X | | | X | | X | |
| Naciemento Lake | X | X | | | X | | X | |
| Naciemento River | X | | X | | | X | | |
| Abbott Lakes | X | X | | | X | | X | |
| Arroyo Seco River | X | X | | | | | X | X |
| Bear Gulch Reservoir | | | | | | X | | X |
| Carmel River | X | | | | | | X | |
| El Estero Lake | X | | X | | X | X | | |

## 10 South Bay to Santa Cruz

| | E | ⛺ | 👫 | 🥾 | 👨‍👩‍👧‍👦 | B | 🎣 | 🌲 |
|---|---|---|---|---|---|---|---|---|
| Pinto Lake | X | X | X | | X | X | | |
| San Lorenzo River | | | | | | | X | X |
| Loch Lomond Reservoir | X | X | X | | X | X | | X |
| Coyote Reservoir | X | X | X | | X | X | X | |
| Anderson Reservoir | X | | | | | X | | |
| Coyote Creek | X | | | | | | | |
| Uvas Reservoir | X | | | | X | X | | |
| Chesbro Reservoir | X | | | | | X | | |
| Calero Reservoir | X | | | | | X | | |
| Almaden Lake | X | | | | | | | |
| Lexington Reservoir | X | | | | | | | |

| | E | ⛺ | 🚻 | 🚶 | 👪 | B | 🎣 | 🌲 |
|---|---|---|---|---|---|---|---|---|
| Vasona Lake | x | | | | | x | x | x |
| Campbell Percolation Ponds | x | | x | | | x | x | |
| Stevens Creek Reservoir | x | | x | | | x | x | |
| Cottonwood Lake | x | | x | | | x | x | |
| Cunningham Lake | x | | x | | | x | x | |
| Joseph D. Grant Park Lakes | x | x | | | | x | | x |

## 11 Foothills (Modesto to Madera)

| | E | ⛺ | 🚻 | 🚶 | 👪 | B | 🎣 | 🌲 |
|---|---|---|---|---|---|---|---|---|
| Tulloch Reservoir | | x | | | | | | x |
| Woodward Reservoir | x | x | x | | | x | x | |
| Stanislaus River (Main) | x | x | | | | | | x |
| Modesto Reservoir | x | x | x | | | x | x | |
| Turlock Reservoir | x | x | | | | x | x | x |
| Don Pedro Reservoir | x | x | | | | x | | x |
| Moccasin Creek | | x | | | | x | | |
| Bean Creek | | | | | | | | |
| Jordan Pond | x | x | x | | | x | x | x |
| Bull Creek | x | x | x | | | | x | |
| Tuolumne River (UF) | x | x | x | | x | x | x | x |
| Tuolumne River (MF) | x | x | x | | | x | x | x |
| Merced River (El Portal) | x | x | | | | | x | |
| Merced River (Indian Flat) | x | x | | | | | | x |
| Merced River (SF) | x | x | | | x | | x | x |
| McClure Reservoir | | x | | | | x | | x |
| McSwain Reservoir | x | x | x | | | x | x | x |
| Merced River (Merced Falls) | x | | x | | | x | | |
| Eastman Lake | x | x | | | | | | x |
| Hensley Lake | x | x | | | | | | x |

## 12 Sonora/Stanislaus River Drainage Region

| | E | ⛺ | 🚻 | 🚶 | 👪 | B | 🎣 | 🌲 |
|---|---|---|---|---|---|---|---|---|
| Deadman Creek | x | x | x | | | x | | x |
| Stanislaus River (MF, Upper) | x | x | | | | x | x | x |
| Stanislaus River (Clark Fork) | x | x | x | | | x | x | x |
| Donnell Reservoir | | | | | | | x | x |
| Herring Creek | x | x | x | | | x | x | x |
| Herring Creek Reservoir | x | x | x | | | x | x | x |
| Pinecrest Lake | x | x | x | | | x | x | x |
| Stanislaus River (SF) | x | x | x | | | x | x | |
| Stanislaus River (MF, Lower) | | x | | | x | | x | |
| Beardsley Reservoir | | | | | | x | x | x |
| Tuolumne River (NF Upper, Long Barn) | x | | x | | | x | x | x |
| Lyons Reservoir | x | | x | | | x | x | |
| Lyons Canal | x | | x | | | x | x | |
| Powerhouse Stream | x | | x | | | x | | |
| Sullivan Creek | x | | x | | | x | | |
| Springfield Trout Farm | x | | x | | | x | x | x |
| Tuolumne River (NF, Basin) | x | x | x | | | x | x | x |
| Basin Creek | x | x | x | | | x | x | x |
| Clavey River | | | | | x | | x | |
| Cherry Lake | x | x | | | | x | x | x |

## 13 Bridgeport to Mono Lake

| | E | ⛺ | 🚻 | 🚶 | 👪 | B | 🎣 | 🌲 |
|---|---|---|---|---|---|---|---|---|
| Walker River (WF, Upper) | x | x | x | | | x | x | x |
| Walker River (Little) | x | x | | | | x | x | x |
| Swauger Creek | | | x | | | | | |
| Buckeye Creek | x | x | | | | x | x | x |
| Robinson Creek | x | x | | | | x | x | x |
| Twin Lakes (Bridgeport) | x | x | x | | | x | x | x |
| Bridgeport Reservoir | x | | | | | x | x | x |
| Green Creek | x | x | x | x | | x | x | x |
| Dynamo Pond | x | x | x | | | x | x | |
| Virginia Creek | x | x | x | | | x | x | x |
| Trumbull Lake | x | x | x | | | x | x | x |
| Virginia Lakes (Big and Little) | x | x | x | | | x | x | x |
| Mill Creek | x | x | x | | | x | x | x |
| Lundy Lake | x | | | | | x | x | x |
| Mono Lake | x | | x | | | x | | x |

| | E | ⛺ | 👫 | 🥾 | 👪 | B | 🎣 | 🌲 |
|---|---|---|---|---|---|---|---|---|
| **14 Yosemite National Park** | | | | | | | | |
| Merced River (Yosemite Valley) | x | x | | x | | | x | x |
| Mirror Lake | x | | | x | | | | x |
| Siesta Lake | x | | | x | | | | x |
| Tenaya Lake | x | | | x | | | x | x |
| Tuolumne River (Tuolumne Meadows) | x | x | | x | x | | x | x |
| Hetch Hetchy Reservoir | | | | x | | | x | x |
| **15 Lee Vining Creek Drainage** | | | | | | | | |
| Saddlebag Lake | x | | x | x | x | x | | x |
| Saddlebag Creek | x | x | x | x | x | x | | x |
| Gardisky Lake | | x | | x | | x | | x |
| Tioga Lake | x | x | x | x | x | x | | x |
| Lee Vining Creek (SF) | x | x | x | x | x | | | x |
| Ellery Lake | x | x | x | x | x | x | x | x |
| Lee Vining Creek | x | x | x | x | x | x | x | x |
| **16 June Lake Loop/Deadman's Summit** | | | | | | | | |
| Walker Lake (Little) | | | | x | x | | | x |
| Grant Lake | x | x | | | | x | | |
| Rush Creek | x | x | x | x | x | x | x | x |
| Silver Lake | x | x | x | x | x | x | x | x |
| Ron's Pond | x | x | | x | | | | |
| Reversed Creek | | | | | | x | | x |
| Waugh Lake | | | | x | | | | x |
| Gem Lake | | | | x | | | x | x |
| Agnew Lake | | | | | x | | | |
| Gull Lake | x | x | x | x | x | x | | x |
| June Lake | x | x | x | x | x | x | x | x |
| Glass Creek | x | x | x | x | x | x | | x |
| Deadman Creek | x | x | x | x | x | x | | x |
| Owens River (Crestview) | x | x | | x | | | x | |
| Alpers Trout Farm | x | x | | x | | | x | |
| **17 Ansel Adams Wilderness** | | | | | | | | |
| Johnston Lake | | x | | x | x | | | x |
| Minaret Creek | | x | | x | x | | | x |
| Olaine Lake | | x | | x | x | x | | |
| Shadow Lake | | x | | x | x | x | | x |
| Shadow Creek | | | | x | | | x | x |
| Cabin Lake | | x | | x | x | | x | x |
| Nydiver Lakes (1-3) | | x | | x | x | | | x |
| Ediza Lake | | x | | x | x | | | x |
| Laura Lake | | x | | x | x | | | x |
| Clarice Lake | | x | | x | x | | | x |
| Garnet Lake | | x | | x | x | x | | x |
| Altha Lake | | x | | x | x | | | x |
| Ruby Lake | | x | | x | x | | | x |
| Emerald Lake | | x | | x | x | | | x |
| Thousand Island Lake | | x | | x | x | | x | x |
| San Joaquin River (Upper) | | x | | x | x | | x | x |
| Badger Lakes (1-6) | | x | | x | x | | | x |
| Summit Lake | | x | | x | x | | | x |
| Clark Lakes (1-5) | | x | | x | x | | | x |
| **18 Silver Pass, Minnow Creek and Fish Creek Drainages** | | | | | | | | |
| Silver Pass Creek | | | | x | | | x | x |
| Silver Pass Lake | | | x | x | x | | x | x |
| Warrior Lake | | | | x | x | | | x |
| Chief Lake | | | | x | x | | | x |
| Pappose Lake | | | | x | x | | | x |
| Lake of the Lone Indian | | | x | x | x | | | x |
| Squaw Lake | | | x | x | x | | | x |
| Wilbur May Lake | | | x | x | x | | x | x |
| Peter Pande Lake | | | x | x | x | | x | x |
| Minnie Lake | | | | x | x | | | x |
| Anne Lake | | | | x | x | | x | x |
| Olive Lake | | | x | x | x | | | x |
| Grassy Lake | | | x | x | x | | | x |

| | E | 🏕 | 👫 | 🥾 | 👪 | B | 🎣 | 🌲 |
|---|---|---|---|---|---|---|---|---|
| Minnow Creek | | X | | X | | X | | X |
| Fish Creek | | X | | X | | X | X | X |
| Purple Lake | | X | | X | | X | | X |

## 19 Mammoth Lakes/Devils Postpile

| | E | 🏕 | 👫 | 🥾 | 👪 | B | 🎣 | 🌲 |
|---|---|---|---|---|---|---|---|---|
| Starkweather Lake | X | | X | | X | X | | X |
| San Joaquin River (MF) | X | X | | X | X | | X | X |
| Sotcher Lake | X | X | X | | X | X | | X |
| Sherwin Creek | X | X | | | X | X | | |
| Sherwin Lakes (1-4) | | X | X | X | X | X | X | X |
| Mammoth Creek | X | | X | | | X | | |
| Twin Lakes (Mammoth) | X | X | X | | X | X | X | X |
| Lake Mary | X | X | X | | X | X | | X |
| Lake George | X | X | X | | X | X | X | X |
| TJ Lake | | X | | X | X | X | | X |
| Barrett Lake | | X | | X | X | | | X |
| Lake Mamie | X | X | X | | X | X | | X |
| Horseshoe Lake | X | | | | | | X | X |
| McLeod Lake | | X | | X | X | X | | X |

## 20 Hot Creek to Rock Creek Drainage

| | E | 🏕 | 👫 | 🥾 | 👪 | B | 🎣 | 🌲 |
|---|---|---|---|---|---|---|---|---|
| Hot Creek | X | | | | | X | | X |
| Convict Lake | X | X | X | | X | X | X | X |
| Convict Creek | X | X | X | | X | X | | X |
| McGee Creek | X | X | X | | X | X | X | |
| Crowley Lake | X | X | X | | X | X | | X |
| Rock Creek (Section II) | X | X | X | | X | X | | X |
| Rock Creek Lake | X | X | X | | X | X | | X |
| Rock Creek (Section III) | X | X | | X | X | X | X | X |
| Rock Creek (JMW) | | X | X | X | X | X | | X |
| Mack Lake | | X | X | X | X | X | | X |
| Marsh Lake | | X | X | X | X | X | | X |
| Heart Lake (Rock Creek) | | X | X | X | X | X | | X |
| Box Lake | | X | X | X | X | X | | X |

## 21 Bishop Region

| | E | 🏕 | 👫 | 🥾 | 👪 | B | 🎣 | 🌲 |
|---|---|---|---|---|---|---|---|---|
| Pine Creek | X | | | | X | X | | X |
| Millpond | X | X | X | | X | X | | |
| Pleasant Valley Reservoir | X | | X | | | X | X | |
| Owens River (Bishop to Big Pine) | X | X | | | | | X | |
| Bishop Creek (Lower) | X | | | | X | X | | |
| Intake II | X | X | X | | X | X | | X |
| North Lake | X | X | X | | X | X | | X |
| Bishop Creek (Middle) | X | X | X | | | X | X | X |
| Lake Sabrina | X | | X | | | X | | X |
| Bishop Creek (South) | X | X | X | | | X | X | X |
| Tyee Lakes (1-6) | | X | | X | | X | | X |
| South Lake | X | | X | | | X | X | X |

## 22 Bishop Pass Region

| | E | 🏕 | 👫 | 🥾 | 👪 | B | 🎣 | 🌲 |
|---|---|---|---|---|---|---|---|---|
| Hurd Lake | | X | | X | | X | | X |
| Marie Louise Lakes | | X | | X | | X | | X |
| Bull Lake | | X | | X | | X | | X |
| Chocolate Lakes | | X | | X | | X | | X |
| Ruwau Lake | | X | | X | | | | X |
| Timberline Tarns Lakes | | X | | X | | X | | X |
| Saddlerock Lake | | X | | X | | | X | X |
| Ledge Lake | | X | | X | | | X | X |
| Bishop Lake | | X | | X | | | X | X |
| Spearhead Lake | | X | | X | | X | | X |
| Margaret Lake | | X | | X | | | | X |
| Long Lake (Bishop) | | X | | X | | X | X | X |

## 23 Sequoia National Park

| | E | 🏕 | 👫 | 🥾 | 👪 | B | 🎣 | 🌲 |
|---|---|---|---|---|---|---|---|---|
| Summit Lake | | X | | X | | X | | X |
| Kaweah River | X | X | | | | | X | X |
| Twin Lakes | | X | | X | | X | | X |
| Rock Creek | | X | | X | | | X | X |
| Rock Creek Lake | | X | | X | | X | | X |

| | E | ⛺ | 👫 | 🚶 | 👪 | B | 🎣 | 🌲 |
|---|---|---|---|---|---|---|---|---|
| Soldier Lake (Lower) | | x | | x | | x | | x |
| Soldier Lake (Upper) | | x | | x | | | x | x |
| Sky Blue Lake | | x | | x | | | x | x |
| Iridescent Lake | | x | | x | | | | x |

## 24 Cottonwood Creek Drainage

| | E | ⛺ | 👫 | 🚶 | 👪 | B | 🎣 | 🌲 |
|---|---|---|---|---|---|---|---|---|
| High Lake | | | | x | | x | | x |
| Long Lake (Cottonwood) | | x | x | x | | x | | x |
| South Fork Lakes (1-3) | | x | x | x | | x | | x |
| Cirque Lake (Cottonwood) | | x | | x | | x | | x |
| Cottonwood Lakes (1-6) | | x | | x | | x | x | x |
| Cottonwood Creek (Upper) | | x | | x | | | x | x |
| Muir Lake | | x | | x | | | | x |
| Hidden Lake (Cottonwood) | | x | | x | | | | x |

## 25 Big Pine to Little Lake

| | E | ⛺ | 👫 | 🚶 | 👪 | B | 🎣 | 🌲 |
|---|---|---|---|---|---|---|---|---|
| Big Pine Creek (Lower & Upper) | x | x | x | x | x | x | x | x |
| Baker Creek | x | x | x | | | x | | |
| Tinnemaha Creek | x | x | x | | | x | | |
| Owens River (Below Tinnemaha) | x | | | | | x | | |
| Shepherds Creek | x | | x | | x | x | | |
| Symmes Creek | x | | | | | | | |
| Independence Creek | x | x | x | | x | x | | x |
| Robinson Lake | | x | | x | | x | | x |
| Goodale Creek | x | x | | | | | | |
| Taboose Creek | x | x | x | | x | x | | |
| Georges Creek | x | | x | | x | x | | |
| Lone Pine Creek (Upper) | x | x | x | | x | x | | x |
| Lone Pine Creek (Lower) | x | x | x | | x | x | | x |
| Tuttle Creek | x | x | | | | | | |
| Diaz Lake | x | x | | | x | x | | |
| Cottonwood Creek | x | | | | | x | x | |
| Haiwee Reservoir | x | | | | | x | | |

# TABLE OF CONTENTS

TABLE OF CONTENTS

TABLE OF CONTENTS

TABLE OF CONTENTS

REGION 1

## BAKERSFIELD/
## LAKE ISABELLA

1 Buena Vista Lakes
2 Hart Park Lake
3 Ming Lake
4 Kern River (L)
5 Erskine Creek
6 Lake Isabella
7 Alder Creek
8 Cedar Creek
9 Woollomes Lake

# BUENA VISTA LAKES

*If you have a boat, your best bet is to troll around the two small islands, or near the shoreline where weeds make fishing impossible for shore anglers.*

| | |
|---|---|
| **Rating:** | 5 |
| **Species:** | Rainbow Trout, Largemouth Bass, Striped Bass, Bluegill, Carp, Sunfish and Channel Catfish |
| **Stock:** | Rainbow Trout weekly by private vendors in the winter. |
| **Facilities:** | Restrooms, Launch Ramps, Snack Bar, Camp Store, Campgrounds, Picnic Areas, Swimming Areas, Playgrounds and Bicycle Paths |
| **Contact:** | Kern County Parks and Recreation (661-868-7000), Campground Reservations (661-868-7050) |
| **Directions:** | From Interstate 5 in Buttonwillow, drive 14 miles south to Highway 119. Turn west and drive two miles to Enos Lane. Turn south and continue 2.5 miles to the lake. |

*Frankie Valli with a rainbow trout.*

Most people living near the Bakersfield area immediately associate water-skiing with the Buena Vista Lakes. Located near Buttonwillow, minutes off Interstate 5, Buena Vista Lakes have always been known as water-ski heaven. However, lake management has worked hard over the last several years to change that image. And they've succeeded by stocking trout into Lake Evans, the smaller of the two lakes. When the California Department of Fish and Game wouldn't bite on the idea of stocking the lake, Mt. Lassen Trout Company did. Now just in its fifth year, the program stocks the lake during the cooler months.

Although the lake is stocked weekly, the fishing isn't always so hot. Overall, catch rates could be higher. Most anglers average two-to-three fish per day, with the bulk being caught on Power Bait doused in garlic scent. You can leave the leadcore at home, because the lake is not only small (86 acres), but also shallow. It averages nine feet deep, with the deepest spots being 14 feet.

Sometimes anglers do get lucky at this desert water hole, catching some huge trout ranging from five to 16 pounds. We saw a little girl land an 11-pound rainbow on a Snoopy Pole. However, once the temperatures begin to flare up in early spring the trout bite expires.

As for the larger Webb Lake (873 acres), it's strictly an evening and nighttime fishery. Water-skiers own it during the day. There are a few bass, bluegill, catfish, stripers and carp, but there's too much boat action to catch them during the day. At night, catfish more 50 pounds are landed every so often, as well as some hefty stripers.

If you plan to make the trip, supplies are available at the lake. There is a day-use and fishing fee.

Also nearby are the Buttonwillow Racetrack and the California Aqueduct.

# HART PARK LAKE

*The lake is stocked with 6,410 rainbow trout by the California Department of Fish and Game throughout late fall and winter, but it never seems to be enough.*

**Rating:** 5
**Species:** Rainbow Trout, Channel Catfish, Carp, Largemouth Bass and Bluegill
**Stock:** 4,000 pounds of rainbow trout.
**Facilities:** Picnic Areas, Restrooms, Snack Bar and a Playground
**Contact:** Kern County Parks and Recreation (661) 868-7000

**Directions:** From the 99 Freeway in Bakersfield, drive east on Highway 178. Continue 10 miles to Alfred Harrell Highway and turn north. Drive approximately four miles to the lake.

*Hart Park Lake*

You live in Bakersfield and you just got off work. You don't have any errands to run and you're sick of watching TV. How about going fishing? Hart Park Lake is less than a 10-minute drive from downtown Bakersfield, and it provides a decently stocked fishery. It's stocked with enough fish that you could come after work and have a fair shot at catching a few. You won't be alone, either. The idea of fishing after work is popular. That's why Hart Park Lake is almost always crowded and often over-fished.

The lake is stocked with 6,410 rainbow trout by the California Department of Fish and Game throughout late fall and winter, but it never seems to be enough. So many people fish the 18-acre lake that many of the trout are caught a few days after a plant. With the lake's murky water, Power Bait seems to work best, and the fish aren't picky which color you use.

As spring approaches and the water becomes too warm for trout, a few catfish and bass are caught. In summer, red worms and mealworms take a fair share of small bluegill. From May though September, fishing takes a back seat to picnicking, and the lake becomes so overcrowded, many anglers ignore it until trout plants resume in late fall. If you plan to make the trip, supplies are available in Bakersfield.

Also nearby are Ming Lake, Kern River and the Kern County Soccer Complex.

# MING LAKE

*It offers just fair trout fishing from October through March for shoreline anglers tossing lures or soaking Power Bait.*

|  |  |
|---|---|
| **Rating:** | 5 |
| **Species:** | Rainbow Trout, Channel Catfish, Carp, Largemouth Bass, Crappie and Bluegill |
| **Stock:** | 2,900 pounds of rainbow trout. |
| **Facilities:** | Boat Launch, Restrooms, Campgrounds and Picnic Areas |
| **Contact:** | Kern County Parks and Recreation (661) 868-7000 |
|  | Bob's Bait Bucket (661) 833-8657 |
| **Directions:** | From the 99 Freeway in Bakersfield, drive east on Highway 178. Continue 10 miles to Alfred Harrell Highway and turn north. Drive approximately two miles to a stop sign and turn northeast. Drive a half-mile to the lake. |

*Ming Lake*

Ming Lake is one of the most popular and well-known boat-racing lakes in the state, which means anglers and Ming Lake usually don't get along. Although the lake is only 108 acres, it specializes in boating triathlon, speedboat, outboard and circle boat races. Boat races even take place in the winter, usually shutting off the bite. To protect recreational boaters, nearly half of the lake's shoreline is closed to fishing from April 1 through September 31. Because of all the recreational boat activity, no boat fishing is permitted. There is so much commotion on the lake, most of the fish are constantly looking for cover, anyway.

The only chance fishermen have at catching fish in the summer is early in the morning before the boaters wake up, or after they leave, just before sunset. Another option is to fish on Tuesday, Thursday or the second weekend of each month, when no boating is allowed. When the lake reopens for fishing in October, the California Department of Fish and Game responds by planting more than 4,300 rainbows, most of which weigh three-quarters of a pound.

About 15 minutes from downtown Bakersfield, Ming Lake is run by Kern County Parks. It offers just fair trout fishing from October through March for shoreline anglers tossing lures or soaking Power Bait. During the warmer months, the trout die off, and sometimes a few anglers attempt to land the bass and catfish in the lake. However, most of the bass hide deep in the thick tules that cover much of the shoreline.

If you plan to make the trip, supplies are available at a gas station at the four way stop sign near the lake. A Kern County boat permit is required to launch at the lake.

Also nearby are Hart Park Lake, Kern County Soccer Complex and the Lower Kern River.

# KERN RIVER (LOWER)

**The best time to fish is from late fall through early spring, when the river looks like a stream and sometimes gets so low that all the fish stackup in pools and are easy to catch.**

**Rating:** 7

**Species:** Rainbow Trout, Channel Catfish, Largemouth Bass, Crappie and Sucker Fish

**Stock:** 14,225 pounds of rainbow trout.

**Facilities:** Picnic Areas, Campgrounds and Restrooms

**Contact:** Bob's Bait Bucket (661) 833-8657

Sequoia National Forest (760) 376 3781

**Directions:** From the 99 Freeway in Bakersfield, drive 16 miles east on Highway 178 to Lower Richbar Campground. Access is available from this point to Lake Isabella.

*As shown above, the Kern River's flows are minimal in the month of December.*

The Lower Kern River can be a pleasure to fish if you arrive at the right time of year, because this section of the Kern River has many different faces depending on the season. When entering the canyon from the Bakersfield area, the face you don't want to see is the one cautioning you to stay away from the river. And there are signs posted with statistics on how many people have drowned here to prove that you should heed this caution well.

During the spring, when Lake Isabella releases a lot of water into the Kern, it looks like a flood here, both dangerous and unfishable. If you recall El Nino back in 1998, people had to be rescued out of the Santa Clara River in Ventura County. Fast moving muddy water carried trees, cars and giant boulders that nearly spilled onto the 101 Freeway before the floodwaters receded. That scene (except for the cars) happens daily in the spring season at the lower Kern. However, once the releases begin to subside in early summer, the river calms and fishing starts to pickup again.

By mid-summer, when the river returns to fishable levels, the California Department of Fish and Game begins stocking more than 28,000 rainbow trout. The best time to fish is from late fall through early spring, when the river looks like a stream and sometimes gets so low that all the fish stackup in pools and are easy to catch.

The best places to fish are upstream from Lower Richbar, Sandy Flat and Hobo Campgrounds and from China Garden to Democrat Beach. Most of these sites have long stretches of slow moving water that the planters hold in. Bright colored Roostertails, yellow Panther Martins and night crawlers are the baits most anglers cast. Fishing for bass, crappie and catfish is also fair in the summer months, but most of them are small.

If you plan to make the trip, supplies are available in Bakersfield and Lake Isabella.

Also nearby are Hart Park Lake, Lake Isabella, Ming Lake and Erskine Creek.

# ERSKINE CREEK

**Because much of this shallow, narrow creek is located on private property and it only has a few pools, it is difficult to fish.**

| | |
|---|---|
| **Rating:** | 2 |
| **Species:** | Rainbow Trout |
| **Stock:** | None |
| **Facilities:** | None |
| **Contact:** | Sequoia National Forest (760) 376-3781 |
| | Contact: Bureau of Land Management (661) 391-6000 |

**Directions:** From the 99 Freeway in Bakersfield, take Highway 178 east 45 miles to the Lake Isabella exit. Turn right and continue to Lake Isabella Road. Turn right and continue to Erskine Creek Road. Turn left and continue 2.5 miles to the stream.

*Erskine Creek is no longer stocked with trout.*

Located just outside of the town of Lake Isabella, Erskine Creek has been transformed from a seasonal put-and-take fishery to a small stream that most anglers do not know exists. Dating back to 1950 and prior to 1994, the creek was stocked with 950 pounds of rainbow trout (about 1,500 fish), however, when budget cuts hit the California Department of Fish and Game hard in the mid-Nineties, Erskine Creek was deleted from the stocking list.

Sounds like a bad thing? To tell you the truth, not many anglers were upset. The creek was mostly fished by locals from Isabella, as most out of town anglers skirted on by up to the Kern River.

Because much of this shallow, narrow creek is located on private property and it only has a few pools, it is difficult to fish. There aren't many fish left in it, anyway. A few wild rainbow trout, perhaps, but all of the stockers have been caught. As for now, Erskine Creek's run as a popular fishery for locals has ended.

If you plan to make the trip, supplies are available in Lake Isabella.

Also nearby are Lake Isabella, Lower Kern River, Hart Park Lake and Ming lake.

**Over the past decade, however, there has been resurgence in large bass.**

| | |
|---|---|
| **Rating:** | 8 |
| **Species:** | Rainbow Trout, Brown Trout, Carp, Channel Catfish, Largemouth Bass, Smallmouth Bass, Chinook Salmon, Crappie and Bluegill |
| **Stock:** | 25,000 pounds of rainbow trout. |
| **Facilities:** | Restrooms, Boat Launches, Lodging, Boat Rentals, Bait & Tackle, Campgrounds, Gas, Food, RV Hookups and Picnic Areas |
| **Contact:** | Sequoia National Forest (760) 379-5646, French Gulch Marina (760) 379-8774 or (888) 333-8167 |
| **Directions:** | From the 99 Freeway in Bakersfield, exit Highway 178 east and continue 45 miles to Lake Isabella. From Lake Isabella, exit Highway 155. The lake can be accessed at several places. |

*Trout congregate near Isabella's dam.*

Marking the tail end of the Sierra Nevada Mountains, at 2,605 feet in the mountains above Bakersfield, Lake Isabella is larger than any reservoir in Southern California. It is also home to a diverse fishery. Despite the fact that the frequently changing weather (with steaming hot summers, mild falls and often-snowy winters) is accompanied by drastic changes of water temperature in this large, yet shallow reservoir, the fish do well here.

In the Eighties, Isabella was referred to as one of the top bass fisheries in the world. Amazing feats were accomplished here. During one tournament in the mid-Eighties, a verified 10-fish limit weighed in at 69 pounds! There was also a 10-fish, 100-plus-pound limit taken.Without official scales, however, that accomplishment never reached the record books.

But the lake's bass record of 18.13 pounds dates back to 1984. What happened to those glory days? For one thing, rumors surfaced that many of these trophy fish were caught illegally, employing outlawed methods such as the use of live trout. So, anglers practicing these unsportsmanlike methods stopped because they were afraid of being caught. As expected, without these unlawful practices, catch rates of giant fish decreased.

The fishery's decline since the Eighties, however, has been caused by more than illegal fishing methods. Over-fishing (300 boats a day once were common), drought, bad winter freezes and a die off of threadfin shad were also detrimental to the fishery. In the early Nineties the situation got so bad, at one bass tournament no fish of legal size were recorded.

Yet, over the past decade there has been a resurgence of large bass. A new cycle began in 1994, when after a few years of drought, the fish were able to successfully spawn in high water. The lake filled in '95, '96, and '98. Because of this high water, populations of shad, bluegill, crawdads, golden shiners, clams, rainbow trout and white-and-black crappie have also increased. The increase in these other fish has provided an excellent food source for the bass to grow.

When the California Department of Fish and Game electrofished the lake in '96, they recorded few fish over 12 inches. By 1998, however, electrofishing showed that those fish had grown more than six inches and were now averaging 18 inches. Within two years, a strong population of young fish in '96 had grown from less than one pound to five and six pounds, putting them in the large fish category.

So yes, Isabella is again being considered as a place to catch bass from 15 to 20 pounds. Providing water levels and food sources remain high, CA DFG biologists speculate that bass over 20 pounds will be found in Isabella in 2002. If these fish achieve normal life expectancies, they ought to live in the lake until at least '05.

Despite recent efforts by the Fish and Game Habitat Club to develop habitat in barren stretches of the lake, fish typically remain in old, established areas of Isabella. Here's a list of spots were fish are found: Boulder Gulch, French Gulch, Main Dam, Auxiliary Dam, Piney Point, Engineer's Point, Camp 9, the North Fork Kern River and the South Fork Kern River inlets, and near Tillie Creek Campground.

Water fluctuation has also been a big problem for Isabella's bass. The lake is typically at full pool in the spring (providing the winter was a wet one) and then drawn down from summer through fall. It's filled up again each winter. In 1999, however, in an effort to protect habitat for the Southwestern Willow Flycatcher, a bird the United States Fish & Wildlife Service placed on the endangered species list in Feb. of '95, an injunction prohibited Isabella from reaching full pool. The reason for the injunction was that the flycatcher's habitat, which consists of willow trees in the South Fork arm of the lake, was being flooded when the lake reached full pool.

*Frankie Valli (Left) and Blake Lezak (Right) show a channel catfish.*

These lower water levels hurt recruitment of young warm-water fish, which in turn means less food for the bass and slower growth rates. The injunction will remain until it can be proved that there will be no net loss of habitat for these birds during high water. The Army Corps of Engineers plans on placing the bird's habitat further upstream to solve the problem.

The lake's bass are partially protected from being over-fished by the natural elements, which can act as a deterrent to anglers. The most significant of these natural defenses is the wind. Deadly winds kick up here year-round. When these winds whip up whitecaps, the lake, which has little cover, becomes unsafe for anglers. When you add in cold temperatures, rain, sleet, hail and snow, few anglers can withstand it when the weather gets nasty here. Prior to the early Nineties, there was a light system that warned boaters of impending wind conditions. Because of liability and costs, however, this system is no longer in use.

At one time, chinook salmon were introduced into the lake to crop a shad population. Unlike most lakes where salmon have been planted, however, anglers haven't had much success catching them here. The last plant took place in 1996. Since these salmon typically don't live more than five to six years, it's expected that most of them have since perished.

Experts are not even certain if Isabella's waters are cold enough to sustain a chinook population for a long period of time. But don't completely write off your chances of catching a chinook here. The CA DFG has verified reports that chinook have been seen spawning up the Kern River as far as the Johnsondale Bridge. Now the question is whether or not that spawn was successful.

Isabella's trout fishery is stable due to heavy plants by the CA DFG. Joining holdovers from years past, more than 42,300 rainbow trout are planted each year, giving anglers who work the dam area, or bank anglers who soak Power Bait off the dam, good prospects for landing 10- 12-inch rainbows. Orange and yellow Power Bait are the top colors.

There are few browns in the lake. The only ones found here swim down from the Kern River, which feeds this 11,400-acre reservoir. But the catfish action has been extraordinary in the last decade, with many cats to 35 pounds being caught in coves on anchovies, shad, mackerel and chicken liver.

Crappie are abundant, as well. But their population depends on water levels. The fishery is phenomenal for a few years, then horrible. The cycle lasts about five years. If the cycle is on the upswing, stick to fishing with crappie jigs near the marina and around trees.

If you plan to make the trip, supplies are available in Lake Isabella. A Kern County boating permit is required to launch at the lake. There are a lot of obstacles in the lake. Use caution when boating.

Also nearby are Lower Kern River and North Fork Kern River.

*Lake Isabella is known as one of the top trophy bass waters in the state.*

LAKE ISABELLA

# ALDER CREEK

**With fish caught in small pools and behind rocks, catch rates tend to be fair for the few anglers who fish here.**

| | |
|---|---|
| **Rating:** | 5 |
| **Species:** | Rainbow Trout |
| **Stock:** | 325 pounds of rainbow trout. |
| **Facilities:** | Campgrounds and Restrooms |
| **Contact:** | Bureau of Land Management (661) 391-6000, Sequoia National Forest (760) 379-5646 |
| **Directions:** | From the 99 Freeway in Bakersfield, drive north to Highway 65. Take Highway 65 north to Highway 155 and turn east. Drive past the town of Glennville to the Alder Creek Campground turnoff. Turn south and drive three miles to the stream. |

*Alder Creek is a good trout fishery in April, before water levels subside.*

Although Alder Creek receives little to no fishing pressure, it has one of the more attractive campgrounds in the region. At approximately 4,500 feet in the Sequoia National Forest, shaded by large pines, it's a great spot for campers who want to dodge the crowds that overrun the Kern River Drainage only a few miles east.

With fish caught in small pools and behind rocks, catch rates tend to be fair for the few anglers who fish here. The creek is usually stocked (with as few as 695 rainbows) in April or early May, before the water levels drop below fish-sustaining levels.

Alder Creek's life doesn't last that long. Fed by a few small streams near the Greenhorn Mountain Range, the stream can be reduced to a mere trickle by early summer. When there is a sufficient amount of water in the stream, you can get away with tossing spinners in some of the larger pools. Smaller pools require Power Bait to fill a stringer.

When you arrive at the creek, you'll see two streams that join downstream from a bridge that provides a crossing into the campground. The stream on the left is Cedar Creek, and Alder Creek is on the right. Cedar Creek is also planted with rainbow trout.

If you plan to make the trip, supplies are available in Glennville and Wofford Heights.

Also nearby are Cedar Creek, Woollomes Lake, Lake Isabella and the Kern River.

# CEDAR CREEK

*There are a lot of good-sized pools the trout hold in, and any color of Power Bait will catch fish.*

|  |  |
|---|---|
| **Rating:** | 5 |
| **Species:** | Rainbow Trout |
| **Stock:** | 325 rainbow trout. |
| **Facilities:** | Campgrounds and Vault Toilets |
| **Contact:** | Bureau of Land Management (661) 391-6000, Sequoia National Forest (760) 379-5646 |

**Directions:** From the 99 Freeway in Bakersfield, drive north to Highway 65 north. Continue on Highway 65 north to Highway 155 and turn east. Drive past the town of Glennville to Cedar Creek Campground, 3.5 miles past the Alder Creek Campground turnoff.

*Cedar Creek is often overlooked by anglers.*

On the western slopes of the Sierra, Alder Creek and Cedar Creek are the only two small streams between Glennville and Wofford Heights that are stocked. Not only is Cedar the larger of the two, but it seems to outdo Alder in every category. Cedar Creek is easier to fish, provides better access, is fed by runoff from more streams, making it inhabitable for fish longer and, okay, it's only stocked with one more fish, but that's still more.

Cedar is fed by snow runoff from the Greenhorn Mountains. Most of this runoff comes from the area surrounding Sunday Peak, which rises 8,295 feet in the Sequoia National Forest. The creek is stocked in two places. The easiest to reach is in Cedar Creek Campground, right off Highway 155. It's planted from the area where the creek flows under the highway down to the cabins situated just past the campgrounds. There are a lot of good-sized pools the trout hold in, and any color of Power Bait will catch fish.

The creek is also stocked near Alder Creek Campground. Cedar Creek merges with Alder Creek just before you cross the bridge that leads into the campground. Although rarely noticed, because both streams are seldom fished, try not to mix them up; Cedar Creek is the left fork, Alder is on the right. In all, 696 fish are planted by the California Department of Fish and Game in Cedar Creek, usually from March to early May. If you get here any later, there won't be any fish left, nor will there be much water.

If you plan to make the trip, supplies are available in Glennville and Wofford Heights.

Also nearby are Alder Creek, Woollomes Lake, Lake Isabella and the Kern River.

# WOOLLOMES LAKE

*Fishing for catfish and bass is always slow. However, for those using mealworms or red worms, the bite on small bluegill can be good in the summer.*

| | |
|---|---|
| **Rating:** | 4 |
| **Species:** | Rainbow Trout, Channel Catfish, Bluegill and Largemouth Bass |
| **Stock:** | 3,600 pounds of rainbow trout. |
| **Facilities:** | Restrooms, Boat Launch, Playgrounds and a Picnic Area |
| **Contact:** | Lake Woollomes (661) 725-9220, Kern County Parks and Recreation (661) 868-7000 |
| **Directions:** | From Bakersfield, drive north on the 99 Freeway to Delano. In Delano, exit Highway 155 east and drive two miles to Driver Road. Turn south and continue one mile to Woollomes Road. Turn east and drive 1.5 miles to the lake. |

*Woollomes Lake is a popular picnic area for Delano residents.*

For the residents of Delano, a small city north of Bakersfield, Woollomes Lake is one of the few places to escape the heat of the southern San Joaquin Valley. More of a local hangout than a fishery, it's almost never visited by out-of-towners, to the satisfaction of the locals. That's probably because it has nothing to offer that anglers can't get somewhere closer to home.

Woollomes doesn't have any trophy-size fish or breathtaking scenery; it's just a county park where people can come to catch a few fish while trying to relax. Fed by water pumped in from the Kern Canal, and located a few minutes from the 99 Freeway in downtown Delano, Woollomes Lake is bisected by Woollomes Road and surrounded by grapevines. The lake offers little-to-no structure for fish.

Fishing for catfish and bass is always slow. However, for those using mealworms or red worms, the bite on small bluegill can be good in the summer. When it's cool enough in the winter, the California Department of Fish and Game stocks rainbow trout. The 500-acre lake gets 5,720 rainbow trout in all, making for fair fishing in the cooler months.

If you plan to make the trip, supplies are available in Delano. A Kern County Boating Permit is required to launch a boat. No gas-powered boats are permitted.

Also nearby are Poso Creek, Cedar Creek and Alder Creek.

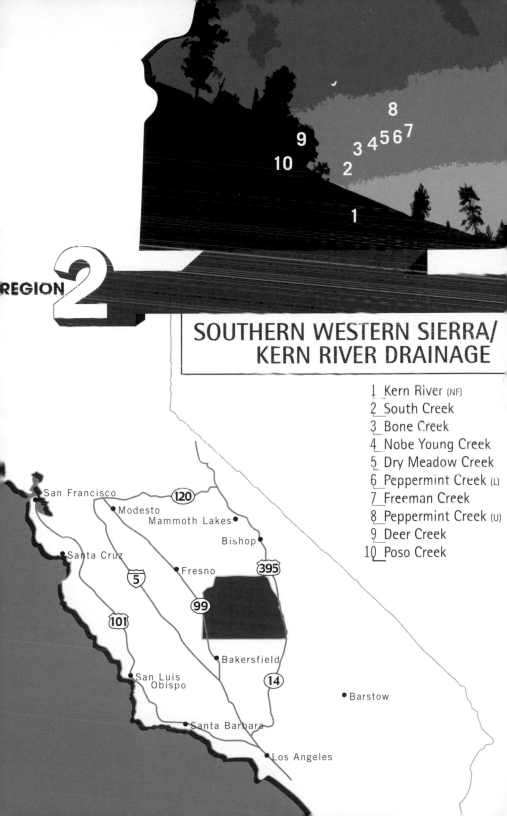

REGION **2**

# SOUTHERN WESTERN SIERRA/ KERN RIVER DRAINAGE

1 Kern River (NF)
2 South Creek
3 Bone Creek
4 Nobe Young Creek
5 Dry Meadow Creek
6 Peppermint Creek (L)
7 Freeman Creek
8 Peppermint Creek (U)
9 Deer Creek
10 Poso Creek

San Francisco
120
Modesto
Mammoth Lakes
Bishop
Santa Cruz
Fresno
5
395
99
101
Bakersfield
San Luis Obispo
14
Barstow
Santa Barbara
Los Angeles

# KERN RIVER (NORTH FORK)

*The river holds fish everywhere, but you may have to work a little to get your limit.*

**Rating:** 9
**Species:** Rainbow Trout, Brown Trout and Sucker Fish
**Stock:** 48,225 pounds of rainbow trout.
**Facilities:** Picnic Areas, Bait & Tackle, Lodging, Gas, Food, and Campgrounds
**Contact:** Sequoia National Forest (760) 379-5646

**Directions:** From the 99 Freeway Bakersfield, take Highway 178 east 45 miles to Lake Isabella. From Lake Isabella, exit Highway 155 and drive 11 miles north to Kernville. In Kernville, turn left on Mountain 99. Access is available directly off the road.

*Kern River (North Fork)*

The North Fork of the Kern River is a large, fast-flowing stretch of water with deep pools, long bends and plenty of fresh mountain air. This section of the river, which is unparalleled in size by any other south of Fresno, flows for 21 miles from the Johnsondale Bridge to Kernville, before emptying into Lake Isabella.

At an elevation that ranges from 2,500 to 4,000 feet, running through Kern and Tulare Counties, this section of the Kern River is set in a remote high-desert canyon that begins with pines, chaparral, willows and manzanita. Beyond this, as you work your way up to higher elevations, there are more pines, digger pines and granite boulders.

I took my friends Rick Spadaro and Brett Ross here on a trip that they'll never forget. Before we'd even taken our poles out of the trunk, they were jazzed to see the kind of scenery you'd expect in Yosemite. "Now, you're sure we're still in California, right?" Brett asked. "Relax," I chuckled, as we rounded the snowy bends of Mountain 99, which followed the river, and we saw some deer, a coyote and two bald eagles. "The best is yet to come -- we're still only at the end of the North Fork of the Kern River, in Kernville. The scenery is going to get much prettier."

In the past, I'd taken my friends to other streams to catch stockers, but here they were going to experience something they wouldn't find anywhere near their homes in Southern California. This was going to be a different kind of trout fishing, where they couldn't see the fish they were targeting. A challenge that would require real fishing knowledge! And, for the first time, they would actually have to work to catch fish.

Trout fishing remains good to excellent year-round in this section of the Kern, with more than 92,852 rainbow trout planted among holdovers, and a healthy population of wild rainbows mixed in with a few browns. However, beginning in the spring and peaking from late June to early July, the river is difficult to fish, because snowmelt pushes it to extremely high levels. From late July to late winter, water levels gradually subside and fishing improves.

*A stocked rainbow trout*

Fishing tends to be productive all day, but the best bite remains near sunrise and sunset. Don't just concentrate on the large pools. The river holds fish everywhere, but you may have to work a little to get your limit. Salmon eggs, Power Bait and crickets are popular, but lures catch fish, too. Fishing access is exceptional here, but to get to the best spots, a good pair of waders is a necessity. Those best spots include Riverside Park in Kernville, near the powerhouse, Limestone Campground, Hospital Flat, Fairview Dam, Camp 3, Corral Creek Picnic Area and where Brush Creek feeds into the Kern.

Each year the river also kicks out browns over five pounds, but they're hard to come by. In early 2000, local merchants teamed up with the California Department of Fish and Game to launch a trophy trout-stocking program with fish up to 10 pounds.

If you're the solitary type, you'd better stay at home. The river gets bombarded daily from late spring through fall, with rafters, kayackers, canoeists and recreationists that brave the elements to find out just how much cold water the body can tolerate. Campers also love to come here, because free camping is offered along the river.

If you plan to make the trip, supplies are available in Kernville, and during the summer at Jonny McNally's near Road's End.

Also nearby are Brush Creek, Lake Isabella, South Creek Falls, Lower Salmon Creek Falls and Peppermint Creek Falls.

*Icicles form along the Kern during winter.*

*Kern River (North Fork)*

**KERN RIVER**

# SOUTH CREEK

**There is some decent fishing below the falls, but access is difficult because of steep cliffs.**

| | |
|---|---|
| **Rating:** | 2 |
| **Species:** | Rainbow Trout |
| **Stock:** | None |
| **Facilities:** | Campgrounds and Restrooms |
| **Contact:** | Sequoia National Forest (760) 376-3781 |

**Directions:** From the 99 Freeway in Bakersfield, exit Highway 178 east and drive 45 miles to Lake Isabella. From Lake Isabella, remain on Highway 178 and drive 11 miles north to Kernville. Turn left on Mountain 99 and drive approximately 19.5 miles (a half-mile past Johnsondale Bridge) to the pullout for South Creek Falls on your left.

*South Creek above South Creek Falls*

A few summers ago, when I was taking pictures of South Creek Falls, I ran into a group of campers with fishing poles. "You guys catch anything?" I asked. "We haven't even seen a fish," one of them said. "We read in a book that this creek is stocked every summer with rainbow trout."

I laughed and asked what book they'd been reading. The funny thing was that the book was printed in 1999 and said it had been completely updated, however, the California Department of Fish and Game stopped planting the creek in 1994. Because of budget cuts, the CA DFG was going to close its Kernville Fish Hatchery in the early Nineties, but instead opted to cut back on its fish plants and delete a few creeks off the stocking list. South Creek was one of them.

No longer stocked with rainbow trout, South Creek's main attraction is South Creek Falls, which you can get to by driving north on Mountain 99 just past Johnsondale Bridge. The waterfall, which flows year-round, is a popular tourist destination.

As for South Creek, there are a few small wild trout left. There is some decent fishing below the falls, but access is difficult because of steep mountainsides. The only way to do it safely is to hike up from Johnsondale Bridge, where the creek empties into the Kern River. Mountain 99 also parallels the creek above the falls, providing access roads that lead down to the creek. This area above the falls offers primitive camping, but holds few fish.

If you plan to make the trip, supplies are available in Kernville. South Creek is closed to fishing from November 16 to the last Saturday in April. In winter call ahead for road conditions. Chains may be required.

Also nearby are North Fork Kern River, Salmon Creek Falls, Brush Creek Falls, Peppermint Creek Falls, Long Meadow Creek Falls, Dry Meadow Creek, Bone Creek, Lower Nobe Young Falls, Nobe Young Creek and Peppermint Creek.

*What Bone Creek lacks in size, it makes up for with beauty.*

| | |
|---|---|
| **Rating:** | 4 |
| **Species:** | Rainbow Trout |
| **Stock:** | 300 pounds of rainbow trout. |
| **Facilities:** | Primitive Campsites |
| **Contact:** | Sequoia National Forest (661) 548-6503 |

**Directions:** From 99 Freeway in Bakersfield, exit Highway 178 east and drive 45 miles to Lake Isabella. Exit Highway 155 and drive 11 miles north to Kernville. Turn left on Mountain 99 and continue approximately 24 miles to a fork in the road. Veer right onto Road 22S82, signed for Camp Whitsett and Lower Peppermint Creek. Continue 1.3 miles to Camp Area No. 1 and veer right on dirt road 22S45. The creek is on your left.

The first thing you'll notice when you arrive at this small stream, located northeast of Johnsondale and the North Fork of the Kern River, 4,000 feet up in the Sequoia National Forest, is that it looks too small for fish. Lucky for you, the California Department of Fish and Game stocks it anyway. However, these plants only occur when enough snowmelt permits the creek to sustain fish. May through June is the best time to fish the creek. That's when the CA DFG plants 627 rainbows, weighing about a half-pound each.

What Bone Creek lacks in size, it makes up for with beauty. Large pine trees overhang the mountain stream, and wildflowers are scattered along its banks. About a half-mile downstream, Bone Creek meets up with Nobe Young Creek, a much larger creek also stocked by the CA DFG. Many anglers work their way down to the confluence in search of better fishing. Now stop reading this and hurry up and get there before it dries up!

If you plan to make the trip, supplies are available in Springville and Kernville. No services or drinking water are available at the creek. Bone Creek is closed to fishing from November 16 to the last Saturday in April.

Also nearby are Nobe Young Creek, Lower Nobe Young Falls, Lower Peppermint Creek, Peppermint Creek Falls, the Trail of 100 Giants, Long Meadow Creek, South Creek, South Creek Falls, North Fork Kern River, Dry Meadow Creek, Freeman Creek and Freeman Creek Falls.

*Bone Creek*

# NOBE YOUNG CREEK

**There are some small pools in the campground, but not many. Most of the fish are caught behind rocks on Power Bait.**

**Rating:** 5
**Species:** Rainbow Trout
**Stock:** 300 pounds of rainbow trout.
**Facilities:** Primitive Campsites
**Contact:** Sequoia National Forest (661) 548-6503

**Directions:** From the 99 Freeway in Bakersfield, exit Highway 178 east and drive 45 miles to Lake Isabella. In Lake Isabella, exit Highway 155 and drive 11 miles north to Kernville. In Kernville turn left on Mountain 99. Take Mountain 99 approximately 24 miles to a fork in the road and veer right onto Road 22S82, signed for Camp Whitsett and Lower Peppermint Creek. Drive two miles to Camp Area No. 3 and Nobe Young Creek.

*Nobe Young Creek*

The Boy Scouts who spend time at Camp Whitsett each summer love Nobe Young Creek, because, without it, they wouldn't be able to use Ida Lake. With the help of water from Bone and Long Meadow Creeks, Ida Lake was formed by damming Nobe Young Creek. The Scouts head down to the lake each year to catch the few rainbow trout planted in Nobe Young that have worked their way down into the lake. When the Scouts leave, the lake is drained for the winter months.

For non-Scouts, Nobe Young provides a decent stocked fishery from early May through June, and as long as the creek's water remains at sufficient levels to hold fish, the California Department of Fish and Game plants 628 rainbows each year. There are some small pools in the campground, but not many. Most of the fish are caught behind rocks on Power Bait. Nobe Young Creek is also stocked were it merges with Dry Meadow Creek, 2.5 miles downstream of Ida Lake.

An added plus is Lower Nobe Young Falls, a group of cascades about a mile upstream. To reach the falls, turn north on a dirt road signed for the Western Divide Highway (just before the turnoff for Camp Whitsett) and continue 1.6 miles to a bridge over Nobe Young Creek. Park in a dirt pullout on the right and proceed to the stream. You can't miss 'em.

If you plan to make the trip, supplies are available in Springville and Kernville. No services or drinking water are available at the creek. Nobe Young Creek is closed to fishing from November 16 to the last Saturday in April. The road to Nobe Young Creek and the Western Divide Highway are usually closed from November to May, and may remain closed later, depending on conditions. Call the Forest Service for updated conditions.

Also nearby are Bone Creek, Lower Nobe Young Falls, Lower Peppermint Creek, Peppermint Creek Falls, the Trail of 100 Giants, Long Meadow Creek, South Creek, South Creek Falls, North Fork Kern River, Dry Meadow Creek, Freeman Creek and Freeman Creek Falls.

# DRY MEADOW CREEK

*In addition to the off-road driving, Dry Meadow Creek provides good rainbow trout fishing.*

**Rating:** 5
**Species:** Rainbow Trout
**Stock:** 800 pounds of rainbow trout.
**Facilities:** Primitive Campsites
**Contact:** Sequoia National Forest (661) 548-6503

**Directions:** From the 99 Freeway in Bakersfield, exit Highway 178 east and drive 45 miles to Lake Isabella. From Lake Isabella, drive 11 miles north to Kernville and turn left on Mountain 99. Continue on Mountain 99 for approximately 24 miles to a fork in the road and veer right onto Road 22S82, signed for Camp Whitsett and Lower Peppermint Creek. Continue approximately four miles to Camp Area No. 4. Turn right on Road 22S53 and continue seven-tenths of a mile to the camp.

Dry Meadow Creek

Most of the people who fish Dry Meadow Creek have four wheel drive vehicles. Dry Meadow Creek has dirt roads that cross the creek numerous times throughout the campground, and those with off-road vehicles have a blast driving in and out of the shallow water. The crossings can get to more than two feet deep, but so far I've never gotten stuck in the stream.

In addition to the off-road driving, Dry Meadow Creek provides good rainbow trout fishing. The creek is stocked with 1,679 rainbows. These stocks occur from the last Saturday in April until water levels become too low to hold fish, in most years by mid-July.

Fishing remains fair throughout the campgrounds, tapering off beyond the point where Dry Meadow Creek meets Nobe Young Creek. This section of where Nobe Young meets Dry Meadow Creek is also planted by the California Department of Fish and Game. There are nice pools along both streams, and as an added incentive both hold wild rainbows as well. The easiest way to catch them is with Panther Martins, but Power Bait is a local favorite.

For those who are confident about their driving skills, just west of where Nobe Young pours into Dry Meadow, there is a four-wheel drive road that takes you almost to the Kern River. If you were to hike along the stream from this crossing to the Kern, rather than following the dirt road, it is about a 1.65-mile hike.

If you plan to make the trip, supplies are available in Springville and Kernville. No services or drinking water are available at the creek. Dry Meadow Creek is closed to fishing from November 16 to the last Saturday in April. Lloyd Meadows Road is closed a few miles past Johnsondale from November through April, depending on snowfall and road conditions. Call the Forest Service for updated conditions.

Also nearby are Nobe Young Creek, Lower Nobe Young Falls, Lower Peppermint Creek, Peppermint Creek Falls, Trail of 100 Giants, Long Meadow Creek, South Creek, South Creek Falls, North Fork Kern River, Bone Creek, Freeman Creek and Freeman Creek Falls.

# PEPPERMINT CREEK (LOWER)

*The lower drop is stunning, cascading 130 feet down into a pool that offers great wild trout fishing, although, most of the fish are only seven to nine inches.*

**Rating:** 6
**Species:** Rainbow Trout
**Stock:** 800 pounds of rainbow trout.
**Facilities:** Campgrounds and Restrooms
**Contact:** Sequoia National Forest (661) 548-6503

**Directions:** From the 99 Freeway in Bakersfield, exit Highway 178 east and drive 45 miles to Lake Isabella. From Lake Isabella, drive 11 miles north on Highway 155 to Kernville and turn left on Mountain 99. Take Mountain 99 approximately 24 miles to a fork and veer right onto Road 22S82, signed for Camp Whitsett and Lower Peppermint Creek. Continue approximately 12 miles to Lower Peppermint Campground.

*Scott Wiessner holds a wild rainbow trout.*

At 5,400 feet in the Sequoia National Forest, Lower Peppermint Creek is a favorite spot for many anglers and campers to enjoy a wide variety of activities without ever having to leave the campgrounds. These activities include swimming, fishing, hiking, butt-sliding and a short hike to a remarkable waterfall.

Lower Peppermint Creek is divided into two sections, with developed campgrounds located on the north side of Lloyd Meadow Road, and free primitive campsites on the south side. When flows are consistent in spring, a plant of about 1,200 rainbow trout is split between these two areas. The pools scattered throughout the campgrounds are large enough for the use of spinners, although, many anglers use Power Bait. The best fishing spot is a swimming pool-sized hole on the side of the road, just below the bridge on Lloyd Meadow Road.

Peppermint Creek's biggest attraction is Peppermint Creek Falls. The falls is easily reached by following the creek to the south end of the primitive campgrounds, and then carefully working your way downstream along the slippery granite rock to the brink of the falls. To reach the base of the falls, scramble down the steep dirt trail just east of the brink. The falls is about 150 feet high and split into two drops.

The upper falls is only about a 20-foot freefall, providing a great swimming and fishing hole at the base, when the water isn't raging. It's usually safe and often warm enough to swim by late June. The lower drop is stunning, cascading 130 feet down into a pool that offers great wild trout fishing, although, most of the fish are only seven to nine inches. A few stockers get flushed over the falls into this pool, as well.

There are two more waterfalls along Peppermint Creek, before it empties into the Kern River two miles downstream, but, since they're on private property, the only way to see them is by rafting or kayaking down the river.

*Peppermint Creek Falls*

For those who like adventure, butt-sliding above the falls is a popular activity. The stream eases over smoothly polished rocks, and you can slide from one pool to the next. There are also small holes that look like craters cut in the granite rock. It's refreshing to wade in them on a hot summer day.

If you plan to make the trip, the road to the creek is closed a few miles past Johnsondale from November through April, depending on snowfall and road conditions. Call the Forest Service for updated conditions. Supplies are available in Springville and Kernville. Lower Peppermint Creek is closed to fishing from November 16 to the last Saturday in April.

Also nearby are the Upper Kern River, Upper Peppermint Creek, Golden Trout Wilderness, Nobe Young Creek, Bone Creek, Dry Meadow Creek, Freeman Creek, Freeman Creek Falls, Lower Nobe Young Falls and Long Meadow Creek Falls.

# FREEMAN CREEK

*If you are headed to Freeman Creek, you don't need to bring much tackle along. The stream is so small you only need a jar of Power Bait.*

**Rating:** 4
**Species:** Rainbow Trout
**Stock:** 200 pounds of rainbow trout.
**Facilities:** Primitive Campgrounds
**Contact:** Sequoia National Forest (661) 548-6503

**Directions:** From the 99 Freeway in Bakersfield, exit Highway 178 east and drive 45 miles to Lake Isabella. From Lake Isabella, drive 11 miles north to Kernville and turn left on Mountain 99. Continue on Mountain 99 approximately 24 miles to a fork in the road and veer right onto Road 22S82, signed for Camp Whitsett and Lower Peppermint Creek. Continue 17.4 miles to Pyles Camp on your right.

*A wild rainbow trout caught below Freeman Creek Falls.*

Located in a remote area of the Sequoia National Forest, Freeman Creek is considered by the California Department of Fish and Game as a "specialty plant," and is therefore only stocked two or three times a year. Originally, it was one of those High Sierra streams that wasn't supposed to be stocked at all, but the politicians thought it would be a good idea for trout to be planted to give a group of underprivileged kids a memorable fishing experience. Sounds great, right? Well, it is, but not for you.

Freeman Creek is stocked in Pyles Boys Camp, a camp for underprivileged kids, which is off-limits to the public. The CA DFG generally stocks the camp only when the boys are present. However, if the camp isn't open during the spring when flows are sufficient, the CA DFG will stock the allotted 450 trout. This stock occurs at Freeman Creek Campground and also where the creek crosses under Lloyd Meadows Road, nine-tenths of a mile past the turnoff for Pyles Camp.

If you are headed to Freeman Creek, you don't need to bring much tackle along. The stream is so small you only need a jar of Power Bait. And, if you made the long trek to the creek, you might as well spend the whole day. The President George Bush Tree, located in the Freeman Grove of sequoia trees, is only a few minutes away. Another option is Freeman Creek Falls, a few miles downstream, but it requires a steep and difficult hike not recommended for children.

If you plan to make the trip, from November through April (depending on snowfall and road conditions), the road to the creek is closed a few miles past Johnsondale. Call the Forest Service for updated conditions. Supplies are available in Springville and Kernville. Freeman Creek is closed to fishing from November 16 to the last Saturday in April.

Also nearby are the Upper Kern River, Peppermint Creek, Golden Trout Wilderness, Nobe Young Creek, Bone Creek, Dry Meadow Creek, Peppermint Creek Falls, Lower Nobe Young Falls and Long Meadow Creek Falls.

*opposite page Freeman Creek Falls*

# PEPPERMINT CREEK (UPPER)

**Concentrate your efforts directly in the campground. The fish tend to stay in the pools in which they are stocked.**

| | |
|---|---|
| **Rating:** | 7 |
| **Species:** | Rainbow Trout |
| **Stock:** | 1,400 pounds of rainbow trout. |
| **Facilities:** | Primitive Campsites and Vault Toilets |
| **Contact:** | Sequoia National Forest (661) 548-6503, Ponderosa Lodge (559) 542-2579 |

**Directions:** From Bakersfield, drive north on the 99 Freeway to Highway 190 east. Drive east on Highway 190 past Porterville and Lake Success to Springville. Continue 28 miles east on Highway 190 past Springville to Peppermint Creek Campground.

*Peppermint Creek*

At 7,200 feet in the Sequoia National Forest, Upper Peppermint Creek is about 10 feet wide and three feet deep, at its deepest. It differs greatly from its lower counterpart, because the upper portion has no waterfalls, gets snowed-in longer and is situated off a heavily used highway.

Upper Peppermint Creek gets heavily fished by campers. Although all of the campsites are primitive, they are located in a piney area that provides a beautiful setting. There are many pools located within the campgrounds, and with the California Department of Fish and Game planting more than 2,000 rainbow trout through early summer, the fishing remains good. Concentrate your efforts directly in the campground. The fish tend to stay in the pools in which they are stocked.

It is only a three-mile walk along Peppermint Creek from the upper to the lower campgrounds. However, to drive from one to the other on paved roads, it's nearly 30 miles, with a 2,000-foot drop in elevation.

If you plan to make the trip, supplies are available at the Ponderosa Lodge. Upper Peppermint Creek is closed to fishing from November 16 to the last Saturday in April. Due to the elevation, the road to the creek isn't always opened by the last Saturday in April when the fishing season begins. At times, depending on the winter's severity, the road doesn't open until Memorial weekend. Call ahead for road conditions. Chains may be required.

Also nearby are the Middle Fork of the South Fork of the Tule River at Camp Nelson and Cedar Slope, the Middle Fork of the Tule River, Tule River Falls, Boulder Creek Falls, the Trail of 100 Giants and the North Fork of the Middle Fork of the Tule River.

**Most of the fish are planted in Leavis Flat Campground, about a half-mile west of the town.**

| | |
|---|---|
| **Rating:** | 5 |
| **Species:** | Rainbow Trout |
| **Stock:** | 375 pounds of rainbow trout. |
| **Facilities:** | Campgrounds, Restrooms, Lodging, RV Sites and a Restaurant |
| **Contact:** | Sequoia National Forest (661) 548-6503, California Hot Springs Resort (661) 548-6582 |

**Directions:**  From Bakersfield, drive north on the 99 Freeway to Highway 65 north. Continue north on Highway 65 to Mt. 56 (Road J-22) and turn east. Drive seven miles to Fountain Springs and veer right onto Hot Springs Road. Continue approximately 20 miles to California Hot Springs The stream is on your right.

*Deer Creek*

Most anglers avoid fishing Deer Creek, but their reason isn't warranted. Driving up the 99 Freeway from Bakersfield, they travel over a portion of Deer Creek that's almost always dry. Most people think that since the creek is dry on the San Joaquin Valley floor, it's also dry in the mountains above. Not so. That's where the fish are planted. The portion people see is almost always dry because the water gets diverted to farms for agricultural use before it reaches the valley floor.

The most popular area of Deer Creek is at California Hot Springs Resort. Actually an RV Park and campground, the resort takes water from the hot springs and pumps it into an outdoor swimming pool that remains at a constant 89 degrees. Water is also pumped to two spas, one stays at 100 degrees and the other remains at 104.

The creek is planted with 788 rainbows, beginning in late April and usually ending in early June, when the stream begins to subside and becomes too low to support trout. Most of the fish are planted in Leavis Flat Campground, about a half-mile from the town. Leavis Flat is a pretty camp shaded by trees in a hot, dry area of the Sequoia National Forest. There are some nice, wide, fairly deep pools in the stream, allowing the use of an array of baits.

If you plan to make the trip, supplies are available in California Hot Springs. Deer Creek is closed to fishing from November 16 to the last Saturday in April.

Also nearby are Upper Peppermint Creek, Boulder Creek Falls and the Trail of 100 Giants.

# POSO CREEK

*Some of the pools are large enough for the use of spinners, but salmon eggs fished on a single salmon egg hook work the best.*

| | |
|---|---|
| **Rating:** | 5 |
| **Species:** | Rainbow Trout |
| **Stock:** | 275 pounds of rainbow trout. |
| **Facilities:** | None |
| **Contact:** | Sequoia National Forest (661) 548-6503 |
| **Directions:** | From the 99 Freeway in Bakersfield, drive north to Highway 65 north. Continue on Highway 65 to Highway 155 and turn north on Jack Ranch Road (just before Glennville). Drive 5.5 miles to Road M-109 (signed for Posey). Turn east and drive 3.5 miles through Posey to Posey Park. You'll cross the stream right before entering the cabin area. |

*Poso Creek*

I like to call Poso Creek "stay on your side of the road creek," because every time I visit I see drivers sneaking into the lane meant for traffic moving in the other direction. The road is a narrow, winding, two-laner that can be dangerous. I flagged a few cars down and asked the drivers why they were edging onto the wrong side of the road. The number one answer was, "I can drive where ever I want. There are never any other cars up here."

Despite the danger from people veering their cars onto the wrong side of the road, Poso Creek is a small, pretty stream that is stocked each spring by the California Department of Fish and Game. There isn't much public access, but with the quantity of fish stocked (574 rainbow trout) not much is needed. The creek is planted in April and May, beginning at the cabins in Poso Park, downstream for about 100 yards. Some of the pools are large enough for the use of spinners, but salmon eggs fished on a single salmon egg hook work the best.

The highlight of the creek is Poso Creek Falls, a set of four waterfalls beginning another 100 yards downstream. There is a trail on the north side that follows the stream to them.

If you plan to make the trip, supplies are available in Delano and California Hot Springs. Call ahead for stream conditions. In poor rain years the stream may not be planted.

Also nearby are Deer Creek, Alder Creek and Cedar Creek.

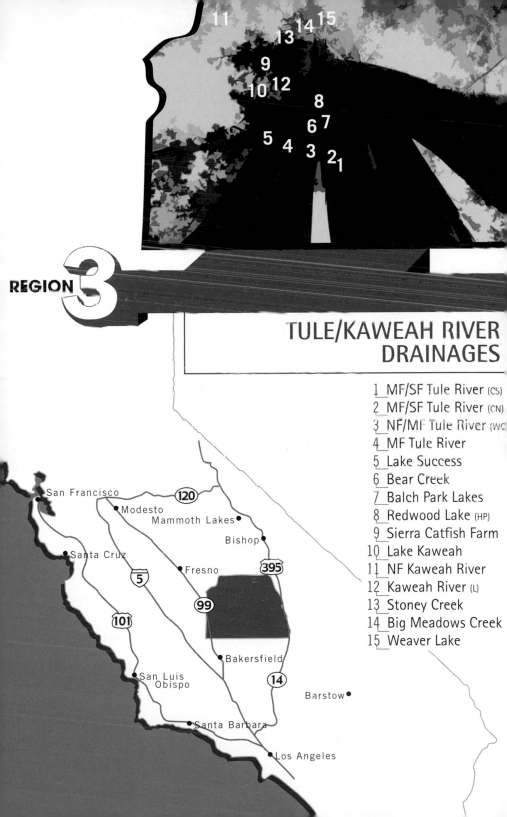

REGION 3

# TULE/KAWEAH RIVER DRAINAGES

1 MF/SF Tule River (CS)
2 MF/SF Tule River (CN)
3 NF/MF Tule River (WC
4 MF Tule River
5 Lake Success
6 Bear Creek
7 Balch Park Lakes
8 Redwood Lake (HP)
9 Sierra Catfish Farm
10 Lake Kaweah
11 NF Kaweah River
12 Kaweah River (L)
13 Stoney Creek
14 Big Meadows Creek
15 Weaver Lake

San Francisco
Modesto
Mammoth Lakes
Bishop
Santa Cruz
Fresno
Bakersfield
San Luis Obispo
Barstow
Santa Barbara
Los Angeles

120
395
5
99
101
14

# MIDDLE FORK OF THE SOUTH FORK
# OF THE TULE RIVER (CEDAR SLOPE)

*There are some large pools here, allowing you to use just about any lure in your box. I've found that these fish hit just about anything.*

| | |
|---|---|
| **Rating:** | 8 |
| **Species:** | Rainbow Trout and Brown Trout |
| **Stock:** | 1,300 pounds of rainbow trout. |
| **Facilities:** | Campgrounds and Restrooms |
| **Contact:** | Sequoia National Forest (559) 539-2607, Mountain Real Estate Cabin Rentals (559) 542-2822 |

**Directions:**  From Bakersfield, drive north on the 99 Freeway to Highway 190 east. Continue on Highway 190 past Porterville and Lake Success to Springville. Continue 14.3 miles east past Springville on Highway 190 to Camp Nelson. Drive another 5.6 miles to Cedar Slope and turn right on unsigned Cedar Drive. Drive three-tenths of a mile to the intersection of Pond and Spring Drive. Veer right and drive one-tenth of a mile to Pond and Redwood. Veer right again, and drive one-tenth of a mile to Redwood and Circle Drive. Veer left and in three-tenths of a mile, where the road changes from pavement to dirt, veer right. Drive eight-tenths of a mile to the end of the road.

*Middle Fork of the South Fork of the Tule River (Cedar Slope)*

By foot, the South Fork of the Middle Fork of the Tule River at Cedar Slope is only 1.1 miles away from Camp Nelson. Yet, because no road follows directly along the river, the distance is nearly 8.5 miles by car. The river near Cedar Slope is almost identical to the downstream section near Camp Nelson. However, Cedar Slope gets less than a quarter of the visitors, partly because anglers can't find their way here. (The Cedar Slope turnoff is difficult to spot.)

Anglers find the best fishing if they hike along the stream from the end of the road near Belknap Camp upstream to the confluence where Boulder Creek empties into the river. Few anglers realize how many of the 2,607 fish planted at Cedar Slope work their way downstream into this area. There are also some wild browns in this section.

This stretch of the Tule River is located in the Sequoia National Forest on the southern end of the Fort Mc Intyre Grove and the northeastern end of the Wheel Meadow Grove. There is also a trail following the Tule that leads to Quaking Aspen. There are some large pools here, allowing you to use just about any lure in your box. I've found that these fish hit almost everything.

If you plan to make the trip, supplies are available in Cedar Slope and Springville. Mountain Real Estate rents cabins near the creek.

Also nearby are the Middle Fork of the South Fork of the Tule River at Camp Nelson, Middle Fork of the Tule River, Tule River Falls, Boulder Creek Falls and the North Fork of the Middle Fork of the Tule River.

**The 17,555 rainbows planted near Camp Nelson amount to 8,650 more trout than are planted in all the other four branches of the river, combined.**

| | |
|---|---|
| **Rating:** | 8 |
| **Species:** | Rainbow Trout and Brown Trout |
| **Stock:** | 8,755 pounds of rainbow trout. |
| **Facilities:** | Campgrounds and Restrooms |
| **Contact:** | Sequoia National Forest (559) 539-2607, Mountain Real Estate Cabin Rentals (559) 542-2822 |
| **Directions:** | From Bakersfield, drive north on the 99 Freeway to Highway 190 east. Continue on Highway 190 past Porterville and Lake Success to Springville. Continue another 14.3 miles east on Highway 190 past Springville to Camp Nelson. Turn right on Nelson Drive and drive 1.5 miles to Belknap Campground where plants are made. The river is also stocked at the end of the road and at Coy Flat. |

*Belknap Campground*

The Middle Fork of the South Fork of the Tule River might seem like a long name to remember, but after you visit it, you wont have a problem remembering it again. Located about an hour's drive from Porterville in an area of the Sequoia National Forest rich with rivers and streams, this section of the Tule River is a hidden gem.

It is the most heavily stocked of all the branches of the Tule. The 17,555 rainbows planted near Camp Nelson amount to 8,650 more trout than are planted in all the other four branches of the river, combined. Most of the plants occur in Belknap Campground.

With giant sequoia trees surrounding Belknap Campground and lining the shores of the stream, this is an ideal place for a family camping trip. The campground is located on Belknap Creek, but if you follow the creek about 50 yards downstream, you'll come to the river and the heart of the Belknap Sequoia Grove. The river is heavily planted here from April through summer, providing good catch rates for anglers fishing with white Roostertails, red Panther Martins and silver Kastmasters.

If you are coming primarily to fish, try to plan your visit after mid-June. Prior to that, the river can be extremely high and difficult to fish. There is no parking at the campground for fishermen, so day-use anglers usually drive to the end of the road (past the camp) and fish near the Fort Mc Intyre Grove. The California Department of Fish and Game also plants this area. There's good access here, but there are also a lot of cabins along this stretch of the river, so you'll have to make sure you're not fishing on private property.

The river is also stocked at Coy Flat. To reach this spot, turn right off Highway 190 onto Nelson Drive. Then, make another right on Linder Drive and continue four-tenths of a mile to Coy Flat. Turn left and drive two-tenths of a mile to the bridge. Concentrate your efforts around the bridge.

If you plan to make the trip, supplies are available in Camp Nelson and Springville. Mountain Real Estate rents cabins near the creek.

Also nearby are the Middle Fork of the South Fork of the Tule River at Cedar Slope, Middle Fork of the Tule River, Tule River Falls, Boulder Creek Falls and the North Fork of the Middle Fork of the Tule River.

*Fishing this section of the Tule can be fun, because it's wide enough to cast lures across the river and watch them get inhaled by trout as you retrieve them.*

| | |
|---|---|
| **Rating:** | 6 |
| **Species:** | Rainbow Trout and Brown Trout |
| **Stock:** | 1,225 pounds of rainbow trout. |
| **Facilities:** | Picnic Areas, Campgrounds and Restrooms |
| **Contact:** | Sequoia National Forest (559) 539-2607 |

**Directions:** From Bakersfield, drive north on the 99 Freeway to Highway 190 east. Take Highway 190 past Porterville and Lake Success to Springville. Continue east on Highway 190 for approximately seven miles to the Camp Wishon turnoff (Road M-208). Turn north and drive three miles to the campground and river.

*North Fork of the Middle Fork of the Tule River (Wishon)*

The North Fork of the Middle Fork of the Tule River near Camp Wishon is a lot like the portion of the same river located in the Golden Trout Wilderness and Mountain Home State Forest. It's heavily forested, has large, deep pools, holds wild rainbow and brown trout, and is seldom fished. However, what's different about this stretch of the river is that the California Department of Fish and Game stocks it. In late spring and early summer, some 2,456 rainbow trout are stocked near Wishon Campground, providing anglers with a quiet place to fish, less than a half-hour drive from Porterville.

Fishing this section of the Tule can be fun, because it's wide enough to cast lures across the river and watch them get inhaled by trout as you retrieve them. For those who enjoy more challenging wild trout fishing, there is a trail that extends from the campground upstream to the Mountain Home State Forest and the Golden Trout Wilderness. There's great fishing up there, and almost no crowds. The creek used to be planted along the cabins east of the campground, but back in the mid-Nineties those plants were stopped because of cutbacks in fish allotments.

If you plan to make the trip, supplies are available in Springville. The North Fork of the Middle Fork of the Tule River is closed to fishing from Nov.16 to the last Saturday in April.

Also nearby are the Middle Tule River, Wishon Falls, Middle Fork of the South Fork of the Tule River near Cedar Slope and Camp Nelson, Lake Success, Balch Park Lakes, Redwood Lake, Boulder Creek Falls and the North Fork of the Tule River.

# TULE RIVER (MIDDLE FORK)

*There are also some small wild trout in the stream, but with the commotion of people swimming, they aren't always inclined to bite.*

| | |
|---|---|
| **Rating:** | 6 |
| **Species:** | Rainbow Trout |
| **Stock:** | 650 pounds of rainbow trout. |
| **Facilities:** | Picnic Areas, Campgrounds, Restrooms, Lodging, Gas, Restaurant, Bait & Tackle and a General Store |
| **Contact:** | Sequoia National Forest (559) 539-2607 |
| **Directions:** | From Bakersfield, drive north on the 99 Freeway to Highway 190 east. Take Highway 190 past Porterville and Lake Success to Springville. Access is available in Springville and further up Highway 190 at Coffee and Upper Coffee Camps. |

*Tule River (Middle Fork)*

The Middle Fork of the Tule River is the most heavily used of all of the Tule River forks. However, it's also the most unattractive and least stocked (excluding the North Fork, which is a wild trout stream and receives no plants). Located in a low-lying, dry area, about an hour northeast of Bakersfield, the banks can be extremely bushy and often pose a major fire hazard by mid-summer.

The Middle Fork flows through Springville and then empties into Lake Success. It is stocked a few miles south of town, in Upper Coffee and Coffee Camps. Because it is so easily accessed and at such close proximity to Porterville, it gets bombarded by both anglers and picnickers.

The 1,322 rainbows planted in the river each spring by the California Department of Fish and Game are nowhere near enough to satisfy its visitors. Most of the fish are caught within a few days after a stock on Power Bait and silver Kastmasters.

There are also some small wild trout in the stream, but with the commotion of people swimming, they aren't always inclined to bite. In my opinion, any of the other forks provide a much better fishing experience. You might as well take the extra 15-minute drive and enjoy the day, instead of battling the crowds at the Middle Fork.

If you plan to make the trip, supplies are available in Springville.

Also nearby are Lake Success, North Fork of the Middle Fork of the Tule River, Middle Fork of the South Fork of the Tule River, Tule River Falls, Balch Park Lakes and Redwood Lake.

# LAKE SUCCESS

**Anglers who jig spoons vertically off the bottom typically catch big bass from mid-January through March.**

| | |
|---|---|
| **Rating:** | 9 |
| **Species:** | Rainbow Trout, Carp, Channel Catfish, Crappie, Bluegill and Largemouth Bass |
| **Stock:** | 13,000 pounds of rainbow trout. |
| **Facilities:** | Boat Launch, Restrooms, Campgrounds, RV Hookups, Marina, General Store and Bait & Tackle |
| **Contact:** | Lake Success (559) 784-0215 |
| **Directions:** | From Bakersfield, drive north on the 99 Freeway to Highway 190 east. Continue five miles on Highway 190 past Porterville to Lake Success. Turn left on Road 284 and drive four-tenths of a mile to Worth Drive. Turn east and continue seven-tenths of a mile to the lake. |

*Lake Success*

Most bass anglers aren't much impressed with Lake Success between August and February. "There can't be many fish in this mud puddle!" is what most of them think. Well, for all you doubters, Lake Success may be the most productive mud puddle in California.

In fact, over the past few years Lake Success has been known as one of California's best bass fisheries. Spring floods have brought an influx of snow and rain runoff, loaded with nutrients for smaller fish. As those smaller fish have thrived, they've provided an excellent food source for the larger fish, like bass. Today, there's such a tremendous population of larval fish and shad, even when the lake gets drained to a mud puddle and thousands of fish crowd into a small area, there's still enough food to go around.

At full pool (which is rarely attained), the lake is 2,406 acres, has a capacity of 82,300-acre-feet and spans 33 miles of shoreline. During most years, however, by summer the lake is drawn down to provide agriculture water to the Central Valley. At minimal pool, it is a mere 5,000-acre-feet, with just three miles of shoreline.

In the spring, when the Tule River pours into Success and the reservoir begins to fill, several occurrences ensure a productive fishery. As water rises, covering dry and dying areas of brush, trees and grass, the water picks up nutrients from that plant life and becomes like a rich soup, providing essential elements for the lake's entire food chain.

Algae absorb these nutrients, and in the process, become more abundant. The algae are ingested by copepods that are in turn eaten by larval fish. The larval fish grow and are eaten by the bass. Because Success is such a large reservoir, it's very important that the bottom rungs of its food chain be bolstered by the inclusion of the nutrients provided by these land plants. Without it, the food supply would not be large enough to maintain Success's stable population of large bass.

Success's flood protection policy requires that its floodgates remain open until March 1, keeping the lake at minimal pool until then. After that, the gates are closed and the lake's

*Jason Higginbotham with a largemouth bass.*

levels begin to rise. Despite its large watershed, the lake can fill up quickly. Success retains these high water levels until summer, when the water is slowly released to meet agriculture needs downstream. Because the lake's size becomes enlarged during the spring spawn, the bass thrive and grow to trophy sizes.

The question remains, will Success continue to be a quality fishery with world-class-sized bass? Unfortunately, there's not an easy answer. Once bass grow to trophy size, they only live a few years, so they constantly need to be replenished. It all boils down to whether the six- and seven-pound bass can continue growing to reach these trophy sizes.

This will depend on several conditions, especially water and food. If both remain available for the fish to grow, Success will continue to be known as a superb trophy-bass lake. If not, the fishery could decline. It's all in Mother Nature's hands.

It helps that in 1998 the California Department of Fish and Game decreased the bass limit from five per day to two. That means more fish will be returned to the lake, enhancing the bass fishery. On the other hand, many anglers don't catch & release the larger fish. Not good.

Anglers who jig spoons vertically off the bottom typically catch big bass from mid-January through March. The idea behind this is that these spoons resemble dying shad, which die in the winter when the water cools. To do this, slowly pick up your jig and let it fall. Live crawdads are a good choice too. The lake record, a 19.3-pound bass, was caught in January of 2001 on a Silver Buddy.

Because the lake is so small during the winter, there are only a few structures to key in on. Try fishing near the boat launch on the west end, behind the marina and around the islands. The big boys are most often caught at night or in low light conditions, early in the morning or just before dusk.

For sheer numbers, hit Success in the spring. Using lizards back in the trees, imitation crawdads and worms work best. In summer stick to fishing the face of the dam, the rock hill on the west shoreline, the Vista Point parking area and the islands on the east shoreline.

While there are a lot of lunkers here, only about 15 fish over 10 pounds are caught annually. Small fish are definitely more plentiful. Twelve- to 14-inch fish are most common. Although catching these smaller fish is pretty easy, the monsters take a lot of work. You'll find it far less frustrating if you keep your expectations in check. Of every 10 fish caught here, only two or three are as large as three pounds. So, you'll be fortunate to catch one over three pounds.

Success hasn't always been a productive bass fishery. There was a period in the Eighties, prior to 1988, that it was one of the worst. The water quality was

*Kevin Heape shows off a pair of largemouths.*

LAKE SUCCESS

very poor, and there were too many carp. There was even a population of white bass. Because the overall condition of the fish population was pretty poor, the lake was chemically treated in December of 1998.

To prepare for this chemical treatment, the CA DFG and volunteers electrofished the lake every night for about a month, attempting to remove all the game fish. Nearly 10,000 game fish were extricated and placed in an adjacent pond that was going to become part of the lake when it filled up in the spring. The purpose of putting the fish in this pond was to spare them the stress of being moved twice.

Almost all the fish left in the lake were killed by this treatment -- 300 tons total -- 98 percent of which were carp and goldfish. Only the remains of a few white bass were found among the exterminated fish. To restock the lake, the CA DFG imported 5,000 fingerling Florida strain largemouth bass, about 80 bass from Upper Otay Reservoir in the three- to 12-pound range, some channel catfish, crappie and bluegill.

An interesting note: prior to the decline in water quality in the Eighties, there were stripers in Success. They were introduced into the lake in the late Seventies and early Eighties, and were known to have reached up to 35 pounds.

As for other species, fishing for trout and catfish can be fair, and crappie are plentiful. While there are hoards of bluegill in the lake, few grow larger than hand size. Red worms and wax worms will catch as many bluegill as you desire, providing you fish the east side of Tule Point.

Rainbow trout are planted from mid-November through April. The CA DFG stocks roughly 21,590 rainbows, all just under a pound. Sounds like a lot? That's nearly half what it used to be! The CA DFG planted 35,500 in 1999. Bows can be caught by shore anglers fishing near the launch ramp with Power Bait or trollers cruising the shoreline with small lures. Trout don't live in the lake year-round. When the water gets warm in the late spring, they swim up the Middle Fork of the Tule River.

No biggie. Target the catfish. There are some nice hefty channel cats in the lake, and if you can get your hands on shad, your chances of catching them in shallow water from shore are good. Can't get a hold of shad? Use anchovies or minnows. Bow hunting on carp

*A threadfin shad*

is also popular here. There's no limit. Take as many as you can!

In the summer, crappie fishing can be exceptional at night in the marina off the back of houseboats. The marina lights attract them. Crappie can also be caught back in the trees in the spring. Full moon nights are the best. Hang a light to attract shad and smaller bait fish, and then jig 1/32-ounce jigs for fish from three-fourths of a pound up to three pounds.

If you plan to make the trip, supplies are available in Porterville. There is a two-fish limit. The bass need to be at least 15 inches to keep.

Also nearby are the Middle Fork of the Tule River, Balch Park Lakes, Redwood Lake and the North Fork of the Middle Fork of the Tule River (Wishon Camp)

*Some stretches of the creek are open to the public, but with all the private property it can be difficult to figure out where you are allowed to fish.*

| | |
|---|---|
| **Rating:** | 3 |
| **Species:** | Rainbow Trout |
| **Stock:** | 150 pounds of rainbow trout. |
| **Facilities:** | Restrooms |
| **Contact:** | Sequoia National Forest (559) 539-2607, Scicon Conservation Camp (559) 539-2642 |

**Directions:** From Bakersfield, drive north on the 99 Freeway to Highway 190. Take Highway 190 east past Porterville and Lake Success to Springville. In Springville turn north on Road J-37 (Balch Park Road) and drive 2.4 miles to Road 220. Turn right and drive approximately three miles to Scicon Camp on the right.

With its deep holes and sufficient flows of clear water, Bear Creek might look like a great place to fish, but unless you're a sixth grader in Tulare County, it's not. It is stocked exclusively at Scicon Conservation Camp, which is used by Tulare County as a place to take students on weeklong field trips, and to teach them about conservation and the environment. These students learn about the ecosystems in a creek, how to identify the trees of the forest, how the Sierra Nevada Mountain range was formed and where the water in the creek comes from. Each year approximately 13,000 students use the 1,100-acre outdoor education center.

Bear Creek flows through the camp for about a mile, and the section where it is planted is not open to the public. It is only stocked with about 80 fish, generally in May, when kids are going to camp. Some stretches of the creek are open to the public, but with all the private property it can be difficult to figure out where you are allowed to fish. Contact the Forest Service for more details.

If you plan to make the trip, supplies are available in Springville. Bear Creek is closed to fishing from November 16 to the last Saturday in April.

Also nearby are Lake Success, the Tule River, Middle Fork, Tule River, North Fork, Balch Park Lakes, Redwood Lake, Hidden Falls and the Golden Trout Wilderness.

# BALCH PARK LAKES

**The lakes are a perfect destination for a family outing or a weekend camping trip.**

| | |
|---|---|
| **Rating:** | 7 |
| **Species:** | Rainbow Trout |
| **Stock:** | 10,050 pounds of rainbow trout. |
| **Facilities:** | Campgrounds, Picnic Areas and Restrooms |
| **Contact:** | Mountain Home State Forest (559) 539-2321 (Summer) or (559) 539-2855 (Winter) |
| **Directions:** | Sequoia National Forest (559) 784-1500, Balch Park (559) 733-6291 |

From Bakersfield, drive north on the 99 Freeway to Highway 190. Take Highway 190 east past Porterville and Lake Success to Springville. In Springville, turn left on Road J-37 (Balch Park Road), and drive 2.4 miles to Road 220 (Bear Creek Road). Turn right, and continue approximately 14 miles to Balch Park. Follow the signs to the lakes.

*Balch Park Lake*

Surrounded by the Sequoia National Forest and Mountain Home State Forest, Balch Park Lakes are located on a small piece of Tulare County land, referred to as Balch Park. The lakes are a perfect destination for a family outing or a weekend camping trip. They are popular, but never get so crowded that it would cause your trip not to be enjoyable.

Although both lakes freeze over in the winter and provide good fishing the rest of the year, they do differ a bit. At two acres, Lower Balch Park Lake is more like a big mud puddle. However, with the California Department of Fish and Game planting 11,020 trout from spring through fall catch rates are high.

Although Lower Balch Park Lake is weedy and extremely shallow, giant sequoia trees that are scattered along the shoreline and provide shade offset those fishing deterrents. There are also large trunks from sawed-off sequoias that anglers use as platforms to fish from. Because of the water's shallowness, many anglers use bobbers to keep their Power Bait or night crawlers from getting stuck on the bottom and in the weeds.

Although planted with the same amount of fish, Upper Balch Lake receives the bulk of the fishing pressure. Half of this lake is actually located within the boundary line of Mountain Home State Forest. It is an acre larger than the lower lake, with clear water, and instead of weeds, tules are scattered along its shoreline. Sequoia trees are also spread out along its banks, making fishing a pleasure. Whether fishing Power Bait, floating night crawlers off the bottom or tossing lures, catch rates remain high. Fishing is good all round the lake, but casting towards a trunk from a sequoia tree in the middle of the lake s always produced the best action for me.

When I first arrived at Upper Balch Park Lake, I saw a kid chasing a group of ducks. And ays thought it was the ducks that harassed the kids. Ironically, the kid was running to a sign that read, "Do Not Catch or Feed Ducks or Frogs". I got a kick out of the park who was sitting in his vehicle laughing at the kid harassing the ducks. "Nice sign

you got here," I said. "Glad the laws are being enforced. Don't work too hard." He wasn't amused, but didn't bother to go after the kid, either.

The geese and ducks aren't the only annoyances to anglers. At times they get in the way of anglers, but the biggest distraction is the bullfrogs. There are hundreds of them, as well as a huge population of pollywogs. I heard so many frogs croaking, I put my pole down and walked around to see if I could find any. Sure enough, there were five bullfrogs all within a few feet of each other, about 10 feet away. I figured since the ranger didn't bust the kid, he wouldn't hassle me, so I caught a few of them, took some pictures and returned them to the lake.

If you plan to make the trip, supplies are available in Springville. There is a day-use fee. The road to Balch Park Lakes is closed in the winter. Call ahead for updated road conditions.

Also nearby are Redwood Lake, Golden Trout Wilderness, North Fork of the Middle Fork of the Tule River, Hidden Falls and Summit Lake.

*Balch Park Lake*

BALCH PARK LAKES

# REDWOOD LAKE (HEDRICK POND)

*I call it "Bobber Lake," because without a bobber it's almost impossible to catch fish.*

| | |
|---|---|
| **Rating:** | 6 |
| **Species:** | Rainbow Trout |
| **Stock:** | 3,650 pounds of rainbow trout. |
| **Facilities:** | Campgrounds and Restrooms |
| **Contact:** | Mountain Home State Forest (559) 539-2321 (Summer) or (559) 539-2855 (Winter) |
| **Directions:** | From Bakersfield, drive north on the 99 Freeway to Highway 190 east. Take Highway 190 past Porterville and Lake Success to Springville. In Springville, turn left on Road J-37 (Balch Park Road) and drive 2.4 miles to Road 220. Turn right and continue approximately 14 miles to Balch Park. Drive through the park to Hedrick Pond. |

*Redwood Lake*

First off, let's get one thing straight: if you come into Mountain Home State Forest looking for Redwood Lake, you're never going to find it. Called "Redwood Lake" on the California Department of Fish and Game's stocking list, it's mostly known as "Hedrick Pond." I don't call it "Redwood Lake" or "Hedrick Pond." I call it "Bobber Lake," because without a bobber it's almost impossible to catch fish.

A dammed portion of Coburn Creek, with sequoia scattered along its shoreline, Redwood Lake is stocked with 6,972 rainbow trout from the CA DFG. This small, one-acre pond in the middle of the state forest is so shallow and weedy that without a bobber to keep your bait off the bottom, chances are your bait will be invisible to the fish. Those who use a bobber to hang Power Bait or night crawlers a few inches below the surface do well. When I was there, every angler was fishing with a bobber. Anglers who try to get away with tossing lures usually end up catching a bundle of weeds.

If you plan to make the trip, supplies are available in Springville. Redwood Lake freezes over in the winter.

Also nearby are Balch Park Lakes, Bear Creek, Golden Trout Wilderness, North Fork of the Middle Fork of the Tule River, Hidden Falls and Summit Lake.

# SIERRA CATFISH FARM

**There are five half-acre ponds open to anglers, all of which are stocked with catfish.**

| | |
|---|---|
| **Rating:** | 7 |
| **Species:** | Channel Catfish |
| **Stock:** | Weekly |
| **Facilities:** | Restrooms, Bait & Tackle, Picnic Areas and a Snack Bar |
| **Contact:** | Sierra Catfish Farms (559) 561-3132 |

**Directions:** From Bakersfield, drive north on the 99 Freeway to Highway 198. Exit east and continue to the city of Visalia. From Visalia, staying on Highway 198, drive 30 miles to Three Rivers. In Three Rivers, turn east on North Fork Road and drive approximately one mile to Kaweah River Drive. Turn right and continue over a bridge that crosses the North Fork of the Kaweah River to the farm on your left.

*James Kiefer with a 22-pound catfish caught at Sierra View Farm in 1996*

Are you sick of fishing lakes for catfish and never catching any? Then head to Sierra Catfish Farm, which raises catfish to sell to the public and local lakes, and opens its rearing ponds to anglers on the weekends. You're almost guaranteed to catch catfish.

There are five half-acre ponds open to anglers, all of which are stocked with catfish. Most of the cats are anywhere from three to 15 pounds, with a few in the twenties. A lake record tipped the scales at over 32 pounds, but giants like that are rarely landed. Chicken liver is a local favorite, although anything that stinks will catch fish. There is no limit, but keep in mind each fish you catch is going to cost you $2.50 a pound. No catch & release is allowed.

The farm is located between the North Fork of the Kaweah River and Lower Kaweah River in Three Rivers, a few miles east of Lake Kaweah. Sierra Catfish Farm mostly raises its fish to sell to private ponds, but it also stocks Lake Kaweah and Plaza Park Pond in Visalia. Another plus is that for a small fee they will fillet the fish for you. For those of you who have ever tried to clean and fillet a catfish, you'd probably appreciate the thought of someone else doing it for you.

If you plan to make the trip, supplies are available in Three Rivers. Sierra Catfish Farm is open on Saturday and Sunday only. No fishing license is required. There is a small admission fee.

Also nearby are North Fork of the Kaweah River, Lake Kaweah, Lower Kaweah River, Kaweah River (Sequoia National Park), Twin Lakes (Sequoia National Park) and Middle Fork Kaweah Falls.

# LAKE KAWEAH

*Each year anglers catch dozens of trophy bass over 10 pounds.*

| | |
|---|---|
| **Rating:** | 7 |
| **Species:** | Rainbow Trout, Channel Catfish, Largemouth Bass, Crappie, Bluegill and Carp |
| **Stock:** | 13,000 pounds of rainbow trout. |
| **Facilities:** | Boat Launch, Boat Rentals, Picnic Areas, Restrooms, Showers, Campgrounds, Marina, Gas, Snack Bar and Bait & Tackle |
| **Contact:** | Lake Kaweah (559) 597-2301 |
| **Directions:** | From the 99 Freeway in Fresno, drive south and exit east on Highway 198. Drive through Visalia and continue to the lake on the left. |

*Lake Kaweah*

Almost every new lake that is stocked with bass turns into a great trophy-bass fishery nearly a decade after it was first stocked. After this first peak, fisheries go in 20-year cycles, swinging from ridge to trough each decade. Although Kaweah was built in 1962, it's currently fishing like a new lake during its first high period, and there's a good explanation for this.

Built just east of Visalia for flood control purposes, this 1,945-acre reservoir was chemically treated in 1987 by the California Department of Fish and Game to remove populations of white bass and carp. The treatment killed 180 tons of fish, including some carp weighing up to 55 pounds. After the treatment, it was stocked with brood stock largemouth from Upper Otay Reservoir and fingerling largemouths. Catfish, bluegill and crappie were also planted.

Shad, however, were not returned to the lake. That's because there were threats from anglers who opposed the treatment, saying they'd reintroduce white bass back into Kaweah. Since shad are a vital source of food for bass, hoping to deter the illegal stocking of white bass, it was decided not to stock shad.

After it was chemically treated, Kaweah became like a new lake, at least from a fishing cycle perspective. And over the last few years the bass have reached their first peak. Each of those years anglers have caught dozens of trophy bass over 10 pounds. A carp fisherman using a dough ball caught the lake record 18-pounder.

In my opinion, however, this fishery will soon begin to slide. The problem is twofold: a lack of water and not enough catch & release being practiced.

Too many of the lunkers caught here are turned into wall ornaments. I was told of an angler who caught a five-fish, 50-plus-pound limit and made a wall mount out of each fish. The fact that anglers have been removing too many big bass from the lake has got to affect the fishery in a negative way. Currently, the lake holds a lot of eight- to 10-pound fish and tons of fish in the nine- to 11-inch class.

Angler harvest, however, is only half the problem here. Low water levels have become another drag. At full pool, Kaweah spans more than 142,000-acre-feet, and with thousands of submerged structures, steep drop-offs and dozens of coves, it has great spawning habitat and hoards of room for fish to grow when the lake is full. But "when" is the key word.

Although water-level fluctuation is inevitable even during the spawning season, because of drastic drawdowns, 10-foot tall trees can be completely submerged one day and have no water around them just a few days later. At low pool, the lake can drop to 3,600-acre-feet.

For most fisheries, these extreme drawdowns would be disastrous to bass; however, at Kaweah the bass have somewhat adapted. Yet, the key to the lake's future remains its water levels. For the lake to continue to be a productive bass fishery, water levels need to remain stable. Now the water's just flushed in and out the way it is in a toilet.

Springtime offers the best bass fishing here. Crankbaits and topwater lures work best in the shallows. Crawdad colors are most effective. Chartreuse spinnerbaits are also a popular choice. As summer approaches and water levels drop and the water warms, fishing turns to a late-night, early-morning affair. Anglers then capitalize on fish feeding in the shallows near submerged trees. As fall comes near, focus turns to purple grubs and brown jigs. Jigging off rock piles and structures works best in winter.

Trout fishing is also good at Kaweah. From winter on into spring, the CA DFG plants 21,030 rainbows here. Because the lake is so shallow and warm in the summer and fall, there are no holdover trout here. The trout that aren't caught swim up the Kaweah River, which feeds the lake. Trolling the dam area or bait fishing both work.

While the lake's pan fish are rarely targeted, the catfish, which are quite abundant, are frequently sought after. Try soaking dead shad in the shallows or dip a night crawler in a jar of Hog Wild for best results

If you plan to make the trip, supplies are available in Visalia. There is a boat launch fee.

Also nearby are North Fork Kaweah River, Kaweah River (Lower), Kaweah River (Sequoia National Park) and Sierra Catfish Farm.

# NORTH FORK KAWEAH RIVER

*In the spring and early summer, this section of the river is stocked by the Department of Fish and Game with 525 rainbow trout, providing decent catch rates for those fishing Power Bait, Super Dupers and Kastmasters.*

**Rating:** 6
**Species:** Rainbow Trout
**Stock:** 375 pounds of rainbow trout.
**Facilities:** None
**Contact:** Bureau of Land Management (661) 291-6000

**Directions:** From Bakersfield, drive north on the 99 Freeway to Highway 198. Exit east and continue to the city of Visalia. From Visalia, continue 30 miles on Highway 198 to Three Rivers. Turn east on North Fork Road and drive approximately 6.2 miles to Paradise Recreation Site.

*North Fork of the Kaweah River at Paradise Recreation Site*

The North Fork of the Kaweah River is almost an exact replica of the Lower Kaweah River, except it is slightly narrower. However, while the Lower Kaweah is bombarded by day-users, the North Fork stays quiet, because its crowds remain at a minimum.

Nearly all of the use occurs at Paradise Recreation Site, which is operated by the Bureau of Land Management. Here, the creek is wide, averaging 10 yards in most places, and it gets as deep as six feet. There are large pools throughout the stream, some bordered by sandy beaches and others by rocks. In the spring and early summer, this section of the river is stocked by the California Department of Fish and Game with 525 rainbow trout, providing decent catch rates for those fishing Power Bait, Super Dupers and Kastmasters.

The North Fork of the Kaweah River's headwaters begin in the southwestern end of Kings Canyon National Park, where they are fed by Woodward and Stoney Creeks. The river then works its way down through Sequoia National Park and converges with the Lower Kaweah near Three Rivers.

This section of the river isn't heavily used or fished, because it is remotely located in the national parks, and also because most of it is surrounded by private property near the town of Kaweah, just southwest of Paradise Recreation Area. If you get here before the water becomes too warm for the stockers in late July, you can use this to your advantage.

If you plan to make the trip, supplies are available in Three Rivers.

Also nearby are Sierra Catfish Farm, Lake Kaweah, the Lower Kaweah River, Kaweah River (Sequoia National Park), Twin Lakes (Sequoia National Park) and Middle Fork Kaweah Falls.

# KAWEAH RIVER (LOWER)

**The best time to fish here is late June, when the water levels begin to subside, just before it gets too warm and the stockers die-off.**

**Rating:** 7
**Species:** Rainbow Trout
**Stock:** 275 pounds of rainbow trout.
**Facilities:** Campgrounds, Restrooms, Lodging, RV Hookups, General Store, Bait & Tackle, Gas, Food, Picnic Areas
**Contact:** McCoy's Mini Mart (559) 597-4115, Kaweah Marina (559) 597-2526

**Directions:** From Bakersfield, drive north on Highway 99 to Highway 198. Exit east and continue to the city of Visalia. From Visalia, continue 30 miles on Highway 198 to Three Rivers. Drive approximately five miles past Three Rivers to the Slick Rock Day-Use area.

*Lower Kaweah River*

A lot like the Tule River near Springville, the lower Kaweah River is a day-user's paradise. Less than a half-hour drive from Visalia, the river provides easy access, decent trout fishing and swimming during the warmer months. Fed from the Marble, Middle, North, East and South Forks of the Kaweah River, the lower portion almost always has enough water to sustain fish. However, it's only cold enough for stocked trout from March through June, when the California Department of Fish and Game plants 535 rainbows into the river.

Concentrate your efforts in Slick Rock Day-Use area, where most of the fish are stocked. This section of the Kaweah River flows westward from the Sequoia National Park boundary to Lake Kaweah. Be alert while fishing this section of the river, because much of it flows through private property.

If targeting the stockers, try using white or Captain America Power Bait, salmon eggs or small spinners. At times, during peak snow runoff, fishing the river can be difficult. The best time to fish here is late June, when the water levels begin to subside, just before it gets too warm and the stockers die-off. Swimming is also popular during the warmer months.

If you plan to make the trip, supplies are available in Three Rivers. Watch out for rattlesnakes.

Also nearby are Moro Rock, the General Sherman Tree, Twin Lakes, Tokopah Valley Falls, Middle Fork Kaweah River, North Fork Kaweah River, Middle Fork Kaweah Falls, Kings Canyon National Park, Sierra Catfish Farm and Lake Kaweah.

# STONEY CREEK

*Most of the fish in this portion of the stream are small, about six to eight inches, half the mass of the stockers, but they fight much better than the stockers do.*

| | |
|---|---|
| **Rating:** | 6 |
| **Species:** | Rainbow Trout |
| **Stock:** | 1,800 pounds of rainbow trout. |
| **Facilities:** | Campgrounds, Restrooms, Lodging, General Store and a Restaurant |
| **Contact:** | Sequoia National Forest (559) 338-2251, Stoney Creek Lodge (559) 565-3909 |

**Directions:** From the 99 Freeway in Fresno, drive 52 miles east on Highway 180 to the entrance to Kings Canyon National Park and continue 1.7 miles to a fork in the road. Veer right onto Generals Highway and drive 12 miles to the creek.

*Stoney Creek*

Located between Kings Canyon and Sequoia National Parks, Stoney Creek is a hidden, but popular, fishing and camping area on a small parcel of Sequoia National Forest land. Along with nearby Woodward and Dorst Creeks, Stoney Creek contributes to the headwaters of the North Fork Kaweah River. The creek borders Kings Canyon National Park to the west, Sequoia National Park to the south and the Jennie Lakes Wilderness to the east.

Located, at 6,000 feet in a heavily pined forest area, the creek is stocked with 3,745 rainbow trout from the last weekend in April through July. The plants are made at Stoney Creek Campground. Once August arrives and there is no longer enough water in the stream for the stockers, hard core anglers work their way downstream towards the confluence of Woodward and Stoney Creeks, about a mile from the campground.

If you take the trail that leads down to the creek, keep an eye out for Stoney Creek Falls, a group of small cascades and freefalls less than a half-mile into your hike. None of them are taller than 15 feet, but they form good swimming holes. Use caution getting down to them; the granite rock is extremely slippery. Most of the fish in this portion of the stream are small, about six to eight inches, half the mass of the stockers, but they fight much better than the stockers do.

If you plan to make the trip, supplies are available in Stoney Creek Village. There is a $10 fee to enter the national park. And yes, even though you aren't staying in the park, you must pay the fee. Stoney Creek is closed to fishing from November 16 to the last Saturday in April.

Also nearby are Big Meadow Creek, Jennie Lake, Sequoia and Kings Canyon National Parks, Hume Lake, Tenmile Creek, Bearskin Creek and Muir Grove.

**Located between Kings Canyon National Park and the Jennie Lakes Wilderness, campers and anglers come to Big Meadows Creek to escape the crowds and enjoy free camping.**

**Rating:** 6
**Species:** Rainbow Trout
**Stock:** 1,500 pounds of rainbow trout.
**Facilities:** Primitive Campgrounds and Restrooms
**Contact:** Sequoia National Forest (559) 338-2251

**Directions:** From the 99 Freeway in Fresno, drive 52 miles east on Highway 180 to the entrance to Kings Canyon National Park. Drive into the park and continue 1.7 miles to a fork in the road. Veer right onto Generals Highway and continue 6.8 miles to Big Meadows Road. Turn northeast and drive approximately four miles to a sign for Big Meadow Campgrounds.

*Big Meadows Creek*

"Do Not Feed the Bears" is the first thing you see when arriving at Big Meadows Creek. Bears visit the campgrounds a lot in the summer and fall, however, they usually don't cause many problems. The big problem that campers have here is catching fish after July. That's because the creek stops flowing and becomes "Big Meadows Pools," as many campers refer to it.

Even worse than trying to catch fish late in the summer, is that the stagnant water attracts more mosquitoes than you could ever imagine trying to swat away. As summer progresses and less snowmelt feeds the creek, it usually ceases to flow by late July, and the water gets trapped in pools. The mosquitoes really love it when this happens.

Located between Kings Canyon National Park and the Jennie Lakes Wilderness, campers and anglers come to Big Meadows Creek to escape the crowds and enjoy free camping. If you're coming to fish, better show up from May through mid-July when the California Department of Fish and Game scatters 3,150 rainbows in and around the campgrounds. You can get away with using small spinners in some of the larger pools, but salmon eggs and night crawlers work best in the smaller ones.

Big Meadows is well known as a starting point into the Jennie Lakes Wilderness, and a back way into Sequoia and Kings Canyon National Parks.

If you plan to make the trip, supplies are available in Grant Grove Village. There is a $10 fee to enter the national park. And yes, even though you aren't staying in the park, you must pay the fee. Big Meadows Creek is closed to fishing from November 16 to the last Saturday in April.

Also nearby are Stoney Creek, Jennie Lake, Sequoia and Kings Canyon National Parks, Hume Lake, Tenmile Creek and Bearskin Creek.

# WEAVER LAKE

*Fly-fishing tends to produce the highest catch rates, especially when the mosquitoes are around.*

| | |
|---|---|
| **Rating:** | 7 |
| **Species:** | Brook Trout and Rainbow Trout |
| **Stock:** | One pound of fingerling brook trout. |
| **Facilities:** | None |
| **Contact:** | Sequoia National Forest (559) 338-2251 |

**Directions:** From the 99 Freeway in Fresno, drive 52 miles east on Highway 180 to the entrance to Kings Canyon National Park and continue 1.7 miles to a fork. Veer right onto Generals Highway and drive 6.8 miles to Big Meadows Road. Turn northeast and drive approximately four miles to a sign on your right for Big Meadow Trailhead. Park in the parking lot.

*Weaver Lake*

Sequoia National Park is one of the most popular backpacking destinations in all of the United States, but what do you do if all the permits to backpack in the park are taken? You go to the Jennie Lakes Wilderness, where only a free campfire permit is required. Not only does it border the park, it also looks and feels just like it. Remote, pretty and uncrowded, Jennie Lakes Wilderness has two things to offer that the high-country lakes of Sequoia National Park can't: stocked fish and an easy hike.

The California Department of Fish and Game airlifts some 2,520 fingerling brook trout to Weaver Lake each spring, in hopes that they'll grow to catchable sizes. There are also holdover trout from years past to ensure that fishing remains consistent at this shallow lake. Plants began in 1953 and rainbows were also planted until 1992.

Most of the fish average seven to nine inches, but some can reach 10 inches. Since the lake is extremely shallow, you'll need to find the deeper areas for catch rates to improve. Just about any small spinner catches fish, however, fly-fishing tends to produce the highest catch rates, especially when the mosquitoes are around.

Unlike most other trails in the region, the one to Weaver Lake is not signed, but it's easy to follow. At the Big Meadow Trailhead, pickup the Big Meadow Trail, heading southeast. After crossing Big Meadow Creek, walk another 1.8 miles to a fork in the trail. Veer right, and you'll hike over Poop Out Pass, which leads to Jennie Lake. Stay to the left, and in about 1.25 miles, you'll run into the lake. Bring along a bathing suit. Since the lake is so small, the water warms quickly, and a dip can be refreshing on a hot summer day.

If you plan to make the trip, supplies are available in Grant Grove Village. Fishing regulations allow you to keep 10 brook trout smaller than 10 inches, in addition to the daily bag limit of five fish. There is a $10 fee to enter the national park. And yes, even though you aren't staying in the park, you must pay the fee.

Also nearby are Big Meadow Creek, Jennie Lake, Sequoia and Kings Canyon National Parks, Hume Lake, Tenmile Creek and Bearskin Creek.

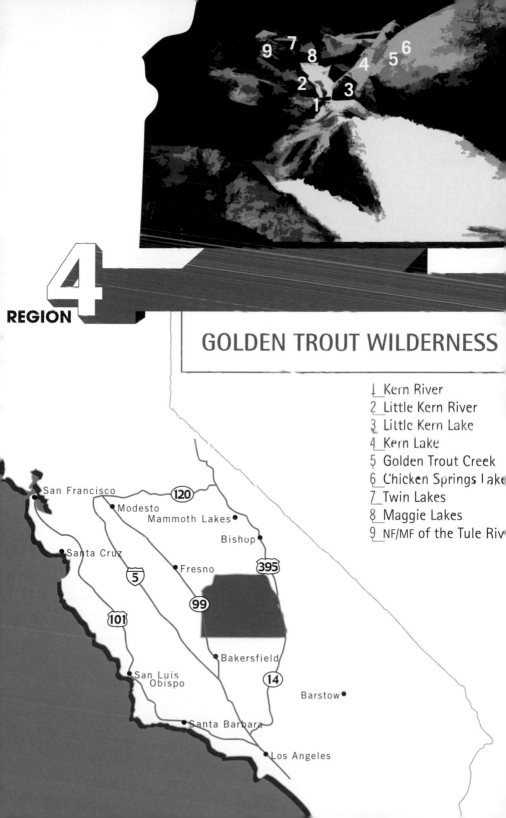

REGION **4**

# GOLDEN TROUT WILDERNESS

1 Kern River
2 Little Kern River
3 Little Kern Lake
4 Kern Lake
5 Golden Trout Creek
6 Chicken Springs Lake
7 Twin Lakes
8 Maggie Lakes
9 NF/MF of the Tule River

San Francisco
Modesto
Mammoth Lakes
Bishop
Santa Cruz
Fresno
395
5
99
101
Bakersfield
San Luis Obispo
14
Barstow
Santa Barbara
Los Angeles
120

# KERN RIVER

*Because of its historical significance, as well as its rarity, the Kern River rainbow trout is on the California and federal "species of special concern" list.*

**Rating:** 7
**Species:** Rainbow Trout and Brown Trout
**Stock:** None
**Facilities:** None
**Contact:** Sequoia National Forest (661) 548-6503

**Directions:** From the 99 Freeway in Bakersfield, exit Highway 178 east and drive 45 miles to Lake Isabella. From Lake Isabella, drive 11 miles north to Kernville and turn left on Mountain 99. Drive approximately 24 miles on Mountain 99 to a fork in the road and veer right onto Road 22S82, signed for Camp Whitsett and Lower Peppermint Creek. Continue approximately 21 miles and veer right just before the end of the road at the sign for the Forks of the Kern Trailhead. Park at the trailhead and walk upstream.

*Kern River (Golden Trout Wilderness)*

Flowing through the Golden Trout Wilderness, this section of the Kern River is one of the most significant waters in California. Only accessible by horse or foot, it is among the last of the waters in the state that hold native trout: specifically, the Kern River rainbow trout.

Because of its biological significance, as well as its rarity, the Kern River rainbow trout is on the California and federal "species of special concern" list. Many precautions have been taken in order to preserve and protect these fish. In addition to being designated a "Wild and Scenic" river, this section of the Kern was also added to the state's designated catch & release waters in the early 1990's. In 1999, it was named as one of the first six Heritage Trout Waters in California. The CA DFG wants not only to preserve these native fish, but also to allow them to grow to trophy sizes.

When I first found out about the efforts to protect these native fish, it occurred to me that the rainbows stocked from Lake Isabella to Johnsondale Bridge could swim upstream and breed with them, ruining their pure gene pool. Ralph Cutter, however, suggests in his book, Sierra Trout Guide, that the stockers can't surmount the waterfall upstream of the Forks of the Kern. I believe he's referring to a waterfall about a quarter-mile upstream of Ninemile Creek on the Kern.

Dave Lentz, of the Heritage Trout Program, told me that when the CA DFG provided biologists from UC Davis with samples of fish from the Kern, results showed that the rainbows downstream of Durwood Creek had different genes than those upstream of Durwood, which is seven miles downstream from Forks of the Kern, where the Heritage River begins. According to Lentz, this suggests that the fish downstream of Durwood have interbred with the stocked rainbows, while those upstream are what are left of the pure-strain native Kern River rainbow trout.

The Heritage section of the river begins at the Forks of the Kern, where the Kern and Little Kern Rivers meet, and continues upstream through the Golden Trout Wilderness and into Sequoia National Park, all the way to Tyndall Creek, a distance of roughly 45 miles. Fishing this section of the Kern can be good after spring runoff subsides in early July. But fishing this fierce-flowing river in May and June is ludicrous, because almost all the river is whitewater.

While some of the river flows gently through meadows, other sections have small waterfalls and rapids; and yes, all are home to many trout. Most are rainbows, with some browns, a few goldens and a smattering of brooks. Remember, this river is governed by special regulations. Only artificial lures with barbless hooks may be used. There is a limit of two rainbow trout (not to exceed 10 inches) per day. Your best bet is using small Panther Martins and Kastmasters. Fly-fishing is also popular.

Reaching this section of the Kern is going to take some effort. It can be accessed from many points, the easiest and closest being the Forks of the Kern Trailhead. From the trail-head, it's a two mile downhill trek to the river. Then it's entirely up to you how far upstream you wish to travel. The river can also be accessed from the Jerky Meadow Trailhead, Camp Nelson, areas of the South Fork of the Kern and through Sequoia National Park and the Eastern Sierra.

If you plan to make the trip, supplies are available in Kernville. The Kern River is closed to fishing from November 16 to the last Saturday in April. A wilderness permit is required for overnight travel in the Golden Trout Wilderness and Sequoia National Park.

Also nearby are Grasshopper Creek Falls, Freeman Creek Falls, Coyote Creek Falls, Volcano Falls, Golden Trout Creek, Kern Lake and Little Kern Lake.

*Kern River (Golden Trout Wilderness)*

KERN RIVER

# LITTLE KERN RIVER

*Although most of the fish are small, they are abundant and can be caught in pools with small Panther Martins, especially in the upper stretches of the river where fishing pressure is extremely light.*

| | |
|---|---|
| **Rating:** | 8 |
| **Species:** | Rainbow Trout, Brown Trout and Golden Trout |
| **Stock:** | None |
| **Facilities:** | None |
| **Contact:** | Sequoia National Forest (661) 548-6503 |

**Directions:** From the 99 Freeway in Bakersfield, exit Highway 178 east and drive 45 miles to Lake Isabella. From Lake Isabella, drive 11 miles north on Highway 155 to Kernville and turn left on Mountain 99. Drive approximately 24 miles on Mountain 99 to a fork in the road and veer right onto Road 22S82, signed for Camp Whitsett and Lower Peppermint Creek. Continue approximately 21 miles to the trailhead at the end of the road.

For at least the last three decades, the California Department of Fish and Game has invested millions of dollars, working around the clock to remove non-native fish from waters where native fish reside. There are numerous ways to remove these non-native fish, including gill nets, fishing, electroshocking and poison. All have been tried.

At one time, the Little Kern River was loaded with a pure strain of golden trout. Their genetic purity, however, was threatened by rainbows and browns swimming up from the Kern River to the Little Kern. Concerned that these non-native fish would mix with the goldens, the CA DFG took a different approach to save California's state fish. This time, biologists decided to attempt to cut off these fish's passageway to the upper reaches of the river. Roughly two-thirds of the way up the Little Kern, where Rifle Creek enters the Little Kern, the CA DFG built an artificial waterfall barrier to block these intruders from swimming further upstream.

This attempt seems to have been successful. The CA DFG is not aware of any rainbows or browns that have been able to surpass this barrier. If they are correct, all the fish upstream of this point are indeed pure goldens. Downstream, on the other hand, it's a different story. Because rainbows and browns are known to be in this section of the river, it's assumed that at least some goldens below Rifle Creek aren't pure. At the end of 2001, another waterfall barrier is planned near Soda Springs.

So, what can anglers expect to catch in the Little Kern? Although most of the goldens are small, they are abundant and can be caught in pools with small Panther Martins, especially in the upper stretches of the river where fishing pressure is extremely light.

With its origin at the Bullfrog Lakes, nearly 11,000 feet up in the Golden Trout Wilderness near the border of Sequoia National Park, the Little Kern flows through the wilderness area for its entire 26-mile length, before merging with the Kern River. For all but its last six miles, a trail parallels the river.

The river isn't accessible with a vehicle. Foot and horseback are your only two options. It's a short two-mile descent from the Forks of the Kern Trailhead to the confluence of the Kern and Little Kern Rivers. The Little Kern can also be accessed via the Jerky Meadow Trailhead, Camp Nelson and Mineral King.

If you plan to make the trip, supplies are available in Mineral King and Kernville. The Little Kern River is closed to fishing from November 16 to the last Saturday in April. Only artificial lures with barbless hooks may be used.

Also nearby are Freeman Creek, Freeman Creek Falls, Kern River, Grasshopper Creek Falls, Kern Lake and Little Kern Lake.

*opposite page Little Kern River*

# LITTLE KERN LAKE

*I had the best luck tossing Kastmasters and Thomas Buoyants, although I had a little bit of trouble getting Panther Martins to sink down to where the fish were.*

**Rating:** 6
**Species:** Rainbow Trout and Brown Trout
**Stock:** None
**Facilities:** None
**Contact:** Sequoia National Forest (661) 548-6503

**Directions:** From the 99 Freeway in Bakersfield, exit Highway 178 east and drive 45 miles to Lake Isabella. From Lake Isabella, drive 11 miles north on Highway 155 to Kernville and turn left on Mountain 99. Take Mountain 99 approximately 24 miles to a fork in the road and veer right onto Road 22S82, signed for Camp Whitsett and Lower Peppermint Creek. Continue approximately 21 miles to the trailhead at the end of the road.

*Backpacking near Jerky Meadow*

At 6,200 feet in the Golden Trout Wilderness, Little Kern Lake is a popular camping and fishing area for those backpacking the Kern River Drainage. With the Kern River flowing less than 50 yards east of the lake, many hikers pass by Little Kern Lake on their way to Kern Lake and Sequoia National Park, yet few stop to enjoy it. Don't make that mistake. Not only is Little Kern Lake a great camping destination, it also offers good fishing. The lake is rich with hard-fighting rainbow trout, not to mention a few browns.

There are steep drop-offs here, and the trout swim up and down the shoreline searching for food, so fishing the lake is pretty simple. The trail side is the easiest to fish. I had the best luck tossing Kastmasters and Thomas Buoyants, although I had a little bit of trouble getting Panther Martins to sink down to where the fish were. With most in the eight to 10-inch class, there are also some rainbows that exceed 14 inches. The browns grow as large as four pounds.

The long journey to Little Kern Lake begins at the Jerky Meadow Trailhead and makes you sweat from the get-go, climbing more than 1,000 feet during the first 1.6 miles. In Jerky Meadow (at the top of the peak), the path leaves the Sequoia National Forest and enters the Golden Trout Wilderness. For the next 1.5 miles, the trail threads through a pine forest, dropping a few hundred feet on the way to Jug Spring, a small stream on the right of the path, which serves as a good place to fill your water bottles. For the next 1.2 miles, the path loses nearly 500 feet, coming to a footbridge, allowing you to cross the wide and otherwise un-passable Little Kern River.

After crossing the bridge, continue along the path, following signs for Trout Meadow. From the bridge, the meadow is 2.5 miles ahead, and the trail gains another 400 feet in elevation. Trout Meadow isn't a lush, green meadow like those you'll see in the high-country of Yosemite National Park; it's filled with tall grass and surrounded by barbed wire fences, still intact from when ranchers grazed cattle and horses, before the wilderness area was created.

In another half-mile, you'll arrive at the Trout Meadow Ranger Station. Now, 7.3 miles from your car, this is a good place to take a rest. There is a spring to refill water rations near a picnic table in front of the ranger station. Then, push on. In two-tenths of a mile, a trail signed for Kern Flat splits off to the right. Stay left. Continuing through Trout Meadow and entering Willow Meadow, the next 2.5 miles are fairly level.

There is another spring in Willow Meadow to refill water and give your knees a chance to rest before descending to the Kern River. The drop is gradual for the first 1.8 miles, taking you to an overlook of the drainage. The Kern looks powerful from here. Its whitewater can be clearly seen even this high above the river.

Roughly 2.5 miles from Willow Meadow, you'll cross Angora Creek and be able to hear the roar of the Kern. Ten minutes after crossing Angora, a junction signed for Hole in the Ground veers off to the right. Continue straight, and 13 miles from the Jerky Meadow Trailhead, with an 800 foot descent from Willow Meadow, you'll cross Leggett Creek, finally reaching the shore of the 50 to 75-foot wide Kern River.

Following the path upstream, parallel the Kern for two-tenths of a mile, where you'll cross another stream. There's a tree here with a sign nailed to it that reads, "Grasshopper Creek." Continue another two-tenths of a mile into Grasshopper Flat and begin looking through the trees on the left. There's a waterfall there called Grasshopper Falls.

Pat yourself on the back. You've come 13.7 miles, and mostly likely it will have taken you almost the whole day. When you add up all the peaks you've climbed, it totals almost 2,700 feet. That doesn't take into account the switchbacks you climbed down, descending some 2,600 feet. So, in one day your knees withstood a total of 5,300 feet of ascending and descending.

But, you aren't done yet. From Grasshopper Flat, continue 1.5 miles up the Kern River to Little Kern Lake. This last stretch may be the toughest. Leaving Grasshopper Flat, the path takes you on some grueling climbs. There are no switchbacks, just a trail that leads uphill. It's going to make you huff and puff. From the top of the hill, you'll finally drop down to Little Kern Lake.

If you plan to make the trip, supplies are available in Kernville. A wilderness permit is required for overnight travel in the Golden Trout Wilderness. Little Kern Lake is closed to fishing from November 16 to the last Saturday in April. Only artificial lures with barbless hooks are permitted.

Also nearby are Coyote Creek Falls, Grasshopper Creek Falls, Kern Lake, Kern River and Little Kern River.

*Tony Abel caught this brown at Little Kern Lake.*

LITTLE KERN LAKE

# KERN LAKE

*Some of the browns are big, too. My friend landed a four-pounder in early May of 2000.*

**Rating:** 7
**Species:** Brown Trout, Brook Trout, Rainbow Trout and Golden Trout
**Stock:** None
**Facilities:** None
**Contact:** Sequoia National Forest (661) 548-6503

**Directions:** From the 99 Freeway in Bakersfield, exit Highway 178 east and drive 45 miles to Lake Isabella. From Lake Isabella, drive 11 miles north on Highway 155 to Kernville and turn left on Mountain 99. Drive on Mountain 99 approximately 24 miles to a fork in the road and veer right onto Road 22S82, signed for Camp Whitsett and Lower Peppermint Creek. Continue approximately 21 miles to the trailhead at the end of the road.

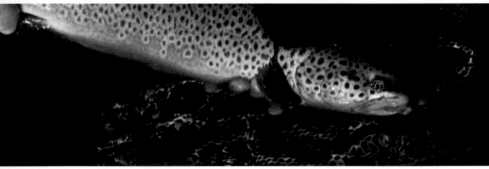

*Large Brown trout can be caught in Kern Lake.*

No matter where you begin your hike, it's a long way to Kern Lake. Also referred to as Big Kern Lake, it is the ideal destination for backpackers who like to avoid crowds, stay out of the high-country and still experience good backcountry fishing.

Located at 6,225 feet in the Golden Trout Wilderness, Kern Lake is set at a relatively low elevation for a backcountry lake, and, therefore, flourishes in mid-spring when most other backcountry lakes are still frozen over. Anglers arrive as early as the trout opener, the last Saturday in April, and begin catching brown trout that cruise the shoreline this time of year.

Kern Lake is small. In reality, it's more of a widening in the Kern River. It provides good access for anglers on its west shoreline. Most of the fish caught are rainbow and brown trout, although a few golden and brook trout are sometimes hooked. Before the Golden Trout Wilderness was created in 1978, Kern Lake was closed to fishing, because it was set aside as a fish nursery for the fish that spawn in the Kern River and use the lake as refuge for their young. Most of the fish that were raised in the lake remain in the Kern River.

Fishing is best in the spring, when the browns and rainbows cruise the shorelines in search of a meal. Some of the browns are big, too. My friend landed a four-pounder in early May of 2000. Rainbows are the most abundant and can be caught tossing Panther Martins, Super Dupers and Kastmasters.

There are only a few campgrounds near the lake, but backpackers take most of them on Friday evening and keep them through the weekend. There are two nice camping sites on the lake's north shore, but all the others are located a short distance north along the Kern River.

To reach Kern Lake from Little Kern Lake, continue north on the Kern River Trail for approximately eight-tenths of a mile to Kern Lake. About five minutes after leaving Little Kern Lake, you'll climb some small switchbacks that will bring you above the lake. Then, you'll slowly descend down to Kern Lake.

If you plan to make the trip, supplies are available in Springville and Kernville. A wilderness permit is required for overnight travel in the Golden Trout Wilderness. Call ahead for updated road conditions. At times Road 22S82 is closed until mid-May. Kern Lake is closed to fishing from November 16 to the last Saturday in April.

# GOLDEN TROUT CREEK

*Like most other places in California where native goldens thrive, the difficult part about fishing the creek is accessing it.*

**Rating:** 8

**Species:** Golden Trout

**Stock:** None

**Facilities:** None

**Contact:** Sequoia National Forest (661) 548-6503, Inyo National Forest (760) 876-6200

**Directions:** From the 99 Freeway in Bakersfield, exit Highway 178 east and drive 45 miles to Lake Isabella. From Lake Isabella, drive 11 miles north on Highway 155 to Kernville and turn left on Mountain 99. Take Mountain 99 approximately 24 miles to a fork in the road and veer right onto Road 22S82, signed for Camp Whitsett and Lower Peppermint Creek. Continue approximately 21 miles to the trailhead at the end of the road.

*Golden trout like this lunker taken from Laurel Lakes are never caught in Golden Trout Creek.*

If I took a survey and asked 10,000 anglers what the California State fish is, chances are fewer than 10 percent would know. For those of you who didn't pay attention in fifth grade when you studied California History, the answer is golden trout. The golden trout is one of the few fish that is native to the state. Most other fish were planted in California's waters by settlers.

With the exception of a few lakes in the Eastern Sierra where goldens were planted, the fish aren't easy to catch. Let me rephrase that: they're easy enough to catch, but you're going to have to work damn hard to get in a position to catch 'em. Goldens can only survive in high mountain rivers, streams and lakes, and one of them's going to have to be your ultimate destination.

In 1978, the golden trout was listed as a threatened species by the US Fish & Wildlife Service; and in 1999, Golden Trout Creek was named as one of the original six Heritage Trout waters, with an eye to protecting the native fish and keeping other types of trout from entering the stream, breeding with the native goldens and destroying their purity. In Golden Trout Creek it's rare to catch a fish longer than eight inches; most average six inches.

Like most other places in California where native goldens thrive, the difficult part about fishing the creek is accessing it. No matter what trailhead you choose, it's a long, grueling hike. You can start at Jerky Meadow or Forks of the Kern Trailheads near the Kern River, or access the river from Camp Nelson or from the Eastern Sierra side. Personally, I've only fished the section of the river directly upstream of Volcano Falls. Here's how you get to that point:

Use the directions in the previous two write-ups to reach Kern Lake. From the east end of Kern Lake, continue 1.5 miles north on the flat trail that parallels the river, to the boundary of Sequoia National Park. Less than one-tenth of a mile after entering the park, walk across a downed tree that acts as a bridge over Coyote Creek. After the stream crossing comes a trail junction. Take the right fork towards the Kern Canyon Ranger Station, Little Whitney Meadow and Funston Meadow. The left fork leads to Coyote Pass.

At the Kern Canyon Ranger Station, 100 yards northeast of Coyote Creek, you'll come to yet another trail junction. Continue straight on the path signed for Funston Meadow. Then, veer right, following signs to Little Whitney Meadow. The trail leaves Sequoia National Park, enters the Golden Trout Wilderness, crosses the Kern River and begins to wind up switchbacks towards Volcano Falls.

While you're here, you might as well keep any eye out for Volcano Falls. It's on the left in the gorge, and in late spring and early summer, you'll hear the falls before seeing it. There's only a window of roughly 100 yards where you can see the falls. When the trail nears the edge of the cliff, look carefully and you should be able to see Volcano spilling off the volcanic rock, falling out of view. Don't expect to be awed.

Pushing on, Golden Trout Creek is a short distance away. Although they do get shorter, there are still more switchbacks ahead. At the top of the peak, you'll come to Natural Bridge, a rock that serves as a footbridge, helping you across Malpias Creek. This point is 2.5 miles and 1,700 feet up from where you crossed the Kern River near the ranger station. Almost there, just 1.2 miles further, now the path crosses Golden Trout Creek; a half-mile from this crossing is Little Whitney Meadow.

You've arrived at the lower section of Golden Trout Creek. If you have the strength, you can trek another 10 miles to Big Whitney Meadow, near Cottonwood Pass and Chicken Springs Lake, where the creek is fed by Stokes Stringer Creek.

If you plan to make the trip, supplies are available in Kernville and Lone Pine. A wilderness permit is required for overnight travel in Sequoia National Park and the Golden Trout Wilderness. Golden Trout Creek is closed to fishing from November 16 to the last Saturday in April. Only artificial lures with barbless hooks are allowed. The road to the trailhead is typically closed until sometime in May. Call the Forest Service for updated conditions.

Also nearby are Chicken Springs Lake, South Fork Kern River, the Miter Basin and the Cottonwood Lakes.

**GOLDEN TROUT CREEK**

*A yellow-bellied marmot*

*As for now, trust me, Chicken Springs Lake is barren of fish, but it is a pretty little lake.*

| | |
|---|---|
| **Rating:** | 1 |
| **Species:** | None |
| **Stock:** | None |
| **Facilities:** | None |
| **Contact:** | Lone Pine Sporting Goods (760) 876-5365, High Sierra Outfitters (760) 876-5020 |
| | Lone Pine Chamber of Commerce (760) 876-4444, Inyo National Forest (760) 876-6200 |
| **Directions:** | From Mojave, drive north on Highway 14 to Highway 395. Drive north on Highway 395 to the town of Lone Pine. In Lone Pine, turn west on Whitney Portal Road and drive three miles to Horseshoe Meadow Road. Turn south and drive approximately 16 miles to the Horseshoe Meadow Trailhead. |

*Chicken Springs Lake*

Walking into Lone Pine Sporting Goods, before heading up to the Golden Trout Wilderness, I came across a picture taken at least 10 years earlier of a kid holding up a four-pound rainbow. It was hanging above the cash register, and the words "Chicken Springs Lake" were written on the bottom of it. While waiting at the Forest Service to pick up my back-packing permits, I found out it was on the way to where I was going. I wondered why it wasn't on the list of the fish populations of lakes given to me by the California Department of Fish and Game. The answer became apparent when the lady behind the counter told me there were no fish in Chicken Springs Lake. Because I've learned not to take everything I hear about fishing holes at face value, I decided to go the lake to find out for myself.

There were two other anglers fishing when I arrived. "Catch anything?" I yelled across the lake. "Not a bite," they replied. "We haven't even seen one. We came up here because we saw a picture of a big trout caught here hanging on the wall in Lone Pine Sporting Goods."

When I called the CA DFG to inquire further, I was told that there used to be fish in the lake, mostly goldens and a few rainbows. However, in the summer of 2000, the CA DFG began poisoning the lake to remove its fish population. The reason given was that Chicken Springs' outlet stream is a tributary of Golden Trout Creek, and since Golden Trout Creek is one of the few streams in California that golden trout are native to, the CA DFG was worried that the non-native goldens from the lake would work their way into the creek and contaminate the native genes.

The kid working the cash register of Lone Pine Sporting Goods who told me there used to be big goldens in the lake proved to be right. But as for now, trust me, Chicken Springs Lake is barren of fish. However, it is a pretty little lake, located at an elevation of 11,242 feet, only four miles from the Horseshoe Meadow Trailhead and three-fourths of a mile from the top of Cottonwood Pass. It's a good destination for a day trip.

To get to the lake, begin hiking from the Horseshoe Meadow Trailhead, working your way through Horseshoe Meadow and over Cottonwood Pass. Just after climbing over the pass, you'll come to a three-way fork in the trail. Follow the right fork to the lake on your right. The middle fork leads to Big Whitney Meadow, and the left fork over Trail and Mulkey Passes.

If you plan to make the trip, supplies are available in Lone Pine. A wilderness permit is required for overnight travel into the Golden Trout Wilderness. Chicken Springs Lake is closed to fishing from November 16 to the last Saturday in April.

Also nearby are Upper and Lower Soldier Lake, Sky Blue Lake, Iridescent Lake, the Cottonwood Lakes, South Fork Lakes, Cirque Lake, Rock Creek, Rock Creek Falls, Sky Blue Falls and Rock Creek Pond.

CHICKEN SPRINGS LAKE          58          *Chicken Springs Lake is barren of fish.*

*There are many great fishing lakes in California named "Twin Lakes," however, the Twin Lakes in the Golden Trout Wilderness are not among them.*

**Rating:** 3
**Species:** Golden Trout
**Stock:** None
**Facilities:** None
**Contact:** Balch Park Pack Station (559) 539-2227 (Summer) or (559) 539-3908 (Winter)
Sequoia National Forest (559) 784-1500

**Directions:** From Bakersfield, drive north on the 99 Freeway to Highway 190 east. Continue on Highway 190 past Porterville and Lake Success to Springville. In Springville, turn left on Road J-37 (Balch Park Road) and drive 2.4 miles to Road 220. Turn right and continue approximately 12 miles to Mountain Home State Forest. Follow signs to the Balch Park Pack Station. The trailhead is just past the pack station.

*Chris Shaffer (Left) and Tim Shew (Right) chat over dinner.*

There are many great fishing lakes in California named "Twin Lakes," however, the Twin Lakes in the Golden Trout Wilderness are not among them. These Twin Lakes have been the subject of controversy since the mid-Nineties, when the California Department of Fish and Game poisoned the lake in an attempt to get rid of the existing brook trout population and establish a new golden trout fishery.

The area's premier packer, Tim Shew, used to bring campers back to the lakes before the CA DFG killed off the self-sustaining brook trout population. Shew said they were two of the best brook trout lakes in the region, and he no longer brings anglers to them, because their fish populations have become nearly extinct. Despite the CA DFG's attempts to establish a golden trout fishery, the goldens haven't been able to spawn. Because many of them had been caught during previous years, and there have not been any recent stocks, most anglers have written-off the lakes. The CA DFG has considered restocking the lake and altering the inlet to allow for spawning, however, nothing has been done as of yet.

Bottom-line, Twin Lakes is a pretty place to camp, but a poor place to fish. There are literally only two fish left, and they probably won't get caught for a long while. These fish have survived countless attempts by thousands of anglers to catch them, and they are extremely smart. Both are goldens, from 12 to 16 inches, and the best way to fool them is to use anything resembling a dragonfly with blue in it. Dragonflies are abundant around the lake, and the goldens make a living feeding on them.

Stay away from the lower lake. It is much too shallow and weedy to be fished and is on its way to becoming a marsh. If fishing the upper lake, work the shoreline opposite the outlet to the lower lake. This far side is much deeper, holds many submerged trees and is more suitable for the two fish. By now they may have been caught!

To get to Twin Lakes from Summit Lake in Sequoia National Park, follow the trail from Summit Lake over Sheep Mountain (the boundary of Sequoia National Park and the Golden Trout Wilderness is on the ridge of Sheep Mountain) down into Peck's Canyon. At the sign for Peck's Canyon, veer right, heading down to the lakes. They can be seen on your right.

If you plan to make the trip, supplies are available in Springville. Twin Lakes is closed to fishing from November 16 to the last Saturday in April. Only artificial lures with barbless hooks are permitted. The trail to Twin Lakes usually isn't snow-free until sometime in June. Call ahead for trail updates.

Also nearby are Summit Lake, Maggie Lakes, North Fork of the Tule River, Summit Lake Falls, North Fork Tule River Falls and Pecker Peak.

*It may take 20 casts before you get hit, but if you catch one here it's going to be well worth it, because goldens are difficult to come by in this area.*

| | |
|---|---|
| **Rating:** | 8 |
| **Species:** | Golden Trout and Rainbow Trout |
| **Stock:** | None |
| **Facilities:** | None |
| **Contact:** | Balch Park Pack Station (559) 539-2227 (Summer) or (559) 539-3908 (Winter) |
| | Sequoia National Forest (559) 784-1500 |
| **Directions:** | From Bakersfield, drive north on the 99 Freeway to Highway 190 east. Continue on Highway 190 east past Porterville and Lake Success to Springville. In Springville, turn left on Road J-37 (Balch Park Road), and drive 2.4 miles to Road 220. Turn right and continue approximately 12 miles to Mountain Home State Forest. Follow signs to the Balch Park Pack Station. The trailhead is just past the pack station. |

*Maggie Lakes provide great fishing opportunities if you can endure the long hike to them.*

Maggie Lakes consists of three separate lakes, all with stable fish populations. Although they compete with Kern Lake and Little Kern Lake, Maggie Lakes are the most popular lakes in the Golden Trout Wilderness. They can be reached either by a 10.5-mile hike from Balch Park or a 12-mile trek from Quaking Aspen.

These lakes are strikingly beautiful. Lodgepole, red fir and silver pines tower overhead, and streams flow in and out of each lake. Better yet, there are minimal crowds, and they are the best fishing lakes in the Golden Trout Wilderness. However, because of the long hike required to reach them, they aren't heavily visited.

Middle Maggie was planted in 1997 and is the only one of the three lakes with an island, and it provides the best and easiest fishing. The lake is so small that you can cast across it, and the water so clear that you can see the bows swimming around. This is the only species found here, and most are from five to nine inches. You might catch one over 10 inches, but that is rare. Try using yellow Panther Martins with a silver blade or a gold Super Duper with a red tip. Another way to catch fish is to climb out on one of the fallen trees that reach over the water, and jig Trout Teasers. The rainbows can't resist 'em.

Most visitors to Lower Maggie come to camp. However, the fishing can be great here, despite the abundance of weeds on the trail side. The best fishing can be found near the lake's two inlets, both of which receive water from one of the other two Maggie Lakes. However, fish can be caught all over the lake. The rainbows here are between six and nine inches and taste great fresh out of a frying pan.

Some of the fish in Lower Maggie, which was last planted in 1995 are a mixed breed of rainbow and golden, but they look just like rainbows. The lakes were originally planted with goldens by the California Department of Fish and Game, but rainbows swam into Lower Maggie from Peck's Creek, corrupting the pure strain of goldens. Many of the pure goldens were caught by anglers over the years, and those that remained interbred with the rainbows, but it's almost impossible to detect the strain of golden in them.

At least four times the size of the other lakes, Upper Maggie last planted in 1995 contains the least, but largest, fish. Because of its size, the upper lake is the most difficult to fish. The best way is with a float tube, but unless you pack trip in, that's almost impossible. The hike is too far to carry a float tube, fins and waders.

Tim Shew, the owner of Balch Park Pack Station, joined us on a pack trip, and we had the time of our lives. Tim and I had a one-hour fishing contest at Middle Maggie, and we each ended up catching and releasing more than 20 rainbows. There are goldens and rainbows as large as two pounds in Upper Maggie, but they're rarely caught.

Upper Maggie has only two quality fishing areas, because the rest of the lake is too shallow. The first is a large boulder on your left just as you reach the lake, which partially juts out of the water about five feet from the shoreline and provides the best fishing. Simply, walk out onto the rock and cast your lures into a deep hole on the other side of it.

The second quality fishing area is on the north shoreline where there's a group of large trees that have fallen into the water. We used them as platforms to get to deeper water, and cast Thomas Buoyants and Panther Martins as far out towards the middle of the lake as we could. It may take 20 casts before you get hit, but if you catch one here it's going to be well worth it, because goldens are difficult to come by in this area. Fishing the lake's outlet stream is the easiest way to catch fish, but you need to be careful not to spook them. Try to sneak up on the pools without letting the fish see you.

Got some extra time? Right above Middle Maggie is Pecker Peak. There is no trail to the top of the peak, but if you start at Middle Maggie and begin climbing, you should make it in less than 40 minutes. At approximately 9,750 feet, Pecker Peak offers breathtaking views of the Little Kern Drainage, Peck's Canyon, Sequoia National Park and a small lake without fish, which can be seen in the distance on the opposite side of Maggie Lakes. As you near the top of the peak, you'll see boulders the size of homes, nestled on top of each other. It feels like you're on top of the world.

*Upper Maggie from Pecker Peak*

*Lower Maggie Lake*

It was on Pecker Peak, my friend Scott Wiessner and I discovered how to fish Maggie Lakes. From this vantage, we realized that because of the lakes drastic changes in depth, only certain areas of the lake are fishable. We'd wondered why we hadn't caught many fish, and we saw that we were fishing in water that was too shallow. This was a key to later catching fish and something I never would have learned without climbing the peak.

To reach Maggie Lakes from Twin Lakes, follow the trail past Frog Lake on your right. You'll cross three feeder streams, one coming out of Twin, the other out of Frog, and the third (which usually dries up by summer) just before reaching Maggie. The trail leads to Lower Maggie Lake. The total distance is 1.70 miles and should take about 15-20 minutes.

If you plan to make the trip, supplies are available in Springville. Maggie Lakes is closed to fishing from November 16 to the last Saturday in April. Only artificial lures with barbless hooks are permitted. The trail to Maggie Lakes usually is snowed-in until sometime in June. Call ahead for trail conditions. There are no fish in Frog Lake. A wilderness permit is required for overnight travel in the Golden Trout Wilderness.

Also nearby are Summit Lake, Twin Lakes, North Fork of the Tule River, Summit Lake Falls, North Fork Tule River Falls and Pecker Peak.

# NORTH FORK OF THE MIDDLE FORK OF THE TULE RIVER

*Although much of the Tule is located in the Golden Trout Wilderness, the river is easily accessible, making for good wild trout fishing or a great family outing.*

**Rating:** 7
**Species:** Rainbow Trout and Brown Trout
**Stock:** None
**Facilities:** None
**Contact:** Balch Park Pack Station (559) 539-2227 (Summer) or (559) 539-3908 (Winter)
Sequoia National Forest (559) 784-1500
**Directions:**
From Bakersfield, drive north on the 99 Freeway to Highway 190 east. Take Highway 190 east past Porterville and Lake Success to Springville. In Springville, turn left on Road J-37 (Balch Park Road) and drive 2.4 miles to Road 220. Turn right and drive approximately 12 miles to Mountain Home State Forest. Follow signs to the Balch Park Pack Station. The trailhead is just past the pack station.

*North Fork of the Middle Fork of the Tule River (Golden Trout Wilderness)*

The fact that the North Fork of the Middle Fork of the Tule River is one of the most special places in California has nothing to do with great fishing. The Mountain Home Grove, located along the river's shoreline in Mountain Home State Forest, is one of the largest groves of prized young sequoia trees in the world. With trees growing right along its shoreline and some even in the river itself, it is an exceptionally picturesque sight.

Although much of the Tule is located in the Golden Trout Wilderness, the river is easily accessible, making for good wild trout fishing or a great family outing. You might even want to try taking a pleasurable horseback ride, the way we did. Tim Shew, owner of Balch Park Pack Station, gave us a guided tour, educating us on the history of the grove.

Even though it's easy to reach, tourists don't heavily use this stretch of the river, because no stocks are made here. It gets much more activity where it's stocked further downstream in the Sequoia National Forest near Camp Wishon. Although most of the fish are small, there are a few large browns pulled out of this stretch of the river each year. Don't try to target the browns, though, because it seems like only those fishing for rainbows catch them. The biggest browns are usually landed in the fall when the water levels subside. Rainbows from six to nine inches are abundant in the river and can be caught on small spinners. Try fishing some of the deeper pools for the larger fish.

The North Fork of the Middle Fork of the Tule is also a great place for waterfall lovers. Three waterfalls, Upper and Lower Hidden Falls, as well as North Fork of the Middle Fork of the Tule River Falls, are all located in this section of the river. Located near the trailhead, Upper and Lower Hidden Falls are accessible by car. However, you have to hike about a half-mile upstream to the North Fork of the Middle Fork of the Tule River Falls.

If you plan to make the trip, supplies are available in Springville. The North Fork of the Middle Fork of the Tule River is closed to fishing from November 16 through the last Saturday in April.

Also nearby are Hidden Falls, Mountain Home State Forest, Balch Park Lake, Redwood Lake, Summit Lake, Twin Lakes, Maggie Lakes and Summit Lake Falls.

REGION **5**

## OAKHURST/SAN JOAQUIN RIVER DRAINAGE

1 Bass Lake
2 NF Willow Creek
3 Nelder Creek
4 Lewis Creek
5 Big Creek (U)
6 Big Creek (FC)
7 Manzanita Lake
8 Corrine Lake
9 Kerckoff Reservoir
10 Redinger Lake
11 Fish Creek
12 Rock Creek
13 Chiquito Creek (WF)
14 Chiquito Creek
15 Mammoth Pool Reservoir
16 Granite Creek

# BASS LAKE

*To pick up trout in the summer you need to be out early before the boaters take over the lake.*

**Rating:** 7
**Species:** Rainbow Trout, Largemouth Bass, Channel Catfish, Kokanee, Crappie, Bluegill and Sunfish
**Stock:** 10,400 pounds of rainbow trout and 155 pounds of fingerling kokanee.
**Facilities:** Boat Launches, Swimming Areas, Picnic Areas, Restrooms, Boat Rentals, Lodging, Gas, Restaurants, Shopping, General Store, RV Hookups, Bait & Tackle and a Ranger Station
**Contact:** Sierra National Forest (559) 877-2218, California Land Management (559) 642-3212
The Forks Resort (559) 642-3737, Bass Lake Boat Tours (559) 642-3121
Pines Marina (559) 642-3565

**Directions:** From the 99 Freeway in Bakersfield, exit Highway 41 north and continue to Oakhurst. Drive through Oakhurst to Road 222 and turn right. Continue approximately four miles to the lake.

*Bass Lake gets bombarded by boaters throughout the summer.*

Bass Lake is one of the great summer recreation spots in California. At 3,500 feet in the Sierra National Forest, it's lushly pined, offers good fishing (depending on the season) and an array of water sports. Surrounded by private residences, resorts and shopping areas, the shores of this pretty 2,500-acre lake are thickly wooded with pine trees, making Bass Lake great for a day trip or a weeklong camping excursion. However you look at it, Bass Lake has something for everyone.

From June through September, when the water creeps up into the mid-seventies, swimmers, water-skiers, wakeboarders and waverunners own the lake. The water turns into one big wake, as every cove and beach becomes over-crowded with hundreds of people looking to have a good time. The highlight of their activities takes place at the Falls Cove, where Willow Creek enters the lake. There's a small cascade that people slide down, using tubes, rafts, boogie boards and even their butts to get into the lake. There is usually a long line at the cascade, as well as a crowd of spectators with video cameras focused on these adventure seekers competing to see who can give the best show.

Because of all the commotion, anglers are limited to catfish fishing in the evenings, unless they have access to leadcore line or a boat with downriggers. Kokanee action can be good in the summer for anglers trolling Needlefish or Hum Dingers behind a set of flashers, or fishing with corn on a hook. To pick up trout in the summer you need to be out early before the boaters take over the lake. There are plenty of trout to be caught.

The California Department of Fish and Game stocks 16,700 trout. More than 50,000 kokanee fingerlings are also planted. The trout grow quite fast and can be caught in the summer by trolling deep. Check with a local tackle store or use your fish finder to meter the fish. After metering the trout, another option is to anchor up and sink Power Bait or night crawlers. It's the easiest way to catch them. There are a lot of two to three pounders in the lake.

As fall approaches, the Pacific Gas & Electric Company begins to gradually draw down the lake, and by early winter it's so low that people who visited in the spring and summer don't recognize it. The best time to fish is in the spring. The trout can be caught from shore, or, even better, toplining with small Rapalas, Kastmasters and Needlefish. There is also a decent bass bite in the spring, but bass aren't a priority here.

If you plan to make the trip, supplies are available at the lake.

Also nearby are Angel Falls, Devils Slide Falls, Willow Creek Falls, Nelder Creek, Whiskey Falls, Manzanita Lake, Willow Creek, Lewis Creek, Big Creek and Fish Camp Falls.

*Bass Lake Falls is popular from June through September.*

BASS LAKE

# NORTH FORK WILLOW CREEK

*The North Fork of Willow Creek offers good fishing for anglers who arrive from late spring through mid-summer, or as long as the creek remains suitable for trout.*

| | |
|---|---|
| **Rating:** | 6 |
| **Species:** | Rainbow Trout |
| **Stock:** | 3,000 pounds of rainbow trout. |
| **Facilities:** | Campgrounds and Vault Toilets |
| **Contact:** | Sierra National Forest (559) 658-7588 |

**Directions:** From the 99 Freeway in Fresno, drive north on Highway 41 to Oakhurst. Continue four miles through Oakhurst to Road 632 and turn right. Drive 8.1 miles to a fork in the road. Veer right, following signs to Soquel Campground, and continue six-tenths of a mile to the campground and stream.

*North Fork Willow Creek*

The North Fork of Willow Creek is close to Yosemite National Park, but with no crowds or traffic jams, its quiet shoreline doesn't feel like you're anywhere near the park. The biggest attraction besides fishing, of course, is a nearby road that takes you to the Bass Lake Overlook. (The turnoff is just before the fork in the road.) However, unless somebody walks the dirt road ahead of you with a giant weed wacker, I don't recommend it.

I made it about a mile, until my car was so scratched up from the trees and bushes overhanging the road, I decided to turn back. The total distance to the overlook was just five miles, but it was a slow road that continued to get narrower as I continued. Save your paint job and concentrate on catching fish in the creek.

Located between Oakhurst and Yosemite National Park at 5,400 feet in the Sierra National Forest, the North Fork of Willow Creek offers good fishing for anglers who arrive from late spring through mid-summer, or as long as the creek remains suitable for trout. The California Department of Fish and Game stocks 6,283 rainbows, a large number relative to the size of the creek.

A little larger than nearby Nelder Creek, Willow is planted along Soquel Campground. Although large trees shade its campground, most of the stream flows through an open meadow. There are some nice-sized pools, but the best fishing can be had for those drifting Power Bait under fallen logs and salmon eggs behind rocks.

If you plan to make the trip, supplies are available in Oakhurst. Willow Creek is closed to fishing from November 16 to the last weekend in April.

Also nearby are Nelder Creek, the Shadow of the Giants Trail, Fresno Dome, Bass Lake, Lewis Creek, the Merced River, Big Creek, Big Creek Falls, Fish Camp Falls and Yosemite National Park.

*The secret to Nelder Creek is not the fishing, but finding the Nelder Grove located about a mile upstream from where the fish are planted.*

**Rating:** 6
**Species:** Rainbow Trout
**Stock:** 700 pounds of rainbow trout.
**Facilities:** Campgrounds and Vault Toilets
**Contact:** Yosemite/Sierra Visitor Bureau (559) 658-7588, Sierra National Forest (559) 877-2218

**Directions:** From the 99 Freeway in Fresno, drive north on Highway 41 to Oakhurst. Continue north four miles past Oakhurst to Road 632 and turn right. Drive 5.4 miles to Gooseberry Flat on the shore of Nelder Creek.

Nelder Creek

Nelder Creek is a quiet, pretty mountain stream between Yosemite National Park and Oakhurst in the Sierra National Forest. With a 3,100-foot elevation gain from the turnoff on Highway 41, the scenery changes dramatically from Oakhurst to Nelder Creek. The stream has relatively few pools and is shaded by alders and pines. Stocked with 1,485 rainbows from the California Department of Fish and Game, its best fishing can be found at Gooseberry Flat. However, anglers can also walk in and fish at private Redwood Camp, just below Gooseberry.

The secret to Nelder Creek is not found in its fishing, but in the Nelder Grove, located about a mile upstream from where the fish are planted. This small grove of sequoias is only a 15-minute drive from the Mariposa Grove in Yosemite National Park, but the two differ drastically. At Mariposa, there is generally no parking available after 8 a.m. because of the huge crowds that can be a problem. Although the Nelder Grove is much smaller, it is rarely visited. The one-mile loop, Shadow of the Giants Trail, leads you through the grove with signs that teach you how to distinguish the different trees in the forest.

On a Thursday morning in late summer, after finding the parking lot full at Mariposa, I drove to Nelder and found myself the only one there. In fact, I had been the first person to visit the grove that day. I knew that because I kept running into spider webs on the trail.

To get to the grove, drive 1.2 miles past Gooseberry Flat to the Nelder Grove turnoff. Follow the signs to Shadow of the Giants Trail.

If you plan to make the trip, supplies are available in Oakhurst. Nelder Creek is closed to fishing from November 16 to the last weekend in April.

Also nearby are Willow Creek (North Fork), Fresno Dome, Bass Lake, Lewis Creek, Merced River, Big Creek, Big Creek Falls, Fish Camp Falls and Yosemite National Park.

# LEWIS CREEK

**Bring along a few jars of Power Bait and some salmon eggs, and the fish will be begging to bite your hook.**

| | |
|---|---|
| **Rating:** | 5 |
| **Species:** | Rainbow Trout |
| **Stock:** | 2,575 pounds of rainbow trout. |
| **Facilities:** | None |
| **Contact:** | Sierra National Forest (559) 658-7588, Yosemite Mountain Sugar Pine Railroad (559) 683-7273 |
| **Directions:** | From the 99 Freeway, drive north on Highway 41 to Oakhurst. Continue 8.8 miles past Oakhurst to Road 630. Turn east and continue eight-tenths of a mile to the creek. |

*Lewis Creek*

You want to take your kids stream fishing for the first time, however, you don't think they're quite ready for a full day's trip. No problem. Take them fishing at Lewis Creek, and after catching a few stocked trout, head over to Yosemite Sugar Pine Railroad where you can take them on a train ride. They'll love it. The old-fashioned steam train, known as the "Logger," is only a few minutes drive from the stream, and it follows daily runs where locomotives used to haul log trains through the Sierra. Both Lewis Creek and the Logger are only a few miles from Yosemite National Park.

At 4,000 feet in the Sierra National Forest, the creek is heavily planted with half-pound rainbow trout. From late spring through summer, the California Department of Fish and Game dumps 5,350 rainbows downstream from access points beginning at Sugar Pine Village, continuing along a six mile stretch of heavily forested and residential areas. Concentrate your efforts at the Old Mill near Sky Ranch, Corlieu Falls, in Cedar Valley, along the Deer Run Trail and at Yosemite Forks Estates.

Best of all, Lewis Creek is only a 45-minute drive from Fresno, providing a relaxing day trip that can be worked into a quick afternoon fishing adventure for those with less time to spare. Bring along a few jars of Power Bait and some salmon eggs, and the fish will be begging to bite your hook.

If you plan to make the trip, supplies are available in Oakhurst. Lewis Creek is closed to fishing from November 16 to the last Saturday in April.

Also nearby are Big Creek (Fish Camp), Fish Camp Falls, Nelder Creek, North Fork Willow Creek, Bass Lake, Yosemite National Park, Big Creek (Upper), Merced River and the Nelder Grove.

# BIG CREEK (UPPER)

*The plants are made at three main access points: Big Sandy Campground, Little Sandy Campground and Fresno Dome Camp.*

**Rating:** 6
**Species:** Rainbow Trout
**Stock:** 2,825 pounds of rainbow trout.
**Facilities:** Primitive Campsites
**Contact:** Sierra National Forest (559) 658-7588

**Directions:** From the 99 Freeway in Fresno, exit north on Highway 41 and continue to Oakhurst. Continue on Highway 41 through Oakhurst for 14.5 miles to Big Sandy Road. Turn east and drive five miles to Big Sandy Campground. The creek is planted from Big Sandy Campground to Fresno Dome Campground.

*Big Creek (Upper)*

Most people who end up camping in the areas that surround Yosemite National Park do so because the campgrounds in the park are full. They find a campsite outside the park and make day trips in. However, visitors who stay at Big Creek (Upper) want nothing to do with the national park. They come to get away from it all. They happily use the primitive campsites, and experience the good fishing that Big Creek offers after plants.

Nearby Fish Camp, and the entrance to Yosemite, Big Creek is a remote stream that receives heavy plants in spring and early summer. This section of the creek ranges from 5,900 to 6,500 feet in the Sierra National Forest. The plants are made at three main access points: Big Sandy Campground, Little Sandy Campground and Fresno Dome Camp. From late April through July, the California Department of Fish and Game stocks Big Creek with 5,830 rainbows, half of which are planted in this upper section, and the other half in Big Creek at Fish Camp.

Big and Little Sandy are situated in large meadows, with some pine shaded areas and large pools. Just below Little Sandy Campground the stream splashes over some granite slabs of rock providing a great area for kids to play.

Big Creek Falls lies between Little Sandy and Fresno Dome. Resembling a large cascade, the falls is about a half-mile from both camps and can be the subject of some great photos when the stream is flowing fast.

If you plan to make the trip, supplies are available in Fish Camp. Big Creek (Upper) is closed to fishing from November 16 to the last Saturday in April.

Also nearby are Big Creek (Fish Camp), Fish Camp Falls, Nelder Creek, North Fork Willow Creek, Bass Lake, Yosemite National Park, Merced River and the Nelder Grove.

# BIG CREEK (FISH CAMP)

*There are also small wild rainbows in the stream, which provide consistent action when the plants cease.*

| | |
|---|---|
| **Rating:** | 6 |
| **Species:** | Rainbow Trout |
| **Stock:** | 2,825 rainbow trout. |
| **Facilities:** | Restrooms and Campgrounds |
| **Contact:** | Sierra National Forest (559) 658-7588 |

**Directions:** From the 99 Freeway in Fresno, drive north on Highway 41 to Oakhurst. Continue east through the city for 15 miles to Fish Camp. Drive another seven-tenths of a mile to Summerdale Campground and stream.

*Big Creek (Fish Camp)*

Most people camp at Big Creek because they couldn't get reservations to stay in Yosemite National Park. They setup camp here and make day trips into Yosemite. Outside of those campgrounds in Yosemite National Park, Big Creek is one of the closest around, and during the summer it is usually full. Few of the creek's visitors come for the fishing, but it can be good in the early summer.

Big Creek empties into the Merced River in Yosemite National Park. Located 4,900 feet up in the Sierra National Forest, the creek is stocked where it calmly meanders through a small meadow in Summerdale Campground. Its pools are long and shallow, and in spring and summer are often surrounded by tall grasses. Generally from late April through July, the California Department of Fish and Game splits its plants of more than 5,830 rainbows between this location and Upper Big Creek.

Casting small Phoebes and Roostertails are your best bets, however, Power Bait takes its share of fish, too. There are also small wild rainbows in the stream, which provide consistent action when the plants cease. About a 45-minute drive from Fresno, the creek is also a good spot for day-users, because most of its campers are off visiting the national park.

If you plan to make the trip, supplies are available in Fish Camp. Big Creek is closed to fishing from November 16 to the last Saturday in April. Although it looks enticing, the pond in Fish Camp is closed to fishing.

Also nearby are Fish Camp Falls, Upper Big Creek, the Merced River, Yosemite National Park, Nelder Creek and the North Fork of Willow Creek.

# MANZANITA LAKE (NORTH FORK)

*Some anglers choose to fish here in a raft or float tube, but the lake is so small it's not really necessary.*

| | |
|---|---|
| **Rating:** | 5 |
| **Species:** | Rainbow Trout |
| **Stock:** | 5,425 pounds of rainbow trout. |
| **Facilities:** | Restrooms and Picnic Areas |
| **Contact:** | Sierra National Forest (559) 877-2218, North Fork Chamber of Commerce (559) 877-2410 |

**Directions:** From the 99 Freeway in Fresno, exit Highway 41 north and drive 28 miles to Road 200 (signed for North Fork). Turn east and continue 19 miles to North Fork. In North Fork, turn north on Road 222 and drive approximately 1.6 miles to lake on your right.

Manzanita Lake

North Fork is a town that promotes itself as being at the exact center of California. Although the town is darn close to the exact center, in reality, the center of California is a few miles away near Redinger Lake. North Fork used to be a logging town, but now provides the last stop for food and supplies to those heading to popular camping destinations in the Sierra National Forest, such as Mammoth Pool Reservoir, Chiquito Creek and Granite Creek.

North Fork locals like to hang out at this 26-acre day-use lake, and escape all the campers and anglers picking up last-minute supplies and chowing down on their final hot meal. Because it's only 1.6 miles from downtown, kids often walk to Manzanita for a day of fishing and swimming. The lake is so shallow that it usually warms enough by mid-June to make swimming comfortable.

From April through November, the lake is stocked with 10,420 rainbow trout, keeping fishing good year-round. Some anglers choose to fish here in a raft or float tube, but the lake is so small it's not really necessary. Shore anglers do just as well tossing lures or dunking Power Bait.

Vacationers driving from the Fresno area often use Manzanita Lake as a rest stop on their way to places higher in the Sierra. They stop, have lunch, make a few casts, catch a few fish and start driving again. It's a lot more fun than just driving straight through.

If you plan to make the trip, supplies are available in North Fork.

Also nearby are Corrine Lake, Bass Lake, Fish Creek, Rock Creek, Rock Creek Falls, Redinger Lake and Kerckoff Reservoir.

# CORRINE LAKE

*With all the anglers who fish towards the end of the week, Power Bait fishing is the only way to go.*

**Rating:** 5
**Species:** Rainbow Trout
**Stock:** 3,125 pounds of rainbow trout.
**Facilities:** Vault Toilets
**Contact:** Sierra National Forest (559) 877-2218

**Directions:** From the 99 Freeway in Fresno, turn north on Highway 41 and continue 28 miles to Road 200 (signed for North Fork). Turn east and continue 16.5 miles to Road 222 (Auberry Road). Turn south and drive approximately 2.4 miles to the unsigned Corrine Lake Road 235 on your left. Turn east onto the dirt road (you'll know it's the correct turnoff because there will be a flume) and continue three miles to the lake.

*Corrine Lake*

Corrine Lake is a local's hangout. I showed up on a Wednesday to fish and there wasn't a soul in sight. I didn't get a bite that day and for a good reason. I showed up the next day to try my luck again and was shocked. It was wall-to-wall anglers.

I walked over to a guy on the shoreline and asked him why all these people where here today when there wasn't anyone yesterday. "You didn't come yesterday, did you?" he chuckled. "There were no fish here yesterday. We caught them all at the end of last week. The truck is coming today." He went on to say that the truck comes every Thursday and sometimes on Fridays. He and most of the other anglers were locals who knew the stocking schedule.

Sure enough, about an hour later the California Department of Fish and Game truck showed up, and the locals cheered as the catching began. Within a few hours, many of the anglers had caught limits. With all the anglers who fish towards the end of the week, Power Bait fishing is the only way to go. If you try tossing spinners, chances are you'll get tangled in others' lines.

Corrine Lake is a small, seven-acre pond near North Fork on a plateau overlooking the San Joaquin River drainage and Kerckoff Reservoir. It gets hot and dry in the summer and there's no shade whatsoever. The shoreline is covered in dry brush and dead grass, but offers good fishing after a stock.

The CA DFG plants 6,230 rainbows from spring through fall. Despite being susceptible to heat and dry conditions, the water usually remains cool enough to plant trout. The key is whether water is being fed to the lake via a flume from Bass Lake and Manzanita Lake. If the flume is transferring water, the lake will stay cool. If they shut it off, the lake will get too warm for the trout. The best area to fish is at the inlet near the Powerhouse.

If you plan to make the trip, supplies are available in North Fork. No boats or float tubes are permitted.

Also nearby are Redinger Lake, Bass Lake, Manzanita Lake and Kerckoff Reservoir.

**Kerckoff isn't known for its great fishing, but it does produce fish for the few regulars who have learned how to fish it.**

| | |
|---|---|
| **Rating:** | 4 |
| **Species:** | Striped Bass, Rainbow Trout, Largemouth Bass, Channel Catfish, Crappie and Bluegill |
| **Stock:** | None |
| **Facilities:** | Vault Toilets, Campgrounds and Picnic Areas |
| **Contact:** | Sierra National Forest (559) 877-2218 |
| | Pacific Gas & Electric Company (800) 743-5000 |
| **Directions:** | From the 99 Freeway in Fresno, turn north on the 41 Freeway and continue 28 miles to Road 200 (signed for North Fork). Turn east and continue 16.5 miles to Road 222 (Auberry Road). Turn south and drive approximately six miles to the lake. |

*Kerckoff Reservoir*

Jet-skiers finally have a place they can call their own, without being bothered by wake boarders and water-skiers or being restricted to a limited recreational area. Kerckoff Reservoir not only allows unlimited jet-skiing, it prohibits all other types of motorized boats. As for the fishermen, they aren't really bothered by the jet-skiers, because they don't even wake up until after the anglers have left.

Located in the San Joaquin River/Bass Lake Recreation Area, just above Millerton Lake and below Redinger Lake, Kerckoff reservoir is a wide, slow moving portion of the San Joaquin River. Along with Redinger Lake, Kerckoff is one of two hydroelectric facilities nearby. Run by Pacific Gas & Electric Company, it is also fed by water from Willow Creek (via Bass Lake).

Kerckoff isn't known for its great fishing, but it does produce fish for the few regulars who have learned how to fish it. The most successful anglers fish the upper end of the lake, just above the bridge, where the river enters the lake.

Although no trout plants occur, there are some wild trout here. Fly-fishermen do best, but those casting lures in the slower moving water catch their share of fish, too. At times striper fishing is also fair. Locals say the stripers swim out of Millerton into Kerckoff, and can be caught by trolling large spoons or still-fishing anchovies from a boat.

Kerckoff hasn't been planted since 1966 when threadfin shad were introduced. Rainbow trout were planted in '50, '51 and '58, largemouth bass in '54 and bluegill in '54.

The lake is also popular for sailboats and canoes. For overnight travelers, Smalley Cove Campground is an option. Keep in mind that it can get hot and dry in the summer here.

If you plan to make the trip, supplies are available in North Fork.

Also nearby are Redinger Lake, Corrine Lake, Manzanita Lake and Millerton Lake.

# REDINGER LAKE

**Redinger Lake is situated in a dry foothill area, has steep banks, and its most abundant fish is... the prized squawfish!**

| | |
|---|---|
| **Rating:** | 3 |
| **Species:** | Rainbow Trout, Brown Trout and Sucker Fish |
| **Stock:** | None |
| **Facilities:** | Picnic Areas, Vault Toilets and Boat Launch |
| **Contact:** | Sierra National Forest (559) 877-2218 |

**Directions:** From the 99 Freeway in Fresno, turn north on Highway 41 and drive 28 miles to Road 200 (signed for North Fork). Turn east and drive 19 miles to North Fork. Turn east, continuing through the town of South Fork, and drive four miles to Italian Bar Road. Turn right and drive 3.8 miles to Redinger Lake Road (Road 235). Turn right and drive 2.1 miles to the launch ramp.

*Redinger Lake*

The most exciting thing about Redinger Lake is that it is almost at the exact geological center of California... not the fishing. Boating is the most popular activity. The lake receives no plants, and the only way for fish to get into it is by swimming down the San Joaquin River. Consequently, most anglers don't catch many fish here.

At a bit more than 1,000 feet in the Sierra National Forrest, near the town of North Fork, 5.5-mile-long Redinger Lake was created in a narrow canyon by a dam that was built in 1950. The most interesting thing we encountered at the lake was a sign at the boat launch, warning visitors to stay away from the buoy area when a siren sounds because the dam gates are about to open. The buoy area is within swimming distance of the boat launch where we were fishing. I was with two kids who were swimming in the lake, and as soon as I saw the sign I pulled them out of the water. I had this vision of the gates opening and the kids getting swept over the dam.

Redinger Lake is situated in a dry foothill area, has steep banks, and its most abundant fish is... the prized squawfish! Not what you wanted to hear? That's what I figured. We tossed small spinners and silver Kastmasters and caught tons of 'em off the boat ramp, some over five pounds.

There are also a few trout in the lake, but they're hard to come by. Your best bet is trolling the shorelines near the lake's inlet. As for shoreline trout fishing, forget about it. Chances are slim you're going to catch anything. In addition to the lack of fish, access is the pits and much of the shoreline is too steep.

There are many other fishing holes nearby. Don't waste your time here. Leave it to the boaters. They deserve a spot where they don't have to deal with anglers.

If you plan to make the trip, supplies are available in North Fork.

Also nearby are Corrine Lake, Bass Lake, Kerckoff Reservoir and Manzanita Lake.

*It's also a great place to teach kids the basics of fishing. The trout are easy to spot darting up and down the shoreline, so you'll be able to point out the fish that they are trying to catch.*

| | |
|---|---|
| **Rating:** | 5 |
| **Species:** | Rainbow Trout |
| **Stock:** | 950 pounds of rainbow trout. |
| **Facilities:** | Picnic Areas, Restrooms and Campgrounds |
| **Contact:** | Sierra National Forest (559) 877-2218 |

**Directions:**    From the 99 Freeway in Fresno, turn north on Highway 41 and continue 28 miles to Road 200 (signed for North Fork). Turn east and drive 19 miles through the town of North Fork. Continue east, heading through the town of South Fork, and drive 19 miles to Fish Creek.

Fish Creek

Heavily shaded Fish Creek is the ideal location to bring the family to spend a few hours in the forest. It's also a great place to teach kids the basics of fishing. The trout are easy to spot darting up and down the shoreline, so you'll be able to point out the fish that they are trying to catch. And since the area doesn't attract hardcore fishermen, it won't be a big deal if your kids end up spooking the fish.

Set at 4,500 feet in the Sierra National Forest, between Mammoth Pool Reservoir and Redinger Lake, Fish Creek is a tiny stream about an hour drive from Fresno. Fish (2,110 of 'em) are planted in the spring and early summer, from the bridge, downstream for about 200 yards. There are no pools large enough for lures, so plan on using salmon eggs and Power Bait. The half-pound rainbows aren't picky; they'll hit just about any color. I brought two 11-year-olds, Dan Sulitzer and Nick Haraden, on their first fishing trip, and they both caught fish. All in all, it's ideal for a first fishing experience.

If you plan to make the trip, supplies are available in North Fork. Fish Creek is closed to fishing from November 16 to the last Saturday in April. The road to Fish Creek closes in winter, so call ahead for updated conditions.

Also nearby are Whiskey Falls, Rock Creek, Rock Creek Falls, Mile High Vista, Mammoth Pool Reservoir, Chiquito Creek Falls, Chiquito Creek, West Fork Chiquito Creek, West Fork Chiquito Creek Slides, Redinger Lake and the San Joaquin River.

# ROCK CREEK

*After taking a dip, grab your pole and head downstream. The pools are loaded with trout, and you'll be so busy filling your stringer, before you know it you'll end up at Rock Creek Campground.*

| | |
|---|---|
| **Rating:** | 7 |
| **Species:** | Rainbow Trout |
| **Stock:** | 1,400 pounds of rainbow trout. |
| **Facilities:** | Restrooms and Campgrounds |
| **Contact:** | Sierra National Forest (559) 877-2218 |

**Directions:** From the 99 Freeway in Fresno, turn north on Highway 41 and drive 28 miles to Road 200 (signed for North Fork). Turn east and drive 19 miles through North Fork. Continue east through the town of South Fork, and drive 23 miles to Rock Creek Campground.

Rock Creek

So, you like to have a little fun while you fish. Maybe do a little swimming, butt-sliding and cliff-jumping in between casts? Not a problem. I have a perfect spot for you. Rock Creek, located at 4,200 feet on the western slopes of the Sierra Nevada Mountains in the Sierra National Forest, is your ideal place.

Here's how it works: park about a half-mile past Rock Creek Campground on a dirt pullout on the right side of the road and walk down to the stream. There are pools here stocked by the California Department of Fish and Game. So, make a few casts, catch a few trout and get ready for some fun.

Downstream, you'll see a large slab of granite with water running over it. Although you won't be able to see them all from this point, there are six cascades from here to the next good fishing pool downstream. Slide down the first four cascades into the pools below. Before reaching the last two cascades, get out of the pool and cross the stream, staying on the left side. You can't go any farther on the right side because of a 15-foot free-fall. (That's why you won't slide down those final cascades. You don't want to get swept over the falls.)

Use caution while walking over the granite rocks; they are extremely slippery. Working your way downstream, just after the freefall you'll come to an inviting swimming pool. The easiest way down to it is to jump off the rocks into the pool. The rocks range from five to 10 feet above the water, and the pool is about eight feet at its deepest, so it's safer to use the smaller rocks to jump off.

Once you've gotten that far (it's about one-eighth of a mile, but you'll be having so much fun it will feel like you came a lot farther), you might as well do a little swimming. After taking a dip, grab your pole and head downstream. The pools are loaded with trout, and you'll be so busy filling your stringer, before you know it you'll end up at Rock Creek Campground. Then, all you'll need to do is walk back up the road to your car. If you ask me,

Nick Harnden (Left) and Dan Sulitzer (Right) enjoy an afternoon at Rock Creek Falls.

this sounds like an ideal day.

For those not inclined to a little adventure, concentrate your efforts in the camp ground. The pools are easily accessible (they're close to your tent if you're camping), and no hiking is required. From the dirt pullout, down though Rock Creek Campground, 2,900 rainbows are planted from May through July, or as long as water levels remain suitable for fish. Most of the pools in the campgrounds are long, shallow and slow moving, making it easy for you to cast small Panther Martins and Roostertails. For those looking to catch wild rainbows, the upper stretch of the creek provides action on smaller fish. Access is available off the road to Whiskey Falls.

Don't confuse this creek with Rock Creek in the Eastern Sierra. This creek is much smaller, less than half the elevation and doesn't receive large crowds.

If you plan to make the trip, supplies are available in North Fork. Rock Creek is closed to fishing from November 16 to the last Saturday in April. The road to Rock Creek closes in winter, so call ahead for updated conditions.

Also nearby are Bass Lake, Whiskey Falls, Fish Creek, Mile High Vista, Mammoth Pool Reservoir, Chiquito Creek Falls, Chiquito Creek, West Fork Chiquito Creek, West Fork Chiquito Creek Slides, Redinger Lake and San Joaquin River.

Phil Freed slides down Rock Creek Falls.

ROCK CREEK

*All methods work, including fly-fishing, tossing spinners and using night crawlers or Power Bait.*

| | |
|---|---|
| **Rating:** | 6 |
| **Species:** | Rainbow Trout |
| **Stock:** | 500 pounds of rainbow trout. |
| **Facilities:** | Primitive and Developed Campsites and Restrooms |
| **Contact:** | Sierra National Forest (559) 877-2218 |

**Directions:** From the 99 Freeway in Fresno, turn north on Highway 41 and drive 28 miles to Road 200 (signed for North Fork). Turn east on Road 200 and continue 19 miles to North Fork. Continue on Road 200 through the town of South Fork and drive 36 miles to Soda Springs Campground.

*Stephen Wiessner butt-slides down West Fork Chiquito Creek Slides.*

With an easily accessible stream, plenty of recreational opportunities and small crowds (except for holiday weekends), the West Fork of Chiquito Creek is a camper's paradise. Located at 4,500 feet in the Sierra National Forest, about 10 minutes from Mammoth Pool Reservoir, the West Fork of Chiquito Creek has it all. There's rafting, swimming, hiking, fishing, butt-sliding and plenty of space to relax. Yet, most tourists head to the more popular Chiquito Creek, ignoring this section of the stream.

Similar to Chiquito Creek, the West Fork is a wide stream. It is stocked with 1,055 rainbow trout (5,395 less than Chiquito). Most campers choose to spend an entire week here, using the creek as a base to make day trips to nearby destinations, such as Mammoth Pool Reservoir, Rock Creek and Granite Creek.

The campers I talked to said that they catch so many fish here, they are able to wait until their last day to stock up with fish to take home. Because of all the fishing that occurs in the Sierra Nevada, it's difficult to find other streams in this mountain range where anglers can catch so many fish. Elsewhere, planted fish are generally yanked out of creeks within a few days after a stock. What surprised me the most is that the anglers who fish here aren't the typically overconfident hard-core fishermen. They are just normal campers who use Snoopy style poles and fish only a few times a year.

With long, shallow pools, grassy shorelines and mostly slow-moving waters, the creek is easy to fish. This is the same stretch where rafters relax on a tube or raft and read a book. If you come here to fish, your options are wide-open. All methods work, including fly-fishing, tossing spinners and using night crawlers or Power Bait.

The West Fork's most prized possession is unknown to most of its campers. The West Fork Chiquito Creek Slides is one of the finest places I've ever visited when it comes to swimming holes. It's like a mini water park with no crowds or admission charges.

West Fork Chiquito Creek

To reach the slides, you can either walk upstream under the highway for about a quarter-mile to the granite rock area, or you can drive. If driving, make a left turn out of Soda Springs Campground and drive to where the West Fork crosses under the road. Immediately after crossing the stream, veer right on an unsigned dirt road and continue about 100 yards until the road ends. Now, follow the trail for 100 yards to the small cascades on the creek. This area is composed of about a dozen swimming holes and small cascades, perfect for swimming and wading.

My favorite spot is an area called Six Craters, just above the two cascades. There are six different craters, all deep enough to wade in. The cool thing is that water rushes down the rocks above (forming the slide) and tumbles into the craters while you are in them. Although they are small, some of the swimming holes are as deep as 10 feet, and, best of all, the water is warm enough that you don't have to jump out as soon as you get it in.

The best time to visit the slides is from May through late July. If you come any later, there might not be enough water for you to enjoy them. Now, be smart and don't tell anybody about this place, because we don't want to turn it into a real amusement park.

If you plan to make the trip, supplies are available in North Fork. West Fork Chiquito Creek is closed to fishing from November 16 to the last Saturday in April. The road to the West Fork of Chiquito Creek closes in winter, so call ahead for updated conditions.

Also nearby are Bass Lake, Whiskey Falls, Rock Creek, Rock Creek Falls, Mile High Vista, Mammoth Pool Reservoir, Chiquito Creek Falls, Chiquito Creek, Fish Creek, Redinger Lake and San Joaquin River

Six Craters along West Fork Chiquito
Creek Slides

CHIQUITO CREEK (WEST)

# CHIQUITO CREEK

*It's a great family destination and, better yet, a must-do spot for weeklong camping trips.*

| | |
|---|---|
| **Rating:** | 8 |
| **Species:** | Rainbow Trout and Brown Trout |
| **Stock:** | 3,100 pounds of rainbow trout. |
| **Facilities:** | Campgrounds and Vault Toilets |
| **Contact:** | Sierra National Forest (559) 877-2218, Campground Reservations (877) 444-6777 |

**Directions:**     From the 99 Freeway in Fresno, turn north on Highway 41 and continue 28 miles to Road 200 (signed for North Fork). Turn east and continue 19 miles to North Fork. Drive past North Fork, through the town of South Fork and continue 40 miles to Road 6S25. Turn south to the campgrounds along the creek.

*Excitement of the Fish and Game stocking truck*

*Dan Sulitzer with his first trout.*

The votes are in, and Chiquito Creek has earned the prize for offering the best drive to stream trout fishing north of the San Joaquin River and south of the Merced River. Located at 4,500 feet in the Sierra National Forest (about an hour-and-45-minute drive from Fresno), Chiquito Creek is much more than just a good place to fish. It's a great family destination and, better yet, a must-do spot for weeklong camping trips.

There is so much to do at the creek and in the surrounding area, you may need more than a week to get it all done. You can bring along a boat and water-ski at Mammoth Pool Reservoir, make day-trips to Jackass Falls and Whiskey Falls, visit the waterslide fun areas at Rock Creek and the West Fork Chiquito Creek Slides, or head up to the high-county at Granite Creek, just to name a few options. At the creek itself, there's swimming, tubing, canoeing, kayaking and rafting. You can't get bored at Chiquito Creek.

Surprisingly, many people don't know about this wonderful place. The creek is stocked with 6,445 rainbow trout scattered among Placer, Sweetwater and Wagner Campgrounds, but there is so much to do it's hard to spend a lot of time fishing. You don't need to spend that much time either, because the fishing remains good for anglers tossing lures throughout the campgrounds.

However, the real highlight is the browns. Many browns are pulled out of the river in June and October, some weighing up to seven pounds. Few anglers know about these browns, but those who find the deepest holes and fish in the late evenings have a good chance at catching one.

If you plan to use Chiquito Creek as a recreational spot, the creek is wide enough and deep enough for canoeing, kayaking and rafting. The best stretch is in Wagner Campground. Just above the camp is a bridge that many campers use as a starting point. My favorite thing to start at the bridge, grab my tube and float down to the end of the campground. Another fun thing to do is start at the bridge and snorkel down to the end of

*Chiquito Creek downstream of Wagner Campground*

the campground. You'll see all sorts of fish you had no idea were in the creek.

There are also a lot of garter snakes hanging out on the bank and swimming in the creek, so try not to get spooked. Bears also stroll through the campgrounds in late summer. They need camper's food to beef up for the winter.

If you plan to make the trip, supplies and gas are available at Wagner's General Store across from Wagner Campground. The road to Mammoth Pool Reservoir closes in winter, so call ahead for updated conditions. Chiquito Creek is closed to fishing from November 16 to the last Saturday in April.

Also nearby are Mammoth Pool Reservoir, West Fork of Chiquito Creek, Chiquito Creek Falls, West Fork Chiquito Creek Slides, Jackass Falls, Granite Creek and Mile High Vista.

*Chiquito Creek being stocked by the CA DFG.*

CHIQUITO CREEK

# MAMMOTH POOL RESERVOIR

*The reservoir is one of a few in the region that allows boat-in camping (at China Bar), and boaters in search of browns sometimes troll the San Joaquin Arm with Rapalas and small Mystics.*

| | |
|---|---|
| **Rating:** | 7 |
| **Species:** | Rainbow Trout and Brown Trout |
| **Stock:** | 5,650 pounds of rainbow trout. |
| **Facilities:** | Campgrounds and Restrooms |
| **Contact:** | Contact: Sierra National Forest (559) 877-2218 |
| **Directions:** | From the 99 Freeway in Fresno, turn north on Highway 41 and drive 28 miles to Road 200 (signed for North Fork). Turn east and drive 19 miles to North Fork. Turn east, heading through the town of South Fork, and continue 40 miles to Road 6S25. Turn south and drive five miles to the reservoir. |

**Mammoth Pool Reservoir from Mile High Vista**

Most lakes and streams are closed to fishing certain times of the year to protect fish populations and spawns. Mammoth Pool Reservoir is a bit different. The reservoir and all of its tributaries close from May 1 through June 15 to protect deer migration, allowing deer to swim across the lake without any distractions from humans.

Mammoth Pool Reservoir is about a two-hour drive from Fresno. Because it is part of the San Joaquin River Hydroelectric Project, it experiences extreme drawdowns that begin in June, and by November, the 1,107-acre reservoir can shrink from 120,000 acre-feet to just 30,000, or nearly one-fourth its total capacity. Sounds brutal? Well, it hurts fishing so badly that many anglers have written the lake off.

The best fishing can be had as soon as the road is free of snow, usually in late April, to the lake's closure in May, and again after the lake reopens until early July. Because it has steep shorelines, there are only a few places shoreline anglers can fish. One option is to drive across the dam and fish off the rocks with night crawlers or Power Bait. Another is to fish near the boat launch. But what I've found to be best is fishing the Chiquito Creek inlet. (The trail to the inlet can be picked up from Mammoth Pool Campground at Site #18.) With all the volume the creek brings into the lake, the fish school up and wait for food to be carried to them.

Fed by the San Joaquin River, Granite Creek, Chiquito Creek, Jackass Creek and water that is diverted via pipelines from Edison Lake, this large reservoir doesn't take long to fill in the spring. And this is the best time to target the lake's browns. The reservoir is one of a few in the region that allows boat-in camping (at China Bar), and boaters in search of browns sometimes troll the San Joaquin Arm with Rapalas and small Mystics. There are surprisingly a lot of browns in the lake, but since not many anglers are aware of them, they aren't heavily targeted.

As for the rainbows, many of them are dinkers. The California Department of Fish and Game plants 24,275 quarter-pounders. There are a sufficient number of holdovers to target. However, because the lake begins to draw down so fast after July, many anglers don't bother fishing for them. Also, that's when the water-skiers begin to attack the lake, driving many anglers away. In the early Seventies coho salmon were introduced with brook trout stocked in the late Seventies and early Eighties.

If you plan to make the trip, supplies and gas are available about a mile from the lake at Wagner's General Store. The road to Mammoth Pool Reservoir closes in winter, so call ahead for updated conditions. Mammoth Pool Reservoir is closed to all traffic (boating, fishing, hiking) from May 1 through June 15.

Also nearby are Chiquito Creek, the West Fork of Chiquito Creek, Chiquito Creek Falls, West Fork Chiquito Creek Slides, Jackass Creek Falls, Granite Creek and Mile High Vista.

*The Chiquito Creek inlet of Mammoth Pool Reservoir*

WOOLOMES LAKE

# GRANITE CREEK

**The drive is at least two hours to the creek from Fresno, and if you're just coming to fish, it might not be worth it.**

| | |
|---|---|
| **Rating:** | 6 |
| **Species:** | Rainbow Trout and Brown Trout |
| **Stock:** | 650 pounds of rainbow trout. |
| **Facilities:** | Campgrounds and Restrooms |
| **Contact:** | Sierra National Forest (559) 877-2218 |

**Directions:** From the 99 Freeway in Fresno, turn north on Highway 41 and drive 28 miles to Road 200 (signed for North Fork). Turn east and continue 19 miles to North Fork. From North Fork continue east heading through the town of South Fork, and drive 40 miles to the junction with Road 6S25. Bear left and drive 10 miles to a sign for Granite Creek. Turn right and continue six miles to the campground.

*Granite Creek*

Granite Creek is the most remote, stocked, drive-to stream east of the Fresno area in the Sierra Nevada Mountain Range. The drive is at least two hours to the creek from Fresno, and if you're just coming to fish, it might not be worth it. Although the creek has a good population of small wild brook, brown and rainbow trout, the California Department of Fish and Game only stocks it with 1,230 rainbows.

Due to high water levels, Granite Creek ironically offers its poorest fishing in the spring when it is planted the heaviest. Most of the fish are planted in the campgrounds. The upper campground is mainly for campers with horses, while car campers use the lower campground. Because of the abundance of mosquitoes in June and early July, many campers wait till mid-summer to come here.

At 7,200 feet near Clover Meadow in the Sierra National Forest, Granite Creek borders the Ansel Adams Wilderness and empties into Mammoth Pool Reservoir. Nearly as wide as Chiquito Creek, it isn't far from Devils Postpile National Monument, however, there are no roads from Granite Creek to lead you to the Postpile, just hiking trails. There is great fishing for wild browns and rainbows from the campgrounds downstream to Mammoth Pool Reservoir. However, the creek meanders though steep and hard to reach granite country, and can only be accessed by those with four-wheel drive vehicles.

If you plan to make the trip, supplies are available in North Fork and at Wagner General Store near Mammoth Pool Reservoir. Granite Creek is closed to fishing from November 16 to the last Saturday in April. The road to Granite Creek is closed from mid-November until May. Call ahead for updated road conditions.

Also nearby are Mammoth Pool Reservoir, Chiquito Creek, the West Fork of Chiquito Creek, Jackass Creek Falls, West Fork Chiquito Creek Slides, Chiquito Creek Falls, Rock Creek, Rock Creek Falls and Fish Creek.

**REGION 6**

## SIERRA NATIONAL FOREST
### (NORTH)

1 Edison Lake
2 Mono Creek
3 Florence Lake
4 San Joaquin River (JM)
5 Ward Lake
6 San Joaquin River (MHS)
7 Portal Forebay
8 College Lake
9 George Lake
10 Twin Lakes (KW)
11 Rancheria Creek
12 Big Creek (H)
13 Tamarack Creek
14 Huntington Lake
15 Shaver Lake
16 Dinkey Creek
17 Courtright Reservoir
18 Wishon Reservoir

# EDISON LAKE

**Back in 1974, the largest brown ever recorded in California was found in Edison.**

| | |
|---|---|
| **Rating:** | 9 |
| **Species:** | Brook Trout, Brown Trout, Rainbow Trout and Golden Trout |
| **Stock:** | 750 pounds of fingerling rainbow trout. |
| **Facilities:** | Campgrounds, Pack Station, General Store, Boat Rentals, Bait & Tackle, Ferry Service, Lodging, Swimming Beach, Restaurant and Boat Launch |
| **Contact:** | Vermilion Resort (559) 259-4000 (Summer) or (559) 855-6558 (Winter), Sierra National Forest (559) 297-0706 or (559) 855-5360, High Sierra Ranger Station (559) 877-7173 (Summer Only), High Sierra Pack Station (559) 285-7225 |
| **Directions:** | From the 99 Freeway in Fresno, drive 72 miles east on Highway 168 to the east end of Huntington Lake. Turn east on Kaiser Pass Road and continue approximately 5.5 miles. After the road becomes one lane, follow it for another 19 miles to Vermilion Resort, staying left at the fork in the road. (The right fork leads to Florence Lake.) |

*The Mono Creek inlet of Edison Lake*

There's only one way to Edison Lake by car - Kaiser Pass Road - and it's one of the most dangerous and frightening paved roads I've ever driven. Only wide enough for one vehicle in most spots, all it would take is one careless driver to cause a major accident. This 19-mile long, winding one lane road, with blind spots and a 10 mph speed limit, is the only obstacle that keeps Edison Lake from being one of the top brown trout fisheries in the country. So many anglers are afraid to drive this road, they pass up fishing Edison Lake. Big mistake, because Edison Lake is one of the best and most consistent fisheries in California.

Aside from the fear of getting hit head-on while traveling up Kaiser Pass Road, many experienced trout anglers say that they shy away from visiting because they have difficulty towing boats up to the lake. I towed a 19-foot boat and it took me more than two-and-a-half hours to safely maneuver it over that 19-mile stretch. The only way to drive safely was to stay under 10 mph and honk my horn at all the blind spots.

Back in 1974, the largest brown ever recorded in California was found in Edison. This trout was hooked a day earlier than it was recorded, and after an exhausting battle, snapped the angler's line. However, the fish was injured by the lure, which got stuck in its gill, and the following day a group of anglers found it struggling to stay alive. When they scooped it up, the fish weighed in at 27.5 pounds, almost a pound bigger than the state record 26.8-pounder that was caught at Upper Twin Lake in 1987.

And that brown wasn't a fluke. Each year at least three browns over 15 pounds are recorded and many more are hooked and lost. When my friend Blake Lezak and I fished the lake in late August of 2000, we hooked into a brown that we estimated to be about 15 pounds. The fish dragged us around the lake for 45 minutes and spit out the hook about 20 yards from our boat. If I had a chance to fight the fish again, there is nothing I would have done differently. Large browns are simply difficult to land.

Blake Lezak with a brown trout caught at Edison.

There are two times each year to hook up on the browns. About a week after ice-out (usually late-April) is the first opportunity. The second occurs from September through November when they are cruising the shorelines looking for a meal to beef up for winter.

To fish the lake in April, you'd better have plenty of extra cash floating around, because it will cost you about the same as it would to fly a four person family to Hawaii. The only easy way in is by helicopter. The Vermilion Resort sponsors two four-day copter trips for anglers specifically targeting the browns. Lodging and food are provided, however, there is a $1,500 fee and it's limited to just nine anglers. If you don't have the money for a copter trip, the only other ways to the lake are by snowmobile or cross-country skiing. However, the snowmobile trail isn't maintained all the way to the lake.

After slowing from June through mid-August, brown trout fishing picks up again as early as late August. Trolling from the dam to the Mono Creek inlet, the bite on browns can be excellent if you stay 50 to 100 yards off the south shoreline. The best bite is in the early morning from about 30 minutes before sunrise to 9 a.m., and then again from 6 p.m. to 30 minutes after dark. Use large Rapalas and rainbow-patterned YO-Zuris.

In addition to the world-class brown trout fishery, the lake offers excellent fishing for rainbow trout. The California Department of Fish and Game plants 75,000 fingerling rainbow trout each summer in this put-and-grow fishery. In 1999, the lake was given an additional 25,000 fingerlings originally allotted for Florence Lake, but they were transferred to Edison because of low water levels at Florence. Now 100,000 are planted each year.

In recent years, the CA DFG and Vermilion Resort have worked together to try to improve the fishery. They closed the lake's three inlets during the spawning period to enable the fish to spawn successfully.

Rainbows grow fast here, feeding on smaller rainbows and browns. The lake record is a 12-pounder, but that's a rarity. You're lucky if you catch one over three pounds, but there are many from one to two pounds and they are fighters.

Catching fish with a boat can be easy, because you can reach areas with steep banks that are otherwise difficult to reach. The surest way to catch a limit is by trolling a night crawler behind a set of flashers, but trolling just about any lure will catch fish. As summer approaches, boat anglers need leadcore line or downriggers to fish the lake, because the fish move to deeper water.

In the spring and early summer, anglers take the water taxi to the Mono Creek inlet to capitalize on fish looking for food that flows into the lake. They catch good numbers, tossing spinners and fishing with night crawlers. Topwater trolling Mystic lures, green Cripplelures and green Repel frogs are also productive.

Shore anglers can also get in on the fun by tossing Power Bait or night-crawlers off the dam, near the boat launch area and off the lake's points.

Surprisingly, there are small goldens in the creek next to the resort, and a few have found their way into the lake. There are also brooks in the lake, but chances of catching either are slim.

Blake Lezak with a brown trout caught at Edison.

EDISON LAKE

Edison Lake is a popular starting point for those heading into the John Muir and Ansel Adams Wilderness. Each morning and evening, a ferry service hauls (for a small fee) hikers and backpackers across the lake to the trailhead. The most popular destinations are Red's Meadow and Yosemite Valley, however, Duck and Virginia Lakes, the Minnow Creek Drainage and Silver Pass Lake also receive their share of visitors.

Set at 7,700 feet in the Sierra National Forest, Edison is the second largest lake in the chain of lakes east of Fresno that are reached via Highway 168. Only Shaver Lake is bigger. Edison releases water into Mono Creek and the Portal Forebay, before emptying into Rancheria Creek and Huntington Lake. Some of its water is also diverted to Mammoth Pool Reservoir.

Not only is the fishing good here, but crime is nearly non-existent because of the lake's remoteness and the lack of crowds. The late Butch Wiggs, who owned Vermilion Resort told me the only thefts that occur are by the bears that sneak into campsites at night and take campers' food.

If you plan to make the trip, supplies are available at the lake. Kaiser Pass Road is closed from the first snowfall (usually in November) to Memorial Weekend (or when snow in the road can be cleared away). During long winters the road may not open until early July. Call ahead for updated conditions. Trailers are not recommended.

Also nearby are Mono Creek, the John Muir Wilderness, Florence Lake, Ward Lake, Portal Forebay, South Fork San Joaquin River at Jackass Meadow and Mono Hot Springs, Mono Hot Springs, Rancheria Creek and Huntington Lake.

*Smart fishermen concentrate their efforts closer to the dam where the water has slowed.*

| | |
|---|---|
| **Rating:** | 7 |
| **Species:** | Rainbow Trout and Brown Trout |
| **Stock:** | 1,750 rainbow trout. |
| **Facilities:** | Campgrounds, Picnic Areas and Vault Toilets |
| **Contact:** | Sierra National Forest (559) 297-0706 or (559) 855-5360 |
| | High Sierra Ranger Station (559) 877-7173 (Summer Only) |

**Directions:** From the 99 Freeway in Fresno, drive 72 miles east on Highway 168 to the east end of Huntington Lake. Turn east on Kaiser Pass Road and drive approximately 5.5 miles until the road becomes one lane. Continue on Kaiser Pass Road past the High Sierra Ranger Station and veer left at a fork in the road. Follow signs to Edison Lake and continue approximately four miles to the Mono Creek Campground turnoff. Turn left to the creek.

*Mono Creek*

When other streams in the region have gone dry or have been reduced to a trickle, Mono Creek is a raging river. Before it was dammed in the mid-Fifties, Mono Creek, located at 7,400 feet in the Sierra National Forest, was a natural stream fed by snow runoff in the Sierra, which flowed freely from the John Muir Wilderness down into the Sierra National Forest. However, after the damn was built, Mono Creek's nature changed.

Presently, and into the foreseeable future, unless Edison Lake's dam is destroyed, Mono Creek's flows will be controlled by releases from Edison Lake. These releases are so great that the creek should be called a river, as it burgeons to 20 yards wide and cannot be crossed. From Edison Dam down to the Mono Diversion Dam, much of the creek is too dangerous to enter because of fast flows and numerous rapids.

Smart fishermen concentrate their efforts closer to the dam where the water has slowed. This is where the California Department of Fish and Game stocks 3,455 rainbows. The best area is just above the diversion dam where the creek begins to slow. There are a lot of fallen trees here for the fish hide under. Three of the fallen trees reach out about 10 yards into the creek, providing platforms for casting.

The creek is best fished with waders. Try casting Panther Martins, Cripplelures or Thomas Buoyants to the far bank, then reel them in across the current. The planters wait for food to flow in through the channel where the creek enters the dam area.

Most anglers who fish the creek are either camping at Edison Lake Campground or at Mono Creek. Don't expect any large crowds.

If you plan to make the trip, supplies are available at Edison Lake. Road restrictions and hazards for Edison Lake also apply to Mono Creek. Mono Creek is closed to fishing from November 16 to the last Saturday in April.

Also nearby are Edison Lake, the John Muir Wilderness, Florence Lake, Ward Lake, Portal Forebay, the South Fork San Joaquin River at Jackass Meadow and Mono Hot Springs, Mono Hot Springs, Rancheria Creek and Huntington Lake.

# FLORENCE LAKE

*I still consider Florence Lake to be a sleeper, partly because of the big browns that do manage to swim down into the lake each year.*

**Rating:** 5

**Species:** Rainbow Trout, Brown Trout and Brook Trout

**Stock:** None

**Facilities:** Picnic Areas, Restrooms, General Store, Bait & Tackle, Water Taxi, Boat Launch and a Pack Station

**Contact:** Sierra National Forest (559) 855-5360, High Sierra Ranger Station (559) 877-7173 (Summer Only), Lost Valley Pack Station and Water Taxi Information (209) 966-3195

**Directions:** From the 99 Freeway in Fresno, drive 72 miles east on Highway 168 to the east end of Huntington Lake. Turn east on Kaiser Pass Road. After approximately 5.5 miles, Kaiser Pass Road becomes one lane. Continue approximately 10.5 miles past the High Sierra Ranger Station to the turnoff for Florence Lake. Veer right and continue to the lake.

*Florence Lake*

Most lakes in the Western Sierra have been on the upturn since the drought years. Florence Lake is an exception. It doesn't have problems receiving the amount of water required to maintain a quality fishery, however, it does have difficulty retaining it.

The problem is that Florence Lake's dam, which was constructed in the 1930's, cannot maintain high water levels when there is a possibility that a cold spell might hit. Because of the dam's early construction, if the lake were to freeze, the ice could crack it. To avoid the risk of losing the dam, each spring the lake is drawn down from 962 acres (assuming it's at full capacity), and by November 1 it dwindles down to a mere two-acre-feet of water. Because of these significant drawdowns, the California Department of Fish and Game decided to stop trout plants at Florence, diverting the fish to Edison Lake.

Prior to 1999, when the CA DFG stocked 25,000 fingerling rainbow trout, the lake was run as a put-and-grow fishery. However, when low water levels occurred, these stocked fish were swept downstream with the water that was released into the South Fork of the San Joaquin River, or they simply swam upstream. Today, the lake must build its fish population from the fish that swim down from the San Joaquin River. There are still some fish in the lake, but with nearby Edison Lake thriving and kicking out trophy fish, fishing at Florence has pretty much become a thing of the past.

I still consider Florence Lake to be a sleeper, partly because of the big browns that do manage to swim down into the lake each year. However, when the water levels are low, they can be difficult to catch, and launching a boat is almost impossible by late summer. If you are going to try to fish the lake, arrive in the spring before the major drawdowns occur. At this time of year, trolling Rapalas and Needlefish is the way to go. Remember there are no stockers, so Power Bait doesn't work well.

It's a shame Florence Lake's fishery has dwindled, because with a granite mountain in its backdrop it is probably the prettiest in the region. That picturesque backdrop has become Florence's main attraction, as fishing has taken a backseat to backpacking.

The lake provides a water taxi to ferry hikers and backpackers across the lake to the Lost Valley Trailhead. The trail follows along the South Fork of the San Joaquin River for a few miles until it meets up with the Pacific Crest and John Muir Trails. At this point you can either veer right, heading toward McClure Meadow and Kings Canyon National Park, or stay to the left and enter the John Muir Wilderness. From here, you can work your way over Piute Pass to Humphrey's Basin and eventually to North Lake.

If you plan to make the trip, supplies are available at the lake. Kaiser Pass Road is closed from the first snowfall (usually in November) to Memorial Weekend (or when the snow on the road can be cleared of snow). During long winters the road may not open until early July. Call ahead for updated conditions. The road to the lake is extremely dangerous. Careful, slow driving is a must. Trailers are not recommended. (See Edison Lake write-up.)

Also nearby are the John Muir Wilderness, Ward Lake, South Fork San Joaquin River at Mono Hot Springs and Jackass Meadow, Mono Creek, Portal Forebay, Edison Lake and Huntington Lake.

# SAN JOAQUIN RIVER
## (JACKASS MEADOW)

**Beginning at the base of Florence Dam and stretching nearly a mile downstream, the river is perfect for fly-fishing.**

| | |
|---|---|
| **Rating:** | 7 |
| **Species:** | Rainbow and Brown Trout |
| **Stock:** | 1,150 pounds of rainbow trout. |
| **Facilities:** | Campgrounds and Vault Toilets |
| **Contact:** | Sierra National Forest (559) 297-0706 or (559) 855-5360 |
| | High Sierra Ranger Station (559) 877-7173 (Summer Only) |

**Directions:** From the 99 Freeway in Fresno, drive 72 miles east on Highway 168 to the east end of Huntington Lake. Turn east on Kaiser Pass Road and continue approximately 5.5 miles until the road becomes one lane. Follow the road approximately 10.5 miles to the High Sierra Ranger Station. Continue past the ranger station to a turnoff for Florence Lake. Veer right and drive 4.5 miles to Jackass turnoff. Turn left and drive approximately one mile to the river.

*San Joaquin River (Jackass Meadow)*

Although there are a few spin-cast fishermen and Power Baiters who fish the South Fork of the San Joaquin River at Jackass Meadow, it's still the most popular fly-fishing spot in the region.

Beginning at the base of Florence Dam and stretching nearly a mile downstream, the river is perfect for fly-fishing. It's wide, slow moving and holds a lot of wild rainbows and browns. Fed by releases from Florence Lake, which is drained almost dry each year, the river always has enough water to keep its fish healthy and happy.

The river is stocked with 2,150 rainbows, but its trout population has been bolstered over the last decade by releases from Florence Lake. Prior to 1999, the California Department of Fish and Game used to plant 25,000 fingerling rainbow trout into the lake, but after drawing it down, most of the fish ended up in the river, so they quit planting the lake.

At 8,000 feet in the Sierra National Forest, Jackass Meadow is a popular camping area, which gets hit pretty hard by day-use anglers. For spin casters, try using Panther Martins or some other kind of lure that doesn't sink too fast. Fly-fishermen should check with the tackle shops in Shaver Lake for the latest hatch. After Jackass Meadow, the river picks up steam as it races through a remote canyon, then opens up again in the Mono Hot Springs area.

If you plan to make the trip, supplies are available at Florence Lake. Kaiser Pass Road is closed from the first snowfall (usually in November) to Memorial Weekend, or as soon as the road can be cleared of snow. During long winters, the road may not open until early July. Call ahead for updated conditions. The road to the lake is extremely dangerous. Careful and slow driving is a must. Trailers are not recommended. (See Edison Lake write-up.) The San Joaquin River, South Fork (Jackass Meadow) is closed to fishing from November 16 to the last Saturday in April.

Also nearby are John Muir Wilderness, Florence Lake, South Fork San Joaquin River at Mono Hot Springs, Ward Lake, Mono Creek, the Portal Forebay, Edison Lake and Huntington Lake.

# WARD LAKE

*It's the kind of place where a father takes his kids out in the canoe, drops lines in the water and paddles around.*

| | |
|---|---|
| **Rating:** | 6 |
| **Species:** | Rainbow Trout and Brown Trout |
| **Stock:** | 5,300 pounds of rainbow trout. |
| **Facilities:** | Campgrounds, Picnic Areas and Vault Toilets |
| **Contact:** | Sierra National Forest (559) 297-0706 or (559) 855-5360 |
| | High Sierra Ranger Station (559) 877-7173 (Summer Only) |
| **Directions:** | |

From the 99 Freeway in Fresno, drive 72 miles east on Highway 168 to the east end of Huntington Lake. Turn east on Kaiser Pass Road and drive approximately 5.5 miles until the road becomes one lane. Follow the road approximately 10.5 miles to the High Sierra Ranger Station. Continue past the ranger station to a turnoff for Florence Lake. Veer right and continue to the lake on the right.

*Bucks are common at Ward Lake*

Ward Lake is almost an exact replica of Mack Lake (Rock Creek Drainage) in the John Muir Wilderness. Anglers love this small, six-acre lake for its abundance of stocked rainbow trout and its stunningly picturesque setting. Ward Lake's advantage is that you can drive to it, as opposed to having to hike to Mack Lake.

At 8,000 feet in the Sierra National Forest, only a few miles from Florence Lake, Ward Lake is a popular camping spot. Stocked weekly by the California Department of Fish and Game, which plants a total of 10,225 rainbow trout, fishing remains good in the summer months. There are also holdovers and small wild browns in the lake. In 1988 the lake was planted with fingerling brook trout so a few may still be around.

This quiet lake with a family atmosphere is a great place to bring children to fish. It's the kind of place where a father takes his kids out in the canoe, drops lines in the water and paddles around. This trolling method is productive here, although, it works even better with an electric trolling motor. No motorized boats are permitted.

Most anglers fish from the shore with Power Bait or walk around the lake, tossing Thomas Buoyants and orange Cripplelures. Others fish from rafts and float tubes. On the north shoreline there are a lot of lily pads, which the trout use as cover. Many anglers hook trout here, but they have trouble landing them, because the fish wrap themselves around the base of the pads to break off the line.

The campground is located on the lakeshore and is commonly visited by bears in the late summer and fall. There are also granite cliffs on the far side. The road to the lake is closed in the winter, although, snowmobiles are permitted. There is a groomed trail to the lake. The lake commonly freezes over in the winter, but remains open to fishing, year-round. Ice fishing anyone?

If you plan to make the trip, supplies are available at Florence Lake. Kaiser Pass Road is closed from the first snowfall (usually in November) to Memorial Weekend, or as soon as the road can be cleared of snow. During long winters the road may not open until early July. Call ahead for updated conditions. The road to the lake is extremely dangerous. Slow and careful driving is a must. Trailers are not recommended. (See Edison Lake write-up.)

Also nearby are John Muir Wilderness, Florence Lake, South Fork San Joaquin River at Mono Hot Springs and Jackass Meadow, Mono Creek, Portal Forebay, Edison Lake and Huntington Lake.

# SAN JOAQUIN RIVER
## (MONO HOT SPRINGS)

**With the CA DFG providing the fish, the resort pitches in all the rest of the amenities necessary for a luxurious outdoor adventure.**

**Rating:** 7

**Species:** Rainbow and Brown Trout

**Stock:** 1,150 pounds of rainbow trout

**Facilities:** Campgrounds, Resort, Picnic Area, Restaurant, General Store, Lodging and Vault Toilets

**Contact:** Sierra National Forest (559) 297-0706, Mono Hot Springs Resort (559) 325-1710
Mile High Ranger Station (559) 877-7173 (Summer Only)

**Directions:** From the 99 Freeway in Fresno, drive 72 miles east on Highway 168 to the east end of Huntington Lake. Turn east on Kaiser Pass Road and drive approximately 5.5 miles until the road becomes one lane. Continue approximately 10.5 miles to the High Sierra Ranger Station. Drive another three miles to the Florence Lake junction and veer left. Drive 1.5 miles to the stream.

*San Joaquin River (Mono Hot Springs)*

When you come to Mono Hot Springs, fishing the South Fork of the San Joaquin River is not the biggest attraction; the hot springs take the prize. There are a series of natural hot springs, which can be reached by a short walk from Mono Hot Springs Resort. The South Fork of the San Joaquin River lies between the hot springs and the resort.

The river is known for stocked trout and also for a fair amount of action on wild rainbows and browns. The California Department of Fish and Game stocks 2,150 rainbow trout, most of which are planted directly under the Kaiser Pass Road Bridge, which crosses over the river. Fishing is good after a stock, below the bridge down to the campgrounds.

At 7,400 feet in the Sierra National Forest, the river gets heavy day-use from visitors coming from both Edison Lake and the Fresno area. With the CA DFG providing the fish, the resort pitches in all the rest of the amenities necessary for a luxurious outdoor adventure.

The river is normally stocked weekly in summer to accommodate the large swarm of visitors. The pool below the bridge is about 100 yards long and as deep as seven feet. People swim in it, but it's damn cold. In addition to the hot springs, there are two lakes that can be reached by short hikes. Tule Lake is a 2.5-mile round-tripper, and Doris Lake is one mile. Both are stocked every few years by the CA DFG with either rainbow or brook trout.

If you plan to make the trip, supplies are available at Mono Hot Springs Resort and at Edison Lake. Kaiser Pass Road is closed from the first snowfall (usually in November) to Memorial Weekend, or as soon as the road can be cleared of snow. During long winters, the road may not open until early July. Call ahead for updated conditions. The road to the lake is extremely dangerous. Careful and slow driving is a must. Trailers are not recommended. (See Edison Lake write-up.) The San Joaquin River, South Fork (Mono Hot Springs) is closed to fishing from November 16 to the last Saturday in April.

Also nearby are the John Muir Wilderness, Florence Lake, South Fork San Joaquin River at Jackass Meadow, Ward Lake, Mono Creek, the Portal Forebay, Edison Lake and Huntington Lake.

# PORTAL FOREBAY

*It is also shallow, so those who can get out into the middle with float tubes, canoes or rowboats have the best catch rates.*

**Rating:** 6
**Species:** Rainbow Trout and Brown Trout
**Stock:** 5,525 pounds of rainbow trout.
**Facilities:** Primitive Campsites, Picnic Areas and Vault Toilets
**Contact:** Sierra National Forest (559) 297-0706 or (559) 855-5360
High Sierra Ranger Station (559) 877-7173 (Summer Only)

**Directions:** From the 99 Freeway in Fresno, drive 72 miles east on Highway 168 to the east end of Huntington Lake. Turn east on Kaiser Pass Road and continue approximately 5.5 miles until the road becomes one lane. Follow the road approximately 7.3 miles to the lake.

*Portal Forebay*

The Portal Forebay is a great place to stop and take a quick breather. Better yet, it's a place you can let your brakes rest. Congratulations, you've made it about halfway to Edison or Florence Lake. This seven-mile trip on a one-lane nightmare of a road is a heart-pounder. For most of the trip you're looking at blind turns, and the only way to approximate a safe drive is by traveling under 5 mph and constantly honking your horn. It's the only road I've ever driven where I've been scared. All it takes is for one jerk to come around a corner too fast, and pow, it's all over.

Because Portal Forebay is a holding facility for water that comes from the Mono Tunnel (Edison Lake) and the Ward Tunnel (Florence Lake), it experiences extreme fluctuations. At 7,177 feet in the Sierra National Forest, the four-acre lake is stocked by the California Department of Fish and Game with 10,440 rainbow trout. In 1966 brook trout were stocked, but none of that plant remains in the lake. The Portal Forebay gets both day-users and overnight campers traveling between Huntington and Edison Lakes.

Most of the lake looks like a small pond, with many pines and some nice primitive campsites along its shorelines. It is also shallow, so those who can get out into the middle with float tubes, canoes or rowboats have the best catch rates. No gas-powered motors are permitted.

Shoreline anglers can also get into the mix by tossing spinners towards the middle of the lake and soaking Power Bait. I was told all of the fish in the lake were pan-sized, but I began to think otherwise when my friend was spooled by a larger fish after casting a Thomas Buoyant.

If you plan to make the trip, supplies are available at Huntington Lake. Kaiser Pass Road is closed from the first snowfall (usually in November) to Memorial Weekend, or as soon as the road can be cleared of snow.

Also nearby are Florence Lake and South Fork San Joaquin River at Mono Hot Springs.

College Lake is smaller than Shamu's tank at Sea World in San Diego. Much smaller!

| | |
|---|---|
| **Rating:** | 5 |
| **Species:** | Brook Trout |
| **Stock:** | None |
| **Facilities:** | None |
| **Contact:** | Eastwood Visitor Center (559) 893-6611(Summer Only) |
| | Sierra National Forest (559) 855-5360 or (559) 297-0706 |
| **Directions:** | |

From the 99 Freeway in Fresno, drive 72 miles east on Highway 168 to the east end of Huntington Lake. Turn east on Kaiser Pass Road and continue approximately 5.5 miles. After the road becomes one lane, continue approximately 4.5 miles to Forest Road 5. Turn left onto the dirt road and drive about two miles to the trailhead and parking area.

*College Lake*

Sometimes I wonder how certain bodies of water qualify to be called a "lakes," especially in the case of College Lake. Size-wise, College Lake is no lake. It's a pond; a small one, at that. It's smaller than Shamu's tank at Sea World in San Diego. Much smaller! Lakes should be larger than ponds, don't you agree? Yet, by strict definition, since lakes are formed by some obstruction of moving water and ponds are "still," College qualifies to be called a "lake." It is fed by an unnamed stream, and was formed by the obstruction of its moving waters.

Because there is no formal trail leading to College Lake, many anglers refrain from fishing it. Although there are brook trout in the lake, they are small, mostly four to eight inches. College is fewer than eight feet deep and one-acre in surface area. Despite its size, at 9,520 feet in the Kaiser Wilderness, College is a pretty high-country lake that doesn't see a lot of fishing pressure.

Commonly iced-over at least until early June, the lake is easy to reach if you follow its outlet stream. To get to it, from the inlet to George Lake walk upstream, traversing small waterfalls, large boulders and dodging trees. There is an informal trail here, but it can be difficult to find. It's roughly a half-mile climb from George to College. Follow the stream and you'll have no problem finding it. Keep in mind the stream may dry up by the end of summer and then you are going to need a good map to get here.

If you plan to make the trip, supplies are available at Huntington Lake. A wilderness permit is required for overnight travel into the Kaiser Wilderness.

Also nearby are Smalls Falls, Upper and Lower Twin Lakes, Campfire Lake and Jewel Lake.

**Surrounded by towering pines and granite boulders, George is a clear, shallow lake where anglers can catch as many fish as desired.**

| | |
|---|---|
| **Rating:** | 7 |
| **Species:** | Brook Trout and Rainbow Trout |
| **Stock:** | None |
| **Facilities:** | None |
| **Contact:** | Eastwood Visitor Center (559) 893-6611 (Summer Only) |
| | Sierra National Forest (559) 855-5360 or (559) 297-0706 |

**Directions:** From the 99 Freeway in Fresno, drive 72 miles east on Highway 168 to the east end of Huntington Lake. Turn east on Kaiser Pass Road and continue approximately 5.5 miles. After the road becomes one lane, continue approximately 4.5 miles to Forest Road 5. Turn left onto the dirt road and drive about two miles to the trailhead and parking area.

*George Lake*

Of all the lakes in the Kaiser Wilderness, George Lake provides some of the best fishing. Nestled below Kaiser Peak between College Lake and Upper Twin Lake, George is planted with 1,000 fingerling rainbow trout. It's the lake's self-sustaining brook trout population, however, that gives anglers the most thrills. With almost a half-mile of shoreline and three islands, brookies are abundant here.

Surrounded by towering pines and granite boulders, George is a clear, shallow lake where anglers can catch as many fish as desired, given that they've brought along a few Panther Martins. Color and size doesn't matter, nor does it make any difference where you cast. Anywhere near drop-offs and points along the shoreline or near the islands produces fish. I caught four brooks for each rainbow that I landed. Although no trophy fish are found here, rainbows and brooks from six to nine inches are plentiful.

It's an easy climb from Upper Twin Lake to George. At the outlet of Upper Twin, follow the George Lake Trail around Upper Twin and through the pine forest. Where the trail bends to the left, after the first three-tenths of a mile of the 1.2-mile trip from Twin to George, George's outlet stream can be seen down in the gorge. Continuing on, a small pond can also be seen down in the canyon. Then, if you look carefully through the trees, the upper end of 20-foot Small's Falls will appear. George is a measly one-tenth of a mile ahead.

If you plan to make the trip, supplies are available at Huntington Lake. A wilderness permit is required for overnight travel into the Kaiser Wilderness.

Also nearby are Smalls Falls, College Lake, Upper and Lower Twin Lakes, Campfire Lake and Jewel Lake.

# TWIN LAKES

**Encompassing 22,700 acres of wilderness, Kaiser was created in 1976. It contains 19 named lakes, most of which are stocked yearly with fingerling trout.**

|  |  |
|---|---|
| **Rating:** | 7 |
| **Species:** | Rainbow Trout |
| **Stock:** | Two pounds of fingerling rainbow trout. |
| **Facilities:** | None |
| **Contact:** | Eastwood Visitor Center (559) 893-6611(Summer Only) |
| | Sierra National Forest (559) 855-5360 or (559) 297-0706 |
| **Directions:** | |

From the 99 Freeway in Fresno, drive 72 miles east on Highway 168 to the east end of Huntington Lake. Turn east on Kaiser Pass Road and continue approximately 5.5 miles. After the road becomes one lane, continue approximately 4.5 miles to Forest Road 5. Turn left onto the dirt road and drive about two miles to the trailhead and parking area.

*Lower Twin Lake (Kaiser)*

In the center of the Sierra National Forest, just north of Huntington Lake, the Kaiser Wilderness is a popular destination for both beginning and experienced backpackers. It is also heavily used by day-hikers. Encompassing 22,700 acres of wilderness, Kaiser was created in 1976. It contains 19 named lakes, most of which are stocked yearly with fingerling trout by the California Department of Fish and Game.

Only six lakes in Kaiser have trails leading to them, while cross-country travel is required to reach all the others. Concerned about getting lost, most hikers and fishermen stay near the lakes with trails. Locating some of the other lakes requires serious route-finding skills. Because Upper and Lower Twin Lakes can be easily reached by well-maintained trails, they are the most popular lakes here.

The hardest thing about getting to these lakes is deciding which trail to take. Five trails access them: Potter Pass, Sample Meadows, California Hiking and Riding, Sample Cutoff and the Idaho Lake Trail. I find the easiest and quickest to be the Sample Cutoff Trail that begins on Forest Road 5, two miles north of Kaiser Pass Road.

The route begins in the Sierra National Forest and within the first 100 yards enters the Kaiser Wilderness. Then, the path descends, crossing Kaiser Creek after a half-mile before curving to the left and crossing Kaiser again. The trail begins to ascend and comes to another stream crossing (of an unnamed stream) 1.7 miles from the trailhead.

Now it's time to do a little climbing. In the next four-tenths of a mile, you'll ascend 350 feet before the path levels out at Round Meadow. Once you reach Round Meadow, a trail signed for Badger Flat breaks off to the left. Stay right, walk through the meadow, briefly reenter the forest, make an easy stream crossing, and three miles from your car, you'll arrive at the outlet of Upper Twin Lake. At Upper Twin, there's a trail junction. For Lower Twin, take the left fork three-tenths of a mile to the lake. The right fork leads around Upper Twin and onto George Lake.

Both lakes provide good fishing for pan-sized rainbows. At 21 acres and a maximum depth of 55 feet Upper Twin also has brook trout. In May and June, fishing near the inlet is best here. Both fly fishermen and spin casters do well. As summer approaches, tossing small spinners anywhere along the shoreline or towards the island works well. The lake is planted by air with fingerling rainbow trout. It also has brooks, but they were last stocked in 1986.

Fishing Lower Twin a seven-acre lake with depths to 17 feet (also known as White Cliff) calls for a little more effort. The lake's west and north shores are extremely shallow and don't harbor many fish. The east and south sides are the most productive; yet, to be successful, you'll need to be able to cast out at least 20 yards. There is a shelf about 10 yards from the shore, and anglers who can present their bait on the downside of the shelf seem to catch the rainbows. To enable yourself to cast out there, use a size 1/16 Panther Martin or a large Kastmaster. Most of the rainbows average seven to nine inches. The lake was last planted in 1996 with brook trout.

If you plan to make the trip, supplies are available at Huntington Lake. A wilderness permit is required for overnight travel into the Kaiser Wilderness.

Also nearby are Smalls Falls, College Lake, George Lake, Campfire Lake and Jewel Lake.

# RANCHERIA CREEK

*In spring and fall, a lot of browns swim up the channel from the lake and are commonly caught by anglers fishing for planted rainbows.*

**Rating:** 7
**Species:** Rainbow Trout and Brown Trout
**Stock:** 850 pounds of rainbow trout.
**Facilities:** Restrooms, Visitor Center, Gas, Food, Lodging and a Marina
**Contact:** Sierra National Forest (559) 855-5360 or (559) 297-0706,
Rancheria Enterprises (559) 893-3234, Eastwood Visitor Center (559) 893-6611 (Summer Only)

**Directions:**

From the 99 Freeway in Fresno, drive 71 miles east on Highway 168 to the east end of Huntington Lake. After crossing over the stream, turn east on Kaiser Pass Road. The road parallels the stream for about a mile. Access is also available upstream near the pack station.

*Water being released out of the Ward Tunnel and into Rancheria Creek.*

Set in the Sierra National Forest, Rancheria, which flows into Huntington Lake, is a deceiving creek that assumes a variety of shapes and forms. Beginning as a small, shallow stream, about the width of two hockey goals, it is fed by snowmelt from the mountains above Huntington Lake. It first trickles down hillsides, before it merges with water being forced out of the Ward Tunnel. This water combines with Rancheria to form a much larger and deeper stream. In fact, now Rancheria no longer looks like a creek or a stream, but a fast flowing river.

The water that joins with Rancheria is transported via pipeline from Edison and Florence Lakes through the Ward Tunnel. Roughly 50 yards above the point where it meets Rancheria, it is forced through a pumping station where hydroelectric power is created. Huntington Lake is located about 200 yards from the point where the water leaves the Ward Tunnel.

The California Department of Fish and Game plants 1,775 rainbows in spring and early summer, from the flume down to the lake. Some fish are also planted in the upper portion of the stream near the pack station, which can be accessed on Kaiser Pass Road, further upstream. Although there aren't a lot of trout stocked in the stream, many of the fish that are planted in Huntington Lake, as well as wild trout from the lake, swim up Rancheria. In spring and fall, a lot of browns also swim up the channel from the lake and are commonly caught by anglers fishing for planted rainbows.

The water from Rancheria and the water pumped from Ward Tunnel offer fish a great food source where they enter the lake, so the fish hang nearby, looking to get in on the feast. This portion of the stream is heavily fished; however, because the current is so swift in this area, it's best to use lures here. When the water gets below the bridge, it slows drastically, and the use of Power Bait and salmon eggs becomes an option.

If you plan to make the trip, supplies are available at Huntington Lake. Rancheria Creek is closed to fishing from November 16 to the last Saturday in April.

Also nearby are Big Creek (Huntington), Tamarack Creek, Rancheria Falls, Huntington Lake, Shaver Lake, Portal Forebay, Mono Creek, Edison Lake, Florence Lake and the San Joaquin River at Mono Hot Springs and Jackass Meadow.

*Rancheria Creek downstream of the Ward Tunnel.*

RANCHERIA CREEK

# BIG CREEK (HUNTINGTON)

*After getting skunked at Huntington, they come to Big Creek where they know they can catch their limit, which is usually pretty easy to come by from late spring through July.*

| | |
|---|---|
| **Rating:** | 6 |
| **Species:** | Rainbow Trout and Brown Trout |
| **Stock:** | 2,275 pounds of rainbow trout. |
| **Facilities:** | Restrooms, Resort and Lodging |
| **Contact:** | Sierra National Forest (559) 855-5360 or (559) 297-0706 Sierra Summit Resort (559) 233-2500, Eastwood Visitor Center (559) 893-6611 (Summer Only) |

**Directions:** From the 99 Freeway in Fresno, take Highway 168 east 70 miles to Sierra Summit Resort. The creek flows next to the resort.

*Big Creek after a winter storm.*

Sorry to disappoint you, but Big Creek isn't that big. Located between Tamarack and Rancheria Creeks, at 7,000 feet in the Sierra National Forest, Big Creek is just another small stream that flows into Huntington Lake. It often gets heavy use from Huntington's anglers. After getting skunked at Huntington, they come to Big Creek where they know they can catch their limit, which is usually pretty easy to come by from late spring through July. If they come any later, they may have trouble finding a pool suitable for fish.

With no other source for its water, the creek gets extremely low after all the snow melts in the mountains above. The California Department of Fish and Game stocks 4,745 rainbows, mostly near Sierra Summit Resort. Rainbow-colored Roostertails and small silver Kastmasters are favorite lures here, however, Power Bait produces limits, too.

In winter Big Creek shifts gears from being a popular fishery to becoming the region's premier ski area. Because Big Creek is located near the base of the slopes, its landscape glistens with snow-capped peaks and glitters with snow-covered towering pines. It's a convenient and pretty spot to relax between ski runs.

If you plan to make the trip, supplies are available at Huntington Lake and in Shaver Lake. Big Creek is closed to fishing from November 16 to the last Saturday in April. In winter call ahead for road conditions. Chains may be required. Big Creek Resort is closed in the summer.

Also nearby are Rancheria Creek, Shaver Lake, Tamarack Creek, Rancheria Falls, Huntington Lake, Shaver Lake, Portal Forebay, Mono Creek, Edison Lake, Florence Lake, San Joaquin River at Mono Hot Springs and Jackass Meadow.

*When the plants are coming, Power Bait is the favorite choice of anglers.*

| | |
|---|---|
| **Rating:** | 6 |
| **Species:** | Rainbow Trout and Brown Trout |
| **Stock:** | 800 rainbow trout. |
| **Facilities:** | Lodging, Restrooms and a General Store |
| **Contact:** | Tamarack Lodge (559) 893-3244, Sequoia National Forest (559) 855-5360 |
| | Eastwood Visitor Center (559) 893-6611 (Summer Only) |

**Directions:** From the 99 Freeway in Fresno, drive 70 miles east on Highway 168 (past Shaver Lake and over Tamarack Ridge) to a bridge over Tamarack Creek.

*Tamarack Creek is often hidden under snow in the winter.*

The ideal way to hit Tamarack Creek is to spend a weekend at Tamarack Lodge. The lodge is less than a quarter-mile from the creek, and after an easy and peaceful walk, you can be at the stream within 10 minutes of leaving your hotel room. Tamarack Creek is one of the few streams in the region with a lodge that remains open during the summer near its banks. Nearby Rancheria Creek doesn't have a lodge and Big Creek's isn't open over the summer.

At 7,000 feet in the Sierra National Forest, Tamarack Creek is about 600 feet below Tamarack Ridge, near Huntington Lake, and offers good fishing for planted trout from May through mid-July. The California Department of Fish and Game stocks 1,675 rainbows near the Highway 168 Bridge that crosses over the creek and along the access road that parallels the creek immediately after the bridge. When the plants are coming, Power Bait is the favorite choice of anglers.

Once August arrives, the stream turns into a trickle. The only shot at catching fish is for those who work the stream in search of tiny wild rainbow and brown trout. There will be a little more water downstream where the South Fork enters, but a few hundred yards beyond, the water gets pumped away to Shaver Lake.

Don't confuse the South Fork of Tamarack Creek with Tamarack Creek. If coming from Shaver Lake, you'll cross the South Fork first, however, no fish are planted there.

If you plan to make the trip, supplies are available at Huntington and Shaver Lakes. Tamarack Creek is closed to fishing from November 16 to the last Saturday in April.

Also nearby are Big Creek (Huntington), Rancheria Creek, Rancheria Falls, Huntington Lake, Shaver Lake, Portal Forebay, Mono Creek, Edison Lake, Florence Lake and San Joaquin River at Mono Hot Springs and Jackass Meadow.

# HUNTINGTON LAKE

*We had one line at 75 feet and the other down at 110. The one at 75 feet got hit, and we fought the fish for about 45 minutes before it dove down to the bottom, wrapped the line around a tree stump and broke free.*

**Rating:** 8

**Species:** Rainbow Trout, Brown Trout and Kokanee

**Stock:** 14,850 pounds of rainbow trout.

**Facilities:** Campgrounds, Picnic Areas, Bait & Tackle, Restrooms, General Store, Gas, Food, Lodging, Boat Launches, Boat Rentals, Full-Service Marinas and Visitor Center

**Contact:** Sierra National Forest (559) 855-5360, Rancheria Enterprises (559) 893-3234, Eastwood Visitor Center (559) 893-6611 (Summer Only), Lakeshore Resort (559) 893-3193

**Directions:** From the 99 Freeway in Fresno, drive 71 miles east on Highway 168 to the east end of Huntington Lake. Turn west on Huntington Lake Road and drive to the lake.

*Huntington Lake*

It's safe to say that Huntington is one of the best sailing lakes in California. Each summer several regattas are held, and even when these competitions aren't taking place, sailboats cover the lake. In the early morning, evenings and in the fall, when the sailboats aren't around, the fishing can be great.

Huntington Lake is a good rainbow and brown trout fishery, and in a few years its kokanee fishing could regain strength. Kokanee fishing used to be good in the mid-Nineties, until too many were planted in the lake. As a result of this overstocking, the adult spawn only grew to about nine inches, too small for anglers.

In 1997, the California Department of Fish and Game stopped planting kokanee. They found that the fish were naturally reproducing and plants were no longer needed. It's going to take a few more years for these fish to reach a size anglers enjoy catching. The CA DFG also plants 26,470 rainbows.

It's no secret that Huntington is home to large browns. However, the best chance of landing them is when conditions are miserable, and there are few that will brave the elements to try their luck. Most of the smart and successful anglers who target browns fish in the late fall or early spring, when the winds are howling, temperatures are freezing and snow is falling. Anglers who can withstand these elements and troll large Rapalas have a good chance at catching one over 10 pounds. A few anglers have landed monster browns in the summer, but the chances are slim. The big browns hang out near the dam, and you have to fish with downriggers to have any shot at all.

My fishing partner Blake Lezak and I fished the lake in late August of 2000. We had one line at 75 feet and the other down at 110. The one at 75 feet got hit, and we fought the fish for about 45 minutes before it dove down to the bottom, wrapped the line around a tree stump and broke free. Lesson learned: there's always a chance at hooking a monster brown, but landing it is another story.

At 7,000 feet in the Sierra National Forest, 1,435-acre Huntington Lake is one of two out of the six lakes in the region that allows personal watercraft and water-skiing. It also has fair rainbow trout fishing. With 14 miles of pine-wooded shoreline, Huntington is popular for day-use and week-long vacations. From Memorial Day to Labor Day it's run as a resort town.

The lake is fed by water from Big Creek, Rancheria Creek, Tamarack Creek and the Ward Tunnel. The Ward Tunnel is comprised of water diverted from the Portal Forebay, the South Fork of the San Joaquin River, Edison Lake and Florence Lake. Fishing near any of these inlets is the best opportunity for shoreline anglers. In the fall, browns are caught from the shores of the inlets. In the spring and fall, toplining with small Rapalas, gold Super Dupers or gold Kastmasters works well. But, as summer approaches, leadcore or downriggers are needed, because the fish congregate in deep water near the dam.

Of the three dams on the lake, numbers two are three provide the most consistent action. The dams are numbered from east to west. In the winter, the lake is drawn down and commonly freezes over. In severe winters, ice fishing is an option, but always check with the Forest Service first before heading out on the ice.

With groomed trails nearby, snowmobile riding is popular during the winter. For photographers, the Huntington Lake overlook is a must. It can be reached by driving one mile up Kaiser Pass Road. The pullout is on your right.

If you plan to make the trip, supplies are available at the lake. In winter, call ahead for road conditions. Chains may be required. Try to work your fishing time around the sail-boaters. They commonly chop off trollers' lines, oblivious to the fact that they're even there.

Also nearby are Big Creek (Huntington), Tamarack Creek, Rancheria Falls, Rancheria Creek, Shaver Lake, Portal Forebay, Mono Creek, Edison Lake, Florence Lake and the San Joaquin River at Mono Hot Springs and Jackass Meadow.

# SHAVER LAKE

*The lake remains quiet on the weekdays, but it can get crowded on the weekends, so fishermen either have to get here early and leave early, or battle the water-skiers and jet-skiers that max-out the 40mph speed limit.*

**Rating:** 7

**Species:** Rainbow Trout, Carp, Channel Catfish, Smallmouth Bass, Kokanee Salmon, Crappie, Bluegill, Bullhead, Brown Trout and Largemouth Bass

**Stock:** 18,050 pounds of rainbow trout and 55 pounds of kokanee salmon.

**Facilities:** Lodging, Picnic Areas, Campgrounds, Boat Launches, Boat, Canoe and Kayak Rentals, Food, Gas, Full-Service Marinas, Bait & Tackle, RV Hookups and Restrooms

**Contact:** Fishing Guide Captain Jack Yandell (559) 841-2522, Sierra Marina (559) 841-3324 Camp Edison (559) 841-3134, Shaver Lake Sports (559) 841-2740

**Directions:** From Highway 99 in Fresno, drive 52 miles east on Highway 168 to the town of Shaver Lake. Continue through the town to the lake.

*Shaver Lake*

With 13 miles of shoreline scattered amongst private and public land, Shaver Lake is fast becoming one of the best kokanee salmon fisheries in Central California. Shaver and Huntington Lakes are the only two lakes that are located between Pine Flat and Mammoth Pool Reservoir in the Big Creek Chain, which hold kokanee salmon.

There used to be a sawmill where Shaver Lake's dam now sits. The dam was constructed in 1927 and the lake was filled by 1929. Today, at 2,177 acres, it's the largest of the five Big Creek lakes in the region, and one of the two lakes in the region that allow water-skiing and fishing.

Each year the lake is planted with 50,000 fingerling kokanee, raised from eggs that are taken from an inlet (called Taylor Creek) to Lake Tahoe. The best bite is from June to early August, trolling in 35 to 70 feet of water near the dam. Needlefish and any of Captain Jack's Specials, fished behind a Sling Blade should do the trick. For better catch rates, try adding a piece of white corn on the tip of the hook. For updates on the kokanee bite, contact fishing guide Captain Jack, the inventor of Captain Jack's Special. He tracks the fish daily.

Whether trolling or bait fishing for planted rainbow trout, the bite remains good from fall through spring. The California Department of Fish and Game stocks 33,470 rainbow trout just under a half-pound.

If trolling, begin at Sierra Marina and work your way across the dam to Shaver Point, which is just before the Shaver Lake Marina. Then, work the shoreline on the other side of the bay. Topwater trolling works best all times of year except summer, when leadcore or downriggers are needed as fish move to deeper water.

Most of the stockers are from 12 to 15 inches, but each year brood stock rainbows to four pounds are also stocked. The lake is maintained as a put-and-take fishery. Because of all the fishing pressure, there aren't many holdovers from years past.

Years ago, there used to be a huge population of crawdads in the lake, but when smallmouth bass were stocked they began to feed on them. For a few years, the smallies flourished. However, when the smallmouths ate most of the crawdads, they ran out of a food source. With the bulk of the crawdads now gone, the lake has a stunted smallmouth population.

There is still a population of both small-mouths and largemouths in the lake, although the CA DFG and local fishermen are trying to get rid of them. Bass clubs have been holding tournaments at the lake and with the help of the CA DFG the bass caught during these tournaments have been transported to other lakes. For example, groups of 500 smallies were taken to Millerton Lake and Diamond Valley Reservoir, near Riverside in Southern California.

*Jo Ann Yandell caught this limit of kokanee*

Carp and bullhead can be caught in grassy areas from mid to late-June. Catfish, which often range from a half-pound to two pounds, are caught during summer. Carp are also caught off docks where people feed bread to ducks and geese; they swoop underneath and nab the bread the birds miss.

The lake remains quiet on the weekdays, but it can get crowded on the weekends, so fishermen either have to get here early and leave early, or battle the water-skiers and jet-skiers that max-out the 40mph speed limit.

If you plan to make the trip, supplies are available in Shaver Lake and at the marinas on the lake.

Also nearby are Huntington Lake, Big Creek (Huntington), Rancheria Creek, Tamarack Creek, Bear Creek Falls, Dinkey Creek, Dinkey Creek Falls, Courtright Reservoir and Wishon Reservoir.

*Four-year old Cary Kent had a great fishing trip at Shaver Lake*

*Captain Jack with a spawning kokanee.*

SHAVER LAKE

# DINKEY CREEK

*At 6,000 feet, between Shaver Lake and Wishon Reservoir, anglers love heavily stocked Dinkey Creek.*

| | |
|---|---|
| **Rating:** | 7 |
| **Species:** | Rainbow Trout and Brown Trout |
| **Stock:** | 5,475 pounds of rainbow trout. |
| **Facilities:** | Picnic Areas, Restrooms, Campgrounds, Café, Bait & Tackle, General Store, Lodging and Gas |
| **Contact:** | Sequoia National Forest (559) 855-5360 or (559) 297-0706 |
| | Dinkey Creek Inn & Chalets (559) 841-3435, Dinkey Ranger Station (559) 841-3404 |
| **Directions:** | From the 99 Freeway in Fresno, take Highway 168 east 51 miles to Dinkey Creek Road. Turn east and drive 12 miles to the creek. |

*Dinkey Creek*

Dinkey Creek is one of the more popular camping and stream-fishing destinations in the Sierra National Forest. At 6,000 feet, between Shaver Lake and Wishon Reservoir, anglers love heavily stocked Dinkey Creek. And the California Department of Fish and Game keeps these anglers happy by dumping 11,345 rainbows into Dinkey's waters.

There are three main sections of the creek: the part that flows through the Dinkey Creek Wilderness, the easily accessible area near the Dinkey Picnic Grounds and the Dinkey Creek Inn, and the lower section near Ross Crossing. Most of the fish are planted near the campgrounds where the creek crosses under Dinkey Creek Road, and also at Ross Crossing.

For best results, most anglers arrive by early August. Show up any later and you'll have trouble finding sections of the creek that flow, because by early August much of the creek dries up and the water gets held in pools. Many anglers stop fishing the creek at this time, but there are still many fish to be caught. The stockers and many small wild rainbow and brown trout hang out in these pools. The pools are also popular for swimmers, so arrive early in the day if you plan on fishing. During the spring and early summer, anglers catch trout with small Panther Martins, bright colored Roostertails or soaking Power Bait.

With class IV rapids, the creek is popular to kayakers in the spring. Another attraction is Dinkey Creek Bridge. Built in 1938, it has great historical interest. It was closed to vehicular traffic in 1965 and is now used as a footbridge.

If you plan to make the trip, supplies are available at Dinkey Creek Inn. Dinkey Creek is closed to fishing from November 16 to the last Saturday in April. In winter call ahead for road conditions. Chains may be required.

Also nearby are Courtright Reservoir, Wishon Reservoir, Big Creek (Kings), the McKinley Grove, Bear Creek Falls, the Dinkey Wilderness and Shaver Lake.

# COURTRIGHT RESERVOIR

**Anglers know Courtright holds browns, but word of the giant ones is seldom heard.**

**Rating:** 7
**Species:** Rainbow Trout and Brown Trout
**Stock:** 15,050 pounds of rainbow trout and 5,000 sub-catchable rainbow trout.
**Facilities:** Campgrounds, A Boat Launch and Vault Toilets
**Contact:** Sierra National Forest (559) 855-5360, Shaver Lake Sports (559) 841-2740

**Directions:** From the 99 Freeway in Fresno, take Highway 168 east 51 miles to Dinkey Creek Road. Turn east and drive 12 miles to McKinley Grove Road (Forest Road 40). Turn east and continue 14 miles. Bear left at the Wishon turnoff onto Courtright Road. Drive eight miles to the reservoir.

*Courtright Reservoir*

In the fall, Courtright Reservoir can be a sleeper. The 1,440-acre reservoir holds a lot of browns, even some lunkers. However, with nearby Edison and Huntington Lakes receiving all the hype, not many anglers give Courtright a chance. Anglers know Courtright holds browns, but word of the giant ones is seldom heard. There are two reasons for this: first, not many people fish the lake for the big browns. Second, those who catch them keep their mouths shut. They know if they tell others it will be much harder to catch other browns because fishing pressure will develop.

The best time to target the browns is in the fall and early spring, after the road to the lake is cleared of snow. In the fall, the lake's size gets greatly reduced by drawdowns, but the browns are still on the prowl. Troll large Rapalas near the dam and at the Helms Creek. In the summer, most of the browns stay in deep water and are rarely caught. From 1959 to '69 only brook and brown trout were planted.

At 8,184 feet in the Sierra National Forest, this deep reservoir is set in a remote granite area with many large buttes in the background. Along its barren shores you can see thousands of tree trunks about two feet tall, that were cut down to build this reservoir that sends water to Wishon Reservoir.

The lake is best known for its rainbow trout fishery that provides consistent catch rates from spring through fall. But most of its trout are small. The California Department of Fish and Game stocks 26,800 rainbows, and Pacific Gas & Electric Company pays the CA DFG to plant some 5,000 rainbow trout sub-catchables.

In the spring and beginning again in late August, the easiest way to catch trout is by toplining. Small Mystics, orange Cripplelures and white Phoebes provide the best action. Trolling anywhere on the lake will catch fish, however, the best spot is near a large boulder that juts out of the water in front of the dam. Bank fishermen can also get in on the action by soaking Power Bait or tossing lures from the boat launch area.

If you plan to make the trip, supplies are available in Shaver Lake. The road to Courtright Reservoir is closed in the winter. Call ahead for road conditions. Chains may be required.

Also nearby are Wishon Reservoir, the McKinley Grove, Dinkey Creek, Big Creek (Kings), Bear Creek Falls, Dinkey Creek Falls, the Dinkey Wilderness and Shaver Lake.

# WISHON RESERVOIR

**For shoreline anglers, your best bet is to fish the cove near the boat launch. There are a lot of fish in the channel, and Power Bait or spinners should land at least a few of them.**

**Rating:** 7
**Species:** Rainbow Trout and Brown Trout
**Stock:** 17,360 pounds of rainbow trout.
**Facilities:** Vault Toilets, Picnic Areas, Boat Rentals and a Boat Launch
**Contact:** Sierra National Forest (559) 855-5360, Shaver Lake Sports (559) 841-2740

**Directions:** From the 99 Freeway in Fresno, take Highway 168 east 51 miles to Dinkey Creek Road. Turn east and drive 12 miles to McKinley Grove Road (Forest Road 40). Turn east and continue 14 miles, bearing to the left at the Wishon turnoff. Continue three miles to the lake.

*Trout like this rainbow squeezed by Christian Perez are caught regularly at Wishon.*

At 6,500 feet in the Sierra National Forest, Wishon Reservoir offers fair trout fishing for those with a boat, but can be difficult for anglers fishing from shore. Wishon is a remote 1,025-acre reservoir with tall granite peaks and buttes in the backdrop. It is stocked with 25,862 rainbow trout from the California Department of Fish and Game and another 3,000 trout paid for by Pacific Gas & Electric Company. Most of these trout are small, but prospects for catching them are good.

Anglers who troll near the dam and off the points always seem to do well, but rarely catch anything to brag about. Try using small red and black Panther Martins, red and gold Thomas Buoyants and silver Kastmasters.

The lake has steep shorelines and can be difficult to fish for those without a boat. For shoreline anglers, your best bet is to fish the cove near the boat launch. There are a lot of fish in the channel, and Power Bait or spinners should land at least a few of them.

As October approaches, fishing for browns becomes an option. Although there are some large browns in the lake, they are rarely targeted. The best area to catch them is where the North Fork of the Kings River comes into the lake. Many hunters take boats here during deer season. They hunt in the early morning and fish for browns in the afternoon. Browns were last planted in 1968 and '70. Brooks were also stocked in 1959 and '68.

Launching a boat can be difficult anytime after July when drawdowns become severe, because the ramp is 100 to 150 yards long and only wide enough for one sports utility vehicle. There's a small turnout about halfway down the ramp, but it's not big enough for larger vehicles to turn around. Good luck.

If you plan to make the trip, supplies are available at Wishon Village. There are a general store and a bar. The road to Wishon closes in the winter. For updated road conditions, contact the Forest Service.

Also nearby are Courtright Reservoir, McKinley Grove, Dinkey Creek, Big Creek (Kings), Bear Creek Falls, Dinkey Falls, Dinkey Wilderness and Shaver Lake.

*next page Wishon Reservoir*

REGION **7**

## KINGS RIVER DRAINAGE/ FRESNO REGION

1 Kings River (SF)
2 Hume Lake
3 Tenmile Creek
4 Bearskin Creek
5 Big Creek (K)
6 Pine Flat Res.
7 Kings River (BPF)
8 Avacado Lakes
9 Kings River (R)
10 Whispering Lakes
11 Millerton Lake
12 San Joaquin River (BFD)
13 Lost Lake
14 Fresno Slough

# KINGS RIVER (SOUTH FORK)

*"I've been coming here for 20 years," he said. "The fish only bite for about two hours after sunrise and from an hour before sunset, to sunset."*

|  |  |
|---|---|
| **Rating:** | 7 |
| **Species:** | Brown Trout and Rainbow Trout |
| **Stock:** | None |
| **Facilities:** | Campgrounds, Picnic Areas, Restaurant, Pack Station, Gift Shop, General Store, Showers, RV Sites, Ranger Station and Vault Toilets |
| **Contact:** | Kings Canyon National Park (559) 565-4307, Cedar Grove Lodge (559) 335-5500, Cedar Grove Pack Station (559) 565-3464 |

**Directions:**  From the 99 Freeway in Fresno, drive 52 miles east on Highway 180 to the entrance to Sequoia/Kings Canyon National Parks. Continue 1.7 miles to a fork in the road. Veer left, heading north, and continue 20 miles on Highway 180 to the bridge at Boyden Cave. The river parallels the road from this point to the end of the road.

*A path parallels the South Fork of the Kings River to Mist Falls.*

Flowing through one of only a few easily accessible parts of Kings Canyon National Park, the South Fork of the Kings River is mostly fished by campers. The river is fast-flowing and wide, and if you don't fish it at the right time of day, don't plan on catching anything.

Luckily, when I arrived at one of the campsites along the river, I picked a spot next to a few fishermen who'd been fishing the river for the last week. It was about 9 a.m. I picked up my rod and started towards the river, when they offered me some advice. "You're not going fishing are you?" asked the fisherman cooking eggs over the fire. "You aren't going to catch anything. You're about an hour too late, pal."

Curious, I walked over and asked him to explain. "I've been coming here for 20 years," he said. "The fish only bite for about two hours after sunrise and from an hour before sunset, to sunset."

I've had fishermen tell me all sorts of stories and fairy tales, so I went out to fish the river for a few hours anyway. Not a bite. "See, I told you," he chuckled, as I walked past his campsite. "The fish are on a schedule up here. Go do some hiking or something and come back about an hour before dark. You'll catch a lot of fish, then."

I took his advice and went to see Roaring River Falls and Boyden Cave, returning just in time for the evening bite. Most of the campers had their poles out, too, and were getting ready for the epic evening bite. Sure enough, the fish cooperated. We had a great time and everybody caught fish. Many of the anglers used fly rods, but I caught plenty of fish with small spinners.

About noon the next day, I put on a mask and snorkel, and floated down the river, searching for the deep holes where fish were said to be hiding during the day. They were in the same places I caught them at night, only they weren't feeding.

The only drawbacks to this river are that most of the rainbow and brown trout are small, and it can be difficult to fish in the spring and early summer when snow runoff swells its waters. From the end of the road downstream to Boyden Cave, there is a two-fish limit. Upstream from the end of the road, only barbless hooks are permitted. It's catch & release only for rainbow trout, and there is a five fish limit for all other species. The California Department of Fish and Game stocked rainbow trout from 1950-72.

If you plan to make the trip, supplies are available at Cedar Grove. In winter, call ahead for road conditions. Chains may be required. The Kings River above Copper Creek is closed to fishing from November 16 to the last Saturday in April. There is a fee to enter Kings Canyon National Park.

Also nearby are Mist Falls, Roaring River Falls, Grizzly Falls, Boyden Cave, Cedar Sequoia Grove, Tenmile Creek, Hume Lake and Bearskin Creek.

# HUME LAKE

*Anglers do well fishing with Power Bait or night crawlers from the shore, or tossing spinners from float tubes.*

| | |
|---|---|
| **Rating:** | 8 |
| **Species:** | Rainbow Trout |
| **Stock:** | 15,650 pounds of rainbow trout. |
| **Facilities:** | Campgrounds, Boat Launch, Picnic Areas, Restrooms, General Store, Gas, Bait & Tackle, RV Hookups, Lodging, Restaurant, Rowboat, Canoe and Kayak Rentals |
| **Contact:** | Sequoia National Forest (559) 338-2251<br>Hume Christian Camp (559) 335-2000 or (559) 251-6043 |

**Directions:** From the 99 Freeway in Fresno, drive 52 miles east on Highway 180 to the entrance to Kings Canyon National Park. Drive through the entrance and continue 1.7 miles to a fork in the road. Veer left and drive 7.6 miles to the Hume Lake turnoff. Turn east and continue 3.2 miles to the lake.

*Hume Lake*

Fishing Hume Lake in late August of 2000, I thought to myself, "There aren't many lakes around here as beautiful as this. Hell, there aren't many lakes around here at all."

A dad walking by with his son ruined my thoughts when I heard him say, "Now, son, that's the dam over there. They haven't started letting any water out yet."

It figured. There was a good reason there weren't any other lakes in the region. This one wasn't supposed to be here either. It is man made. The Hume-Bennett Lumber Company built the dam in 1908 along Tenmile Creek, and used it to power a lumber mill. After the mill closed, the Forest Service purchased the land in 1935. Currently, Hume Lake is visited by anglers and campers, as well as visitors to its Christian camp and conference center.

Located at 5,300 feet between Sequoia and Kings Canyon National Parks, surrounded by tall pines in the Sequoia National Forest, 85-acre Hume Lake is a small, pretty high-mountain lake. The east shore of this family-style lake is packed with public campsites, while the south shore is run by the Christian Camp. The Christian Camp opens its services to the public as well as its visitors.

The lake is excellent for trout fishing. The California Department of Fish and Game stocks 26,350 rainbows from spring through summer. Anglers do well fishing with Power Bait or night crawlers from the shore, or tossing spinners from float tubes.

Trolling is also popular, however, only electric trolling motors are permitted. Concentrate on the dam area and the middle of the lake. Topwater trolling is your best bet. Leadcore or downriggers aren't needed.

If you plan to make the trip, supplies are available at the lake. Rentals are only available during the warmer months. No gas-powered motors are permitted. In winter call ahead for road conditions. There is a fee to enter Sequoia/Kings Canyon National Parks.

Also nearby are Tenmile Creek, Bearskin Creek, Stoney Creek, Big Meadows Creek, Kings River (South Fork), Roaring River Falls, Mist Falls and Grizzly Falls.

*Leaves change color in the fall at Hume.*

# TENMILE CREEK

*Half of the fish are dumped in pools above Hume Lake near Tenmile Campground, and the rest are released into pools near Barton's Resort.*

| | |
|---|---|
| **Rating:** | 6 |
| **Species:** | Rainbow Trout and Brown Trout |
| **Stock:** | 2,525 pounds of rainbow trout. |
| **Facilities:** | Campground, Lodging and Restrooms |
| **Contact:** | Sierra National Forest (559) 338-2251, Kings Canyon Lodge (559) 335-2405 |

**Directions:** From the 99 Freeway in Fresno, drive 52 miles east on Highway 180 to the entrance of Sequoia/Kings Canyon National Parks and continue 1.7 miles to a fork. Veer right, following Generals Highway for 3.5 miles to Quail Flat Road. Turn left and drive approximately five miles to another fork. Veer right (away from the Bearskin Grove) to the campgrounds along Tenmile Creek. Fish are planted in the campgrounds and at access sites along the road. The creek is also planted near Cedar Grove.

*Quail Flat Road*

For campers staying in Kings Canyon National Park, Tenmile Creek is the place to go for easy fishing. It is the only creek near the Cedar Grove end of the national park that is stocked by the California Department of Fish and Game. The CA DFG stocks 5,220 rainbow trout from late April through July, or as long as the stream has enough water to support the planters.

Tenmile Creek is located on a small parcel of national forest land in the Sequoia National Forest. The creek is fed by runoff from the mountains above Tenmile Sequoia Grove. The runoff forms Upper Tenmile Creek, which empties into Hume Lake. It's then released into Lower Tenmile Creek and finishes its run in the Kings River. Both Upper and Lower Tenmile Creek are planted. Half of the fish are dumped in pools above Hume Lake near Tenmile Campground, and the rest are released into pools near Barton's Resort.

To reach Barton's Resort (now called Kings Canyon Lodge) and Lower Tenmile Creek, veer left at a fork in the road, just after entering the national park. Continue approximately 14 miles (it's 6.5 miles past the Hume Lake turnoff) to the Highway 180 bridge crossing over the creek. The creek plants take place immediately upstream from the bridge and continue downstream a few hundred yards to Barton's Resort. Salmon eggs seem to entice the most fish, but small spinners also work well.

If you plan to make the trip, supplies are available at Hume Lake and at Barton's Resort. Tenmile Creek is closed to fishing from November 16 to the last Saturday in April. In winter, call ahead for road conditions. Chains may be required. There is a fee to enter Sequoia/Kings Canyon National Parks.

Also nearby are Hume Lake, Bearskin Creek, the Bearskin Sequoia Grove, Stoney Creek, Big Meadows Creek, the Kings River (South Fork), Roaring River Falls, Mist Falls and Grizzly Falls.

# BEARSKIN CREEK

*The main reason Bearskin Creek is planted is because it's situated next to Bearskin Diabetes Camp. The 520 rainbows dumped into the creek are meant to give camp visitors' something to do between seminars.*

**Rating:** 6
**Species:** Rainbow Trout
**Stock:** 250 pounds of rainbow trout.
**Facilities:** Primitive Campsites
**Contact:** Sierra National Forest (559) 338-2251

**Directions:** From the 99 Freeway in Fresno, take Highway 180 east for 52 miles east to the entrance of Sequoia/Kings Canyon National Parks. Continue 1.7 miles past the entrance to a fork in the road. Veer right, following Generals Highway 3.5 miles to Quail Flat Road. Turn left and continue approximately five miles to a fork in the road. Veer left and drive a half-mile to the creek.

Bearskin Creek

A sequoia trunk

A small creek in the Sequoia National Forest, Bearskin only provides limited fishing opportunities for anglers in late spring. The creek is planted near the Bearskin Sequoia Grove, but the time frame to get in on the action is narrow. The creek is a tributary to Tenmile Creek and because it's fed by a small watershed there is usually only enough water to support the stockers in May and early June. Also, the allotment is small. The creek is stocked with less trout than any other stream in the region.

The main reason Bearskin Creek is planted is because it's situated next to Bearskin Diabetes Camp. The 520 rainbows dumped into the creek are meant to give camp visitors something to do between seminars. This very small stream is best fished with Power Bait. The creek is also stocked just north of the ball field.

The principal attraction here is the Bearskin Sequoia Grove. It is notable because in 1975 the Sequoia National Forest first attempted to genetically alter the reproduction of sequoia trees in this grove. If you show up, you'll be able to see if they were successful.

If you plan to make the trip, supplies are available at Hume Lake. Bearskin Creek is closed to fishing from November 16 to the last Saturday in April. In winter call ahead for road conditions. Chains may be required. There is a fee to enter Sequoia/Kings Canyon National Parks.

Also nearby are Hume Lake, Tenmile Creek, Bearskin Sequoia Grove, Stoney Creek, Big Meadows Creek, Kings River (South Fork), Roaring River Falls, Mist Falls and Grizzly Falls.

# BIG CREEK (KINGS)

*Because it has large pools and is easily accessed by the CA DFG truck, one of the best spots to fish is where Duff Creek pours into Big Creek.*

| | |
|---|---|
| **Rating:** | 6 |
| **Species:** | Rainbow Trout |
| **Stock:** | 1,025 pounds of rainbow trout. |
| **Facilities:** | None |
| **Contact:** | Sierra National Forest (559) 855-5360 |
| **Directions:** | From the 99 Freeway in Fresno, turn north on Highway 180 to Belmont Ave. Turn east and drive 20 miles to Trimmer Springs Road. Turn northeast and continue 21 miles to Trimmer. Continue for seven miles past Trimmer, skirting around Pine Flat Reservoir, to USFS Route 9. Turn north. The road parallels the stream. |

*Big Creek (Kings)*

For those spending time at Pine Flat Reservoir, Big Creek can be a great escape from the houseboats, speedboats and jet-skiers. A tributary to that reservoir, Big Creek is in a remote area of the Sierra National Forest, about a 45-minute drive from Fresno.

Big Creek has two distinct portions. The upper stretch is in a pretty, heavily pined area, while the lower section is a lot like the terrain surrounding the reservoir: dry and hot, without much shade. Big Creek isn't heavily stocked; it receives less than 2,190 rainbow trout, when water levels are suitable, but it can provide good fishing while the trout plants are in progress.

In both the upper and lower sections, there are long, wide and sometimes deep pools, allowing anglers to fish with lures, Power Bait or salmon eggs. Because it has large pools and is easily accessed by the CA DFG truck, one of the best spots to fish is where Duff Creek pours into Big Creek. Big Creek is loaded with nice pools that hold fish, even when the creek stops flowing in late July. However, it isn't talked up as a good trout stream, because there are no services here. For example, all the campsites are primitive. I couldn't even find any restrooms.

The creek is best used as a day-use area. If you have a little extra time, there is a small waterfall on the lower stretch. It's exactly 3.2 miles from Trimmer Springs Road.

If you plan to make the trip, supplies are available at Pine Flat Reservoir. Big Creek (Kings) is closed to fishing from November 16 to the last Saturday in April.

Also nearby are the upper Kings River, Pine Flat Reservoir, Big Creek Falls and the lower Kings River.

# PINE FLAT RESERVOIR

*So, even though those giant spots we used to hear about simply got old and died, it's expected that by 2004 anglers can begin catching giant spots again.*

**Rating:** 7

**Species:** Largemouth Bass, Smallmouth Bass, Spotted Bass, Rainbow Trout, Brown Trout, White Catfish, Channel Catfish, Kokanee, Chinook Salmon, Bluegill, Carp, Sacramento Pike Minnow and Crappie

**Stock:** 26,300 pounds of rainbow trout, 424 pounds of fingerling rainbow trout and 498 pounds of kokanee.

**Facilities:** Boat Launch, Food, Showers, General Store, Boat Rentals, Restrooms, Full-Service Marinas, RV Hookups, Bait & Tackles, Campgrounds, Picnic Areas and Houseboat Rentals

**Contact:** Sierra National Forest (559) 855-5360

**Directions:** From the 99 Freeway in Fresno, take the Belmont Avenue exit east and drive 20 miles to Trimmer Springs Road. Turn northeast and drive 21 miles to Trimmer. There are several access sites here and around the lake.

*Biologist Larry Hanson with a spotted bass.*

Only a handful of years ago, Pine Flat Reservoir was recognized as one of the top spotted bass lakes in the world, a proven producer of giant spotted bass. When the first "spot" over 10 pounds was caught here (a 10.27-pounder was landed in spring of 2000), it became a state, national and world record. The previous record was a 9.9-pound spot also taken from Pine Flat in 1996. There are still some big spots in the lake, but the number is way down. Don't be too alarmed, though, because it's all a normal part of nature's cycle, with a little help from some outside human sources trying to get things back on track.

One example of nature's cycle, which helped to thin the spotted bass population, is that mature spotted bass eat the small spotted bass. The thinning of the spotted bass population was also exacerbated by what was thought to be a die off of the lake's shad population during a cold winter in the late-Nineties. In fact, the shad just waited for warmer weather and spawned in the summer instead of the spring. During this period, the feeding pattern of the spots was disrupted, slowing their overall growth rates. Added to these problems, for a handful of years prior to 1998, there was a lower occurrence of smaller shad in the lake, which gave the spots less forage.

There were still plenty of larger shad that love to snack on small spotted bass. To thin the population of larger shad that eat fingerling-sized largemouth and spotted bass, beginning in 1997, chinook salmon were introduced into the 6,300-acre reservoir. It was hoped that they would help stabilize the spotted bass population by eating the larger shad. When chinook are planted as fingerlings, however, they only grow at about a pound per year. So, additional plants of chinook took place in '98, '99 and 2001.

These efforts were designed to maintain a delicate balance that would increase the population of large spotted bass. Maintaining the right quantity of shad is one example of how this delicate balance works. You need a fair number of large shad so they can reproduce smaller shad, a primary food source for the spots in the lake. On the other hand, you don't want too many shad spawning in the winter. Even though that will create an abundance of small shad for spots to eat, there will also be more big shad, which tend to eat bass fry. The chinook seem to have been the right ingredient in this delicate balance, because they have successfully begun to keep the shad population in check.

Another human factor that added to the spots problems was inadvertently caused by the Army Corps of Engineers. Prior to this century, unaware of fish-spawning habits, they would draw down the lake quite substantially (up to 200 vertical feet) beginning on March 1, which hurt the spotted bass's spawns. A few years ago, Fish and Game biologist Jim Houk attended a meeting at which the water releases were discussed, and he asked if these releases could be held back a month or so to allow bass to spawn successfully.

Houk explained that the lake was being drawn down just two weeks after the bass spawn, and the water that was receding at two feet per day was exposing their eggs to air. Houk asked if these releases could be postponed until at least the end of April. The Army Corps, however, had to balance the needs of the spots with other concerns about the danger of flood and irrigation requirements. If there were no threat of flood, and irrigation needs could be met, the Army Corps agreed to try to meet Houk's request. Houk says the Army Corps has done a great job of keeping the lake levels stable during spawn.

So, what's the current state of Pine Flat Reservoir in 2001? Although the spotted bass fishery is on a normal downside stage of its cycle, things are looking pretty good. Even though there aren't a lot of giant spots currently in the lake, there are tons of small spots that grow fast, faster than largemouth bass. Also, in 1998-99, the larger spotted bass began eating the smaller spots, and that's a sign of a renewed cycle. So, even though those giant spots we used to hear about simply got old and died, it's expected that by 2004 anglers can begin catching giant spots again.

A lot of attention is given to Pine Flat's spotted bass, but the reservoir is much more than just a spotted bass fishery. Kokanee, chinook, largemouth bass, channel catfish, white catfish, smallmouth bass, sunfish, rainbow trout, brown trout and crappie all thrive here.

Pine Flat's largemouth bass don't get huge; a seven-pounder would be a lunker. Although the reservoir has plenty of food for the largemouths to eat, including bluegill, sunfish, crappie, suckers, squawfish, shad and redear, the lake's structure and the intense competition for food hinders their growth. In the Central Valley, largemouths aren't known to grow big in lakes that are extremely deep, anyway.

Smallmouth bass used to flourish here, but their population has diminished because spots and largemouth have taken over the lake. Most of the smallies are caught near the Kings River inlet or up in the river arm. The majority is smaller than 12 inches.

The lake's chinook have grown to adult sizes, and anglers are enjoying success catching them. Many of the chinook are now in the three- to four-pound range and can be caught in deep water; in the summer, most likely near the dam or down the lake's main channel. From March through June, trollers catch chinook, working Needlefish and small shad imitation lures in the top five feet of water. Although kokanee were also planted in 1998, overharvest diminished their overall population. With kokanee stocking planned for the future, the population is expected to stabilize. More than 100,000 fingerlings were stocked in 2000.

Anglers who arrive within a few days after a rainbow trout stock do awfully well. The 41,210 fish are planted at three launch ramps around the lake and tend to stay near the ramps for a few days before moving into deeper water. Those who float Power Bait or toss lures get in on the action. Also, nearly 160,000 fingerling rainbows are planted. Since anglers rarely target the wild rainbows and browns that enter the lake through the Kings River, you don't hear much about them.

If you plan to make the trip, supplies are available at the lake and at the Doyle's store just below the dam. There is a day-use fee to access some of the launch ramps and day-use areas.

Also nearby are King River, Big Creek (Kings), Big Creek Falls (Kings), Kings River (below Pine Flat Reservoir) and Avocado Lake.

opposite page Pine Flat Reservoir experiences drastic drawdowns.

# KINGS RIVER (BELOW PINE FLAT RES)

*Fish are planted at 12 access sites along the river, but the bulk of the plants are made at Winton, Choinumni Recreation Area, the handicap access area just above Choinumni and above the bridge just below the dam.*

**Rating:** 7

**Species:** Rainbow Trout, Largemouth Bass, Bluegill and Channel Catfish

**Stock:** 21,110 pounds of rainbow trout and 1,277 pounds of fingerling rainbow trout.

**Facilities:** Campgrounds, Picnic Areas and Vault Toilets

**Contact:** Fresno County Parks (559) 488-3004

**Directions:** From the 99 Freeway in Fresno, exit Belmont Avenue east and drive 15 miles to Academy Avenue. Turn south and drive one mile to Highway 180. Turn east onto Highway 180 and drive five miles to Piedra Road. Turn north and continue 8.6 miles to Winton Recreation Area.

*Kings River below Pine Flat*

The Kings River below Pine Flat Reservoir is mostly fished by Fresno residents. Heavily planted by the California Department of Fish and Game from the base of Pine Flat Dam downstream to Winton Recreation Area, the river is stocked with more than 32,000 rainbow trout, not including 24,724 fingerlings. All the plants make for good fishing and high catch rates.

Fish are planted at 12 access sites along the river, but the bulk of the plants are made at Winton, Choinumni Recreation Area, the handicap access area just above Choinumni and above the bridge just below the dam.

To access Choinumni Recreation Area, continue east on Piedra Road (past Winton) and turn north on Trimmer Springs Road. Drive eight-tenths of a mile on Trimmer Springs Road to Pine Flat Road and turn south. The recreation area is on your right.

To get to the bridge below the reservoir, continue about a mile south on Pine Flat Road. Flowing through dry, flat areas below Pine Flat Reservoir, the Kings River is wide and fast flowing here when water has been released from the reservoir. Stocks usually take place year-round, with the majority of the plants just below the reservoir. An array of baits will do the trick, including night crawlers, Power Bait, salmon eggs, small Panther Martins and Roostertails.

If you plan to make the trip, supplies are available in Piedra and at Pine Flat Reservoir. There is a day-use fee charged at most of the access sites. On weekends, the river can get pretty crowded, so plan on arriving early.

Also nearby are Avocado Lake, Pine Flat Reservoir, Kings River (Reedley) and Big Creek (Kings).

**None of the fish in the lake have any size to speak of, but during the week it's a great place to get in a little fishing without having to drive too far.**

| | |
|---|---|
| **Rating:** | 5 |
| **Species:** | Rainbow Trout, Channel Catfish, Bluegill and Largemouth Bass |
| **Stock:** | 8,200 pounds of rainbow trout. |
| **Facilities:** | Picnic Areas, Restrooms, Swimming Area and a Boat Launch |
| **Contact:** | Fresno County Parks (559) 488-3004 |
| **Directions:** | From the 99 Freeway in Fresno, exit Belmont Avenue. Turn east and drive 15 miles to Academy Avenue. Turn south and drive one mile to Highway 180. Turn east and continue five miles to Piedra Road. Turn north and drive 5.3 miles to the park entrance. |

*Avocado Lake*

For Fresno area residents who are sick of having to drive a few hours up into the mountains for some good lake trout fishing, Avocado Lake is just what the doctor ordered. Located in a county park less than a half-hour drive from Fresno, 83-acre Avocado Lake is heavily stocked with rainbow trout. The California Department of Fish and Game plants more than 13,520 rainbows from October to May, with most weighing in at just over a pound. During the summer the water becomes too warm for trout.

Shore anglers do well fishing with Power Bait, floating night crawlers off the bottom and tossing lures. Boat anglers fool trout by trolling small Panther Martins and Kastmasters down the middle of the lake. No gas-powered motors are permitted, but in the summer anglers have been known to bring float tubes and fish for the few bass and bluegill out near the tules. In the evenings, using mackerel, night crawlers or anchovies will catch catfish.

None of the fish in the lake have any size to speak of, but during the week it's a great place to get in a little fishing without having to drive too far. Come on the weekend and you might be disappointed by too many people.

If you plan to make the trip, supplies are available in Sanger. There is a day-use fee.

Also nearby are Pine Flat Reservoir, Kings River (below Pine Flat Reservoir) and Kings River (Reedley).

# KINGS RIVER (REEDLEY)

*Except for the early morning or late evening, the river can be difficult to fish because of water-skiers and jet-skiers.*

| | |
|---|---|
| **Rating:** | 4 |
| **Species:** | Rainbow Trout, Largemouth Bass, Channel Catfish, Carp, Bluegill and Crappie |
| **Stock:** | 500 pounds of rainbow trout. |
| **Facilities:** | Restrooms, Picnic Areas and a Boat Launch |
| **Contact:** | City of Reedley (559) 637-4203, Reedley Chamber of Commerce (559) 638-3548 |
| **Directions:** | From the 99 Freeway in Fresno, drive 12 miles south and exit Manning Avenue. Drive 12 miles east on Manning to Reedley. In the city of Reedley, turn south on Reed Avenue and drive one mile to Olsen Avenue. Turn west and drive two-tenths of a mile to Cricket Hollow Park. |

For most of the year, the Kings River in the city of Reedley is only about two feet deep. However, each summer, as soon as flows increase enough to aid farmers with desperately needed water and allotments for farming are met, the river begins to pick up speed and gain depth. Then, the California Department of Fish and Game responds by stocking rainbow trout, about 50 pounds (approximately 80 fish) each week, usually from June to August, or as long as the water remains suitable.

All the plants take place at Cricket Hollow Park, the only section of the river near Reedley that does not run through private property and is open to the public. Maintained by the City of Reedley, Cricket Hollow Park is a popular boating, swimming and picnic area for the residents of Reedley, most of whom haven't yet caught on to the trout plants. Consequently, not many people fish here.

In fact, the Kings River near Reedley isn't a great place to fish. It's more popular as a picnic area. Except for the early morning or late evening, the river can be difficult to fish because of water-skiers and jet-skiers. But, if you're up here anyway, and have a little time to fit a bit of fishing into your schedule, why not give it a try? Your best bet is tossing small spinners from shore.

If you plan to make the trip, supplies are available in Reedley.

Also nearby are Kings River (below Pine Flat Reservoir), Avocado Lake and Pine Flat Reservoir.

# WHISPERING LAKES

**It's a place you can take your kids and be certain they'll catch fish.**

| | |
|---|---|
| **Rating:** | 6 |
| **Species:** | Rainbow Trout, Bluegill, Largemouth Bass and Channel Catfish |
| **Stock:** | Weekly |
| **Facilities:** | Restrooms, Bait & Tackle and a Picnic Area |
| **Contact:** | Whispering Waters Fishing Lakes (559) 787-2625 |

**Directions:** From the 99 Freeway in Fresno, exit Belmont Avenue and turn east. Drive 15 miles to Academy Avenue and turn south. Drive one mile to Highway 180 and turn east. Continue five miles to Piedra Road. The lakes are on your right just before the turnoff for Piedra Road.

*Whispering Lakes*

If you can't catch any fish in the nearby Kings River or at Pine Flat Reservoir, why not head over to Whispering Waters Fishing Lakes? It offers the highest catch rates in the region

The lakes, which are opened to the public for fishing on Saturday and Sunday only, are a series of rearing ponds for trout, catfish, bass and bluegill. No fishing license is required, but, as with all private ponds, there is a fee. Although, the entrance fee will be the least of your worries when you see how expensive the fish are. Trout and bass cost $3.99 per pound, catfish runs $3.59 per pound and bluegill are $2.59 per pound.

With two large ponds surrounded by grass and shaded by tall trees, Whispering Lakes is a pretty little place. But, most importantly, it's a place you can take your kids and be certain they'll catch fish. Just make sure to bring your wallet.

If you plan to make the trip, supplies are available in Piedra. There is an admission fee, but no fishing license is required. Call ahead for updated fishing hours.

Also nearby are Avocado Lake, Kings River (Reedley), Kings River (Below Pine Flat Reservoir), Pine Flat Reservoir, Big Creek (Kings) and Big Creek Falls.

# MILLERTON LAKE

*Although these stripers do take skill to catch, at an average size of 16 pounds, they are worth targeting.*

**Rating:** 7

**Species:** Smallmouth Bass, Largemouth Bass, Striped Bass, Sturgeon, Channel Catfish, White Catfish, Bluegill, Crappie, American Shad, Rainbow Trout and Carp

**Stock:** 2,000 pounds of striped bass.

**Facilities:** RV Hookups, Campgrounds, Restrooms, Marina, Boat Rentals and Launches, Picnic Areas, Showers and Swimming Areas

**Contact:** Millerton Lake (559) 822-2332, Millerton Lake North Shore (559) 822-2225
Camping Reservations (800) 444-7275

**Directions:** From the 99 Freeway in Fresno, take the 41 Freeway toward Yosemite to Road 145. Turn east, drive three miles and turn south on Road 206. Continue to the lake.

*A goldfish*

Located 578 feet up in the foothills east of Fresno, Millerton Lake was built in 1947. In 1955, the California Department of Fish and Game began stocking stripers into the 4,900-acre lake. The plants were considered a trial run and continued until 1987 when they were suddenly halted. Although the experiment initially worked, it had begun to backfire. The striper population grew too large, and these predatory fish were eating most of the available food sources, causing other species to suffer dearly.

While the stripers flourished for a few decades without being replenished, anglers began to notice a downfall in the early Nineties. This reduction in population was caused by over-fishing and a lack of reproduction. In 1996, the California Striped Bass Association was granted a permit to plant stripers into Millerton. After 13 years of no plants, 1,000 fish were stocked, and now yearly plants of pound-sized fish have been slated into the foreseeable future. These stocks are expected to bring the number of stripers back up to where they were before plants ceased.

Despite adequate numbers, stripers aren't easy to catch in Millerton. Not only are they difficult to locate in this long, deep lake, but also because of clear water they are easily spooked when you do find them. Added to that, fluctuating water levels turn the bite on and off.

Although these stripers do take skill to catch, at an average size of 16 pounds, they are worth targeting. Caught in 1998, Roger George holds the lake record at 50.3 pounds. The official weigh-in came a full day after the fish was caught. Unofficially, the fish was 55 pounds. There are several ways to catch these stripers; but to catch giant stripers over 20 pounds, you need to put in some time.

Your best bet is fishing the San Joaquin River arm in the spring when stripers swim to the channel in search of food. Anglers respond by anchoring in the current and either casting hair-raiser jigs, using spoons or soaking anchovies. The "log jam" is the best spot when water is flowing into the lake; otherwise don't fish this area. If there's no water coming into the lake, this stretch, which is normally seven miles long, can be reduced to four, and it becomes too shallow for boats.

Trolling can also be a hit or miss proposition. If you're going to try it, use broken-back Rapalas or any lure that resembles a trout or shad. Silver or silver-and-black Rapalas work best. On sunny days, go to a more muted color or your lure will be too bright and scare off the fish. As the sun goes down, switch to a silver color. Fishing shad boils is popular in the mornings and evenings during the spring.

There are three other areas to target, which stripers use as "highways," swimming from one channel to another in search of food and cover. Winchell Cove is good in the morning; Squaw Cove (Dumma Cove) near the Madera Launch Ramp and Fine Gould also hold a lot of fish.

Here are some other tips when you're targeting stripers here: First, approach the area you plan to fish quietly (stripers are easily spooked, especially in clear water) and anchor at least 50 yards from where you plan to fish. Then use equipment that allows you to cast far. An eight-foot rod minimum is best.

Remember, because they get easily spooked, it's highly unlikely that stripers are going to be under your boat. So, you'll need to be able to cast a great distance to reach them. In clear water especially, ensure that you can cast at least 50 yards. Finally, use gear that allows you to fight a big fish. At least 17-pound test is recommended, but 25-pound test is better for the larger fish.

According to the CA DFG, Millerton's American shad population is the only known reproducing population of that species in any reservoir in the US. When flows are high from April through June, the shad spawn up the San Joaquin River arm. Although most of these fish average 16 inches, some can grow to 22 inches and reach four pounds. Typically, the shad are caught on small shadflies; however, mini jigs, Hopkins spoons and small silver Kastmasters garner their share.

Rainbows used to be planted in the lake, but that was stopped years ago when a copepod was found in one of the trout. With the San Joaquin River Fish Hatchery a short distance downstream from the dam, it was feared that in a high rain year a rainbow could get washed over the dam and spread the parasite to the fish there. There are some rainbow trout left in the lake, but they are rarely caught.

Of late, a few anglers have wondered if they've hooked a sturgeon. Yet, no angler can say for sure if they've really seen one. Although the CA DFG did plant 17 sturgeons into the lake in 1958, biologists are unsure if the fish have reproduced. Also, the sturgeon used to migrate up the San Joaquin River and may have been trapped when the dam was constructed.

*Brenda Kopperdahl with a hefty channel catfish from Millerton.*

133

How would you know if you'd actually hooked a sturgeon? The original planters could still be alive, but according to normal growth rates that would put them in the 300-pound range! That's why anglers who think they've hooked one can't be sure. At that size, they'll break your line, and you'll never get to take a close look at what's on the other end.

If they did exist, sturgeon would be hard to target in a lake this size. Many anglers have described fish they thought were sturgeon to fishing guides who catch them for a living. Because of the way they fought the guides told them that they definitely were.

Bass fishing here is also hit or miss. Either you'll get skunked or catch 20. There's no doubt that there are thousands of bass here, however, they aren't always inclined to bite. Clear water, boaters and too many bass tournaments have made them skittish.

The lake used to have a plentiful population of smallmouth bass, but when the spotted bass were introduced in the early Eighties they began to overtake areas inhabited by the smallies. There are a few smallies left in the lake. The spots, on the other hand, have exploded. George told me that when he tosses a seven-inch plug tied onto 20-pound test he catches spotted bass all the time. Largemouth, on the other hand, are few and far between.

If you plan to make the trip, supplies are available in Friant. There is a day-use fee. It is not permitted to take bass between 12-15 inches.

Also nearby are San Joaquin River (below Friant Dam), Lost Lake and Kerckoff Reservoir.

*Biologist Walt Beer and Eric Guzman display bass caught and released electrofishing at Millerton.*

# SAN JOAQUIN RIVER
## (BELOW FRIANT DAM)

**Although there are some largemouth bass, bluegill and catfish, most anglers come for the trout, and they are pretty easy to catch, year-round.**

**Rating:** 7

**Species:** Rainbow Trout, Brook Trout, Channel Catfish, Largemouth Bass and Bluegill

**Stock:** 19,875 pounds of rainbow trout, 2,220 pounds of fingerling rainbow trout, 900 pounds of brook trout and 69 pounds of fingerling brook trout.

**Facilities:** Picnic Areas, Restrooms, Campgrounds and Recreational Facilities

**Contact:** Fresno County Parks (559) 488-3004

**Directions:** From the 99 Freeway in Fresno, exit north on Highway 41 and drive 10 miles to Friant Road. Turn east and continue 15 miles east to Lost Lake Recreation Area.

*San Joaquin River below Pine Flat*

Although the San Joaquin River below Friant Dam provides good trout fishing year-round for the residents of the Fresno area, ironically, many anglers living in this area have no idea this consistent fishery exists. The thought of trout fishing in the summer months in a region where temperatures top 100 daily seems unusual to most anglers. However, the water released into the river comes from the bottom of Millerton Lake, so it's cool enough during the summer to hold trout.

The California Department of Fish and Game used to plant both rainbow and brook trout in this stretch of the river, but with the San Joaquin Hatchery no longer raising brooks, only rainbows are now planted. More than 33,310 rainbows weighing over a half-pound, and an additional 336,042 fingerlings, 2,700 brooks and 46,368 fingerling brooks were stocked in 2000.

The river is fairly wide, about 20 yards in most places, and provides good access. Although there are some largemouth bass, bluegill and catfish, most anglers come for the trout, and they are pretty easy to catch, year-round.

The best area is just below Friant Dam, which can be reached by following signs from Friant. More trout are planted here than anywhere else in this part of the river. White Roostertails, small Blue Foxes and orange Cripplelures work best for spin casters. Anglers who can find slower pockets of water do well using Power Bait. Although brookies are no longer planted, some are still left in the stream. There isn't a big population, but they have begun to naturally reproduce.

If you plan to make the trip, supplies are available in Friant. There is a day-use fee charged.

Also nearby are Lost Lake, Millerton Lake, Eastman Lake and Hensley Lake.

# LOST LAKE

**Because no special techniques are required to catch fish here, it's an excellent spot to bring kids to learn how to fish.**

| | |
|---|---|
| **Rating:** | 6 |
| **Species:** | Brook Trout, Brown Trout, Channel Catfish, Bluegill and Largemouth Bass |
| **Stock:** | 19,875 pounds of rainbow trout, 2,220 pounds of fingerling rainbow trout, 900 pounds of brook trout and 69 pounds of fingerling brook trout. |
| **Facilities:** | Picnic Areas, Restrooms, Campgrounds, Boat Launch and Recreational Facilities |
| **Contact:** | Fresno County Parks (559) 488-3004 |
| **Directions:** | From Highway 99 in Fresno, exit north on Highway 41 and drive 10 miles to Friant Road. Turn east and continue 15 miles to Lost Lake Recreation Area. |

*Lost Lake*

Located below Millerton Lake inside the Lost Lake Recreation Area, Lost Lake is actually the portion of the San Joaquin River below Friant Dam, where the river slows and appears to become a narrow canal. It's a great location to come to fish during the few hours after work before the sun goes down. It is so heavily stocked, chances are you won't go home without catching a few.

Because no special techniques are required to catch fish here, it's an excellent spot to bring kids to learn how to fish. There are also plenty of open grassy areas along the shoreline without any trees, so you can teach them how to cast without worrying about getting snagged.

Fishing for rainbows is good year-round. The California Department of Fish and Game stocks more than 40,000 rainbows, along with 336,000 fingerlings and 2,700 brooks with 46,000 fingerlings. Although brook trout will no longer stocked, they have begun to reproduce naturally. The stocks are split between Lost Lake and the river below Friant Dam (just below the lake). Another plus is that you can fish from canoes, rowboats, float-tubes and kayaks. No motorized boats are permitted.

In the summer, anglers who fish with anchovies or night crawlers during the twilight hours are often successful for catfish. There are some campsites along the river, allowing anglers to fish overnight while camping. If staying overnight, use caution, because there's been some problems with gang activity over the past few years. Be safe and don't come alone at night.

If you plan to make the trip, supplies are available in Friant. There is a day-use fee.

Also nearby are Millerton Lake, Hensley Lake, Eastman Lake and San Joaquin River (below Friant Dam).

*Most anglers come at night when the catfish are on the prowl.*

| | |
|---|---|
| **Rating:** | 7 |
| **Species:** | Largemouth Bass, Striped Bass, Channel Catfish, Crappie, Carp and Bluegill |
| **Stock:** | None |
| **Facilities:** | Restrooms, Boat Launch, Bait & Tackle, Campgrounds, RV Hookups and Restaurant |
| **Contact:** | Mendota Wildlife Refuge (559) 655-4645, Bruce's Bait (559) 655-2336 |

**Directions:** From the junction of the 99 and 41 Freeways in Fresno, drive north and exit Highway 180 (Whites Bridge Avenue). Drive west through the town of Kerman to Whites Bridge, roughly 100 yards after crossing the railroad tracks.

Fresno Slough

And I always thought it was dogs that chased chickens! On the way from the 99 Freeway to the Fresno Slough, I was proven wrong.

A few miles from the freeway, I made a left turn and saw a congregation of about 10 dogs sitting on a street corner in front of a small, grassy lot. They reminded me of a bunch of kids hanging out in New York City. But these were definitely dogs, ranging in size from miniature poodles to golden retrievers. They all had that loopy kind of happy look that dogs get when they're thirsty, dry tongues drooping from their mouths. I wondered if they were pets. But not one looked groomed. Knotted hair was the rule.

Then, from around the corner came a group of a dozen or so roosters and chickens racing toward the dogs, chasing them away. They chased the dogs all the way around the corner, until they all vanished from sight.

Now, I've seen a lot of bizarre things, but I've never seen anything like this. It was a hot day, well over 100. Was I dreaming? I looked over at my friend who also had a puzzled look on his face. "Did you see that?" he said.

We discussed it for a while, and agreed that we'd seen dogs chase chickens in movies, mostly in third world countries, of course. But, neither of us had ever seen chickens chasing dogs anywhere in the world!

A few miles up the street, we stopped at Bill's Bait and Tackle Shop on Highway 180. We walked in, picked up a container of 12 night crawlers and a package of stink bait. Bill looked at me kind of smug-like. "Fellers, you aren't going to catch anything with those," he uttered, wiping the sweat off his forehead with a white handkerchief. The heat and humidity had already drenched most of his white t-shirt. I couldn't tell for sure how much, because it was partially covered by a pair of blue overalls. "Anchovies. That's what they're eating right now. Anchovies." Bill seemed pretty sure of himself that the fish were in the mood for anchovies. So, I figured I better follow his advice.

Located outside the little town of Mendota, near the Mendota Wildlife Refuge between Fresno and Los Banos, the Fresno Slough is a remote body of water that holds a lot of fish. Ultimately, the canal's water comes from Lake Shasta. Released from Shasta Dam, the water flows down the Sacramento River to the city of Tracy, where it is pumped into the California Aqueduct. From the Aqueduct, some water is diverted into the Delta-Mendota Canal and ends up at the Mendota Pool. The Fresno Slough is the portion of the canal south of Whites Bridge, located on Highway 180.

If there are so many fish in the Slough why isn't it well known to anglers? The answer is "human nature." Anglers like to brag about their catch. We all know they'd sooner brag about one big fish than 20 small ones, and there are no trophy-sized fish here. The Slough is constantly fed with largemouth bass, carp, bluegill, crappie, channel catfish and stripers from the Aqueduct. But, because it's flushed like a toilet every two years and kept dry while work is being done on the dam at the Mendota Pool, the fish are never given the opportunity to grow to trophy size.

When there is water in the Slough, fishing can be excellent. Most anglers come at night when the catfish are on the prowl. The Slough is roughly 20 yards wide and has an average depth of seven feet. Boating is allowed and is the preferred method to fish at night, when fishermen anchor up and toss out cut baits, night crawlers or chicken liver for the cats, which average two to four pounds. Stripers, largemouth bass, crappie, bluegill and carp are also abundant in the Slough. The hottest bait seems to be live minnows. Most of the stripers and largemouths are in the one to five-pound class. The best fishing occurs on full moon nights.

If you plan to make the trip, supplies are available at Jack's Resort, located on the northeast corner of Whites Bridge. There is a boat launch fee. Fishing is permitted 24 hours a day, seven days a week and 365 days a year. If using a boat in the Slough, use caution; the water is extremely shallow.

Also nearby is the Mendota Pool.

*Catfish like this one, caught by Skyler Teitelbaum, is common at the Slough.*

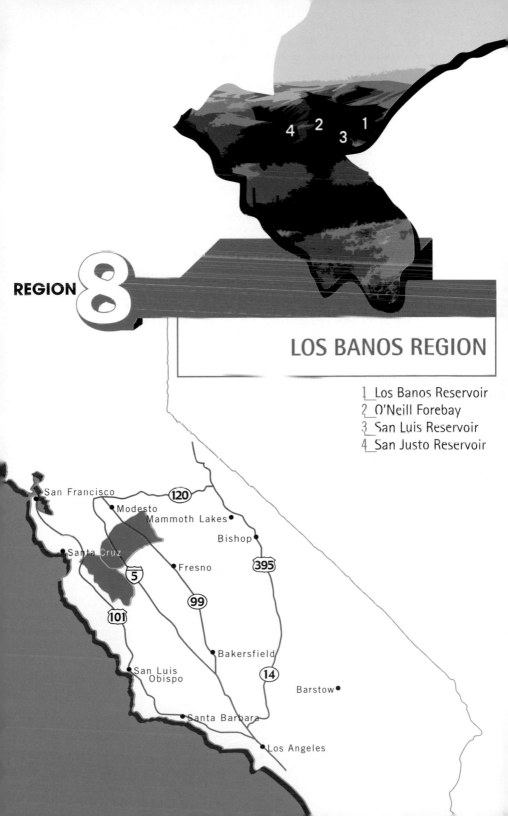

**REGION 8**

# LOS BANOS REGION

1 Los Banos Reservoir
2 O'Neill Forebay
3 San Luis Reservoir
4 San Justo Reservoir

San Francisco
120
Modesto
Mammoth Lakes
Bishop
Santa Cruz
5
Fresno
395
99
101
Bakersfield
San Luis Obispo
14
Barstow
Santa Barbara
Los Angeles

# LOS BANOS RESERVOIR

**Although not known as a bass lake, recently Los Banos has kicked out many bass to 15 pounds.**

**Rating:** 7
**Species:** Rainbow Trout, Channel Catfish, Bluegill, Crappie and Largemouth Bass
**Stock:** 6,000 pounds of rainbow trout.
**Facilities:** Picnic Areas, Campgrounds, Launch Ramp, Restrooms and Hiking Trails
**Contact:** California State Parks, Four Rivers District (209) 826-1196

**Directions:** From Interstate 5 in Los Banos, exit Highway 152 and drive east to Volta Road. Turn right to Pioneer Road. Turn left and continue to Canyon Road. Turn right and drive to the reservoir.

*Los Banos Reservoir*

Prior to the Sixties, the city of Los Banos was highly susceptible to flash floods during rare strong winter storms. Although the town didn't flood yearly, it happened enough to cause authorities to take measures to protect nearby ranches, farmlands and the aqueduct against a possible deluge. In 1965, a joint effort by the Bureau of Reclamation and the California Department of Water Resources to complete a 154-foot high dam along Los Banos Creek made the locals feel much more comfortable. Now part of the Los Banos Creek Reservoir State Recreation Area, the 470-acre lake has not only put a stop to the flooding, but has also provided a nice recreation area on the leeward side of the coastal mountains east of Gilroy in the Central Valley.

With extremely steep shorelines, the lake is best fished from a boat; however, shoreline anglers can access the water near the boat launch and dam area. Although not known as a bass lake, recently Los Banos has kicked out bass to 15 pounds. While crappie and bluegill are rarely targeted, catfish fishing from June through October is good. Towards dusk, those fishing in coves tend to land the larger cats. Traditional methods work well, but the majority of fish from 20-30 pounds are caught on whole mackerel.

When the warm water fishery slows in the winter, the California Department of Fish and Game hurries to the lake to stock 10,100 rainbows from December to February. The half-pound trout can be caught trolling small silver and blue Kastmasters, Needlefish and green Cripplelures. Bank fishermen, hanging out near the dam and launch ramp, float night crawlers off the bottom or cast spinners off points.

A 5 mph speed limit keeps water-skiers off the lake and anglers happy. The sky above the lake can get crowded on weekends with model airplanes; flying them is a popular activity here.

If you plan to make the trip, supplies are available in Los Banos. There is a day-use fee. Waterfowl hunting is permitted during hunting season.

Also nearby are San Luis Reservoir and O'Neill Forebay.

# O'NEILL FOREBAY

*Yet, when a breeze develops and a chop hits the water, the fish become vulnerable.*

**Rating:** 8
**Species:** Largemouth Bass, Crappie, Channel Catfish, Bluegill, and Striped Bass
**Stock:** None
**Facilities:** Boat Launch, Restrooms, Campgrounds, RV Hookups and Picnic Areas
**Contact:** San Luis Reservoir State Recreation Area (209) 826-1196, Reservoir Information Hotline (800) 346-2711, Campground Reservations (800) 444-7275

**Directions:** From Interstate 5 in Santa Nella, drive four miles south and exit west on Highway 152. Drive five miles to the sign for O'Neill Forebay on the right.

*Lee Haskin is one of the Forebay's top fly-fishermen.*

When it comes to the size of stripers, San Luis Reservoir and the O'Neill Forebay kick out near replicas. Yet, even though giant stripers are taken each year from both reservoirs, the chance of catching one at O'Neill is much greater. It all has to do with fish concentration.

In San Luis, fish have 12,520 acres and depths of up to 274 feet to roam and dodge anglers. O'Neill, on the other hand, located at 225 feet in the foothills of the Diablo Mountain Range, has only 2,700 acres, with a maximum depth of 40 feet. The fish have less space to wander here, with fewer spots to hide, and are therefore more prone to being caught.

Truthfully, even with O'Neill's conditions, catching these stripers is not that easy. Many of these fish have smartened up over the years. But when a breeze develops and a chop hits the water, the fish do become more vulnerable.

Boating is permitted in O'Neill, so trolling is also an option. Try the inlet and outlet areas and use large trout and shad imitation lures. But fishing from the shore can be just as productive, because anglers can cast into areas near the inlet where the stripers stack up waiting for food to be pushed into the reservoir. Although some anglers choose to bait fish with anchovies and sardines, tossing Castaic Trout Lures, silver Rapalas with a black stripe and large Krocodiles usually catches the largest fish. The state record a 67.8-pound striper was caught here in May of 1992.

Like San Luis, winds are a big problem here. When the winds kick up (50 mph gusts are common), you can forget about fishing. For those who aren't inclined to fish for stripers, catfish thrive in the lake. Try night fishing with minnows, night crawlers or liver. Using floating lights help, but it's not a necessity.

If you plan to make the trip, supplies are available in Los Banos and Santa Nella. There is a day-use fee.

Also nearby are San Luis Reservoir, Los Banos Reservoir and Aqueduct.

# SAN JUSTO RESERVOIR

**The lack of stripers allows the California Department of Fish and Game to stocks hoards of rainbow trout into the lake.**

| | |
|---|---|
| **Rating:** | 6 |
| **Species:** | 13,000 pounds of rainbow trout. |
| **Stock:** | Rainbow Trout, Channel Catfish, Crappie, Bluegill and Largemouth Bass |
| **Facilities:** | Restrooms, Boat Rentals, Bait & Tackle, Boat Launch, Snack Bar, Fishing Piers, Picnic Areas and Hiking Trails |
| **Contact:** | San Justo Reservoir (831) 638-3300, San Benito County Parks (831) 636-4170 |
| **Directions:** | From the 101 Freeway in Salinas, drive north to Highway 156 and exit east. Continue seven miles east on Highway 156 to Union Road and turn south. Drive 1.6 miles to the parking entrance on the left. |

*Fish getting released from the stocking truck.*

When most anglers living in Central California think of striper fishing, the San Luis Reservoir and O'Neill Forebay are usually the first two lakes that come to mind. Considering that San Luis feeds San Justo Reservoir, shouldn't that mean San Justo would also be among the great striper fisheries. No!

Although San Justo receives water piped in from San Luis, fish screens were attached to the pipe outlets to prohibit the stripers from getting into San Justo. If a fish were to slip through the screen, chances of it living after being sucked through turbines are slim. Bottom-line, there are no stripers in San Justo.

The lack of stripers allows the California Department of Fish and Game to stocks hoards of rainbow trout into the lake. The CA DFG unloads some 22,600 half-pound rainbows each year, keeping anglers satisfied from January through July, when the fish are planted. Traditional techniques, including trolling, using a sliding sinker night crawler rig and dousing Power Bait, work well here.

While trout fishing thrives in the spring, so does the bass bite. Chartreuse spinnerbaits are the anglers choice, however, in 2000, a fisherman landed a 13-pound bass using a night crawler from shore. Rumor has it when Coyote Reservoir was drained more than a decade ago, the bass from Coyote were dumped into San Justo, starting-up what has become a fairly good bass fishery. There is also a sprinkling of catfish, crappie and bluegill in the lake.

Closed on Monday and Tuesday, this 250-acre lake, which is 125 feet deep, is run by a private concessionaire who is under contract from San Benito County. San Justo's primary purpose is not for recreation; it's a holding reservoir, used for irrigation and to provide municipal needs to Hollister. Water is pumped uphill from San Luis and then gravity fed in San Justo.

If you plan to make the trip, supplies are available in Hollister. There is a day-use fee. No boats over 18 feet and no gas-powered boats are permitted.

Also nearby are San Luis Reservoir, O'Neill Forebay and Los Banos Reservoir.

# SAN LUIS RESERVOIR

*Don't get me wrong, there are still some 30- to 40-pound giants in the lake.*

**Rating:** 8
**Species:** Kokanee,Largemouth Bass, Channel Catfish, Bluegill, Striped Bass and Chinook Salmon
**Stock:** None
**Facilities:** Campgrounds, Boats Launches, Picnic Areas, Visitor Center, Showers, Restrooms, RV Hookups
**Contact:** San Luis Reservoir State Recreation Area (209) 826-1196,
Reservoir Information Hotline (800) 346-2711, Campground Reservations (800) 444-7275

**Directions:** From Interstate 5 in Santa Nella, drive four miles south and exit west on Highway 152. Drive five miles to the park headquarters sign on the left. The lake can be accessed here or by continuing on Highway 152.

San Luis Reservoir

Because of the rich supply of fish that were once pumped in from The Delta that feeds it, for decades San Luis Reservoir was known as one of the world's best freshwater striper fisheries. Several records were set here, and while huge fish continue to be landed, it sure doesn't happen as often as it used to.

San Luis' ups and downs as a striper fishery are directly related to The Delta. From the early Nineties up until the wanning months of 2001, the California Department of Fish and Game ceased any striper plants in San Luis, other than the relatively small amount of stripers that run up the Sacramento River from the Pacific Ocean each year, the only way stripers get into San Luis is by those fish being pumped out of The Delta into the aqueduct and the reservoir.

San Luis' striper fishery was hurt by a series of events that occurred in The Delta, beginning in the early-Nineties. These events include new and improved fish screens that were added to The Delta's pump plants to keep stripers from passing through, a change in the pumping schedule out of the Delta, angler harvest and the cessation of striper stocking in the Delta.

The biggest crisis to have an adverse long-term affect (I'll explain later how it initially bolstered San Luis' striper fishery) on San Luis's stripers occurred in the mid-Nineties, when three species that live in the Delta were placed on either the endangered or threatened species list. The Delta smelt was placed on the threatened species list (March 1993), the winter run chinook on the endangered species list (April 1990) and the spring run chinook was placed on the threatened species list (1999). Because stripers further endanger these fish, the decision was made that the stripers would no longer be stocked in the Delta. When the population of stripers in the Delta decreased, fewer stripers were pumped out of the Delta into San Luis.

Although improved fish screens were put on the pumps in The Delta to avoid pumping the endangered and threatened species into the aqueduct system, their smallest fish fry

143

can still pass through. Stripers could pretty easily get past the old fish screens, but these new screens remain on at all times, and although some stripers have been able to slip through the gates, their numbers are greatly diminished.

The authorities changed the pumping schedule in an effort to pump more water into the aqueduct when the endangered and threatened species weren't spawning in the Delta. They prefer to pump water in the winter, rather than in the spring when the fish are in the larva stages of reproduction and can easily slip through the screens.

There's a limit to the number of endangered and threatened species that are allowed into the aqueduct each year. The officials actually monitor the fish that get trapped in the large screens intended to keep protected fish from being pumped into the aqueduct. When these protected fish are trapped in the screens, they are picked up and put back into the Delta. If a fish passes through a screen, it's considered "take" (or caught) by the United States Fish & Wildlife Service.

It took a while for these above precautions to hurt San Luis' striper fishery, and in the meantime, things actually improved for a while before they got worse. The CA DFG decided rather than discarding 10 million stripers initially allotted for the Delta, they would dump them into San Luis Reservoir and O'Neill Forebay, and that was a definite short-term boon to San Luis' striper fishery. Added to those stripers, millions that had been planted in the Delta prior to the mid-Nineties were pumped into the aqueduct and later into San Luis Reservoir.

Because the reservoir was rich with goldfish, shad, smaller stripers, chinook salmon, small catfish and Sacramento blackfish, the stripers grew to enormous proportions, filling their bellies with these smaller fish. Word of San Luis' huge stripers spread, and not just Californians, but people from all over the country, came here for that big chance of catching a monster striper. So, while these temporary striper riches were being overharvested, far fewer stripers were entering San Luis, and the result was the diminished striper fishery we see today.

Don't get me wrong, there are still some 30- to 40-pound giants in the lake; but because the number of big fish in the lake is way down, huge lunkers simply aren't caught as often as they used to be. The decrease in large fish is in great part due to the fact that the number of stripers in the aqueduct have been greatly reduced, and also that the numbers of stripers in the Delta are way down.

So how do you catch the monster stripers that are still left? The most consistent method is using sardine wraps near the dam, tossing large shad imitation lures and trolling Rapalas. Anything that resembles an injured fish should work. Other methods include monitoring the fish on depth finders and then jigging silver spoons. Using seagulls to locate striper boils also helps. One of the best places for stripers is a cove near the dam. If you come upon a striper boil, try casting large white Roostertails or Rat-L-Traps into the boils.

Help may have arrived for the stripers. The Striped Bass Association has worked out an agreement with the CA DFG giving them excess stripers that were slated for plants in other waters. The Association raises the fish in pens at San Luis and releases them when they grow to appropriate sizes. In Sept. 2001, 70,000 six- to eight-inch fish were released. The project is funded by the Striped Bass Stamp Fund and the goal is to stock 100,000 stripers each year.

In April of 2001, the CA DFG had 120,000 excess kokanee, and instead of destroying them, state biologists came up with the idea of attempting to introduce these fish in San Luis. Although there was some opposition concerned that the stripers would eat the kokanee before they could grow to adult sizes, recent studies have shown that many of the kokanee have survived.

With a reduction in the number and size of stripers, the population of chinook has begun to increase. And while the stripers are difficult to catch without a boat, the lake's bass and catfish are more available. From June through October, catfish offer a good bite to anglers soaking stink baits in the coves. Bass fishing can also be good during the spring spawn.

San Luis is one of the state's largest reservoirs. In fact, in the United States, it's the largest reservoir filled with water from a source other than its natural watershed. With 65 miles of shoreline, 12,520 acres and a maximum depth of 274 feet, windsurfers, boaters and others also enjoy this massive lake. Ultimately, San Luis is a storage facility for water headed to Southern California, San Joaquin Valley and San Benito and Santa Clara Counties.

One thing that's important to consider when you're planning a visit to San Luis is that the winds howl here. I mean howl! A warning siren used to sound when conditions become too dangerous, however, that system is no longer used. Check the weather report before launching your boat. Here's a rule of thumb to follow: If it's cold on the coast and hot in the San Joaquin Valley, the winds are probably going to howl.

If you plan to make the trip, supplies are available in Los Banos and Santa Nella. Call ahead to check on weather conditions. When the winds howl, you don't want to be on the lake.

Also nearby are O'Neil Forebay and the Aqueduct.

*Stripers like this lunker, landed by Lee Haskin, can be caught in San Luis by anglers willing to put the time in.*

145            SAN LUIS RESERVOIR

REGION **9**

## CENTRAL COAST REGION

1 Lopez Lake
2 Laguna Lake
3 Santa Margarita Lake
4 Whale Rock Res
5 Atascadero Lake
6 San Antonio Lake
7 Lake Naciemento
8 Naciemento River
9 Abbott Lakes
10 Arroyo Seco River
11 Bear Gulch Res
12 Carmel River
13 El Estero Lake

San Francisco

Modesto

Mammoth Lakes

120

Santa

Bishop

5

Fresno

395

99

101

Bakersfield

Barstow

San Luis
Obispo

14

Santa Barbara

Los Angeles

# LOPEZ LAKE

*Lopez is also notorious for its bluegill and crappie fishing.*

| | |
|---|---|
| **Rating:** | 7 |
| **Species:** | Channel Catfish, Rainbow Trout, Largemouth Bass, Crappie, Bluegill and Smallmouth Bass |
| **Stock:** | 18,950 pounds of rainbow trout. |
| **Facilities:** | Boat Launch, Restrooms, Campgrounds, Bait & Tackle, General Store, Boat Rentals, Fish Cleaning Station, RV Hookups, Gas, Grocery Store, Waterslide and a Laundry Mat |
| **Contact:** | Lopez Lake (805) 788-2381, Lopez Lake Marina and Store (805) 489-1006 |
| **Directions:** | From the 101 Freeway in Arroyo Grande, take the Lopez Lake/Highway 227 exit and drive approximately nine miles to the lake entrance on the left. |

Situated in the foothills above the city of Arroyo Grande, with steep, rocky shorelines, Lopez Lake is a great family destination. With 22 miles of shoreline and 950 surface acres, the lake presents several activity options, including camping, boating and fishing. Added to that, it's an ideal place for catching smallmouth bass. And with the California Department of Fish and Game dumping more than 39,000 trout each year, trout fishing can be good. Anglers also catch largemouth bass, crappie, red ear and catfish during the summer.

If you're a newcomer to the lake, try perfecting the trout fishery first. Stocks take place from late fall through spring. Within a few days after a trout plant, shore anglers can nab easy limits, averaging seven to nine inches. But shortly after the plants, the rainbows leave the marina area and dart towards deeper water and the dam. Lopez's dam was built in 1969 for the purpose of providing water to the Five Cities area. Because of the lake's depth, trout can live here year-round. In the summer, however, many anglers have a difficult time catching them without downriggers or leadcore line.

As the water warms in March, action on the large and smallmouth bass picks up. The lake-record largemouth tipped the scales at more than 13 pounds. Lopez is also notorious for its bluegill and crappie fishing. In summertime, action explodes on these pan fish. Anglers using Jumper European night crawlers have been known to catch as many fish as they please. In summer, however, the real attention turns to the catfish.

The official lake record for a catfish is 40 pounds. But Jerry Weatherly, who operates the marina at Lopez Lake, swears by a 76-pound cat that he says was pulled from the lake in the late Nineties. Weatherly said an elderly man caught the giant cat and brought it into the marina to be weighed. Unfortunately the marina's scales didn't have the capacity to weigh something that big, they took it into Arroyo Grande and weighed it at EC Loomis. Since the scale wasn't certified, it wasn't classified as a lake record.

Keep an eye out for wild turkeys at the lake. When I drove through the entrance kiosk a few turkeys darted in front of my car. There are also a lot of deer and buzzards at the lake. The wildlife is as diverse as the fishing.

If you plan to make the trip, supplies are available at the lake. There is a day-use and boat lunch fee.

Also nearby are Big Falls, Little Falls and Santa Margarita Lake.

**With the maritime influence stirring up afternoon breezes, Laguna is ideal for windsurfing and sailing.**

**Rating:** 5

**Species:** Largemouth Bass, Channel Catfish and Bluegill

**Stock:** None

**Facilities:** Picnic Areas, Restrooms, Playground, Hiking Trails and Fishing Piers

**Contact:** San Luis Obispo County Parks (805) 781-7300

**Directions:** From the 101 Freeway in San Luis Obispo, exit Madonna Road and drive west to the park entrance.

Laguna Lake

Leave it to the windsurfers! With no stocks, a small fish population and half of the lake bordered by private homes, Laguna Lake isn't a popular fishing lake. Located in San Luis Obispo, down the street from the Madonna Inn, the 60-acre lake is set in rolling hill country just a few miles from the Pacific Ocean. With the maritime influence stirring up afternoon breezes, Laguna is ideal for windsurfing and sailing. Swimming is also popular.

With only a sprinkle of largemouth bass and catfish in the lake, the only reason to come here with a rod in hand would be to catch bluegill. Few have any size, but there are plenty of small ones to go around. Use pieces of night crawlers, red worms or white crappie jigs. There are many tules along the shoreline; fish near them and you should do well.

In the early Nineties, Laguna was a promising rainbow trout fishery; however, when plants were halted because of a combination of low water levels, poor water quality and a lack of oxygen in the lake, the California Department of Fish and Game opted to suspend trout stocking for the foreseeable future. There are no trout left in the lake today.

If you plan to make the trip, supplies are available in San Luis Obispo. No gas-powered motors are permitted. Only electric trolling motors with less than a one-horse power motor are allowed.

Also nearby are Lake Naciemento, Naciemento River, Lake San Antonio, Lopez Lake and Naciemento Falls.

# SANTA MARGARITA LAKE

**The lake is rich with bass from two to three pounds, with the largest largemouths peaking at roughly seven pounds.**

| | |
|---|---|
| **Rating:** | 8 |
| **Species:** | Rainbow Trout, Channel Catfish, Bluegill, Largemouth Bass, Striped Bass and Crappie |
| **Stock:** | 15,900 pounds of rainbow trout. |
| **Facilities:** | Boat Launches, Boat Rentals, Fish Cleaning Station, Full Service Marina, Bait & Tackle, Gas, Restrooms, Campgrounds, Picnic Areas, Playground and a Swimming Pool |
| **Contact:** | Santa Margarita Lake (805) 788-2397, Santa Margarita Marina (805) 438-4682 Camping Reservations (805) 438-5485 |
| **Directions:** | From the 101 Freeway in San Luis Obispo, drive eight miles north to Highway 58. Drive four miles east on Highway 58 to Pozo Road. Turn south and drive seven miles on Pozo Road to Santa Margarita Lake Road. Turn left and drive two miles to the lake. |

*Saladin Patterson fooled this black crappie at Santa Margarita.*

*Jerome Clayton is one of Santa Margarita's top crappie fisherman.*

Santa Margarita Lake, which is used as a reservoir to provide the city of San Luis Obispo with water, is one of the best bass fishing lakes in Central California. Yet, it doesn't come up much in conversation when bass anglers chatter about what lake they are planning to fish next. This is because Santa Margarita lacks trophy-sized fish, which causes many anglers to refrain from fishing it.

What Santa Margarita does offer, however, is consistency. The lake is rich with bass from two to three pounds, with the biggest largemouths peaking at roughly seven pounds. The lake record is a 10.12-pound bass that was landed before the drought in the early Nineties, which pretty much obliterated the bass fishery for the next several seasons. The lake was nearly dry during the drought, but Santa Margarita is poised to make a comeback and once again become a trophy bass fishery. Although it's not quite there, Santa Margarita is definitely on its way.

Bass fishing is typically best in March and April, when anglers use crankbaits, spinner-baits and plastics in the back of coves. In May, anglers target the weed lines along the lake, before the bass move off points and into deeper water in July.

In the mid-Seventies, striped bass were introduced, however, most of them were also killed during the drought. A 32-pounder was once landed, but there are only a few stripers left in the lake. Only one or two of that ilk are caught each year.

Santa Margarita is also a quality trout fishery. From November through April, the California Department of Fish and Game mercifully dumps 32,550 rainbow trout into the 800-acre lake, giving anglers a noble shot at catching a rainbow from 10 to 12 inches. Each season the CA DFG adds a few hundred trout, weighing two to four pounds, providing anglers with an added incentive to fish the lake.

Trolling down the middle of the lake and along the shorelines is your best bet. While trolling Kastmasters or small Rapalas for trout, it's highly likely that you'll land a bass.

Shore fishermen commonly soak Power Bait near the marina and boat launch areas.

As summer approaches and the trout bite dwindles, the catfish begin to prowl, swallowing up mackerel, anchovies, chicken liver and night crawlers from anglers fishing coves from late afternoon through the twilight hours. The bluegill bite also flourishes in the summer. Tossing out red worms or bits of night crawlers will land as many palm-sized fish as desired. In February, March and early April, there is a fair bite on crappie for those using live shiners.

If you plan to make the trip, supplies are available at the lake. There is a day-use and boat launch fee. No water sports are allowed on the lake.

Also nearby are Lopez Lake, Santa Margarita Falls and Atascadero Lake.

*Jared Fearon admires this crappie from Santa Margarita. (Right) Black Crappie*

# SANTA MARGARITA LAKE

**Despite the recovering steelhead population, officials report that only 50 are caught each year.**

| | |
|---|---|
| **Rating:** | 5 |
| **Species:** | Steelhead, Brown Bullhead, Suckers and Bluegill |
| **Stock:** | None |
| **Facilities:** | Restrooms |
| **Contact:** | San Luis Obispo County Parks (805) 781-5930 |

**Directions:**   From Highway 1 in San Luis Obispo, drive north to the town of Cayucos and exit Old Creek Road. Turn right and continue to the reservoir on the left.

*Whale Rock Reservoir*

Prior to 1961, there was a lot of controversy surrounding the construction of Whale Rock Reservoir in San Luis Obispo County. Proponents of the reservoir argued that it would benefit a growing population in San Luis Obispo. Opponents, on the other hand, said the reservoir would prohibit the steelhead from spawning when they made their run from the Pacific Ocean up Old Creek. Despite the opponents' concerns, the reservoir was completed in 1961, and the steelhead indeed did stop running up Old Creek, theoretically wiping out their population in Whale Rock Reservoir.

But, was the steelhead population in Whale Rock really destroyed? When Whale Rock was constructed, part of the contractual obligation agreed upon by SLO County and the California Department of Fish and Game stipulated that SLO County would be responsible for planting rainbow trout in Whale Rock. The reason for these plants was to reestablish fishing opportunities that were taken away by the cessation of the steelhead runs.

But those rainbow stocks never occurred, because when the dam was built, several steelhead were trapped in the reservoir before they had a chance to return to the ocean. Since these steelhead successfully spawned, the CA DFG told the county not to stock rainbow trout, because they did not want to corrupt the genetic purity of these rare steelhead.

Using Old and Cottontail Creeks as spawning grounds, the steelhead flourished in Whale Rock for nearly two decades. When their population began to dwindle in the Eighties, however, biologists discovered that suckers had been introduced into the lake. According to lake officials, an angler was using a sucker for bait and incorrectly put it on his hook, allowing it to escape into the lake. At least two suckers must have squiggled off his hook, because they reproduced and populated the lake.

The reason suckers harm steelhead is that they follow behind as steelhead swim up creek inlets to spawn, and the suckers eat their eggs. Unable to exterminate the suckers without poisoning the lake, the Whale Rock Project decided the answer to the problem

*Whale Rock Reservoir*

was to trap the steelhead when they spawn to protect their eggs from the suckers.

After successfully trapping the steelhead, their eggs were given to the CA DFG, who hatched and reared them until they were four to six inches and returned them to the lake. Although the suckers had drastically reduced the number of steelhead in the lake, the CA DFG has been successful in its effort to bring the population back. In 1992, the first group of steelhead that were stocked into the lake totaled 22,000; in 1994 there were another 12,000; and 7,455 were planted in 2000.

Despite the recovering steelhead population, officials report that only 50 are caught each year. That's because a series of regulations and restrictions make catching steelhead here pretty tough. First, only shoreline fishing is permitted, because Whale Rock supplies water to Cal Poly San Luis Obispo, Cayucos and the city of San Luis Obispo. To make matters worse, fishing on the lake is restricted to Wednesdays through Sundays, from April 29 through November 15, and on legal holidays. During most of this time, trout typically stay in deep water and are difficult to catch from shore.

The best method of catching steelhead here is by tossing inflated night crawlers from the shore. The fish average 12-16 inches, but steelhead up to 28 inches, weighing nearly six pounds, have been recorded.

If you plan to make the trip, supplies are available in Cayucos. Whale Rock Reservoir is closed to fishing from November 16 to April 29. Anglers may not use live baitfish. There is a day-use fee.

Also nearby are Laguna Lake, Lopez Lake and Santa Margarita Lake.

*In spring and summer, there's a decent bite on carp, catfish, bluegill and bass.*

| | |
|---|---|
| **Rating:** | 5 |
| **Species:** | Rainbow Trout, Channel Catfish, Largemouth Bass, Carp and Bluegill |
| **Stock:** | 7,400 pounds of rainbow trout. |
| **Facilities:** | Picnic Area, Restrooms, Playground, Fishing Piers, Swimming Area, Zoo, Paddle Boat Rentals and a Baseball Diamond |
| **Contact:** | City of Atascadero (805) 461-5000 |
| **Directions:** | From the 101 Freeway in San Luis Obispo, drive 16 miles north to Atascadero and exit west on Highway 41. Continue one-mile to the lake on the left. |

*Atascadero Lake*

There isn't much to do in the small city of Atascadero. During the winter and spring, however, the California Department of Fish and Game stocks the small, urban lake with rainbow trout every other week, giving residents a popular local activity.

Although the water clarity can be bad, catch rates are fair from December through April for those using Power Bait or dunking night crawlers from the shore. For a day or two after each stock, it's productive to toss small silver Kastmasters, red and gold Super Dupers and Phoebes from the shore near where the fish were planted. With 15,210 rainbows spilled into the lake, there are plenty of fish to go around.

The City of Atascadero has done a tremendous job keeping all the facilities up to par and the park's lawns green and trash-free. It's an ideal place to spend the day. There's a small zoo and playground, as well as a path around the lake, perfect for running, walking and biking. In spring and summer, there's a decent bite on carp, catfish, bluegill and bass.

If you plan to make the trip, supplies are available in Atascadero. No gas-powered boats are permitted. There is a 5 mph speed limit.

Also nearby are Santa Margarita Lake, Naciemento Lake and Naciemento River.

# SAN ANTONIO LAKE

*In 1999 and 2000, 25-fish limits of two- to three-pound crappie were common for anglers trolling three-inch broken-back minnows or using mini jigs.*

**Rating:** 6

**Species:** Striped Bass, Large and Smallmouth Bass, Red Ear Sunfish, Bluegill, Crappie, Carp, Channel Catfish

**Stock:** None

**Facilities:** Campgrounds, RV Hookups, Restrooms, Fish Cleaning Stations, Picnic Areas, Visitor Center, Storage Facilities, Showers, Lodging, Food, Bait & Tackles, Boat Rentals, Launches and Tours, Playgrounds, Gas

**Contact:** San Antonio Resort (800) 472-2313, Lake San Antonio (805) 472-2311

**Directions:** From Highway 101 in San Luis Obispo, drive approximately 27 miles north to the city of Paso Robles and exit Naciemento Lake Drive (Road G-14). Drive 23 miles west (Naciemento Lake Drive becomes Interlake Road) to San Antonio Road and turn north. Continue four miles to the lake.

Stripers were abundant in San Antonio in the Eighties.

Mike McMahon (Left) and Jeff Parlet (Right) with a double limit of bass caught in 1972.

Driving along the 99 Freeway in Central California, signs that read "Food grows where water flows" dot the road. That statement is also true of fish. Fish also grow where water flows. And to prove that point, over the last decade, fish populations in San Antonio Reservoir have fluctuated with water levels. Unfortunately, since El Nino in 1998, water levels have been down at San Antonio. And so has the bass fishing in this narrow 18-mile-long, 5,720-acre lake with 67 miles of shoreline.

From the Seventies through the mid-Eighties, San Antonio was known as one of the best bass lakes in California. Limits came fast, sometimes five fish in 30-minutes, with 25-pound limit norms. But that's all in the past now.

After the drought of the late-Eighties, the lake remained at minimum pool for three years, and the bass population dwindled. The drought did, however, do a few positive things for the lake in the long run. The exposed lake bottom became a forest of cotton-wood and willow trees, growing among brush, grass, mustard plants and tumbleweeds. These trees grew as high as 20 feet, becoming a nursery for birds, deer, pigs and other animals. When rain finally returned in the early Nineties and the lake once again filled up, water covered the forest, which loaded the lake with nutrients and created a perfect spawning habitat.

Although the bass fishery rebounded for a few years, because of unstable water levels through the Nineties, the fishery has been unable to make a full recovery. Added to the water-level problems, the lake has hosted far too many bass tournaments. Because anglers in these tournaments pull fish out of their spawning beds to take them to weigh-ins, many bass are never returned to their nests, and that obviously harms the population.

Currently, San Antonio's bass are fighting low water levels, and while there are still many bass in the lake, catch rates are way down. The best bite occurs in the spring, in coves and off points and ledges, with salt-and-pepper worms taking the most fish.

The California Department of Fish and Game wrote a report in the mid-Eighties, which cited a number of reasons for the decline in San Antonio's bass fishery. Included were the bass' competition with stripers for food, a profusion of carp and goldfish, over-fishing and tournament pressure. The report also mentioned the fact that cattle grazing killed vegetation around the lake.

Another setback for the lake's bass fishery occurred in the early Nineties. A commercial electrofishing boat that harvested non game fish was slowly thinning out the carp population. This was good for the bass because carp eat bass eggs and diminish water quality. Unfortunately, when wardens caught these fishermen taking game fish in the mid-Nineties, their license was revoked.

Stripers were introduced into San Antonio in 1971 to control an over-abundant shad population. The CA DFG didn't expect these stripers to reproduce. When they discovered they were reproducing, however, plants were halted in 1984. It seems these stripers were able to reproduce in high-water years, when the San Antonio River's flows were strong. The high-water flows kept their eggs buoyant, and they didn't sink to the bottom where they would become covered in sediment and suffocate.

Because of the lake's striper population, the CA DFG made the decision not to stock trout in the lake. Monterey County, on other hand, attempted to plant bows here in the mid-Eighties. They thought this would attract anglers in the winter, but the stripers inhaled the bows before anglers could get their lines in the water. Not wanting to pass up an opportunity, striper anglers anchored near where the bows were released and tossed rainbow-color Pencil Poppers and Hopskin spoons to catch the feeding stripers. When the

**Caught in 1980, Amy McMahon's first striper was a whopping 10 pounds.**

**Mike McMahon caught limits of stripers at San Antonio with little effort in the Eighties.**

county realized they were only paying for anglers to catch more stripers, bow plants were stopped the following year.

Rangers told me they haven't seen many stripers caught in the last 10 years, but that's because no one seems to be targeting them. The senior ranger at San Antonio also told me that no park ranger has seen a juvenile striper in more than a decade, which could mean that reproduction has ceased. When stripers are landed they average 22-25 pounds.

The crappie fishery here has been something to brag about of late, however, over-fishing has taken its toll on these fish, too. In 1999 and 2000, 25-fish limits of two- to three-pound crappie were common for anglers trolling three-inch broken-back minnows or using mini jigs. There is still a substantial number of crappie, even though the numbers are way down.

San Antonio's catfish shouldn't be ignored either. In the summer they can be found in two places: in coves at night and suspended near the dam in 50-70 feet of water in this 200-foot deep lake. If you drop dead shad down into that zone, expect to catch cats in the three- to 10-pound range.

If you plan to make the trip, supplies are available at the lake. There is a day-use and boat launch fee. Also nearby are Lake Naciemento, Naciemento Falls and Naciemento River.

*Naciemento is notorious for its white bass fishery.*

| | |
|---|---|
| **Rating:** | 8 |
| **Species:** | White Bass, Largemouth Bass, Smallmouth Bass, Bluegill, Crappie, Carp and Channel Catfish |
| **Stock:** | None |
| **Facilities:** | Boat Launch, Boat Rentals, RV Hookups, Campgrounds, Picnic Areas, Lodging, Restrooms, Bait & Tackle, Gas, Food, General Store, Recreation Areas, Swimming Beach and a Swimming Pool |
| **Contact:** | Lake Naciemento Resort (800) 323-3839 |
| **Directions:** | From Paso Robles, drive north on the 101 Freeway to Road G-14. Exit G-14 and drive 16 miles west to the lake. |

*Wildflowers blanket Naciemento's shoreline in the spring.*

Naciemento is one of California's premier vacation lakes. Its 165 miles of shoreline get swarmed year-round by water-skiers, jet skiers, boaters, anglers and vacationers just looking to lie out on the beach and get a tan.

With floating marinas, hundreds of coves and resorts, Naciemento is a lot like Lake Shasta in Northern California; it offers something for everyone. It's best to visit the lake in late winter through spring when the surrounding hillsides are green, wildflowers color the lake's shoreline and the temperatures are still bearable.

Naciemento has three main sections: the main body of water, coves and the Narrows. If you plan to fish, stay away from the main water body. Boaters rule this area; however, a 5 mph speed limit keeps them from spooking fish in coves and the Narrows. Yet, anglers aren't totally secluded, even in the coves and Narrows. Others enjoy them, too.

Naciemento is one of the most attractive areas for young fun seekers to vacation. Cliff diving, rock jumping, rope swinging and various water activities in the clear water attract teenagers from all over California to the Narrows. It can get really crowded. That's why anglers are encouraged to arrive during the week or early in the morning when the youngsters are still recovering from last night's hangover.

Naciemento is notorious for its white bass fishery. Generally in March, the white bass spawn at one of the lake's inlets. If you've never seen thousands of fish spawning at once, you should come take a peek. It's the best fishing anglers could ask for. It's typical for anglers tossing white Roostertails, Yellow Vibrax spinners, Kastmasters and worms to catch 50 to 100 fish on an outing. Trolling for the white bass is also an option, however, if they aren't schooled up they can be difficult to catch. During the spawn, fish near the inlets of Dry and Gould Creeks and the Naciemento River.

In the spring, action on small and largemouth bass can be good for those fishing off points and in coves. There is also an overabundance of carp in the lake. I went snorkeling near the Gould Creek inlet and saw one in excess of 50 pounds, not to mention a few 30-pounders in the same group. Try using corn, bread or dough for the carp.

As summer approaches, this place turns into a blazing inferno, the fishing slows and boaters take over the lake. The only chance you have then is dousing anchovies or mackerel in the coves in the evening, hoping a catfish will swim by and inhale the bait.

If you plan to make the trip, supplies are available at the lake. There is a day-use and boat launch fee.

Also nearby are Naciemento Falls, Lake San Antonio and the Naciemento River.

# NACIEMENTO RIVER

*Downstream from Lake Naciemento, the river can provide good trout fishing for eight to nine-inch fish, although a fishing permit must be obtained before entering the base.*

**Rating:** 5

**Species:** Rainbow Trout, Channel Catfish, Carp, Bluegill, Largemouth Bass and White Bass

**Stock:** 6,500 pounds of rainbow trout.

**Facilities:** Restrooms

**Contact:** California Department of Fish and Game (707) 944-5500

**Directions:** From San Luis Obispo, drive north on the 101 Freeway, continuing approximately 12 miles past Paso Robles, and exit west at the Fast Garrison Exit. Continue to Camp Roberts.

*Sid Poe holds one of the Eagle Lake trout that are planted into the Naciemento River.*

Have you ever fished on an army base? Well, here's your chance. The Naciemento River is stocked by the California Department of Fish and Game on Camp Roberts Army/National Guard Training Post, just a short drive from Paso Robles. In all, 11,720 rainbows are planted from spring through summer. There are also largemouth bass, white bass, catfish and bluegill in the stream.

Downstream from Lake Naciemento, the river can provide good trout fishing for eight to nine-inch fish, although a fishing permit must be obtained before entering the base. The base is only opened to fishing on weekends and holidays. With no trout planted at nearby Lake Naciemento, the river gives anglers in these parts their best shot at catching a limit of trout. Power Bait, salmon eggs and small spinners all work equally well.

If you plan to make the trip, supplies are available in Paso Robles. There is a day-use fee.

Also nearby are Naciemento Falls and San Antonio Lake.

# ABBOTT LAKES

*In spite of its stable fish population, catch rates can be fairly low because these fish need to be "enticed," as the locals refer to it.*

| | |
|---|---|
| **Rating:** | 5 |
| **Species:** | Channel Catfish, Bluegill and Largemouth Bass |
| **Stock:** | None |
| **Facilities:** | Restrooms, Campgrounds and Picnic Areas |
| **Contact:** | Rocky Mountain Recreation Company (831) 674-5726, Camping Reservations (877) 444-6777, Los Padres National Forest (831) 385-5434 |
| **Directions:** | From the 101 Freeway in San Luis Obispo, drive north approximately 90 miles and exit County Road G16 (Elm Street). Turn west and continue to the junction with Arroyo Seco Road. Drive west on Arroyo Seco Road to the lakes. |

Abbott Lakes

For most anglers who fish the Central Coast, Abbott Lakes don't exist. With bass lakes like Lake Naciemento and San Antonio only a short drive away, who would want to fish these two small ponds with no trophy-size fish, called Abbot Lakes? Simple, locals who can't stand crowds and don't own their own fishing boats, nor hundreds of dollars worth of fishing gear. In other words, mostly the residents of Soledad come here.

It's silly to ask if there are really fish here, because there are tons. However, since it gets so little attention and is rarely publicized, most anglers believe there are no fish. In spite of its stable fish population, catch rates can be fairly low because these fish need to be "enticed", as the locals refer to it. The reason is that the water is so clear that the fish need to be tricked into biting. Those who are skilled enough catch quality fish on a regular basis.

The lake's most targeted fish are its largemouth bass, which have been recorded up to eight pounds. Believe it or not, the most popular bait is night crawlers. There are also sunfish, bluegill, bullhead and channel catfish in the lake, but most of them are on the small side. Those with a rowboat, float tube or canoe do the best. No gas-powered boats are allowed. Shoreline fishing can be difficult because of heavy weed growth.

If you plan to make the trip, there is a day-use fee. Supplies are available in Soledad.

Also nearby are the Arroyo Seco and Soledad Rivers.

**For those who take time to fish the 20-yard wide river, whose depth can reach more than 10 feet, the chance of hooking into a rainbow trout is good.**

| | |
|---|---|
| **Rating:** | 5 |
| **Species:** | Rainbow Trout and Steelhead |
| **Stock:** | None |
| **Facilities:** | Campgrounds, Picnic Areas and Restrooms |
| **Contact:** | Rocky Mountain Recreation Company (831) 674-5726, Camping Reservations (877) 444-6777 Los Padres National Forest (831) 385-5434 |
| **Directions:** | From the 101 Freeway in San Luis Obispo, drive north approximately 90 miles and exit County Road G16 (Elm Street). Turn west and continue to the junction with Arroyo Seco Road. Drive west on Arroyo Seco Road to the river. |

*Arroyo Seco River*

A lot like nearby Abbott Lakes, the Arroyo Seco River is often overlooked by Central California anglers. Why? Most probably because there are special fishing regulations and no trout plants.

These regulations are so confusing they scare a lot of anglers away. Arroyo Seco is opened to fishing only on Saturday, Sunday, Wednesday and legal holidays, from November 16 to February 28. Also, only barbless hooks may be used and all fish caught must be returned to the water. These regulations are in effect beginning at the bridge near the US Forest Service Ranger Station and range 3.5 miles upstream to the waterfall. Above the waterfall, the river is opened to fishing from the last Saturday in April through Nov 15.

Did you get all that? Here's the logic behind the regulations: they are designed to protect native steelhead runs. Since it's unlikely that the fish will swim upstream above the waterfall, it's not necessary for the restrictions to be as stringent there.

For those who take time to fish the 20-yard wide river, whose depth can reach more than 20 feet, the chance of hooking into a rainbow trout is good. Rainbows to 14 inches are plentiful here, especially in the large, deep pools. Try using small spinners or Wholly Buggers.

Accessing the river can be a little tricky. It's possible to follow the river upstream from the bridge, however, most anglers walk up the dirt road from the parking area. The road parallels the river, but stays well above it for the first 2.5 miles. At this point, keep an eye out on the right for a trail that leads down the canyon to the river. The path guides you to where Willow Creek meets the Arroyo Seco. There is a bridge here to help you cross the Arroyo.

If you plan to make the trip, supplies are available in Greenfield. There is a day-use fee. Fishing regulations are subject to change. Check with the California Department of Fish and Game in advance.

Also nearby are Pine Valley Falls and Abbott Lakes.

# BEAR GULCH RESERVOIR

**Although fishing is still allowed at the reservoir, few people fish here, for the simple reason that there are no fish.**

| | |
|---|---|
| **Rating:** | 1 |
| **Species:** | None |
| **Stock:** | None |
| **Facilities:** | Restrooms and a Visitor Center |
| **Contact:** | Pinnacles National Monument (831) 389-4485 |
| **Directions:** | From Gilroy, drive south on the 101 Freeway to Highway 25. Drive south on Highway 25 to Highway 146. Turn west on Highway 146 and continue approximately five miles to the park visitor center. (It may look easier to access the park through Soledad on the west side, but the reservoir can only be accessed from the east, because no roads traverse the park.) |

*Pinnacles National Monument*

There is no place left to fish in Pinnacles National Monument. It was created in 1908 to preserve the unique pinnacle rock formations from which the park took its name. At the time of its creation, because of its dry and rugged location, the park had little water running through it, far less than was required to sustain fish. However, for the purposes of fighting fires, a rock dam was built along Bear Gulch Creek in 1937, creating Bear Gulch Reservoir on the park's lands.

Prior to the mid-Eighties, when camping was still allowed along the creek, in order to provide added activities for its visitors, the monument's caretakers allowed channel catfish to be stocked in Bear Gulch Reservoir. However, those plants were discontinued in the early Nineties. Because the remaining fish were not native to the park's natural habitat, the monument chose to poison the lake and remove them.

Although fishing is still allowed at the reservoir, few people fish here, for the simple reason that there are no fish. There are, however, plenty of other activities to keep you busy in the park. Numerous hiking trails exist, including those that lead to caves and to the top of the pinnacles.

If you plan to make the trip, supplies are available in Soledad and Kings City. There is a fee to enter Pinnacles National Monument.

Also nearby are Bear Gulch Cascades, Condor Gulch Creek, Bear Gulch Cave, Balconies Caves and Chalone Creek.

*opposite page Bear Gulch Reservoir*

# CARMEL RIVER

*Although there is a chance at catching a native steelhead here, catches are few and far between.*

| | |
|---|---|
| **Rating:** | 3 |
| **Species:** | Steelhead |
| **Stock:** | None |
| **Facilities:** | Restrooms |
| **Contact:** | Monterey Peninsula Regional Park District (831) 659-4488 |

**Directions:** From Highway 1 in Carmel, turn south on Carmel Valley Road and continue 8.6 miles to Garland Ranch Regional Park on the right.

*Carmel River*

The city of Carmel is known for its extravagant and high-class coastal setting, which also includes posh dining and shopping. Tourists from all over California also venture to Carmel to golf, relax and enjoy the ocean setting. Don't expect a similarly extraordinary experience when attempting to fish the Carmel River. While Carmel by the Sea is scenic and awe-inspiring, the river doesn't offer the same magnificent beauty. Not even close. Spending a day at the coast and then moving inland to fish the river is just asking for disappointment.

And the scenery doesn't make up for the bad fishing at the Carmel River. They're both the pits. Although there is a chance at catching a native steelhead here, catches are few and far between. In order to protect the native steelhead, there are no trout plants, and special regulations are enforced.

The steelhead run typically occurs from December through April, however, the river is closed to fishing from sundown on February 28 through November 15. During the open season, you can only fish on Saturday, Sunday, Wednesday, legal holidays and opening and closing days. Only artificial lures with barbless hooks can be used. These regulations are in effect below the bridge at Robles Del Rio/Esquiline Roads (Rosie's Bridge). The river is closed to fishing upstream of the bridge to Los Padres Dam.

If you plan to make the trip, supplies are available in Carmel. Call the California Department of Fish and Game before arriving. The river is also closed to fishing if the water drops below 135 cubic feet per second. The river is best accessed at Garland Ranch Park.

Also nearby are Garland Ranch Falls, Pine Falls and Monterey.

# EL ESTERO LAKE

**For better fishing access, there are fishing piers around the lake.**

| | |
|---|---|
| **Rating:** | 6 |
| **Species:** | Rainbow Trout, Channel Catfish and Bluegill |
| **Stock:** | 7,600 pounds of rainbow trout. |
| **Facilities:** | Picnic Areas, Fishing Piers, Paddle Boat Rentals, Playgrounds, Snack Bar, Baseball Diamond, Restrooms and a Skate Park |
| **Contact:** | El Estero Park Snack Bar (831) 372-8446, El Estero Boat Rentals (831) 375-1484 |
| **Directions:** | Driving north on Highway 101 in Monterey, exit Aquajito Road and turn left. The lake is located less than a mile from the highway on the left side of the road. If driving south on the 101 Freeway, there is no Aquajito Road off ramp. Take the exit signed for Monterey and turn right. |

Monterey is one of the most visited tourist spots in all of Central California. The Monterey Aquarium, Cannery Row, Pebble Beach, 17 Mile Drive and Fisherman's Wharf are bombarded daily, much like Disneyland. Saltwater fishing is popular here, however, freshwater angling opportunities are difficult to find. There is Del Monte Lake, but it's located on military land and there are few fish in its waters.

Located at sea level in the city of Monterey, El Estero Lake offers the best chance in the Monterey area to catch freshwater fish. Rainbow trout are stocked in the spring and summer months. The California Department of Fish and Game plants more than 12,045 rainbows, which anglers can easily land using Power Bait or floating night crawlers off the lake's bottom. Tossing small lures can also be productive right after a stock.

The lake is shaped like a "C," and has bridges that extend over the water where Third Street crosses over the lake. No fishing is permitted from these bridges. However, for better fishing access, there are fishing piers around the lake.

With Fisherman's Warf located less than a half-mile away, and Monterey State Beach situated along Monterey Bay just across the street, it can be difficult to keep your mind on fishing. To help keep your mind focused on fish, the fresh smell of the nearby commercial fishing operations permeates the air.

As for the amenities, they couldn't be better. The park is an ideal family destination for nearby residents with children, as well as for out-of-towners. Located inside the park, Dennis the Menace Playground is a place your kids will never forget. There is a retired locomotive for them to play on and pretend that they are conductors. There are also numerous bridges and various recreation equipment that provide great childhood memories. A skate park for skateboarders and rollerbladers borders the lake. And, as an added plus, the park is well taken care of and always clean. The surroundings are impressive, too. Grassy lawns line most of the lake's 20-acre shoreline, and cypress trees are scattered throughout the park.

If you plan to make the trip, supplies are available in Monterey. The park is open for day-use only.

Also nearby are the Monterey Aquarium, 17 Mile Drive, Fisherman's Wharf and Cannery Row.

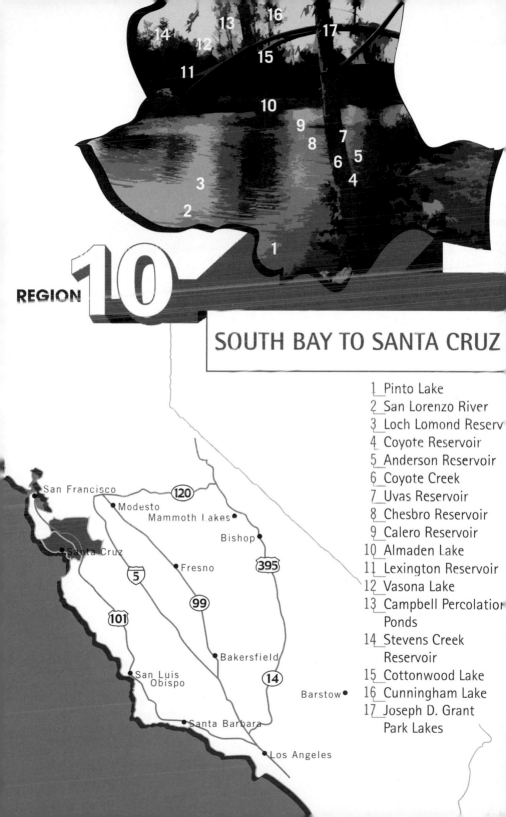

REGION **10**

# SOUTH BAY TO SANTA CRUZ

1 Pinto Lake
2 San Lorenzo River
3 Loch Lomond Reserv
4 Coyote Reservoir
5 Anderson Reservoir
6 Coyote Creek
7 Uvas Reservoir
8 Chesbro Reservoir
9 Calero Reservoir
10 Almaden Lake
11 Lexington Reservoir
12 Vasona Lake
13 Campbell Percolatior
Ponds
14 Stevens Creek
Reservoir
15 Cottonwood Lake
16 Cunningham Lake
17 Joseph D. Grant
Park Lakes

# PINTO LAKE

*In the winter and spring, when the wind isn't howling, trout fishing can be fair.*

**Rating:** 5
**Species:** Rainbow Trout, Channel Catfish, Crappie, Bluegill and Carp
**Stock:** 17,600 pounds of rainbow trout.
**Facilities:** Restrooms, Boat Launch, Baseball Diamond, Volleyball Court, RV Hookups, Campground and Picnic Areas
**Contact:** Pinto Lake (831) 722-8129

**Directions:** From Highway 1 in Watsonville, exit Airport Blvd. and drive 2.1 miles northeast to Green Valley Road. Turn north and drive a half-mile to Pinto Lake Park on the left.

*Anglers await the stocking of Pinto Lake.*

I was on my way through Castroville, the Artichoke Capital of the World, just a few miles south of Watsonville on Highway 1, when I stopped at a stand to purchase a few artichokes.

The cashier saw fishing poles in the back of my car. "Going fishing?"

"Well, I'm not sure. Are there any good places to catch trout around here?" I was kind of distracted, checking out this giant replica of an artichoke in front of the restaurant next door.

"There's always Pinto Lake, up the road. Me and the boys catch trout there all the time."

Banking on Pinto being a great fishing lake, I decided to drive up Pacific Coast Highway to find it. With a bag of fresh artichokes in hand, I got back in my car and searched for Pinto, figuring it was going to be easy to spot since it was just "up the road." I quickly learned that "up the road" has a different meaning when you live in Castroville. The lake was at least 20 miles north.

When I found it, I also learned that Pinto Lake Park is not just for anglers. (Not even close!) In fact, the park is Watsonville's premier recreation area. There's a top-notch baseball diamond, volleyball courts, nature trails, a campground, picnic area, and, of course, the 67-acre lake.

In the winter and spring, when the wind isn't howling, trout fishing can be fair. The California Department of Fish and Game dumps more than 29,500 rainbows in the lake, which is surrounded by bushy shores with lots of trees encroaching on its waterline. If you can avoid getting tangled by the hundreds of ducks and geese that are quacking everywhere, soaking Power Bait is your best bet. For a few days after a stock, tossing small silver Kastmasters or silver and red Super Dupers works well, too.

As summer approaches, the trout die off, and anglers focus on the evening catfish bite, which is best on night crawlers dipped in Hog Wild sauce, or cut mackerel. The bluegill bite is also fair in the summer, however, few grow larger than pan size.

If you plan to make the trip, supplies are available in Watsonville. There is a 5 mph speed limit.

Also nearby are San Justo Reservoir, Loch Lomond Reservoir and San Lorenzo River.

| | |
|---|---|
| **Rating:** | 4 |
| **Species:** | Rainbow Trout and Steelhead |
| **Stock:** | None |
| **Facilities:** | Restrooms |
| **Contact:** | California Department of Fish and Game (831) 649-2870 |

**Directions:** From Highway 1 in Santa Cruz, exit Highway 9 and drive north to several access points along the road.

*San Lorenzo River*

Like many rivers along the California coast, at one time the San Lorenzo River, near Santa Cruz, was rich with steelhead during seasonal spawning periods.Over the last few decades, several factors, including floods, drought, sediment buildup, water diversion and dams, brought devastation on the fishery. The steelhead is now on the endangered species list, and the seasonal runs have dwindled. So, most anglers have simply given up on fishing the river.

Hatchery reared steelhead, however, have also been planted in the San Lorenzo. If you want to give it a try, the runs can start as early as October and last until April, although the bulk of the run takes place from mid-December through March. Concentrate your efforts near tributaries to the San Lorenzo; Zianne Creek is the best.

Coho salmon also used to inhabit the river, but their population is now non-existent. In the early Nineties, the California Department of Fish and Game stocked some young coho, but the program was deemed unsuccessful. In November of 1996, the US Fish & Wildlife Service added the coho to the list of endangered species.

If you plan to make the trip, supplies are available in Santa Cruz. The San Lorenzo River is open to fishing from November 16 through February 28, on Saturday, Sunday, Wednesday, legal holidays and opening and closing days. Only barbless hooks may be used, and one hatchery trout or steelhead may be kept.

Also nearby are Loch Lomond Reservoir and Big Basin State Park.

# LOCH LOMOND RESERVOIR

*While the trout population is maintained through stocking, the largemouths fluctuate with the lake's crawdad population.*

| | |
|---|---|
| **Rating:** | 8 |
| **Species:** | Rainbow Trout, Bluegill, Largemouth Bass, Channel Catfish and Sculpin |
| **Stock:** | 12,250 pounds of rainbow trout. |
| **Facilities:** | Picnic Areas, Boat Launch, Bait and Tackle, Restrooms, Boat Rentals, Snack Bar, Fishing Piers |
| **Contact:** | Loch Lomond Reservoir (831) 420-5320 or (831) 335-7424 |
| **Directions:** | From Santa Cruz, drive east on Highway 17 to the Mt. Herman exit. Turn west and drive four miles to Zayante Road. Turn north, continue 3.2 miles, and bear left onto Lompico Road. Follow signs to the reservoir. |

*Loch Lomond Reservoir*

To many residents along the Central Coast, Loch Lomond Reservoir offers a lot more than just the water it supplies to the cities of Santa Cruz and Capitola. Surrounded by tall pines and fresh mountain air, it also offers good fishing, for starters. Added to that, Loch Lomond is one of only a few places in the region that give anglers that "wilderness feeling."

Loch Lomond hasn't always been a great fishing hole. Drought kept the lake closed to the public from 1988-91. The water got so low that the 87-acre lake, which today averages 100 feet deep, was reduced to a stream flowing down its middle and a small pool near the dam. It was a true mud puddle. The fish populations also took a big hit, but have since made a great recovery.

The lake has a good population of rainbow trout, bluegill and largemouth bass, as well as a small population of channel catfish. While the trout population is maintained through stocking, the largemouths fluctuate with the lake's crawdad population. When there are a lot of crawdads, the bass population grows. Bass weighing more than 12 pounds have yet to be caught here, however, if the lake's levels remain high for the next few years, a chance of a new lake record is possible. Bluegill are caught by the dozens in coves in the summer, and a 2.5 pounder is the current lake record.

Most anglers fish Loch Lomond for trout. At 700 feet in the Santa Cruz Mountains, the climate is ideal for rainbows. It doesn't get too hot or too cold. It's only snowed twice here in the last two decades (December 1990 and February 2001), and it doesn't become a summer inferno like many of the lakes to the east near Gilroy.

The lake is deep enough to sustain trout year-round. The California Department of Fish and Game keeps catch rates consistent by dumping 20,990 trout in the lake from March through June. No trout plants are made after July 1. Standard topwater trolling techniques work great from March to June, but as the water warms in July, the trout move to deeper water, and the use of leadcore or downriggers is required.

Shore anglers do well fishing for the rainbows, too. Dunking Power Bait off points and in coves produces good catch rates. Try not to fish the lake right after a powerful storm hits the coast. Storms cause the lake's inlets to swell, which brings in dirt and debris, turning the water brown and shutting off the trout bite.

Shortly after the dam was completed in 1963, channel catfish were introduced into the lake, but they haven't faired well because there is no spawning habitat. Lake staff told me that since the mid-Nineties they've seen only one catfish checked in per year. The few cats left in the lake are big; a 32-pound lake record proves that.

Because it's a drinking water reservoir, no body contact with the lake is permitted, and Lock Lomond is drawn down each year. Part of the agreement that allowed the dam to be built was that the lake would maintain a minimum release year-round, in order to maintain a sufficient amount of water in Newell Creek, which is a tributary to the San Lorenzo River where native steelhead runs occur.

Sculpin are also found in the reservoir, but are in no way considered a game fish. They are native to coastal streams and rarely grow longer than four inches. Anglers somehow catch them from time to time. They feed on pieces of night crawlers.

If you plan to make the trip, supplies are available in Felton. There is a day-use fee. Due to low visitation, Lock Lomond is closed from September 16 through February. No gas-powered motors are permitted.

Also nearby are San Lorenzo River, Sempervirens Falls and Big Basin State Park.

# COYOTE RESERVOIR

*To date, a 16-pounder caught in May of 2001 is the largest bass recorded, however, the lake has a ton of 12 inchers.*

| | |
|---|---|
| **Rating:** | 6 |
| **Species:** | Rainbow Trout, Largemouth Bass, Channel Catfish, White Catfish, Bluegill and Crappie |
| **Stock:** | 18,950 pounds of rainbow trout. |
| **Facilities:** | Restrooms, Boat Launch, Campgrounds, Picnic Areas and Fish-Cleaning Stations |
| **Contact:** | Coyote Lake (408) 842-9798 |
| **Directions:** | From the 101 Freeway in Gilroy, exit Leavesley Road. Drive east 1.8 miles to New Avenue and turn north. Drive six-tenths of a mile to Roop Road. Turn east and drive 3.3 miles to Coyote Lake Road. Turn north and drive 2.2 miles to the lake. |

*Coyote Reservoir*

Is Coyote Reservoir the best largemouth bass fishery in Santa Clara County? Depends on who you ask. Not wanting to spread the news too widely, the park rangers will quietly tell you yes. Experienced bass anglers will almost always tell you no, because they're smart enough not to leak the word and risk other anglers encroaching on their territory. As for those who fish the lake on occasion, they can't seem to make up their minds. And the California Department of Fish and Game couldn't tell me much of anything. Seems the last time they surveyed the lake was in 1981, and nearly all the fish sampled at that time have since perished.

At 688 acres, Coyote is large enough to be a viable bass fishery; it also has the right ingredients, including a healthy insect population, trout stocks, crawdads, minnows and shad. Black crappie and bluegill fry are also abundant and provide the bass with the forage they need to grow quickly. To date, a 16-pounder caught in May of 2001 is the largest bass recorded, however, the lake has a ton of 12-inchers. Anglers seem to do best with anything that has a flashy blade.

Set at 1,000 feet in the foothills of the Mount Hamilton Mountain Range, Coyote, which was constructed in 1936, may also be the best trout fishery in the county. In addition to 23,385 half-pound rainbows spilled into the lake by the California Department of Fish and Game from March through June, Santa Clara County pays Mt. Lassen Trout Farms to stock another 7,000 pounds of rainbows, many weighing three to 10 pounds. Those fish join a handful of holdovers from years past.

Fishing can be difficult in the summer when water-skiers and other boaters bombard the water. But there are two no-wake zones, one on the north end and another on the south. Each covers about a mile of space and offers anglers calm water.

If you plan to make the trip, supplies are available in Gilroy. There is a day-use fee. In fall, call ahead for launching conditions. Low water commonly forces the closure of the ramp during this period.

Also nearby are Anderson Reservoir and Coyote Creek.

# ANDERSON RESERVOIR

*Anglers come to Anderson to bass fish, and unfortunately that's also been pretty crappy over the past decade.*

**Rating:** 5

**Species:** Rainbow Trout, Channel Catfish, Crappie, Bluegill, Largemouth Bass and Carp

**Stock:** None

**Facilities:** Launch Ramp, Picnic Areas and Restrooms

**Contact:** Anderson Reservoir (408) 779-3634

**Directions:** From the 101 Freeway in Gilroy, drive north to Morgan Hill and exit Cochran Road. Turn right and continue three miles to the lake.

*Anderson Reservoir*

Because the California Department of Fish and Game doesn't stock 1,600-acre Anderson Reservoir with trout, many anglers are curious where the trout they catch here come from. Since it's a known fact that trout can't reproduce in Anderson, you'd think it would be easy to guess, right?

Because there's a dam that inhibits fish from swimming upstream out of Coyote Creek into the lake, there's only one other place the trout could be coming from: Coyote Reservoir, the lake's main water source. But, are there trout in Coyote? Yup: tons of 'em. The CA DFG stocks thousands of trout in Coyote each year, many of which get washed down into Anderson.

Okay, enough for the trout caught in Anderson; the population is minimal, and they aren't hooked that often. Anglers come to Anderson to bass fish, and unfortunately that's also been pretty crappy over the past decade.

Anderson's unimpressive bass fishery is directly related to a lack of forage and extreme drawdowns. There are a handful of smaller one- to three-pound fish in the lake, but few over five pounds are ever caught. And the lack of bigger fish has discouraged many anglers from fishing here. There is a decent crappie bite in the spring, but your best bet is carp fishing, and not many angers are into that.

If you plan to make the trip, supplies are available in Gilroy. There is a day-use fee.

Also nearby are Coyote Reservoir, Coyote Creek, Uvas Reservoir and Chesbro Reservoir.

# COYOTE CREEK

*Some pools are large enough for casting small lures, but drifting salmon eggs and Power Bait are your best bets.*

**Rating:** 6
**Species:** None
**Stock:** Rainbow Trout
**Facilities:** Picnic Areas and Restrooms
**Contact:** Santa Clara County Parks and Recreation (408) 358-3741

**Directions:** At the junction of the 101 Freeway and Interstate 680 in San Jose, drive 18 miles south on the 101 to Cochran Road. Drive 1.2 miles northeast to the county park on the left. Coyote Creek is visible from the road.

*Coyote Creek*

When it comes to urban fishing, Santa Clara County has done a tremendous job providing anglers with dozens of lakes to fish, however, stream fishing sites are hard to come by. From San Jose to Gilroy, and throughout the South Bay Area, Coyote Creek is the only creek stocked with rainbow trout. There are other streams in the region with enough water suitable for trout, but most of them have been set aside for native steelhead to make their seasonal runs upstream. Biologists don't want stocked trout to breed with the steelheads, so the streams aren't planted.

Fed by water released from Anderson Reservoir, Coyote Creek provides anglers with a good fishery for planted fish. Ranging from five to 10 feet wide, the creek was last stocked with 9,015 trout in 1999. These stocks by the California Department of Fish and Game were spread out from April through September and have been stopped to protect native steelhead runs.

Some pools are large enough for casting small lures, but drifting salmon eggs and Power Bait are your best bets. Stick to fishing the one-mile section downstream from Anderson. The rest of the creek isn't planted.

If you plan to make the trip, supplies are available in Morgan Hill. There is fee if you park in the day-use county park. Parking alongside the road is free.

Also nearby are Uvas Reservoir, Anderson Reservoir, Coyote Lake, Chesbro Reservoir and Calero Reservoir.

# UVAS RESERVOIR

*The largemouth bass fishery at Uvas Reservoir was hit hard during the drought years of the early Nineties.*

| | |
|---|---|
| **Rating:** | 4 |
| **Species:** | Largemouth Bass, Channel Catfish, Crappie, Bluegill and Carp |
| **Stock:** | None |
| **Facilities:** | Boat Launch, Restrooms and Picnic Area |
| **Contact:** | Uvas Reservoir (408) 779-9232, Santa Clara County Parks and Recreation (408) 358-3741 |
| **Directions:** | From the 101 Freeway in Gilroy, drive north to Morgan Hill and exit Cochran. Drive west on Cochran to Monterey Highway and turn south. Drive to Watsonville Road and turn west. Take Watsonville to Uvas Road (G8) and turn north to the reservoir. |

*Uvas Reservoir*

The largemouth bass fishery at Uvas Reservoir was hit hard during the drought years of the early Nineties. The reservoir nearly dried up, killing off most of the bass. Those anglers who fished throughout the low water years, however, have turned out to be the most successful today. By studying Uvas' shoreline when it wasn't submerged, they now know where the fallen trees, deep holes and structures lie, and continually find fish while other anglers struggle to locate the bass.

Uvas still hasn't recovered from the drought years; few fish over seven pounds exist, and park rangers tell me that the locals who fish here don't practice catch & release when they land larger bass. Most of the bass average three- to five-pounds. In 2000, there was a good population of crappie in the lake, however, that population has since dwindled. Although there are some small bluegill, the population is also thin. Catfish fishing is fair in the evenings for anglers tossing cut baits into coves.

If you plan to make the trip, supplies are available in Morgan Hill. No gas-powered motors are permitted. There is a 5 mph speed limit.

Also nearby are Chesbro Reservoir, Calero Reservoir and Uvas Park Falls.

# CHESBRO RESERVOIR

**Like Uvas, Chesbro was hurt by the drought years of the early Nineties, so it rarely kicks out bass larger than six pounds.**

**Rating:** 4
**Species:** Largemouth Bass, Channel Catfish, Crappie, Bluegill and Carp
**Stock:** None
**Facilities:** Boat Launch and Restrooms
**Contact:** Chesbro Reservoir (408) 779-9232, Santa Clara County Parks and Recreation (408) 358-3741

**Directions:** From the 101 Freeway in Gilroy, drive north to Morgan Hill and exit Cochran. Drive west on Cochran to the Monterey Highway and turn south. Drive to Watsonville Road and turn west. Take Watsonville to Uvas Road (G8) and turn north to the reservoir.

*Chesbro Reservoir*

Chesbro was constructed in 1955 to provide the growing population of Santa Clara County with an adequate water supply. With the exception of a boat launch and a few vault toilets, there are no facilities at this 269-acre lake. The 5 mph speed limit, which limits recreational activities, as well as the lack of facilities, deters most potential visitors. So, aside from a few die-hard anglers, just about everyone stays away.

Chesbro is almost an exact replica of nearby Uvas Reservoir, offering pretty much the same fishing experience. Like Uvas, Chesbro was hurt by the drought years of the early Nineties, so it rarely kicks out bass larger than six pounds. The best action is near the dam and boat launch. While there is a fair chance of hooking bass in the two- to five-pound range, your best bet is to fish the twilight hours for catfish up to 15 pounds.

If you plan to make the trip, supplies are available in Morgan Hill. No gas-powered motors are permitted.

Also nearby are Uvas Reservoir, Calero Reservoir and Uvas Park Falls.

*Ironically, these unsafe mercury levels have directly led to Calero becoming a quality bass fishery.*

| | |
|---|---|
| **Rating:** | 8 |
| **Species:** | Largemouth Bass, Channel Catfish, Crappie, Carp and Bluegill |
| **Stock:** | None |
| **Facilities:** | Boat Launch, Restrooms, Picnic Area, Equestrian Staging Area, Visitor Center and Hiking Trails |
| **Contact:** | Santa Clara County Parks and Recreation (408) 358-3741 |
| | Calero Visitor Center (408) 268-3883, Calero Entrance Kiosk (408) 927-9144 |
| **Directions:** | From the 101 Freeway in Gilroy, drive north to Cochran Road and exit west. Continue to Monterey Highway and turn right. Drive to Bailey Road and turn left. Continue to the lake. |

*Calero Reservoir*

When you arrive at Calero Reservoir, near Morgan Hill, the first thing that will most likely catch your attention is dozens of signs posted around the reservoir warning anglers not to eat the fish they catch. Because Calero has no natural watershed, it's fed from the Almaden Reservoir via a canal that is contaminated with mercury. In turn, Calero is also contaminated.

Almaden Creek and Silver Creek's watershed passes over mercury mines. Although the mercury that fills their waters is absorbed by the fish, it does not kill them. It does, however, make them unsafe for human consumption. Ironically, these unsafe mercury levels have directly led to Calero becoming a quality bass fishery, because 90 percent of Calero's fishermen catch & release, leaving the lake with a good fish population.

Since the California Department of Fish and Game and Santa Clara County don't want to waste their time stocking trout that aren't going to be edible, anglers come for the bass and pan fish. Bass fishing is phenomenal in the spring when the fish move into shallow areas to spawn. And each year, the size of bass in the lake increases. In the winter of 1999, an 11.25-pounder was landed; a 12.5-pound lunker in the winter of 2000; and a 13.5-pounder in the winter of 2001. An array of spinnerbaits and plastics works well.

Crappie and bluegill fishing remain hot in the spring for anglers using red worms or jigs in coves. If you enjoy catching crappie and bluegill, make sure you arrive at the lake before summer. During the summer, a weed bed spans from the shoreline out about 30 feet into the lake, keeping the fish out of reach of shoreline anglers.

Recently, the park staff was stoked when an angler fishing from a float tube was dragged around the lake by what was thought to be a giant catfish. When the angler landed the fish and weighed it in, however, it turned out to be an 18-pound striper. That is the only striper ever reported to be taken from the lake. With water coming in from San Luis Reservoir, the possibility of more stripers sneaking in through the pipes is good.

If you plan to make the trip, supplies are available in Morgan Hill. There is a day-use fee. Also nearby are Uvas Reservoir, Uvas Park Falls, Coyote Creek, Coyote Lake, Anderson Reservoir and Chesbro Reservoir.

**What draws visitors to the lake is a swimming beach, which is only opened during the summer.**

| | |
|---|---|
| **Rating:** | 4 |
| **Species:** | None |
| **Stock:** | Largemouth Bass, Carp, Crappie and Bluegill |
| **Facilities:** | Swimming Beach, Restrooms, Picnic Areas and a Launch Ramp |
| **Contact:** | Almaden Lake (408) 277-5130 |
| **Directions:** | From the junction of the 101 and 85 Freeways in San Jose, drive northwest on the 85 Freeway to Almaden Expressway and exit south. Continue to Coleman Avenue and turn left. Drive to Winfield and turn right to the lake. |

*Almaden Lake*

Almaden Lake is one of the poorest fisheries in the San Jose area. Because it receives no trout or catfish plants, it has to rely on its bass population to satisfy anglers.

Almaden shouldn't be confused with nearby Almaden Reservoir. The lake is operated by the City of San Jose and the reservoir by Santa Clara County. What draws visitors to the lake is a swimming beach, which is only opened during the summer. Almaden is one of the few urban lakes in the region that does allow swimming.

With the fishing as poor as it is, few anglers fish the lake. Those that do, however, target the lake's bass population, which consists mostly of one to three pounders. While the fishing is fairly boring, there is an interesting side note about the lake. Fed by the Guadalupe River at the north end and Los Alamitos Creek on the south end, steelhead sometimes use the fish ladder at the dam to enter the reservoir. But, few steelhead are ever caught.

The best fishing is for pan fish, carp and catfish. Fishing at dusk provides the best action. To avoid getting frustrated with a poor fishing day, leave your rod at home and stick to swimming.

If you plan to make the trip, supplies are available in San Jose. No gas-powered motors or boats over 16 feet are permitted on the lake.

Also nearby are Almaden Reservoir, Guadalupe Reservoir, and Calero Reservoir.

# LEXINGTON RESERVOIR

**Dammed in 1952 where the towns of Lexington and Alma were once located, Lexington is used as a holding facility for water released into Los Gatos Creek.**

**Rating:** 5

**Species:** 16,600 pounds of rainbow trout.

**Stock:** Channel Catfish, Largemouth Bass, Rainbow Trout, Crappie and Bluegill

**Facilities:** Boat Launch, Hiking Trails, Restrooms and a Picnic Area

**Contact:** Lexington Reservoir (408) 356-2729

**Directions:** From San Jose, drive south on the 17 Freeway and exit Bear Creek Road. Follow the road across the overpass and get back on the 17 Freeway heading north. Exit Alma Bridge Road, turn right and continue to the lake.

*Lexington Reservoir*

Situated off Highway 17 between Los Gatos and Santa Cruz, Lexington Reservoir is the perfect example of how a fishery can suffer from low water levels. When I arrived to fish Lexington in March, it had already been drawn down more than 50 vertical feet, not good for the bass that were preparing to soon spawn.

I figured the drawdown was directly related to a poor rainy season, however, when I spent the rest of the day chatting with anglers they assured me I was wrong. They all told me it was like this every year.

Dammed in 1952 where the towns of Lexington and Alma were once located, Lexington is used as a holding facility for water released into Los Gatos Creek. Despite the dramatic drawdowns, there are still bass, catfish, bluegill and crappie in the lake; but most anglers have written off the lake, anyway.

In the spring, the 450-acre reservoir is best fished for bass in coves, and during the summer months catfish fishing is most productive. Regulations prohibit gas-powered motors, although, I saw two motorboats working with a crew team that appeared to be practicing on the lake. If the water levels were kept high for a few years, this fishery could rebound. For now, keep it on the backburner unless you are a trout lover. More than 23,675 rainbows are stocked by the California Department of Fish and Game and 3,000 pounds of bows by Santa Clara County.

If you plan to make the trip, supplies are available in Los Gatos. There is a day-use fee.

Also nearby are the San Lorenzo River, Lock Lomond Reservoir, Vasona Lake and Campbell Relocation Ponds.

# VASONA LAKE

*Fishing is not the most popular activity at Vasona Lake, not even close.*

**Rating:** 4
**Species:** Rainbow Trout, Channel Catfish, Largemouth Bass, Carp and Bluegill
**Stock:** 9,250 pounds of rainbow trout and 3,000 pounds of channel catfish.
**Facilities:** Restrooms, Bike Path, Picnic Areas, Boat Launch, Boat Rentals, Playground, Volleyball Court
**Contact:** Vasona and Los Gatos Creek Park (408) 356-2729

**Directions:** From San Jose, drive south on the 17 Freeway and exit east on Lark Avenue. Continue to Los Gatos Blvd. and turn right. Drive to Blossom Hill Road and turn right. Drive to the entrance on the right.

*Vasona Lake*

Fishing is not the most popular activity at Vasona Lake, not even close. Operated by the County of Santa Clara, Vasona is a popular park with a bike path, picnic areas, playgrounds, well-maintained green lawns and many heavily shaded areas. Although anglers do come here, they are far outnumbered by bike riders, roller bladders, joggers and walkers. A 14-mile multiuse path, starting at Lexington Reservoir and ending in San Jose, cuts through Vasona, and many exercisers begin their routines here.

While the fishing at Vasona never goes off the Richter scale, the South Bay Fishing in the City program plants nearly 20,000 rainbow trout in the winter and channel catfish in the summer, giving anglers some incentive to show up. Although the fish aren't raised by the California Department of Fish and Game, the CA DFG funds the program. Fed by Los Gatos Creek, there is also a smidgen of bass, bluegill and carp in the lake. Power Bait is best for the trout. Catfish seem to be keen on night crawlers and anchovies.

If you plan to make the trip, supplies are available in the nearby urban community. No gas-powered boats are permitted. There is a day-use fee.

Also nearby are Lexington Reservoir, Campbell Percolation Ponds and Los Gatos Creek.

# CAMPBELL PERCOLATION PONDS

**Most anglers bring a lounge chair, pick a spot on the lake, cast out a line with either an inflated night crawler or Power Bait and read a book while waiting for a nibble.**

**Rating:** 5
**Species:** 6,500 pounds of rainbow trout.
**Stock:** Rainbow Trout, Bluegill, Crappie, Largemouth Bass, Carp and Channel Catfish
**Facilities:** Picnic Areas, Fishing Piers, Restrooms, Bike Path and a Playground
**Contact:** Santa Clara County Parks and Recreation (408) 358-3741

**Directions:** From the 85 Freeway in Campbell, exit Winchester Road and drive north to Hacienda. Turn right and drive to Dell. Turn left to Los Gatos Park on the right.

*Campbell Percolation Ponds*

What the heck is a percolation pond? Chances are, if you live in Santa Clara County, you've seen dozens but don't know what they're used for. A percolation pond is a holding pond that is used to replenish the area's ground water supply In the case of Campbell Percolation Ponds, water can be received from any of three reservoirs, Anderson, Lexington or San Luis. Water released from Lexington enters the ponds from Los Gatos Creek. Water from Anderson or San Luis is channeled through the Almaden Valley Pipeline. Once at Campbell, the water percolates, or seeps through the ground, until it reaches the underground water supply deep below the earth's surface. After permeating the soil, water from the ponds helps to fill the underground supply.

Campbell is also used for recreation. There are picnic areas, five fishing lakes, two small fly-casting ponds to tune up your casting, and a bike and runner's path that parallels the lake. The fly-casting ponds can be a lot of fun. These two shallow ponds have targets in the middle of them, allowing anglers to practice casting hookless flies at targets. This gives them a chance to work on their accuracy before moving on to fishing rivers and lakes.

For fishing, there are three larger ponds and two smaller ones. All of the 8,400 rainbows that are planted by the California Department of Fish and Game get dumped in lake No. 1, which can be seen from the park access road. Located alongside the 17 Freeway in Campbell and run by Santa Clara County, this lake is part of Los Gatos Creek Park. The South Bay Fishing in the City project also plants 1,500 pounds of rainbows.

Most anglers bring a lounge chair, pick a spot on the lake, cast out a line with either an inflated night crawler or Power Bait and read a book while waiting for a nibble. Because the lake is only eight acres, catch rates are usually good. In the summer when the trout bite slows, anglers arrive in the evening with anchovies and mackerel for a chance at hooking a catfish.

If you plan to make the trip, supplies are available in Campbell. There is a day use fee.

Also nearby are Vasona Lake, Stevens Creek Reservoir and Lexington Reservoir.

# STEVENS CREEK RESERVOIR

*Despite its steep shorelines, the reservoir is a popular winter and springtime trout fishery.*

**Rating:** 6
**Species:** Largemouth Bass, Crappie, Bluegill, Channel Catfish and Rainbow Trout
**Stock:** 9,500 pounds of rainbow trout.
**Facilities:** Boat Launch, Restrooms and a Picnic Area
**Contact:** Santa Clara County Parks (408) 358-3741

**Directions:** From Highway 280 in Cupertino, exit Foothill Expressway and drive approximately three miles west on Foothill Blvd. to the lake on the left. (Just after it crosses McClellan, Foothill becomes Stevens Canyon Road.)

*Stevens Creek Reservoir*

Fed by Swiss and Stevens Creeks, 92-acre Stevens Creek Reservoir is set in the foothills between Cupertino and Saratoga. Despite its steep shorelines, the reservoir is a popular winter and springtime trout fishery, also offering anglers the option of catching bass and catfish in the warmer months.

The hot ticket when it comes to catching the rainbows is dousing Power Bait off the dam or casting small Kastmasters near the launch ramp for a few days after a stock. Most of the more than 16,000 trout planted by the California Department of Fish and Game are in the nine to 12-inch class.

When the water warms in early May, anglers turn their attention to catfish. Though catch rates suffer because no night fishing is permitted, plenty are caught in coves in the summer months. Catfish and bass used to be planted in the lake, but the plants were suspended. Both species, however, have begun to successfully reproduce in the lake. Since most of the bass are small, few anglers fish for them. A three-pound bass would be a whopper. There is also a sprinkling of bluegill and crappie, but hardly any grow larger than pan size.

Aside from fishing, the reservoir is popular with wind surfers, because afternoon winds are common here. Float tubing is also popular on the lake. In all but drought years, the lake is spared from drastic drawdowns.

If you plan to make the trip, supplies are available in Saratoga. There is a day-use fee to park in the parking area. It's free to park alongside the highway. No gas-powered motors are permitted.

Also nearby are Campbell Relocation Ponds and Vasona Lake.

# COTTONWOOD LAKE

*Cottonwood is the best place in the Bay Area to watch cormorants catch helpless stocked rainbow trout.*

| | |
|---|---|
| **Rating:** | 5 |
| **Species:** | Rainbow Trout, Largemouth Bass, Channel Catfish, Carp and Bluegill |
| **Stock:** | 12,500 pounds of rainbow trout and 1,000 pounds of catfish. |
| **Facilities:** | Restrooms, Boat Launch, Picnic Areas, Volleyball Court, Horseshoes and a Playground |
| **Contact:** | Coyote Hellyer Park (408) 225-0225<br>Santa Clara County Parks (408) 358-3741 |
| **Directions:** | From the 101 Freeway in San Jose, drive south and exit west on Capital Expressway. Drive to Senter Road and turn left. Continue to Hellyer Avenue and turn left. Drive to the park entrance on the right. |

*Cottonwood Lake*

What is little 13-acre Cottonwood Lake, located in Coyote Hellyer Park, most known for? That it has a nice picnic area? Or its good fishing? Being a pretty urban lake? That some of the grassy areas that surround the lake were once dumpsites or rock quarries utilized to build the 101 Freeway. Nope! Cottonwood is the best place in the Bay Area to watch cormorants catch helpless stocked rainbow trout. The lake's structure makes it easy for the cormorants to nab the rainbows.

Here's what the birds do: swimming in groups of up to 40, some swim under water, others on the surface, all with the same goal, to force the rainbows into a cove near the shoreline. At its deepest point the lake is eight feet, but the birds corral the rainbows into a shallow cove, pushing them up against the shore, and attack, swallowing them whole. It makes for a great show. The anglers, however, don't enjoy it. It frustrates them to see the birds eating the fish they are trying to catch. Of the more than 9,750 half-pound rainbows planted by the California Department of Fish and Game, anglers catch less than half. More than 6,000 pounds are planted by the Fishing in the City Project.

Used to irrigate lawns in nearby South Bay communities, Cottonwood is fed by Coyote Creek. The lake is so small you can cast across it with a heavy lure, but most anglers fish with Power Bait. Nearly all anglers who fish the lake live in the communities that surround it. Most of the lake's regulars are seniors who get free parking passes.

While the trout make a delicious lunch for the birds, the catfish and carp are too big for them to eat. Roughly 750 catfish are planted yearly, and a good number are one to four pounds. Catfish to 10 pounds are caught on traditional baits from June to August. Anglers commonly catch large carp while fishing for the cats. The lake-record, a 33-pound carp, was caught by an angler fishing for catfish. The lake's bass are rarely targeted.

If you plan to make the trip, supplies are available in San Jose. No gas-powered boats are permitted. There is a day-use fee.

Also nearby are Cunningham Lake and Joseph D. Grant Park Lakes.

# CUNNINGHAM LAKE

**For those not interested in the theme park, the CA DFG also stocks catfish from May to September.**

| | |
|---|---|
| **Rating:** | 6 |
| **Species:** | Carp, Rainbow Trout, Bluegill, Sunfish and Channel Catfish |
| **Stock:** | 14,675 pounds of rainbow trout and 4,000 pounds of channel catfish. |
| **Facilities:** | Boat Launch, Restrooms, Picnic Area, Boat Rentals and Hiking Trails |
| **Contact:** | Lake Cunningham (408) 277-4319 |

**Directions:** At the junction of the 101 Freeway and Interstate 680 in San Jose, drive south to Capital Expressway and exit east. Continue on Capital Expressway to Tully and turn right to the lake.

*Cunningham Lake*

With Raging Waters Theme Park on its west shoreline, it's hard for most people to spend a day fishing Cunningham Lake, when they'd rather be having fun at the park. In the winter, however, when Raging Waters shuts down, anglers come back to Cunningham. It's perfect timing, too, because the California Department of Fish and Game plants Cunningham with half-pound rainbow trout from October to mid-April. More than 25,000 fish are planted between the CA DFG and the South Bay Fishing in the City Project.

It's ideal for visitors; they can enjoy the water rides during the warmer months and fish during the cooler ones. Because the 50-acre lake is so small, fishing from the shoreline is as good as from a boat. The best time to catch the fish is within a few days after a stock, tossing small white Phoebes or silver Kastmasters near where the fish were stocked. Often, however, fishermen have to fight cormorants for the trout.

For those not interested in the theme park, the CA DFG also stocks catfish from May to September. Bass were stocked in the lake years ago; however, with no structure and bedding grounds, they were unable to reproduce. Over the years nearly all of the bass have been caught. Ironically, the bluegill that were put in the lake as bass food have begun to reproduce. Although few are larger than the palm of your hand, you can catch dozens of 'em all around the 11-foot deep lake.

Designed for flood control, Cunningham, unlike most other lakes, has no streams, canals or aqueducts that feed it; its sole source of water is rain runoff. Because the lake has a clay bottom, it doesn't lose water to seepage. Most of its water loss is by evaporation. On a positive note for anglers, the lake isn't drawn down. It fluctuates a mere foot all year.

Sailing clubs from San Jose State and Hawaiian paddling crew teams also use Cunningham to practice. Watercraft is limited to non-gas powered motors.

If you plan to make the trip, supplies are available in San Jose. There is a day use fee. No night fishing is allowed.

Also nearby are Joseph D. Grant Park Lakes and Cottonwood Lake.

# JOSEPH D. GRANT PARK LAKES

**An angler can get that woodsy feeling and a lot more at this 9,522-acre regional park.**

**Rating:** 5
**Species:** None
**Stock:** Largemouth Bass, Channel Catfish, Crappie and Bluegill
**Facilities:** Campgrounds, Restrooms, Hiking Trails and Picnic Areas
**Contact:** Joseph D. Grant Park (408) 274-6121

**Directions:** From the junction of the 101 Freeway and Interstate 680 in San Jose, drive north on Interstate 680 and exit east on Alum Rock Avenue. Continue to Mt. Hamilton Road. Drive to the park entrance and pick up a free map.

*McCreery Lake*

The Santa Clara County Parks and Recreation Department has done a phenomenal job providing its urban residents with places to fish; however, few of the parks are far enough from the city to give sportsmen a wilderness feeling. In the foothills above San José, Joseph D. Grant Park has no residential neighborhoods, freeways, airports, high rises, bridges or traffic lights nearby. An angler can get that woodsy feeling and a lot more at this 9,522-acre regional park. Surrounded by rolling hills sprinkled with oak trees, there are three ponds in the park, giving anglers a shot at catching largemouth bass, catfish, crappie and bluegill.

Grant, the largest of the lakes, is small, but you wouldn't call it a "pond." Formerly known as the Bernal Lagoon, Grant can offer surprisingly good fishing for its size. Most of the bass are in the one to three-pound range. There are a few larger ones, but they can take a little effort to catch. There is a lot of structure in the lake, fallen trees, weed lines, tules, etc., which can make landing fish difficult. During spring, night crawlers and white spinnerbaits work well, but we had the highest catch rates on plastics.

Located up the road from Grant, McCreery and Bass Lakes are true farm ponds. Each was created by damming a small, seasonal stream. They're both smaller than five acres, but that's not to say there aren't fish in them. The fish are like those found in Grant; they just don't grow as large. Bluegill fishing is best at McCreery and Bass.

While Grant is easily spotted from the road, you'll need to pick up a park map to spot the other two. There's a small sign on the left side of the highway marking the trailhead to McCreery. (It's only a 50-yard walk.) There is no trail to Bass Lake, nor is there a signed turnoff. Driving past McCreery, look for a call box on the right side of the road. Next to the call box, park in the dirt pullout and walk down to the lake, which is located at the base of the hill on the right.

If you plan to make the trip, supplies are available in San Jose.

Also nearby are Cunningham Lake, Cottonwood Lake and Raging Waters.

*next page Pinto Lake*

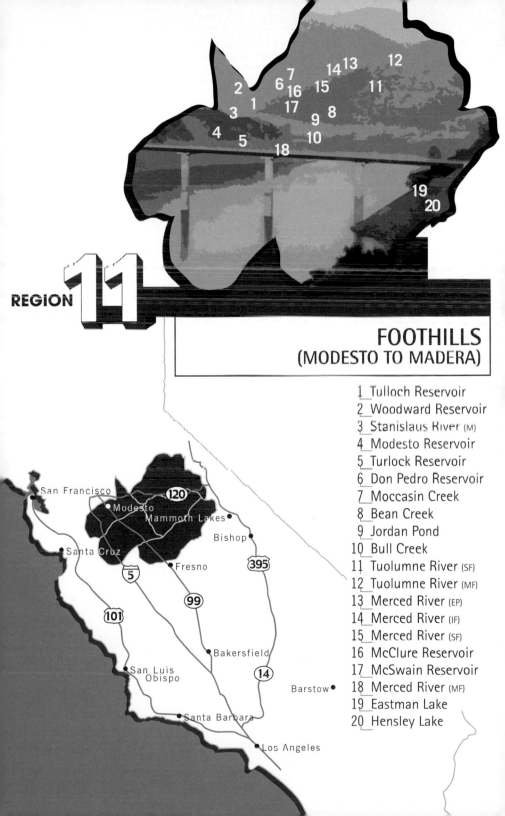

REGION 11

## FOOTHILLS
### (MODESTO TO MADERA)

1 Tulloch Reservoir
2 Woodward Reservoir
3 Stanislaus River (M)
4 Modesto Reservoir
5 Turlock Reservoir
6 Don Pedro Reservoir
7 Moccasin Creek
8 Bean Creek
9 Jordan Pond
10 Bull Creek
11 Tuolumne River (SF)
12 Tuolumne River (MF)
13 Merced River (EP)
14 Merced River (IF)
15 Merced River (SF)
16 McClure Reservoir
17 McSwain Reservoir
18 Merced River (MF)
19 Eastman Lake
20 Hensley Lake

# TULLOCH RESERVOIR

*Some of the brood stocks are still in the lake and can be caught in the winter and spring by anglers trolling from the surface to 20 feet deep.*

| | |
|---|---|
| **Rating:** | 6 |
| **Species:** | Rainbow Trout, Brown Trout, Channel Catfish, Largemouth Bass, Smallmouth Bass, Crappie, Bluegill |
| **Stock:** | 5,700 pounds of rainbow trout. |
| **Facilities:** | RV Hookups, Campgrounds, Picnic Areas, Restrooms, Boat Launch, Lodging, Restaurant, Marina, Gas, Boat Rentals and Swimming Areas |
| **Contact:** | South Lake Tulloch RV Campground and Marina (209) 881-0107 or (800) 894-2267 Tulloch Lake (209) 785-3838, Bev's Boat Rentals (209) 847-8586 or (888) 760-8600 |
| **Directions:** | From the 99 Freeway in Modesto, take Highway 108 east to Oakdale. At the junction of Highway 108 and Highway 120 in Oakdale, drive east for 15 miles to Tulloch Road. Turn north and drive five miles to the lake entrance. |

*Tulloch Reservoir*

Tulloch Reservoir's best asset is that it isn't drawn down as drastically as other reservoirs in the region. In September and October, the 1,260-acre reservoir normally gets drawn down only eight vertical feet, much less than nearby Don Pedro, New Melones and Mc Clure Reservoir.

From May to October, boaters rule the lake. Anglers concentrate on working the lake from late October to April. Beginning in early November and continuing through April, the California Department of Fish and Game stocks 11,150 rainbow trout. Most of the fish are about a half-pound, but in the mid-Nineties, the CA DFG surprised anglers with a load of brood stocks weighing more than four pounds each. Some of the brood stocks are still in the lake and can be caught in the winter and spring by anglers trolling from the surface to 20 feet deep.

To catch trout in the summer, downriggers or leadcore line are needed. In the spring, bass anglers attempt to fool the lake's smallmouth bass population, but fishing is hit or miss. Bass fishing isn't as consistent as it is at Don Pedro or New Melones.

Not only does Tulloch offer great recreational opportunities, it's also home to many private residences on the north shore. Located between Sonora and Oakdale, the reservoir is situated in two crisscrossing canyons that form its waters into an "X"-like pattern. The reservoir is fed by water from New Melones Lake.

If you plan to make the trip, supplies are available at the lake. There is a day-use and a boat launch fee.

Also nearby are New Melones Reservoir, Don Pedro Reservoir, Moccasin Creek, Mc Swain Reservoir, Woodward Reservoir and Mc Clure Reservoir.

# WOODWARD RESERVOIR

*Whether trolling or fishing from the shore with Power Bait, fishing remains fair for these planters throughout the winter and early spring.*

**Rating:** 6

**Species:** Rainbow Trout, Channel Catfish, Largemouth Bass, Smallmouth Bass, Crappie and Bluegill

**Stock:** 2,400 pounds of rainbow trout.

**Facilities:** Boat Launch, Campgrounds, Picnic Areas, Restrooms, Boat Rentals, RV Hookups, General Store

**Contact:** Bait Barn (209) 874-3011, Auto Life Bait & Tackle (209) 538-1111
Woodward Reservoir (209) 847-3304, Woodward Marina (209) 847-3129

**Directions:** From the 99 Freeway in Modesto, take Highway 108 east to Oakdale. At the junction of Highways 108 and 120 in Oakdale, turn north on Highway 120 and drive 1.8 miles to 26 Mile Road. Turn north and continue 3.5 miles to the signs for the lake. Turn east to the lake.

*Woodward Reservoir*

During the winter when temperatures cool in the upper San Joaquin Valley, senior citizens make it a habit to come to Woodward Reservoir. Because water-skiers and jet-skiers overrun the lake in the summer, and, more importantly, trout plants are only made in the winter, seniors adjust their schedule to arrive at the right time.

Located 20 minutes from Modesto, about 200 feet above sea level, Woodward is a large, 2,427-acre reservoir set among farmland and ranches. For anglers, the lake is most popular in the winter when the California Department of Fish and Game stocks 4,220 rainbow trout. Whether trolling or fishing from the shore with Power Bait, action remains fair for these planters throughout the winter and early spring. Anytime thereafter, if you want to catch any trout, you'll have to fish the inlet where the water is cooler.

The lake is fed by water from Tulloch Reservoir, which in turn receives its water from New Melones Reservoir. The result is that there are also small and largemouth bass in the lake, which were originally planted into New Melones and have since been pumped into Woodward.

Although a nine-pound largemouth and seven-pound smallmouth have been caught in the lake, it has yet to become a trophy fishery because of the severe drawdowns. The lake is almost completely drained every three to four years, forcing the fish downstream into farm ponds.

Keep your eye out in the future for news about the lake. Currently, there are ongoing court battles. The lake is now used for irrigation, but opponents are working towards making it a drinking facility, which could help do away with the water-skiers and improve the fishing.

If you plan to make the trip, supplies are available at the lake. There is a day-use fee. If water-skiing or jet-skiing, watch out for the islands. They are all over the lake.

Also nearby are Tullock Reservoir, Turlock Reservoir, New Melones Reservoir, Don Pedro Reservoir and Modesto Reservoir.

**During the fall run, which typically occurs in late September, salmon can reach 50 pounds or more.**

| | |
|---|---|
| **Rating:** | 7 |
| **Species:** | Striped Bass, Smallmouth Bass, Largemouth Bass, Channel Catfish, Rainbow Trout, Chinook Salmon, Steelhead, Bluegill and Crappie |
| **Stock:** | None |
| **Facilities:** | Visitor Center, Campgrounds, Picnic Areas and Restrooms |
| **Contact:** | Stanislaus River Parks, US Army Corps of Engineers (209) 881-3517 |
| **Directions:** | From the junction of Highway 120/108 in Oakdale, drive about four miles east to Orange Blossom Road and turn left. Continue to the river. For the upper section, continue east on Highway 120/108 to Knights Ferry or Tulloch Lake Road and turn left. Both provide river access. |

*Stanislaus River just below Goodwin Dam*

The recovery of salmon runs in the Stanislaus River has been fantastic! Because of record-low fish counts in the early Nineties, the California Department of Fish and Game nearly eliminated fishing on the river. In 1992, a mere 250 salmon swam out of the Pacific Ocean through The Delta and the San Joaquin River into the Stanislaus. The main reason for the pitiful runs was mostly because of drought; however, fish habitat was also a factor.

The San Joaquin Salmon Project was created by the CA DFG to improve fish habitat. Where spawning gravel was poor it was replaced. Old mining pits were filled in and shore-line vegetation was enhanced to keep the river cooler. Although the retrofit is still in process, the salmon fishery has rebounded, partially due to wetter weather. In 2000, an estimated 8,000 salmon spawned in the Stanislaus.

The runs take place in the fall and spring. During the fall run, which typically occurs in late September, salmon can reach 50 pounds or more. The spring run begins when salmon swim upriver in the spring. It continues as they hold in the water in the summer and then spawn in the fall. Those fish rarely reach more than 25 pounds.

Fishing for salmon is catch & release only. The best fishing is from Orange Blossom Bridge to Goodwin Dam. There is a fish ladder at Goodwin Dam, but it's not a good place to target. Striped bass and steelhead runs also take place in the Stanislaus. The number of steelhead participating in the run, which usually occurs in February and March, is on the small side. Unfortunately, the steelhead don't get more than five pounds. Steelhead are also catch & release only. The striped bass run takes place in the spring, but the fish normally don't move upstream past Knights Ferry. Stick to soaking anchovies or pile worms.

If you plan to make the trip, supplies are available in Oakdale. No motors are allowed from Goodwin Dam to Horseshoe Road Recreation Area. The Stanislaus River from Goodwin Dam downstream to Highway 120 is closed to fishing from Oct. 16 through Dec.31. Also nearby is Tulloch Lake.

# MODESTO RESERVOIR

*Trout are the only reason to fish this lake. They can be caught by tossing spinners near the inlet or soaking Power Bait near the dam.*

**Rating:** 6

**Species:** Rainbow Trout, Channel Catfish, Bluegill, Crappie, Largemouth Bass and Smallmouth Bass

**Stock:** 2,400 pounds of rainbow trout.

**Facilities:** Restrooms, Campgrounds, Picnic Areas, Boat Launch, RV Hookups, Bait & Tackle, General Store

**Contact:** Bait Barn (209) 874-3011, Auto Life Bait & Tackle (209) 538-1111
Modesto Reservoir (209) 874-9540, Modesto Marina (209) 874-1340

**Directions:** From the 99 Freeway in Modesto, exit Highway 132 east and drive 13 miles to Waterford. Continue 4.3 miles past the intersection of Road J-9 and Highway 132 to Reservoir Road. Turn north and drive a half-mile to the park entrance.

Modesto Reservoir

Of the three reservoirs built on the floor of the San Joaquin Valley in Stanislaus County, 3,800-acre Modesto Reservoir provides the best and most consistent trout fishery, but it's not worth a minute of a bass fisherman's time. Modesto looks almost identical to nearby Woodward Reservoir, however, Woodward has many more islands and submerged trees, making for a little better bass fishing. Modesto could become a better bass fishery if the lake didn't get so severely drawn down, sweeping most of the fish out of the reservoir.

As for the local residents, they've written-off fishing the lake for anything but stocked trout. "That lake is worthless. Nobody fishes there," said a local tackle shop owner. "You need to go to the bigger lakes up in the foothills for bass. Modesto is a recreation lake, and it's too damn shallow."

The reservoir's most consistent fishing takes place near the inlet where water enters from Don Pedro Lake. Of the 4,020 rainbow trout planted by the California Department of Fish and Game, most of them end up in this area, because the water is cooler.

Although trout don't reproduce in the lake, they can live in it year-round, and grow surprisingly fast. Fish that were planted as half-pounders in the winter are commonly over a pound by summer. Trout are the only reason to fish this lake. They can be caught by tossing spinners near the inlet or soaking Power Bait near the dam. As for the weekends, fishermen beware: boaters own it.

If you plan to make the trip, supplies are available at the lake. There is a day-use and a boat launch fee. Now that Modesto Reservoir supplies drinking water to the city of Modesto, only MTBE-free fuel is permitted.

Also nearby are Woodward Reservoir, Turlock Lake, Don Pedro Reservoir, Mc Swain Reservoir and McClure Reservoir.

# TURLOCK RESERVOIR

*Because cold water from Don Pedro Lake is diverted down a canal from the Tuolumne River to Turlock Reservoir, trout fishing remains consistent year-round.*

| | |
|---|---|
| **Rating:** | 5 |
| **Species:** | Rainbow Trout, Channel Catfish, Largemouth Bass, Smallmouth Bass and Bluegill |
| **Stock:** | 4,900 pounds of rainbow trout. |
| **Facilities:** | Boat Launch, Picnic Areas, Vault Toilets and a Campground |
| **Contact:** | Bait Barn (209) 874-3011, Auto Life Bait & Tackle (209) 538-1111 |
| | Turlock Lake (209) 874-2056, Turlock Community Services (209) 668-5550 |
| **Directions:** | From the 99 Freeway in Modesto, exit Highway 132 and drive 13 miles east to Waterford. Continue eight miles on Highway 132, past the intersection of Road J-9 and Highway 132, to Roberts Ferry Road. Turn east and continue 1.2 miles to the lake entrance. |

*The Tuolumne River feeds Turlock Reservoir with cold water.*

Situated in a hilly area of the San Joaquin Valley, Turlock Reservoir has yet to emerge as a quality fishery. Although the reservoir provides good prospects for trout, there aren't enough big smallmouth or largemouth bass to get anglers' attention. Run by Stanislaus County, there is a free fishing access area on the east side of the lake. The majority of the facilities are located near the south shore, which is part of a State Recreation Area, and a day-use fee is charged.

Because cold water from Don Pedro Lake is diverted down a canal from the Tuolumne River to Turlock Reservoir, trout fishing remains consistent year-round. However, when water is raging into the lake from the inlet, the rushing current is often so swift that it can be difficult to anchor up and fish. It's better to wait for the releases to subside and then fish.

From late fall through winter, the California Department of Fish and Game stocks 9,150 rainbow trout to perk up the action. Even though Turlock is heavily stocked, there aren't a lot of anglers attracted here, and fishing pressure isn't a problem.

Turlock is more of a boater's lake than a fishing hole. During the week, recreational boating is light on this 3,267-acre reservoir, although, some boaters do come after work. On the weekends, it can get crowded with boats.

There is also a pleasant, heavily shaded campground next to the lake. The campsites are located along the Tuolumne River.

If you plan to make the trip there is a day-use fee. Supplies are available at nearby Modesto Reservoir.

Also nearby are Mc Swain Reservoir, Mc Clure Reservoir, Don Pedro Reservoir, Merced River (Merced Falls) and Woodward Reservoir.

# DON PEDRO RESERVOIR

**Although the lake was once known as one of the state's best largemouth bass fisheries, its prime has passed.**

**Rating:** 8

**Species:** Rainbow Trout, Brook Trout, Brown Trout, Chinook Salmon, Kokanee Salmon, Largemouth Bass, Spotted Bass, Smallmouth Bass, Channel Catfish, Crappie, Carp and Bluegill

**Stock:** 2,500 fingerling largemouth bass, 25,000 pounds of rainbow trout, 450 pounds of fingerling rainbow trout, 2,000 pounds of brook trout, 2,230 pounds of sub-catchable brook trout and 554 pounds of kokanee.

**Facilities:** Houseboat Rentals, Boat Rentals, Gas, Marinas, Boat Launches, Restrooms, Swimming Areas, Showers, Visitor Center, Campgrounds, Picnic Areas, General Store, Bait & Tackle and RV Sites

**Contact:** Moccasin Point Marina (209) 989-2206, Lake Don Pedro Marina (209) 852-2369

**Directions:** From Oakdale on Highway 108/120, drive 21 miles east and turn south on La Grange Road (Road J-59). Continue 10 miles to Bonds Flat Road and turn east. Continue to the turnoff on the left for Fleming Meadows Recreation Area.

*Don Pedro Reservoir's bass are hurt by extreme drawdowns.*

At 12,960 acres, Don Pedro Reservoir is the second largest reservoir in Central California, runner-up only to San Luis Reservoir. Although the lake was once known as one of the state's best largemouth bass fisheries, its prime has passed. The days of 10-fish, 60-pound limits are as long gone as most Bob's Big Boy restaurants and drive-in movie theatres. And unfortunately, none of the above will return unless a miracle happens.

During its prime, from the mid- to late-Eighties, Don Pedro was a tremendous fishery, but it was hurt by several factors, including the loss of shad and structure, as well as the drought. Several bass anglers blame the downfall of the fishery on certain cold-water species of fish, namely trout and salmon. Can those allegations be correct? I don't think so. And here's why:

Don Pedro Lake was first formed by damming a portion of the Tuolumne River in 1923. Later, the old lake was flooded and new Don Pedro Lake was created in '71. According to some bass anglers, it was the introduction of cold-water fish when the new lake was created that hurt the bass fishery. But that can't be correct, because the cold-water fish were already present.

Prior to 1923, when the building of a concrete dam along the river created the Old Don Pedro Reservoir, native runs of salmon and steelhead already took place here. Wild runs of kokanee salmon also took place, and wild rainbow and brown trout inhabited the river.

When the first dam was built, salmon, steelhead and trout were trapped in Old Don Pedro Lake. Then, in the Fifties and Sixties, kokanee, brook trout and rainbow trout were planted by the California Department of Fish and Game. In fact, the CA DFG made a substantial effort to create a quality warm water fishery.

In the early Eighties, brood stock largemouths were taken from Lower Otay Reservoir in San Diego County and planted here. Then in '82, 7,500 fingerling bass were trucked in from Alabama. In '75, 300 adult white crappie were planted, with plants of channel catfish coming in '79, '80 and '81. The only new species introduced was coho salmon, which were stocked from 1972-80.

And despite all those cold-water fish, the bass stocks proved successful. From 1984-89 bass fishing was superb. Each of those years the average catch in tournaments went up nearly two pounds, with the largest catches also continuously increasing from year to year.

So, what in fact did happen to the bass fishery? First and foremost, a terrible drought caused low water conditions from the late-Eighties until the mid-Nineties. When the lake was low, there were fewer hiding places for juvenile bass, and it became easier for the larger bass to feed on the smaller fish. During the drought, each year's new crop of fish became smaller because of predation. In short, the larger fish were eating the future big bass in the lake.

A lack of structure also played a vital role. When the new lake was built, areas of trees, grass and brush were flooded, providing fish with excellent habitat. By the time two decades passed, however, nearly all the trees and vegetation had died, leaving the fish with little cover and few spawning areas.

Although the CA DFG and spawning clubs have worked together to add habitat in the lake, unfortunately most of these attempts have been unsuccessful. With drawdowns as severe as 110 vertical feet, it's nearly impossible to get down to the bottom of the lake to plant vegetation.

The only way Don Pedro's fishery could make a comeback is if there were a severe drought for eight to 10 years. This would allow grass, willow trees and brush to grow along the newly exposed lake bottom. When the water rose again, it would give fish the habitat needed to provide cover for juvenile fish to survive and result in the return of a tremendous fishery.

*Gary Coe (Left) and Phil Johnson (Right) with limits of kokanee and kings from Don Pedro.*

Presently, there are still a number of big bass in Don Pedro; however, their numbers are way down. Because of the cooler weather, the lake also has a shorter growing season than other big bass lakes in Southern California. A 17.12-pound largemouth established a new lake record in '97. With 160 miles of shoreline, there are hundreds of coves in the lake, but as I've said above, there's very little structure in them.

Another problem that's hurt the lake's bass fishery is drastic water fluctuations. Water levels swing radically during the spawning season. Yet, since this is an irrigation reservoir, it's hard to complain.

The lake wasn't built for fish. It's managed by the Don Pedro Recreation Agency, which consists of the City and County of San Francisco and the Turlock and Modesto Irrigation Districts. San Francisco uses the lake for water storage, while Turlock and Modesto tap into it for irrigation needs. To provide for anglers' needs, the agency uses money from gate receipts to pay for the stocking of 2,500 three- to four-inch fingerling Florida largemouth bass. These plants have been continuous since the early Eighties.

If targeting bass, fish the back of coves in April. The most consistent areas are the Woods Creek Arm, Rodger's Creek, Rough and Ready Creek, and from Jenkins Hill on north to Hatch Creek. Red and green plastic worms work best. Crankbaits are best from April through July. In summer and fall, topwater lures are the hot ticket. Crawdads work well year-round. There are a few spotted bass in the lake, and also some smallmouths. The lake record smallmouth is 4.12 pounds.

Don Pedro's cold-water fishery is doing just fine. In the early Nineties, there were problems with copepods found on rainbow trout. The copepod is also known as an anchor worm or learnea. It looks like a worm attached to the fish, and can cause sores to break out on rainbows.

Since the copepod can't attach to brook or brown trout, in an effort to rid the lake of the parasite, rainbows weren't stocked from 1994-97. Plants of rainbows resumed in '98. Rainbows are still quite available in the lake, and many in the two three-pound class are caught. The fishery is managed as both a put-and-take and a put-and-grow fishery. In addition to 14,700 fingerlings, more than 41,400 half-pound bows are stocked each year. The lake record is 11.8 pounds.

Brook trout were last stocked in 2000, and most likely won't be planted again in the future. It's possible that the brooks are reproducing. If they're not, either due to harvest or old age, anglers will most likely stop catching brooks by 2004.

While fingerling browns have been planted every year since '95, they don't show up in anglers' creels. There's a strong presence of trophy browns (the lake record is 13.6 pounds), yet few are caught, most likely because they aren't targeted. The best time to catch them is in the spring, where the Tuolumne enters the lake.

The lake's chinook population remains strong. Fish to 15 pounds have been reported, but the official lake record stands at 12.12 pounds. Most average five to seven pounds. Chinook were introduced to provide a trophy element to the lake's cold-water species. There are no longer coho salmon in the lake.

There is a self-sustaining population of kokanee here. Although recently passed up by New Melones and Indian Valley Reservoir, prior to '99 Don Pedro was known as the best kokanee lake in the state. In '92, seven kokanee weighing from 4.0-4.25 pounds were caught. Currently, the fish are peaking at two pounds. Deep water trolling techniques with Apex lures or flies produces fish to 15 inches.

If you plan to make the trip, supplies are available at the lake. At some locations there is a day-use fee. There are also several boat-in campsites.

Also nearby are Moccasin Creek and New Melones Reservoir.

*House boats are popular on Don Pedro.*

DON PEDRO RESERVOIR

# MOCCASIN CREEK

*Because it's so easy to plant, the creek receives fish nearly every week, from the opening of fishing season in late April through the end of the season in mid November.*

| | |
|---|---|
| **Rating:** | 7 |
| **Species:** | Rainbow Trout |
| **Stock:** | 4,000 rainbow trout. |
| **Facilities:** | Restrooms |
| **Contact:** | California Department of Fish and Game (559) 243-4005 |
| **Directions:** | From the 99 Freeway in Modesto, take Highway 132 east for approximately 54 miles to Highway 49. Turn north and drive approximately nine miles to the Moccasin Creek Fish Hatchery. (It's just before you come to Highway 120.) Access to the creek is available through the hatchery. |

*Moccasin Creek Fish Hatchery*

Employees at the Moccasin Creek Fish Hatchery love to stock Moccasin Creek. They don't even have to load the fish in a truck, because Moccasin Creek flows right next to the hatchery. California Fish and Game employees simply grab a bucket of fish out of the holding tanks and walk them over the stream. It's almost effortless.

Because it's so easy to plant, the creek receives fish nearly every week, from the opening of fishing season in late April through the end of the season in mid November. The CA DFG plants 7,797 fish, most of which are about a half-pound.

The best access is available from the hatchery. Accessing the creek from its east side can be tricky because of steep banks and overgrown trees. Moccasin Creek is planted from the base of the dam downstream to a few hundred yards above Don Pedro Reservoir.

Moccasin Creek's flows are at the mercy of Moccasin Dam, which is part of the Hetch Hetchy Water Project. Most of the time the creek is low, but when they let water out, it can become a torrent. Sometimes, it's even a bit dangerous. However, there are always pools deep enough to toss spinners and soak Power Bait.

The hatchery is a great place to bring kids. You can show them how trout are raised, and then take them over to the creek to catch a few.

If you plan to make the trip, supplies are available in Sonora. Moccasin Creek is closed to fishing from November 16 to the last Saturday in April.

Also nearby are Don Pedro Reservoir, Lake McClure, Tuolumne River (South Fork) and Rainbow Pool Falls.

# BEAN CREEK

*Now that the trout plants are gone, the biggest attraction around is the jackrabbits.*

**Rating:** 2
**Species:** Rainbow Trout
**Stock:** None
**Facilities:** None
**Contact:** Stanislaus National Forest (209) 962-7825

**Directions:** From Coulterville at the junction of Highway 49-132, take Greeley Hill Road (Road J 20) east for 6.3 miles to Greeley Hill Market. Just after the market, turn south at Holtzel Road. Drive 2.7 miles to Dogtown Road and turn northeast. Continue 1.5 miles to Red Cloud Ranch and Bean Creek.

*Bean Creek*

Bean Creek is no longer stocked by the California Department of Fish and Game. The creek used to be planted in Red Cloud Ranch, but after reports from anglers in the mid-Nineties that the owner began kicking anglers off his ranch, the allotments were cancelled. The creek was also planted in the stream behind Greeley Hill Market, but the entire allotment was transferred to nearby Jordan Pond.

Bean Creek is a small, shallow stream that runs through Red Cloud Ranch in the Stanislaus National Forest, with few fish left in it, if any. With the stocking halted in 1996 and few wild trout in the stream, it would be wise not to fish here. Plants began in 1958. The stream is overgrown by brush and there is little public access in the area, anyway. There is some access on a Forest Service Road (Road 2518) that parallels the creek on the other side of the ranch, but you need a high clearance vehicle to drive on it.

Now that the trout plants are gone, the biggest attraction around here is the jackrabbits. There are thousands of them and they jump in front of your car when you least expect it. Keep your eyes opened for them!

If you plan to make the trip, supplies are available at Greeley Hill Market. In the winter and spring, a four-wheel drive vehicle is recommended. The road can get extremely muddy and unsafe in wet weather.

Also nearby are Jordan Pond, Bull Creek, Diana Falls, Rainbow Pool Falls, the Merced River (Indian Flat) and the Tuolumne River (South Fork).

# JORDAN POND

*In the spring, fishing for trout can be quite good for anglers tossing small spinners or fishing Power Bait, but most of the fish get nabbed soon after a stock.*

| | |
|---|---|
| **Rating:** | 4 |
| **Species:** | Rainbow Trout, Bluegill, Largemouth Bass and Channel Catfish |
| **Stock:** | 200 pounds of rainbow trout. |
| **Facilities:** | Vault Toilets |
| **Contact:** | Stanislaus National Forest (209) 962-7107 |

**Directions:** From Groveland, drive east on Highway 120 to Smith Station Road and turn east. Drive to Jordan Road and turn left (it may be signed as Jordan Stables). Continue 3.2 miles to the lake.

*Jordan Pond*

Anglers who fish Jordan Pond love the fact that nearby Bean Creek was deleted from the stocking list in the mid-Nineties, because all the fish slated for Bean Creek now get put into Jordan Pond. The 380 rainbow trout that are planted each spring don't sound like a lot, but it's enough to satisfy the few locals who fish here.

Jordan is a small, eight-acre pond that also holds catfish, bass and bluegill. In the spring, fishing for trout can be quite good for anglers tossing small spinners or fishing Power Bait, but most of the fish get nabbed soon after a stock. The spring-fed pond only stays cool enough for trout until mid-June, when the focus turns to bluegill, catfish and bass. None of them have any size to speak of, but they are fun for the local kids to catch on a hot summer's day.

The pond used to be half on the Linkletter Ranch and half on Forest Service Land, and the property line ran right down the middle. But the Forest Service acquired the entire lake in 1990. Prior to 1990, the 800-acre ranch was owned by the son of the famous TV star Art Linkletter, who starred in the hit show "Kids Say The Darndest Things." Linkletter's son used the ranch as a mountain retreat.

When the Forest Service bought the land they also gained access to Diana Falls and Bower Cave. The cave you can see is more of a grotto, but there are underground caverns filled with water.

If you plan to make the trip, supplies are available in Greeley Hill. A permit is required to visit Bower Cave. They are available from the Forest Service.

Also nearby are Bull Creek, Bean Creek, Diana Falls and Bower Cave.

**Keep in mind that the creek is only planted in May and early June, and the dirt road that leads there may require a high clearance vehicle in the spring, due to muddy conditions.**

| | |
|---|---|
| **Rating:** | 3 |
| **Species:** | Rainbow Trout |
| **Stock:** | 500 pounds of rainbow trout. |
| **Facilities:** | Primitive Campgrounds and Vault Toilets |
| **Contact:** | Stanislaus National Forest (209) 962-7825 |

**Directions:** From Coulterville at the junction of Highway 49-132, take Greeley Hill Road (Road J-20) east 10 miles. Bear south, staying on Greeley Hill Road as it veers away from Road J-20. Drive 4.5 miles on Greeley Hill Road, veering left at the fork in the road in 4.1 miles. (At this point, the road changes name to Bull Creek Road.) Continue to Bull Creek Crossing and turn east on Road 2S02, following signs to Anderson Flat.

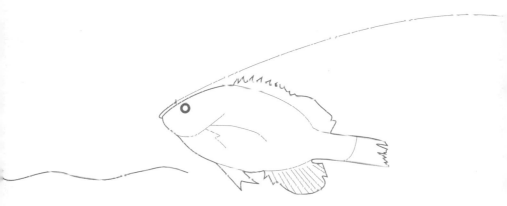

Bull Creek is a small, hard to reach stream that most out-of-towners don't come to fish, probably because they get lost trying to find it. In other words, locals rule the place.

Located at 3,300 feet in the Stanislaus National Forest, this secluded stream can only be reached by a long, slow drive on dirt roads. If you look on a map, Bull Creek looks like it can be reached more easily from Highway 140. Don't even try it. I tried to go that way, and three hours later I ended up back in the same place I 'd started. I'd only driven five miles, but the roads seemed like they were meant for motorcycles, not a Suburban. None of the roads were signed, either.

Providing there is enough water in the stream, the California Department of Fish and Game stocks 950 rainbow trout during the spring, all in the vicinity of Anderson Flat Campground. The fishing at Anderson Flat is fair for the few locals who come, but the stream is so small you need to use salmon eggs or Power Bait.

Keep in mind that the creek is only planted in May and early June, and the dirt road that leads there may require a high clearance vehicle in the spring, due to muddy conditions. Also remember, only primitive campsites are provided, and other services are at least an hour's drive away.

If you plan to make the trip, supplies are available at Greeley Hill Market. Bull Creek is closed to fishing from November 16 to the last Saturday in April.

Also nearby are Diana Falls, Rainbow Pool Falls, Bean Creek, Jordan Pond, the Merced River (Indian Flat) and the Tuolumne River (South Fork).

# TUOLUMNE RIVER (SOUTH FORK)

**A well-kept secret is that the South Fork holds some surprisingly large browns.**

| | |
|---|---|
| **Rating:** | 7 |
| **Species:** | Rainbow Trout and Brown Trout |
| **Stock:** | 4,110 pounds of rainbow trout. |
| **Facilities:** | Campgrounds, Picnic Areas, RV Hookups, Showers, Lodging, General Store and Vault Toilets |
| **Contact:** | Stanislaus National Forest (209) 962-7825, Berkeley Tuolumne Camp (510) 981-5140 |
| | Yosemite Pines (800) 368-5386 |
| **Directions:** | From Modesto, drive approximately 50 miles east on Highway 120 to the junction with Highway 108. Veer right, staying on Highway 120, and continue to Groveland. From Highway 120 in Groveland, drive east 13 miles to the Rainbow Pool turnoff. Continue a quarter-mile to the river. |

*Rainbow Pool Falls*

The South Fork of the Tuolumne River is the nearest you can get to Yosemite National Park without having to fight all the tourists for fishing space. The fishing is also much better at the South Fork than it is in the park. Between Groveland and Carlon Falls (just west of the Yosemite Park Line), there is good fishing for both planted and wild trout. Joining wild browns and rainbows the California Department of Fish and Game stocks 8,163 rainbows in the river.

There are public campgrounds and day-use areas along the river, but private resorts and RV parks dominate the river's shorelines. Yosemite Pines RV Park and Berkeley Tuolumne Camp are two of the larger private camps. The CA DFG plants along both of them, but public access is allowed for foot traffic only. To better provide for rafting, tubing, swimming and fishing opportunities, the private camps along the river have done a lot of work building small dams to slow the river and make it deeper.

A well-kept secret is that the South Fork holds some surprisingly large browns. The area just below the stretch between Yosemite Pines RV Park and Rainbow Pool Falls is the best place to catch these browns, because it is remote, hard to reach, and not many anglers fish it. Each summer browns up to eight pounds are pulled from the river.

The best place for day-users is Rainbow Pool Falls. Fish are planted above and below the waterfall, but it can get crowded with drunken teenagers, so try to plan your trip in the early morning before they arrive.

If you plan to make the trip, supplies are available at Yosemite Pines RV Park. The South Fork of the Tuolumne River is closed to fishing from November 16 to the last Saturday in April.

Also nearby are Carlon Falls, Rainbow Pool Falls, Middle Fork of the Tuolumne River, Yosemite National Park and Hetch Hetchy Reservoir.

# TUOLUMNE RIVER (MIDDLE FORK)

**Most anglers fish with bright colors of Power Bait, but those who use small Roostertails and Kastmasters also do well.**

**Rating:** 6
**Species:** Rainbow Trout and Brown Trout
**Stock:** 5,920 pounds of rainbow trout.
**Facilities:** Campgrounds, Picnic Areas and Vault Toilets
**Contact:** Stanislaus National Forest (209) 962-7825

**Directions:** From the 99 Freeway in Modesto, drive approximately 50 miles east on Highway 120 to the junction with Highway 108. Veer right, staying on Highway 120, and continue to Groveland. From Groveland, drive 25 miles east to Evergreen Road and turn north. Continue five miles to Middle Fork Campground.

*Tuolumne River (Middle Fork)*

In a region mostly visited by tourists heading to Hetch Hetchy Reservoir, there is also good fishing to be found just outside the western boundary of Yosemite National Park. Because the California Department of Fish and Game stocks it with rainbow trout, the Middle Fork of the Tuolumne River offers much better fishing than is found in Yosemite National Park. From late spring through early summer, or as long as the water temperatures remain suitable, the CA DFG plants 11,756 rainbow trout, keeping fishing hot both for campers and day-users.

Most of the anglers work the area around the Middle Fork Campground, which is only opened for day-use. The water is so clear that you can see the fish from the Middle Fork Bridge. This section of the river is more the size of a creek, but has many nice pools and holes where fish hang out. Most anglers fish with bright colors of Power Bait, but those who use small Roostertails and Kastmasters also do well.

The river is also planted near San Jose Camp. About a half-mile after the turnoff for Rainbow Pool Falls, turn left at the sign for Cherry Oil Road and continue another half-mile to a dirt road on your right. Turn right and follow the dirt road to the river. There are primitive campsites here, as well as plenty of fish.

If you plan to make the trip, supplies are available in Groveland. The Middle Fork of the Tuolumne River is closed to fishing from November 16 to the last Saturday in April.

Also nearby are Hetch Hetchy Reservoir, Cherry Lake, Rainbow Pool Falls and South Fork of the Tuolumne River.

# MERCED RIVER (El Portal)

**Anglers who can drift bait below the boulders do well, and spin casters fishing some of the larger pools also experience their share of success.**

| | |
|---|---|
| **Rating:** | 6 |
| **Species:** | Rainbow Trout and Brown Trout |
| **Stock:** | None |
| **Facilities:** | Campgrounds, Restaurant and Bar, Lodging, Gas, Restrooms and a Grocery Store |
| **Contact:** | Yosemite View Lodge (209) 379-2681, Sierra National Forest (559) 297-0706, Stanislaus National Forest (209) 962-7825, Mariposa Chamber of Commerce (209) 966-2456 |
| **Directions:** | From the 99 Freeway in Fresno drive north and exit east on Highway 140 and continue to Mariposa. In Mariposa, drive 31 miles east past El Portal to the Yosemite National Park boundary. |

*Merced River (El Portal)*

Located between the Merced River in Yosemite National Park and the Merced around Indian Flat, the section of the Merced flowing through El Portal offers anglers a different taste of fishing than other parts of the river. The section referred to as "El Portal" isn't bombarded daily by campers and fishermen the way the other portions of the river are. It isn't stocked with rainbow trout either. As a matter of fact, this section is home to those who enjoy fishing for wild trout.

This part of the river flows for four miles from the park boundary downstream to Foresta Bridge. Plentiful with both rainbows and browns, most of which are small, the river is opened to fishing year-round, but is governed by special regulations. Only artificial lures with barbless hooks are permitted. There is a five fish limit on browns, however, no rainbow trout may be kept.

Removed from the tourist hot spots in the park and the river rafting adventures downstream of here, the El Portal section is less fished than its neighbors. Most of the anglers who fish here are experienced fly-fishermen in search of a place away from the crowds.

After the river begins to subside in early July, catch rates increase greatly. This portion of the river, which mostly flows through the Sierra National Forest, is wide and has some deep holes with large boulders that fish use for cover. Anglers who can drift bait below the boulders do well, and spin casters fishing some of the larger pools also experience their share of success.

One piece of advice is to get to the river early in the morning or late in the evening. The fish don't seem to feed when the sun hits the water. I guess it's just a trout thing.

If you plan to make the trip, supplies are available in El Portal.

Also nearby are Foresta Falls, Merced River (Indian Flat), Merced River (Yosemite) and Yosemite National Park.

# MERCED RIVER (INDIAN FLAT)

**If you see people rafting, it's a good indication that you shouldn't be fishing, because the river will be flowing too fast.**

**Rating:** 6
**Species:** Rainbow Trout, Largemouth Bass and Brown Trout
**Stock:** 2,430 pounds of rainbow trout.
**Facilities:** Picnic Areas, Campground, RV Hookups, Restrooms, Showers and Lodging
**Contact:** Indian Flat RV Park (209) 379-2339, Bureau of Land Management (209) 966-3192, Mariposa Chamber of Commerce (209) 966-2456, Sierra National Forest (559) 297-0706, California Whitewater Rafting Adventures (800) 750-2386, ARTA River Trips (800) 323-2782

**Directions:** From Highway 140 in Mariposa, drive 22 miles east to Savage Trading Post State Historical Site. This portion of the river parallels the road from the trading post upstream six miles to Foresta Bridge.

*Merced River (Indian Flat)*

The Merced River around Indian Flat is the easiest section of the Merced River to fish, and it provides the most consistent catch rates. From Foresta Bridge downstream to where the South Fork enters the main river, the California Department of Fish and Game stocks 4,939 rainbow trout from April through August. This is the only stretch of the river from Yosemite Valley to McClure Reservoir that is stocked. Most of this stretch of the river parallels Highway 140, giving anglers easy access.

Though the river can be difficult to fish from April through June, due to high water from snowmelt. Catch rates improve as summer approaches. Most anglers fish with spinners, but fly-fishing is also popular. From the last Saturday in April through November 15, there is a five fish limit. However, at any other time of the year only two fish may be kept. In addition to the planters, there are also wild rainbow and brown trout, and largemouth bass. Few have any size, but they fight much harder than the planters.

In the spring, this section of the Merced is popular for white-water rafting. The trips begin near Foresta Bridge and progress downstream. If you see people rafting, it's a good indication that you shouldn't be fishing, because the river will be flowing too fast.

If you plan to make the trip, supplies are available in El Portal and Mariposa.

Also nearby are Merced River (El Portal), Merced River (Yosemite), Bull Creek, Bean Creek and the Tuolumne River (Middle Fork).

# MERCED RIVER (SOUTH FORK)

**Although the fishing is poor in the river around Wawona, it improves near Highway 140 where the South Fork meets the main stem of the river.**

| | |
|---|---|
| **Rating:** | 4 |
| **Species:** | Brown Trout and Rainbow Trout |
| **Stock:** | None |
| **Facilities:** | Campgrounds and Vault Toilets |
| **Contact:** | Yosemite National Park (209) 372-0200, Campground Reservations (800) 436-7275 |

**Directions:** From the 99 Freeway in Fresno, take Highway 41 north to Oakhurst. From the junction of Highways 41 and 49 in Oakhurst, continue 34 miles north on Highway 41 to Wawona. Stay on Highway 41through Wawona, until you arrive at the Wawona Campground. The river parallels the campground.

*Coyotes are common near Wawona Campground.*

People come to Yosemite National Park for its beauty, not for it's fishing. And of the many forks of the Merced River, the South Fork is the least fished. Most anglers have no idea it exists. With all of the possible distractions facing tourists here, the majority drive through Wawona, slowing just enough to see deer grazing on the Wawona Golf Course. Eager to get to popular tourist attractions in Yosemite Valley, they cross over the Merced River and don't think twice about stopping.

For serious anglers, not stopping is probably a good idea. One of the park rangers told me he's been working in Yosemite for more than 10 years and has never seen a fish pulled out of the river. I don't know if the fishing is that bad, but with no stocks and few anglers standing on its banks, it could be. Most of the anglers who do fish this stretch of the river are campers at Wawona Campground.

Although the fishing is poor in the river around Wawona, it improves near Highway 140 where the South Fork meets the main stem of the river. Access is available near Savage Trading Post State Historical National Monument. The rest of the river runs through remote, hard to reach places that are rarely fished.

The most important piece of advice I can give you is not to fish the river in the spring. Snowmelt swells the river and makes it nearly impossible. The river does have some large, deep pools that hold fish, but you have to work hard to get to them. For the few anglers who do catch rainbow and brown trout, the fish rarely peak over 10 inches.

If you plan to make the trip, supplies are available in Wawona and El Portal. The creek can also be accessed via the Iron Creek Trailhead. The South Fork of the Merced River is closed to fishing from November 16 to the last Saturday in April.

Also nearby are Alder Creek Falls, Chilnualna Falls, Fish Camp Falls, the Wawona Dome, the Mariposa Grove, Big Creek (Upper) and Big Creek (Fish Camp).

# MCCLURE RESERVOIR

*Frequently, people fishing for the rainbows catch chinook salmon, also known as king salmon.*

**Rating:** 8

**Species:** Rainbow Trout, Brown Trout, Brook Trout, Smallmouth Bass, Carp, Chinook Salmon, Largemouth Bass, Spotted Bass, Bluegill, Crappie and Channel Catfish

**Stock:** 22,000 pounds of rainbow trout, 2,150 pounds of sub-catchable brook trout.

**Facilities:** RV Sites, Campgrounds, Picnic Areas, Gas, Showers, General Store, Swimming Areas, Playgrounds, Restrooms, Boat Rentals, Marina, Houseboat Rentals, Boat Launch and Bait & Tackle

**Contact:** Lake Mc Clure (209) 378-2521, A-1 Bait & Tackle (209) 563 6505
Barrett Cove Marina (209) 378-2441, Camping Reservation (800) 468-8889

**Directions:** From Highway 49 in Sonora, drive 28 miles south to Coulterville and turn west on Highway 132. Drive 30.4 miles to Merced Falls Road and turn south. Continue 3.4 miles to Barrett Cove Road. Turn east and drive one mile to the recreation area.

*Water fluctuation can be embarrassing to the fishery at Mc Clure.*

A lot like nearby Don Pedro and New Melones Reservoirs, 7,147-acre Mc Clure Reservoir is a huge multi-recreational lake that is used each year by thousands of Central California residents. Even with all the hammering its 80 miles of shoreline gets, it still offers good year-round fishing for a wide variety of species. The lake is set in two narrow canyons. Fed by the roaring Merced River and multiple creeks, it is quite popular for houseboats.

There are largemouth, smallmouth and spotted bass in the lake. The smallmouth population used to predominate, but most of the fish now caught are spotted bass. There are also trophy-size largemouths in the lake. A new lake record was recently established when a 15.7-pound largemouth was landed. In the spring, the best action for those working crankbaits or salt-and-pepper plastics with chartreuse tails can be found near the Copper and Temperance Creek inlets. As summer approaches, the fish can be caught by jigging spoons in 20 feet of water off points and rocky areas, or by bouncing minnows off the bottom.

Although anglers' techniques differ, trout fishing remains good for all year-round. The California Department of Fish and Game plants 38,000 rainbow trout and 13,975 sub-catchable brook trout. In 1999, 63,546 chinook salmon were stocked. In late winter and spring, trollers do best toplining small lures near the shoreline.

As the water warms and the trout begin to move deeper, the trollers move towards Exchequer Dam and drag Needlefish and spoons or night crawlers behind a set of flashers. Trout fishing remains good near any of the creek inlets year-round. Frequently, people fishing for the rainbows catch chinook salmon, also known as king salmon. Most of the kings average one to three pounds, but sometimes fish to five pounds are landed. Anglers who troll frozen shad behind a set of flashers catch the most kings.

If you plan to make the trip, supplies are available at the lake. There is a day-use and boat launch fee. No bass between 12 to 15 inches may be kept.

Also nearby are Mc Swain Reservoir, the Merced River (Merced Falls), Don Pedro Reservoir and Moccasin Creek.

# McSwain Reservoir

**Rating:** 8

**Species:** Rainbow Trout, Brown Trout, Brook Trout, Smallmouth Bass, Largemouth Bass, Spotted Bass, Bluegill, Crappie and Catfish

**Stock:** 15,650 pounds of brook trout, 4,500 pounds of rainbow trout and 16,000 pounds of brook trout (by Calaveras).

**Facilities:** RV Sites, Campgrounds, Picnic Areas, Gas, Showers, General Store, Swimming Areas, Playgrounds, Restrooms, Boat Rentals, Marina, Boat Launch and Bait & Tackle

**Contact:** Lake Mc Swain (209) 378-2521, McSwain Marina (209) 378-2534

**Directions:** From Highway 49 in Sonora, drive 28 miles south to Coulterville and turn west on Highway 132. Drive 10.4 miles to Merced Falls Road and turn south. Continue 12.5 miles to Hornitos Road and turn east. Drive 1.2 miles to the lake entrance.

*Rainbow trout like this one caught by Phil Freed are common at Mc Swain.*

Located between Fresno and Stockton, Mc Swain Reservoir is one of the easiest and most popular places in the foothills of the Sierra Nevada to catch trout. Heavily stocked by both the California Department of Fish and Game and Calaveras Trout Farm, Mc Swain Reservoir's waters remain cool enough to maintain excellent trout fishing year-round. Its 10 mph speed limit on boats also guarantees calm water.

The Merced Irrigation District runs this reservoir that serves as a holding pool for water from Mc Clure Reservoir. Used for irrigation and hydroelectric power, the 300-acre Mc Swain Reservoir is more like a dammed-up river whose waters never fluctuate more than two to three feet. In fact, so much water is pumped in and out the reservoir each day, if the lake were totally dry, it would only take three days to refill it.

The cold water that enters from the bottom of Mc Clure does put a damper on bass fishing at Mc Swain. With water temperatures as cold as they are, the fish tend to hide out in coves where the water is warmer, and their metabolisms become so slow they are hard to entice. For this reason, the smallmouth, largemouth and spotted bass can be difficult to catch.

Bass fishing might be a challenge here, but the main attraction, trout fishing, isn't. Trout fishermen benefit from a deal worked out between Calaveras and the MID, which stipulates that Calaveras is allowed to use water that comes out of Mc Swain to raise trout, providing they stock a certain amount of fish back into the lake. No money changes hands, but Calaveras stocks Mc Swain with about 16,000 pounds of brook trout (averaging a pound) throughout the course of the year.

The weeks Calaveras doesn't make trout plants, the CA DFG does, planting a total of 29,780 brook trout and 8,390 rainbows. In 2001, the CA DFG planted rainbows and brooks, but in the future only rainbow are slated for plants. Calaveras showed up in the summer of 2000 with a bonus plant of 1,000 pounds of brown trout ranging from three to four pounds, surprising appreciative anglers. With all these plants, fishing tends to remain

*John Kemper and a limit of trout from McSwain.*

good throughout the year.

Trollers do well with flashers and night crawlers, while bank fishermen use Power Bait, inflated night crawlers or a marshmallow/mealworm combo. Bank fishermen need to keep their bait off the bottom, because there are numerous crawdads and squawfish that will steal it. Most bank fishermen fish near the marina, but the area gets fished-out pretty fast after a stock. Those who walk across the dam and fish the far side of the lake get the better results. For the biggest fish, try trolling in the spring. There are a lot of holdovers in the lake, and rainbows to seven pounds are caught regularly.

Fishing pressure all depends on the report the marina gives to the Fresno Bee. If the report says that fishing is good, the lake will be packed, otherwise it will be empty. I guess fishermen move in schools too.

If you plan to make the trip, there is a day-use and boat launch fee. Supplies are available at the lake.

Also nearby are Mc Clure Reservoir, the Merced River (Merced Falls), Don Pedro Reservoir and Moccasin Creek.

*Brett Ross with a rainbow trout.*

McSWA

# MERCED RIVER (MERCED FALLS)

**Those who are willing to battle the dry brush and overgrown trees on the shoreline can also get in on the action by tossing Panther Martins and Blue Foxes, or by soaking Power Bait.**

**Rating:** 6

**Species:** Rainbow Trout, Brook Trout and Brown Trout

**Stock:** 1,700 pounds of rainbow trout, 3,300 pounds of brook trout, 2,200 sub-catchable brook trout.

**Facilities:** Vault Toilets

**Contact:** California Department of Fish & Game (559) 243-4017

**Directions:** From Highway 49 in Sonora, drive 28 miles south to Coulterville and turn west on Highway 132. Drive 10.4 miles to Merced Falls Road and turn south. Continue 12.5 miles to Hornitos Road and turn east. The river is on the right.

*Merced River (Merced Falls)*

Are you sick of catching stocked rainbow trout in the streams you fish? Are you looking for a place to catch stocked brook trout, but having trouble finding it? Well, then you've been searching in the wrong places. Since the latter Nineties, the Merced River below Lake Mc Swain has been stocked exclusively with brook trout.

In the mid-Nineties, this section of the Merced was planted exclusively with rainbow trout, but after a parasite problem with the rainbows, the hatcheries that raised them converted to brook trout, because the parasite dies when it attaches itself to brooks. In effect, the brook trout serve as a biological filter that helps to get rid of the parasite.

With all these brook trout growing in the hatchery, the California Department of Fish and Game needed somewhere to put them before they got too big for the holding tanks. Most of the brooks they've planted in this section of the Merced River are just over a pound. After the parasite problem is cured, the CA DFG plans to stock half brooks and half rainbows in the river for one final year before they begin stocking all rainbows again. So, you'd better get to the river and catch some brooks before they stop stocking them. In ?00, 5,780 half-pound brooks, 14,300 sub-catchable brookies and 3,050 rainbow trout ?e planted.

? 320 feet, located seven miles from the town of Snelling, the river is planted in a ? referred to as "Merced Falls." More like a small lake than a river, this section is best ?ith a canoe or float tube. Access is available directly at Rivers Edge Fishing Access ?cific Gas & Electric Company. Those who are willing to battle the dry brush and ? trees on the shoreline can also get in on the action by tossing Panther Martins and ?xes, or by soaking Power Bait.

? to make the trip, supplies are available in Snelling.

?re Mc Swain Reservoir, Mc Clure Reservoir, Modesto Reservoir, Turlock ?on Pedro Reservoir.

# EASTMAN LAKE

*While there are tons of 15- to 19-inch bass in the lake, those larger lunkers that were common in the early- and mid-Nineties are hard to come by.*

**Rating:** 7

**Species:** Largemouth Bass, Rainbow Trout, Channel Catfish, White Catfish, Bluegill, Crappie, Redear Sunfish, Carp

**Stock:** 5,000 pounds of rainbow trout.

**Facilities:** Visitor Center, Restrooms, Launch Ramps, Campgrounds, Picnic Areas, RV Hookups, Fish Cleaning Stations

**Contact:** Eastman Lake (559) 689-3255

**Directions:** From the 99 Freeway in Fresno, drive north to Chowchilla and exit east on Robertson Blvd. Continue 11 miles on Avenue 26 (Robertson Blvd. becomes Avenue 26) to a T in the road. Make a left on Road 29 and continue seven miles to the lake.

Rudy Hernandez and a 16.5 pound bass

Biologist George Edwards with a channel catfish.

Hydrilla is a weed you definitely don't want in your lake. For years, Eastman Lake in the foothills of the Sierra Nevada, about a 20-minute drive from Madera, was free of it. Although it's uncertain how hydrilla made its way into Eastman, this much is known for sure: this weed changed Eastman's fishery.

Although hydrilla is believed to have spread from private property upstream from the lake, the exact spot is unknown. It worked its way down the Chowchilla River, which feeds the lake, and eventually found its way into Eastman.

So what's the big deal about some weed getting into a lake? Hydrilla isn't your average weed! It can wreak havoc on lakes. Not only does it grow prolifically, taking over a lake in a short period of time, but it also decreases water quality by raising pH levels. This in turn reduces the lake's oxygen supply and increases water temperature. Also, by clogging intake pipes, hydrilla has been known to damage water delivery systems and hydroelectric power plants.

The Army Corps of Engineers who run Eastman took this weed seriously. They knew that hydrilla can get into boats' pump systems and be transferred into other lakes. In order to keep hydrilla from being introduced into other lakes, Eastman was closed to all traffic, including shore fishing, in June of 1989.

Although there were a few other contributing factors, hydrilla is the single most important reason for the downfall of Eastman's trophy bass fishery. After being closed for three years because of hydrilla, the west side of the lake was reopened to shoreline fishing only in August of 1992. On that opening day, creel surveys taken by the California Department of Fish and Game showed more than 3,000 bass taken from the lake. At the time, there was a five-fish limit on bass at least 12 inches long, and few anglers practiced catch & release, so we're talking about a lot of anglers who took bass home.

Hearing there were tons of lunkers, anglers hit Eastman hard. Many caught their five-fish limit (totaling up to 35 pounds) in the morning and came back to take another limit in the evening. Eventually, the fishing pressure took its toll on the lake, and most of those large bass are now in anglers' bellies or hanging on their walls.

To counter the depletion of the fishery, the CA DFG implemented new regulations: now only one fish measuring at least 22 inches can be taken by each angler. While there are tons of 15- to 19-inch bass in the lake, those larger lunkers that were common in the early- and mid-Nineties are hard to come by. The lake record, a 16.5-pound largemouth was taken in 2001, yet fish like that are rarely seen today. Because now the fish average only one-and-a-half to three pounds (substantially smaller than in the past), many anglers have lost interest in Eastman.

For those who are still interested in Eastman, here are your best bets for catching bass: During the spring spawn, use shad-colored spinnerbaits in the shallows. In the summer, Eastman becomes an early-morning/late-evening fishery. Buzzbaits and Zara Spooks work well right after the spawn. Although jigging works year-round, it's especially productive in the winter, off points, rock piles and other structure. Just pop 'em and let 'em fall. Crawdads and worms are a hit all year.

While Eastman's bass are heavily targeted, the other species aren't. There are crappie, redear sunfish and bluegill, but hungry bass have diminished their populations. With no shad in the lake, these pan fish have become the main food source (along with a few minnows). Every few years the crappie surprise anglers by showing up in schools near the dam or around trees near the inlet. In June of 2001, the lake was opened to 24-hour fishing, so anglers now have a better shot at targeting catfish. Crappie and bluegill were stocked in November of 2001.

Of the 8,750 rainbows planted by the CA DFG, all weigh more than a half-pound and are pretty easy to catch from late fall through spring, when the fish are near the surface. As summer approaches, the trout stay near the dam. They can live year-round if enough oxygen remains.

*Charles Villafonia handles a rare crappie from Hensley.*   *Eastman Lake*

At times in the summer, when the Chowchilla runs dry and temperatures level out near 100, the lake's oxygen levels get low. Since the Chowchilla isn't a year-round river, low water levels have also been a problem here. Fed by 80 percent rain runoff, the river can dry up by summer. Consequently, in the summer, this 1,780-acre reservoir can drop from 150,000 acre-feet of water to just 15,000 acre-feet, a 90 percent decrease! When this happens, the lake becomes a large mud puddle, scaring off most anglers until winter returns.

The lake was reopened to boating in 1995, although at the present time, one-third of it remains closed because hydrilla was found on the east end. This area will not be reopened until it remains free of hydrilla for five years.

While at Eastman, keep an eye out for bald and golden eagles. Both are year-round residents and nest about a mile from each other. Ranger Keith told me if you were lucky you'd get to see them take part in aerial battles. As you guessed, the bald and golden eagles don't like each other.

Another interesting side note: Before Eastman was built, salmon spawned up the Chowchilla. Funny thing is, a few years ago three salmon got lost and ended up at the base of Eastman's dam. Someone must have forgotten to tell them when it was built!

If you plan to make the trip, supplies are available in Madera.

Also nearby is Hensley Lake.

EASTMAN LAKE

# HENSLEY LAKE

*One credible angler told me that in order to catch a fish over six pounds, he has to work the lake hard for six to eight months.*

**Rating:** 7
**Species:** Largemouth Bass, Rainbow Trout, Crappie, and Bluegill
**Stock:** 5,500 pounds of rainbow trout.
**Facilities:** Boat Launch, Restrooms, RV Hookups, Fish Cleaning Stations, Campgrounds, Picnic Areas, Nature Trails
**Contact:** Hensley Lake (559) 673-5151

**Directions:** From the 99 Freeway in Fresno, exit north on Highway 41 and continue to Highway 145. Turn left on Highway 145 and continue approximately 10 miles to Road 33. Drive one-mile to Road 400 and turn right. Continue approximately seven miles to the lake.

*Hensley Lake*

I think it's funny the way some anglers have the audacity to call the California Department of Fish and Game to complain that there are no fish in a lake. Nearly every drive-to lake in California has fish in it, but you've gotta remember the sport is called "fishing," not "catching." So, in most lakes it takes at least a sprinkling of effort and a dash of skill to catch fish.

How much fun would it be if you caught a fish on every cast? Where's the challenge? CA DFG biologist Jim Houk has told me numerous stories of anglers calling and whining because they went fishing and didn't catch any fish at 1,520-acre Hensley Lake. While I've heard conflicting reports about the lake, some good, others bad, Houk assured me there was only one way for me to get the truth and invited me on an "electrofishing" trip to the lake.

In order to monitor fish populations and ensure that the fish in reservoirs are healthy, the CA DFG attempts once a year to electrofish most reservoirs. Using sophisticated equipment that consists of a generator, pulsation unit and amperage control, they create a pulsating electrical current that attracts fish. The pulsation unit sends from 20 to 120 pulsating charges per second into the water. These charges immobilize muscles on the fish, and while not harming them, make it difficult for them to swim, so they end up surfacing. The fish are netted, weighed, measured and returned to the water unscathed. I personally witnessed a sampling of more than 500 fish over a three-day period, all of which were safely put back into the lake.

While working with Houk, I learned that a lot like its neighbor Eastman Lake, Hensley has a large population of bass, however, the fish in the two lakes differ in size. Fed by the Fresno River, Hensley's bass are mostly small, in the 10- to 14-inch range, averaging about a pound.

Although many anglers have complained that a lack of food for the bass in Hensley has resulted in a population of stunted fish, the CA DFG begs to differ. It's true that there are no shad in the lake, but there are plenty of crappie, rainbow trout, bluegill and redear for the bass to feed on.

Also, over a 14-year period from 1984 to 1997, a slot limit was implemented to remove some of the smaller fish. This limit restricted anglers to no more than five fish, one over 15 inches and four under 12 inches, while nothing between 12-15 inches could be kept. The CA DFG lifted this limit because aging techniques proved the fish were growing at normal rates, and examinations showed the bass were now plump, rather than long and slim.

While the CA DFG claims the fish are growing well, the number of anglers fishing the lake has dropped off. A senior ranger told me that over the last two decades he's seen a massive decline in shore anglers. Anglers with bass boats mostly fish the lake. Shore anglers that fish during the spring spawn and anglers who troll for trout in the spring are the exceptions.

The ranger said it's a lack of sizeable bass that's deterred anglers from coming here. I'm convinced, however, that the fish are growing well. While electrofishing, I saw many bass greater than 15 inches with my own eyes. There are just a lot of bass in the lake, and when there are higher concentrations of fish, it takes them a bit longer to grow to satisfying sizes. The unofficial lake record is 14 pounds. One credible angler told me that in order to

*A hybrid warmouth*                    *Biologist Jim Houk and a five-pound largemouth*

catch a fish over six pounds, he has to work the lake hard for six to eight months. Fishing the spawning beds in the spring is the best way to get in on the action here.

Trout seekers typically troll the lake from March to April for fish in the 10- to 14-inch range. Although discouraged by drastic drawdowns (the lake is sucked down from 90,000-acre-feet at full pool to 7,000-acre-feet), the trout still bite. During the summer, trout anglers should fish in the deepest water they can find. Using deep trolling methods near the dam is best. It's common to catch 18- to 20-inch trout. The CA DFG plants 8,640 half-pound rainbows each year.

If you plan to make the trip, supplies are available in Chowchilla. There is a day-use fee.

Also nearby are Eastman Lake and Millerton Lake.

*A bluegill*

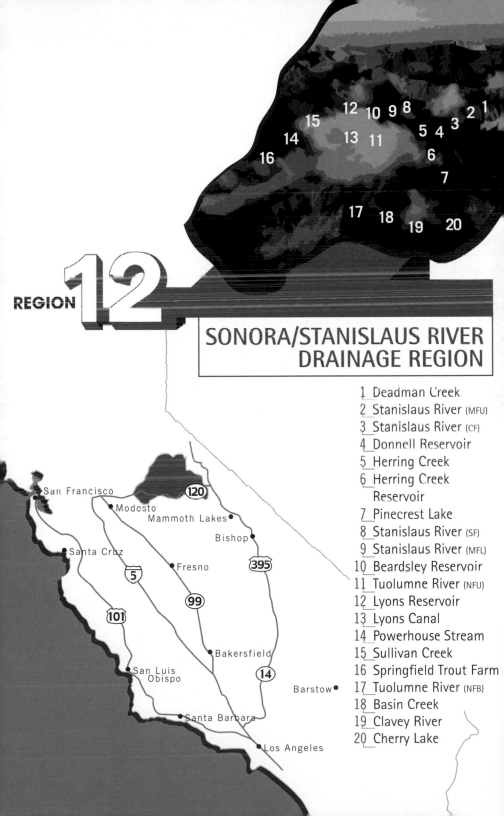

REGION **12**

# SONORA/STANISLAUS RIVER DRAINAGE REGION

1 Deadman Creek
2 Stanislaus River (MFU)
3 Stanislaus River (CF)
4 Donnell Reservoir
5 Herring Creek
6 Herring Creek Reservoir
7 Pinecrest Lake
8 Stanislaus River (SF)
9 Stanislaus River (MFL)
10 Beardsley Reservoir
11 Tuolumne River (NFU)
12 Lyons Reservoir
13 Lyons Canal
14 Powerhouse Stream
15 Sullivan Creek
16 Springfield Trout Farm
17 Tuolumne River (NFB)
18 Basin Creek
19 Clavey River
20 Cherry Lake

# DEADMAN CREEK

*If you have a jar of Power Bait, it's also an easy spot to catch stockers.*

| | |
|---|---|
| **Rating:** | 7 |
| **Species:** | Rainbow Trout and Brown Trout |
| **Stock:** | 1,000 pounds of rainbow trout. |
| **Facilities:** | Restrooms, Campgrounds, Pack Station, Restaurant, Bait & Tackle, Saloon, General Store |
| **Contact:** | Stanislaus National Forest (209) 965-3434, Kennedy Meadows Resort and Pack Station (209) 965-3900, Dardanelle Resort (209) 965-4355 |
| **Directions:** | From Modesto, drive east on Highway 120 approximately 50 miles to the junction with Highway 108. Veer left onto Highway 108 and continue nine miles to Sonora. Drive through Sonora and continue east approximately 60 miles to Kennedy Meadows. Turn south and drive nine-tenths of a mile to the bridge over Deadman Creek. |

*Deadman Creek is seldom fished like these backcountry waters.*

South of Sonora Pass there are two Deadman Creeks in the Sierra Nevada, both of which are stocked, but differ greatly. Deadman Creek near Mammoth is a small, shallow stream, while Deadman Creek near Kennedy Meadows in the Stanislaus National Forest is much wider, a bit deeper and has some nice pools for good fishing.

Deadman Creek near Kennedy Meadows is a tributary to the upper Middle Fork of the Stanislaus River. It provides decent trout fishing in the spring and early summer when the California Department of Fish and Game stocks 2,065 rainbows. The plants are made directly above and below the bridge. If you have a jar of Power Bait, it's also an easy spot to catch stockers.

Kennedy Meadows is a popular starting point for backpackers heading into the Emigrant Wilderness and it's a good spot to rest the night before heading out on your journey. Some anglers fish here because they can walk to the saloon and have a drink after catching a few trout. Whatever floats your boat.

If you plan to make the trip, supplies are available in Kennedy Meadows and Dardanelle. Deadman Creek is closed to fishing from November 16 to the last Saturday in April.

Also nearby are Lyons Canal, Lyons Reservoir, Pinecrest Lake, Herring Creek, Stanislaus River (Middle Fork, Upper), Stanislaus River (Clark Fork), Stanislaus River (South Fork), Stanislaus River (Middle Fork, Lower), Herring Creek Reservoir, Donnell Reservoir, Beardsley Reservoir and Tuolumne River (Long Barn).

# STANISLAUS RIVER
## (MIDDLE FORK, UPPER)

*Grasshoppers are one of the best baits to use. They are found in grassy areas along the riverbed, and the trout can't resist 'em.*

**Rating:** 8
**Species:** Rainbow Trout and Brown Trout
**Stock:** 14,400 pounds of rainbow trout.
**Facilities:** Campgrounds, Vault Toilets, General Store, Picnic Areas, Saloon, Lodging, Restaurant, Bait & Tackle and a Pack Station
**Contact:** Stanislaus National Forest (209) 965-3434, Dardanelle Resort (209) 965-4355 Kennedy Meadows Resort and Pack Station (209) 965-3900

**Directions.** From Modesto, drive approximately 50 miles east on Highway 120 to the junction with Highway 108. Veer left onto Highway 108 and continue nine miles to Sonora. Drive east approximately 53 miles to Dardanelle. The road parallels the stream from here to Kennedy Meadows.

*Anglers got their wish on this August morning.*

When most people try to find the Stanislaus River (Middle Fork, Upper) on a map, they pinpoint the town of Dardanelle, because it's one of just two towns in the region along the river. You will probably be shocked (as I was) when you see the town of Dardanelle, especially when you see the sign that says, "Dardanelle Population 2". In fact, there is no town; Dardanelle is a resort. It used to have two year-round residents, but one of them has since passed away, which brings the present population down to one. The last time I passed through town the population had been removed from the sign.

The resort no longer stays open year-round, either. The lack of services, summer cabins, homes and civilization, in general, is what makes the river such a special place to visit. Yet, even with the lack of local folks, this remains a friendly place to visit.

For example, when I first arrived, I saw a sign that said, "DFG, please plant fish here." It was hanging from a pine tree near the river, directly behind a few campsites. And the wish was granted, too. I saw the DFG truck toss fish right where the campers had expressed their desire.

This pretty section of the river is remote and less fished than the nearby South Fork. There is a 10-mile stretch, flowing from 6,200 to 5,800 feet in the Stanislaus National Forest, that is stocked. It has great access and consistent fishing.

If you're coming from the west, the river is first stocked in Boulder and Brightman Flat Campgrounds, and then, from Dardanelle to Pigeon Flat Picnic Area. Directly upstream, the river is planted in the Eureka Valley Campground and Douglas Picnic Area. Finally, the stretch of water from Baker Campground to the pack station at Kennedy Meadows is also planted.

Sounds like a lot of places to stock? Get this -- the California Department of Fish and Game plants nearly 29,000 rainbows into this section of the river. It's stocked from the last week of April through mid-September. One drawback is that there aren't many trophy-size fish here. However, the fishing is still worth it, if for no other reason than the fact that

215

*Stanislaus River, Middle Fork Upper*

there aren't heavy crowds, as there are in the Eastern Sierra and Yosemite National Park.

Wide, with consistent flows, deep pools and long bends, like the Kern River, this stretch of the Stanislaus is similar to the South Fork of the Kings River in Kings Canyon National Park near Cedar Grove. Also like the Kern, it's difficult to fish due to snow runoff in the spring.

The Upper Middle Fork offers fishing for every type of angler. Power Bait fishing can be productive, fishing lures or salmon eggs works well, and anglers with waders and fly rods catch their share of trout. There are also wild rainbows and browns.

The best place to target these fish is between Pigeon Flat and Eureka Valley Campground. However, it may be difficult to find access here, because the river flows through a narrow gorge. Yet, many of the larger fish are caught here, because it is hard to reach and less fished. Grasshoppers are one of the best baits to use. They are found in grassy areas along the riverbed, and the trout can't resist 'em. Anglers who fish behind the large boulders and under fallen trees seem to catch the most fish.

If you plan to make the trip, supplies are available in Kennedy Meadows and Dardanelle. The Stanislaus River (Middle Fork, Upper) is closed to fishing from November 16 to the last Saturday in April.

Also nearby are Lyons Canal, Lyons Reservoir, Pinecrest Lake, Herring Creek, Deadman Creek, Stanislaus River (Clark Fork), Stanislaus River (South Fork), Stanislaus River (Middle Fork, Lower), Herring Creek Reservoir, Donnell Reservoir, Beardsley Reservoir and Tuolumne River (Long Barn).

# STANISLAUS RIVER

*Stanislaus River near Eureka Valley Campground*

# STANISLAUS RIVER (CLARK FORK)

**Most of the plants are made at Sand Flat Campground, but fish are also stocked at Cottonwood Picnic Area, Clark Fork Camp and at other access sites along the road.**

| | |
|---|---|
| **Rating:** | 7 |
| **Species:** | Rainbow Trout and Brown Trout |
| **Stock:** | 6,400 pounds of rainbow trout. |
| **Facilities:** | Campgrounds, Picnic Areas, RV Hookups and Vault Toilets |
| **Contact:** | Stanislaus National Forest (209) 965-3434 |

**Directions:** From Modesto, drive approximately 50 miles east on Highway 120 to the junction with Highway 108. Veer left onto Highway 108 and drive nine miles to Sonora. Continue east through Sonora and drive approximately 49 miles to Clark Fork Road. Turn north and drive six miles to Sand Flat Campground. The road parallels the river from here to the road's end.

*Stanislaus River (Clark Fork) near Iceberg Meadow*

The Clark Fork of the Stanislaus River is heaven for those with RV's. This section of the river is easy to bring an RV. It's also pretty, with small crowds and good fishing.

At 6,000 feet in the Stanislaus National Forest, the Clark Fork is a wide river in a remote area, stocked with 12,910 rainbow trout in the spring and early summer. Most of the plants are made at Sand Flat Campground, but fish are also stocked at Cottonwood Picnic Area, Clark Fork Camp and at other access sites along the road. An array of baits will catch fish, including white Power Bait, salmon eggs, small Panther Martins and silver Kastmasters.

The end of Clark Fork Road is a popular starting point for backpackers heading into the backcountry of the Stanislaus National Forest. They begin at Iceberg Meadow and follow Disaster Creek to the Pacific Crest Trail and Half Moon Lake.

If you arrive in the spring, keep an eye out for the Clark Fork Cascades. It is on your right at the second bridge after taking the Clark Fork turnoff. It can be powerful in the spring when the snow is melting.

If you plan to make the trip, supplies are available in Dardanelle. The Stanislaus River (Clark Fork) is closed to fishing from November 16 to the last Saturday in April.

Also nearby are Lyons Canal, Lyons Reservoir, Pinecrest Lake, Herring Creek, Deadman Creek, Stanislaus River (Middle Fork, Upper), Stanislaus River (South Fork), Stanislaus River (Middle Fork, Lower), Herring Creek Reservoir, Donnell Reservoir, Beardsley Reservoir and Tuolumne River (Long Barn).

# DONNELL RESERVOIR

**Fishing this lake is only for the adventurous and physically fit.**

| | |
|---|---|
| **Rating:** | 5 |
| **Species:** | Rainbow Trout and Brown Trout |
| **Stock:** | None |
| **Facilities:** | None |
| **Contact:** | Stanislaus National Forest (209) 965-3434 |

**Directions:** From Modesto, drive east on Highway 120 for approximately 50 miles to the junction with Highway 108. Veer left onto Highway 108 and continue nine miles to Sonora. Drive past Sonora and continue east for approximately 36 miles to Forest Service Road 5N02. Turn north, take the second right (Road 5N06) and drive for approximately 11.5 miles to a locked gate. Park and walk a half-mile to the dam.

*Donnell Reservoir*

At 4,920 feet in the Stanislaus National Forest, Donnell Reservoir is a remote, hard to reach body of water. It requires a slow 11-mile drive on a dirt road and then some boulder hopping just to get down to the lake. Getting to Donnell Reservoir is tough even for the most physically fit. The access is horrible, and you aren't going to make it unless you know what you're doing.

Boats are allowed, but good luck getting one in. There is no launch and no shoreline access to walk your boat down to the water. A few anglers have managed to get boats on the lake, but they haven't figured out how to get them off. They just leave them on the water.

Some of the boat owners who've left their boats on the lake have gotten sick of people borrowing them without asking, so as payback they've put small holes in the boats. That way, when the "borrowers" begin to paddle, they start to sink. The owners keep the exact size plugs with them, so they can still use the boats.

The "in thing" is to bring float tubes or kayaks because they are much lighter than boats, but I suggest you take a drive to the lake to see what you're up against before you try to launch. Fishing this lake is only for the adventurous and physically fit. It's best to go to the Donnell Reservoir Overlook first to see the lake before you decide to try bringing a boat down to the lake. After seeing the steep banks and narrow canyon, many anglers give up.

The reservoir which was last planted in 1963 with 30,000 fingerling rainbow trout no longer receives any plants from the California Department of Fish and Game, however, many wild trout get into in the clear, narrow lake by way of the Middle Fork of the Stanislaus River. There are many nice-sized browns and rainbows, but not many anglers there to catch 'em. You might try bringing an electric trolling motor and "borrowing" one of the lake's permanent boats. Just make sure you bring enough plugs to ensure you'll be able to plug the hole, or instead of catching fish, you'll be swimming with them.

If you plan to make the trip, supplies are available in Strawberry. In winter call ahead for road conditions. Chains may be required. To get to Donnell Reservoir Overlook, drive 11 miles north of the Beardsley Lake turnoff to the vista point on your left. A high-clearance vehicle is recommended to get to the lake.

Also nearby are Lyons Canal, Lyons Reservoir, Pinecrest Lake, Herring Creek, Deadman Creek, Stanislaus River (Middle Fork, Upper), Stanislaus River (South Fork), Stanislaus River (Middle Fork, Lower), Herring Creek Reservoir, Stanislaus River (Clark Fork), Beardsley Reservoir and Tuolumne River (Long Barn).

# HERRING CREEK
*It can be fun to fish its small pools until late July.*

| | |
|---|---|
| **Rating:** | 5 |
| **Species:** | Rainbow Trout |
| **Stock:** | 980 pounds of rainbow trout. |
| **Facilities:** | Campgrounds and Vault Toilets |
| **Contact:** | Stanislaus National Forest (209) 965-3434 |

**Directions:** From Modesto, drive approximately 50 miles east on Highway 120 to the junction with Highway 108. Veer left onto Highway 108 and continue nine miles to Sonora. Continue east through Sonora approximately 29 miles to Herring Creek Road (Forest Service Road 4N12), and turn right. Drive northeast for seven miles to a "y" in the road. Bear right and continue to the stream and campground.

*Herring Creek*

Fed by Herring Creek Reservoir, Herring Creek is a small, remote stream at 5,800 feet in the Stanislaus National Forest. Of all the planted streams east of Sonora and west of Bridgeport along Highway 108, Herring Creek is the least fished. The creek is planted with nearly 2,014 rainbows from late spring through early summer. It can be fun to fish its small pools until early July. If you come any later, fishing is nearly impossible, because the stream quits flowing and its water gets trapped in pools and becomes stagnant.

Herring Creek is a lot like Big Meadows Creek in the Sierra National Forest: bears commonly stroll through the primitive campsites at night, campers rather than day-users generally fish the creeks, and Power Bait is the best way to catch fish at both places.

If you plan to make the trip, supplies are available in Strawberry. Herring Creek Road is closed in the winter because of snow. Herring Creek is closed to fishing from November 16 to the last Saturday in April.

Also nearby are Lyons Canal, Lyons Reservoir, Pinecrest Lake, Herring Creek Reservoir, Deadman Creek, Stanislaus River (Clark Fork), Stanislaus River (Middle Fork, Lower), Stanislaus River (Middle Fork, Upper), Stanislaus River (South Fork), Donnell Reservoir, Beardsley Reservoir and Tuolumne River (Long Barn).

# HERRING CREEK RESERVOIR

*Fly-fishing is also popular here, but most anglers just toss spinners or fish Power Bait from the shoreline.*

**Rating:** 6

**Species:** Rainbow Trout, Brown Trout and Brook Trout

**Stock:** 1,460 pounds of rainbow trout.

**Facilities:** None

**Contact:** Stanislaus National Forest (209) 965-3434

**Directions:** From Modesto, drive approximately 50 miles east on Highway 120 to the junction with Highway 108. Veer left onto Highway 108 and continue nine miles to Sonora. Continue east through Sonora for approximately 29 miles to Herring Creek Road (Forest Service Road 4N12), and turn right. Drive northeast and drive for seven miles to a "y" in the road. Bear right and drive through the campground for about a mile to the reservoir.

*Herring Creek Reservoir*

Herring Creek Reservoir is a drive-to lake, but it gives you the feeling you're at a small high-country lake. It's quiet, with minimal crowds, lots of mosquitoes and offers good fishing.

Herring Creek Reservoir is a small, shallow 15-acre reservoir, located at 5,900 feet in a remote, seldom-used area of the Stanislaus National Forest. Only a few miles from Pinecrest Lake, this reservoir receives little to no pressure. It's a quiet little fishing hole that many locals use to dodge crowds.

In addition to wild trout, the California Department of Fish and Game stocks 2,998 rainbows. The best way to fish the lake is with waders, a float tube or canoe. No gas-powered motors are allowed, but electric trolling motors are permitted. Those who are able to find the deeper water find the best fishing. Fly-fishing is also popular here, but most anglers just toss spinners or fish Power Bait from the shoreline.

Although I didn't catch any, the locals tell me there are some brooks and browns in the lake. They're not planted, but they swim into the reservoir from Herring and Willow Creeks.

If you plan to make the trip, supplies are available in Strawberry. The road to Herring Creek Reservoir is closed in the winter due to snow.

Also nearby are Lyons Canal, Lyons Reservoir, Pinecrest Lake, Herring Creek, Deadman Creek, Stanislaus River (Clark Fork), Stanislaus River (Middle Fork, Lower), Stanislaus River (Middle Fork, Upper), Stanislaus River (South Fork), Donnell Reservoir, Beardsley Reservoir and Tuolumne River (Long Barn).

# PINECREST LAKE

**The average trout angler can come to the lake for the first time and do well.**

| | |
|---|---|
| **Rating:** | 9 |
| **Species:** | Rainbow Trout, Brook Trout, Brown Trout and Channel Catfish |
| **Stock:** | 32,200 pounds of rainbow trout. |
| **Facilities:** | Lodging, General Store, Boat Launch, Boat, Kayak and Sailboat Rentals, Restaurant, Campgrounds, Picnic Areas, Gas, Restrooms, Bait & Tackle and a Marina |
| **Contact:** | Stanislaus National Forest (209) 965-3434, Pinecrest Lake Resort (209) 965-3411 Pinecrest Lake Marina (209) 965-3333 |
| **Directions:** | From Modesto, drive approximately 50 miles east on Highway 120 to the junction with Highway 108. Veer left onto Highway 108 and drive nine miles to Sonora. Continue east 24 miles through Sonora to Pinecrest Road and turn northeast. Drive 1.5 miles to the lake. |

*Pinecrest Lake*

Located at 5,600 feet in the Stanislaus National Forest, Pinecrest Lake is a vacationer's paradise. Surrounded by tall pines and a picturesque backdrop of granite outcroppings, Pinecrest is the best all-around lake along Highway 108 between Sonora to Bridgeport. It's a premier family destination that offers boating, fishing, swimming, and peace and quiet, all at the same time. About an hour-and-a-half drive from the Stockton area, this is a must-visit lake.

Most of the lake's visitors drive from the Bay Area to vacation here. With snow covering its shorelines in the winter and water temperatures in the mid-seventies in the summer, Pinecrest has something for everyone, year-round. Highlighting the winter attractions, Dodge Ridge Ski Area and snow-play areas are only a few minutes from the lake. Summer is home to kayakers, swimmers, sailboaters and anglers. Good news for fishermen, no water-skiing, tubing or any activity where a rope is attached to the back of a boat is allowed. There is a 20 mph speed limit on the lake.

Pinecrest is an easy lake to fish. Although techniques differ by season, fishing remains good year-round. The average trout angler can come to the lake for the first time and do well. The only downside is, with the exception of a few caught in the two to three-pound range, most of the rainbows are small, about a half-pound.

Each year the California Department of Fish and Game stocks more than 63,810 trout into the 300-acre lake. The best time to fish is in late spring when toplining small Rapalas, silver Kastmasters and Needlefish anywhere on the lake produces limits. As summer approaches, the fish move to deeper water, and either leadcore or a downrigger is needed to get in on the action. Fall again brings the fish towards the surface, and toplining and Power Bait fishing from shore will catch fish.

During the winter, the lake is drawn down, and it's impossible to launch a boat. Only a few anglers can withstand the cold this time of year, but those who have the tolerance experience good fishing by tossing lures from the shoreline. There is a trail that circumferences the lake, which is nearly encompassed by private cabins.

There are also some browns and brooks that enter the lake via the South Fork of the Stanislaus River, but not many are caught. Most anglers concentrate on fishing for the planters. Many people think that with the amount of fish that are stocked into the lake there would be a lot of holdovers, but it's not the case. The lake is so heavily fished that most of the stocked trout are caught each year. Then, the few holdover rainbows swim up the Stanislaus River each winter.

A little known fact is that the lake is also home to some large catfish. They can be caught during the summer, however, are rarely targeted. In winter when the lake is drawn down, the catfish live in the mud.

If you plan to make the trip, supplies are available at the lake. In winter, call ahead for road conditions. Chains may be required. Launching your boat and camping are free.

Also nearby are Lyons Canal, Lyons Reservoir, Herring Creek, Herring Creek Reservoir, Deadman Creek, Stanislaus River (Clark Fork), Stanislaus River (Middle Fork, Lower), Stanislaus River (Middle Fork, Upper), Stanislaus River (South Fork), Donnell Reservoir, Beardsley Reservoir and Tuolumne River (Long Barn).

*Fingerling golden trout*

PINECREST LAKE

# STANISLAUS RIVER (SOUTH FORK)

*Anglers who wait until late June often do extremely well fishing salmon eggs, gold Kastmasters or white Roostertails.*

| | |
|---|---|
| **Rating:** | 7 |
| **Species:** | Rainbow Trout, Brook Trout and Brown Trout |
| **Stock:** | 4,110 pounds of rainbow trout. |
| **Facilities:** | Campground and Vault Toilets |
| **Contact:** | Stanislaus National Forest (209) 965-3434 |

**Directions:** From Modesto, drive approximately 50 miles east on Highway 120 to the junction with Highway 108. Veer left onto Highway 108 and continue nine miles to Sonora. Drive east approximately 30 miles past Sonora to Fraser Road (Forest Service Road 4N01) and turn north. Drive three miles to Fraser Flat Campground.

*Stanislaus River (South Fork)*

With the exception of the Lower Middle Fork, anglers bombard all parts of the Stanislaus River daily, and the South Fork is no exception. Both campers and day-use anglers heavily fish the South Fork of the Stanislaus River. In fact, so many anglers come here, if you don't arrive a few days after a stock, there might not be any planters left.

The river is planted weekly, from the last week of April through July, with the California Department of Fish and Game dumping a total of 8,163 rainbows, but it doesn't seem to be enough. You've got to figure about 750 fish are planted each week, and with more than 50 anglers fishing this stretch daily, all it takes is for 140 of the 350 anglers who fish the river each week to catch their limits, and there are no more stockers left.

Catching fish is usually easy right after a plant. The fish are planted in many large pools, and since rock walls have been constructed around the pools in the Fraser Flat Campground, the fish are easy to catch, because they can't get out. The stream is planted from the campground upstream past the bridge on Fraser Road, all the way to Strawberry.

Access to the river is also available by following a dirt road that parallels the river for four miles to the town of Strawberry. The dirt road can be picked up just before you reach Fraser Flat Campground, however, only high clearance vehicles are recommended. Other good spots for access are where Old Strawberry Road crosses over the river close to town and near where Highway 108 meets the river in Strawberry.

Because of high flows from snow runoff, the river can be difficult to fish in the spring and early summer. Anglers who wait until late June often do extremely well fishing salmon eggs, gold Kastmasters or white Roostertails. Mixed in with the planters are wild brook, rainbow and brown trout, but they are harder to catch.

If you plan to make the trip, supplies are available in Strawberry. The Stanislaus River (South Fork) is closed to fishing from November 16 to the last Saturday in April.

Also nearby are Stanislaus River (Middle Fork, Upper).

# STANISLAUS RIVER
## (MIDDLE FORK, LOWER)

*This section of the river is designated as a wild trout stream and holds the largest fish in the region.*

**Rating:** 8

**Species:** Rainbow Trout, Brook Trout and Brown Trout

**Stock:** None

**Facilities:** Campgrounds and Vault Toilets

**Contact:** Stanislaus National Forest (209) 965-3434

**Directions:** From Modesto, drive approximately 50 miles east on Highway 120 to the junction with Highway 108. Veer left onto Highway 108 and continue nine miles to Sonora. Continue east approximately 30 miles to Fraser Road (Forest Service Road 4N01) and turn north. Drive three miles to Fraser Flat Campground. Continue nine miles past Fraser Flat Campground to Sand Bar Flat.

*Like these glaciers near Big Pine, the Stanislaus River Middle Fork (Lower) can't be reached without effort to reach it.*

The Stanislaus River (Middle Fork, Lower) provides the best wild trout fishing of all the forks of the river, but the question is, do you have the patience to drive there? The access road to this remote, hard-to-reach section of the river is only 10 miles, but it will take you more than an hour to drive it. Rough and winding, it requires slow, careful driving, but those who make the trip are usually happy they did. This section of the river is designated as a wild trout stream and holds the largest fish in the region. Rainbow and brown trout are abundant, with the occasional brook.

The river is governed by special regulations. From the Beardsley Dam downstream to the US Forest Service footbridge at Spring Gap, there is a two fish limit. Each fish must be at least 14 inches in total length, and only artificial lures with barbless hooks are allowed. Below the footbridge to New Melones Reservoir, there is also a two fish limit.

Access is easy to Spring Gap, with a trail leading from Beardsley, however, the trail stops there. For further travel downstream, rock-hopping is required, and access becomes much more difficult. Two other popular spots are in Beardsley Afterbay and the Sand Bar Forebay. Access is also available at the Spring Gap Powerhouse and at Beardsley Lake. Call the Forest Service for the specifics.

Although most anglers fly-fish this section of the river, spin casters do well, too. I found small Panther Martins to be best.

If you plan to make the trip, supplies are available in Strawberry. The Stanislaus River (Middle Fork, Lower) is closed to fishing from November 16 to the last Saturday in April.

Also nearby are Lyons Canal, Lyons Reservoir, Pinecrest Lake, Herring Creek, Deadman Creek, Stanislaus River (Clark Fork), Stanislaus River (South Fork), Stanislaus River (Middle Fork, Upper), Herring Creek Reservoir, Donnell Reservoir, Beardsley Reservoir and Tuolumne River (Long Barn).

# BEARDSLEY RESERVOIR

*Because there is a stable population of large browns, the ideal thing would be to attempt to catch one of the larger browns in the lake.*

**Rating:** 7

**Species:** Rainbow Trout and Brown Trout

**Stock:** 9,000 pounds of rainbow trout and 2,250 pounds of sub-catchable brown trout.

**Facilities:** Boat Launch, Swimming Area, Picnic Area and Vault Toilets

**Contact:** Stanislaus National Forest (209) 965-3434

**Directions:** From Modesto, drive east on Highway 120 for approximately 50 miles to the junction with Highway 108. Veer left onto Highway 108 and continue nine miles to Sonora. From Sonora, continue east for approximately 36 miles to Forest Service Road 5N02. Turn north and drive 8.8 miles to the lake.

*Beardsley Reservoir*

At 3,405 feet in the Stanislaus National Forest, Beardsley Reservoir is a long, narrow, clear 720-acre reservoir that holds the largest trout in the region. Depending on when they arrive, Beardsley Reservoir can either be a delight for anglers or their worst nightmare. During the week, the lake is empty and perfect for fishing. However, on the weekends, boaters and water-skiers own it, and frighten the fish so much, they won't bite.

Prior to 1995, the lake held only rainbow trout. However, due to a parasite problem that occurred in the rainbow population in the mid-Nineties, in 1995 the California Department of Fish and Game chose to reduce the rainbow population, and stopped planting rainbow trout. Since browns are less likely to get this parasite that shows up as visible sores on the side of the fish, from 1995-97 only browns were planted. Though the problem with the parasites never totally went away, currently both browns and rainbows are planted in the lake. The CA DFG stocks 18,500 half-pound rainbows and 20,250 sub-catchable browns.

Both species prosper in the lake and are best caught by trollers. Because the lake's shoreline is steep, it's hard for shoreline anglers to get in on the action. However, shore fishing can be productive near the boat launch and swimming areas. Trollers generally parallel the shorelines or work the middle of the lake. In spring and fall when the trout are near the surface, top-lining works best, but downriggers or leadcore are needed in the summer when the trout move to deeper water.

Most anglers catch half rainbows and half browns. However, because there is a stable population of large browns, the ideal thing would be to attempt to catch one of the larger browns in the lake. Yet, most anglers choose to fish for the smaller planters because they are easier to catch. The larger browns can take some work to hook. If targeting the large browns the best time is in the early spring and late fall, with the finest bite coming about an hour before sunset to an hour after sunrise. Try using the largest Rapalas you can find.

*Mathew Mitchell handles a brood stock rainbow trout, which are planted into Beardsley at times.*

For those content with catching stockers, use Needlefish, Thomas Buoyants, Kastmasters and small Mystics.

If you plan to make the trip, supplies are available in Strawberry. Beardsley Lake is drawn down in the winter and launching can be difficult. Call the Forest Service for updated launching conditions. In winter, chains may be required.

Also nearby are Lyons Canal, Lyons Reservoir, Pinecrest Lake, Herring Creek, Deadman Creek, Stanislaus River (Clark Fork), Stanislaus River (South Fork), Stanislaus River (Middle Fork, Lower), Herring Creek Reservoir, Donnell Reservoir, Stanislaus River (Middle Fork, Upper) and Tuolumne River (Long Barn).

*Rainbow trout*

*A redwood sorrel*

# TUOLUMNE RIVER
## (NORTH FORK, UPPER)

*It's about a mile walk from the road down to all the camps, but I'd head to Hull's Crossing.*
*The fishing is better and the access is easier.*

| | |
|---|---|
| **Rating:** | 7 |
| **Species:** | Rainbow Trout and Brown Trout |
| **Stock:** | 1,700 pounds of rainbow trout. |
| **Facilities:** | Picnic Areas and Vault Toilets |
| **Contact:** | Stanislaus National Forest (209) 965-3434 |

**Directions:** From Modesto, drive approximately 50 miles east on Highway 120 to the junction with Highway 108. Veer left onto Highway 108 and continue nine miles to Sonora. From Sonora, drive approximately 21 miles east on Highway 108 to Long Barn Road. Turn right and drive one-tenth of a mile to Merrill Springs Road. Turn left and continue two miles to the North Fork Picnic Area.

*Tuolumne River (North Fork, Upper)*

Located at 5,200 feet in the Stanislaus National Forest, the weather and water levels can make it difficult for the California Department of Fish and game to stock the Upper North Fork of the Tuolumne River. The river opens to fishing the last Saturday in April, however, because it's usually thick with mud and snow, planting can be difficult, and may not even take place until conditions improve. Then, by early July, the water can become too low for the trout to survive, so you'll need to arrive sometime between mid-May and early July to be successful. If everything is right, the fishing will be good.

The CA DFG dumps 2,830 rainbow trout at the North Fork Picnic Area (also known as Hull's Crossing), at Camp High Sierra and at the pond at Jenness Park Christian Camp. Public access to both camps is limited to walk-in traffic only. It's about a mile walk from the road down to all the camps, but I'd head to Hull's Crossing. The fishing is better and the access is easier.

The Upper North Fork has less volume than the Lower North Fork, but offers some beautiful scenery. The river flows through meadows and past towering pines. Most of the pools are small and shallow, so using salmon eggs and Power Bait is your best bet.

If you plan to make the trip, supplies are available in Long Barn. The Upper North Fork of the Tuolumne River is closed to fishing from November 16 to the last Saturday in April.

Also nearby are Lyons Canal, Lyons Reservoir, Pinecrest Lake, Herring Creek, Deadman Creek, Stanislaus River (Middle Fork, Upper), Stanislaus River (South Fork), Stanislaus River (Middle Fork, Lower), Herring Creek Reservoir, Donnell Reservoir, Beardsley Reservoir and Stanislaus River (Clark Fork).

# LYONS RESERVOIR

*Although catching fish was simpler when boating was allowed, anglers are still successful soaking Power Bait, floating night crawlers off the bottom or tossing lures.*

| | |
|---|---|
| **Rating:** | 6 |
| **Species:** | Rainbow Trout, Largemouth Bass and Channel Catfish |
| **Stock:** | 4,000 pounds of rainbow trout. |
| **Facilities:** | Vault Toilets and Picnic Area |
| **Contact:** | Stanislaus National Forest (209) 586-3234 |
| **Directions:** | From Modesto, drive approximately 50 miles east on Highway 120 to the junction with Highway 108. Veer left onto Highway 108 and continue nine miles to Sonora. From Sonora, continue approximately 14 miles east on Highway 108 to Forest Service Road 3N14. Turn left and drive two miles north on the dirt road to the lake. |

*Lyons Reservoir*

Lyons Reservoir has gone through some drastic changes over the last decade. In direct response to problems with rowdies urinating in the water and spilling beer into the lake, as well as a general lack of responsibility by boaters, the reservoir has been closed to boating and swimming. Camping has also been prohibited. Because the lake is used as a domestic water supply, taking away these user privileges was the only way to keep the water from getting polluted.

Located at 4,226 feet in the Stanislaus National Forest and surrounded by tall pine trees, this 170-acre reservoir can be a beautiful fishing spot if you arrive before drawdowns begin. And without the rowdies, Lyons Reservoir is now a calm and quiet place. Run strictly as a day-use area, the roads leading to the lake are locked after sunset.

The California Department of Fish and Game stocks 7,750 rainbows to keep the lake's largemouth bass and catfish company, but anglers don't target the bass and catfish much. The lake also has a few browns that enter through the South Fork of the Stanislaus River. However, the easiest fish to catch are definitely the rainbows. Although catching fish was simpler when boating was allowed, anglers are still successful soaking Power Bait, floating night crawlers off the bottom or tossing lures.

The best area to catch trout is near the lake's inlet, but many anglers don't fish here because it's a 1.7-mile walk, and they're simply too lazy to hike it. There is an off-road vehicle trail that goes around the lake, but it's for green-stickered vehicles only.

If you plan to make the trip, supplies are available in Sierra Village. Lyons Reservoir is closed to fishing from November through April.

Also nearby are Lyons Canal, Herring Creek Reservoir, Pinecrest Lake, Herring Creek, Deadman Creek, Stanislaus River (Clark Fork), Stanislaus River (Middle Fork, Lower), Stanislaus River (Middle Fork, Upper), Stanislaus River (South Fork), Donnell Reservoir, Beardsley Reservoir and Tuolumne River (Long Barn).

# LYONS CANAL

| | |
|---|---|
| **Rating:** | 5 |
| **Species:** | Rainbow Trout and Channel Catfish |
| **Stock:** | 4,330 pounds of rainbow trout. |
| **Facilities:** | None |
| **Contact:** | Stanislaus National Forest (209) 586-3234 |

**Directions:** From Modesto, drive approximately 50 miles east on Highway 120 to the junction with Highway 108. Veer left onto Highway 108 and continue nine miles to Sonora. At the junction of Highway 49 and 108 in Sonora, continue another 11 miles east on Highway 108 to Twain Harte Drive. Turn north, drive 1.7 miles to Joaquin Gully Road and turn northeast. Drive one mile to Middle Camp Road and turn east. Drive one-tenth of a mile and turn north on South Fork Road. Continue four-tenths of a mile to the fishing access site on the left. The road parallels the canal for the next few miles.

*Lyons Canal*

Lyons Canal is a flume created by water released from Lyons Reservoir. At 3,500 feet, near the town of Twain Harte in the Stanislaus National Forest, the canal is only about five-feet wide, but it is stocked by the California Department of Fish and Game with 8,520 rainbow trout.

To make fishing easy, the Pacific Gas & Electric Company has established a readily accessible dirt parking area with direct access to the canal. It's a great place for anglers who love to fish streams but aren't in physical shape to do rock-hopping or hiking. At the fishing access site, there is one main canal and a smaller overflow canal, both of which hold fish.

The best way to catch the rainbows is to drift Power Bait under the small bushes that hang over the streambed, which the trout use as cover. Under many of the branches are small cave-like holes that allow the trout to save energy by staying out of the fast moving water.

Word has it that there are also small catfish in the overflow stream. None of them weigh more than a pound, with most running about eight inches. I ran into an older gentleman who catches them all the time. He said night crawlers are the hot ticket.

If you plan to make the trip, supplies are available in Twain Harte. Lyons Canal is closed to fishing from November 16 to the last Saturday in April.

Also nearby are Sullivan Creek, Lyons Reservoir, Pinecrest Lake, Herring Creek Reservoir, Herring Creek, Stanislaus River (South Fork) and Stanislaus River (Middle Fork, Lower).

# POWERHOUSE STREAM

**Shaded by oaks and pines, the stream usually flows pretty fast and is difficult to fish without salmon eggs or Power Bait.**

| | |
|---|---|
| **Rating:** | 5 |
| **Species:** | Rainbow Trout |
| **Stock:** | 1,500 pounds of rainbow trout. |
| **Facilities:** | None |
| **Contact:** | California Department of Fish and Game (559) 243-4005, The Sportsman (209) 532-1716 |

**Directions:** From East Sonora on Mono Way (Old Highway 108), turn north on Greenley Way. Drive 1.1 miles to the end of the road. Turn right on Lyons-Bald Mountain Road and drive 3.8 miles to a fork. Veer right and drive six-tenths of a mile to the stream.

*Powerhouse Stream is a drive to stream, unlike the streams shown here that are invisible to the eye.*

Powerhouse Stream and Sullivan Creek are two small trout streams fished almost exclusively by Sonora residents. Powerhouse Stream flows into Phoenix Lake, a private lake in Sonora, while Sullivan Creek flows out of it.

Powerhouse Stream is not a place out-of-towners often come to. First of all, the stream is so small there isn't a lot of room to fish. Also, locals usually fish it out before the weekend comes. The ones who live along Lyons-Bald Mountain Road have an advantage – they can see the California Department of Fish and Game truck coming. As soon as it passes, they head to the creek to fill their stringers.

The stream is planted with 2,953 rainbow trout, beginning at the Powerhouse that the Pacific Gas & Electric Company uses to create power, and continuing for a distance of about 100 yards downstream to the barbed wire fence just below the bridge. Stay in this area, because everywhere else is private property. The most consistent spots are behind the mailboxes and just below the Powerhouse. Shaded by oaks and pines, the stream usually flows pretty fast and is difficult to fish without salmon eggs or Power Bait.

If you plan to make the trip, supplies are available in Sonora. Powerhouse Stream is closed to fishing from November 16 to the last Saturday in April.

Also nearby are Springville Trout Farm and Sullivan Creek.

# SULLIVAN CREEK

*If there is a lot of water in the stream, you can get away with casting lures, but most of the time, using salmon eggs produces the highest catch rates.*

| | |
|---|---|
| **Rating:** | 5 |
| **Species:** | Rainbow Trout |
| **Stock:** | 1,200 pounds of rainbow trout. |
| **Facilities:** | None |
| **Contact:** | The Sportsman (209) 532-1716 |

**Directions:** From Modesto, drive approximately 50 miles east on Highway 120 to the junction with Highway 108. Veer left onto Highway 108 and continue nine miles to Sonora. In East Sonora, turn left on Phoenix Lake Road and drive 1.3 miles to Meadow Brook Drive. Turn north and drive four-tenths of a mile to Alder Lane. Turn left and continue one-tenth of a mile to the bridge and creek.

*Sullivan Creek*

Sullivan Creek is an urban stream in Sonora, dependent on releases from Phoenix Lake. Shaded by alders, the creek flows through residential areas of Sonora. The black and red berries that are abundant along its shoreline may be Sullivan Creek's best assets. I was so busy picking and eating them I didn't get to do much fishing.

The California Department of Fish and Game begins planting the stream with rainbow trout the last weekend in April, and by the end of May, it usually completes stocking 2,245 fish. Anytime thereafter, water levels subside and the creek becomes too warm for the trout. If there is a lot of water in the stream, you can get away with casting lures, but most of the time, using salmon eggs produces the highest catch rates. Because the stream has a rocky and sandy bottom, salmon eggs stick out well. Concentrate your efforts directly above and below the bridge. The fish seem to stay in this area.

If you plan to make the trip, supplies are available in Sonora. Sullivan Creek is closed to fishing from November 16 to the last Saturday in April.

Also nearby are Powerhouse Stream, Springfield Trout Farm, Lyons Canal and Lyons Canyon Reservoir.

# SPRINGFIELD TROUT FARM

**Catching fish is easy. They aren't fed, so they're always hungry and they'll eat anything.**

**Rating:** 8
**Species:** Rainbow Trout
**Stock:** Weekly
**Facilities:** Fish Cleaning Station, Bait & Tackle, Restrooms and Picnic Area
**Contact:** Springfield Trout Farm (209) 532-4623

**Directions:** From Modesto, drive approximately 50 miles east on Highway 120 to the junction with Highway 108. Veer left onto Highway 108 and continue nine miles to Sonora. Exit Highway 49 and drive north through Sonora. Turn right on Shaws Flat Road and drive nine-tenths of a mile to the trout farm on your left.

*David Brown (Left) and his grandson Cody Denton caught these trout at Springfield.*

Every angler dreams of catching a trout over five pounds, but not many get to experience that feat. Yet, at Springfield Trout Farm near Sonora, it happens every day. It doesn't require that you be an experienced fisherman. You don't even need a fishing pole or a license. They provide old-fashioned fly-fishing reels and bait for you. (You can bring your own gear if you want.) Springfield Trout Farm raises the trout themselves and stocks them in a shallow pool.

Located on a private residence, the attractive grounds are heavily shaded, with two small streams (fed by water pumped from springs located elsewhere on the property) that meander through the grassy hills. The trout farm is a great family destination. It's the kind of place you'll want to bring your kids to catch their first fish. Mom and grandma can sit on the benches next to the pond and get nervous when the kids get too close to the water.

Catching fish is easy. They aren't fed, so they're always hungry and they'll eat anything. The only catch is that there is no catch & release, so it costs money to catch 'em. However, Springfield Trout Farm's prices are much less expensive than most trout farms in the state, and there's no admission charge.

The prices range anywhere from $1.25 for a seven-incher to $5 for anything more than 14 inches. That means you can catch a five-pound rainbow trout for $5! At most other trout farms, a five-pound trout would cost at least $25. There's no limit. You can catch as many lunkers as your heart desires. You'd better hurry up and get there before someone else catches your dream fish.

If you plan to make the trip, supplies are available in Sonora. During the summer the trout farm is open daily. All other times of the year, it's only open from Fri. through Sun.

Also nearby are Powerhouse Stream, Sullivan Creek and the Sonora Wineries.

# TUOLUMNE RIVER
## (NORTH FORK, LOWER)

*This section of the Tuolumne River doesn't get the attention it deserves, but the anglers who fish it would like to keep it that way. More fish for them.*

| | |
|---|---|
| **Rating:** | 6 |
| **Species:** | Rainbow Trout and Brown Trout |
| **Stock:** | 1,700 pounds of rainbow trout. |
| **Facilities:** | Picnic Areas, Campgrounds and Showers |
| **Contact:** | Stanislaus National Forest (209) 586-3234, River Ranch Campground (209) 928-3708 |

**Directions:** From Modesto, drive approximately 50 miles east on Highway 120 to the junction with Highway 108. Veer left onto Highway 108 and drive nine miles to Sonora. From the junction of Highway 49 and 108, drive another four miles east on Highway 108 to Tuolumne Road (Road E 17). Turn southeast and drive 6.8 miles to Tuolumne City. Turn north on Carter Street and drive three-tenths of a mile to Buchanan Road. Turn east and drive approximately five miles to a dirt road on your right, just after you cross over the bridge. Turn north and continue to the creek.

*Tuolumne River (North Fork, Lower)*

Located at 2,200 feet in the Stanislaus National Forest, the Tuolumne River (North Fork, Lower) is only six miles from Tuolumne City, however, most of the city's residents have no idea it exists. It's sad, but true. This section of the Tuolumne River doesn't get the attention it deserves, but the anglers who fish it would like to keep it that way. More fish for them.

The Lower North Fork is best accessed where it meets Basin Creek in River Ranch Campground. There is no hiking required, and when water levels are sufficient and the water is cool enough, the California Department of Fish and Game plants 2,830 rainbow trout to spice up the fishing in the spring and early summer. Fishing tends to be good for anglers drifting Power Bait behind boulders and tossing lures in the large pools or slow moving stretches of the river.

The river also has many wild browns and rainbows. Heavily shaded by large pines, it is half the size of Chiquito Creek in the Sierra National Forest, but has the same characteristics, with a rock and sand bottom and long, wide pools. Campers also spend time rafting and tubing on both rivers. The water can get quite warm, making swimming enjoyable when the fishing dies down in the summer.

If you plan to make the trip, supplies are available in Tuolumne City. The Tuolumne River (North Fork, Lower) is closed to fishing from November 16 to the last Saturday in April.

Also nearby are Basin Creek, Cherry Lake, Cherry River and Clavey River.

*The best fishing in the stream isn't for stocked trout. There are a great number of small wild browns in the stream that few anglers target.*

**Rating:** 5
**Species:** Rainbow Trout and Brown Trout
**Stock:** 300 pounds of rainbow trout.
**Facilities:** Picnic Areas, Campgrounds and Showers
**Contact:** Stanislaus National Forest (209) 586-3234, River Ranch Campground (209) 928-3708

**Directions:** From Modesto, drive east on Highway 120 for approximately 50 miles to the junction with Highway 108. Veer left onto Highway 108 and continue nine miles to Sonora. From the junction of Highway 49 and 108, drive east four miles to Tuolumne Road (Road E 17). Turn southeast and drive 6.8 miles to Tuolumne City. Turn north on Carter Street and drive three-tenths of a mile. Turn east on Buchanan Road and drive approximately five miles to a dirt road on your right, just after you cross over the bridge. Turn north and continue to the creek.

*Basin Creek*

Basin Creek is a tributary to the North Fork of the Tuolumne River (Lower). The creek is rarely fished, but offers surprisingly good fishing for small wild brown trout. The creek is stocked in late spring by the California Department of Fish and Game, however, the 595 rainbows aren't enough to excite most anglers to make the trip. Located in River Ranch Campground, the creek is heavily shaded and produces good catch rates for anglers who fish Power Bait or salmon eggs behind boulders and in small pools.

The best fishing in the stream isn't for stocked trout. There are a great number of small wild browns in the stream that few anglers target. These browns are mixed in with the planters, but are harder to catch, because they are far more wary of anglers and get easily spooked.

Basin Creek used to be the site of the region's fish hatchery, but when the Moccasin Creek Fish Hatchery opened in the early Fifties, it took the place of Basin's hatchery, which has been closed ever since. Its only remains are a few concrete blocks from some of the old fish runs.

Basin Creek can play tricks on your eyes. Many anglers believe that it has more water than the Tuolumne, however it only appears that way. Because Basin Creek is much narrower and runs down a slope, the water flows faster, which makes it look like it has more volume than the wider, slower Tuolumne. In fact, the Tuolumne has at least twice the amount of water, though most of it is trapped in pools.

If you plan to make the trip, supplies are available in Tuolumne City. Basin Creek is closed to fishing from November 16 to the last Saturday in April.

Also nearby are North Fork of the Tuolumne River (Lower), Cherry Lake, Cherry River and Clavey River.

# CLAVEY RIVER

*The Clavey River is one of six Heritage waters in the state and is home to the coastal rainbow trout.*

| | |
|---|---|
| **Rating:** | 10 |
| **Species:** | Rainbow Trout and Brown Trout |
| **Stock:** | None |
| **Facilities:** | None |
| **Contact:** | Stanislaus National Forest (209) 532-3671 |

**Directions:** From Modesto, drive approximately 50 miles east on Highway 120 to the junction with Highway 108. Veer left onto Highway 108 and drive nine miles to Sonora. From the junction of Highways 49 and 108, drive another four miles east on Highway 108 to Tuolumne Road (Road E 17). Turn southeast and drive 6.8 miles to Tuolumne City. Turn north on Carter Street and drive three-tenths of a mile to Buchanan Road. Turn east and drive approximately 18 miles to a bridge over the river. Park and climb carefully down the steep slopes to the river.

*Clavey River*

Very few anglers have heard of the Heritage Trout Program. Established by the California Department of Fish and Game in 1998, the Heritage Trout Program was created to protect California's native trout populations, which include fish that existed in these waters prior to modern fish-stocking efforts. The program is aimed at restoring these waters to their pristine state, preserving and caring for the native fish and their natural habitat.

The Clavey River is one of six Heritage waters in the state and is home to the coastal rainbow trout. Many biologists consider the Clavey to be one of the last rivers in the state that has not been altered by civilization, so the fish can reproduce in a totally natural environment. There are no dams or other artificial obstructions built along the Clavey. In fact, it's one of the last free-flowing rivers in the state.

The Clavey's coastal rainbows are in good shape. They are plentiful here, though few anglers fish the river. Those who do can expect to catch hoards of small trout, most of which are yanked out of large, deep pools. Size 1/64 Panther Martins, white trout jigs and small silver Kastmasters all work well here.

The Clavey begins at 6,000 feet in the Stanislaus National Forest, where Lily and Bell Creeks meet. The river then meanders 29 miles through a narrow gorge, before emptying into the Tuolumne River. Most of the river is located in a remote canyon, especially the lower section; however, a few roads cross the upper section of the river, and some four-wheel drive roads parallel it.

If you plan to make the trip, supplies are available in Sonora. The Clavey River is closed to fishing from November 16 to the last Saturday in April. For other roads that lead to the river call the Forest Service.

Also nearby are Cherry Lake, Tuolumne River, North Fork (Lower) and Basin Creek.

*For the few anglers who fish here, the reservoir is heavily stocked.*

| | |
|---|---|
| **Rating:** | 6 |
| **Species:** | Rainbow Trout and Brown Trout |
| **Stock:** | 11,000 pounds of rainbow trout, one pound of fingerling rainbow trout and 362 pounds of fingerling brook trout. |
| **Facilities:** | Boat Launch, Campgrounds and Vault Toilets |
| **Contact:** | Stanislaus National Forest (209) 962-7825 |

**Directions:** From Modesto, drive east on Highway 120 approximately 50 miles to the junction with Highway 108. Veer right on Highway 120 and continue to Groveland. From Highway 120 in Groveland, drive east 14 miles to Road 1N07 (Cherry Oil Road). Turn north and continue 26 miles to the lake.

*Cherry Lake loses its beauty as the lake's level begins to drop.*

On my way from the Clavey River to Cherry Lake, I had only driven a few miles on the winding road from the river when I came around a blind curve and saw something large and black about 20 yards dead-ahead in the middle of the road. I slammed on the brakes, and my car screeched to a halt, only inches from hitting it head-on.

"What the hell are you doing?" I hollered at this Angus that took up my whole side of the road. "Get out of the road," I yelled. "You're going to kill someone." She had nothing to say for herself except, "Mmuurrrr." Eventually I got tired of waiting for this stubborn cow to move, so I drove around her.

After that frustrating experience, I was eager to move on and do some fishing at Cherry Valley in this beautiful reservoir I'd heard about. When I got there, what I saw was an unsightly muddy shoreline littered with rocks and dirt. It sloped down steeply from a ragged-looking line of pine trees that I could tell once shaded the shoreline before the lake was drawn down. I could imagine that it would have been a stunning sight at full pool, with the crystal blue reservoir framed by giant granite mountains in the distance.

At 4,700 feet in the Stanislaus National Forest, directly adjacent to Yosemite National Park, this 1,765-acre reservoir is in a remote area bordered by the Emigrant Wilderness. For the few anglers who fish here, the reservoir is heavily stocked. The California Department of Fish and Game plants 22,200 rainbow trout, in addition to more than 60,400 fingerling rainbows. That's a lot of fish, but catch rates don't reflect the heavy plants. Also, 70,000 fingerling brook trout were dumped in.

The lake is best fished in the spring when water levels are high. Try trolling down the middle of the lake or along the shorelines with Needlefish, Kastmasters and Cripplelures. Because of the lake's steep shorelines, it can be difficult for bank anglers to get in on the action. There are also a few browns that find their way into the reservoir by way of Cherry Creek, but they are rarely caught. Nearly 10,000 browns were planted in 1986. Here are a

few interesting facts: In 1990, cutthroats were introduced, in '72, '74, '75, and '76 coho salmon were planted and kokanee were stocked in '76.

Fishing picks up again in the fall after the action slows in the summer, but not many anglers show up to try their luck. Most people who come to Cherry Lake use it as a base to hike into Yosemite National Park and the Emigrant Wilderness.

If you plan to make the trip, supplies are available in Groveland. In winter call ahead for road conditions. Chains may be required. After July it can be difficult to launch a boat. Call the Forest Service for updates on launching conditions.

Also nearby are the Cherry River, Clavey River, the Emigrant Wilderness, Basin Creek, the Lower North Fork of the Tuolumne River, South Fork of the Tuolumne River and Middle Fork of the Tuolumne River.

*A lupine*

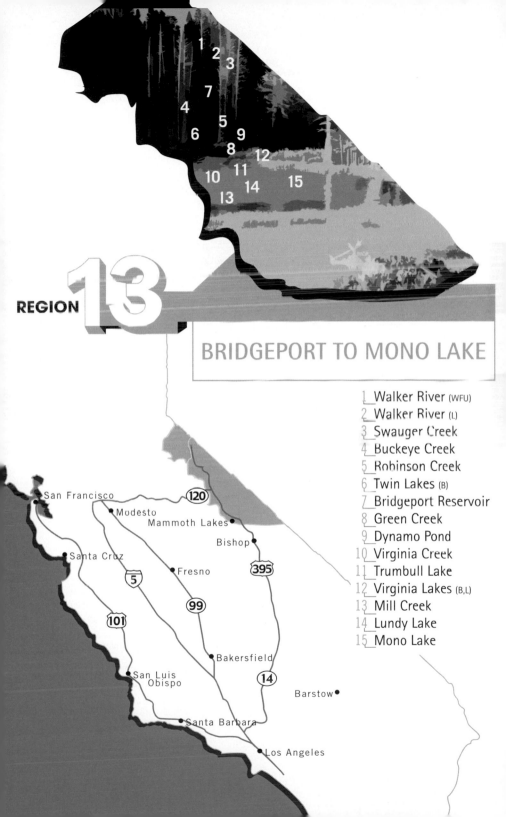

REGION **13**

## BRIDGEPORT TO MONO LAKE

1 Walker River (WFU)
2 Walker River (L)
3 Swauger Creek
4 Buckeye Creek
5 Robinson Creek
6 Twin Lakes (B)
7 Bridgeport Reservoir
8 Green Creek
9 Dynamo Pond
10 Virginia Creek
11 Trumbull Lake
12 Virginia Lakes (B,L)
13 Mill Creek
14 Lundy Lake
15 Mono Lake

# WALKER RIVER (WEST FORK, UPPER)

*Although there aren't many browns to go around, anglers fly-fishing the river for wild rainbows have been known to catch a few hefty ones.*

| | |
|---|---|
| **Rating:** | 7 |
| **Species:** | Rainbow Trout, Brown Trout, Brook Trout and Cutthroat Trout |
| **Stock:** | 18,398 pounds of rainbow trout and 10,010 sub-catchable cutthroat trout. |
| **Facilities:** | Campgrounds, Picnic Areas, RV Hookups and Restrooms |
| **Contact:** | Toiyabe National Forest (760) 932-7070 |
| **Directions:** | From Highway 395 in Bridgeport, drive 17 miles north to Highway 108 and turn left. Continue 2.1 miles to the Sonora Bridge. The river is stocked from the bridge upstream to Leavitt Campground. |

Walker River (West Fork, Upper)

On the extreme north end of the Eastern Sierra Nevada Mountains, the Upper West Fork of the Walker River is rich with both planted and wild trout. This six-mile stretch of alternately slow- and fast-moving water begins where the river flows under Highway 395 and stretches upstream past Leavitt Campground. It is complete with long runs and deep holes and sometimes offers shorelines covered with tall grass or shaded by towering pines.

This section of the river that flows through the Toiyabe National Forest is replete with stocks of Alpers from three to eight pounds and 31,844 half-pound California Department of Fish and Game rainbows. The CA DFG also adds another 10,010 sub-catchable cutthroats. While the planters are easy enough to catch with any small spinner, Power Bait and salmon eggs, the real challenge is catching the wild fish.

Recently the cutthroat stocks haven't been too successful. During one year, low water levels caused a big die off; on another occasion, the CA DFG stocking truck had a problem with warm water in one of its tanks, causing the whole stock of fish to go belly up. This may sound discouraging, but there is still a stable population of cutts.

Although there aren't many browns to go around, anglers fly-fishing the river for wild rainbows have been known to catch a few hefty ones.

If you plan to make the trip, supplies are available in Bridgeport. The Upper West Fork of the Walker River is closed to fishing from November 16 to the last Saturday in April.

Also nearby are the Little Walker River, Topaz Lake, Bridgeport Reservoir and Swauger Creek.

*There's plenty of casting room for everyone, and so many deep pools that each angler can have his own.*

| | |
|---|---|
| **Rating:** | 7 |
| **Species:** | Rainbow Trout, Brook Trout and Brown Trout |
| **Stock:** | 6,778 pounds of rainbow trout. |
| **Facilities:** | Campgrounds |
| **Contact:** | Toiyabe National Forest (760) 932-707 |

**Directions:** From Bridgeport, drive 16.5 miles north on Highway 395 to Little Walker Road and turn left. Continue on the dirt road to a fork at Obsidian Camp and veer right. Three and six-tenths miles from Highway 395 you'll come to a bridge over the river.

*Walker River (Little)*

Of all the sections of the Walker River, the Little Walker is the least fished, but that's not because there are less fish here. This is the least fished section of the Walker because there are few, if any, trophy fish here.

While many sections of the Walker are governed by special regulations, the Little Walker has none. You can fish with any lure you choose -- use night crawlers, Power Bait, cheese or even fly-fish -- and expect to do well. This is because the California Department of Fish and Game keeps the river loaded with rainbow trout by dumping in a total of 12,983 half-pound fish each season.

The Little Walker is one of the few rivers in the Eastern Sierra where you don't have to battle anglers for space. There's plenty of casting room for everyone, and so many deep pools that each angler can have his own. The streambed is comprised of boulders, mostly the size of basketballs, but some larger ones are the size of wheel barrels.

At 6,300 feet in the Toiyabe National Forest, the Little Walker is also rich with wild rainbow, brown, brook and cutthroat trout. To target these fish, walk a few-hundred yards upstream from the bridge and then begin fishing upstream from this point. The river can be difficult to fish in the spring when snow runoff keeps water levels high.

If you plan to make the trip, supplies are available in Walker and Bridgeport. The Little Walker River is closed to fishing from November 16 to the last Saturday in April.

Also nearby are the West Fork of the Walker River, Bridgeport Reservoir, Swauger Creek and Buckeye Creek.

# SWAUGER CREEK

*Swauger gets 1,977 rainbows from late April through July and is strictly a Power Bait and salmon egg-fishing creek.*

| | |
|---|---|
| **Rating:** | 3 |
| **Species:** | Rainbow Trout, Brook Trout and Brown Trout |
| **Stock:** | 1,034 pounds of rainbow trout. |
| **Facilities:** | Restrooms and Campgrounds |
| **Contact:** | Toiyabe National Forest (760) 932-7070 |
| **Directions:** | From Highway 395 and Twin Lakes Road in Bridgeport, drive four miles north to an unsigned dirt road on the right. Turn right and follow the road to the stream. |

*Swauger Creek*

From Lone Pine to the Sonora Junction, there are more than 40 streams that are planted by the California Department of Fish and Game. In my mind the worst stream to fish is Swauger Creek. A few miles north of Bridgeport, Swauger runs along the east side of Highway 395, and its minuscule size prohibits the California Department of Fish and Game from stocking large quantities of fish into its shallow waters.

Swauger is planted along a half-mile stretch that runs through Swauger Campground. At 6,750 feet, the creek flows through a landscape of desert brush; no pines are found along its shoreline, just overgrown bushes. The scenery is the pits! Swauger gets 1,977 rainbows from late April through July and is strictly a Power Bait and salmon egg-fishing creek. Because of low water levels, Swauger isn't planted after late July.

If you plan to make the trip, supplies are available in Bridgeport. Swauger Creek is closed to fishing from November 16 to the last Saturday in April.

Also nearby are Bridgeport Reservoir, Buckeye Creek, Twin Lakes and Little Walker River.

# BUCKEYE CREEK

*Although the section of the stream that is planted isn't located in the forest, the upper reaches of Buckeye, which are plentiful with rainbow and brown trout, run through the Toiyabe National Forest.*

| | |
|---|---|
| **Rating:** | 6 |
| **Species:** | Rainbow Trout and Brown Trout |
| **Stock:** | 2,183 pounds of rainbow trout. |
| **Facilities:** | Campgrounds and Restrooms |
| **Contact:** | Toiyabe National Forest (760) 932-7070 |

**Directions:** From Highway 395 in Bridgeport, drive 7.3 miles west on Twin Lakes Road to Buckeye Road and turn right. Continue 2.7 miles, until the road crosses over Buckeye Creek.

Buckeye Creek

Sometimes you don't need to work hard to catch fish, and that is definitely the case at Buckeye Creek. Catching limits often occurs at Buckeye, and some anglers don't even bother to stray more than a few feet from their car to catch 'em.

One of the best places to fish is from the bridge, where this tributary to Robinson Creek crosses under Buckeye Road. I would have driven right past this hole if it weren't for a father and son fishing from the bridge, who refused to get out of my way.

I parked the car and walked over to see what they were doing. I wondered what could have distracted them from a courtesy as common as stepping off to the side of the road so I could pass. The creek must have just been stocked, because from the bridge you could see about a dozen trout schooled up, just itchin' for some angler to drift Power Bait their way. Fortunately, those two caught their limit pretty quick, so I didn't have to wait long to pass.

Ten miles from Bridgeport, at about 7,000 feet, Buckeye is a pretty stream, shaded by pines and home to some small rocky pools. Throughout the fishing season, the California Department of Fish and Game stocks the creek weekly with a total of 4,289 fish. The plants begin at Buckeye Campground and range two miles downstream. Although the section of the stream that is planted isn't located in the forest, the upper reaches of Buckeye, which are plentiful with rainbow and brown trout, run through the Toiyabe National Forest.

If you plan to make the trip, supplies are available in Bridgeport. Buckeye Creek is closed to fishing from November 16 to the last Saturday in April.

Also nearby are Robinson Creek, Twin Lakes (Bridgeport), Bridgeport Reservoir and Swauger Creek.

**The stream is at least 15 feet wide in most places and has both deep pools and long runs.**

| | |
|---|---|
| **Rating:** | 8 |
| **Species:** | Rainbow Trout and Brown Trout |
| **Stock:** | 23,812 pounds of rainbow trout. |
| **Facilities:** | Campgrounds, RV Hookups, General Store, Bait & Tackle and Restrooms |
| **Contact:** | Toiyabe National Forest (760) 932-7070 |
| **Directions:** | From Highway 395 in Bridgeport, turn west on Twin Lakes Road and drive five miles to the stream. |

*Robinson Creek*

Situated in the mountains above Bridgeport, at 7,000 feet in the Toiyabe National Forest, Robinson Creek is one of the best and easiest to fish streams in the Sierra. What makes it the best? Where should I start? Stocks for one: the California Department of Fish and Game mercifully plants 45,994 rainbows into the stream, 150 of which are in the three- to five-pound class. Robinson receives these stocks weekly, over a six-mile stretch of water.

Wild rainbows and browns also inhabit the stream. And Robinson's size makes the fishing even better. The stream is at least 15 feet wide in most places and has both deep pools and long runs. With jagged, snow-capped peaks in the backdrop and pine trees lining the shoreline, at times the scenery at Robinson can distract you from fishing.

The best access areas are found at four campgrounds Paha, Robinson Creek, Honeymoon Flat and Sawmill. Because of the stream's size, it can be fished with several different baits, including Power Bait, night crawlers, salmon eggs and small spinners. Fly-fishing is also popular here. Concentrate your efforts in the campgrounds and where the creek crosses under the road.

If you plan to make the trip, supplies are available at Twin Lakes and in Bridgeport. Robinson Creek is closed to fishing from November 16 to the last Saturday in April.

Also nearby are Twin Lakes, Bridgeport Reservoir, Buckeye Creek and Swauger Creek.

# TWIN LAKES (BRIDGEPORT)

*These lakes still remain a place where anglers show up with the fantasy of catching a monster brown, but most leave with a stringer full of planters.*

**Rating:** 9

**Species:** Brown Trout, Rainbow Trout and Cutthroat Trout

**Stock:** 52,560 pounds of rainbow trout and 228 pounds of fingerling rainbow trout (Lower Twin).

**Facilities:** Boat Launch, Bait & Tackle, RV Hookups, Lodging, Food, Campgrounds, Picnic Areas, Restrooms

**Contact:** Ken's Sporting Goods (760) 932-7707, Mono Village (760) 932-7071
Twin Lakes Resort (877) 932-7751

**Directions:** From Highway 395 in Bridgeport, turn west on Twin Lakes Road. Continue 10 miles to Lower Twin or 13.7 miles to Upper Twin.

*Trout like this two pounder are common at Twin Lakes.*

I was in Lake Tahoe when I first learned about the brown trout fishery at Bridgeport's Twin Lakes. A group of fishing guides were talking about the lakes and how illegal sewage was being dumped into them to fatten the browns to trophy sizes in record time. These fellers had no idea who I was as I walked the isles of a local tackle shop in South Lake Tahoe. I strolled up and down the next isle just to listen to their conversation.

"You know we have a lot of browns in Tahoe," said one of the younger guys. "We should think about doing the same thing. People have no idea there are a lot of browns here. If we can grow them huge, we'd have people paying us to catch them browns too. Not just mackinaw."

"Our browns are huge already. You just have to know how to catch them. We don't want to pollute our lake like they do theirs," said one of the older guides.

Acting like I was a typical weekend visitor, I walked up to the counter and asked them to explain to me about the sewage being dumped into the lake. Although they refused to elaborate much, they were willing to tell me that a reliable source had been tipping them off for years that people were dumping tons of sewage into Twin Lakes in an effort to grow huge browns.

A month later I ventured to Twin Lakes to do a little investigating. I stopped by the tackle shop in Mono Village and asked a guy who worked there if the rumors were true. "Those guys are jealous. They just don't want anglers to come here (to Twin Lakes). They want them to stay in Tahoe and catch little two- to four-pound mackinaw. Who told you that anyway? Tell me who they are so I can go up there and kick their ass. That's absurd."

I walked around the shops, cabins and campgrounds of both Upper and Lower Twin Lakes that day and failed to get anyone to talk to me about the sewage ordeal. Whatever was happening here was sure working, though. Over the last few decades Twin Lakes has been known as one of the best world-class brown trout fisheries in the country. In April of

1987, a 26.8-pound brown was taken from Upper Twin, and that still stands as the California record.

I called the California Department of Fish and Game to see if I could get some answers. The biologist with whom I talked (and who asked to remain nameless) chuckled when I asked the question. "That sure is a great question. I've heard that too, and I don't really know how to answer it," I was told. "I know sewage in the form of grazing (cow turds) has entered Upper Twin for years. A lot of grazing takes place near the stream that feeds the lake, but I don't know about other forms of sewage. It's possible, but I really don't know what has taken place." I was further informed that the browns could eat the nutrients coming into the lake from the grazing, and that could cause them to grow quickly.

I was also told a few other things that made sense, about several factors that have contributed to Twin becoming a world-renown brown fishery. Actually, there are seven

*Twin Lakes from the air.*

factors: chubs, rainbow trout, suckers, kokanee, mountain whitefish, deep water and lots of space. Browns need loads of space and deep water to flourish. Twin has both.

A reliable food source (if not a few reliable food sources) is also vital to the development of hefty browns. Twin has many of these sources, the most abundant of which is stocked rainbow trout. Joining tens of thousands of holdovers from years past, the CA DFG plants nearly 50,000 half-pound rainbows into both Upper and Lower Twin. And many serve as growing pellets for the browns. Anglers target others. For decades, chubs and mountain whitefish, which are native to the lake, were a big food source; however, many of them have grown too large for most of the browns to eat.

Despite these perfect conditions, the number of large browns caught here has declined drastically. Curtis Milliron, associate fisheries biologist for the region, attributes the weakening of the brown fishery to a poor support system. Nearly every successful brown trout fishery has a strong nursery of fish that come from a hatchery. Prior to 1986, the Mt. Whitney strain of brown trout, which was used as brood stock to produce fingerlings for Eastern Sierra lakes, was a strong fish that did well when planted in reservoirs. Unfortunately, whirling disease was discovered and the CA DFG chose to destroy them all. To take their place, the CA DFG imported strains of browns from Utah and Shasta, as well as trying to breed browns from the Pleasant Valley spawn channel, to use as brood stock. None of these strains worked; they all died. The problem is that when fish are taken out of the wild and put in a hatchery environment, they don't do well.

The CA DFG finally decided to look for a new source of fish by returning to the headwaters of Oak Creek, where they found Twin Lakes' original strain of browns. Typically, it takes at least 10 generations for the offspring of brood stock fish to become strong enough to survive in the wild as fingerlings. While the old strain of Mt. Whitney browns showed remarkable survival rates, the new strain appears weak. The majority has not survived.

Although the CA DFG previously planted more than 100,000 browns each year into

Twin Lakes, presently none are being planted, because their survival rates are so low. With less fish being introduced into the lake, and the ones that are already present being harvested by anglers, the lake's brown population is declining.

Despite the fact that fewer fish will be planted, Twin's fisheries are expected to improve over the next decade. First, there is a plan afoot to restore cutthroats, which, unlike the rainbows, are native to the drainage. If the plan is successful, the CA DFG would stop planting rainbows altogether.

Rather than attempting to net or poison the rainbows to rid the lake of them, the plan is to just let angler harvest take its natural course. Over time, all the rainbows will be caught. Because cutthroats and browns occupy different depths of the lake and don't interbreed, they can coexist and thrive in Twin. The overall goal is for Twin to become a trophy fishery for both cutthroats and browns.

Upper Twin is 110 feet deep and 265 acres; Lower is 285 feet deep and 375 acres. At 7,080 feet in the Toiyabe National Forest, these lakes still remain a place where anglers show up with the fantasy of catching a monster brown, but most leave with a stringer full of planters. If you're coming for the browns, don't come on a clear, sunny day. They bite when conditions are miserable, i.e. wind, rain, snow, choppy waves. Troll big Rapalas or Storm Lures.

What Twin is best known for is its good rainbow trout fishing. In addition to 1,700 pounds of Alpers, the CA DFG dumps more than 98,000 half-pound rainbows and 440 brood fish each year. Lower was planted with 10,005 fingerling bows. So there's great shoreline fishing with Power Bait and also good trolling for anglers toplining small spinners.

If you plan to make the trip, supplies are available at the lakes. Twin Lake is closed to fishing from November 16 to the last Saturday in April.

Also nearby are Robinson Creek, Buckeye Creek and Bridgeport Reservoir.

*Lower Twin Lake*

TWIN LAKES

# BRIDGEPORT RESERVOIR

*The average size of fish here is definitely larger than most other lakes, with a one- to four-pound range common.*

**Rating:** 9

**Species:** Rainbow Trout, Brown Trout and Cutthroat Trout

**Stock:** 15,500 pounds of rainbow trout and 1,236 fingerling brown trout.

**Facilities:** Boat Launch, Restrooms, Marina, Boat Rentals and Bait & Tackle

**Contact:** Fishing Guide Keith Mount (760-932-7128), Ken's Sporting Goods (760) 932-7707

**Directions:** From the junction of Highways 395 and 182 in Bridgeport, take Highway 182 approximately five miles north to the reservoir.

*A brood stock rainbow trout*

Many anglers complain that Bridgeport Reservoir is difficult to fish in the summer because of an abundance of weed overgrowth. Those anglers are right. Yet, without the weeds, Bridgeport Reservoir wouldn't be the productive fishery it is.

Those weeds serve as the habitat of the San Juan worm, freshwater shrimp and various snails, all of which are primary food sources for the fish in this 3,000-acre reservoir (when full, which it rarely is). While the weeds do indeed make fishing more difficult, they also help to develop an extremely abundant food source for the fish in the reservoir; and the fish in turn grow at an accelerated rate because of that abundance.

Smart anglers don't fish Bridgeport in the summer. They concentrate on the spring and fall, when the weeds are not as dense. In the spring, the best area to fish is on the west end, where the East Walker River, Robinson Creek and Buckeye Creek spill into the lake. Anglers who anchor in these shallow waters, dangling night crawlers off the bottom or using Power Bait, experience high catch rates. The problem with fishing the inlets, however, is that the fish only stack up here in the spring. By the 4th of July, when the inlets have subsided, the fish relocate to the east end of the lake.

Something else to take into consideration when fishing here is the water level. The Walker River Irrigation District pretty much sucks the lake dry most years, which does hurt the fishing. At capacity, the reservoir is only 40 feet deep, and it's one of the few lakes in the state where most of the trout are hooked in less than 15 feet of water.

Although most anglers tend to catch rainbows here, there are also stable populations of browns and cutthroats. The California Department of Fish and Game dumps in 25,810 half-pound rainbows and 415 brood fish each year, joining thousands of holdovers from previous years. The CA DFG also stocks 25,000 fingerling browns and 1,700 pounds of Alpers from three to 12 pounds. So, there are a lot of fish to go around! With a one- to four-pound range common, the average size of fish here is definitely larger than in most other lakes.

Fishing for browns is popular in the fall, when some hefty ones are caught. Trolling Rapalas works best, however, some anglers choose to drag flasher/night crawler combos. To avoid getting caught in the weeds, try not to troll between the 4th of July and October 1, or be prepared to check your lures every five minutes.

If you plan to make the trip, supplies are available in Bridgeport. Bridgeport Reservoir is closed to fishing from November 16 to the last Saturday in April.

Also nearby are the East Walker River, Swauger Creek, Robinson Creek, Buckeye Creek, Green Creek and Twin Lakes (Bridgeport).

*Fishing guide Keith Mount after a successful day at Bridgeport Reservoir.*

# GREEN CREEK

*The 10-foot wide stream, which meanders through peaceful meadows sparkling with an assortment of wildflowers, also offers anglers a rare sense of serenity.*

| | |
|---|---|
| **Rating:** | 7 |
| **Species:** | Rainbow Trout |
| **Stock:** | 5,178 pounds of rainbow trout. |
| **Facilities:** | Campgrounds |
| **Contact:** | Toiyabe National Forest (760) 932-7070 |

**Directions:** From Highway 395 in Bridgeport, drive approximately five miles south to Green Lakes Road and turn right. Continue six miles to the stream.

*Green Creek*

At roughly 6,500 feet in the Toiyabe National Forest, Green Creek is different than most other drive-to streams in the Sierra. For starters, there are no resorts built along its banks, no pack stations, not a lot of developed campsites or general stores. Green is situated in a primitive area on a four-mile stretch of water along Green Creek Road, and offers no services except vault toilets and one campground.

This lack of development is what makes Green Creek so special, and because most anglers desire a small amount of amenities, fewer fish here than at most other streams in the region. Yes, that means you don't have to fight for fishing space, because there is plenty of it to go around. The 10-foot wide stream, which meanders through peaceful meadows sparkling with an assortment of wildflowers, also offers anglers a rare sense of serenity.

More importantly, the fishing here is often good, too. In addition to wild rainbow and brown trout, the California Department of Fish and Game drops 10,144 rainbows into the stream. Fishing at Green is productive with flies, lures and Power Bait. Take your pick.

If you plan to make the trip, supplies are available in Bridgeport. Green Creek is closed to fishing from November 16 to the last Saturday in April.

Also nearby are Virginia Lakes, Virginia Creek, Bridgeport Reservoir, Lundy Lake and Mill Creek.

# DYNAMO POND

*Since much of the pond is shallow and marshy, waders are necessary to fish it correctly.*

**Rating:** 5
**Species:** Rainbow Trout and Brown Trout
**Stock:** None
**Facilities:** None
**Contact:** Toiyabe National Forest (760) 932-7070

**Directions:** From Highway 395 in Bridgeport, drive approximately five miles south to Green Lakes Road and turn right. Continue approximately five miles to the stream and pond on the right.

*Dynamo Pond*

In the 1890s, the creation of Dynamo Pond established Bodie as a thriving mining town. It was October of 1893 when the Standard-Consolidated Mining Company completed a hydroelectric plant that sent power from the pond to their Stamp Mill 13 miles away in Bodie. Now little remains of the plant. I only saw a historical point of interest sign near the entrance to the pond.

Today the pond is a dammed portion of Green Creek and is a good fishing spot for anglers interested in a shot at catching rainbow and brown trout in the Inyo National Forest. Although browns are rarely caught here, rainbows are frequently landed. Upstream from the pond in Green, the California Department of Fish and Game stocks rainbows from spring through fall, and many of these fish end up in Dynamo.

Since much of the pond is shallow and marshy, waders are necessary to fish it correctly. The best way to hit the pond is with a fly rod when bows are combing the surface in search of the most recent insect hatch.

If you plan to make the trip, supplies are available in Bridgeport. Dynamo Pond is closed to fishing from November 16 to the last Saturday in April.

Also nearby are Virginia Lakes, Virginia Creek, Bridgeport Reservoir, Lundy Lake and Mill Creek.

# VIRGINIA CREEK

**Offering anglers that unspoiled high-country feeling, Virginia flows through meadows and heavily forested areas, where the creek has both large pools and fast moving sections.**

| | |
|---|---|
| **Rating:** | 7 |
| **Species:** | Rainbow Trout and Brown Trout |
| **Stock:** | 7,060 pounds of rainbow trout. |
| **Facilities:** | Bait & Tackle, Restaurant, Lodging, Picnic Areas, Campgrounds, General Store, Restrooms |
| **Contact:** | Toiyabe National Forest (760) 932-7070, Virginia Lakes Resort (760) 647-6484 |
| **Directions:** | From Highway 395 in Lee Vining, drive 12.5 miles north to Virginia Lakes Road and turn left. There are several access points from this intersection to Virginia Lakes. |

*Virginia Creek*

When it comes to camping, few destinations are as good as Virginia Creek. There are three heavily stocked lakes (Big Virginia, Little Virginia, and Trumbull), dozens of backcountry lakes that are easy to reach, and Virginia Creek itself is planted over an eight-mile stretch. The services here are also a plus. In addition to campgrounds, there are cabins, a restaurant, general store and bait & tackle shop. So, why wouldn't you come here? Well, I hope you do, because you won't be disappointed.

In addition to the great fishing and full amenities, at 8,500 feet in the Toiyabe National Forest, the scenery is also exceptional. Offering anglers that unspoiled high-country feeling, Virginia flows through meadows and heavily forested areas, where the creek has both large pools and fast moving sections.

With the California Department of Fish and Game making weekly appearances to stock the stream, the fishing remains good throughout the season. In all, 13,847 rainbows are planted. While Virginia Lakes Road does parallel the creek, it doesn't access it. For access to the creek, take the turnoff signed for Road 139, which follows the stream.

If you plan to make the trip, supplies are available at Virginia Lakes Resort. Virginia Creek is closed to fishing from November 16 to the last Saturday in April. Call ahead for road conditions. Virginia Lakes Road may not open until sometime in June.

Also nearby are the Hoover Wilderness, Mill Creek, Lundy Lake and Green Creek.

*A 13.6-pound brown hangs on the wall of the Virginia Lakes Resort General Store as a testament to Trumbull's lunkers.*

| | |
|---|---|
| **Rating:** | 8 |
| **Species:** | Rainbow Trout, Brown Trout and Brook Trout |
| **Stock:** | 5,292 pounds of rainbow trout. |
| **Facilities:** | Restrooms and Campgrounds |
| **Contact:** | Toiyabe National Forest (760) 932-7070, Virginia Lakes Resort (760) 647-6484 |

**Directions:** From Highway 395 in Lee Vining, drive 12.5 miles north to Virginia Lakes Road and turn left. Continue six miles and veer right at the sign for Trumbull Lake.

*Deer rely on the meadows near Trumbull for food.*

Flanked by a meadow dappled with wildflowers on one side and tall mountains on the other, surrounded by pine trees, Trumbull is one of the few drive-to lakes in the Sierra that offers the special high-country feeling normally associated with a backcountry lake. At 12 acres, Trumbull isn't big enough to accommodate large crowds, and the scarcity of people seems to invite the many deer that spend time chewing on grass in the meadow each morning and evening.

But don't let this fabulous scenery keep you from the great fishing. Because of heavy plants by the California Department of Fish and Game, and the fact that the fish are concentrated in such a small area, the action rarely slows. Both float tubing and shoreline fishing can be exceptional; however, the lake is too small for boats.

Most anglers think that the fishing at Trumbull is good simply because of the 10,011 half-pound and 45 brood fish that are stocked. That's a false perception. There are brooks and browns, too. A 13.6-pound brown hangs on the wall of the Virginia Lakes Resort General Store as a testament to Trumbull's lunkers.

If you plan to make the trip, supplies are available at Virginia Lakes Resort. Trumbull Lake is closed to fishing from November 16 to the last Saturday in April. No gas-powered motors are permitted.

Also nearby are Virginia Lakes, Virginia Creek, Mill Creek, Lundy Lake, Green Creek and the Hoover Wilderness.

# VIRGINIA LAKES

*At 110 feet deep, Big Virginia has much larger holes than Little, so if you're going to target the browns during summer, plan on fishing deep.*

| | |
|---|---|
| **Rating:** | 9 |
| **Species:** | Rainbow Trout, Brown Trout and Brook Trout |
| **Stock:** | 21,086 pounds of rainbow trout. |
| **Facilities:** | Boat Launch, Restrooms, Lodging, Bait & Tackle, General Store, Food and Campgrounds |
| **Contact:** | Toiyabe National Forest (760) 932-7070, Virginia Lakes Resort (760) 647-6484 |
| **Directions:** | From Highway 395 in Lee Vining, drive 12.5 miles north to Virginia Lakes Road and turn left. Continue 6.5 miles to Little Virginia. Big Virginia is just up the road. |

*Big Virginia Lake*

While out-of-towners refer to these lakes as "The Virginia Lakes," locals and those who frequent the lakes call them "Big" and "Little." Nestled in the mountains northwest of Mono Lake, these are some of the prettiest lakes and offer some of the best fishing in the Sierra. Besides great fishing for rainbows (which is true of nearly all Sierra lakes), the Virginias are also great brown trout fisheries and give anglers an outside chance at hooking a brook.

At 27-acres (Big) and 10-acres (Little), both lakes provide good fishing. Weekly plants of rainbow trout keep the action hot all season. The California Department of Fish and Game dumps 11,162 half-pound rainbows into Big Virginia and 15,755 into Little. Also, 3,200 pounds of Alpers and 105 brood fish are also dispersed between the two lakes.

With a lake-record brown at a tad over 19 pounds, Little kicks out some big browns. Because of its size, shoreline fishing is best; boats aren't needed. Float tubing the 15-foot deep lake is also a good idea. Shoreline anglers do best with night crawlers.

At 110 feet deep, Big Virginia has much larger holes than Little, so if you're going to target the browns during summer, plan on fishing deep. Trollers commonly catch browns from five to 15 pounds early in the season, or from the last week of August through October..

Big Virginia used to be an exceptional brook trout fishery. A flood in the early Nineties, however, ruined the spawning habitat in the stream that feeds the lake, and the brookies are no longer a hit. A four-pound brook landed here now hangs on the wall in the resort as a testament to the brookies the lake used to kick out.

If you plan to make the trip, supplies are available at Virginia Lakes Resort. Virginia Lakes are closed to fishing from November 16 to the last Saturday in April. No gas-powered motors are permitted.

Also nearby are Trumbull Lake, Virginia Creek, Mill Creek and Lundy Lake.

*One big plus is that Mill doesn't get bombarded by anglers the way most other streams in the region do.*

| | |
|---|---|
| **Rating:** | 5 |
| **Species:** | Rainbow Trout |
| **Stock:** | 1,373 pounds of rainbow trout. |
| **Facilities:** | Campgrounds and Restrooms |
| **Contact:** | Mono Basin Scenic Forest Visitors Center (760) 647-3044 |

**Directions:** From Lee Vining, drive 7.1 miles north on Highway 395 and turn left on Lundy Lake Road. Continue 3.8 miles to Lundy Dam Road and turn left. The road parallels the stream.

*Browns like this one from the East Walker River held by Curtis Milliron are too big to be found in Mill Creek.*

Flowing out of Lundy Lake, Mill Creek is a small stream in the Inyo National Forest, just north of Lee Vining. Too narrow and overgrown with trees and bushes to use lures, Mill is a great place to use Power Bait and salmon eggs.

The California Department of Fish and Game plants a total of 2,692 fish each season along a three-mile section of Mill Creek. The planted rainbows are about a half-pound each.

At 7,500 feet, Mill is heavily shaded by pines and quaking aspens. One big plus is that Mill doesn't get bombarded by anglers the way most other streams in the region do.

If you plan to make the trip, supplies are available in Lee Vining. Mill Creek is closed to fishing from November 16 to the last Saturday in April.

Also nearby are Lundy Lake, Virginia Lakes, Virginia Creek, Trumbull Lake, Mono Lake and Green Creek.

# LUNDY LAKE

**Most of the big browns that come of out Lundy are in the eight- to 13-pound class, although there also are many smaller fish.**

| | |
|---|---|
| **Rating:** | 7 |
| **Species:** | Rainbow Trout and Brown Trout |
| **Stock:** | 20,056 pounds of rainbow trout. |
| **Facilities:** | Lodging, Food, Boat Rentals, Boat Launch, Restrooms and Campgrounds |
| **Contact:** | Mono Basin Scenic Forest Visitors Center (760) 647-3044 |
| **Directions:** | From Highway 395 in Lee Vining, drive 7.1 miles north to the signed turnoff for Lundy Lake. Turn left and drive five miles to the lake. |

*A brown trout*

It was a breezy mid-October late afternoon. Four friends and I had left our campground on the shore of Lee Vining Creek and headed for Lundy Lake in search of that big brown trout we were told was lurking there.

Leaving Highway 120, we made a left onto Highway 395. Obeying the 25 mph speed limit through the town of Lee Vining, I checked my rearview mirror and saw a California Highway Patrol vehicle going in the opposite direction turn on his siren and make a quick u-turn. "Damn! That guy's in a hurry," I said to my pals. "There must be an accident or something."

Or not! He was coming after me! For a change I was actually driving the speed limit, but I still got pulled over. I tried to remain calm as the officer headed to the front passenger window, taking his time as he scoped out our boat and new Excursion. While he was looking at the poles near the bow of the boat, I tried to unlatch my seat belt so I could lean over and get my license out of the glove compartment. That's when I realized why I'd been pulled over: My seatbelt wasn't on, and when I looked over at my co-pilot, neither was his. Uh-oh.

"Do you know why I pulled you over?" he asked.

"I have no idea, sir. I was driving the speed limit," I told him.

He quickly got to the part about my not wearing a seat belt, before moving on to more important items, asking if we liked our boat! "Where are you guys going fishing?" He was thrilled when I told him Lundy Lake. "That's a great spot," he told us, proceeding to tell us how to fish the lake.

"Wait!" he interrupted his fishing talk as he was studying my registration. "Whose truck and boat is this? It's registered under Shafdog Publications, not under your name." I told him Shafdog was my company. He was lost. "So your company has a truck and boat?"

Everything got clearer when I explained to the officer that I write books on fishing, and I was headed to Lundy Lake in search of a big brown. "You sure don't need my help then," he said as he abruptly stopped describing the lake and how the fish stack up at the inlet

*Lundy Lake*

waiting for food.

Taking my license with him, he went back to his car to write my ticket. Luckily another call came in. He rushed back to our car, gave back my license, told me to wear my seatbelt and catch a lot of fish, then raced back to his vehicle and sped away.

We never caught our desired brown that night, but Lundy has often produced big ones. In most Sierra lakes, the bigger browns are caught at the end of October, but Lundy seems to be most productive in the spring, right after ice-out. We were only five months off! There are lots of big browns here, but there's no chance of a state record, as there is in most other big brown lakes of the Sierra.

Most of the big browns that come of out Lundy are in the eight- to 13-pound class, although there also are many smaller fish. The big boys are typically caught before the sun rises by trollers working large Rapalas. If conditions are crappy (i.e. wind, snow, rain) they can be caught all day. But they're smart, so use thin line and put your lines out farther than normal.

To many anglers, Lundy Lake, at 7,815 feet in the Inyo National Forest, just north of the town of Lee Vining, is a great fishery that offers a good chance at catching brown trout, but most come for the planters. At 110 acres, Lundy is a long, narrow lake that is heavily stocked by the California Department of Fish and Game, giving shoreline anglers who fish the north side of the lake a good chance at catching half-pound trout. Power Bait and night crawlers work best. The CA DFG plants 32,605 half-pound rainbows and 377 brood fish in addition to 1,700 pounds of Alpers from five to 12 pounds.

If you plan to make the trip, supplies are available in Lee Vining. Lundy Lake is closed to fishing from November 16 to the last Saturday in April. Call ahead for lake conditions. The lake may be frozen over at the start of the fishing season.

Also nearby are Mill Creek, Mono Lake, Virginia Lakes, Trumbull Lake, Virginia Creek and Lee Vining Creek.

LUNDY LAKE

# MONO LAKE

*Although Mono Lake doesn't have any fish, it's a must-see tourist attraction for anglers fishing the surrounding areas.*

| | |
|---|---|
| **Rating:** | 1 |
| **Species:** | None |
| **Stock:** | None |
| **Facilities:** | Picnic Areas, Restrooms, Boat Launch and Visitor Center |
| **Contact:** | Mono Basin Scenic Forest Visitors Center (760) 647-3044 |
| | Mono Lake Tufa State Reserve (760) 647-6331 |
| **Directions:** | From Highway 395 in Mammoth, drive north approximately 10 miles past the turnoff for June Lake to the lake on your right. |

*Tufa towers at Mono Lake*

The Eastern Sierra Nevada is renown for some of the best fishing in California, however, Mono Lake doesn't share this reputation. In fact, Mono Lake has no fish! At more than 700,000 years old, Mono Lake is one of the oldest lakes in North America. It's also one of the saltiest. With no present water outlets, it has become two-and-a-half times as salty as the Pacific Ocean.

Over the years, the lake has been the center of controversy. In 1941, the City of Los Angeles began diverting water off four of the lake's five inlets. Subsequently, the lake dropped 40 feet and doubled in salinity. After lengthy court battles, a decision was arrived at to restore some of the lake's diverted water and enable it to begin to rise again.

Although Mono Lake doesn't have any fish, it's a must-see tourist attraction for anglers fishing the surrounding areas. It's only 13 miles from the eastern boundary of Yosemite National Park, and a short drive from Mammoth and June Lakes.

There is some life in the lake. Brine shrimp and alkali flies feed on the algae that are at the bottom of the food chain. There are more than four trillion shrimp in the lake and millions of flies buzzing around it. More than 80 species of birds come here to feed on the shrimp and flies. Yum!

The lake's main attraction is its tufa towers that peek out of the water. (Tufa is a form of limestone.) Boating, hiking, photography, kayaking, swimming and canoeing are also popular activities. My favorite one is water-skiing on the lake. Not many people do, but it is allowed. If you want to try it, remember to be careful not to hit the tufas.

If you plan to make the trip, supplies are available in Lee Vining.

Also nearby are Bodie Ghost Town, Yosemite National Park, Tioga Lake, Ellery Lake, Lee Vining Creek, June Lake Loop and Mammoth Lakes.

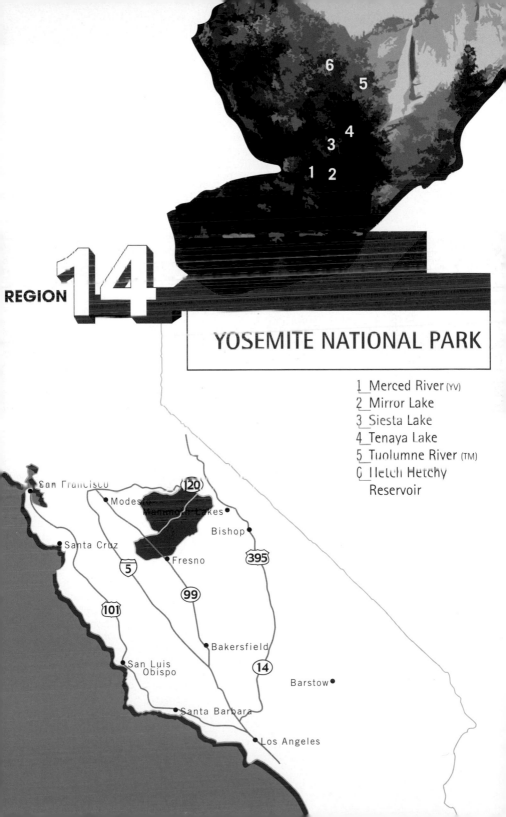

REGION **14**

# YOSEMITE NATIONAL PARK

1_Merced River (YV)
2_Mirror Lake
3_Siesta Lake
4_Tenaya Lake
5_Tuolumne River (TM)
6_Hetch Hetchy
  Reservoir

*These trout are smart. They've seen nearly every lure and fly in creation, and have become wary of fishing lines.*

| | |
|---|---|
| **Rating:** | 3 |
| **Species:** | Rainbow Trout and Brown Trout |
| **Stock:** | None |
| **Facilities:** | Restrooms, Picnic Areas and Campgrounds |
| **Contact:** | Yosemite Valley Visitor Center (209) 372-0299 |

**Directions:** From the 99 Freeway in Fresno, take Highway 41 north to Oakhurst. Drive 33 miles through Oakhurst to Wawona. Continue on Highway 41 to Yosemite Valley. Once in Yosemite Valley, the road parallels the river.

*Merced River (Yosemite Valley)*                    *Yosemite Falls*

The Merced River in Yosemite Valley is among the most heavily fished waters in the state. Fishing this section of the Merced is relaxing and enjoying, but not productive. The river has been so heavily fished, there aren't many wild trout left, and it's not stocked.

If you have any luck here, you're damn good. These trout are smart. They've seen nearly every lure and fly in creation, and have become wary of fishing lines. If you use heavier than four-pound test, you won't get a bite.

At 4,000 feet, flowing mostly through meadows, this section of the river is governed by special regulations. From the Happy Isles Bridge downstream to the western boundary of the park, only artificial lures with barbless hooks are allowed. You may keep five browns but no rainbows.

With spectacular views of Yosemite Falls, Ribbon Falls, Staircase Falls, Bridalveil Falls, the Royal Arch Cascades, Half Dome, El Capitan, and refreshing, lush green meadows filled with deer grazing along the river's banks, fishing Yosemite can be rewarding. However, because this is the area that most local campers fish, it receives way too much fishing pressure.

Your best bet is to fish west of Valley View, working your way downstream where there are fewer anglers. Surprisingly, the river has some large rainbow and brown trout, but they are rarely caught. They've gotten used to seeing artificial lures and choose not to be cooked on a grill. This section of the Merced River is for tourists, not anglers.

If you plan to make the trip, supplies are available in Curry and Yosemite Villages. The Merced River (Yosemite Valley) is closed to fishing from Nov. 16 to the last Saturday in April.

Also nearby are the Merced River (El Portal), the waterfalls of Yosemite National Park and the South and Middle Forks of the Tuolumne River.

# MIRROR LAKE

*The fishing is terrible.*

| | |
|---|---|
| **Rating:** | 3 |
| **Species:** | Rainbow Trout and Brown Trout |
| **Stock:** | None |
| **Facilities:** | Restrooms |
| **Contact:** | Yosemite National Park (209) 372-0200, Yosemite Valley Visitor Center (209) 372-0299 |

**Directions:** From the 99 Freeway in Fresno, exit Highway 41 and drive north to the entrance of Yosemite National Park. Remaining on Highway 41, drive into the park and continue 30.6 miles to the day-use parking area at Curry Village. (Highway 41 becomes Southside Drive near Bridalveil Falls). Pick up the shuttle and ride it to stop No. 17.

*Mirror Lake*

There is no question that Mirror Lake is the most popular lake in Yosemite National Park. During peak visitation season, thousands of hikers walk the paved trail to the lake to see the mirrored reflections it offers in the morning hours. Relaxing along the shoreline provides you with a magnificent view of Half Dome, Basket Dome and Mt. Watkins. While you will definitely see hundreds of people with cameras and water bottles, chances are you won't see anybody with a fishing pole at Mirror. The fishing is terrible.

Mirror Lake, which is in the process of becoming a marsh, is a dammed portion of Tenaya Creek. Fairly shallow, the lake is fewer than 10 feet deep. (I know this because a friend swam across it a few years ago.) As for the fishing, no plants are made. There are wild rainbow and brown trout in Tenaya Creek which flows in and out of Mirror Lake, but they are difficult to catch. Fishing is much better in deep pools above or below the lake. Some of the trout in Tenaya run into the three-pound class, however, the overall population in the creek is small.

You can get to Mirror Lake in a wheelchair; the half-mile path is paved the entire way. In summer there is a free shuttle that stops at the Tenaya Creek Bridge (stop #17). In winter you have to walk from North or Upper Pines Campground. The roads are well marked, but are not opened to vehicles. From the Tenaya Creek Bridge, follow the path on either side of the stream to the lake. The trail on the north side is paved; the south side is dirt.

If you plan to make the trip, supplies are available in Curry and Yosemite Villages. There is a fee to enter Yosemite National Park.

Also nearby are Three Chute Falls, Snow Creek Falls, Merced River, Staircase Falls, Royal Arch Cascades and Yosemite Falls.

# SIESTA LAKE

*Located on a heavily traveled stretch of Highway 120, Siesta Lake has no fish in it.*

**Rating:** 1
**Species:** None
**Stock:** None
**Facilities:** None
**Contact:** Yosemite National Park (209) 372-0200

**Directions:** From Highway 120 at the Big Oak Flat entrance to Yosemite National Park, drive 7.6 miles east to Tioga Pass Road. Turn northeast, staying on Highway 120, and continue 13.8 miles to the lake on the right.

*Siesta Lake*

Although many lakes in Yosemite National Park are barren of fish, tourists still visit them. Sightseers are drawn to their natural beauty, crystal-clear water, sparkling reflections and pine-covered shorelines.

Located on a heavily traveled stretch of Highway 120, Siesta Lake has no fish in it, but that doesn't stop travelers from screeching their brakes to snap a few pictures. In fact, most anglers don't know there aren't any fish here and can be seen tossing lures into the shallow lake in search of a hungry trout.

Siesta Lake is a two-acre dying pond. According to the information board beside the lake, Siesta was formed during the last ice age, when a moraine that blocked a small stream caused Siesta to fill with water. Dependent on snow for its water, Siesta is known as a meltwater lake. Gradually being filled in with dirt, twigs and leaves, it's on its way to becoming a marsh. Eventually it will become a meadow and then part of the forest.

If you plan to make the trip, supplies are available at Crane Flat. There is a fee to enter Yosemite National Park. Tioga Pass Road is closed from winter through at least mid-spring. Call ahead for updated road conditions.

Also nearby are South Fork Tuolumne River Falls, Tioga Pass Falls, Tenaya Lake and Tenaya Lake Falls.

# TENAYA LAKE

*Well, if you fish the lake when the trout are spawning, most of them will be swimming in Tenaya Creek, upstream of the lake.*

**Rating:** 4
**Species:** Rainbow Trout
**Stock:** None
**Facilities:** Picnic Areas and Restrooms
**Contact:** Yosemite National Park (209) 372-0200, Tuolumne Meadows Visitor Center (209) 372-0263

**Directions:** From the Big Oak Flat Entrance Station at Yosemite National Park, drive approximately eight miles east on Highway 120 to Tioga Pass Road. Turn left on Tioga Pass Road and continue approximately 30.2 miles to the lake on the right.

*Tenaya Lake*

When you're talking about high-country lakes, there is no way to pinpoint the exact month trout are going to spawn. Several conditions, including water temperature, snowmelt, elevation and the type of fish, contribute to when the spawn occurs. When fishing Tenaya Lake, make sure you don't arrive during the spawn, or chances are you won't be successful.

How do you know when the spawn is going to take place? Bank on it being around the same time Tioga Pass opens. The opening of the road typically coincides with the spawning period, which normally is in late May or early June. Why should you care about the spawn, anyway? Well, if you fish the lake when the trout are spawning, most of them will be swimming in Tenaya Creek, upstream of the lake. There will be few fish in the lake.

At 8,150 feet in Yosemite National Park, Tenaya is a popular drive-to lake, not just for anglers, but also for sightseers, tour buses and picnickers. This scenic lake, surrounded by granite domes, gets heavily fished. Although there is a self-sustaining rainbow trout population, the population is small; and these fish are smart and not overwhelmingly willing to bite your line. They've managed to live a number of years in this heavily fished lake, and they've learned what bait is. There are a few fish to 14 inches; however, most tend to be in the seven to 10-inch class. Your best chance at hooking a trout is by tossing Panther Martins near the Tenaya Creek inlet.

If you plan to make the trip, there is a fee to enter Yosemite National Park. Tioga Pass Road closes in the winter and may not reopen until sometime in May or June. Call the park for updated road conditions.

Also nearby are Pywiack Dome Falls, Olmsted Point, Tuolumne River (Tuolumne Meadows) and Cathedral Lakes.

# TUOLUMNE RIVER
## (TUOLUMNE MEADOWS)
*Downstream from the bridge can get over-fished pretty easily.*

**Rating:** 6
**Species:** Rainbow Trout, Brown Trout and Brook Trout
**Stock:** None
**Facilities:** Visitor Center, Restrooms, Gas, Food, Lodging and Campgrounds
**Contact:** Yosemite National Park (209) 372-0200. Tuolumne Meadows Visitor Center (209) 372-0263

**Directions:** From the Big Oak Flat Entrance Station at Yosemite National Park, drive approximately eight miles east on Highway 120 to Tioga Pass Road. Turn left on Tioga Pass Road (also known as Highway 120) and continue approximately 39 miles until the river crosses under the road.

*Tuolumne River (Tuolumne Meadows)*

It's no secret that Tuolumne Meadows in Yosemite National Park is one of the prettiest drive-to areas in California. Snow-capped mountain peaks in all directions, colorful wildflower-filled meadows, pristine high-county rivers and streams, and clear blue skies guarantee a wonderful outdoor experience. There is a secret, however, that has been kept pretty quiet in this popular neck of Yosemite National Park. While fishing in most of the park's rivers and streams is poor, anglers who correctly fish the Tuolumne experience staggeringly good catch rates.

The biggest obstacle here is your fellow anglers. Because of its close proximity to the road, this river gets heavily fished in the summer, and, for the most part, few of the anglers are experienced trout fishermen. Most are weekend warriors who fish once or twice a year, using ocean poles and bass lures to catch trout.

In fact, what these novice anglers are doing is making it difficult for the hardcore fishermen to catch fish. I like to compare these fish to the deer in Yosemite Valley. Just as the deer have become accustomed to seeing people, so have the fish. And just the way the deer no longer get spooked when they see humans, neither do the fish. While most wild trout scatter for cover when humans arrive, these brave rainbows and brooks stay put. They've seen so many lures and hooks over their lifetime that they've learned to ignore them.

So, how can you be successful? The best way is to try to target areas of the river that aren't near the road and to use some kind of bait that the fish haven't seen before, which rules out most lures. Fly fishermen do best. Those who can properly present a Panther Martin, however, should also experience good catch rates.

Fishing tends to be better for anglers who fish upstream from where the river crosses under the bridge. Where Lyell and Dana Forks of the Tuolumne merge, roughly 100 yards upstream, just above the small pond-like section of the river, is one good fishing spot.

Downstream from the bridge can get over-fished pretty easily. Most of the fish average six to nine inches.

If you plan to make the trip, supplies are available in Tuolumne Meadows. There is a fee to enter Yosemite National Park. Call ahead for road conditions. Some years Tioga Pass can remain closed into July. The Tuolumne River is closed to fishing from November 16 to the last Saturday in April.

Also nearby are Tenaya Lake, Olmsted Point, Tuolumne Meadows, Cathedral Lakes and the Pywiack Dome Falls.

*Tuolumne River with Cathedral Peak in the backdrop.*

TUOLUMNE RIVER

**At 1,860 acres, Hetch Hetchy is one of only a few man-made reservoirs in the park.**

| | |
|---|---|
| **Rating:** | 4 |
| **Species:** | Rainbow Trout and Brown Trout |
| **Stock:** | None |
| **Facilities:** | None |
| **Contact:** | Yosemite National Park (209) 372-0200 |

**Directions:** From Modesto, drive approximately 50 miles east on Highway 120 to the junction with Highway 108. Veer right, staying on Highway 120, and continue to Groveland. From Groveland, drive 25 miles east to Evergreen Road and turn north. Drive about seven miles to the town of Mather. Turn right on Hetch Hetchy Road and continue to the end of the road at Hetch Hetchy Reservoir.

*Hetch Hetchy Reservoir with Tueeulala and Wapama Falls.*

Because the National Park Service learned that most of the lakes in Yosemite National Park had no trout prior to early pioneers stocking them years ago, most trout plants in the park were halted in the late Seventies. The idea was to return many of the park's rivers and lakes to their pristine state. They thought that if they stopped stocking the waters, the combination of angler harvest and a lack of spawning grounds for reproduction would cause the trout to eventually die-off. In many waters this plan has worked, however, Hetch Hetchy Reservoir has remained full of fish. The reason? Hetch Hetchy is fed by the large, fast flowing Tuolumne River, which provides grounds for the rainbows and browns to spawn.

Yet, many anglers believe that there are very few fish in Hetch Hetchy. This misconception is partly promoted by their knowledge that the reservoir is not stocked. Apparently, they're not aware that a lake doesn't have to be stocked to have a productive fishery. Also, a lot of anglers get skunked here because they fish the wrong areas. The key to Hetch Hetchy is learning where to fish.

So, let's work on where to fish. At 1,860 acres, Hetch Hetchy is one of only a few man-made reservoirs in the park. Because of its relatively low elevation (3,800 feet), it can be fished year-round; and there are a few areas that are always productive. These include the Tueeulala Falls inlet, Falls Creek inlet, Tiltill Creek inlet, Rancheria Creek inlet and the Tuolumne River inlet.

These creek inlets carry a lot of food into the lake and the fish stack up to wait for it. Most anglers who fish off the dam and near the parking area won't catch fish, but those who take the time to walk around the lake to any one of the inlets should do fine if casting white trout jigs, Kastmasters and Thomas Buoyants. The south shoreline is mostly inaccessible because of steep cliffs. Hetch Hetchy has both rainbow and brown trout, most eight to nine inches.

If you plan to make the trip, supplies are available in Groveland. There is a fee to enter Yosemite National Park.

Also nearby are Tueeulala Falls, Wapama Falls, Cherry Lake, Tuolumne River (Middle Fork) and Rainbow Pool Falls.

REGION **15**

(1-7)

## LEE VINING CREEK DRAINAGE

1_Saddlebag Lake
2_Saddlebag Creek
3_Gardisky Lake
4_Tioga Lake
5_Lee Vining Creek (SF)
6_Ellery Lake
7_Lee Vining Creek

San Francisco
Modesto
120
Mammoth Lakes
Bishop
Santa Cruz
5    Fresno
395
99
101
Bakersfield
San Luis
Obispo
14
Barstow
Santa Barbara
Los Angeles

# SADDLEBAG LAKE

**As the summer progresses and water levels drop, anglers who wade near the dam do well catching planted fish.**

| | |
|---|---|
| **Rating:** | 5 |
| **Species:** | Rainbow Trout and Brook Trout |
| **Stock:** | 15,754 pounds of rainbow trout. |
| **Facilities:** | Boat Launch |
| **Contact:** | Inyo National Forest (760) 647-3044 |

**Directions:** From Highway 395 in Lee Vining, drive approximately 12 miles west on Highway 120 to Saddlebag Lake Road. Turn right and drive 2.5 miles to the lake.

*Backcountry lakes are planted by air.*

Located at 10,066 feet in the Inyo National Forest, Saddlebag is mostly used by hikers taking the water ferry across the lake to the 20 Lakes Basin. It is one of the few lakes in the Eastern Sierra region that doesn't get hammered by anglers. And there's an easy explanation why: there are no trophy-sized fish here.

While most lakes in the region are planted with giant trout, Saddlebag isn't. But there are no trophy-sized wild trout here either. Yet, there are hoards of smaller stockers to go around. The California Department of Fish and Game tosses 29,735 half-pound rainbows and 75 brood stock fish into the 325-acre lake.

There are a few places where anglers can expect to catch planted trout. The best is in the spring at the lake's inlet, which is on the side of the lake opposite the dam and the dam area itself. It's best fished with a float tube, although shore anglers catch fish here, too. As the summer progresses and water levels drop, anglers who wade near the dam do well catching planted fish.

Trolling anywhere on the lake can be phenomenal, providing you go less than 2 mph. Don't waste your time using any large lures. Stick with the smaller ones like Needlefish, Kastmasters and Cripplelures. Another positive note, there are thousands of holdover trout in Saddlebag, so the chance of catching pound-sized fish is good.

If you plan to make the trip, supplies are available in Lee Vining. Saddlebag Lake is closed to fishing from November 16 to the last Saturday in April. Call ahead for launch conditions. The launch is often closed because of low water levels.

Also nearby are Saddlebag Creek, Lee Vining Creek, Lee Vining Creek (South Fork), Gardisky Lake, Ellery Lake and Tioga Lake.

# SADDLEBAG CREEK

*Despite the confusion surrounding its name, Saddlebag Creek can be productive for anglers looking to catch some of the 2,389 half-pound rainbows that are planted here.*

**Rating:** 5
**Species:** Rainbow Trout and Brook Trout
**Stock:** 1,218 pounds of rainbow trout.
**Facilities:** Campgrounds
**Contact:** Inyo National Forest 760) 647-3044

**Directions:** From Highway 395 in Lee Vining, drive approximately 12 miles west on Highway 120 to Saddlebag Lake Road. Turn right; the creek parallels the road.

*Saddlebag Creek*

For many anglers, finding Inyo National Forest's Saddlebag Creek is much more difficult than catching fish in it. On most maps Saddlebag Creek is listed as Lee Vining Creek; however, the California Department of Fish and Game lists it as Saddlebag Creek. Although the name of the creek differs depending on the map you're looking at, for the purposes of this book we're going to stick with Saddlebag Creek, especially since the CA DFG uses the name "Saddlebag Creek" in newspapers when informing anglers of its stocking schedule.

At about 10,000 feet, Saddlebag Creek begins at the outlet of Saddlebag Lake and terminates 2.75 miles downstream, after nearly a 500-foot drop in elevation, where it merges with the South Fork of Lee Vining Creek. Despite the confusion surrounding its name, Saddlebag Creek can be productive for anglers looking to catch some of the 2,389 half-pound rainbows that are planted here. There are also hundreds of wild brook trout to be caught, although few grow larger than nine inches.

The CA DFG disperses rainbows from Junction Campground for about a mile upstream to the point in the creek near where Saddlebag Lake Road begins to climb up the mountain to the lake. Power Bait is your best bet, unless you're fly-fishing, which is also popular.

If you plan to make the trip, supplies are available in Lee Vining and at the Tioga Pass Resort. Saddlebag Creek is closed to fishing from Nov. 16 to the last Saturday in April. Call ahead for updated road conditions. Highway 120 may not open until sometime in June.

Also nearby are Saddlebag Lake, Lee Vining Creek, Lee Vining Creek (South Fork), Tioga Lake and Ellery Lake.

# GARDISKY LAKE

*Because the lake is so shallow, it's best fished with waders, although most hikers don't want to drag them up.*

**Rating:** 7
**Species:** Brook Trout
**Stock:** None
**Facilities:** None
**Contact:** Mammoth Lakes Visitor Center (760) 647-3044

**Directions:** From Bishop, drive north on Highway 395 to the town of Lee Vining and turn west on Highway 120. Continue approximately 10 miles to Saddlebag Lake Road on the right. Turn right and drive 1.2 miles to the trailhead and parking area on the left.

*Gardisky Lake remains frozen over through June most years.*

When many anglers on their way to Saddlebag Lake drive by the trailhead sign for Gardisky Lake and read that it's only 1.25 miles, they change their plans, park their cars and begin the short walk to Gardisky. Ironically, most of these anglers never make it to the lake. What the sign doesn't tell them is that there is also a 720-foot elevation gain, most of which occurs during the first three-fourths of a mile. This steep climb proves to be too much for many anglers. Those, however, who climb the demanding switchbacks slowly, taking their time, enjoy the light crowds at the lake.

Set in its own little basin below Tioga Peak, at 10,483 feet in the Inyo National Forest, the shallow 25-acre lake is home to a good population of brook trout. Most of the brookies are six to nine inches, but a few manage to grow to 12 inches. Because the lake is so shallow, it's best fished with waders, although most hikers don't want to drag them up. Being successful at Gardisky requires casting to deeper water. Don't bother using bait here. The brookies respond well to anglers fly fishing or using lures.

To reach Gardisky, park in the signed parking area near the trailhead, cross Saddlebag Lake Road and begin walking up the butt-kicking switchbacks through a heavily forested area. You'll cross a small, unnamed stream; walk parallel to it to the lake. Once you climb over the mountain and enter Gardisky's basin, the trees disappear and the path levels out. Continue through the meadows to the lake.

If you plan to make the trip, supplies are available at Tioga Resort on Highway 120. Gardisky is closed to fishing from November 16 to the last Saturday in April. Gardisky typically remains at least partially frozen until sometime in June.

Also nearby are Saddlebag Lake, Saddlebag Creek, Tioga Lake and Ellery Lake.

**The most successful anglers fish from float tubes with fly rods, right after ice-out.**

**Rating:** 7
**Species:** Rainbow Trout
**Stock:** 15,512 pounds of rainbow trout.
**Facilities:** Restrooms and Campgrounds
**Contact:** Mono Basin Scenic Forest Visitor Center (760) 647-3044

**Directions:** From Bishop, drive north on Highway 395 to the town of Lee Vining and turn left on Highway 120. Continue approximately 11 miles to the lake on the left.

Tioga Lake

Tioga Lake is equally popular among both tourists and anglers. Situated at 9,500 feet in a basin just east of Tioga Pass and the boundary of Yosemite National Park, the lake is one of the prettiest drive-to lakes in the Sierra.

About 100 yards from the park's entrance station, there's an overlook with a view of Tioga Lake. Although it offers fabulous photo opportunities year-round, I am most awed by the lake's appearance in late May and early June. Snow keeps the road inaccessible through at least mid-May and some years into July, but as soon as the snow is plowed and road repairs are made, you can take spectacular shots of Tioga Lake, either completely or partially frozen over. Even those who don't appreciate the outdoors are inspired by these vistas and come away filled with the beauty of the Inyo National Forest.

Fishing at 73-acre Tioga Lake is best right after ice-out. As soon as the ice begins to thaw, the larger rainbows go on the prowl, trying to make up for the lack of food during the long winter under ice. The most successful anglers fish from float tubes with fly rods, right after ice-out.

As summer progresses, the California Department of Fish and Game plants rainbow trout every other week through the end of the fishing season in October. In addition to 250 rainbows from two to four pounds, the CA DFG plants 35,700 half-pound fish. These plentiful plants make for great shoreline fishing throughout the fishing season. With no boat launch, anglers are pretty much limited to launching canoes and small car-top boats.

If you plan to make the trip, supplies are available down the road at Tioga Resort. Tioga Lake is closed to fishing from November 16 to the last Saturday in April.

Also nearby are Ellery Lake, Yosemite National Park, Saddlebag Lake, Saddlebag Creek, Gardisky Lake and Ellery Lake Falls.

# LEE VINING CREEK (SOUTH)

*All of the 8,000 half-pound rainbows planted here are best fooled with white mini jigs and the smallest silver Kastmaster you can find.*

| | |
|---|---|
| **Rating:** | 6 |
| **Species:** | Brown Trout, Rainbow Trout and Brook Trout |
| **Stock:** | 4,088 pounds of rainbow trout. |
| **Facilities:** | Campgrounds, Lodging, Food, Bait & Tackle and Restrooms |
| **Contact:** | Inyo National Forest (760) 647-3044 |
| **Directions:** | From Highway 395 in Lee Vining, drive approximately 13 miles west on Highway 120 to Tioga Lake. The creek flows downstream to Ellery Lake. |

*Lee Vining Creek (South Fork)*

Just east of both Tioga Pass and Yosemite National Park's eastern boundary, the South Fork of Lee Vining Creek offers the beauty of the national park without the $20 entrance fee. Although smaller in width than the Dana Fork of the Tuolumne River, which is tucked just inside the park boundary, the South Fork is nearly an exact replica of the Dana Fork; both meander through gentle meadows and wind through pine forests. The South Fork, however, is stocked with trout, while all the fish in the Dana Fork are wild.

Flowing through the Inyo National Forest, the South Fork begins 9,630 feet high at Tioga Lake's dam and extends 1.5 miles to Ellery Lake. One benefit of the South Fork is that no hiking is required to reach it; all access to the creek is available directly off paved Highway 120.

Here are a few spots to try: just upstream from the Tioga Pass Resort; where Saddlebag Creek and the South Fork meet; and in Ellery Lake Campground. All of the 8,796 half-pound rainbows planted here are best fooled with white mini jigs and the smallest silver Kastmaster you can find.

If you plan to make the trip, supplies are available in Lee Vining and at the Tioga Pass Resort. Lee Vining Creek (South Fork) is closed to fishing from November 16 to the last Saturday in April. Call ahead for updated road conditions. Highway 120 may not open until sometime in June.

Also nearby are Saddlebag Lake, Lee Vining Creek, Saddlebag Creek, Tioga Lake and Ellery Lake.

# ELLERY LAKE

**With the California Department of Fish and Game stocking the lake every five to 10 days from June through October, the action rarely slows here.**

**Rating:** 7
**Species:** Rainbow Trout and Brown Trout
**Stock:** 10,270 pounds of rainbow trout.
**Facilities:** Restrooms and Campgrounds
**Contact:** Mammoth Lakes Visitor Center (Mono Basin Scenic Forest Visitor Center) (760) 647-3044

**Directions:** From Bishop, drive north on Highway 395 to the town of Lee Vining and turn west on Highway 120. Continue approximately nine miles to the lake on the right.

*Ellery Lake*

Although a few acres smaller than its neighbor Tioga Lake, 68-acre Ellery Lake offers the same stunning beauty and wonderful fishing as Tioga. At 9,477 feet in the Inyo National Forest, about a mile and a half from the boundary of Yosemite National Park, Ellery gets heavily fished, yet most anglers appear to go home satisfied.

With the California Department of Fish and Game stocking the lake every five to 10 days from June through October, the action rarely slows here, especially for those dousing Power Bait from the shoreline or tossing lures off points. In addition to nearly 19,900 half-pounders, the CA DFG spices up the fishing by planting 260 rainbows in the one- to four-pound class.

The moment ice-out occurs, which is typically sometime in mid-May (but can come as late as late June, if a lot of snow fell in the winter), the smart anglers rush to the Lee Vining Creek inlet. Here, they float night crawlers off the bottom or toss Thomas Buoyants in search of the browns that inhabit the lake.

As the rest of the lake begins to thaw, success can be had fishing Power Bait off the north shore near Highway 120. Because the south shore of the lake has two miles of steep shoreline, it is not usually fished from shore. The lake also has a few nice coves on the west end that can be productive for those tossing Panther Martins.

The best way to fish the lake is with a boat. It has to be a small one, of course, because there is no boat launch, so canoes and small rowboats are ideal.

If you plan to make the trip, supplies are available in Lee Vining and at Tioga Resort just up the road. Ellery Lake is closed to fishing from November 16 to the last Saturday in April. The road to Ellery is closed in the winter and early spring.

Also nearby are Tioga Lake, Ellery Lake Falls, Saddlebag Creek, Gardisky Lake, Saddlebag Lake and Yosemite National Park.

# LEE VINING CREEK

**Bring an arsenal, because Power Bait, salmon eggs, night crawlers, small spinners, crickets and mini jigs all work.**

| | |
|---|---|
| **Rating:** | 8 |
| **Species:** | Rainbow Trout, Brown Trout and Brook Trout |
| **Stock:** | 21,483 pounds of rainbow trout. |
| **Facilities:** | Campgrounds, Picnic Areas and Restrooms |
| **Contact:** | Inyo National Forest 760) 647-3044 |

**Directions:** At the junction of Highways 395 and 120 in Lee Vining, drive 3.5 miles east on Highway 120 to Poole Power Plant Road and turn left. The creek can be accessed off this road.

*Lee Vining Creek*

When you pick up a newspaper, flip to the sports section and browse the outdoors pages that show up once a week, the reports for the Eastern Sierra are spilt into five regions: Lone Pine to Big Pine, Bishop Creek Drainage, Mammoth Area, June Lake Loop and Bridgeport. This upsets me a little, because they're forgetting one of the best drainages in California: Lee Vining Creek.

Often-overlooked, Lee Vining Creek drains the 20 Lakes Basin, areas of Yosemite National Park, the Ansel Adams Wilderness, Ellery, Saddlebag and Tioga Lake, as well as numerous other small lakes and streams. With all of these waters feeding it, you can bet it offers great trout fishing. In addition to hoards of wild rainbow trout mixed in with a few brooks and browns, the California Department of Fish and Game keeps a six-mile stretch of the river chock-full of rainbows by dumping more than 40,818 half-pounders into the creek. That makes Lee Vining the second most heavily stocked creek in Mono County.

With its headwaters at the outlet of Ellery Lake, Lee Vining Creek in the Inyo National Forest is a delight to fish. Most impressive in the fall when the aspen trees that line its shoreline turn golden, yellow and orange, this creek can take on a variety of personalities. In some areas there are frothy white rapids punctuated by lively waterfalls; other stretches, the creek meanders slowly through meadows.

Although campers and day users hit the creek hard, limits are still common. Concentrate your efforts in the campgrounds. Fish are planted weekly at Big Bend, Aspen, Upper, Lower and Cattleguard Campgrounds. There are also easy access sites along Poole Power Plant Road and at the Power Pool just above the Forest Service ranger station.

If you plan to make the trip, supplies are available in Lee Vining. Lee Vining Creek is closed to fishing from November 16 to the last Saturday in April.

Also nearby are Lee Vining Creek (South Fork), Saddlebag Creek, Saddlebag Lake, Tioga Lake and Ellery Lake.

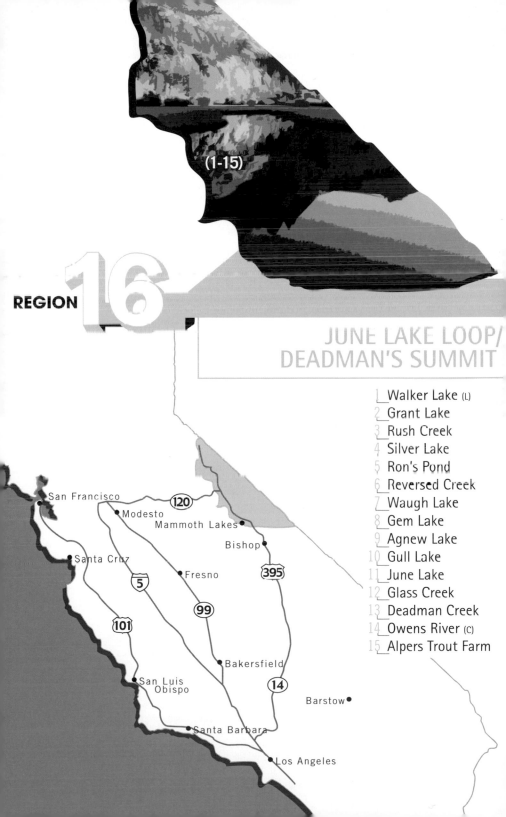

**REGION 16**

(1-15)

## JUNE LAKE LOOP/ DEADMAN'S SUMMIT

1 Walker Lake (L)
2 Grant Lake
3 Rush Creek
4 Silver Lake
5 Ron's Pond
6 Reversed Creek
7 Waugh Lake
8 Gem Lake
9 Agnew Lake
10 Gull Lake
11 June Lake
12 Glass Creek
13 Deadman Creek
14 Owens River (C)
15 Alpers Trout Farm

*Each season some lucky angler will hook into a monster brown while fishing for rainbow trout, so be prepared for a fight.*

| | |
|---|---|
| **Rating:** | 6 |
| **Species:** | Rainbow Trout, Brown Trout and Brook Trout |
| **Stock:** | 3,477 pounds of rainbow trout. |
| **Facilities:** | None |
| **Contact:** | Inyo National Forest (760) 647-3044 |
| **Directions:** | From Highway 395 in Bishop, drive 66 miles north to the second turnoff for the June Lake Loop (Highway 158). Turn left and drive approximately 1.5 miles to a signed turnoff on the right for Parker and Walker Lakes. Veer right onto the dirt road and continue six-tenths of a mile to a fork in the road. Follow the sign toward Walker Lake (veering away from the arrow for Parker Lake), veer right and drive a half-mile to a sign for the Walker Trail. Veer left and drive 2.7 miles to the trailhead. |

**Walker Lake (Little)**

At 7,500 feet in the Inyo National Forest, Walker is a productive drive-to lake for some anglers; for others, fishing it requires a short, yet grueling hike to the shore. Unfortunately, the latter will be the case for most readers of this book. Only members of the Walker Lake Land Company are permitted to drive to the lake and use the cabins, boat house, docks and launch ramp on Walker's east end.

The Walker Land Company has owned the land on the east end of the lake since a land ordinance went into effect in the Thirties. Its members, who are all from Southern California, control the land all the way to the shoreline. So, do everyone a favor and stay away from the east end of the lake. The west end of this 87-acre lake offers better fishing anyway.

A plus for the hikers who walk the half-mile trail to Walker is that the fish are much larger here than they are at most other hike-to lakes. Also, since anglers only catch a portion of the 6,313 half-pound trout that are planted each year, many holdover fish in the pound range can be landed.

Although Walker can be a productive fishery, since only members of the Walker Lake Land Company are permitted to drive boats to the lake, other anglers are limited by the methods available to them. Although the trail is too steep to carry in a boat, it's possible to carry in a float tube, which would allow you to fish the deeper water in the middle of the lake. Shoreline access is good on the south end where anglers set up lines with Power Bait and float night crawlers off the bottom.

Casting larger Thomas Buoyants and Kastmasters yield good catch rates for those walking up and down the shoreline. Each season some lucky angler will hook a monster brown while fishing for rainbow trout, so be prepared for a fight. If you're looking to catch brook trout, try fishing near the inlet on the west side of the lake.

If you plan to make the trip, supplies are available in June Lake and Lee Vining. Walker Lake is closed to fishing from November 16 to the last Saturday in April.

Also nearby are Grant Lake, Mono Lake and Rush Creek.

# GRANT LAKE

*What makes Grant special is that it has an astonishing number of wild brown trout.*

| | |
|---|---|
| **Rating:** | 7 |
| **Species:** | Rainbow Trout, Brown Trout, Brook Trout and Cutthroat Trout |
| **Stock:** | 28,041 pounds of rainbow trout. |
| **Facilities:** | Launch Ramp, Campgrounds, Marina, Bait & Tackle and Restrooms |
| **Contact:** | Ernie's Tackle Shop (760) 648-7756, Grant Lake Marina (760) 648-7964 |

**Directions:** From Highway 395 in Bishop, drive 66 miles north to the second turnoff for the June Lake Loop (Highway 158). Turn left and drive five miles to the lake.

*Kuyvon Kudjui caught this quality Alpers on opening day of 1999.*

Of the four lakes on the June Lake Loop, June, Silver and Gull fall into one category: We'll call it the heavily fished group. And let's not forget to mention that they're profusely stocked, with immense concentrations of fish. Then there's the fourth, Grant Lake, which is much different than the rest.

At 1,095 acres, Grant is a long lake, with a deep channel down its middle, steep shore-lines and a mostly sandy bottom. More than twice the size of all the other lakes on the loop combined, Grant also gets planted with a lot of fish, but because of its size they are far less concentrated, which is why anglers don't swarm Grant the way they do those other lakes.

What makes Grant special is that it has an astonishing number of wild brown trout. In fact, Grant has the most browns on the loop. The California Department of Fish and Game enhances this fishery even further by adding 10,000 fingerling browns each July in most years. (None were planted in 2000.)Yet, while there are a lot of browns here, they aren't caught as frequently as they could be.

So, what's the problem with snagging these browns? The best time to catch browns is in the fall when they leave the depths of the lake and cruise the surface to fill their bellies to prepare for the lake's icing over in the coming winter. And with the season closing on November 16, the last two weeks in October are prime time for targeting them. But Grant Lake Marina closes during this two-week window (typically by the second weekend in October), and the launch ramp shuts down with it. So, you're pretty much stuck with shore fishing. In a way, it almost seems as if lake management is protecting the brown population.

Without a boat to properly troll the lake, fishing for the browns can be a real drag. And the fact that anglers are painfully aware of all the lunkers in this lake frustrates them even further. The lake record, a 20-pounder caught in 1991, stands as a testament for the need to keep that launch ramp open longer.

Right now, anglers' best bet is to troll the lake just after ice-out (providing the ramp is opened). If you can somehow get a boat on the water (a few locals are good at launching from the beach near the inlet, but it's really muddy and there is no ramp), here's what to do: Troll a No. 9 or a No. 13 brown trout Rapala in Rattlesnake Cove, down the middle of the lake or near the Rush Creek inlet.

In addition to 1,700 pounds of Alpers ranging from five to 12 pounds each, the California Department of Fish and Game bolsters Grant's fish population by spilling 51,205 half-pound bows and 61 brood fish in the lake. Because the fish are not that concentrated, trolling small lures works best, although anglers soaking Power Bait off dropoffs and points also do okay.

Most anglers are unaware of it, however Grant also has a stable population of cutthroats. They aren't stocked into the lake; rather, they swim out of Rush Creek into Grant. Few are caught, simply because they aren't targeted. Most of the cutts stay deep, in 70-100 feet, and are about a pound. But it's not uncommon to catch these fish in the two- to four-pound range. Try using Needlefish.

If you plan to make the trip, supplies are available in June Lake. There is a launch fee. Call ahead for lake conditions. The lake can remain iced over after the fishing season begins, and the launch ramp tends to close while the season is still on. Grant Lake is closed to fishing from November 16 to the last Saturday in April.

Also nearby are June Lake, Gull Lake, Rush Creek, Reversed Creek, Silver Lake, Walker Lake and the Ansel Adams Wilderness.

GRANT LAKE

*Grant Lake*

# RUSH CREEK

*One of the secrets to success here is sneaking up to the shore without spooking the fish.*

**Rating:** 7
**Species:** Rainbow Trout, Brown Trout and Brook Trout
**Stock:** 10,471 pounds of rainbow trout.
**Facilities:** None
**Contact:** June Lake Chamber of Commerce (760) 648-7584, Ernie's Tackle Shop (760) 648-7756

**Directions:** From Bishop, drive about 60 miles north on Highway 395 to Highway 158 (signed for the June Lake Loop) and turn left. Drive seven miles to a dirt pullout on the left. Park here and walk across the highway to the creek.

*Rush Creek*

There are two streams in the June Lake Loop, Rush Creek and three-mile-long Reversed Creek, a tributary to Rush. Rush Creek, which is much wider and longer, also has far more public access and gets planted with a lot more fish.

At 12,000 feet in the Ansel Adams Wilderness, Rush Creek originates from melting glaciers just above the Marie Lakes. It then flows into and out of Waugh, Gem and Agnew Lakes. After being released from Agnew's dam, Rush Creek feeds Rush Creek Falls and then flows into and out of Silver and Grant Lakes, before terminating at Mono Lake.

The California Department of Fish and Game keeps fishing hot here from spring through fall by dumping 19,884 rainbows. In addition, fish that were planted in Grant and Silver Lakes swim between the two lakes via Rush.

One of the secrets to success is sneaking up to the shore without spooking the fish. So many anglers stomp along the shore here, the fish get spooked pretty easily. Because there are deep pools, long runs, swift currents and pockets of rapids, any assortment of bait works. Although most anglers use rainbow Power Bait and rainbow-patterned Roostertails, skilled anglers who know how to properly drift flies catch the most fish. Access to the creek is available off Highway 158 from Silver Lake to Grant Lake.

If you plan to make the trip, supplies are available in June Lake. Rush Creek is closed to fishing from November 16 to the last Saturday in April.

Also nearby are June Lake, Reversed Creek, Silver Lake, Grant Lake, Agnew Lake and Gem Lake.

# SILVER LAKE

**Your best bet is to set up rods on the west shore and toss Power Bait or night crawlers as far from the shore as you can.**

| | |
|---|---|
| **Rating:** | 7 |
| **Species:** | Rainbow Trout, Brown Trout and Cutthroat Trout |
| **Stock:** | 15 pounds fingerling cutthroat trout, 385 pounds of sub-catchable cutthroat trout and 25,000 pounds of rainbow trout. |
| **Facilities:** | Bait & Tackle, Boat Rentals, Boat Launch, Lodging, Fish Cleaning Station, RV Hookups, Restrooms, Food and Campgrounds |
| **Contact:** | Silver Lake Resort (760) 648-7525, Ernie's Tackle Shop (760) 648-7756 |
| **Directions:** | From Highway 395 in Bishop, drive 60 miles north to the Highway 158/June Loop turnoff. Turn left and drive 6.5 miles to the lake on the right. |

*The mountains above Silver Lake make for great sunrise photos.*

At 110 acres, Silver Lake is about one-third the size of nearby June Lake, but its gets stocked with more than half the amount of fish. Whereas the Department of Fish and Game stocks June with 82,200 rainbows, Silver gets 46,102 and 15,000 fingerling cutthroats and 5,005 sub-catchables. Both are blessed with 1,700 pounds of Alpers from four to 15 pounds.

If you think about these plants in relationship to the lakes' sizes, Silver Lake is stocked with more fish per acre. So, you'd think the fishing should be better at Silver, because the fish are much more concentrated, right? Yet, that's not necessarily true. Aside from the lakes' relative sizes, there are two other factors that take a few points away from Silver's fishery. The most important is Rush Creek. Rush flows into and out of Silver, and many of the fish that are stocked in the lake swim out into the creek. Also, Silver's holdover fishery doesn't compare to June's.

June might retain more fish than Silver, but that's not to say Silver isn't a quality fishery, because it is. Shoreline fishing is superb here. While private residences crowd the east shoreline, the west shore is loaded with public access. The south shore, on the other hand, is very shallow and doesn't hold many fish. Your best bet is to set up rods on the west shore and toss Power Bait or night crawlers as far from the shore as you can. Limits of half-pound bows are common for anglers shore fishing. Trolling works well too, however, the lake is so small that with even just a few boats out there isn't much space left to troll.

There's much more than just stocked trout at Silver; other fish include wild brown trout and cutthroats. In an area that is best fly-fished, most of the browns and cutts are caught at the Rush Creek inlet, however, this section of the lake is hard to fish because much of it is on private property. With million-dollar houses bordering the east side of Rush Creek, out-of-towners have difficulty distinguishing between public and private property, so you pretty much have to be a local to know how to fish the inlet area properly. Browns and cutts can also be caught in the lake's main channel, which has a maximum depth of 55 feet.

If you plan to make the trip, supplies are available in June Lake. Silver Lake is closed to fishing from November 16 to the last Saturday in April. In winter call ahead for conditions. The lake may be iced over at the start of fishing season.

Also nearby are Gull Lake, June Lake, Grant Lake, Reversed Creek, Rush Creek and the Ansel Adams Wilderness.

# RON'S POND

*When the fishing at the June Lake Loop is bad (which rarely happens), there's a place nearby where the fishing is almost always good.*

| | |
|---|---|
| **Rating:** | 4 |
| **Species:** | Rainbow Trout |
| **Stock:** | Periodically with Alpers trout. |
| **Facilities:** | Lodging, Fitness Center, Spa, Pool and a Restaurant |
| **Contact:** | Double Eagle Resort (760) 648-7004 |
| **Directions:** | From Bishop, drive north on Highway 395 past Mammoth to the June Lake turnoff (Highway 158). Turn left and drive 5.5 miles to the Double Eagle Resort on the left. |

*Ron's Pond*

Sometimes when the bite is off, no matter how good a fisherman you are, the fish just won't cooperate. We've all been through those times. But you know what they say, "A bad day fishing is better than a good day working."

When the fishing at the June Lake Loop is bad (which rarely happens), there's a place nearby where the fishing is almost always good. Little Ron's Pond (approximately a quarter-acre), which was named after the owner of the resort, is stocked with Alpers from one to two pounds.

The bite may always be on at Ron's, but it will also take a bite out of your pocketbook, so it's not for everyone. Although fishing the pond is free for guests at the resort (there are about 100 fish in it), visitors are charged $15 an hour, with a two-hour minimum. Only fly-fishing with barbless hooks is permitted.

Located on the June Lake Loop, between Silver and Gull Lakes, Ron's Pond is opened to fishing until the pond freezes over in winter. The resort also has a fishing guide who gives fly-fishing lessons.

If you plan to make the trip, supplies are available in June Lake. There is a fishing fee. No license is required.

Also nearby are Rush Creek, Reversed Creek, Grant Lake, Silver Lake, June Lake, Gull Lake and Rush Creek Falls.

*Reversed Creek originates near Gull Lake and terminates at Silver Lake, and a variety of fish commonly enter the creek from both of these lakes.*

| | |
|---|---|
| **Rating:** | 6 |
| **Species:** | Rainbow Trout, Brown Trout and Brook Trout |
| **Stock:** | 681 pounds of rainbow trout. |
| **Facilities:** | None |
| **Contact:** | June Lake Chamber of Commerce (760) 648-7584 |
| **Directions:** | From Bishop, drive about 60 miles north on Highway 395 to Highway 158 (signed for the June Lake Loop) and turn left. Drive three miles to the turnoff for Gull Lake. Reversed Creek begins near Gull and runs to Silver Lake. |

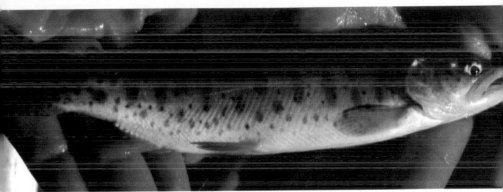

*A cutthroat trout*

A tad longer than three miles, Reversed Creek is one of the shortest named streams in the entire Sierra. With the California Department of Fish and Game planting a mere 1,250 fish each year, it's also one of the least stocked; but that's not to say there aren't tons of fish here. Reversed Creek originates near Gull Lake and terminates at Silver Lake, and a variety of fish commonly enter the creek from both of these lakes, including brook, rainbow and brown trout, all of which can be caught here.

The stream is mainly productive near its inlet to Silver Lake. Fifteen feet wide and a few feet deep in most places, this section of the stream meanders through delicate meadows and is a favorite spot for the fish to hang. Another good area is a few hundred yards upstream from Silver Lake, where Rush Creek crosses under the highway and meets up with Reversed Creek.

Because of its clear water, anglers have no trouble spotting fish in the creek. Since the water clarity allows the fish to see anglers, too, they can get easily spooked. Small lures, such as Kastmasters and Panther Martins, work best, but some anglers would rather drift Power Bait under fallen logs and overhanging brush. Reversed Creek is only stocked prior to the trout opener and Memorial weekend.

If you plan to make the trip, supplies are available in June Lake. Reversed Creek is closed to fishing from November 16 to the last Saturday in April.

Also nearby are June Lake, Rush Creek, Grant Lake, Agnew Lake and Gem Lake.

# WAUGH LAKE

*There is an outside chance of catching fish in the early summer when the lake is full, however, the opportunities are much greater at any of the other lakes in the region.*

**Rating:** 3
**Species:** Rainbow Trout and Brook Trout
**Stock:** None
**Facilities:** None
**Contact:** Mammoth Lakes Visitors Center (760) 924-5500, Inyo National Forest Wilderness Permits (760) 873-2483l, Frontier Pack Station (760) 873-7971 (Winter) or (760) 648-7701 (Summer)

**Directions:** From Bishop, drive north on Highway 395 to the turnoff for the June Lakes Loop. Turn left and drive approximately seven miles to the trailhead located across from Silver Lake.

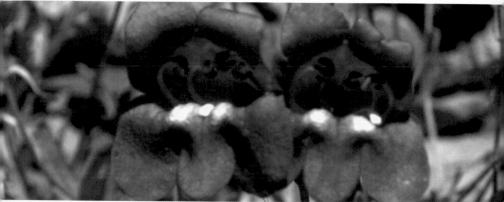

*Wildflowers*

From the west side, Waugh Lake looks like a perfect jewel, an ideal high-country lake with crystal-clear water, surrounded by pine-covered mountains, stunning scenery and fresh air; you can just imagine it brimming with fish. If you hike to it from the east, however, you'll discover a different, more unsettling view of the lake.

Although it is located in the backcountry, many hikers, backpackers and anglers think Waugh Lake is a fraud and they refuse to give it the status of a backcountry lake, because it was created by a man-made dam. You might expect to find a lake formed by a dammed creek in a metropolitan reservoir, but not in the high country. Formerly known as Upper Rush Meadow, Waugh Lake was formed in 1919, when a dam was constructed to sustain Gem Lake's (located just below Waugh Lake) water levels and to generate hydroelectric power.

At 9,442 feet in the Ansel Adams Wilderness, Waugh Lake is just a bit smaller than nearby Garnet Lake, but it doesn't provide anywhere near as consistent a fishery. No plants are made, and the only ways fish are able to enter the lake are through Upper Rush Creek and the outlet streams from Rodgers Lakes and Davis Lakes.

Bottom line, there are not enough fish in the lake to warrant anglers to fish it, and few do. There are wild trout in both Upper Rush Creek and Gem Lake. But, Waugh Lake is drawn so low (virtually dry by fall), its few fish either end up in Rush Creek or Gem Lake.There is an outside chance of catching fish in the early summer when the lake is full, however, the opportunities are much greater at any of the other lakes in the region.

To reach Waugh Lake from Gem Lake, continue west on the trail around the lake to tiny Billy Lakes. Veer right, away from the pass, just after Billy Lakes, and continue 1.7 miles to the lake.

If you plan to make the trip, supplies are available at Silver Lake. A wilderness permit is required for overnight travel in the Ansel Adams Wilderness. Waugh Lake is closed to fishing from November 16 to the last Saturday in April.

Also nearby are Rush Creek, Gem Lake, Agnew Lake, Gem Lake Falls, Clark Lakes, Weber Lake and Sullivan Lake.

**The area that most consistently produces fish is the Rush Creek inlet.**

| | |
|---|---|
| **Rating:** | 5 |
| **Species:** | Rainbow Trout and Brook Trout |
| **Stock:** | 10 pounds of fingerling rainbow trout. |
| **Facilities:** | None |
| **Contact:** | Mammoth Lakes Visitors Center (760) 924-5500, Inyo National Forest Wilderness Permits (760) 873-2483I, Frontier Pack Station (760) 873-7971 (Winter) or (760) 648-7701 (Summer) |
| **Directions:** | From Bishop, drive north on Highway 395 to the turnoff for the June Lakes Loop. Turn left, and drive approximately seven miles to the trailhead located across from Silver Lake. |

*Gem Lake*

Gem Lake is a natural backcountry lake that was dammed in the early 1920s to provide hydroelectric power to nearby cities. The dam also enlarged its size, but Gem is still a real high-country lake. It's just a little larger than it was before.

At 9,050 feet in the Ansel Adams Wilderness, Gem Lake doesn't provide great catch rates, even though both rainbow and brook trout inhabit the lake (10,000 fingerlings are air lifted in). Most of the trout remain on the small side, but few anglers seem to mind. The scenery offered by the lake and its surrounding wilderness makes up for the fishes' lack of size.

With 4.2 miles of shoreline, the lake is quite large and provides a lot of water to fish. The area that most consistently produces fish is the Rush Creek inlet. The trout stack up here waiting for food to be dropped into the lake. In addition to Thomas Buoyants and Kastmasters, fly & bubble combos also work well. The east and south shores are difficult to fish because of steep banks, so concentrate on the north side of the lake near the trail.

For those who are impressed with natural beauty, Gem Lake offers some stunning vistas. For example, from Clark Lake No. 1, walk east for approximately four-tenths of a mile and look to the left: you'll get a great view of Gem Lake and Gem Lake Falls. Even better, look off towards the June Lake Loop. Mono Lake looks huge from here.

To reach Gem Lake from the Silver Lake Trailhead, ascend for 2.2 miles to Agnew Lake. Continue 2.5 miles to Gem Lake.

If you plan to make the trip, supplies are available at Silver Lake. A wilderness permit is required for overnight travel in the Ansel Adams Wilderness. Gem Lake is closed to fishing from November 16 to the last Saturday in April.

Also nearby are Agnew Lake, Waugh Lake, Clark Lakes, Sullivan Lake, Weber Lake and Billy Lakes.

# AGNEW LAKE

*For the few who do take time out to fish, there are some rainbow and brook trout to be caught.*

**Rating:** 4
**Species:** Rainbow Trout and Brook Trout
**Stock:** Five pounds of fingerling rainbow trout.
**Facilities:** None
**Contact:** Mammoth Lakes Visitors Center (760) 924-5500, Inyo National Forest Wilderness Permits (760) 873-2483, Frontier Pack Station (760) 873-7971 (Winter) or (760) 648-7701 (Summer)

**Directions:** From Bishop, drive north on Highway 395 to the turnoff for the June Lakes Loop. Turn left and drive approximately seven miles to the trailhead, located across from Silver Lake.

*The view of Mono Lake from Agnew Lake's dam.*

Agnew Lake is one of the ugliest hike-to lakes you'll ever see. There are no trees around, no vegetation of any kind for that matter, no beautiful snow capped peaks overhead, and the fishing isn't too hot either. As you can tell, Agnew Lake isn't one of the more spectacular backcountry lakes, but it does have some value to the local communities.

Agnew Lake is vital to the communities of Lee Vining, June Lake and Mammoth. Before its dam was built in the early 1920's, Agnew Lake was a natural lake. When a dam was constructed to produce hydroelectric power, it also increased the size of the lake, which in turn enabled the production of hydroelectric power throughout added months of the year. Agnew Lake's dam is the last in a series of three dams run by Southern California Edison. The two that precede it are at Waugh and Gem Lakes.

The whole process is interesting. A winch-cable tram is used to transfer workers and supplies from the June Lake Loop to Agnew Lake. Then, workers and supplies are transferred to a barge that carries them across the lake to another winch-cable system that hauls them up to Gem Lake's Dam.

As for the fishing, few anglers come here. With steep shorelines around the entire lake, access is poor. For the few who do take time out to fish, there are some rainbow and brook trout to be caught. The California Department of Fish and Game airlifts 5,000 fingerling rainbow trout each year.

At 8,500 feet in the Inyo National Forest, Agnew Lake is just outside the border of the Ansel Adams Wilderness. Getting to it is like walking on a railroad track. The rocks on the trail are the size of softballs and are very loose. Be careful not to sprain an ankle. To reach Agnew Lake from the Silver Lake Trailhead, continue 2.2 miles to the lake.

If you plan to make the trip, Agnew Lake is closed to fishing from November 16 to the last Saturday in April.

Also nearby are Gem Lake, Waugh Lake, the Clark Lakes, Sullivan Lake, Weber Lake and the Billy Lakes.

# GULL LAKE

**At 65 acres, Gull is the smallest lake in the June Lake Loop.**

**Rating:** 8

**Species:** Rainbow Trout, Brown Trout, Cutthroat Trout and Brook Trout

**Stock:** 22,370 pounds of rainbow trout, 385 pounds of sub-catchable cutthroat trout and 15 pounds of fingerling cutthroat trout.

**Facilities:** Restrooms, Launch Ramp, Bait & Tackle, General Store, Lodging, Campgrounds and Boat Rentals

**Contact:** Gull Lake Lodge (800) 631-9081, Gull Lake Marina (760) 648-7539, June Lake Chamber of Commerce (760) 648-7584, Mono Basin Scenic Forest Visitor Center (760) 647-3044

**Directions:** From Bishop, drive about 60 miles north on Highway 395 to Highway 158 (signed for the June Lake Loop) and turn left. Drive 2.7 miles to the turnoff for Gull Lake and turn right. At a fork in the road, veer right and continue to the lake.

*Gull Lake*

At 65 acres, Gull is the smallest lake in the June Lake Loop. In Gull's case, however, its small size can be considered a good thing. The fish are more concentrated, and you don't have to be a skilled angler to catch fish here. Trolling, still fishing from a boat and bank fishing are all productive.

Good fishing is directly related to stocking numbers. Spreading them out in weekly plants, the California Department of Fish and Game mercifully dumps 38,556 rainbow trout, 287 of which are three pounds or more, 5,005 sub-catchable cutthroat trout and 15,000 fingerling cutthroat trout. Gull Lake Marina also plants 1,700 pounds of Alpers trout. With all these fish, it's obvious why catch rates tend to be high.

If trolling, there's no need to target a specific area. Start by working the shoreline, then down the middle of the lake, and if that doesn't work, crisscross the lake. Just about any Rapala, Needlefish, Z-Ray or red and gold Thomas Buoyant works well.

If still fishing in a boat, there are two popular areas: the first is a large rock formation directly across the marina. There is a steep drop-off here, and those soaking Power Bait seem to easily fool the rainbows. The other spot is roughly 50 yards to the right of the rock where reeds make up the shoreline. Floating night crawlers off the bottom work well here. Shoreline anglers can also do well, setting up almost anywhere around the lake.

At 7,650 feet in the Inyo National Forest, Gull is also home to some wild brooks and browns. While the browns aren't frequently caught, a few lunkers are checked in each season. Although a brook more than six pounds was landed years ago, brooks have become rare over the last decade. Cutthroats to three pounds are also caught regularly.

If you plan to make the trip, supplies are available in June Lake. Gull Lake is closed to fishing from November 16 to the last Saturday in April. There is a boat launch fee.

Also nearby are June Lake, Silver Lake, Grant Lake, Reversed Creek and Walker Lake.

# JUNE LAKE

*Whether you're an angler who fishes one weekend a year or every weekend, or even an experienced angler who targets fish that are difficult to catch, June has something for you.*

**Rating:** 9

**Species:** Rainbow Trout, Brown Trout and Cutthroat Trout

**Stock:** 15 pounds of fingerling cutthroat trout, 385 pounds of sub-catchable cutthroat trout and 55,000 pounds of rainbow trout.

**Facilities:** Bait & Tackle, Boat Rentals, Boat Launch, Lodging, Fish Cleaning Station, RV Hookups, Restrooms, Food and Campgrounds

**Contact:** June Lake Marina (760) 648-7726, Boulder Lodge (760) 648-7533 or (800) 458-3556 June Lake Motel and Cabins 760-648-7547 or (800) 648-6835

**Directions:** From Highway 395 in Bishop, drive 60 miles north to the Highway 158/June Loop turnoff. Turn left, drive 2.6 miles and turn right on Knoll Road. Continue one-tenth of a mile to Brenner Street and turn right. Drive to the June Lake Marina.

*Mornings at June Lake can be inspiring.*

Nestled at 7,650 feet up in the Inyo National Forest, glacier-carved, spring-fed June Lake is one of the Eastern Sierra's top fisheries. At 320 acres, June is the second largest lake on the June Loop. And with depths to 140 feet, it is also the most popular and one of the most frequently fished bodies of water in the Sierra.

While crowds develop here, massive amounts of stocked fish keep the limits coming. The California Department of Fish and Game mercifully spills more than 85,000 half-pound rainbows and 281 brood fish in the four- to six-pound class into the lake, in addition to 10,000 fingerling-sized cutthroats and 5,000 sub-cutts. A special co-op program also benefits June. Each year the CA DFG provides June Lake Marina with at least 10,000 (and up to 24,000) fingerling rainbow trout. The marina then raises them in rearing pens in the lake and releases them throughout the season when the fish reach at least a pound, but they can also grow to two pounds before being set free. Another 1,700 pounds of Alpers ranging from five to 12 pounds are also stocked.

Whether you're an angler who fishes one weekend a year or every weekend, or even an experienced angler who targets fish that are difficult to catch, June has something for you. There's the easy-to-catch half-pound planters, the larger holdover rainbows, trophy-sized Alpers trout, wild brown trout and cutthroats that were put in the lake at just a few inches, but have since grown to adult sizes.

If you're a beginner, target the stockers. They're easy to catch, even for those who don't have a clue how to fish. There are several places where anglers always seem to catch fish, so don't try to go out and find your own secret spot. Stick to these places: the tules on the west side of the lake, a large rock that juts out on the north side of the lake, the shoreline east of Boulder Lodge, and the beach area. In the spring and fall, night crawlers work best; however, green, yellow and rainbow Power Bait are the ticket in the summer months.

While larger fish are sometimes caught on the west end in the reeds, most fish are landed near the beach. Boaters anchor off the beach on a ledge with a steep drop-off. Catching the

A cutthroat trout

Geoff Gullards with a rainbow trout

larger Alpers and the holdovers is all about luck. In the summer, only a few fish larger than five pounds get landed each week. Yet in the months of April, May, June, September and October, it's common to see more than three fish a day over five pounds caught.

Because of the heat, August is the worst month to fish June. Most of the big fish are caught on Power Bait, which frustrates anglers who troll large Rapalas, looking to catch bigger fish. Using small Rapalas, Thomas Buoyants and silver Kastmasters works well for trollers zigzagging across the lake or cruising down the middle and along the shoreline.

While the rainbows are easy to catch, the cutthroats take a little bit more effort, and depending on the season, you'll most likely need downriggers or leadcore to hook them. The cutthroats typically stay in water anywhere from 25 to 60 feet deep. In the spring and fall, try trolling anything silver or a Needlefish in 25 to 45 feet of water. During the warmer months when the fish move into 40 to 60 feet of water, try trolling down the lake's main channel. The best troll is across the width of the lake, beginning near Boulder Lodge. The cutthroats average a half-pound to a pound, but the lake record stands at 8.5 pounds.

Browns are the most difficult trout to catch in June. Although I've seen browns to 20 pounds swimming in the shallows, it's rare for one to be caught. Much of the problem has to do with the tremendous amount of fishing pressure on the lake, which spooks the browns. I've personally never caught a brown here, although I've worked my butt off trying to accomplish the feat. They're just hard to catch, and while there are only a few in the lake, it's worth targeting them because a state record could be landed here.

If you plan to make the trip, supplies are available at June Lake. June Lake is closed to fishing from November 16 to the last Saturday in April. In winter call ahead for lake conditions. The lake may be iced over at the start of fishing season.

Also nearby are Gull Lake, Silver Lake, Grant Lake, Reversed Creek, Rush Creek and the Ansel Adams Wilderness.

# GLASS CREEK

*Because of its size, the stream is only fished with Power Bait.*

| | |
|---|---|
| **Rating:** | 5 |
| **Species:** | Rainbow Trout |
| **Stock:** | 1,532 pounds of rainbow trout. |
| **Facilities:** | Vault Toilets and Primitive Campsites |
| **Contact:** | Mammoth Lakes Visitors Center (760) 924-5500, Rick's Sports Center (760) 934-3416 |

**Directions:** From Highway 395 in Bishop, drive north 46 miles to Glass Creek Road. Turn left and continue two-tenths of a mile to the campground.

*A wildflower*

Glass Creek is one of the smallest but most popular streams in the Eastern Sierra. However, its popularity doesn't stem from fishing. People mostly come here to camp. Camp for free, that is. Glass Creek, along with nearby Deadman Creek, are two of only a handful of free campsites in the Eastern Sierra. These are primitive campsites, meaning no services are provided except for vault toilets.

Located at 8,000 feet in the Inyo National Forest between Mammoth and June Lake, Glass Creek's campgrounds allow campers to save money by not paying for campsites. Yet, they can still remain only a 10-minute drive from all the lakes in both the June Lake and Mammoth Lake Loops.

As for fishing at the creek, most anglers prefer not to. The creek is pitiful. It's as wide as the distance between my legs when I'm doing the splits, and as deep as the bathtub when I have the shower on. The stream is stocked weekly with rainbow trout from the California Department of Fish and Game. However, the 124 fish planted each week (more than 2,993 throughout the season) usually aren't enough to satisfy anglers. Because of its size, the stream is only fished with Power Bait. Concentrate your efforts in the campgrounds.

If you plan to make the trip, supplies are available in June Lake and Mammoth. Glass Creek is closed to fishing from November 16 to the last Saturday in April.

Also nearby are Mono Lake, Deadman Creek, the Mammoth Lakes, June Lake Loop, Mammoth Creek, Sherwin Creek and Reversed Creek.

*With its popularity among campers who also sometimes fish, many of the fish are caught by Friday, leaving nothing for weekend visitors.*

**Rating:** 4
**Species:** Rainbow Trout
**Stock:** 839 pounds of rainbow trout.
**Facilities:** Vault Toilets and Primitive Campsites
**Contact:** Mammoth Lakes Visitors Center (760) 924-5500, Rick's Sports Center (760) 934-3416

**Directions:** From Highway 395 in Bishop, drive north approximately 46 miles to Deadman Creek Road. Turn west and continue three miles on the dirt road to the campground.

*All Ross Schwartzberg needed was a salmon egg to entice this rainbow trout.*

Along with its nextdoor neighbor Glass Creek, Deadman Creek isn't a popular fishing area. Its visitors come mainly for the camping. Free camping is popular wherever it is offered in the Sierra, and Deadman Creek is one of the few campgrounds that do offer it.

The creek also provides trout fishing. Stocked with 1,644 rainbow trout, it receives about half the allotment of Glass Creek. If it were stocked weekly, as scheduled, the California Department of Fish and Game would plant about 68 fish each week. With its popularity among campers who mostly fish, many of the fish are caught by Friday, leaving nothing for weekend visitors. The stream is small with minimal pools, so the use of salmon eggs and Power Bait is your only option.

At 8,000 feet in the Inyo National Forest, between the towns of June Lake and Mammoth, snow can remain along the stream's banks until late May. However, crowds don't usually form until July, and generally leave by mid-September. Plan your trip accordingly.

If you plan to make the trip, supplies are available in June Lake and Mammoth. Deadman Creek is closed to fishing from November 16 to the last Saturday in April.

Also nearby are Mono Lake, Glass Creek, Mammoth Lakes, June Lake Loop, Mammoth Creek, Sherwin Creek and Reversed Creek.

# OWENS RIVER (CRESTVIEW)

**Regulations only permit artificial lures with barbless hooks, so fly-fishing dominates.**

| | |
|---|---|
| **Rating:** | 5 |
| **Species:** | Rainbow Trout and Brown Trout |
| **Stock:** | 1,100 pounds of rainbow trout. |
| **Facilities:** | Restrooms and Campgrounds |
| **Contact:** | Inyo National Forest (Mammoth Lakes Visitors Center) (760) 924-5500 |
| | Rick's Sports Center (760) 934-3416 |

**Directions:**   From the junction of Highways 395 and 203 in Mammoth, drive seven miles north to Owens River Road and turn right. Continue two miles to Big Springs Campground on the left.

*Owens River (Crestview)*

Many anglers who plan a trip to the Eastern Sierra truly believe that they're going to catch a huge trout. And due to extensive stocking, it is common for even inexperienced anglers to land lunkers in the Eastern Sierra. But don't expect to catch any big fish in this section of the Owens, although fishing for pan-sized trout is typically fair.

At 7,800 feet in the Inyo National Forest, this stretch of the river, known as Crestview, extends from the Owens' headwaters downstream to where the river crosses under Owens River Road. It is stocked by Alpers Trout Farm with 2,200 half-pound Alpers, which join hundreds of wild rainbow trout. The California Department of Fish and Game does not pay Alpers to plant fish here, however, citing "hygiene" reasons, Tim Alpers says he does it for free. Because the river runs through his ranch, he doesn't want CA DFG-raised fish entering his rearing ponds and mixing with his fish.

Fishing this section is not for everyone. Regulations only permit artificial lures with barbless hooks, so fly-fishing dominates. Although it's possible to use lures, fly-fishermen tend to give dirty looks to spin casters. They think of this as their territory!

If you plan to make the trip, supplies are available in Mammoth. Owens River (Crestview) is closed to fishing from November 16 to the last Saturday in April. There is a two-fish limit, and no fish greater than 16 inches may be kept. Check updated regulations for changes.

Also nearby are Alpers Trout Farms, Deadman Creek, Glass Creek and the Mammoth Lakes.

# ALPERS TROUT FARM

*Raised in water diverted off various springs and the Owens River, the Alpers Ranch produces more than 60,000 pounds of fish each year.*

|  |  |
|---|---|
| **Rating:** | 10 |
| **Species:** | Rainbow Trout and Brown Trout |
| **Stock:** | Periodically. |
| **Facilities:** | Bait & Tackle, Restrooms and Lodging |
| **Contact:** | Alpers Trout Farm (760) 648-7334 |

**Directions:** From Highway 395 in Bishop, drive approximately 40 miles north to the Mammoth Lakes turnoff (Highway 203). Continue 7.3 miles past the turnoff for Highway 203 to Owens River Road and turn right. Drive three miles to the ranch on the left.

People visit Las Vegas to gamble, Yosemite National Park for its breathtaking waterfalls, the Napa Valley to see to the wine country and Monterey for spectacular views of the coast. Anglers, however, come to the Eastern Sierra for a chance to catch the prized Alpers trout.

What is so special about Alpers? Their size for one. Most Alpers stocked in the Sierra are between three and 12 pounds, and although they are raised in a hatchery, they look like wild trout and fight like wild trout. They are an angler's dream fish, and while most anglers think they need to plan an expensive trip to Alaska to land that "once in a lifetime fish," they are wrong; it can happen all along the Sierra.

The Alpers trout is the work of Tim Alpers, who raises the fish on a 210-acre ranch along the Owens River, between Mammoth and June Lake. Raised in water diverted off various springs and the Owens River, the Alpers Ranch produces more than 60,000 pounds of fish each year.

Here's a brief description of the process: Tim locates eggs from the prettiest and largest brood stock fish he can find in the Western United States. After purchasing these eggs, he hatches roughly 120,000 of them a year, and they grow in troughs until they reach three to four inches. At four inches they are held in a small pond that accommodates 80,000 fish, until they grow to six inches, which typically takes about a year.

Now, it's on to the next pond, where 40,000 fish are kept until they grow from six inches to 1.5 pounds. Still not large enough to be planted in streams, these rainbows are then moved into larger fish-holding ponds ("runs"), where they have more room to grow until they are sold. Fed three times a week, it takes three to four years for the trout to reach 10 to 12 pounds. There are 10 runs and one fishing pond on the property.

A better appreciation of the Alpers Ranch requires a quick history lesson. Tim's grandfather bought the ranch in 1906 for the purpose of grazing cattle. Aquaculture (the science of cultivating fish) was practiced here as early as the Teens; however, it was halted during the Depression of the Thirties. In 1952, Tim's father purchased the ranch from his grandfather. Tim was raised as an outdoorsman and went on to study aquaculture, specializing in fisheries, at the University of Nevada, Reno.

For his senior thesis in 1971, Tim designed a fish hatchery, and in August of '71, he began its construction. Shortly after he started work on the hatchery, Tim was given an offer to be the assistant basketball coach at the University of Tulsa and jumped at the opportunity. Soon after his father passed away, Tim returned home in the summer of '79, determined to build the ultimate fish hatchery.

In spring of '84, Tim's dream came true when he stocked 100 two-pound rainbow trout into June Lake, the first Alpers Trout available commercially. From that day on, Alpers Trout have been the ultimate symbol of Eastern Sierra trout fishing. Alpers have helped attract tourists to the region and stimulated the local economy. Inyo and Mono Counties, the Cities of Bishop and Mammoth, Adopt a Creek, various private vendors and resorts all purchase Alpers. They are also served in a few restaurants.

What most anglers don't know is that there is also a 4.75-acre pond on the ranch that is opened to the public. This pond is filled with 50 brown trout, ranging from one to 15 pounds, and 200 to 300 rainbows, most of which are between seven and 12 pounds. The lake record is a 22-pound rainbow.

To fish in the pond, a reservation is required, and there is a $40 fee to fish for a three-hour block of time; however, only float tube fishing with barbless flies is allowed. Fishing is catch & release only. Alpers Creek, which flows through the ranch, is also opened to fishing, and it is stocked with one to two-pound rainbows.

If you plan to make the trip, supplies are available in Mammoth. Reservations are required. No fishing license is required. The ranch is closed in the winter. Call ahead for specific dates.

Also nearby are Owens River (Crestview), Deadman Creek, Glass Creek, Mammoth Lake Loop and June Lake Loop.

ALPERS TROUT FARM

*Tim Alpers poses with one of his Alpers trout.*

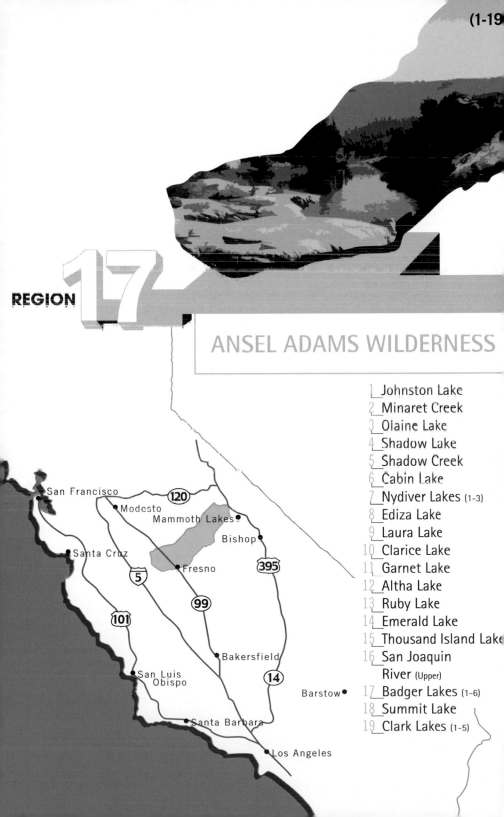

# REGION 17

## ANSEL ADAMS WILDERNESS

1 Johnston Lake
2 Minaret Creek
3 Olaine Lake
4 Shadow Lake
5 Shadow Creek
6 Cabin Lake
7 Nydiver Lakes (1-3)
8 Ediza Lake
9 Laura Lake
10 Clarice Lake
11 Garnet Lake
12 Altha Lake
13 Ruby Lake
14 Emerald Lake
15 Thousand Island Lake
16 San Joaquin
    River (Upper)
17 Badger Lakes (1-6)
18 Summit Lake
19 Clark Lakes (1-5)

San Francisco
Modesto
120
Mammoth Lakes
Bishop
Santa Cruz
395
Fresno
5
99
101
Bakersfield
14
San Luis
Obispo
Barstow
Santa Barbara
Los Angeles

# JOHNSTON LAKE

*A great spot for a picnic, Johnston Lake is a short, pleasant day-hike from the Postpile.*

| | |
|---|---|
| **Rating:** | 3 |
| **Species:** | Rainbow Trout |
| **Stock:** | None |
| **Facilities:** | None |
| **Contact:** | Mammoth Lakes Visitors Center (760) 924-5500, Devil's Postpile National Monument (760) 872-4881 (Winter) or (760) 934-2289 |
| **Directions:** | From Highway 395 in Mammoth, turn west on Mammoth Lakes Road and drive three miles to Minaret Road. Turn north and drive 11.8 miles on Minaret Rd. to the Devils Postpile turnoff. Veer right and continue four-tenths of a mile to the river. The trail can be picked up next to the Visitor's Center. |

*Wildflowers*

While I was having a bite to eat in the Mule House Café at Red's Meadow, the locals began to laugh when I asked how the fishing was at Johnston Lake. "Nobody goes up there. There's too much to do down here," said one man, wearing a "Mule Days" t-shirt and smoking an old pipe. "That place is like a damn swamp." The park ranger at Devils Postpile agreed. "You mean Mosquito Lake," he said jokingly. "I don't even think there are any fish in there."

Despite all the negative comments I'd heard, I hiked to the lake to find out for myself. The locals were right. The tiny, five-acre lake had few trout. Located approximately 8,200 feet in the Ansel Adams Wilderness, about the size of Arrowbear Lake in the San Bernardino National Forest, and Doane Pond in Palomar State Park near San Diego, Johnston Lake is seldom fished.

The far side of the lake is all tules, marshland and weeds. You'd need waders and a mosquito net over your head to fish it. The mosquitoes are thick and nearly unbearable through July. Only the trail side of the lake is fishable. Concentrate on fishing it with small spinners. Anything with blue in it will give you a chance at catching fish.

Johnston Lake is a short, pleasant day-hike from the Postpile, and a great spot for a picnic. To get to it, pick up the trail at the Devils Postpile Visitor Center and follow the trail west towards the Postpile. After about 300 yards, veer right, following signs to Minaret Falls. You'll walk over a bridge on the San Joaquin River and then parallel the river before veering left at the junction with the John Muir Trail. (If you choose to go right, you'll end up at Minaret Falls.) Follow the JM Trail uphill for eight-tenths of a mile to another trail junction. The left spur takes you to Beck Lake. Go right. It's signed for Minaret Lake. About 10 minutes (seven-tenths of a mile) after you cross Minaret Creek, the lake will be on your left. Minaret Creek flows just behind the lake, but doesn't make contact with it.

If desired, you can also reach the lake by taking the right fork at the JM Trail leading to Minaret Falls. There is a small, steep, un-maintained trail on the west side of the falls. If you're an experienced hiker, take this trail above the falls to the Minaret Creek crossing, where you'll pick up the JM Trail. Use caution on this trail. It is very steep and dangerous. If you lose the trail, don't worry. Simply follow the stream to the crossing.

If you plan to make the trip, supplies are available at Red's Meadow Resort. Johnston Lake is closed to fishing from November 16 to the last Saturday in April. Minaret Road generally doesn't open until late June. Call ahead for updated road conditions. No vehicular traffic is permitted from 7:30 a.m. to 5:30 p.m.. Exceptions apply only to those who have campground reservations or reservations at Red's Meadow Resort. Those who arrive during the restricted hours must ride a shuttle into the valley. There is a fee to ride the shuttle and enter the park. Road restrictions are enforced from late June through Labor Day.

Also nearby are Starkweather Lake, Sotcher Lake, Ansel Adams Wilderness, Minaret Falls, Rainbow Falls, San Joaquin River (Middle Fork), Devils Postpile, Minaret Creek and Sotcher Lake Falls.

*Johnston Lake*

JOHNSTON LAKE

My friend and I caught and released more than 20 brookies in less than 10 minutes, using small red and black, yellow, and silver Panther Martins.

| | |
|---|---|
| **Rating:** | 6 |
| **Species:** | Rainbow Trout and Brook Trout |
| **Stock:** | None |
| **Facilities:** | None |
| **Contact:** | Mammoth Lakes Visitors Center (760) 924-5500 |
| | Devil's Postpile National Monument (760) 872-4881 (Winter) or (760) 934-2289 |

**Directions:** From Highway 395 in Mammoth, turn west on Mammoth Lakes Road and continue three miles to Minaret Road. Turn north and drive 11.8 miles on Minaret Rd. to the Devils Postpile turnoff. Veer right and drive four-tenths of a mile to the river. The trail can be picked up next to the visitor center.

*A wild rainbow trout caught at Minaret Creek.*

For those who are sick of fighting the crowds at the San Joaquin River (Middle Fork), Minaret Creek provides an option where the fish might be a lot smaller, but you'll have a lot more elbow room to land 'em. Located in the Ansel Adams Wilderness, this section of the creek is about as wide as Chiquito Creek in the Sierra National Forest, but nowhere near as deep, and stretches from the top of Minaret Falls to Johnston Lake. It offers great fishing for small wild brook trout mixed in with a few rainbows.

With the creek receiving little to no pressure, the fish will hit just about anything. My friend and I caught and released more than 20 brookies in less than 10 minutes, using small red and black, yellow, and silver Panther Martins. The stream has some good-sized pools, but your best bet is fishing under one of the many fallen logs laying half submerged in the water. The pools just above Minaret Falls (below where the John Muir Trail crosses the stream) provide great fishing, but the banks are too steep for most anglers.

To get to Minaret Creek, pick up the trail at the Devils Postpile Visitor Center and follow it west towards the Postpile. After about 300 yards, veer right, following signs to Minaret Falls. You'll walk over a bridge on the San Joaquin River and then parallel the river. Then, veer left at the junction with the John Muir Trail. (If you choose to go right, you'll end up at Minaret Falls.) Follow the JM Trail uphill for eight-tenths of a mile to another trail junction. The left spur takes you to Beck Lake. Take the right path, which is signed for Minaret Lake. It takes about three minutes to walk to the creek.

If you plan to make the trip, supplies are available at Red's Meadow Resort. Minaret Creek is closed to fishing from November 16 to the last Saturday in April. Trailhead access restrictions for Johnston Lake also apply to Minaret Creek.

Also nearby are Starkweather Lake, Sotcher Lake, the Ansel Adams Wilderness, Minaret Falls, Rainbow Falls, the San Joaquin River (Middle Fork), Devils Postpile, Johnston Lake and Sotcher Lake Falls.

# OLAINE LAKE

*The only reason anglers bother with it at all is rainbow trout. There are plenty of them to go around, however, size is a problem.*

| | |
|---|---|
| **Rating:** | 4 |
| **Species:** | Rainbow Trout |
| **Stock:** | Two pounds of fingerling rainbow trout. |
| **Facilities:** | None |
| **Contact:** | Mammoth Lakes Visitors Center (760) 924-5500, Devil's Postpile National Monument (760) 872-4881 (Winter) or (760) 934-2289, Red's Meadow Pack Station (760) 934-2345 or (800) 292-7758, Inyo National Forest Wilderness Permits (760) 873-2483 |
| **Directions:** | From Highway 395 in Mammoth, turn west on Mammoth Lakes Road and drive three miles to Minaret Road and turn right. Continue approximately 7.9 miles on Minaret Rd. to the trailhead on your right. |

*Olaine Lake*

At 8,120 feet in the Ansel Adams Wilderness, Olaine Lake is one of the lowest hike-to lakes in the Eastern Sierra, but its usage doesn't reflect the easy walk to its shores. Despite the fact that Olaine Lake is easy to get to, it is one of the least popular high-county lakes in the region, and few anglers fish it.

The only reason anglers bother with it all is rainbow trout. There are plenty of them to go around, however, size is a problem. Most of the fish are dinkers, anywhere from six to nine inches. Few grow to larger proportions.

This heavily shaded seven-acre lake, surrounded by blooming wildflowers in spring and early summer, is really more of a pond. Weeds cover most of its shoreline, allowing anglers little access. Although there are a few small openings on the south shoreline, the best access is on the lake's southwest shore. Providing anglers with a nearby option the San Joaquin River runs directly behind the lake, but the two don't connect.

To reach Olaine Lake, begin at the Agnew Meadow Trailhead, staying above the San Joaquin River. Follow the Shadow Trail, crossing two small streams. In four-tenths of a mile you'll come to a junction. The left fork takes you to Red's Meadow. Stay right and continue 1.2 miles to the lake. (You'll pass another trail junction that also takes you to Red's Meadow.)

If you plan to make the trip, supplies are available at Red's Meadow Resort and Mammoth Lakes. Trailhead access restrictions for Johnston Lake also apply to Olaine Lake. A wilderness permit is required for overnight travel in the Ansel Adams Wilderness.

Also nearby are Shadow Creek, Shadow Creek Falls, Shadow Lake, Ediza Lake, Cabin Lake, the Nydiver Lakes, Shadow Lake Falls, Nydiver Lake Falls, Devils Postpile National Monument and Starkweather Lake.

# SHADOW LAKE

**The lake is stocked with 20,000 fingerling rainbow trout each year, not to mention holdovers from years past and a stable brook trout population.**

| | |
|---|---|
| **Rating:** | 7 |
| **Species:** | Rainbow Trout and Brook Trout |
| **Stock:** | 20 pounds of fingerling rainbow trout. |
| **Facilities:** | None |
| **Contact:** | Mammoth Lakes Visitors Center (760) 924-5500, Devil's Postpile National Monument (760) 872-4881 (Winter) or (760) 934-2289, Red's Meadow Pack Station (760) 934-2345 or (800) 292-7758, Inyo National Forest Wilderness Permits (760) 873-2483 |

**Directions:** From Highway 395 in Mammoth, turn west on Mammoth Lakes Road and drive three miles to Minaret Road. Turn north and drive approximately 7.9 miles on Minaret Rd. to the trailhead on your right.

*Shadow Lake*

The moment you get your first glimpse of Shadow Lake, you'll know why people come to the Ansel Adams Wilderness, and why it's so hard to obtain a wilderness permit to back pack in this area. With clean air, clear blue water, pine trees all around, towering snowcapped peaks in the distance, and a small waterfall tumbling into the lake, this majestic wilderness is what hikers call heaven. Best of all, it's close enough for day-hikers to make an easy trip or for a family picnic.

At 8,800 feet, this 51-acre lake is only a three-mile hike with a 460-foot elevation gain from the Agnew Meadow Trailhead. As for the fishing, it doesn't get as much attention as it deserves. Most anglers pass on it, thinking the lake's too close to the trailhead for good fishing. They usually continue on to more popular fishing lakes such as Ediza, Garnet and the Thousand Island Lakes.

Don't pass it up too quickly! The lake is stocked with 20,000 fingerling rainbow trout each year, not to mention holdovers from years past and a stable brook trout population. Your best bet is to start fishing the inlet and work your way around the shoreline. Try Thomas Buoyants or Kastmasters.

To reach Shadow Lake from Olaine Lake, take the Shadow Lake Trail past a small stream, until you come to a trail junction. Stay left, veering away from the River Trail. Walk over a bridge across the San Joaquin River and begin to climb up some fairly easy switchbacks. As you reach the top of the switchbacks, you'll get a close glimpse of Shadow Lake Falls on your left. The lake is just past the falls.

If you plan to make the trip, supplies are available at Red's Meadow Resort and in Mammoth Lakes. Trailhead access restrictions for Johnston Lake also apply to Shadow Lake. A wilderness permit is required for overnight travel in the Ansel Adams Wilderness.

Also nearby are Shadow Creek, Shadow Creek Falls, Ediza Lake, Olaine Lake, Cabin Lake, Nydiver Lakes, Shadow Lake Falls, and Nydiver Lake Falls.

*next page Shadow Lake*

**The majority of the fish you'll catch are brooks, with a few rainbows mixed in.**

| | |
|---|---|
| **Rating:** | 5 |
| **Species:** | Rainbow Trout and Brook Trout |
| **Stock:** | None |
| **Facilities:** | None |
| **Contact:** | Mammoth Lakes Visitors Center (760) 924-5500, Devil's Postpile National Monument (760) 872-4881 (Winter) or (760) 934-2289, Red's Meadow Pack Station (760) 934-2345 or (800) 292-7758, Inyo National Forest Wilderness Permits (760) 873-2483 |
| **Directions:** | From Highway 395 in Mammoth, turn west on Mammoth Lakes Road and continue three miles to Minaret Road. Turn north and drive approximately 7.9 miles on Minaret Road to the Agnew Meadow Trailhead on your right. |

*The Shadow Creek Drainage upstream of Shadow Lake*

Shadow Creek is nearly a replica of its neighbor Minaret Creek. Both are fed by high-country lakes, both end in waterfalls before emptying into the San Joaquin River, and both are located in the Ansel Adams Wilderness and seldom fished, but loaded with brook and rainbow trout. One difference, Minaret Falls located on Minaret Creek is far more popular than Shadow Lake Falls located on Shadow Creek.

Shadow Creek is rarely fished throughout the 3.3-mile stretch from Ediza Lake to the San Joaquin River. Much of the neglect is due to the fact that there are so many other streams, as well as a handful of popular lakes, to fish in the area. Similar to Minaret Creek, some portions of Shadow Creek are unfishable, particularly where it flows through steep, narrow canyons, such as the one between Shadow Lake and the San Joaquin River. Don't even bother trying to fish it.

Concentrate your efforts from Shadow Lake upstream to Ediza Lake. This section of the river has waterfalls, large pools, fast moving water and slow moving sections, which meander through large meadows. The majority of the fish you'll catch are brooks, with a few rainbows mixed in. Few of the fish are over eight inches, but there are plenty to be caught by anglers tossing size 1/16 Panther Martins.

If you plan to make the trip, supplies are available at Red's Meadow Resort and in Mammoth Lakes. Trailhead access restrictions for Johnston Lake also apply to Shadow Creek. Shadow Creek is closed to fishing from November 16 through the last Saturday in April. A wilderness permit is required for overnight travel in the Ansel Adams Wilderness.

Also nearby are Minaret Creek, Shadow Creek Falls, Shadow Lake, Ediza Lake, Cabin Lake, Nydiver Lakes, Shadow Lake Falls, Olaine Lake, Nydiver Lake Falls, Devils Postpile National Monument and Starkweather Lake.

# CABIN LAKE

**Cabin's only six-acres and hard to find, but it's the least-fished lake in the Shadow Creek Drainage, so it can offer good fishing for pan-sized goldens, particularly because it is so seldom fished.**

| | |
|---|---|
| **Rating:** | 7 |
| **Species:** | Golden Trout |
| **Stock:** | Two pounds of fingerling golden trout. |
| **Facilities:** | None |
| **Contact:** | Mammoth Lakes Visitors Center (760) 924-5500, Devil's Postpile National Monument (760) 872-4881 (Winter) or (760) 934-2289, Red's Meadow Pack Station (760) 934-2345 or (800) 292-7758, Inyo National Forest Wilderness Permits (760) 873-2483 |
| **Directions:** | From Highway 395 in Mammoth, turn west on Mammoth Lakes Road and continue three miles to Minaret Road. Turn north and drive approximately 7.9 miles to the Agnew Meadows Trailhead on your right. |

*Cabin Lake*

If you don't have good route-finding skills, then don't bother coming to Cabin Lake. At 9,520 feet in the Ansel Adams Wilderness, just northwest of Shadow Lake, Cabin Lake can be difficult to find even for experienced hikers and backpackers. The lake should really be called "Hidden Lake," because it is so well hidden in a small basin 500 feet above Shadow Creek. There is no trail to the lake, either. It can only be reached by locating its outlet stream and following it up to the lake.

That's not to say that we were successful on our first try. We found two streams running down the steep mountainside, but couldn't figure out which one was Cabin Lake's outlet stream, and we ended up walking up to the Nydiver Lakes. Because the Nydiver Lakes are at a higher elevation than Cabin Lake, we could see the entire Cabin Lake from the outlet of Lower Nydiver Lake. From this point, at 10,100 feet, it was also obvious that Cabin Lake was still frozen over, even though it was in the middle of July.

Finding the lake without first spotting it from Lower Nydiver Lake can be tricky. Begin at Shadow Lake and continue to the north end. Coming to a junction where the Shadow Lake Trail joins with the John Muir Trail, the left fork leads to Rosalie Lake, Johnston Lake and Devil's Postpile National Monument. Stay right, following the JM Trail for a mile to another trail junction. This time, veer left onto the Ediza Lake Trial, hiking away from the JM Trail. Just past the trail junction, a small stream can be seen tumbling down the mountain on the other side of Shadow Creek. This stream comes from a small glacier, not Cabin Lake. The next stream that flows down the far mountainside is Cabin Lake's outlet stream. When you see it, carefully cross Shadow Creek (it will be difficult until late August), and follow the stream uphill to the lake.

Cabin and Iceberg Lakes are the only two in the drainage that have golden trout. Cabin was last stocked with 2,000 fingerling golden trout in 2000. Cabin's only six-acres and hard to find, but it's the least-fished lake in the Shadow Creek Drainage, so it can offer good fishing for pan-sized goldens, particularly because it is so seldom fished. The best time is right after ice-out, usually sometime from mid- to late-July. Just about any small spinner will work.

If you plan to make the trip, supplies are available at Red's Meadow Resort and in Mammoth Lakes. Call ahead for lake conditions. After severe winters, the lake can remain frozen-over until early August. Minaret Road usually doesn't open until late June. Call ahead for updated road conditions. No vehicular traffic is permitted from 7:30 a.m. to 5:30 p.m. Exceptions apply only to those who have campground reservations or reservations at Red's Meadow Resort. Those who arrive during the restricted hours must ride a shuttle into the valley. There is a fee to ride the shuttle and enter the park. Road restrictions run from late June through Labor Day.

Also nearby are Shadow Creek, Shadow Creek Falls, Ediza Lake, Olaine Lake, Nydiver Lakes, Shadow Lake, Shadow Lake Falls, Nydiver Lake Falls, Devils Postpile National Monument and Starkweather Lake.

*Cabin Lake still frozen over in July of 2000*

CABIN LAKE

# NYDIVER LAKES

**Because they are located off the John Muir and Pacific Crest Trail, and there is no formal trail to the lakes, visitor usage remains low.**

**Rating:** 7
**Species:** Brook Trout
**Stock:** None
**Facilities:** None
**Contact:** Mammoth Lakes Visitors Center (760) 924-5500, Devil's Postpile National Monument (760) 872-4881 (Winter) or (760) 934-2289, Red's Meadow Pack Station (760) 934-2345 or (800) 292-7758, Inyo National Forest Wilderness Permits (760) 873-2483

**Directions:** From Highway 395 in Mammoth, turn west on Mammoth Lakes Road and drive three miles to Minaret Road and turn right. Continue approximately 7.9 miles on Minaret Rd. to the Agnew Meadow Trailhead on your right.

*Wildflowers found only at high elevations.*

When I first arrived at the Nydiver Lakes, I couldn't believe what I saw. "Is this really California?" I asked myself. It was the second week of July and the lake was partially frozen-over. There were chunks of ice that looked like small icebergs bobbing up and down all around the lake. The surrounding mountain peaks and the lake's shoreline were still covered in snow.

At 10,100 feet in the Ansel Adams Wilderness, the picturesque Nydiver Lakes offer breathtaking views of the surrounding drainage. If you walk to the top of any mountain south of the lakes, you'll get a view you'll never forget. Cabin Lake is directly across, hidden in a small hard-to-see basin, and it is one of a few lakes in the drainage that has golden trout. To your right will be Ediza Lake; above Ediza is Iceberg Lake, which remains frozen until late July; and Shadow Lake on the left. I used an entire roll of film here, as I'm sure you will, too.

Nydiver Lakes are a set of three small lakes that, unlike most lakes in the region, aren't bombarded by visitors. Because they are located off the John Muir and Pacific Crest Trail, and there is no formal trail to the lakes, visitor usage remains low. Fishing is fair for the self-sustaining population of brook trout that inhabit all of the lakes. No other species are present.

Like the panoramas viewed from the mountains that surround them, the vistas from the lakes are also spectacular, with Banner Peak (12,936 feet) and Mt. Ritter (13,143 feet) directly in front of you. The tops of these peaks mark the boundary between the Sierra and Inyo National Forests.

Six-acre Lower Nydiver is the smallest and narrowest of the three lakes. It has some steep drop-offs and a shallow inlet. If you walk to the lake's outlet, you can see Mammoth Mountain in the distance. Due to snow, the west side is usually inaccessible until early August. Because the lake is so small, you don't need to use larger lures to reach its deeper waters. Try using silver Kastmasters, Panther Martins and Phoebes.

Located just above the lower lake, Middle Nydiver, at eight acres, has a long outlet channel in which the brookies swim back and forth searching for food. The lake is shaped like a foot, and its channel is shaped like an ankle leading to that foot

Thirteen-acre Upper Nydiver, situated at the base of Mt. Ritter and Banner Peak, usually doesn't begin to thaw until mid-July. There are many small glaciers between the lake and the peaks above, giving the mountains a snow-capped look year-round. The peaks look so close you could touch them, but, in reality, they are a difficult climb away.

Instead of walking the easier, more traveled, longer (4.6 miles) route to Garnet Lake, another popular thing to do is to take the shorter, less traveled, more adventurous route. I think it's actually easier than taking the maintained trail, and it's four miles shorter. Garnet is located just over the ridge northeast of the Nydiver Lakes. All you need to do is walk over the smaller, less-steep mountains to the east (no, not Banner Peak) above Upper Nydiver Lake. When you get to the top, you'll be able to see Garnet Lake. Then, simply make the descent to the lake and you'll have saved yourself a few hours.

To reach the Nydiver Lakes from Shadow Lake, continue to the north end of Shadow Lake, where you will come to a junction with the John Muir Trail. The left fork takes you to Rosalie Lake, Johnston Lake and Devil's Postpile National Monument, however, you want to stay right, where the Shadow Lake Trail joins with the John Muir Trail. Follow the JM Trail for about a mile to another junction. This time you'll veer left onto the Ediza Lake Trail, walking away from the JM Trail. Parallel Shadow Creek and climb over two small mountains, each with short switchbacks, before coming to your first stream crossing. This is Nydiver Creek. From this point to the lakes, you'll continue on a faint trail that fades in and out throughout your journey to the lakes. There is no formal trail.

The easiest and best way to avoid getting lost is to follow the creek to the lakes. After 10 minutes of following it, the stream forks. Take the left fork that passes by the three (Lower, Middle and Upper) Nydiver Falls, and in just over a half-mile you'll come to Lower Nydiver Lake. Middle and Upper Nydiver Lakes are directly above.

If you plan to make the trip, supplies are available at Red's Meadow Resort and Mammoth Lakes. Call ahead for lake conditions. After severe winters, the lake can remain frozen-over until early August. Minaret Road usually doesn't open until late June. Call ahead for updated road conditions. No vehicular traffic is permitted from 7:30 a.m. to 5:30 p.m. Exceptions apply only to those who have campground reservations or reservations at Red's Meadow Resort. Those who arrive during the restricted hours must ride a shuttle into the valley. There is a fee to ride the shuttle and enter the park. Road restrictions run from late June through Labor Day. A wilderness permit is required for overnight travel in the Ansel Adams Wilderness.

Also nearby are Shadow Creek, Shadow Creek Falls, Ediza Lake, Olaine Lake, Cabin Lake, Shadow Lake, Shadow Lake Falls, Nydiver Lake Falls, Devils Postpile National Monument and Starkweather Lake.

NYDIVER LAKES

*It appears on postcards, brochures, at tourist bureaus and hangs on the walls of restaurants.*

| | |
|---|---|
| **Rating:** | 7 |
| **Species:** | Rainbow Trout and Brook Trout |
| **Stock:** | Five pounds of fingerling rainbow trout. |
| **Facilities:** | None |
| **Contact:** | Mammoth Lakes Visitors Center (760) 924-5500, Devil's Postpile National Monument (760) 872-4881 (Winter) or (760) 934-2289, Red's Meadow Pack Station (760) 934-2345 or (800) 292-7758, Inyo National Forest Wilderness Permits (760) 873-2483 |

**Directions:**  From Highway 395 in Mammoth, turn west on Mammoth Lakes Road and continue three miles to Minaret Road. Turn north and drive approximately 7.9 miles on Minaret Rd. to the trailhead on your right.

*The view of Ediza Lake from Lower Nydiver Lake*

To both anglers and hikers, Ediza Lake is the most well known lake in the Shadow Creek Drainage. Many hikers pass by Ediza on their way to less-fished lakes like Iceberg and Cecile Lake. Ediza is also the most photographed lake in the region. It appears on post-cards, brochures, at tourist bureaus and hangs on the walls of restaurants. And, as you guessed, it also gets crowded.

At 25 acres, Ediza is half the size of Shadow Lake, and at 9,300 feet in the Ansel Adams Wilderness, it also a popular spot for bears and mosquitoes. Bears do their grocery shopping in backpacker's packs at night, but the mosquitoes attack all day and can be unbearable in late June and July. You need a net over your head and gloves to fend off of the mosquitoes.

The fishing can be as good as the photo opportunities. The lake is stocked with 7,000 fingerling rainbows that join holdovers from years past. Ediza also has a stable brook trout population. Most of the fish are pan-sized, with the best bite coming in the evenings near the inlets and outlet.

To reach Ediza Lake from Shadow Lake, continue to the north end of the lake, where you'll come to a junction with the John Muir Trail. The left fork leads to Rosalie Lake, Johnston Lake and Devil's Postpile National Monument. Stay right, following the JM Trail for about a mile to another trail junction. Veer left onto the Ediza Lake Trail, walking away from the JM Trail. The trail parallels Shadow Creek and climbs over two small mountains with short switchbacks before coming to its first stream crossing at Nydiver Creek. Shortly after crossing the creek, you'll come to a fallen tree that will act as a bridge to get you across Shadow Creek. After walking over the tree, loop around a mountain and you'll come to the lake. Total distance from Shadow Lake is three miles.

If you plan to make the trip, supplies are available at Red's Meadow Resort and in Mammoth Lakes. Minaret Road usually doesn't open until late June. Call ahead for updated road conditions. No vehicular traffic is permitted from 7:30 a.m. to 5:30 p.m. Exceptions apply only to those who have campground reservations or reservations at Red's Meadow Resort. Those who arrive during the restricted hours must ride a shuttle into the valley. There is a fee to ride the shuttle and enter the park. Road restrictions run from June through Labor Day.

Also nearby are Shadow Creek, Shadow Creek Falls, Cabin Lake, Olaine Lake, Nydiver Lakes, Shadow Lake, Shadow Lake Falls, Nydiver Lake Falls, Devils Postpile National Monument and Starkweather Lake.

# LAURA LAKE

**Plan on bringing along a small frying pan. Rarely does a fish over nine inches come out of the lake.**

| | |
|---|---|
| **Rating:** | 6 |
| **Species:** | Rainbow Trout |
| **Stock:** | None |
| **Facilities:** | None |
| **Contact:** | Mammoth Lakes Visitors Center (760) 924-5500, Devil's Postpile National Monument (760) 872-4881 (Winter) or (760) 934-2289, Red's Meadow Pack Station (760) 934-2345 or (800) 292-7758, Inyo National Forest Wilderness Permits (760) 873-2483 |
| **Directions:** | From Interstate 395 in Mammoth, turn west on Mammoth Lakes Road and drive three miles to Minaret Road. Turn north and drive approximately 7.9 miles on Minaret Rd. to the trailhead on your right. |

*Laura Lake from above*

Laura is a small lake in the Ansel Adams Wilderness, to which horse packers love to bring customers. It has some nice large open dirt areas shaded by pines, which are ideal for camping. Because few others can even find the lake, those who come here on pack trips are almost the only ones to use these areas. There are no signs or formal trails leading here, and that's one of the reasons there are not a lot of visitors. This provides anglers with a definite opportunity to dodge crowds and catch small rainbow trout.

At 9,600 feet in Madera County near Clarice Lake, mountains border the north side of Laura Lake. There is good access for anglers, who mostly fish with small white Panther Martins and blue Roostertails along the trail side of the lake. Plan on bringing along a small frying pan. Rarely does a fish over nine inches come out of the lake.

To reach Laura Lake from the junction of the Ediza Lake Trail and John Muir Trails, veer right, following the John Muir Trail uphill for about 30 minutes. Keep an eye out for a small, unnamed stream on the right side of the trail. (It may be dry by late summer.) After crossing over the stream, veer right again, following the stream. The foot-warn but unsigned trail begins after you cross the stream. The only way to know if you are on the right path is by looking for horse tracks and/or horse droppings. After following the trail for roughly three-tenths of a mile, you'll come to a small meadow overlooking the San Joaquin River Drainage. Descend down through an area heavily shaded by trees. Laura Lake is less than two-tenths of a mile ahead.

If you plan to make the trip, supplies are available at Red's Meadow Resort and in Mammoth Lakes. Trailhead access restrictions for Ediza Lake also apply to Laura Lake.

Also nearby are Ruby Lake, Emerald Lake, Clarice Lake, Altha Lake, Garnet Lake, Thousand Island Lake, Shadow Lake, Garnet Lake Falls and Shadow Creek Falls.

# CLARICE LAKE

*The lake is home to a few trout, but most are tiny, anywhere from six to nine inches. Try using any small spinner.*

|  |  |
|---|---|
| **Rating:** | 5 |
| **Species:** | Rainbow Trout |
| **Stock:** | None |
| **Facilities:** | None |
| **Contact:** | Mammoth Lakes Visitors Center (760) 924-5500, Devil's Postpile National Monument (760) 872-4881 (Winter) or (760) 934-2289, Red's Meadow Pack Station (760) 934-2345 or (800) 292-7758, Inyo National Forest Wilderness Permits (760) 873-2483 |
| **Directions:** | From Highway 395 in Mammoth, turn west on Mammoth Lakes Road and continue three miles to Minaret Road. Turn north and drive approximately 7.9 miles on Minaret Rd. to the trailhead on your right. |

*Clarice Lake with Mt. Ritter and Banner Peak in the backdrop*

The best thing Clarice Lake has to offer is the view from its surrounding mountains; that is, if you have the endurance to climb above the lake to get a glimpse of these spectacular vistas. From this lofty perspective, Clarice Lake looks minuscule compared to Garnet Lake, Laura Lake, Mammoth Mountain and the San Joaquin River Drainage, all framed by magnificent panoramas.

Anglers rarely fish this five-acre lake, mostly because they can't find it. At 9,925 feet in the Ansel Adams Wilderness, the hard-to-find shallow lake is well hidden between four mountains. The lake is home to a few trout, but most are tiny, anywhere from six to nine inches. Try using any small spinner.

Many anglers dispute the type of trout that inhabit the lake. I talked to a few who insist they caught golden trout, while others say they caught rainbows. I couldn't get any of them to bite, so I can't add my two-cents to the argument.

There are two ways to reach Clarice Lake from Laura Lake. The first way is to walk to the top of the mountain directly behind Laura Lake, and then proceed down the mountain to Clarice Lake. The second way is to walk over the mountains just east of Laura Lake, and from the top you'll get a clear view of Clarice. Both ways only require about 100 yards of uphill climbing and neither includes trails. Its sounds difficult, but it's not. There is really no easier way to get to the lake. I was told there is a trail that veers off from the path to Laura Lake, but I looked carefully and had no luck locating it. Good luck.

If you plan to make the trip, supplies are available at Red's Meadow Resort and in Mammoth Lakes. Trailhead access restrictions for Ediza Lake also apply to Clarice Lake. A wilderness permit is required for overnight travel in the Ansel Adams Wilderness.

Also nearby are Ruby Lake, Emerald Lake, Laura Lake, Altha Lake, Garnet Lake, Thousand Island Lake, Shadow Lake, Garnet Lake Falls and Shadow Creek Falls.

# GARNET LAKE

*There are seven separate chains on the lake, comprising more than 100 tiny islands.*

| | |
|---|---|
| **Rating:** | 10 |
| **Species:** | Rainbow Trout and Brook Trout |
| **Stock:** | 20 pounds of fingerling rainbow trout. |
| **Facilities:** | None |
| **Contact:** | Mammoth Lakes Visitors Center (760) 924-5500, Devil's Postpile National Monument (760) 872-4881 (Winter) or (760) 934-2289, Red's Meadow Pack Station (760) 934-2345 or (800) 292-7758, Inyo National Forest Wilderness Permits (760) 873-2483 |
| **Directions:** | From Highway 395 in Mammoth, turn west on Mammoth Lakes Road and continue three miles to Minaret Road. Turn north and drive approximately 7.9 miles on Minaret Rd. to the trailhead on your right. |

*Garnet Lake*

Along with nearby Thousand Island Lake, Garnet is one of the premier lakes in the region. Offering great scenery for photo opportunities, good fishing and hiking, it excels in just about every category.

At 9,840 feet in the Ansel Adams Wilderness, 212-acre Garnet is the second largest lake in the region. Only 320-acre Thousand Island Lake is larger. Garnet is also heavily stocked, receiving 18,000 fingerling rainbow trout, the same as Shadow Lake, but 9,000 less than Thousand Island Lake.

These hefty plants make for fair to good fishing. With the bountiful stocks, many trout peak in the 14-inch class. The lake also holds many brook trout. Try fishing off the points or in coves with larger spinners, such as Thomas Buoyants.

The lake is also known for its islands. There are seven separate chains on the lake, comprising more than 100 tiny islands.

To reach Garnet Lake, hike to the north end of Shadow Lake, where you'll come to a junction with the John Muir Trail. The left fork leads to Rosalie Lake, Johnston Lake and Devil's Postpile National Monument. Stay right, following the JM Trail for about a mile to another trail junction. Where the Shadow Lake Trail joins with the John Muir Trail, veer right, staying on the JM Trail, and ascend 2.5 miles to the lake's outlet, where you'll find yourself in a small cove on the southeast shore. Walk over a small wooden bridge, and continue on the trail to the main body of the lake. From here, you'll get spectacular views of Banner Peak and Mt. Ritter. They don't even look like the same mountains that are also seen from the Nydiver Lakes.

If you plan to make the trip, supplies are available at Red's Meadow Resort and in Mammoth Lakes. Trailhead access restrictions for Ediza Lake also apply to Garnet Lake.

Also nearby are Ruby Lake, Emerald Lake, Clarice Lake, Laura Lake, Altha Lake, Thousand Island Lake, Shadow Lake, Garnet Lake Falls and Shadow Creek Falls.

**The lake only holds rainbow trout, but the evening bite is incredible in the summer.**

| | |
|---|---|
| **Rating:** | 6 |
| **Species:** | Rainbow Trout |
| **Stock:** | None |
| **Facilities:** | None |
| **Contact:** | Mammoth Lakes Visitors Center (760) 924-5500, Devil's Postpile National Monument (760) 872-4881 (Winter) or (760) 934-2289, Red's Meadow Pack Station (760) 934-2345 or (800) 292-7758, Inyo National Forest Wilderness Permits (760) 873-2483 |
| **Directions:** | From Highway 395 in Mammoth, turn west on Mammoth Lakes Road and continue three miles to Minaret Road. Turn north and drive approximately 7.9 miles on Minaret Rd. |

*Altha Lake at sunset*

Although Altha and Garnet Lakes are only three-tenths of a mile apart, they differ greatly in size and popularity. Garnet is much larger and is visited by a lot more anglers. In fact, Altha has traditionally been one of the least popular lakes in the region.

However, recent changes in Garnet Lake's camping regulations have forced backpackers to open their eyes to nearby Altha Lake. With heavy restrictions placed on camping at Garnet, backpackers have begun to discover that Altha is a quiet spot with attractive campgrounds. What used to be a seldom-visited lake can now get crowded in the evenings when Garnet's overflow comes looking for a place to camp.

At 9,680 feet in the Ansel Adams Wilderness, the 14-acre lake provides good fishing to its visitors. The lake only holds rainbow trout, but the evening bite is incredible in the summer. Each time I retrieved my lure, I saw at least half-a-dozen rainbows fighting over which would be first to get the next bite. This was the only lake in the Sierra where I couldn't get the rainbows to bite Panther Martins. They were only interested in silver and gold Kastmasters, and red and gold Thomas Buoyants.

To reach Altha Lake from the Garnet Lake outlet, veer right off the John Muir Trail, walking away from the lake. A small outlet pool and Garnet Lake Falls will be on your left. In a tad more than one-tenth of a mile, at the base of the falls, veer right again on a small trail spur that leads to the lake, a quarter-mile ahead. The lake can also be reached by a short 15-minute hike from Laura Lake. From Laura Lake, walk north, staying between the tall mountains on your left and the drop-off for the San Joaquin River Drainage on your right.

If you plan to make the trip, supplies are available at Red's Meadow Resort and in Mammoth Lakes. Trailhead access restrictions for Ediza Lake also apply to Altha Lake.

Also nearby are Ruby Lake, Emerald Lake, Clarice Lake, Laura Lake, Garnet Lake, Thousand Island Lake, Shadow Lake, Garnet Lake Falls and Shadow Creek Falls.

# RUBY LAKE

*If you need to take a quick rest here, it might be worth making a few casts.*

| | |
|---|---|
| **Rating:** | 7 |
| **Species:** | Rainbow Trout |
| **Stock:** | One pound of fingerling rainbow trout. |
| **Facilities:** | None |
| **Contact:** | Mammoth Lakes Visitors Center (760) 924-5500, Devil's Postpile National Monument (760) 872-4881 (Winter) or (760) 934-2289, Red's Meadow Pack Station (760) 934-2345 or (800) 292-7758, Inyo National Forest Wilderness Permits (760) 873-2483 |
| **Directions:** | From Highway 395 in Mammoth, turn west on Mammoth Lakes Road and continue three miles to Minaret Road. Turn north and drive approximately 7.9 miles on Minaret Rd. to the trailhead on your right. |

*Ruby Lake*

I was a little disappointed when I got my first glimpse of Ruby Lake. Because of the name "Ruby," I was expecting a beautiful lake in a picturesque setting, but my expectations weren't totally satisfied. There were no awe-inspiring views of a surrounding wilderness or towering snow-capped peaks overhead.

Ruby Lake is almost identical in size and appearance to nearby Laura, Clarice and Altha Lakes. Located just below 10,000 feet in the Ansel Adams Wilderness, this small (10-acre) lake offers fair fishing for small rainbow trout. Because it's along the John Muir Trail, near Emerald Lake between Thousand Island and Garnet Lakes, hundreds of backpackers walk by daily, but few stop to fish it.

Only the trail side of the lake is fishable. The far side is made up of steep cliffs that are mostly covered with snow until early August. If you need to take a quick rest here, it might be worth making a few casts. Try tying on a Kastmaster or any lure that will sink fast. The lake has steep drop-offs, and many of the fish stay in deeper water.

To reach Ruby Lake from Garnet Lake, walk north on the John Muir Trail, climbing up some short switchbacks. Don't forget to take note of the stunning view of the lake. At the top of the mountain, you'll lose site of Garnet Lake and descend towards Ruby Lake. It's visible through the trees, and after a few short switchbacks, you'll arrive there. The entire trip is about three-quarters of a mile.

If you plan to make the trip, supplies are available at Red's Meadow Resort and in Mammoth Lakes. Minaret Road usually doesn't open until late June. Trailhead access restrictions for Ediza Lake also apply to Ruby Lake. A wilderness permit is required for overnight travel in the Ansel Adams Wilderness.

Also nearby are Garnet Lake, Emerald Lake, Clarice Lake, Laura Lake, Altha Lake, Thousand Island Lake, Shadow Lake, Garnet Lake Falls and Shadow Creek Falls.

# EMERALD LAKE

**Only a quarter-mile from Thousand Island Lake, Emerald sees a lot of traffic during the day, so concentrate on fishing in the early morning or late evening.**

| | |
|---|---|
| **Rating:** | 6 |
| **Species:** | Rainbow Trout |
| **Stock:** | One pound of fingerling rainbow trout. |
| **Facilities:** | None |
| **Contact:** | Mammoth Lakes Visitors Center (760) 924-5500, Devil's Postpile National Monument (760) 872-4881 (Winter) or (760) 934-2289, Red's Meadow Pack Station (760) 934-2345 or (800) 292-7758, Inyo National Forest Wilderness Permits (760) 873-2483 |
| **Directions:** | From Highway 395 in Mammoth, turn west on Mammoth Lakes Road and continue three miles to Minaret Road. Turn north and drive approximately 7.9 miles on Minaret Rd. to the trailhead on your right. |

*Emerald Lake*

Emerald Lake is visited for the same reason as nearby Altha Lake: its camping spots. With new restrictions put on camping at Thousand Island Lake, many backpackers head to Emerald Lake in search of a place to stake their tent for the night. In addition to the camping spots, anglers find fair rainbow trout fishing in the evenings.

At 9,880 feet in the Ansel Adams Wilderness, this seven-acre lake is shallow and seldom fished. It is shaped like a ghost costume worn on Halloween night. There is a small head on the east end, with two small islands (like holes for eyes), and the main body of the lake is like a sheet dangling from a head.

Although ghosts don't spook the lake at night, bears do. They visit in search of people food almost every night in the summer and fall, so be sure to use proper food storage methods.

Only a quarter-mile from Thousand Island Lake, Emerald sees a lot of traffic during the day, so concentrate on fishing in the early morning or late evening.

To reach Emerald Lake from Ruby Lake, hike east on the John Muir Trail, gradually climbing uphill for the first one-tenth of a mile. At the top of the hill, you'll get your first glimpse of the lake. Then, descend over the next three-tenths of a mile to the lake.

If you plan to make the trip, supplies are available at Red's Meadow Resort and in Mammoth Lakes. Minaret Road usually doesn't open until late June. Call ahead for updated road conditions. No vehicular traffic is permitted from 7:30 a.m. to 5:30 p.m. Exceptions apply only to those who have campground reservations or reservations at Red's Meadow Resort. Those who arrive during the restricted hours must ride a shuttle into the valley. There is a fee to ride the shuttle and enter the park. Road restrictions run from late June through Labor Day.

Also nearby are Garnet Lake, Ruby Lake, Clarice Lake, Laura Lake, Altha Lake, Thousand Island Lake, Shadow Lake, Garnet Lake Falls and Shadow Creek Falls.

# THOUSAND ISLAND LAKE

**With more than six miles of shoreline, the lake can take a while to fish if you try to walk all the way around it.**

| | |
|---|---|
| **Rating:** | 9 |
| **Species:** | Rainbow Trout and Brook Trout |
| **Stock:** | 30 pounds of fingerling rainbow trout. |
| **Facilities:** | None |
| **Contact:** | Mammoth Lakes Visitors Center (760) 924-5500, Devil's Postpile National Monument (760) 872-4881 (Winter) or (760) 934-2289, Red's Meadow Pack Station (760) 934-2345 or (800) 292-7758, Inyo National Forest Wilderness Permits (760) 873-2483 |
| **Directions:** | From Highway 395 in Mammoth, turn west on Mammoth Lakes Road and drive three miles to Minaret Road. Turn north and drive approximately 7.9 miles to the trailhead on your right. |

*Thousand Island Lake is one of the best fisheries in the Ansel Adams Wilderness.*

When I first arrived at Thousand Island Lake, I was left with an empty feeling in my stomach. "This is it?" I asked my hiking partner. "Are you sure? Check the map again. This can't be it." Sure enough, it was, and I was thoroughly disappointed.

Thousand Island Lake is one of the most hyped-up, hike-to lakes in all the Sierra. It may be that it's extremely large for a high county lake; at 320 acres, it's equal in size to June Lake and bigger than any of the lakes on the Mammoth Lake Loop. (An interesting side note is that the lake marks the headwaters of the San Joaquin River.)

Also, as its name implies, Thousand Island Lake is known for hundreds of islands that are scattered around its waters, but most can't be reached without a swim. You can get great pictures of the islands with Mt. Ritter and Banner Peak in the background. Don't forget a camera.

With more than six miles of shoreline, the lake can take a while to fish if you try to walk all the way around it. Your best bet is to fish off the points or in one of the many coves.

In addition to a population of brook trout, the lake also has a ton of rainbows. Each year the California Department of Fish and Game airlifts some 30,000 fingerling trout into the lake, joining holdovers from years past.

Fly-fishing is popular in the spring and early summer, when mosquitoes infest the lake. The rest of the summer through the fall, anglers casting Thomas Buoyants, Kastmasters and Panther Martins do best.

To reach Thousand Island Lake from Garnet Lake, continue north on the John Muir Trail for 2.4 miles (past Ruby and Emerald Lakes) to the lake. It can also be reached by following the Pacific Crest or River Trails from Agnew Meadow.

If you plan to make the trip, supplies are available at Red's Meadow Resort. Trailhead access restrictions for Emerald Lake also apply to Thousand Island Lake. A wilderness permit is required for overnight travel in the Ansel Adams Wilderness.

Also nearby are Garnet Lake, Ruby Lake, Altha Lake and Emerald Lake.

# SAN JOAQUIN RIVER (UPPER)

*To be successful, you need to find sections of the river that have pools or stretches where the water slows as it turns around bends.*

**Rating:** 6

**Species:** Rainbow Trout, Brook Trout and Brown Trout

**Stock:** None

**Facilities:** None

**Contact:** Mammoth Lakes Visitors Center (760) 924-5500, Rick's Sports Center (760) 934-3416, Devil's Postpile National Monument (760) 872-4881 (Winter) or (760) 934-2289, Red's Meadow Pack Station (760) 934-2345 or (800) 292-7758, Inyo National Forest Wilderness Permits (760) 873-2483

**Directions:** From Highway 395 in Mammoth, turn west on Mammoth Lakes Road and drive three miles to Minaret Road. Turn north and drive approximately 7.9 miles on Minaret Rd. to the trailhead on your right.

San Joaquin River (Upper)

Finally, a section of the San Joaquin River that is easily accessible and isn't bombarded by anglers!

Beginning at the outlet of Thousand Island Lake and ending near the Agnew Meadow Trailhead, this stretch of the river changes drastically as it flows through the Ansel Adams Wilderness. In just over six miles, it loses nearly 1,900 feet, as it flows through meadows, cascades over rocks, accelerates rapidly in some spots and slows down in others. In the spring and early summer, many sections of the river cannot be fished because of high water levels. To be successful, you need to find sections of the river that have pools or stretches where the water slows as it turns around bends.

The best stretch is at Thousand Island Lake near the mouth of the river. Here, where the river goes through transition zones, water flows out of the lake into large pools. Some anglers wait until the fall season, when the river has slowed drastically, because they think they have a chance at catching browns. However, the majority of the fish caught are rainbows and a sprinkle of brooks, with the highest catch rates coming to fly-fishermen.

With all the easily accessible lakes in the region, this section of the San Joaquin River receives little pressure, because it commonly kicks out smaller fish than the lakes. It can be reached by following the River Trail from the Agnew Meadow Trailhead, which parallels the river to Thousand Island Lake.

If you plan to make the trip, supplies are available at Red's Meadow Resort and in Mammoth Lakes. Trailhead access restrictions for Emerald Lake also apply to the San Joaquin River. The San Joaquin River is closed to fishing from November 16 through the last Saturday in April. A wilderness permit is required for overnight travel in the Ansel Adams Wilderness.

Also nearby are Thousand Island Lake, Garnet Lake, Altha Lake and Olaine Lake.

# BADGER LAKES

**Some of the trout reach 10 inches, but most are in the seven to nine-inch class.**

| | |
|---|---|
| **Rating:** | 6 |
| **Species:** | Rainbow Trout |
| **Stock:** | None |
| **Facilities:** | None |
| **Contact:** | Mammoth Lakes Visitors Center (760) 924-5500, Devil's Postpile National Monument (760) 872-4881 (Winter) or (760) 934-2289, Red's Meadow Pack Station (760) 934-2345 or (800) 292-7758, Inyo National Forest Wilderness Permits (760) 873-2483 |
| **Directions:** | From Highway 395 in Mammoth, turn west on Mammoth Lakes Road and continue three miles to Minaret Road. Turn north and drive 7.9 miles on Minaret Rd. to the trailhead on your right. |

*Badger Lakes don't provide good fishing.*

Badger Lakes are a series of six small pond-sized lakes, five of which are barren of fish. At 9,600 feet in the Ansel Adams Wilderness, the lakes are a great place to dodge crowds and learn a little about the food chain, consisting in this case of garter snakes and ducks, Pacific Tree Frogs and pollywogs. As a matter of fact, Badger Lakes are among a handful of places in the wilderness where you can see thousands of pollywogs.

For our purposes, we'll call the first lake you come to from Thousand Island Lake, Lake No. 1. We numbered the lakes in order of how you would view them from the trail walking from Thousand Island, beginning with the first lake that is visible from the trail. Lake No. 1 and 2 are both next to each other on the right side of the trail. They have no fish and only a few pollywogs.

Lake No. 3, directly across from Lake No. 2 on the opposite side of the trail, is loaded with pollywogs. They swim in schools, desperately trying to avoid being eaten by the garter snakes and ducks. The ones that don't get eaten turn into Pacific Tree Frogs. It's an education watching this whole food chain at work.

Continuing around the bend, you'll see Lake No. 4 on your right. It doesn't have any fish, either. If you leave the trail and walk past the lake over a small hill, you'll see a swimming pool-sized pond to the left. (It's not one of the Badger Lakes and also has no fish.) Then, in the distance, about one-tenth of a mile away, you'll see Lake No. 5. You should be able to follow horse tracks to it from Lake No. 4, because packers bring a lot of customers to these lakes. At last, a lake with fish!

Airplanes last stocked Lake No. 5 in 1999 with fingerling rainbow trout from the California Department of Fish and Game, keeping fishing good throughout the summer and fall. Some of the trout reach 10 inches, but most are in the seven to nine-inch class. They are eager to strike small Panther Martins and Thomas Buoyants. Lake No. 6 is situated just west of Lake No. 5 and is also barren of fish.

To reach the Badger Lakes from the junction of the Pacific Crest and John Muir Trail at Thousand Island Lake, take the PCT to the right and continue for one mile to the junction with the River Trail. Stay left, continuing on the High Trail (PCT) for four-tenths of a mile to another junction. Veer right, away from the Clark Lakes, staying on the PCT. In less than two-tenths of a mile you'll come to the first of the six Badger Lakes.

If you plan to make the trip, supplies are available at Red's Meadow Resort and in Mammoth Lakes. Minaret Road usually doesn't open until late June. Call ahead for updated road conditions. No vehicular traffic is permitted from 7:30 a.m. to 5:30 p.m. Exceptions apply only to those who have campground reservations or reservations at Red's Meadow Resort. Those who arrive during the restricted hours must ride a shuttle into the valley. There is a fee to ride the shuttle and enter the park. Road restrictions run from late June through Labor Day. A wilderness permit is required for overnight travel in the Ansel Adams Wilderness.

Also nearby are Ruby Lake, Emerald Lake, Clarice Lake, Laura Lake, Altha Lake, Thousand Island Lake, Summit Lake, Garnet Lake Falls and the Clark Lakes.

*This Badger Lake is barren of fish.*

BADGER LAKES

# SUMMIT LAKE

*Summit Lake provides good angler access, but it has steep drop-offs, so you'll need to use a heavier lure to get down to the fish.*

| | |
|---|---|
| **Rating:** | 6 |
| **Species:** | Brook Trout |
| **Stock:** | One pound of fingerling golden trout. |
| **Facilities:** | None |
| **Contact:** | Mammoth Lakes Visitors Center (760) 924-5500, Inyo National Forest Wilderness Permits (760) 873-2483l, Frontier Pack Station (760) 873-07971 (Winter) or (760) 648-7701 (Summer) |
| **Directions:** | From Highway 395 in Bishop, drive 60 miles north to the Highway 158/June Loop turnoff. Turn left and drive 6.5 miles to Silver Lake. The trailhead is opposite of the lake. |

*Summit Lake (Madera)*

Just inside the border of Madera County near the Clark Lakes and Gem Lake, Summit Lake in the Ansel Adams Wilderness is a lot like Summit Lake in Sequoia National Park. Both are small lakes located at the top of mountain peaks, and both are home to good brook trout fishing. The California Department of Fish and Game lists the lake as also being stocked with golden trout, but I had no luck catching any. All I caught were brooks. I thought it might have been bad luck that I could catch any goldens until the owner of Frontier Pack Station (who brings anglers to the lake daily during the fishing season) told me he's never seen any goldens, either.

At the top of Agnew Pass, Summit Lake is mostly used as a rest stop for hikers heading to Thousand Island, Waugh and Gem Lakes. Because there are too many better fishing lakes in the region, most of these visitors pass the small lake by.

Summit Lake provides good angler access, but it has steep drop-offs, so you'll need to use a heavier lure to get down to the fish. The lake's best asset may be its great views from the top of Agnew Pass; you can take in the San Joaquin Drainage and Mammoth Mountain.

To reach Summit Lake from the outlet of Clark Lake No. 2, continue approximately two-tenths of a mile south on the trail signed for Agnew Pass to the lake.

If you plan to make the trip, supplies are available in June Lake. A wilderness permit is required for overnight travel in the Ansel Adams Wilderness.

Also nearby are Clark Lakes, Thousand Island Lake, Gem Lake, Agnew Lake, Gem Lake Falls, Billy Lake, Sullivan Lake, Weber Lake, Upper Rush Creek and Waugh Lake.

# CLARK LAKES

*Because of the great fishing, Frontier Pack Station brings anglers to the lakes to teach them how to fly fish, and to build up their confidence before continuing on to the Alger Lakes to catch golden trout.*

**Rating:** 9
**Species:** Brook Trout
**Stock:** None
**Facilities:** None
**Contact:** Mammoth Lakes Visitors Center (760) 924-5500, Devil's Postpile National Monument (760) 872-4881 (Winter) or (760) 934-2289, Inyo National Forest Wilderness Permits (760) 873-2483l, Frontier Pack Station (760) 873-07971 (Winter) or (760) 648-7701 (Summer)

**Directions:** From Highway 395 in Mammoth, turn west on Mammoth Lakes Road and continue three miles to Minaret Road. Turn north and drive approximately 7.9 miles on Minaret Rd. to the trailhead on your right.

*Clark Lake No. 2 from the Clark Lakes Overlook*

Although seldom visited by anglers, the Clark Lakes offer some of the best brook trout fishing in the Ansel Adams Wilderness. The Clark Lakes consist of five lakes located just inside the border of Mono County, between Gem and Summit Lakes. All of the lakes are loaded with nice-sized brook trout that can be caught (and released) by the hundreds if desired. Because of the great fishing, Frontier Pack Station brings anglers to the lakes to teach them how to fly-fish, and to build up angler confidence before continuing on to the Alger Lakes to catch golden trout. My fishing partner and I caught and released our limit in less than five minutes. In 1999, a total of three pounds of fingerling golden trout (in lakes three, four and five only) were planted.

The lakes are surrounded by dry meadows that provide ideal camping spots. They are numbered from east to west, with lake No. 1 being closest to Agnew Lake. Lake No. 1 is shallow, and because weeds cover its shorelines, it's difficult to fish it while remaining dry. If you don't mind getting your feet wet, limits are common for both fly-fishermen and those tossing small spinners.

At 9,800 feet, with more than a half-mile of shoreline, Lake No. 2 is the largest of the Clark Lakes, and holds the biggest and most fish. Whether you fish the narrow channel near the lake's outlet, or the main body of the lake, it's easy to catch fish. It's almost like a brook trout farm.

Tucked in behind the west shore of Lake No. 2, Lake No. 3 is the smallest of the lakes and holds the least fish. It's smaller than an Olympic swimming pool, weedy and rarely fished.

To reach Lakes No. 4 and 5, begin at the trail junction near the outlet of Lake No. 2. If you are facing Lake No. 2, the left fork leads back to Lake No. 1. The path directly ahead will take you to Summit Lake and Agnew Pass. The route directly behind goes to Gem Lake. You'll want to turn right, following signs for the Clark Lakes. In less than five minutes, a trail veers off to the left. It passes by Lake's No. 4 and 5, before merging with the Pacific Crest Trail.

The California Department of Fish and Game lists the Clark Lakes as being planted with golden trout, however, after fishing the lakes thoroughly and consulting with packers who fish the lakes daily, neither I, nor anyone I've talked to, have ever seen any. The consensus seems to be that the goldens get eaten by the larger brooks before they can grow to catchable sizes.

Before you leave, climbing up to the Clark Lake Overlook is a must. It's right on top of the hill, due north of Summit Lake, and gives you priceless views of Lakes No. 2 and 3 and the surrounding wilderness.

To reach the Clark Lakes from Agnew Meadow, follow the Shadow Creek Trail past Olaine Lake to the junction with the River Trail. Veer right along the River Trail, and continue to another junction 2.5 miles ahead. Veer right again, away from Thousand Island Lake, and in approximately one mile turn right on the Pacific Crest Trail. In three-tenths of a mile, veer right, leaving the PCT, and follow the signs to Agnew Pass. Climb over the pass -- it's easy and doesn't require the strenuous climbing that most passes do -- to Summit Lake. Continue past the lake, descending down to Clark Lake No. 2. The lakes can also be reached by a trailhead near Silver Lake, but the climb is a butt-kicker. At the top of Agnew Pass be sure to turn around and take in the view of Mt. Ritter, Banner Peak, the San Joaquin River Drainage and Mammoth Mountain.

If you plan to make the trip, supplies are available at Red's Meadow Resort and in Mammoth Lakes. Minaret Road usually doesn't open until late June. Call ahead for updated road conditions. No vehicular traffic is permitted from 7:30 a.m. to 5:30 p.m. Exceptions apply only to those who have campground reservations or reservations at Red's Meadow Resort. Those who arrive during the restricted hours must ride a shuttle into the valley. There is a fee to ride the shuttle and enter the park. Road restrictions run from late June through Labor Day. A wilderness permit is required for overnight travel in the Ansel Adams Wilderness. The Clark Lakes are closed to fishing from November 16 to the last Saturday in April.

Also nearby are Agnew Pass, Summit Lake, Thousand Island Lake, Gem Lake, Agnew Lake, Gem Lake Falls, Billy Lake, Sullivan Lake, Weber Lake, upper Rush Creek and Waugh Lake.

**CLARK LAKE**

*Clark Lake No. 2*

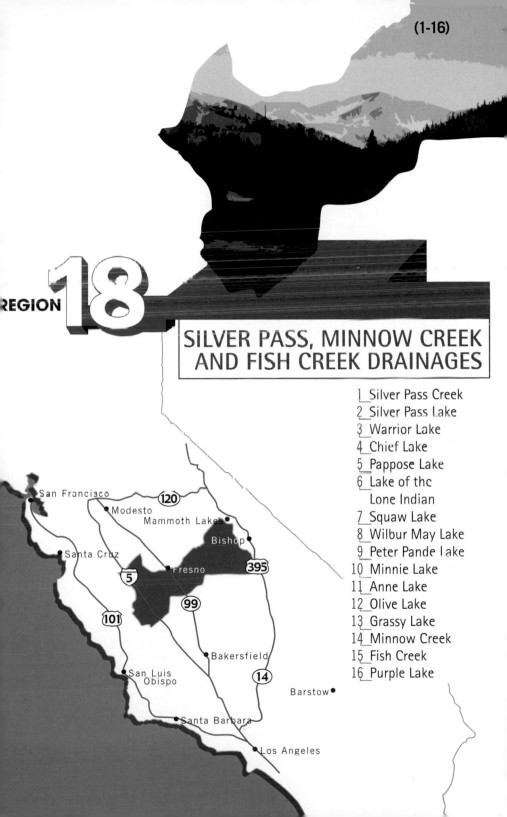

(1-16)

REGION 18

# SILVER PASS, MINNOW CREEK AND FISH CREEK DRAINAGES

1 Silver Pass Creek
2 Silver Pass Lake
3 Warrior Lake
4 Chief Lake
5 Pappose Lake
6 Lake of the
   Lone Indian
7 Squaw Lake
8 Wilbur May Lake
9 Peter Pande Lake
10 Minnie Lake
11 Anne Lake
12 Olive Lake
13 Grassy Lake
14 Minnow Creek
15 Fish Creek
16 Purple Lake

# SILVER PASS CREEK

*Most of Silver Pass Creek is inaccessible to anglers, however, the part of the creek that is accessible holds some small golden, rainbow and brook trout.*

**Rating:** 5

**Species:** Rainbow Trout, Golden Trout and Brook Trout

**Stock:** None

**Facilities:** None

**Contact:** Vermilion Resort (559) 259-4000 (Summer) or (559) 855-6558 (Winter), Sierra National Forest (559) 297-0706 or (559) 855-5360, High Sierra Ranger Station (559) 877-7173 (Summer Only)

**Directions:** From the 99 Freeway in Fresno, drive 72 miles east on Highway 168 to the east end of Huntington Lake. Turn east on Kaiser Pass Road and continue approximately 5.5 miles until the road becomes one lane. Follow the road for another 19 miles to Vermilion Resort, staying left at the fork. (The right fork leads to Florence Lake.) Continue about a half-mile past the resort to the trailhead.

*A delicate meadow just above Silver Pass Falls*

Most of Silver Pass Creek is inaccessible to anglers, however, the part of the creek that is accessible holds some small golden, rainbow and brook trout. The creek's entire length is only two miles, beginning at 10,300 feet at the outlet of Silver Pass Lake, and terminating downstream at its confluence with the North Fork of Mono Creek, at 8,800 feet. Unfortunately, only about half of the creek is fishable. The rest cascades down cliffs and becomes Silver Pass Falls.

The best stretch of the river is directly upstream from the meadow above the Silver Pass Falls. There are some nice pools in this area. Most of the fish are golden trout that swim out of Silver Pass Lake. Each summer, thousands of anglers begin at Edison Lake and walk by the creek on their way to the John Muir and Pacific Crest Trail, but few ever stop to fish it. There just aren't enough fish to attract most anglers, and there are too many other more productive places to fish in the region. It might be a good idea for you to skip it, too. Use the directions in the next write-up to Silver Pass Lake to access the creek.

If you plan to make the trip, supplies are available at Vermilion Resort. A wilderness permit is required for overnight travel in the John Muir Wilderness. If visiting in June or July, bring along lots of insect repellent. The mosquitoes are nearly unbearable. Kaiser Pass Road is closed from the first snowfall (usually in November) to Memorial Weekend, or as soon as the road can be cleared of snow. During long winters the road may not open until early July. Call ahead for updated conditions. Trailers are not recommended.

Also nearby are Edison Lake, Mono Creek, the Minnow Creek Drainage, Silver Pass Falls, Papoose Lake, Chief Lake, Lake of the Lone Indian, Silver Pass Lake, Warrior Lake and Squaw Lake.

**The best fishing can be found on the north side where the creek inlets flow.**

| | |
|---|---|
| **Rating:** | 6 |
| **Species:** | Golden Trout |
| **Stock:** | Five pounds of fingerling golden trout. |
| **Facilities:** | None |
| **Contact:** | Vermillion Resort (559) 259-4000 (Summer) or (559) 855-6558 (Winter), Sierra National Forest (559) 297-0706 or (559) 855-5360, High Sierra Ranger Station (559) 877-7173 (Summer Only) |

**Directions:** From the 99 Freeway in Fresno, drive 72 miles east on Highway 168 to the east end of Huntington Lake. Turn east on Kaiser Pass Road and continue approximately 5.5 miles until the road becomes one lane. Follow the road for another 19 miles to Vermilion Resort, staying left at the fork. (The right fork leads to Florence Lake.) Continue about a half-mile past the resort to the trailhead.

*Looking south from Silver Pass Lake*

You want to be alone? Have a little privacy in the backcountry? A little solitude? Then you'd better not plan on staying at Silver Pass Lake. Located only 11 miles from the trail head (with a 2,800-foot elevation gain), at 10,375 feet in the John Muir Wilderness, Silver Pass is the first lake hikers come to on the popular hiking trip from Edison Lake to Red Meadow. The only way around it is by hiking over Goodale Pass from Edison Lake. Because it's located along the ever-so-popular John Muir and Pacific Crest Trails, the lake is heavily visited.

On a more positive note, this small, shallow lake is one of the few in the region that holds golden trout, and it also offers great views and a good rest area for hikers. There are no trees around the lake, just a large meadow and some tall cliffs on its west side.

The best fishing can be found on the north side where the creek inlets flow. The lake has a gravel and dirt bottom, so you won't need to worry about getting snagged. Most of the fish are small, about six to eight inches, however, a few to 10 inches show up from time to time. Similar to most high-country lakes, fishing is either hit or miss. Either the fish will hit any lure you throw at them or they won't even look at a perfectly presented lure.

Begin the trip to Silver Pass Lake at Edison Lake. The Mono Creek Trail follows the north shore of Edison, beginning with a bridge that crosses over a stream, and continuing with a series of short switchbacks, before coming to the Mono Creek inlet. (This part of the hike can be bypassed by taking the water taxi from Vermilion Resort.)

Now, having left Edison Lake, you'll parallel Mono Creek for just over six-tenths of a mile, until you come to Quail Meadow. Filled with tall trees and covered by grasses, this pretty meadow offers wooden footbridges, which allow you to walk through it without getting covered in the mud.

Continuing on towards Pocket Meadow, you'll cross the North Fork of Mono Creek. After crossing the stream a trail takes off to the right, but you'll want to stay left, heading

*Campgrounds with cover are rare at Silver Pass Lake*

towards Pocket Meadow. You will now be on the Pacific Crest/John Muir Trail.

After a small climb, you'll come to Pocket Meadow. (It's 2.8 miles from the stream-crossing to the end of Pocket Meadow.) This long, lovely meadow filled with wildflowers can be used as a resting spot. Take a look at the cliffs ahead, and Silver Pass Falls can be seen. It looks far away, but that's where you'll end up in about a half-hour.

At the end of Pocket Meadow, cross the North Fork of Mono Creek for the last time, and here you'll be presented with another choice. The right spur leads to seldom-visited Mott Lake. Take the left fork, cross the creek, and begin the climb up Silver Pass. (The stream crossing can be difficult through July.) This is by far the toughest part of the trip. Enduring what seems like an endless amount of switchbacks, taking you to the top of Silver Pass Falls, you actually walk across the middle portion of the falls. Don't forget to look over your left shoulder for stunning views of the backcountry.

Next, you'll come to a large meadow, which Silver Pass Creek meanders through. Follow the trail as it curves to the right and gradually works its way to Silver Pass Lake. It's 2.7 miles from the turnoff to Mott Lake to Silver Pass Lake, and a 1,400-foot elevation gain.

If you plan to make the trip, supplies are available at Vermilion Resort. There is a fee to ride the water taxi, which makes one run in the morning and another in the evening. A wilderness permit is required for overnight travel in the John Muir Wilderness. If visiting in June or July, bring along lots of insect repellent. The mosquitoes are nearly unbearable. Kaiser Pass Road is closed from the first snowfall (usually in November) to Memorial Weekend, or as soon as the road can be cleared of snow. During long winters, the road may not open until early July. Call ahead for updated conditions. Trailers are not recommended.

Also nearby are Edison Lake, Mono Creek, the Minnow Creek Drainage, Silver Pass Falls, Papoose Lake, Chief Lake, Lake of the Lone Indian, Silver Pass Creek, Warrior Lake and Squaw Lake.

# SILVER PASS LAKE

*Silver Pass Lake*

*I tried some lures that I never use, including an orange Blue Fox and a rainbow patterned Kastmaster, and the fish hit them the moment they touched the water.*

| | |
|---|---|
| **Rating:** | 6 |
| **Species:** | Brook Trout |
| **Stock:** | None |
| **Facilities:** | None |
| **Contact:** | Vermilion Resort (559) 259-4000 (Summer) or (559) 855-6558 (Winter), Sierra National Forest (559) 297-0706 or (559) 855-5360, High Sierra Ranger Station (559) 877-7173 (Summer Only) |
| **Directions:** | From the 99 Freeway in Fresno, drive 72 miles east on Highway 168 to the east end of Huntington Lake. Turn east on Kaiser Pass Road and continue approximately 5.5 miles until the road becomes one lane. Follow the road another 19 miles to Vermilion Resort, staying left at the fork. (The right fork leads to Florence Lake.) Continue about a half-mile past the resort to the trailhead. |

*Silver Pass remains covered in snow into July.*

*Warrior Lake*

Standing atop Silver Pass you get a extraordinary view. At 10,880 feet, this pass marks the boundary line of the Silver Divide and provides picturesque outlooks over the backcountry of Yosemite National Park to the north and Goodale Pass to the left. To the right is Warrior Lake, Chief and Papoose are on the left. Although the view may be unforgettable, unfortunately, I can't say the same for the fishing.

At 10,650 feet in the John Muir Wilderness, Warrior has no trees around it and few spots to camp. Because it is adjacent to the Pacific Crest/John Muir Trail, Warrior gets bombarded by anglers and that is why the fish are not able to grow to worthy sizes. Even though the lake is loaded with brook trout, they rarely grow over eight inches.

The brookies often swim in schools and attack just about any lure that hits the water. I tried some lures that I never use, including an orange Blue Fox and a rainbow patterned Kastmaster, and the fish hit them the moment they touched the water.

The west side of the lake is extremely shallow, whereas, the east side has some steep drop-offs. The water is clear, allowing anglers to see the fish. The bottom is composed of granite rock, so there's little concern about getting snagged. Because the fish are so small, my advice would be to take a few casts, catch a few brookies and move on. There are larger fish to be caught in the nearby Minnow Creek Drainage.

To get to Warrior Lake from Silver Pass Lake, follow the JM/PCT Trail for about a mile to the top of Silver Pass. (You'll pass a small pond on your left, but it has no fish.) Then follow a side spur down to the lake on your right. Snow usually covers Silver Pass until late July.

If you plan to make the trip, supplies are available at Vermilion Resort. A wilderness permit is required for overnight travel in the John Muir Wilderness.

Also nearby are Edison Lake, Mono Creek, the Minnow Creek Drainage, Silver Pass Falls, Papoose Lake, Chief Lake, Lake of the Lone Indian and Silver Pass Lake.

# CHIEF LAKE
*Because the south shore is steep, the most easily accessible area is along the northeast shore where the trail makes its way down to the water.*

**Rating:** 6
**Species:** Brook Trout
**Stock:** None
**Facilities:** None
**Contact:** Vermilion Resort (559) 259-4000 (Summer) or (559) 855-6558 (Winter), Sierra National Forest (559) 297-0706 or (559) 855-5360, High Sierra Ranger Station (559) 877-7173 (Summer Only)

**Directions:** From the 99 Freeway in Fresno, drive 72 miles east on Highway 168 to the east end of Huntington Lake. Turn east on Kaiser Pass Road and continue approximately 5.5 miles until the road becomes one lane. Take the road another 19 miles to Vermilion Resort, staying left at the fork. (The right fork leads to Florence Lake.) Continue about a half-mile past the resort to the trailhead.

*Chief Lake*

Located at 10,500 feet in the John Muir Wilderness, Chief Lake is the largest in the chain of lakes (including Warrior, Squaw, Lone Indian and Papoose) below Silver Pass. Like its neighboring lakes, it suffers from over-fishing and usually remains frozen from November through May. These long freezes leave the fish only five months to feed and grow, which explains why they are so small. Often fish that are six years old will only be six inches long.

Because of the over-fishing that occurs in this 20-acre lake, many of the fish get caught and cooked before they have a chance to grow. And the fish are so hungry (as they are in nearby Warrior Lake), they attack lures with a vengeance. Just about any Panther Martin or Roostertail will work.

All of the fish in Chief Lake are brooks, most in the six to eight-inch range, although a few 10-inchers are caught each summer. Fishing is consistent all around the lake. Because the south shore is steep, the most easily accessible area is along the northeast shore where the trail makes its way down to the water.

Surprisingly, the outlet stream and pond usually offer better fishing than the lake. One sure hot spot is next to a rock that is the same size as my parents' Ford Explorer. It juts out of the water just west of the outlet stream. There is a little hole on the far side of the rock that the brooks like to hang in.

To get to Chief Lake from Silver Pass, follow the trail past Warrior Lake to Chief Lake. Total distance from the pass is seven-tenths of a mile.

If you plan to make the trip, supplies are available at Vermilion Resort. A wilderness permit is required for overnight travel in the John Muir Wilderness. Kaiser Pass Road is closed from the first snowfall (usually in November) to Memorial Weekend, or as soon as the road can be cleared of snow. During long winters the road may not open until early July.

Also nearby are Warrior Lake, Chief Lake, Pappose Lake and Squaw Lake.

# PAPOOSE LAKE

*There's no way around catching small brookies at this five-acre lake.*

| | |
|---|---|
| **Rating:** | 6 |
| **Species:** | Brook Trout |
| **Stock:** | None |
| **Facilities:** | None |
| **Contact:** | Vermilion Resort (559) 259-4000 (Summer) or (559) 855-6558 (Winter), Sierra National Forest (559) 297-0706 or (559) 855-5360, High Sierra Ranger Station (559) 877-7173 (Summer Only) |
| **Directions:** | From the 99 Freeway in Fresno, drive 72 miles east on Highway 168 to the east end of Huntington Lake. Turn east on Kaiser Pass Road and continue approximately 5.5 miles until the road becomes one lane. Follow the road for another 19 miles to Vermilion Resort, staying left at the fork. (The right fork leads to Florence Lake.) Continue about a half mile past the resort to the trailhead. |

*Chief and Papoose Lake from Silver Pass*

By the time I'd hiked from the top of Silver Pass to Papoose Lake, I'd grown tired of catching six to eight-inch brook trout. Don't expect anything different from Papoose Lake. At 10,300 feet in the John Muir Wilderness, Papoose Lake may be pretty, but it's best used as a rest area or a good place to have lunch. It doesn't hold any quality fish.

Situated at the end of the Goodale Pass Trail, close to the Pacific Crest/John Muir Trail, Papoose gets fished by hordes of anglers. Anglers commonly limit on small brook trout in less than an hour. My partner and I each caught and released a limit in less than 15 minutes, but failed to land a fish greater than nine inches. I even used larger lures like Thomas Buoyants and Cripplelures, trying to avoid catching smaller fish, but they attacked the big lures, too. There's no way around catching small brookies at this five-acre lake.

Unlike nearby Warrior and Chief Lakes, there are trees along Papoose's shoreline, making for a good resting spot. Hikers and anglers can enjoy lunch in a shaded environment.

To reach Papoose Lake from the top of Silver Pass, follow the trail for one mile, down past Warrior and Chief Lakes to a three-way fork. The right fork follows the JM/PCT Trail and the left fork is signed for Goodale Pass. Veer left and continue four-tenths of a mile to the lake on your left.

If you plan to make the trip, supplies are available at Vermilion Resort. A wilderness permit is required for overnight travel in the John Muir Wilderness. If visiting in June or July, bring along lots of insect repellent. The mosquitoes are nearly unbearable. Kaiser Pass Road is closed from the first snowfall (usually in November) to Memorial Weekend, or as soon as the road can be cleared of snow. During long winters the road may not open until early July. Call ahead for updated conditions. Trailers are not recommended.

Also nearby are Edison Lake, Mono Creek, the Minnow Creek Drainage, Silver Pass Falls, Chief Lake, Warrior Lake, Lake of the Lone Indian, Silver Pass Creek, Silver Pass Lake and Squaw Lake.

*Next page Papoose Lake*

329

# LAKE OF THE LONE INDIAN

*In July, when the bugs are thick, the only way to get in on the action is with a fly rod or a fly & bubble combo. Lures don't begin to work until sometime in August.*

**Rating:** 7
**Species:** Brook Trout
**Stock:** None
**Facilities:** None
**Contact:** Vermilion Resort (559) 259-4000 (Summer) or (559) 855-6558 (Winter), Sierra National Forest (559) 297-0706 or (559) 855-5360, High Sierra Ranger Station (559) 877-7173 (Summer Only)

**Directions:** From the 99 Freeway in Fresno, drive 72 miles east on Highway 168 to the east end of Huntington Lake. Turn east on Kaiser Pass Road and drive approximately 5.5 miles until the road becomes one lane. Follow the road for another 19 miles to Vermilion Resort, staying left at the fork. (The right fork leads to Florence Lake.) Continue about a half-mile past the resort to the trailhead.

*Lake of the Lone Indian*

When I first arrived at Lake of the Lone Indian, I thought it was raining, because there were rings of water all over the lake. When I looked overhead and saw that the clouds were still too far away to rain on us, I realized all those rings were fish surfacing and feeding on mosquitoes. I knew without a fly rod I was going to have trouble catching these fish, but I gave it a try anyway. Sure enough, I got skunked. I tried every lure I had with me and couldn't get a bite. The fish were destined to feed only on the mosquitoes.

Of all the lakes in the region below Silver Pass, Lake of the Lone Indian provides the best scenery and the largest fish. The inlet area is shallow and can be difficult to fish, but there is a trail that leads you around the lake, allowing you to reach some of the deeper holes. In July, when the bugs are thick, the only way to get in on the action is with a fly rod or a fly & bubble combo. Lures don't begin to work until sometime in August. Most of the fish are brooks, but a few rainbows are caught every so often.

The lake overlook is a must-see for everyone. Coming down from Papoose Lake, you can first see parts of the Lake of the Lone Indian through the trees, but as you continue, the view begins to broaden and becomes inspiring. You see Papoose Lake's outlet stream cascading down lush, green meadows and Lone Indian's sparkling waters just beyond the outlet stream, not to mention the shimmering pines in the mountains above. I unloaded an entire roll of film here.

Reaching Lake of the Lone Indian is easy from the top of Silver Pass. Follow the John Muir/Pacific Crest Trail for one mile down past Warrior and Chief Lakes to a three-way fork. The right fork follows the JM/PCT Trail. The left fork is signed for Goodale Pass. Veer left and continue four-tenths of a mile to Papoose Lake on your left. One-tenth of a mile past the lake, make a right at the junction with the Goodale Pass Trail. Lake of the Lone Indian in three-tenths of a mile ahead.

If you plan to make the trip, supplies are available at Vermillion Resort. A wilderness permit is required for overnight travel in the John Muir Wilderness. If visiting in June or July, bring along lots of insect repellent. The mosquitoes are nearly unbearable. Kaiser Pass Road is closed from the first snowfall (usually in November) to Memorial Weekend, or as soon as the road can be cleared of snow. During long winters, the road may not open until early July. Call ahead for updated conditions. Trailers are not recommended.

Also nearby are Edison Lake, Mono Creek, the Minnow Creek Drainage, Silver Pass Falls, Chief Lake, Warrior Lake, Papoose Lake, Silver Pass Creek, Silver Pass Lake and Squaw Lake.

# SQUAW LAKE

**Rating:** 5
**Species:** Brook Trout
**Stock:** None
**Facilities:** None
**Contact:** Vermilion Resort (559) 259-4000 (Summer) or (559) 855-6558 (Winter), Sierra National Forest (559) 297-0706 or (559) 855-5360, High Sierra Ranger Station (559) 877-7173 (Summer Only)

**Directions:** From the 99 Freeway in Fresno, drive 72 miles east on Highway 168 to the east end of Huntington Lake. Turn east on Kaiser Pass Road and drive approximately 5.5 miles until the road becomes one lane. Follow the road for another 19 miles to Vermilion Resort, staying left at the fork. (The right fork leads to Florence Lake.) Continue about a half-mile past the resort to the trailhead.

Squaw Lake

Of all the lakes near Silver Pass, Squaw is the least fished, but it provides a good resting spot for hikers and anglers on their way to Virginia, Duck or Purple Lake. At five acres, it's also the smallest around, but unlike many of the other nearby lakes, it holds rainbow trout in addition to brooks. Both species are small, running mostly between five and eight inches.

Located directly below Warrior Lake, at 10,250 feet in the John Muir Wilderness, this shallow lake has only three-tenths of a mile of shoreline, and there are no secret spots to fish. Your best bet is to walk around the lake casting medium-sized Panther Martins and Roostertails; Thomas Buoyants and Cripplelures are too big.

To reach Squaw Lake from Silver Pass, take the John Muir/Pacific Crest Trail north, descending past Warrior Lake on your right and Chief Lake on the left. In approximately one mile, you'll come to a trail junction. The left fork takes you to Goodale Pass or to the Minnow Creek Drainage, but you'll want to veer right and continue four-tenths of a mile to the lake.

If you plan to make the trip, supplies are available at Vermilion Resort. A wilderness permit is required for overnight travel in the John Muir Wilderness. If visiting in June or July, bring along lots of insect repellent. The mosquitoes are nearly unbearable. Kaiser Pass Road is closed from the first snowfall (usually in November) to Memorial Weekend, or as soon as the road can be cleared of snow. During long winters, the road may not open until early July. Call ahead for updated conditions. Trailers are not recommended.

Also nearby are Edison Lake, Mono Creek, the Minnow Creek Drainage, Fish Creek, Purple Lake, Purple Lake Falls, Minnow Creek Falls, Virginia Lake, Silver Pass Falls, Chief Lake, Warrior Lake, Lake of the Lone Indian, Silver Pass Creek and Silver Pass Lake.

# WILBUR MAY LAKE

**Rainbows can be caught all over the lake, but the most consistent area is towards the back where a creek inlet enters.**

**Rating:** 8
**Species:** Rainbow Trout and Brook Trout
**Stock:** One pound of fingerling rainbow trout.
**Facilities:** None
**Contact:** Vermilion Resort (559) 259-4000 (Summer) or (559) 855-6558 (Winter), Sierra National Forest (559) 297-0706 or (559) 855-5360, High Sierra Ranger Station (559) 877-7173 (Summer Only)

**Directions:** From the 99 Freeway in Fresno, drive 72 miles east on Highway 168 to the east end of Huntington Lake. Turn east on Kaiser Pass Road and continue approximately 5.5 miles until the road becomes one lane. Follow the road another 19 miles to Vermilion Resort, staying left at the fork. (The right fork leads to Florence Lake.) Continue about a half-mile past the resort to the trailhead.

*Wilbur May Lake*

It's no secret that to catch larger fish in the high-country it's necessary to get away from the more popular lakes located near (or directly on) heavily used trails. After visiting the lakes on both sides of Silver Pass along the John Muir and Pacific Crest Trails, my hiking companion and I quickly got bored with catching bite-sized brook trout.

I scanned our topo map, looking for a lake off the beaten path. Realizing the nearby Minnow Creek Trail is less used, I looked for what we thought would be the least-fished lake in the drainage. We immediately counted out Grassy Lake, because it was right on the trail. Anne, Minnie, Peter Pande and Olive Lake were all grouped together, and I figured most anglers would plan on fishing them, because they would be able to setup camp and be in short walking distance to all those lakes. The only other lake in the basin was Wilbur May, and it turned out to be the right choice.

At 9,980 feet in the John Muir Wilderness, Wilbur May Lake provides the best fishing in the Minnow Creek Drainage, and the fish are far larger than the ones in the other lakes near Silver Pass. Twice the acreage of nearby Chief Lake, but shallower, Wilbur May holds some nice-sized rainbows. It's not uncommon for them to reach a pound-and-a-half. The lake was first planted by air in 1954 and has been planted a total of nine times, the latest coming in 2000.

Rainbows can be caught all over the lake, but the most consistent area is towards the back where a creek inlet enters. (There are a total of three inlets.) There is a sandy beach where this creek comes in, and the rainbows wait for food to enter the lake here. Black Thomas Buoyants with yellow spots, as well as white Panther Martins with black spots and shades of pink, proved to be the best lures.

Opposite this creek inlet, there is a waterfall that skips off the cliff into the lake, but it only runs in June and July. There are rocks and branches that protrude from the water here, hinting at other fish hideouts. Along the lakes' north shore in an area heavily covered by tall trees, there are some nice campsites shaded by tall pines. Don't leave without fishing the lake's outlet stream. There are a lot of small brooks and rainbows in it.

To get to Wilbur May Lake, pick up the Minnow Lake Trail at the middle of the west shoreline of Lake of the Lone Indian. It can be difficult to find, because it is unsigned. The easiest landmark to use is a small stream that enters the lake. The trail follows this stream, gradually climbing uphill for three-tenths of a mile to a small open sandy area. Then, the trail winds to the left and descends below the tree line. If you look to your right, you'll get your first view of Grassy Lake. Continuing downhill through some switchbacks, you'll come to a stream crossing. Just after this crossing, there's a sign for Wilbur May Lake on a tree. The trail veers to the left and continues gradually uphill for four-tenths of a mile to the lake.

If you plan to make the trip, supplies are available at Vermilion Resort. A wilderness permit is required for overnight travel in the John Muir Wilderness. If visiting in June or July, bring along lots of insect repellent. The mosquitoes are nearly unbearable. Kaiser Pass Road is closed from the first snowfall (usually in November) to Memorial Weekend, or as soon as the road can be cleared of snow. During long winters the road may not open until early July. Call ahead for updated conditions. Trailers are not recommended.

Also nearby are Minnow Creek, Grassy Lake, Peter Pande Lake, Olive Lake, Minnie Lake, Anne Lake, Peter Pande Falls, Anne Lake Falls, Minnow Creek Falls, Fish Creek and Silver Pass Drainage.

*Stephen Wiessner caught this nice rainbow at Wilbur May.*

# WILBUR MAY LAKE

# PETER PANDE LAKE

*It's easiest to fish in the early morning and late evenings, when the fish are surfacing.*

**Rating:** 7

**Species:** Rainbow Trout, Brook Trout and Brown Trout

**Stock:** One pound of fingerling rainbow trout.

**Facilities:** None

**Contact:** Vermilion Resort (559) 259-4000 (Summer) or (559) 855-6558 (Winter), Sierra National Forest (559) 297-0706 or (559) 855-5360, High Sierra Ranger Station (559) 877-7173 (Summer Only)

**Directions:** From the 99 Freeway in Fresno, drive 72 miles east on Highway 168 to the east end of Huntington Lake. Turn east on Kaiser Pass Road and drive approximately 5.5 miles until the road becomes one lane. Follow the road for another 19 miles to Vermilion Resort, staying left at the fork. (The right fork leads to Florence Lake.) Continue about a half-mile past the resort to the trailhead.

*Peter Pande Lake*

With its two waterfalls and crystal-clear water, Peter Pande is the most beautiful lake in the Minnow Creek Drainage. Peter Pande Falls can only be seen from the Minnow Creek Trail near Olive Lake, but Anne Lake Falls, which flows into the west end of the lake, can be seen from all around the lake and is quite remarkable in early summer.

Anne Lake Falls is made up of three separate tiers with slopes that increase with intensity as they get closer to the lake below. The upper tier is the longest and least sloped, with water that flows gently over its granite rocks. The middle tier begins to slope more aggressively and causes the stream to pickup speed. The lower tier slopes the most dramatically, as the water cascades over it, splashing into Peter Pande Lake.

The lake needs to be fished differently, depending on the time of day. It's easiest to fish in the early morning and late evenings, when the fish are surfacing. However, if you arrive during the day, the fish move to deeper water. To be successful mid-day, concentrate on one of the lake's two inlets, located at Anne Lake Falls and at a small stream about 50 yards northeast of the falls. There are mostly rainbows in the lake, but a few browns and some brooks are also caught.

At 10,000 feet in the John Muir Wilderness, Peter Pande Lake has 1.55 miles of shoreline, and the entire south shore is difficult to fish because of steep banks and no trail. Fishing is easier from the north side of the lake. It has a trail that parallels the shoreline. Most of the fish are in the nine to 10-inch range, but a few to 14 inches are landed each year. Along with Anne Lake, Peter Pande Lake kicks out the largest fish in the drainage.

To reach Peter Pande Lake from Grassy Lake, walk south towards Wilbur May Lake for a morsel more than four-tenths of a mile to the turnoff for Peter Pande Lake. Follow the turnoff to the right until you come to a small stream. A lot of hikers get lost here, because the path is not clearly marked. The best way to stay on the correct path is to look for horse tracks and horse droppings. A lot of pack trips come to these lakes and know exactly where the path is. Shortly after crossing the stream, begin to walk up some switchbacks. The switchbacks get shorter near the top, which opens into a large meadow where you can see the lake. Halfway across the meadow, cross over a stream and begin your descent to the lake.

This stream becomes a small waterfall that can be viewed from Peter Pande Lake, however, from the trail, you can't tell there's a waterfall below you. The stream originates at a small, unnamed lake one-tenth of a mile away. As you near that lake, prepare to get your feet wet. You'll have to cross another stream, this one being Peter Pande's outlet stream (the headwaters of Minnow Creek), which is about 10 yards wide. In late July, the stream is typically low enough to use small rocks as stepping stones, but they are submerged from June to mid-July. Looking on a map, people often plan to fish the large, unnamed pond due-east of the lake, but don't waste your time. It's has few fish and looks more like a meadow.

If you plan to make the trip, supplies are available at Vermilion Resort. A wilderness permit is required for overnight travel in the John Muir Wilderness. If visiting in June or July, bring along lots of insect repellent. The mosquitoes are nearly unbearable. Kaiser Pass Road is closed from the first snowfall (usually in November) to Memorial Weekend, or as soon as the road can be cleared of snow. During long winters the road may not open until early July. Call ahead for updated conditions. Trailers are not recommended.

Also nearby are Wilbur May Lake, Minnow Creek, Minnie Lake, Olive Lake, Grassy Lake, Anne Lake, Peter Pande Falls, Anne Lake Falls, Minnow Creek Falls, Fish Creek and the Silver Pass Drainage.

*Peter Pande's outlet pool*

PETER PANDE LAKE

# MINNIE LAKE

**Minnie Lake may be small, but it sure has the most aggressive fish in the region.**

| | |
|---|---|
| **Rating:** | 8 |
| **Species:** | Rainbow Trout, Brook Trout and Brown Trout |
| **Stock:** | One pound of fingerling rainbow trout. |
| **Facilities:** | None |
| **Contact:** | Vermilion Resort (559) 259-4000 (Summer) or (559) 855-6558 (Winter), Sierra National Forest (559) 297-0706 or (559) 855-5360, High Sierra Ranger Station (559) 877-7173 (Summer Only) |
| **Directions:** | From the 99 Freeway in Fresno, drive 72 miles east on Highway 168 to the east end of Huntington Lake. Turn east on Kaiser Pass Road and drive approximately 5.5 miles until the road becomes one lane. Follow the road for another 19 miles to Vermilion Resort, staying left at the fork. (The right fork leads to Florence Lake.) Continue about a half-mile past the resort to the trailhead. |

*Minnie Lake*

I was jigging my lure less than three feet from shore in two feet of water, trying to get the blade spinning properly, when a fish came darting towards it and whacked it with a vengeance. "Did you see that?" I asked my fishing partner. "That fish looked right at me and he still bit my lure." My friend didn't believe me, so he did the same thing. His blade wasn't even spinning when a fish came and hit his lure. Minnie Lake may be small, but it sure has the most aggressive fish in the region.

Located at 10,300 feet in the John Muir Wilderness, just north of Anne Lake's outlet stream in the Minnow Creek Drainage, Minnie Lake is a measly three acres, but provides good fishing. Most anglers catch rainbows, but there are also brooks and a few browns in the lake. The majority of the fish are between six and 10 inches, although a few to 12 inches are landed each summer.

We found that black Panther Martins with yellow spots and silver Panther Martins caught the largest fish, although all the lures we tried worked. Fly-fishing is also popular across the entire drainage in the late spring and early summer, when the fish are feeding on mosquitoes and other insects.

To reach Minnie Lake from Anne Lake, follow the outlet stream for about 50 yards to a small pond. Make sure you're on the north side of the stream. When you get to the pond, walk over the tiny hill above it and you'll be at the lake.

If you plan to make the trip, supplies are available at Vermilion Resort. A wilderness permit is required for overnight travel in the John Muir Wilderness. Kaiser Pass Road is closed from the first snowfall (usually in November) to Memorial Weekend. During long winters, the road may not open until early July. Trailers are not recommended.

Also nearby are Wilbur May Lake, Minnow Creek, Peter Pande Lake, Olive Lake, Grassy Lake, Anne Lake, Peter Pande Falls, Anne Lake Falls, Minnow Creek Falls, Fish Creek and the Silver Pass Drainage.

# ANNE LAKE

*Trout often take cover in the channel's numerous deep holes next to large boulders. However, enticing the fish to come out of these holes can be as simple as tossing large Panther Martins and Thomas Buoyants.*

**Rating:** 7
**Species:** Rainbow Trout, Brook Trout and Brown Trout
**Stock:** One pound of fingerling rainbow trout.
**Facilities:** None
**Contact:** Vermilion Resort (559) 259-4000 (Summer) or (559) 855-6558 (Winter), Sierra National Forest (559) 297-0706 or (559) 855-5360, High Sierra Ranger Station (559) 877-7173 (Summer Only)

**Directions:** From the 99 Freeway in Fresno, drive east on Highway 168 for 72 miles to the east end of Huntington Lake. Turn east on Kaiser Pass Road and drive approximately 5.5 miles until the road becomes one lane. Continue on the road for another 19 miles to Vermilion Resort, staying left at the fork. (The right fork leads to Florence Lake.) Continue about a half-mile past the resort to the trailhead.

*Anne Lake's outlet pool*

Anne Lake may not look that big on a map, but it can easily take half a day to fish. With 1.65 miles of shoreline, including many coves and steep slopes, Anne is a large high-country lake that holds many fish, most of which are rainbow trout.

Situated at 10,250 feet in the John Muir Wilderness, in the back of the Minnow Creek Drainage, Anne Lake holds larger rainbows than most lakes in the region. Most weigh about three-fourths of a pound, but fish up to a pound-and-a-half are caught each summer. There are also brookies and some browns in the lake. Each fall a few browns over three pounds are landed, but not many anglers target them. They are usually caught accidentally by anglers fishing for rainbows.

The best fishing occurs in the lake's outlet channel. In July, many of the fish swim in and out of this channel searching for food. Trout often take cover in the channel's numerous deep holes next to large boulders. However, enticing the fish to come out of these holes can be as simple as tossing large Panther Martins and Thomas Buoyants. Fly-fishermen also do well in the outlet channel. Fishing off points in any of the lake's coves is also productive.

If you plan to make the trip, supplies are available at Vermilion Resort. A wilderness permit is required for overnight travel in the John Muir Wilderness. If visiting in June or July, bring along lots of insect repellent. The mosquitoes are nearly unbearable. Kaiser Pass Road is closed from the first snowfall (usually in November) to Memorial Weekend, or as soon as the road can be cleared of snow. During long winters the road may not open until early July. Call ahead for updated conditions. Trailers are not recommended.

Also nearby are Wilbur May Lake, Minnow Creek, Minnie Lake, Olive Lake, Grassy Lake, Peter Pande Lake, Peter Pande Falls, Anne Lake Falls, Minnow Creek Falls, Fish Creek and the Silver Pass Drainage.

# OLIVE LAKE

*There is a shelf that extends anywhere from 10 to 30 feet out from the shoreline, and the water is less than a foot deep before it begins to drop-off. You need to cast beyond that shelf into the deeper water to catch fish.*

| | |
|---|---|
| **Rating:** | 7 |
| **Species:** | Rainbow Trout and Brook Trout |
| **Stock:** | None |
| **Facilities:** | None |
| **Contact:** | Vermilion Resort (559) 259-4000 (Summer) or (559) 855-6558 (Winter), Sierra National Forest (559) 297-0706 or (559) 855-5360, High Sierra Ranger Station (559) 877-7173 (Summer Only) |
| **Directions:** | From the 99 Freeway in Fresno, drive 72 miles east on Highway 168 to the east end of Huntington Lake. Turn east on Kaiser Pass Road and continue approximately 5.5 miles until the road becomes one lane. Follow the road another 19 miles to Vermilion Resort, staying left at the fork. (The right fork leads to Florence Lake.) Continue about a half-mile past the resort to the trailhead. |

*Olive Lake*

Getting to Olive Lake can be as much fun as fishing it. If you take the off-trail route from Minnie Lake, the trip is a real adventure. Most people fish Peter Pande, Minnie and Anne Lakes as a group, and then fish Olive Lake. Instead of walking 5.3 miles from Minnie Lake back out towards Grassy Lake and then up the Minnow Lake Trail to Olive Lake, why not take the easier, shorter route? It may look nearly impossible when you study the contour lines on your topo map, but it's not. It's a fun, adventurous, seldom-traveled route that allows you to test your trailblazing skills and get some great pictures, while you're at it. It's an easy trip, even though most hikers shy away from taking the 92-percent shorter route, because there is no formal trail. Ready to try it?

It's best to start from Minnie Lake, which also gives you a chance to fish the other lakes in the area. Begin on the north shore and walk directly over the small mountain to the northwest. From the top of the mountain, you'll be able to see a small pond below. Walk along the pond (it's barren of fish), and follow its outlet stream down a few small hills to a three-way fork in the stream. Take the right fork, keeping your eyes open for a small waterfall on the left (it may dry up by early August), and continue past the falls for one-tenth of a mile to a spectacular view of Olive Lake. This is a great spot for photos. There's a magnificent view of Olive Lake, the John Muir Wilderness and the Ansel Adams Wilderness in the background. Now, follow the creek down to Olive Lake. There is no trail, but hikers have placed markers to keep you from getting lost.

At 9,700 feet in the John Muir Wilderness, peaceful, pretty Olive Lake is home to both rainbow and brook trout. However, it can be difficult to fish without a reel that allows you to cast far. There is a shelf that extends anywhere from 10 to 30 feet out from the shoreline, and the water is less than a foot deep before it begins to drop-off. You need to cast beyond that shelf into the deeper water to catch fish.

Another option is to walk the shoreline (there is a trail on the north shoreline) in search off drop-offs, fallen trees, boulders or any other kind of structure that looks like it could attract fish. Most of the fish are rainbows between six and nine inches, with the rare 10 to 12-inch fish caught every so often. Panther Martins seem to be the best lure. We had trouble catching fish on Thomas Buoyants and Cripplelures.

Olive Lake can also be reached from Grassy Lake. Follow the trail north from Grassy Lake, down a small hill, crossing over its outlet stream. In about 20 yards you'll veer left onto the Olive Lake Trail. Continue walking past some tall cliffs on your left, and you'll get your first view of Peter Pande Falls, also on your left. The cataract comes from Peter Pande Lake and is impressive in late spring and early summer. After tumbling over the cliffs, the water freefalls halfway down the mountain where it hits the cliff side and branches into two drops. A half-mile past the falls, you'll come to the lake.

If you plan to make the trip, supplies are available at Vermilion Resort. A wilderness permit is required for overnight travel in the John Muir Wilderness. If visiting in June or July, bring along lots of insect repellent. The mosquitoes are nearly unbearable. Kaiser Pass Road is closed from the first snowfall (usually in November) to Memorial Weekend, or as soon as the road can be cleared of snow. During long winters the road may not open until early July. Call ahead for updated conditions. Trailers are not recommended.

Also nearby are Wilbur May Lake, Minnow Creek, Minnie Lake, Anne Lake, Grassy Lake, Peter Pande Lake, Peter Pande Falls, Anne Lake Falls, Minnow Creek Falls, Fish Creek and the Silver Pass Drainage.

*Olive Lake from above*

OLIVE LAKE

# GRASSY LAKE

*The lake is loaded with eager rainbow and brook trout. I caught 25 fish on my first 25 casts.*

| | |
|---|---|
| **Rating:** | 8 |
| **Species:** | Rainbow Trout and Brook Trout |
| **Stock:** | None |
| **Facilities:** | None |
| **Contact:** | Vermilion Resort (559) 259-4000 (Summer) or (559) 855-6558 (Winter), Sierra National Forest (559) 297-0706 or (559) 855-5360, High Sierra Ranger Station (559) 877-7173 (Summer Only) |

**Directions:** From the 99 Freeway in Fresno, drive 72 miles east on Highway 168 to the east end of Huntington Lake. Turn east on Kaiser Pass Road and continue approximately 5.5 miles until the road becomes one lane. Follow the road for another 19 miles to Vermilion Resort, staying left at the fork. (The right fork leads to Florence Lake.) Continue about a half-mile past the resort to the trailhead.

*Stephen Wiessner with an average size rainbow from Grassy.*

At 9,500 feet in the John Muir Wilderness, located in the Minnow Creek Drainage, Grassy Lake is a angler's dream. Catching fish on every cast is expected. Although most of the fish are small, Grassy Lake provides the most consistent fishing in the region.

Grassy Lake also provides spectacular views. The best photo opportunity is from the lake's east shore. You can capture parts of Grassy Lake and its meadow, the pine trees in the mountains above the lake and the snow-capped peaks in the distance. It's one of the best views in the Sierra.

It's hard to decide which is better, the fishing or the vistas. The lake is loaded with eager rainbow and brook trout. I caught 25 fish on my first 25 casts. You can fish anywhere around the lake with any lure and be successful. We caught the biggest fish with rainbow colored Thomas Buoyants and silver Panther Martins. Interestingly, there are two different strains of rainbows in the lake.

To get to Grassy Lake from the junction of the Minnow Creek Trail and the trail to Wilbur May Lake, hike north for eight-tenths of a mile. First, you'll pass the turnoff for Peter Pande Lake and then you'll come to a large meadow before reaching the lake. There are also some exceptional campsites around.

If you plan to make the trip, supplies are available at Vermilion Resort. A wilderness permit is required for overnight travel in the John Muir Wilderness. If visiting in June or July, bring along lots of insect repellent. The mosquitoes are nearly unbearable. Kaiser Pass Road is closed from the first snowfall (usually in November) to Memorial Weekend, or as soon as the road can be cleared of snow. During long winters the road may not open until early July. Call ahead for updated conditions. Trailers are not recommended.

Also nearby are Wilbur May Lake, Minnow Creek, Peter Pande Lake, Olive Lake, Minnie Lake, Anne Lake, Peter Pande Falls, Anne Lake Falls, Minnow Creek Falls, Fish Creek and the Silver Pass Drainage.

*I've found that size 1/16 Panther Martins have enticed the most fish, but any small spinner should work.*

| | |
|---|---|
| **Rating:** | 7 |
| **Species:** | Rainbow Trout and Brook Trout |
| **Stock:** | None |
| **Facilities:** | None |
| **Contact:** | Vermilion Resort (559) 259-4000 (Summer) or (559) 855-6558 (Winter), Sierra National Forest (559) 297-0706 or (559) 855-5360, High Sierra Ranger Station (559) 877-7173 (Summer Only) |

**Directions:** From the 99 Freeway in Fresno, drive 72 miles east on Highway 168 to the east end of Huntington Lake. Turn east on Kaiser Pass Road and drive approximately 5.5 miles until the road becomes one lane. Follow the road for another 19 miles to Vermilion Resort, staying left at the fork. (The right fork leads to Florence Lake.) Continue about a half-mile past the resort to the trailhead.

*Minnow Creek*

Most anglers who fish the Minnow Creek Drainage come strictly for the lakes. They figure the creeks in the drainage are too small and ignore them. Big mistake! Although the streams are small and narrow, they are loaded with rainbow and brook trout.

Of all the streams in the drainage, Minnow Creek especially offers the best fishing. Located in the John Muir Wilderness, fed by runoff from Anne, Olive, Minnie, Peter Pande, Wilbur May and Grassy Lakes, Minnow Creek always has enough water in it for fish, and never seems to disappoint the few anglers who take time to fish it.

In most areas, the creek is about a foot deep and 10 feet wide, with pools holding both rainbow and brook trout. The majority of the trout range from five to eight inches, but a few up to 10 inches are caught each summer. The creek has a lot of brush, bushes and overhanging trees along the shoreline, so use caution not to get snagged. I've found that size 1/16 Panther Martins have enticed the most fish, but any small spinner should work. Attaching flies to your line also catches fish.

The creek's headwaters are created by Peter Pande Falls, just south of the trail to Olive Lake. The creek is best accessed from the trail to Olive Lake or downstream in Jackson Meadow. In Jackson Meadow, the creek widens and becomes easier to fish. Further downstream, the creek runs through steep slopes and moves far too fast to fish. Just below Jackson Meadow, it pours off the mountainside, creating Minnow Creek Falls, and empties into Fish Creek.

If you plan to make the trip, supplies are available at Vermilion Resort. A wilderness permit is required for overnight travel in the John Muir Wilderness. Kaiser Pass Road is closed from the first snowfall to Memorial Weekend, or as soon as the road can be cleared of snow. During long winters, the road may not open until early July.

Also nearby are Wilbur May Lake, Grassy Lake, Peter Pande Lake, Olive Lake, Minnie Lake, Anne Lake, Peter Pande Falls, Anne Lake Falls, Minnow Creek Falls, Fish Creek.

# FISH CREEK

*If you have a video camera and want to get some great fishing footage, this is the ideal place to bring it along. I had my cameraman film a spot where we knew there were fish and the video looked like a highlight film.*

**Rating:** 6
**Species:** Rainbow Trout and Brook Trout
**Stock:** None
**Facilities:** None
**Contact:** Vermilion Resort (559) 259-4000 (Summer) or (559) 855-6558 (Winter), Sierra National Forest (559) 297-0706 or (559) 855-5360, High Sierra Ranger Station (559) 877-7173 (Summer Only)

**Directions:** From the 99 Freeway in Fresno, drive 72 miles east on Highway 168 to the east end of Huntington Lake. Turn east on Kaiser Pass Road and continue approximately 5.5 miles until the road becomes one lane. Follow the road for another 19 miles to Vermilion Resort, staying left at the fork. (The right fork leads to Florence Lake.) Continue about a half-mile past the resort to the trailhead.

Fish Creek

There is a reason Fish Creek is called "Fish Creek." And yes, you guess it, it's because it's loaded with fish. The fish are almost all brook trout, mixed in with a few rainbows. But there is one downfall: they are all small. Most are in the four to eight-inch class. You'd be lucky to catch anything bigger.

No matter which way you come, it's a long hike to Fish Creek, a 15-mile trek from Edison Lake, and 16 miles from Red's Meadow. There's no way around it, and it's a butt-kicker. The upside is you can expect to catch fish on every cast, and it's a great place to take someone to learn to fly-fish. Although most of the fish are found near the tall grass along the shore, in back eddies and under fallen logs, you don't have to concentrate on these specific areas. There are fish all over the creek.

Fish Creek flows for approximately 19 miles, beginning at over 11,000 feet from Red and White Lake, continuing just below McGee Pass to the Middle Fork of the San Joaquin River, and finally terminating at Mammoth Pool Reservoir. If you have a video camera and want to get some great fishing footage, this is the ideal place to bring it along. I had my cameraman film a spot where we knew there were fish and the video looked like a highlight film. When we brought it home, my fishing buddies who didn't make the trip got sick of seeing us catching fish. It's a problem I can live with.

Much of the stream is difficult to reach, with the easiest access coming to anglers in Cascade Valley. To reach the creek from Squaw Lake, northeast of Silver Pass, follow the John Muir/Pacific Crest Trail for 2.3 miles to a fork. Veer left, turning away from the JM/PCT. The creek parallels the trail into Cascade Valley. Other popular areas from which to reach the creek are Second Crossing, First Crossing and Fox Meadow.

If you plan to make the trip, supplies are available at Vermilion Resort. A wilderness permit is required for overnight travel in the John Muir Wilderness. Fish Creek is closed to fishing from November 16 to the last Saturday in April.

Also nearby are Purple Lake Falls and Minnow Creek Falls.

# PURPLE LAKE

*About an hour before sunset, the lake comes alive with surfacing rainbow trout willing to snatch almost any lure or fly worked near the surface.*

**Rating:** 8
**Species:** Rainbow Trout
**Stock:** 10 pounds of fingerling golden trout.
**Facilities:** None
**Contact:** Mammoth Lakes Visitors Center (760) 924-5500, Rick's Sports Center (760) 934-3416, Red's Meadow Pack Station (760) 934-2345 or (800) 292-7758, Inyo National Forest Wilderness Permits (760) 873-2483

**Directions:** From Highway 395 in Mammoth, turn west on Mammoth Lakes Road and drive three miles to Minaret Road. Turn north, drive 12.2 miles and veer left at the sign for Sotcher Lake. Continue past Sotcher Lake to Red's Meadow Resort. The trail can be picked up at the resort and general store at the end of the road.

*Red Cones along the path to Purple Lake*

Situated between Edison Lake and Red's Meadow, pines encroach upon the rocky shoreline and crowd the hillsides above Purple Lake. At 9,860 feet in the John Muir Wilderness, it is the only lake in this small basin, and its 50 acres of water are loaded with rainbow trout! One of the most heavily visited water holes along the John Muir/Pacific Crest Trail, the evening trout bite is among the best in the Sierra. More than 10,000 fingerling rainbow trout were plucked into Purple in 2000.

During late spring and early summer, fly fishermen do the best, but spin casters can do well, too. About an hour before sunset, the lake comes alive with surfacing rainbow trout willing to snatch almost any lure or fly worked near the surface. We found solid black to be the best color, but anything that has shades of black should catch a quick limit.

To reach Purple Lake from Red's Meadow Resort, begin at the Red's Meadow Store and pickup the John Muir/Pacific Crest Trail. At first you'll walk through a pine forest. Then, you'll enter some fire-charred areas before reentering the pine forest. After crossing a stream, you'll come to a large spring about the size of a wading pool, with a sandy bottom that looks like quicksand. Many hikers do various experiments, including tossing stones and throwing tree branches into the spring, trying to figure out if the sand below is indeed quicksand. (It's not.)

After passing the spring, you'll begin to climb up the first of two switchbacks. The first one is short, but the second is long. Look north to get a great view of the Ansel Adams Wilderness and the San Joaquin River Drainage, much of which was charred in the Rainbow Fire of 1992. Three-and-a-half miles from the trailhead, you'll come to the Red Cones. It's part of a volcanic mountain with red sand and no trees. It makes you feel like you're on Mars.

Enter Crater Meadow, passing a trail on your left that leads over Mammoth Pass to McCloud Lake. At Upper Crater Meadow you'll pass another junction that also leads over

Purple Lake

Mammoth Pass. (It merges with the first trail just before going over the pass.) Follow small feeder streams that parallel the trail, past the meadow to some more large open meadows.

In just over six miles from where you began the trip, you'll cross Deer Creek and walk through a wildflower-filled meadow that is adjacent to the stream. Shortly after, the trail begins to bend to the left, and for the next five miles you'll parallel Cascade Valley. At more than 2,000 feet above the valley floor, there are some great views of Fish Creek below. When the trail begins to turn to the left, you'll be getting close to the turnoff for Duck Lake, which comes about 11.5 miles from where you saw your last bathroom at Red's Meadow. (You'll cross over Duck Creek just before the junction.) After a brief straightaway and a little climbing, the trail bends to the left, and in 13.75 miles you'll come to the Purple Lake outlet.

If you plan to make the trip, supplies are available at Red's Meadow Resort. Minaret Road usually doesn't open until late June. Call ahead for updated road conditions. No vehicular traffic is permitted from 7:30 a.m. to 5:30 p.m. Exceptions apply only to those who have campground reservations or reservations at Red's Meadow Resort. Those who arrive during the restricted hours must ride a shuttle into the valley. There is a fee to ride the shuttle and enter the park. Road restrictions run from late June through Labor Day.

Also nearby are Purple Lake Falls, Fish Creek, Minnow Creek Falls, Duck Lake and Virginia Lake.

## PURPLE LAKE

*Charred forest from the Rainbow Fire.*

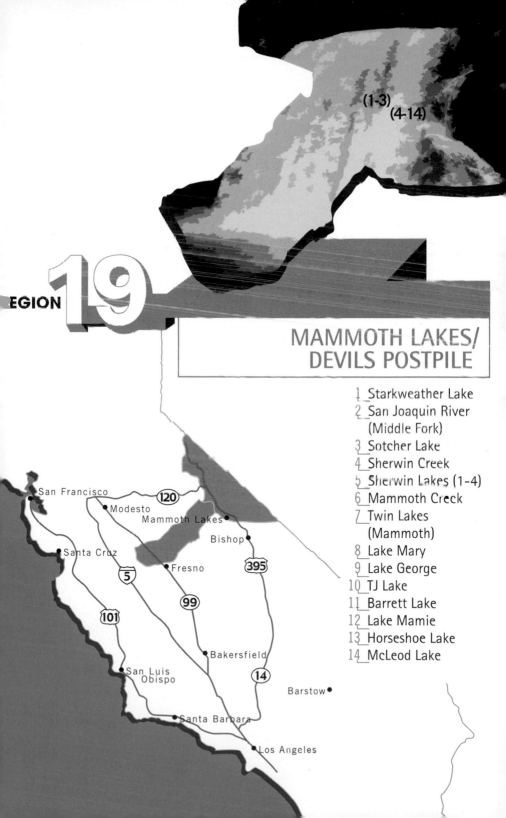

(1-3)
(4-14)

REGION 19

# MAMMOTH LAKES/
# DEVILS POSTPILE

1_Starkweather Lake
2_San Joaquin River
   (Middle Fork)
3_Sotcher Lake
4_Sherwin Creek
5_Sherwin Lakes (1-4)
6_Mammoth Creek
7_Twin Lakes
   (Mammoth)
8_Lake Mary
9_Lake George
10_TJ Lake
11_Barrett Lake
12_Lake Mamie
13_Horseshoe Lake
14_McLeod Lake

San Francisco
Modesto
Mammoth Lakes
Bishop
120
Santa Cruz
Fresno
395
5
99
101
Bakersfield
San Luis
Obispo
14
Barstow
Santa Barbara
Los Angeles

# STARKWEATHER LAKE

*For the best fishing, walk to the far side of the lake where a few fallen trees can be seen poking their limbs out of the water.*

| | |
|---|---|
| **Rating:** | 7 |
| **Species:** | Rainbow Trout |
| **Stock:** | 8,011 pounds of rainbow trout. |
| **Facilities:** | Picnic Areas |
| **Contact:** | Mammoth Lakes Visitors Center (760) 924-5500, Rick's Sports Center (760) 934-3416 Devil's Postpile National Monument (760) 872-4881 (Winter) or (760) 934-2289 |
| **Directions:** | From Highway 395 in Mammoth, turn west on Mammoth Lakes Road and continue three miles to Minaret Road. Turn right and drive 9.2 miles on Minaret Rd. to the lake on your right. |

*Starkweather Lake*

Most people first see and hear about Starkweather Lake on a shuttle bus. If you arrive after between 7:30 a.m. and 5:30 p.m., the only way to get past Minaret Summit and Starkweather Lake to Devils Postpile National Monument and Red's Meadow is by taking a shuttle. The road is closed daily to public vehicular traffic, unless you have a reservation at one of the campgrounds or Red's Meadow. Starkweather Lake is the first body of water the shuttle passes.

The driver points out the lake to his passengers and tells them the lake is stocked weekly by the California Department of Fish and Game. Then, the bus usually stops for a few seconds to showcase the lake. The tourists commonly see fish swimming in the clear water, and instead of getting off the shuttle where they had planned, many anglers take the shuttle back to their cars so they can get their poles. They get back on the next shuttle and go fishing at Starkweather.

At 7,800 feet in the Inyo National Forest, Starkweather is a 3.5-acre lake located between Red's and Agnew Meadow, just outside the boundary for Devil's Postpile National Monument. This small, shallow lake is on its way to becoming a swamp (it wont happen in our lifetime), but it still provides good fishing to both vacationers and day-users.

The roadside shoreline is only a foot deep. For the best fishing, walk to the far side of the lake where a few fallen trees can be seen poking their limbs out of the water. There are steep drop-offs here, where most of the fish hold. Keep an eye out for where the fish are feeding. If they are surfacing, which is more often than not the case, then cast and retrieve your lure without letting it sink. If you don't see fish breaking water, you'll have to let you lure sink for a few seconds before retrieving it.

Super Dupers and Thomas Buoyants are the best lures to catch the 10,708 planted rainbows, 122 of which weigh over three pounds. Alpers (2,500 pounds) from three to nine pounds are sporadically stocked throughout the summer. Starkweather Lake is heavily fished during the summer, so if you don't arrive early, you might have trouble finding a spot.

If you plan to make the trip, supplies are available in Mammoth Lakes and at Red's Meadow. Minaret Road usually doesn't open until late June. Call ahead for updated road conditions. There is a fee to ride the shuttle and enter the park. Road restrictions run from late June through Labor Day.

Also nearby are the Ansel Adams Wilderness, Sotcher Lake, the San Joaquin River, Devil's Postpile National Monument, Rainbow Falls, Minaret Falls and Johnston Lake.

*Devils Postpile*

STARKWEATHER LAKE

# SAN JOAQUIN RIVER
## (MIDDLE FORK)

*The best way to fish the river is with waders, because the biggest fish lie in hard to reach places.*

| | |
|---|---|
| **Rating:** | 7 |
| **Species:** | Rainbow Trout, Brook Trout, Golden Trout and Brown Trout |
| **Stock:** | 10,071 pounds of rainbow trout. |
| **Facilities:** | Picnic Areas, Campgrounds, A Visitor Center and Restrooms |
| **Contact:** | Lakes Visitors Center (760) 924-5500, Rick's Sports Center (760) 934-3416 <br> Devil's Postpile National Monument (760) 872-4881 (Winter) or (760) 934-2289 |
| **Directions:** | From Highway 395 in Mammoth, turn west on Mammoth Lakes Road and drive three miles to Minaret Road. Turn right and drive 11.8 miles on Minaret Rd. to the Devils Postpile turnoff. Veer right and continue four-tenths of a mile to the river. |

*San Joaquin River (Middle Fork)*

Anglers used to consider the San Joaquin River a great fishery, but constant fishing pressure has prompted many anglers to stop fishing it. This section of the river, which stretches from Shadow Creek near the Agnew Meadow Trailhead to about a mile below Rainbow Falls in Devils Postpile National Monument, gets hammered by anglers from late June through Labor Day weekend. And the fishing obviously suffers. Even the 19,524 rainbows planted (122 are three or more pounds) aren't enough to accommodate all of the pressure. Within a few days of a stock, most of the planters have been caught.

The river is planted weekly from late spring through early fall. Most of the fish are planted at Minaret Campground, just upstream from the Postpile. In addition to the planters, there are numerous wild rainbows, browns and a few brooks and goldens. But, with all the tourists who fish the river, to be successful, you have to find an area where these inexperienced anglers haven't spooked all the wild fish. The best time to fish the river is from late September through October, when the fishing pressure pretty much disappears. This is also the best time to land the larger browns.

Ranging from 7,400 to 8,000 feet, this section of the river flows through areas of the Ansel Adams Wilderness, Devils Postpile National Monument and the Inyo National Forest, winding through meadows, racing through narrow, hard to reach canyons, cascading over waterfalls and experiencing a variety of drastic changes.

The best way to fish the river is with waders, because the biggest fish lie in hard to reach places. Two of the best spots are in the pool below Rainbow and Lower Rainbow Falls. Fly-fishing is popular in a stretch of the river adjacent to the Devils Postpile Visitor Center.

If you plan to make the trip, supplies are available at Red's Meadow Resort. The San Joaquin River (Middle Fork) is closed to fishing from November 16 to the last Saturday in April. Trailhead access restrictions for Starkweather Lake also apply to the San Joaquin River. Also nearby are Starkweather Lake, Sotcher Lake, Rainbow Falls and Sotcher Lake Falls.

**The largest fish are usually landed by anglers who troll down the middle of the lake in late June and in October.**

| | |
|---|---|
| **Rating:** | 8 |
| **Species:** | Rainbow Trout and Brown Trout |
| **Stock:** | 8,020 pounds of rainbow trout. |
| **Facilities:** | Picnic Areas, Restrooms and Campgrounds |
| **Contact:** | Mammoth Lakes Visitors Center (760) 924-5500, Rick's Sports Center (760) 934-3416 |

**Directions:** From Highway 395 in Mammoth, turn west on Mammoth Lakes Road and continue three miles to Minaret Road. Turn right, drive 11.8 miles to a split in the road. Stay left and continue four-tenths of a mile to the lake on the left.

*Jason McLean poses at the Sotcher Lake Overlook.*

Don't let the pictures hanging in Red's Meadow General Store and the Mule House Café deceive you. These photographs of huge browns pulled out of Sotcher Lake were all taken at least 10 years ago. Some are more than 25 years old. Nowadays, most of them have been fished-out, and a big brown is caught perhaps once a year.

The 22-acre lake, located close to the Ansel Adams Wilderness and Devil's Postpile National Monument, at 7,600 feet in the Inyo National Forest, was named after Red Sotcher. As the story goes, Sotcher was a farmer who raised vegetables in the meadow adjacent to the lake (now called Red's Meadow) and traded these along with horses and cattle to the mining community in Mammoth. Sotcher Lake also has one of the worst bear problems in the region.

The best fishing can be had along the drop-offs on the north shore. However, much of this area is inaccessible by foot because of steep banks. Anglers who troll down the middle of the lake in late June and October typically land the biggest fish. The only way to do this is with electric trolling motors, because no gas-powered motors are allowed. Float tubing is also popular, allowing anglers to cast into areas that are nearly impossible to reach for shore anglers. If trolling or casting on the south shore, you need to be careful not to get snagged. In 1986 there was an avalanche on the south side of the lake, which sent 1,400 cords of wood tumbling into the water.

The California Department of Fish and Game stocks 12,184 rainbows each season, approximately 150 of which are more than three pounds. Holdovers from years past also join these fish and 2,000 pounds of Alpers from three- to 12-pounds are also planted. Sotcher isn't fished much by day-users. Most of its anglers are campers staying at nearby Devils Postpile National Monument or at Red's Meadow Campground.

If you plan to make the trip, supplies are available at Red's Meadow Resort. Road restrictions for Starkweather Lake also apply to Sotcher Lake.

Also nearby are Starkweather Lake, San Joaquin River and Rainbow Falls.

# SHERWIN CREEK

*Although overgrown trees and bushes can make fishing difficult for beginners, Sherwin is a great place to bring youngsters to learn how to stream fish.*

**Rating:** 5
**Species:** Rainbow Trout and Brown Trout
**Stock:** 2,252 pounds of rainbow trout.
**Facilities:** Campgrounds and Restrooms
**Contact:** Mammoth Lakes Visitors Center (760) 924-5500. Rick's Sports Center (760) 934-3416

**Directions:** From Highway 395 in Bishop, drive approximately 38 miles north and exit west on Highway 203 (Mammoth Lakes turnoff). Continue 2.7 miles and turn left on Old Mammoth Road. Drive nine-tenths of a mile, and just after crossing Mammoth Creek, turn left on Sherwin Creek Road. Continue 1.9 miles to Sherwin Campground.

*Sherwin Creek*

When it comes to large streams with trout, the Mammoth Lakes area isn't rich with them. If you're just looking to catch fish, however, and aren't concerned with being able to cast and retrieve spinners, then Mammoth has a great place for you. Fed by the Sherwin Lakes, Sherwin Creek is a small stream loaded with both wild and stocked trout. The weekly stocks typically take place from Memorial weekend through Labor Day, when the California Department of Fish and Game tosses in 5,451 half-pound rainbow trout.

Where can you get in on the action? Stick to the area where Sherwin Creek crosses under Sherwin Lakes Road. Most of the plants begin at this point and range roughly a half-mile downstream through Sherwin Campground. Although overgrown trees and bushes can make fishing difficult for beginners, Sherwin is a great place to bring youngsters to learn how to stream fish. There are some small pools throughout the stream, where floating Power Bait or using salmon eggs can almost assure you a bite.

If you plan to make the trip, supplies are available in Mammoth. Sherwin Creek is closed to fishing from November 16 to the last Saturday in April.

Also nearby are Sherwin Lakes, Laurel Lakes, the Mammoth Lakes Loop, Mammoth Creek, Mammoth Creek Falls and Twin Falls.

**All but one of the lakes is full of rainbow and brook trout, with a sprinkling of browns.**

**Rating:** 7
**Species:** Rainbow Trout, Brown Trout and Brook Trout
**Stock:** Three pounds of fingerling rainbow trout.
**Facilities:** None
**Contact:** Mammoth Lakes Visitors Center (760) 924-5500, Rick's Sports Center (760) 934-3416

**Directions:** From Highway 395 in Bishop, drive approximately 38 miles north and exit west on Highway 203 (Mammoth Lakes turnoff). Continue 2.7 miles and turn left on Old Mammoth Road. Drive nine-tenths of a mile, and just after crossing Mammoth Creek, turn left on Sherwin Creek Road. Continue 1.4 miles and turn right on a dirt road signed for Sherwin Lakes Trail and Motocross. Drive four-tenths of a mile to the trailhead and parking area.

*Sherwin Lake*

There are thousands of high-county lakes in the Sierra, but because of their high elevations, few are accessible until sometime in mid-June. Those at elevations higher than 10,600 feet usually remain at least partially frozen until sometime in July. The Sherwin Lakes, however, are normally ice-free by Memorial Weekend. Located at 8,700 feet in the Inyo National Forest, these lakes thaw much more quickly than most others in the region. When the snow pack in the Mammoth Lakes region is below average, the lakes may even be visited as early as the first week in May.

While the Sherwin Lakes are small (none larger than five acres), there are plenty of fish to be caught. All but one of the lakes is full of rainbow and brook trout, with a sprinkling of browns. The California Department of Fish and Game airlifts a total of 3,500 fingerling rainbow trout into the lakes each year, where they join holdovers from a self-sustaining population of brook trout.

The browns here are wild trout, and because they aren't often caught, they grow to trophy sizes. I've seen browns to eight pounds. They are extremely skittish and smart enough not to be fooled by lures and other artificial baits. The only time the browns are active is right after ice-out, when their bellies are empty and they go into feeding mode for a few days. While the browns grow large, the rainbows and brookies don't (an eight-incher would be big), but catching them requires no effort.

All the effort comes on the hike to the lake, which meanders through a high desert landscape and then a forested area. The path begins at the Sherwin Lakes Trailhead and leads south, crossing Sherwin Creek before entering a pine forest. For the duration of the trek to the Sherwin Lakes Basin, you'll be forced to zigzag through dozens of gradual switchbacks, ascending more than 850 feet over the 2.2 miles to Sherwin Lake No. 1.

At 8,700 feet, it's difficult to miss this lake, which can be seen on the right side of the trail, about 200 yards after climbing over a ridge and entering the basin. Some anglers think of Lake No. 1 as two lakes, because it's shaped like a pair of sunglasses with two lens-shaped bodies of water. Roughly two acres each, they are joined by a narrow channel (resembling the bridge on sunglasses) about 20 yards long and 10 yards wide.

Because this channel is where Sherwin Creek enters the lake, it is one of the best places to catch rainbows and browns. The fish pile up here waiting for food to enter the lake. Small Panther Martins work best. Anything larger tends to spook the fish. Although trout can be found all around the lake, they can be difficult to catch away from the channel. Elsewhere, the water is shallow and there are numerous boulders in the lake that are easy to get snagged on. Sherwin Creek used to flow from Lake No. 1 to No. 2. Now, however, the creek dries up before reaching Lake No. 2, which is less than a half-acre.

Although Lake No. 3 is a quality fishery, because there is no trail leading to it, it isn't often fished. To find Lake No. 3, here's what you'll need to do: first, go to the lakeside opposite where Sherwin Creek enters Lake No. 1 and look for an outlet stream. This can be a little tricky, because the outlet stream begins underground, and its waters can't actually be seen leaving the lake. You'll need to look for a dry streambed. There are three of them, and they all lead to the actual stream, which then descends to Lake No. 3.

At fewer than four feet deep, this lake is extremely shallow. Because of marshy conditions, it's worthless to fish the inlet area. Instead, walk to the outlet, which is clearly visible and is productive for anglers targeting small brooks. The real secret here, however, is the browns. Usually taking cover on the west shore of this one-acre lake, there are three of them between five and eight pounds.

*Brett Ross with a brookie caught at Sherwin.*  *An average size brook from Sherwin*

Reaching the fourth lake is a cakewalk. Located at 8,775 feet, it can be seen from Lake No. 3's outlet stream and is fewer than 30 yards away. Fishing is exceptional here. Rainbows and brooks can be caught by the dozens, if you use the right bait. Small spinners work, but there's a better way. Walk to the inlet, sit on one of the rocks and toss out a small rubber mini jig. Let it sit in the current and give your pole a slight jerk every few seconds. A fish will be pulling back on your line within seconds.

I brought two friends here for their first high-country fishing experience, and each caught and released a limit of rainbow and brook trout in about 10 minutes. About 10 yards from where Sherwin Creek enters four-acre Lake No. 4, there is a steep drop-off where the larger fish tend to hang. The coves and points around the entire lake also produce high catch rates.

If you plan to make the trip, supplies are available in Mammoth Lakes. Call ahead for trail conditions. In heavy snow years, the trail may not be snow-free until sometime in June. Sherwin Lakes are closed to fishing from November 16 to the last Saturday in April.

Also nearby are Sherwin Creek, Valentine Lake, Mammoth Creek and the Mammoth Lakes Loop.

*The stream is too small and narrow for casting and retrieving. But if you have Power Bait or salmon eggs, you're in business. Plan on catching an easy limit.*

| | |
|---|---|
| **Rating:** | 4 |
| **Species:** | 10,332 pounds of rainbow trout. |
| **Stock:** | Rainbow Trout, Brown Trout and Brook Trout |
| **Facilities:** | None |
| **Contact:** | Mammoth Lakes Visitors Center (760) 924-5500, Rick's Sports Center (760) 934-3416 |

**Directions:** From Highway 395 in Bishop, drive approximately 38 miles north and exit west on Highway 203 (Mammoth Lakes turnoff). Continue 2.7 miles and turn left on Old Mammoth Road. Drive nine tenths of a mile, and just after crossing Mammoth Creek, turn left on Sherwin Creek Road. The creek is planted from here on downstream at access sites.

*Mammoth Creek*

Let's just say that Mammoth Creek doesn't totally live up to its name. Associated with a town that almost every outdoorsman has heard of and looks forward to visiting, you'd figure Mammoth Creek to be one of the best fishing holes in the region. But it's not exactly what you'd expect. Mammoth Creek is a small stream located a few minutes drive from downtown Mammoth. It has only a few of the breathtaking characteristics of other streams in the Eastern Sierra. However, it does have good fishing.

This stream doesn't have deep inviting pools, nor are there hundreds of pine trees towering over its shorelines. It's not even surrounded by serene meadows. To give credit where credit is due, looking west at mountaintops in the John Muir and Ansel Adams Wildernesses, and east overlooking the upper Owens Valley, it does have some nice scenery. And, an added incentive to fish the stream is that most anglers overlook it, trying their luck at more popular streams, such as Rock Creek, Convict Creek and Bishop Creek. So, if you're mostly out to catch fish, this is a good thing.

The California Department of Fish and Game stocks more than 15,748 trout in the 10-12-inch class, and another 110 two-pounders. The creek is also planted with 2,200 pounds of Alpers trout in the one to two pound range. With most anglers sinking their bait elsewhere, somebody has to catch these fish. Bring along lures and it won't be you. The stream is too small and narrow for casting and retrieving. But if you have Power Bait or salmon eggs, you're in business. Plan on catching an easy limit.

If you plan to make the trip, supplies are available in Mammoth. Mammoth Creek is closed to fishing from November 16 to the last Saturday in April.

Also nearby are Lake Mamie, Lake Mary, Horseshoe Lake, Twin Lakes Mammoth, Lake George, Twin Falls, Mammoth Mountain, Hot Creek, Sherwin Creek and Devils Postpile National Monument.

# TWIN LAKES (MAMMOTH)

*During the dry fly hatch, know-hows can catch more than 60 fish each morning.*

| | |
|---|---|
| **Rating:** | 7 |
| **Species:** | Rainbow Trout, Brook Trout and Brown Trout |
| **Stock:** | 12,300 pounds of rainbow trout. |
| **Facilities:** | Boat Rentals, Food, Boat Launch, Bait & Tackle, General Store, Campgrounds, Picnic Areas and Lodging |
| **Contact:** | Mammoth Lakes Visitors Center (760) 924-5500, Rick's Sports Center (760) 934-3416 |
| **Directions:** | From the junction of Highways 395 and 203 near Mammoth, take Highway 203 west 3.7 miles to Lake Mary Road. Veer left and drive 2.3 miles to Twin Lakes on the right. |

*Twin Lakes from Twin Falls*

Contrary to popular belief, Mammoth's Twin Lakes is not just a put-and-take fishery. Twin is also a great wild trout fishery for brooks and rainbows, with an outside shot at hooking a brown.

The bows and brookies landed here are up to three pounds. Browns can reach five pounds, but they are scarce. The window of opportunity to cash in on the wild trout is short, generally from mid-June through July, when the lake-born Callibaetis mayfly hatch takes place. During the dry fly hatch, know-hows can catch more than 60 fish each morning. But this terrific fly-fishing is best done from a float tube or boat near vegetation and aquatic plants.

The wild trout fishery aside, Twin is your typical Mammoth area lake. The California Department of Fish and Game plants 21,425 half-pound rainbows here, as well as another 50 brood stock bows. Another 1,200 pounds of Alpers from five to 10 pounds are also stocked.

Unfortunately, these small, shallow lakes (Twin Lakes is actually three small lakes), at 8,600 feet in the Inyo National Forest, are fished so hard that most of the fish get caught within a few days of being planted. Any-and-every shoreline technique works, including Power Bait, lures and night crawlers. Just be prepared for crowds.

If you plan to make the trip, supplies are available in Mammoth. Twin Lakes is closed to fishing from November 16 to the last Saturday in April. No gas-powered motors are permitted.

Also nearby are Mammoth Creek, Mammoth Creek Falls, Twin Falls, Lake Mary, Lake Mamie, Lake George, Horseshoe Lake and Mc Cloud Lake.

**No special techniques are required: just a hook and some bait.**

| | |
|---|---|
| **Rating:** | 8 |
| **Species:** | Rainbow Trout and Brown Trout |
| **Stock:** | 21,500 pounds of rainbow trout. |
| **Facilities:** | Lodging, Campgrounds, Picnic Areas, Boat Launch and Restrooms |
| **Contact:** | Mammoth Lakes Visitors Center (760) 924-5500, Rick's Sports Center (760) 934-3416 |

**Directions:** From the junction of Highways 395 and 203 near Mammoth, take Highway (203) west 3.7 miles to Lake Mary Road. Veer left, drive 3.7 miles and turn left at the sign for Lake Mary.

Lake Mary

Lake Mary is a perfect example of a successful put-and-take fishery. At 140 acres, the largest of the lakes on the Mammoth Lakes Loop, Mary is also the most heavily planted. In addition to 4,500 pounds of Alpers from three to 12 pounds, the California Department of Fish and Game spills 33,109 rainbows into the lake, 297 of which are in the two- to five-pound class. Although that may sound like a lot of fish, most of them are caught, and caught fast. The CA DFG estimates that anglers catch more than 75 percent of the fish planted in Mary each year.

Lake Mary is an easy place to catch fish. No special techniques are required: just a hook and some bait. Because it's a shallow lake, no leadcore or downriggers are needed here. As a matter of fact, you really don't need a boat at all. Although topwater trolling is productive, shore fishing is just as good. Setting up anywhere around the lake, and either tossing Kastmasters or Cripplelures, or simply floating Power Bait, night crawlers or cheeses, works well.

If you plan to make the trip, supplies are available in Mammoth. There is a boat-launch fee. Lake Mary is closed to fishing from November 16 to the last Saturday in April.

Also nearby are Barrett Lake, Crystal Lake, Twin Lakes, Lake Mamie, Lake George, Twin Falls and Mammoth Creek Falls.

# LAKE GEORGE

*The rainbows are such easy pickings, most anglers would rather have a blast catching stockers than spend all day fishing their butts off, trying to land one of the scarce big browns.*

**Rating:** 8
**Species:** Rainbow Trout, Brook Trout and Brown Trout
**Stock:** 14,242 pounds of rainbow trout.
**Facilities:** Campgrounds, Boat Rentals, Restrooms, Bait & Tackle and Boat Launch
**Contact:** Mammoth Lakes Visitors Center (760) 924-5500, Rick's Sports Center (760) 934-3416

**Directions:** From the junction of Highways 395 and 203 near Mammoth, take Highway 203 west 3.7 miles to Lake Mary Road. Veer left, drive 3.9 miles and turn left at the sign for George Lake. Continue three-tenths of a mile and turn right. Continue to the lake on the right.

*Lake George with Crystal Crag in the backdrop*

Most of the lakes in the Mammoth Lakes Loop are extremely shallow. With a maximum depth of 218 feet, however, Lake George is an exception. George also has some deep holes, which is the reason that prized brown trout thrives here. It therefore seems peculiar that few browns have been caught in George, but the explanation is actually simple.

With the California Department of Fish and Game spilling from their trucks 24,243 rainbow trout into the lake, the focus is on the easy catching. The rainbows are such easy pickings, most anglers would rather have a blast catching stockers than spend all day fishing their butts off, trying to land one of the scarce big browns. Chances of catching a brown really are pretty slim, unless you show up within a few days after ice-out or during the last few weeks of fishing season, when Rapalas have been known to entice a few.

Fishing for the rainbows is as easy as passing PE in high school. With all the trout that are stocked into this relatively small 38-acre lake, the rainbows are so concentrated they don't require special techniques to catch. To entice more anglers to fish the Mammoth area, 2,000 pounds of Alpers from two to 12 pounds are also stocked in George.

Shore and boat fishing are both productive. If you have a boat, troll red and gold Thomas Buoyants. Shore anglers station themselves all around the pine-shaded shoreline, but the most consistent areas are near the inlets on the back side. There is also a large boulder that offers great fishing between the inlets. There's a steep drop-off here where the fish tend to hang.

At 9,120 feet in the Inyo National Forest, George freezes over in the winter and isn't normally ice-free until sometime in June.

If you plan to make the trip, supplies are available in Mammoth. There is a boat launch fee. Lake George is closed to fishing from November 16 to the last Saturday in April.

Also nearby are Barrett Lake, Crystal Lake, Twin Lakes, Lake Mary and Lake Mamie.

*TJ does hold rainbow and brook trout, yet none grow to trophy sizes.*

**Rating:** 6
**Species:** Rainbow Trout and Brook Trout
**Stock:** 2 pounds of fingerling rainbow trout.
**Facilities:** None
**Contact:** Mammoth Lakes Visitors Center (760) 924-5500, Rick's Sports Center (760) 934-3416

**Directions:** From the junction of Highways 395 and 203 near Mammoth, take Highway 203 west 3.7 miles to Lake Mary Road. Veer left, drive 3.9 miles and turn left at the sign for Lake George. Drive three-tenths of a mile and turn right. Continue to the parking area at Lake George.

*TJ Lake*

Tucked away in a small basin, just a few hundred feet above Lake George, TJ Lake is one of the easiest to reach high-country lakes in the Sierra. At 9,250 feet in the Inyo National Forest, TJ (also known as Tee Jay Lake) is a popular destination for those camping at Lake Mary and Lake George.

TJ provides a less-crowded option, and anglers don't have to beat their bodies up to reach it. With a 1.6-mile roundtrip hike, and only a 285-foot elevation gain, you don't need to be in great shape to fish TJ. Even when it's taken slowly, the eight-tenths of a mile is easy to complete in about a half-hour.

The trail is easy to follow. The trailhead, which begins at the parking area for Lake George, is clearly visible. The path parallels George's south shore, before crossing its outlet stream. It then follows about 100 yards along the north shoreline, arriving at a trail junction. The right fork continues around the lake, while the left, which you'll need to follow, leads uphill, where it gains nearly all of its elevation over the next two-tenths of a mile, bringing you to Barrett Lake. The trail splits at Barrett. Take the right fork, which leads along Barrett's shoreline, before reaching another junction. Passing by signs for Emerald Lake, stay right, climbing over a small hill and finally arriving at TJ.

Don't expect to catch any lunkers here. TJ does hold rainbow and brook trout, yet none grow to trophy sizes. The California Department of Fish and Game plants 2,000 fingerling rainbows each year, and because of heavy fishing pressure, most are caught before they reach nine inches. Work the entire shoreline, tossing spinners, and you should do just fine. The outlet area may be your best bet.

If you plan to make the trip, supplies are available in Mammoth. TJ Lake is closed to fishing from November 16 to the last Saturday in April. Call ahead for road conditions. The road to Lake George may be closed till late May.

Also nearby are Barrett Lake, Crystal Lake, Lake Mary and Lake George.

# BARRETT LAKE

*Barrett is barren of fish. That's right, no fish live here.*

| | |
|---|---|
| **Rating:** | 1 |
| **Species:** | None |
| **Stock:** | None |
| **Facilities:** | None |
| **Contact:** | Mammoth Lakes Visitors Center (760) 924-5500, Rick's Sports Center (760) 934-3416 |

**Directions:** From the junction of Highways 395 and 203 near Mammoth, take Highway 203 west 3.7 miles to Lake Mary Road. Veer left, drive 3.9 miles and turn left at the sign for Lake George. Continue three-tenths of a mile and turn right. Continue to the parking area at Lake George.

*Barrett Lake*

As you may have figured by looking at this book's low rating, Barrett Lake isn't a great fishing lake. Actually, if you end up fishing it at all, we need to talk. Just between us, Barrett is barren of fish. That's right, no fish live here. None. So, why is it even in this book? Well, because every time I pass by the lake on my way to TJ Lake, I see people fishing it, complaining about how slow the bite is.

Barrett is not stocked by the California Department of Fish and Game and has no inlet stream, so there is no way for fish to enter it. There is a tiny outlet stream, but a logjam prohibits fish from entering that way. When I called the CA DFG to inquire about why the lake isn't planted (since most lakes in the region are), the most reasonable response I got was in reference to the size and depth of the lake. At about two acres, it is almost guaranteed to freeze solid each year, which obviously would kill all the fish. Fewer than seven feet deep, and with no water flowing in, Barrett can freeze damn fast.

Don't waste your time fishing here; instead, use the lake as a picnic area or a pretty place in the Inyo National Forest to read a book. If you don't believe me about the lack of fish here, walk around the lake yourself. The water is so clear you can see the bottom all the way out to the middle. To reach Barrett follow the directions on the previous write-up to TJ Lake.

If you plan to make the trip, supplies are available in Mammoth. Barrett Lake is closed to fishing from November 16 to the last Saturday in April. Call ahead for road conditions. The road to Lake George may be closed till late May.

Also nearby are TJ Lake, Crystal Lake, Lake Mary and Lake George.

*The only downfall here is that this shallow (10-foot deep) lake has extremely clear water, and although you can see the lake's bottom, the planters can also see you trying to catch them.*

| | |
|---|---|
| **Rating:** | 6 |
| **Species:** | Rainbow Trout |
| **Stock:** | 7,267 pounds of rainbow trout. |
| **Facilities:** | Campgrounds, Lodging, Boat Rentals, Restrooms and Bait & Tackle |
| **Contact:** | Mammoth Lakes Visitors Center (760) 924-5500, Rick's Sports Center (760) 934-3416 |

**Directions:** From the junction of Highways 395 and 203 near Mammoth, take Highway 203 west 3.7 miles to Lake Mary Road. Veer left and drive 4.3 miles to the lake on the left.

*Lake Mamie*

Part of the Mammoth Lakes Loop, Lake Mamie is not known for its spectacular fishing. Most people come here to take in the outstanding view from Mammoth Creek, Mamie's outlet stream, which rushes over a spillway, crosses under Lake Mary Road and becomes Twin Falls, cascading 250 feet down into Twin Lakes. From the brink of the falls, which is about 30 yards from the lake, visitors get a breathtaking view of all three Twin Lakes and the bridges that connect them.

As for Mamie itself, at 8,960 feet in the Inyo National Forest, although the smallest and shallowest lake on the loop, it does offer good fishing. The good fortune that anglers experience at this 19-acre lake is a direct result of the 11,697 half pounders and 50 brood fish rainbows that are planted by the California Department of Fish and Game. Mamie also gets 1,200 pounds of Alpers, ranging from two to 12 pounds.

The only downfall here is that this shallow (10-foot deep) lake has extremely clear water, and although you can see the lake's bottom, the planters can also see you trying to catch them. The rainbows bite Power Bait and night crawlers anyway, but don't expect to fool the Alpers so easily. Shoreline fishing is exceptional here, and an abundance of shade makes it an enjoyable experience.

If you plan to make the trip, supplies are available in Mammoth. There is a boat launch fee. Lake Mamie is closed to fishing from November 16 to the last Saturday in April.

Also nearby are Barrett Lake, Crystal Lake, Twin Lakes, Lake Mary, Lake George, Twin Falls and Mammoth Creek Falls.

# HORSESHOE LAKE

*A simple piece of advice: Don't waste your time fishing here.*

**Rating:** 2
**Species:** Cutthroat Trout
**Stock:** None
**Facilities:** Restrooms
**Contact:** Mammoth Lakes Visitors Center (760) 924-5500, Rick's Sports Center (760) 934-3416

**Directions:** From the junction of Highways 395 and 203 near Mammoth, take Highway 203 west 3.7 miles to Lake Mary Road. Veer left and drive 4.8 miles to the lake on the left.

*Horseshoe Lake*

Located at the base of the Mammoth Mountain Volcano, Horseshoe Lake is an unhealthy place for anglers because of dangerous $CO_2$ levels. This gas is responsible for killing off plant life and has created an unsafe environment for humans. After renewed seismic activity began in the Mammoth Lakes area in 1989, sightseers discovered hundreds of dead trees in the area around the lake, which alerted scientists to the problem.

Because $CO_2$ is odorless and cannot be detected by our senses, measurement devises were required to detect it and monitor its levels. After extensive research, the United States Geological Survey determined that seismic activity was responsible for the creation of underground fissures, and $CO_2$ was seeping through these fissures into the air. While normal levels are less the one percent, instruments have shown that the $CO_2$ gas levels in the soil are between 20 and 95 percent around Horseshoe. According to the USGS, these high concentrations of $CO_2$ come from underground magma, which releases gas through fissures. $CO_2$ is also released from surrounding limestone that the magma overheats.

At last count, at least 170 acres of trees were killed by high concentrations of $CO^2$. Although plants produce oxygen from $CO_2$ through photosynthesis, a fact sheet provided by the USGS explains how these trees are dying: "The high $CO_2$ concentrations in the soil on Mammoth Mountain are killing trees by denying their roots oxygen and by interfering with nutrient uptake."

I know you are all asking yourselves (and it's a damn good question) if there are any fish in the lake. It's hard to believe, but yah. Despite the fact that Horseshoe was purposely dried up twice in the Nineties in an effort to discourage visitors, there are still fish in it. The lake was dried by diverting its inlet streams, which normally carry fish from Mc Cloud Lake and an unnamed stream near Bottomless Pit.

At 8,950 feet in the Inyo National Forest, Horseshoe hasn't been stocked with fish for more than a decade. Although some fish are still able to enter it from Mc Cloud, there isn't a large population here. Can the fish live with the $CO_2$ emissions? In the summer, yes; the $CO_2$ rises up through the lake and is released into the air. In winter, however, when the lake freezes, the fish are put into danger, because the ice traps $CO_2$ that can kill them.

A simple piece of advice: don't waste your time fishing here. The dangers far outweigh the benefits of getting a shot at the cutthroat trout.

If you plan to make the trip, supplies are available in Mammoth. Posted in the parking area and all around the lake are precautionary warning signs. It is okay to walk through the area, provided you don't fall asleep on the ground and remain there for extended periods of time. Also, you are cautioned to keep your head above ground level and not to enter any holes, fissures or cracks. If you or anyone in your party becomes dizzy, nauseated or faint, seek medical attention immediately. Horseshoe Lake is closed to fishing from November 16 to the last Saturday in April.

Also nearby are Mc Cloud Lake, Lake Mamie, Twin Lakes (Mammoth), Lake George, Twin Falls, Lake Mary and Mammoth Creek Falls.

*$CO_2$ emissions at Horseshoe can be hazardous to humans.*

HORSESHOE LAKE

# MC LEOD LAKE

*There is one lake in the Mammoth Lakes region where you can catch the rare cutthroat trout, and the hike won't leave your legs sore for weeks after.*

| | |
|---|---|
| **Rating:** | 8 |
| **Species:** | Cutthroat Trout |
| **Stock:** | Three pounds of fingerling cutthroat trout. |
| **Facilities:** | None |
| **Contact:** | Mammoth Lakes Visitors Center (760) 924-5500, Rick's Sports Center (760) 934-3416 |
| **Directions:** | From the junction of Highways 395 and 203 near Mammoth, take Highway 203 west 3.7 miles to Lake Mary Road. Veer left and drive 4.8 miles to the trailhead and parking area. |

McLeod Lake

A cutthroat trout

There is one lake in the Mammoth Lakes region where you can catch the rare cutthroat trout, and the hike won't leave your legs sore for weeks after. At 9,250 feet in the Inyo National Forest, near Horseshoe Lake, Mc Leod Lake (also known as McCloud Lake) offers some great fishing.

Just a short half-mile trek through a pine forest, Mc Leod holds only cutthroats. In order to maintain a stable fish population, the California Department of Fish and Game plants 3,000 fingerlings each year. Most of the fish that get landed here are from six to eight inches, but many over 12 inches have been recorded. There are special regulations at McLeod: fishing is catch & release only, and only barbless hooks are permitted.

Anglers who don't take time to learn the lake's structure don't do well here. For example, because the first 10 yards of the lake is shallow, it's necessary to cast further out to be successful. Most of the fish hang where the underwater shelf drops-off.

Most people fly-fish Mc Leod, but I stuck with small spinners. The cutthroats wouldn't hit any of the larger lures like Cripplelures or Thomas Buoyants and were even pickier with the Panther Martins. But as soon as I found the color they liked, the action heated up. Try using all silver or gold. They shine extremely well in the sparkling clear water.

Getting to 9.5-acre Mc Leod is like a walk in the park (actually in the forest). The path starts at the parking area of Horseshoe Lake and gradually climbs 300 feet on a well-signed trail to the lake on the left.

If you plan to make the trip, supplies are available in Mammoth. Mc Leod Lake is closed to fishing from November 16 to the last Saturday in April. The road to Horseshoe Lake is sometimes closed into June.

Also nearby are Horseshoe Lake, Lake Mary, Lake Mamie, Twin Lakes and Lake George.

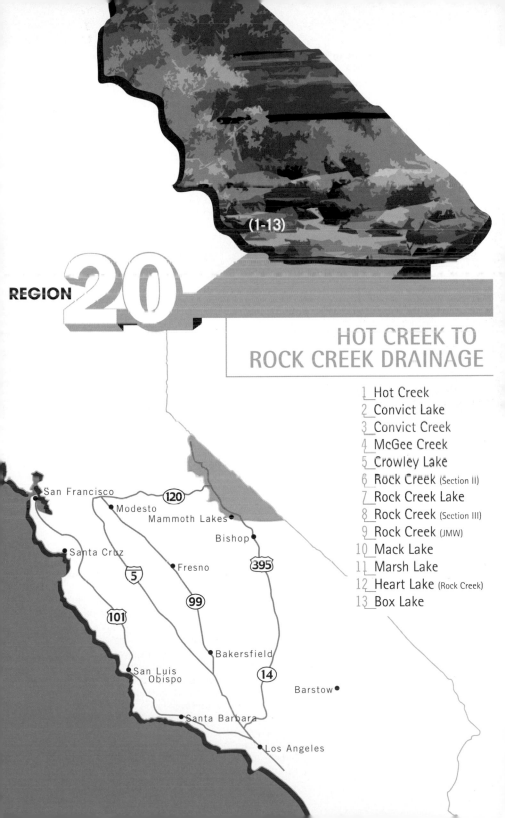

REGION 20

(1-13)

## HOT CREEK TO
## ROCK CREEK DRAINAGE

1_Hot Creek
2_Convict Lake
3_Convict Creek
4_McGee Creek
5_Crowley Lake
6_Rock Creek (Section II)
7_Rock Creek Lake
8_Rock Creek (Section III)
9_Rock Creek (JMW)
10_Mack Lake
11_Marsh Lake
12_Heart Lake (Rock Creek)
13_Box Lake

# HOT CREEK

*Don't you dare do anything illegal here! Anglers take care of this stream and won't tolerate unlawful methods.*

| | |
|---|---|
| **Rating:** | 10 |
| **Species:** | Rainbow Trout and Brown Trout |
| **Stock:** | None |
| **Facilities:** | Restrooms and Lodging |
| **Contact:** | Hot Creek Ranch (888) 695-0774, Mammoth Lakes Visitor Center (760) 924-5599 Rick's Sports Center (760) 934-3416 |
| **Directions:** | From the junction of Highway 395 and 203 in Mammoth, drive 3.5 miles south on Highway 395 to Hot Creek Road and turn left. Continue past the airport and turn right on a dirt road just before the cattle guard. Continue 2.3 miles to access points along the creek. |

*Hot Creek*

What is the finest trout stream in California? Many would argue Hot Creek, near Mammoth. While a few anglers might put up a defense for some other favorite wild trout stream, no knowledgeable one will dispute Hot Creek's fantastic fishery.

The tremendous fishing pressure Hot Creek receives is a testament to how many fish are here. In fact, at its peak in the Nineties, studies showed more than 11,000 fish inhabited each mile of the stream. In recent years, the population has fluctuated from 5,000 to 10,000 fish per mile.

What makes Hot Creek the world-class trout fishery it is? Several factors. Unlike many streams in the Eastern Sierra, stable water temperatures keep the creek from freezing over in the winter. This means shoreline and aquatic vegetation won't die, which sets the stage for year-round hatches of bugs and flies. More fish food!

Also, the Hot Creek Hatchery, which is located just upstream, flushes lots of nutrients into the creek. Consistent annual flows keep plenty of water for the fish, and, most importantly, the creek is designated as a wild trout stream, which means it's catch & release only. Because no take is permitted, the fish are kept in the system. Only artificial flies with barbless hooks are allowed. Bait dunkers and spin casters are not welcome here.

Though some rainbows reside here, Hot is primarily brown trout water. And while browns to six pounds have been caught, this isn't a trophy fishery. The majority of browns average eight to 12 inches. Two-pound fish are common, yet anything bigger is rare. Fish more than two pounds have usually smartened up and are tricky to land.

Hot Creek is one of the few waters in the state that remains free from poaching. Because wardens frequently patrol the creek, it's virtually non-existent. Don't you dare do anything illegal here! Anglers take care of this stream and won't tolerate unlawful methods.

The only downfall here is access. A mere one-mile section of the river is fishable. Upstream from this section is private Hot Creek Ranch, and downstream is the thermal hot springs area, where temperatures are too warm for fish.

If you plan to make the trip, supplies are available in Mammoth. Hot Creek is closed to fishing from November 16 to the last Saturday in April. Check sport-fishing regulations.

Also nearby are McGee Creek, Crowley Lake, Sherwin Creek and the Upper Owens River.

*Hot Creek is one of the best wild trout fisheries in the West.*

HOT CREEK

# CONVICT LAKE

*Six escapees from a prison break in Mono County took refuge at Convict Lake in 1871.*

| | |
|---|---|
| **Rating:** | 8 |
| **Species:** | Rainbow Trout and Brook Trout |
| **Stock:** | 24,424 pounds of rainbow trout. |
| **Facilities:** | Campgrounds, Boat Launch, Restrooms, Restaurant, General Store, Boat Rentals, Picnic Areas, RV Hookups and Lodging |
| **Contact:** | Convict Lake Resort (760) 934 - 3800 |
| **Directions:** | From Highway 395 in Bishop, drive approximately 35 miles north to Convict Lake Road. Turn left and drive two miles to the lake. |

*Convict Lake was formally known as Monte Diablo Lake.*

According to a story I was told by a Forest Service ranger, six escapees from a prison break in Mono County took refuge at Convict Lake in 1871. Prior to that, the lake was known as Monte Diablo. Shortly after the convicts set up camp, they had a gunfight with the authorities. Two convicts were killed in the battle and the rest fled. Soon after Monte Diablo Lake was renamed Convict Lake, it became a favorite fishing hole for many anglers. And now more than a century later, when most people have forgotten how it got its name, Convict is still considered a great place to fish.

At 7,580 feet in the Inyo National Forest, between Mammoth and Bishop, the lake's beauty is well known among anglers and it's the reason why so many of them visit here. Surrounded by towering snow-capped mountain peaks, this glacier-carved, crystal-clear lake is nearly a mile long and half a mile wide, with depths of up to 140 feet.

Good fishing is maintained with weekly stocks from the California Department of Fish and Game, totaling more than 43,000 trout each year. With the additional plants of 1,700 pounds of Alpers from five to 12 pounds, the chance of catching a lunker is excellent. The most consistent area is the Convict Creek inlet at the back of the lake. The absolute best spot is a half-submerged tree at the back of the lake, but shore fishing with Power Bait is productive everywhere, especially off points, near the spillway and at the boat launch. Trolling the shoreline or zigzagging the lake also works well.

If you plan to make the trip, supplies are available at Convict Lake Resort. Convict Lake is closed to fishing from November 16 to the last Saturday in April. Call ahead for lake conditions. The lake may be iced over at the start of the fishing season.

Also nearby are Rock Creek, Rock Creek Lake, Convict Creek, Crowley Lake and McGee Creek.

**To catch the fish of a lifetime, like one of these lunkers, you may have to spend all day here.**

| | |
|---|---|
| **Rating:** | 7 |
| **Species:** | Brown Trout, Brook Trout and Rainbow Trout |
| **Stock:** | 10,257 pounds of rainbow trout. |
| **Facilities:** | RV Hookups, Campgrounds and Restrooms |
| **Contact:** | Mammoth Lakes Visitors Center (760) 924-5500, Rick's Sports Center (760) 934-3416 |
| **Directions:** | From Highway 395 in Bishop, drive 34 miles north to Convict Lake Road. Turn left and continue to the stream. |

Convict Creek

Convict Creek doesn't get the same hype as Convict Lake, but it does get a lot of fishing pressure. Located eight miles south of Mammoth Lakes, Convict Creek is fed by Convict Lake's outlet. It's a medium-sized stream, much larger than the creeks in Lone Pine and Independence, but smaller than Bishop Creek. It usually yields high catch rates, but after weekends (or whenever fishing pressure is high) the fish aren't always so cooperative.

The few campgrounds scattered along Convict Creek are all heavily stocked on a weekly basis by the California Department of Fish and Game. The CA DFG dumps 19,914 half-pound bows and another 30 over three pounds. There are also wild rainbows and browns in the stream.

The most popular spot, a large pool located at 7,600 feet just below Convict Lake's spillway, ironically has low catch rates. However, there is no better place along the creek to try to catch a five to 10-pounder, because the big ones always seem to be here. On an average day, more than 75 anglers fish this pool, keeping the fish wary and timid. These fish have seen almost every lure invented, so you have to be patient or get lucky.

Most anglers who fish this pool do so for about 15 minutes and leave, because they aren't getting any action. To catch the fish of a lifetime, like one of these lunkers, you may have to spend all day here. Remember, these fish have to eat sometime.

If you are going to fish Convict Creek, you'll need to bring along an arsenal of equipment. Lures work best in some spots, but you might want to try using flies, Power Bait or salmon eggs in others. For the highest catch rates, target your efforts near the campgrounds and where the river crosses under the road.

If you plan to make the trip, supplies are available at Convict Lake. Convict Creek is closed to fishing from November 16 to the last Saturday in April.

Also nearby are Convict Lake, Hot Creek, Hot Creek Fish Hatchery, Rock Creek, Rock Creek Lake and the Mammoth Lakes Loop.

# MCGEE CREEK

| | |
|---|---|
| **Rating:** | 7 |
| **Species:** | Rainbow Trout and Brown Trout |
| **Stock:** | 5,687 pounds of rainbow trout. |
| **Facilities:** | Pack Station, Campgrounds and Restrooms |
| **Contact:** | Mammoth Lakes Visitors Center (760) 924-5500, Rick's Sports Center (760) 934-3416, \cGee Pack Station (760) 935-4324 (Summer) or (760) 878-2207 (Winter) |

**Directions:** From Highway 395 in Bishop, drive 28 miles north to McGee Creek Road. Turn left and continue one-quarter of a mile south on Old Highway 395 to McGee Pack Station Road. The stream is planted off access roads from Old Highway 395 to the upper campground.

*McGee Creek in December of 2001*

McGee Creek is a favorite spot for salmon egg anglers, who often experience high catch rates there. Because of a lack of pools, the creek can be difficult to fish with spinners, but those with salmon eggs can lift their bait into places where spin fishermen can't. Fishing with either a single salmon egg hook or a treble hook work well.

McGee Creek is a small stream located at 7,000 feet in the Inyo National Forest just north of the town of Tom's Place, and one of its largest draws is the McGee Pack Station located at the end of the road. This pack station specializes in taking hikers and anglers into the John Muir Wilderness, Hilton Lakes Basin, Upper McGee Creek and over McGee Pass.

Although the creek is small, the California Department of Fish and Game gives anglers incentive to stop here, dumping 11,063 bows into the stream. An added treat is that McGee Creek isn't heavily fished like many nearby streams, such as Rock and Convict Creeks. It's a great place to come and dodge the crowds at more popular destinations in the Eastern Sierra.

If you plan to make the trip, supplies are available in Tom's Place, Mammoth and Bishop. McGee Creek is closed to fishing from November 16 to the last Saturday in April.

Also nearby are Convict Creek, Convict Lake, McGee Falls, Crowley Lake and the Rock Creek Drainage.

*There are a few-hundred-thousand fish caught during the first three months of the fishing season here, and as many as 80,000 are reportedly landed on opening weekend.*

**Rating:** 10

**Species:** Rainbow Trout, Brown Trout, Cutthroat Trout, Golden Trout and Sacramento Perch

**Stock:** 30,950 pounds of sub-catchable, 28,125 pounds of rainbow trout, 4,358 pounds of fingerling rainbow trout, 140 pounds of fingerling brown trout, 40 pounds of fingering golden trout and 2,500 pounds of sub-catchable cutthroat trout.

**Facilities:** Boat Launch, Boat Rentals, Restrooms, Marina, Gas, Snack Bar, Bait & Tackle, Campgrounds and Fish Cleaning Stations

**Contact:** Sierra Drifters Guide Service (760) 935-4250, Crowley Fish Camp (760) 935-4301

**Directions:** From Highway 395 in Bishop, drive 31 miles north and turn east on Crowley Lake Road. Drive four-tenths of a mile to the lake.

*Roughly 300 brood stock rainbows are released into Crowley each year.*

For most anglers who visit Crowley Lake, it's the site of their annual opening day fishing trip to the Eastern Sierra, the last Saturday in April. During each opener, approximately 10,000 anglers fish here, and most catch limits in only a few hours. There are a few-hundred thousand fish caught during the first three months of the fishing season here, and as many as 80,000 are reportedly landed on opening weekend.

How is it possible that so many anglers catch so many fish? It's called "stocking." It's estimated that at the start of each season there are nearly one million fish in Crowley. Added to a large population of wild brown and rainbow trout, as well as thousands of holdover rainbows, the California Department of Fish and Game stocks nearly 700,000 trout into Crowley each year. Also, 1,700 pounds of Alpers from five to 10 pounds are planted.

Many anglers think this man-made 5,280-acre lake is the most productive trout lake in California, maybe even in the country. Fish growth rates here are staggering. In fact, the lake is run as a put-and-grow fishery. That's why only a small number of catchable size fish are planted. They don't really need to be reared in hatcheries, because they can grow here on their own.

So, most of the fish planted here are fingerlings and sub-catchables. The CA DFG believes that if possible it's preferable to let fish grow where they're planted, rather than transplanting them from a hatchery. Not only is it more cost-effective, the fish develop more of the characteristics of wild fish, which makes them an all around better product.

Why is Crowley so productive? There are three main reasons: 1) a plentiful supply of food; 2) excellent structure; 3) numerous tributaries.

A lake's food source is obviously the most important ingredient for a healthy fish population. The key to Crowley's food chain is phosphorous, which is an essential nutrient for plant growth. Big Springs, the headwaters of the Upper Owens River, Crowley's largest tributary, provides a lot of the lake's phosphorous.

Because algae, which is at the foundation of the lake's food chain, thrives on this phosphorous, it provides a stable food source for a plethora of larger organisms in the lake. The trout then feed on these larger organisms, the most abundant of which is an aquatic insect species called the midge (also known as chironomids). In the same class as mosquitoes, these insects look pretty much like small mosquitoes. Amazing as it might seem when you strain your eyes to see one of these tiny critters, the fish here grow very quickly on a diet of these little guys.

Crowley develops excellent structure because it is a large body of water that is relatively shallow. Sunlight (there are no trees on the shoreline to block the sun) and shallow water are the perfect ingredients for vegetation growth underwater. Although its deepest point (90 feet) is in the middle of the lake where the Old Owens River channel runs, this deep water takes up just a fraction of the lake's space. Overall, the lake only averages 30 feet deep, and there are plenty of shallow areas near the shore that are productive. That's because submerged aquatic vegetation and rooted plants make great fish habitat and spawning areas.

Crowley has numerous subsystems that feed it. Several tributaries not only bring a lot of water to the lake, but also deliver nutrients and food. Sherwin, Mammoth, Deadman, Hot and Glass Creek feed the lake via the Upper Owens on the north shore. McGee, Convict (a tributary to McGee) Hilton and Whiskey Creek enter on the west end. These inlets also keep cool water coming into the lake, which is vital for trout.

Unlike most other lakes, Crowley is planted with three strains of rainbow trout, the Kamloops, Coleman and Eagle Lake trout, maintaining a diverse rainbow fishery. Coleman

Biologist Curtis Milliron is proud of this giant Sacramento perch.

Michele Loe displays a three-pound rainbow caught at Crowley.

and Eagle Lakes are planted from August through October as sub-catchables, which means there are 10 fish in each stocked pound. The Kamloops are stocked as catchables, or three to a pound. Kamloops are typically found near the shore and Colemans in open water. Anglers usually don't catch the Eagle Lake trout until their second year in the lake, so these fish have a chance to develop and contribute to the lake's trophy-fish population.

Prior to 1985, Crowley was closed to fishing on August 1, offering anglers only a three-month window to fish the lake. The lake closed in August to allow for stocking. As long as water quality was up to par and the water was cool enough, stocking took place right after the lake's closing. This allowed the fish nine months to grow without anglers harassing them. And because of the ideal conditions here, the fish got a lot bigger than they would have in a hatchery.

The lake, however, has been managed differently since 1985, following more traditional Eastern Sierra-fishery seasonal patterns. One exception here is that special regulations take affect August 1. Only artificial lures with barbless hooks can be used. The limit is also reduced to two fish, and each must be at least 18 inches in total length. These regulations are to protect the newly stocked fish.

Unfortunately, the days are long gone when Crowley possibly held the state record for browns. Prior to the Nineties, there were a lot of browns over 20 pounds. At that time, 100,000 browns of both sub-catchable and catchable size were being stocked each season, and the lake was loaded with them. Even though a lot of browns were caught and others died of old age, there always seemed to be plenty of them that survived year after year.

The downfall of Crowley's brown trout fishery began in 1986, when -- in response to an infection of whirling disease -- the CA DFG destroyed the entire strain of browns in their hatchery. To replace them, wild browns were taken from nearby Oak Creek in Inyo County and were raised as the next group of brood stock to provide fingerling trout for Eastern Sierra reservoirs.

This new strain of fish, however, has proven to be a dud. Since 1987, the CA DFG has yet to stock fish larger than fingerling size. And although the fingerlings can survive in the hatchery, most have been unable to live in the lake. Predators have taken most of them. Overall, stocking of browns has been reduced by more than 60 percent. Don't get me wrong, there are still some large browns in the lake, as well as thousands of wild rainbows, but they aren't growing to the enormous sizes they used to. More than 116,000 fingerling browns are planted annually. A credible CA DFG biologist estimates that today there are roughly 100,000 wild brown and rainbow trout in Crowley and its tributaries.

While Crowley is known for its rainbow and brown trout, cutthroats have begun to flourish here during the last few years. Although the CA DFG has planted cutts into Crowley for some time now, when they were planted as fingerlings they didn't survive, most likely because adult fish ate them. So, the CA DFG changed strategies, and instead of planting fish 30-40 per pound, in the late Nineties they decided to stock sub-catchables, which come 10 to the pound. It worked. The cutts are now well represented with many four- to six-pound fish. Biologists soon expect cutts weighing in double digits to be caught. More than 15,200 sub-catchable cutts are planted each year.

The locals will tell you if you can't catch fish at Crowley, give it up! More than 100,000 half-pound rainbows, 323,585 subs and 139,172 fingerlings are planted. In 2000, 36,000 fingerling golden trout were also planted. While the pressure during the first three months of the season is tremendous, the numbers of fish caught is also staggering. Whether boating, fishing in any of the coves with night crawlers, tossing Power Bait from the shore, trolling the middle of the lake and off the points, or fly-fishing a midge (chironomid) under a strike indicator, nearly everyone catches limits. Tiny 16- to 20-size midges are best. If using lures, stick to olive, red and black colors, resembling various stages of the midge hatch.

*Tom Loe caught this brown while guiding at Crowley.*

CROWLEY LAKE

Over the years, Crowley's Sacramento perch fishery has also become world class. Although the CA DFG is unsure how the fish got into the lake, they know it happened in September of 1965 and that they were illegally introduced. It's estimated there are a few-hundred-thousand perch here. On an average day, anglers catch 10-50. The state record 3.10-pounder was landed here in 1987.

At 6,780 feet in the Inyo National Forest, Crowley has the potential to remain one of the best and most productive trout fisheries in the continental United States. The reservoir, however, was constructed in 1941 for the primary purpose of storing water for Southern California. And we all know what a huge issue water has become in California.

Currently the lake is allowed to fill in the winter and early spring, before water is released in the summer to create hydroelectric power and provide for the domestic needs of Southern California residents. If the decision is made, however, to take more water from the lake, the fishery could go downhill. At low water levels, the lake's temperature will rise and its oxygen levels will become dangerously low. In turn, this could cause algae blooms. In short, lower water levels could mean a doomed fishery. We'll just have to wait and see.

If you plan to make the trip, supplies are available in Mammoth and Bishop. Crowley Lake is closed to fishing from November 16 to the last Saturday in April. Special restrictions apply from August 1 through October 31. Call ahead before opening day, because some years the lake can be iced over. Call ahead for weather conditions. Nasty winds develop here.

Also nearby are Convict Lake, Hot Creek, Convict Creek, Rock Creek and Rock Creek Lake.

CROWLEY LAKE

*Crowley Lake is a mix of ice and snow in the winter.*

**When we fished the stream just before sunset, we could see more than 20 trout jump out of the water, all vying to catch flies.**

| | |
|---|---|
| **Rating:** | 8 |
| **Species:** | Rainbow Trout, Brown Trout and Brook Trout |
| **Stock:** | 18,744 pounds of rainbow trout. |
| **Facilities:** | Campgrounds, RV Hookups, Lodging, Restaurant, Bait & Tackle and Restrooms |
| **Contact:** | Rock Creek Resort (760) 935-4311, Camping Information (877) 444-6777 Inyo National Forest (760) 873-2400 |
| **Directions:** | From Highway 395 in Bishop, drive 20 miles north to Tom's Place. Turn left on Rock Creek Road to the stream. The stream is stocked from Iris Meadow Campground to Rock Creek Lodge. |

*Jason McLean (Left) and Brett Ermilio (Right) build a fire to stay warm at Rock Creek.*

It was 4:45 in the morning. We'd already been warned about the bear problem in this area, but, to tell you the truth, we were staying here because I really wanted to see a bear. I'd seen them before, but I wanted my friends Brett Ermilio and Jason McLean to see one.

I told them we should leave some food out for the bears. While I was building the fire, I instructed them to leave a trail of food from the creek to our tent, but when I glanced over neither had moved an inch.

"What are you guys doing?" I tried not to show a smile. "Hurry, we have to build the trail before it gets dark, or the bears won't come."

When I went to the car to get some lighter fluid, I heard Brett whisper to Jason. "Do you think he's serious? Wouldn't a bear attack us? I don't think we should do it."

I told them later that I was kidding. I didn't think they were really going to do it. Anyway, Jason was too smart to listen to me. His dad was an L.A. County Sheriff who'd raised him to think before acting. My telling them that didn't help; I'd already gotten them paranoid. Jason and Brett made me put all our food two campsites away. Then, they tried to scrub the scent of food off the table.

As luck would have it, the bear found our trash hanging from the tree and woke us up, slurping on a Snickers candy bar wrapper. I hurried out of my sleeping bag to see it, but by the time I got there the bear was gone. Brett said it was a baby, but I was happy he got to see his first bear. That was a great experience, but the previous night's fishing was even better.

With green meadows, deep pools and wild trout, the lower portion of Rock Creek, just below Rock Creek Lake, has many of the same characteristics as Upper Rock Creek. When we fished the stream just before sunset, and could see more than 20 trout jump out of the water, all vying to catch flies. Most of them were small, but it was a sight to see.

Lower Rock Creek gets a lot of visitors, but it also gets a lot of fish. It's planted with some 36,311 rainbows from the California Department of Fish and Game, and that's on top of the wild trout already present in the stream. Fly-fishing works well in the crystal-clear water, as do spinners, salmon eggs and Power Bait. Work on fishing in the campgrounds, where the creek crosses under the road, and just below Rock Creek Lake. These areas are planted weekly from late spring through fall.

If you plan to make the trip, supplies are available in Tom's Place and at Rock Creek Lodge. Rock Creek is closed to fishing from November 16 to the last Saturday in April.

Also nearby are Rock Creek Lake, Upper Rock Creek, Little Lakes Valley, Owens River, McGee Creek, Pine Creek, Crowley Lake and Hilton Creek.

376

*Due to snow and ice Rock Creek can be difficult to fish in May.*

# ROCK CREEK LAKE

*The lake is heavily planted, receiving 40,000 rainbow trout from the California Department of Fish and Game, including some more than three pounds.*

**Rating:** 9
**Species:** Rainbow Trout, Brown Trout and Brook Trout
**Stock:** 21,883 pounds of rainbow trout.
**Facilities:** Campsites, Restrooms, Restaurant, Lodging, Bait & Tackle, Boat Rentals and Launch Ramp
**Contact:** Rock Creek Resort (760) 935-4311, Camping Information (877) 444-6777
Inyo National Forest (760) 873-2400

**Directions:** From Highway 395 in Bishop, drive 30 miles north to the town of Tom's Place and turn left on Rock Creek Road. Continue eight miles to Rock Creek Lake.

*Rock Creek Lake from above*

Rock Creek Lake is the ideal family destination for a week in the outdoors. It offers something for everyone and can be used as a base camp for nearby activities in the Eastern Sierra. The crowds don't mob Rock Creek Lake the way they do nearby Crowley Lake or the Mammoth and June Lake Loops. Nor, does the wind blow frantically as it does at nearby Convict Lake.

Located at 8,000 feet in the Inyo National Forest, Rock Creek is one of the most scenic lakes in the Sierra. Sounds good? Even better are your choices for day trips: there's Hot Creek, Devils Postpile National Monument, Rock Creek, Mammoth Lakes, June Lakes, Mammoth Mountain and the John Muir Wilderness, to name but a few. Staying at the lake isn't a bad idea either, because the fishing is superb and the scenery is unforgettable.

Good fishing can be had throughout the fishing season. The lake is heavily planted, receiving nearly 40,000 rainbow trout from the California Department of Fish and Game, including some more than three pounds and 1,000 pounds of Alpers from five to 10 pounds. Red and gold Thomas Buoyants, silver Kastmasters, as well as fly & bubble combos produce the best catch rates. Trolling can also be productive, but at only 55 acres, there's not a lot of lake for your boat to explore.

Most importantly, with snow-capped peaks towering above the tall pines that surround the lake, and the peace and quiet infused with the freshness of clean, crisp mountain air, there is a wonderful serenity about Rock Creek Lake. Many people come just to relax and enjoy these surroundings. Whether you're here for the fishing or not, you won't be disappointed.

If you plan to make the trip, supplies are available at Rock Creek Lake Resort. Rock Creek Lake is closed to fishing from November 1 to the last Saturday in April. Call ahead for road conditions. Chains may be required. At times the lake doesn't thaw until early June.

Also nearby are Rock Creek (Sections II & III, Rock Creek (JM Wilderness), Little Lakes Valley, John Muir Wilderness, Convict Lake, Convict Creek, Crowley Lake and Mammoth Lakes Loop.

**In addition to the planted fish, wild rainbows, browns and brook trout are already present.**

| | |
|---|---|
| **Rating:** | 7 |
| **Species:** | Rainbow Trout, Brown Trout and Brook Trout |
| **Stock:** | 2,412 pounds of rainbow trout. |
| **Facilities:** | Primitive Campsites, Restrooms, Restaurant, Lodging and Bait & Tackle |
| **Contact:** | Rock Creek Resort (760) 935-4311, Camping Information (877) 444-6777 |
| | Inyo National Forest (760) 873-2400 |
| **Directions:** | From Highway 395 in Bishop, drive 30 miles north to the town of Tom's Place and turn left on Rock Creek Road. Drive eight miles to Rock Creek Lake and veer right. The creek is stocked at the Mosquito Flat Trailhead and also near it's inlet to Rock Creek Lake. |

*Rock Creek near the Mosquito Flat Trailhead*

Rock Creek, between Rock Creek Lake and the John Muir Wilderness, is amazing. Beginning at 10,300 feet and ending at 8,000 feet at Rock Creek Lake, this section of the stream in the Inyo National Forest offers to its visitors the beauty of the John Muir Wilderness, just a step away from their car.

The stream is mostly fished by anglers on their way to the Little Lakes Valley. They park at the Mosquito Flat Trailhead, the starting point of one of the most popular trails in the Sierra. There are primitive campsites with restrooms at the trailhead, allowing hikers to get a good night's rest before heading out into the backcountry.

The fishing remains good partly because the California Department of Fish and Game stocks some 4,700 trout in the 10-12 inch class. In addition to the planted fish, wild rainbows, browns and brook trout are already present. Power Bait and just about any lure will do the trick. Because of the elevation, the stream usually isn't fishable until it thaws in June.

Bring along a camera. This stream offers some amazing shots. The creek winds through meadows with pines towering overhead, and, if you're lucky, a bear or a few deer will stay in the frame long enough for you to snap a quick shot.

If you plan to make the trip, supplies are available at Rock Creek Resort. Check road conditions ahead of time. At times the road isn't snow-free until May. Rock Creek is closed to fishing from the November 1 until the last Saturday in April.

Also nearby are Little Lakes Valley, Rock Creek Lake and lower Rock Creek.

*Rock Creek above Rock Creek Lake*

# ROCK CREEK
## (JOHN MUIR WILDERNESS)

*It's one of the few streams in the West where on every cast you have a chance of hooking a rainbow, brown, brook or golden trout.*

| | |
|---|---|
| **Rating:** | 10 |
| **Species:** | Rainbow, Brook, Brown and Golden Trout. |
| **Stock:** | None |
| **Facilities:** | None |
| **Contact:** | Mammoth Lakes Visitors Center (760) 924-5500, Rick's Sports Center (760) 934-3416 |

**Directions:** From Highway 395 in Bishop, drive 30 miles north to Tom's Place. Turn west on Rock Creek Road and drive eight miles. Just before Rock Creek Lake, veer right at the fork and continue to the Mosquito Flat Trailhead (about a mile from the lake). Park in the parking lot and follow the trail to the creek. The creek is next to the trail.

*Rock Creek between Mack and Marsh Lakes*

There are so many Rock Creeks in this state that you could get confused about where they all are, but if you ever visit Rock Creek in the John Muir Wilderness, you'll never forget where it is. Located between Mammoth and Bishop in the Eastern Sierra Nevada Mountain Range, this Rock Creek is one of the state's most beautiful streams, and it offers some of the best stream fishing in the high country. Although this is considered a high-country destination, you can relax, because your car does most of the work for you. One of the highest paved roads in the Western United States the road climbs over 10,000 feet to the Mosquito Flat Trailhead, which leads to the creek.

The Rock Creek Drainage is one of the best-known fishing areas in the California. However, most anglers concentrate on Lower Rock Creek below Rock Creek Lake and the upper stretch of the creek alongside the parking lot near the trailhead. Surprisingly, few anglers make the effort to hike into the John Muir Wilderness where the best fishing is found. The hike only takes a few minutes. More of a walk, it climbs gradually uphill on a smooth dirt trail, allowing people of all ages to enjoy nature's beauty.

The creek originates in the 14,000-foot peaks between Mt. Abbot and Mt. Dade, before it drains into the Treasure Lakes at 11,175 feet. Then, in the Little Lakes Valley, it winds in and out of Long, Box, Heart, Marsh and Mack Lakes, finally emptying into Rock Creek Lake. The scenery along its course is breathtaking. Most of the way, the creek flows through lush green meadows sprinkled with wildflowers and meanders beneath snow-capped peaks towering west, south and north. Bears and deer are commonly seen sipping water from the creek in the early mornings and late evenings.

As for the fishing, it's hard to find a better place. It's one of the few streams in the West where on every cast you have a chance of hooking a rainbow, brown, brook or golden trout. Ironically, with all the fish in the creek, many anglers have difficulty catching them. That's because they're used to fishing for stockers, not wild trout. When wild fish see them, they dart for cover. These anglers walk to the bank and wonder where all the fish went. Experienced anglers who don't let the fish see them do a lot better.

This stretch of the creek has many different personalities. There's deep, clear pools in some places, fast moving waters in others, and a variety of rocky, sandy, dirt and grassy bottoms. Fly-fishing is extremely popular here, but small spinners and Wholly Buggers are also productive. Most importantly: pack in – pack out. This area is worth preserving. If possible, use barbless lures and hooks to protect the fish and save them from injury.

If you plan to make the trip, supplies are available in Tom's Place, Bishop and Mammoth. Rock Creek is closed to fishing from November 1 to the last Saturday in April. Check trail and weather conditions ahead of time. The trail can be covered in snow until July. A wilderness permit is required for overnight travel in the John Muir Wilderness.

Also nearby are the lakes in the Little Lakes Valley, Ruby Lake, Hilton Lakes and Lower Rock Creek.

*Rock Creek west of the Mosquito Flat Trailhead*

ROCK CREEK (JMW)

# MACK LAKE

*There was no trash, no people, just me and a crystal-clear, calm, mirror-like lake. At 10,470 feet, surrounded by animals, wildflowers, green meadows and wild trout, I was amazed.*

**Rating:** 9
**Species:** Rainbow Trout, Brook Trout and Brown Trout
**Stock:** None
**Facilities:** None
**Contact:** Mammoth Lakes Visitors Center (760) 924-5500, Rock Creek Resort (760) 935-4311 Camping Information (877) 444-6777, Inyo National Forest (760) 873-2400

**Directions:** From Highway 395 in Bishop, drive 30 miles north to the town of Tom's Place and exit Rock Creek Road. Turn west and continue eight miles to Rock Creek Lake. Veer right and continue approximately one mile to the Mosquito Flat trailhead. Park and follow the trail for one-fourth of a mile to the lake on your left-hand side.

*Mack Lake*

While camping at Rock Creek just below Rock Creek Lake, my friend Brett Ermilio woke me at 4:45 a.m. to tell me he'd heard something walking around our campground. We hadn't bothered sleeping in a tent, and because the zipper on his sleeping bag was broken and unable to be zipped up, the frigid temperatures kept him awake all night. Now, Brett's not what you'd call a regular outdoorsman, and his ears pricked with every rustling leaf. He was a little spooked even before he heard these noises. When I got up to see what all the ruckus was about, sure enough, he was right: there was a small bear going through our trash. But, when I marched over to greet the intruder, he ran off before I could get a good look at him.

It was August and the temperatures were in the upper 20's, too cold to get back to sleep. We got in the car and drove a few miles up the road to Mosquito Flat Trailhead, where I hit the jackpot. And I owe it all to that bear. If he hadn't awakened me that morning, I would have never found this wonderful place. As for Brett, who stayed in the car instead of joining me on the trail, well, I think that was the worst decision he'd ever made.

I had no idea where I was going, but as soon as I hit the trailhead, the beauty overwhelmed me. I walked for 10 minutes before I left the Inyo National Forest and entered the John Muir Wilderness. Shortly came Mack Lake, the first of many lakes in the Little Lakes Valley. There was no trash, no people, just me and a crystal-clear, calm, mirror-like lake. At 10,470 feet, surrounded by deer, marmots, colorful wildflowers, lush green meadows and wild trout, I was amazed at this majestic place.

This small, narrow lake is filled with rainbow, brown and brook trout. Your best bet is fly-fishing or fishing with small spinners. Best spot is where Rock Creek enters the lake.

If you plan to make the trip, supplies are available at Rock Creek Resort. Call ahead for trail conditions. During bad winters, Mack Lake can remain frozen until mid-July. Mack Lake is closed to fishing from November 1 to the last Saturday in April. A wilderness permit is required for overnight travel in the John Muir Wilderness.

Also nearby are Rock Creek and Rock Creek Lake.

*Fly-fishing is superb, especially in early July when mosquitoes are the thickest.*

| | |
|---|---|
| **Rating:** | 7 |
| **Species:** | Brown Trout, Rainbow Trout and Brook Trout |
| **Stock:** | None |
| **Facilities:** | None |
| **Contact:** | Mammoth Lakes Visitors Center (760) 924-5500, Rick's Sports Center (760) 934-3416 |
| **Directions:** | From Highway 395 in Bishop, drive 30 miles north to the town of Tom's Place and exit Rock Creek Road. Turn west and continue eight miles to Rock Creek Lake. Veer right and continue about a mile to the Mosquito Flat trailhead. |

*Steve Heimlich weights fingerling trout to be stocked in the high country.*

Nearly all of the lakes above the Rock Creek Lake provide great fishing and stunning scenery. However, there are so many within such a close proximity to the trailhead, not all the lakes get the respect they deserve. Marsh Lake is one that is definitely undervalued

Of all the lakes in the drainage, Marsh is probably the least fished. Because it looks more like a large pond than a lake, many anglers simply pass it by without making any casts, but the neglect isn't warranted. This lake is loaded with rainbow and brook trout, has a sprinkle of browns, and you even have an outside chance of catching a golden trout here.

At 10,420 feet in the John Muir Wilderness, because the four-acre lake is less than a mile (with only a 200-foot elevation gain) from the Mosquito Flat Trailhead, it is one of the easiest high-country lakes to reach in the Sierra. The lake is less than one-tenth of a mile east of Heart Lake and a quarter-mile west of Mack Lake. Rock Creek flows in and out of all three lakes, allowing fish to swim out Mack and Heart and into Marsh.

Although trout can be caught anywhere around the lake by tossing Panther Martins, the bulk of anglers arrive with fly rods. Fly-fishing is superb, especially in early July when mosquitoes are the thickest. Most of the fish range from six to 10 inches. Because tall grasses and marshy shorelines surround the lake, it is best fished with waders. Many people wouldn't even consider hauling a pair into the high country, but the hike to Marsh Lake is short and easy, so why not give it a try?

If you plan to make the trip, supplies are available in Mammoth and Bishop. Check trail conditions before you leave. At times, the trail isn't snow-free until July. A wilderness permit is required for overnight travel in the John Muir Wilderness. Marsh Lake is closed to fishing from November 1 to the last Saturday in April.

Also nearby are Heart Lake, Long Lake, Box Lake, Chickenfoot Lake, Rock Creek Lake and Rock Creek.

# HEART LAKE

*They'll hit just about any lure you throw, and they love flies.*

| | |
|---|---|
| **Rating:** | 8 |
| **Species:** | Rainbow Trout, Brown Trout and Brook Trout |
| **Stock:** | Three pounds of fingerling rainbow trout. |
| **Facilities:** | None |
| **Contact:** | Mammoth Lakes Visitors Center (760) 924-5500 |

**Directions:** From Highway 395 in Bishop, drive 30 miles north to the town of Tom's Place. In Tom's Place, turn west on Rock Creek Road and continue to Rock Creek Lake. Veer right at a fork in the road and continue about a mile to the Mosquito Flat trailhead.

*Heart Lake*

Heart Lake is one of the best examples of what the John Muir Wilderness has to offer: beauty, clean air, wildlife, great scenery and fantastic fishing. It is the third major lake you'll encounter along the Mosquito Flat Trailhead, whose path begins at 10,300 feet, just above Rock Creek Lake. By the time you reach the 10,500-foot elevation, where this eight-acre lake is situated, you might be so distracted by the beautiful scenery, you won't be in the mood for fishing.

There are hundreds of wildflowers blossoming along Heart Lake's shoreline, and an abundance of wildlife roaming the woods around the two crystal-clear lakes that lie within five minutes of each other. There are spectacular views whose glossies pay the salaries of numerous photographers that return here year after year. You'll also find beautiful Rock Creek flowing through green meadows, into and out of Heart Lake. Then, if you take a moment to stop and stare, you'll see towering peaks in the distance.

What else can Heart Lake possibly offer? A lot! The lake has a self-sustaining population of brook trout, is planted with rainbows and even holds a few browns. Size? None of them get big; but quantity, yes! There are always enough fish to go around. And the fish are willing, too.

With the lake frozen over from December to June, and even later during long winters (it was frozen over the July 4th weekend following the El Nino of the mid-Nineties), the fish have a small time frame in which to feed and take advantage of the ice-free surface. They'll hit just about any lure you throw, and love flies. Fishing anywhere around the shoreline is productive. However, the Rock Creek inlet produces the most consistent action, because the fish stackup where the water comes in, waiting for food to come in with it.

Leaving Heart Lake, I took a little more time to appreciate the scenery. I realized this was the most beautiful place I'd been, next to Lake Placid, New York. I instantly became attached to the John Muir Wilderness and the Little Lakes Valley. Let's just say I'll be back again next year, and I'm sure you'll feel the same.

If you plan to make the trip, supplies are available in Mammoth and Bishop. Check trail conditions before you leave. At times, the trail isn't snow-free until July. Heart Lake is closed to fishing from November 1 to the last Saturday in April.

Also nearby are Box Lake, Long Lake, Chickenfoot Lake, Rock Creek Lake and Rock Creek.

*The scenery is superb at Heart Lake*

HEART LAKE

# Box Lake

*Most of the fishing pressure occurs along the trail side of the lake, so the fish are less skittish on the far side.*

| | |
|---|---|
| **Rating:** | 7 |
| **Species:** | Brown Trout, Rainbow Trout and Brook Trout |
| **Stock:** | None |
| **Facilities:** | None |
| **Contact:** | Mammoth Lakes Visitors Center (760) 924-5500, Rick's Sports Center (760) 934-3416 |
| **Directions:** | From Highway 395 in Bishop, drive 30 miles north to the town of Tom's Place. In Tom's Place, turn west on Rock Creek Road and continue to Rock Creek Lake. Veer right and continue about a mile to the Mosquito Flat trailhead. |

*Box Lake*

At 10,590 feet in the John Muir Wilderness, just over the hill from Heart Lake, Box Lake is the fourth lake you come to in the Rock Creek Drainage. With less than a 245-foot elevation gain along the 1.7-mile hike from the Mosquito Flat Trailhead, this 13-acre lake, which is almost completely surrounded by small mountains decorated with large boulders rather than large meadows such as many other lakes in the drainage, has the same sparkling clear water as all of its neighboring lakes in the drainage.

The lake holds both brown and brook trout. Many of the fish are pan-size, and seem more than willing to hit red and gold Thomas Buoyants and silver Kastmasters. Like most of the lakes elevated above Rock Creek Lake, Box Lake usually doesn't thaw until sometime in late June or early July. After rough winters it can remain partially frozen-over through July, leaving the fish a small window in which to feed and grow. That's why fishing is so much better from the latter half of July through October.

The best way to approach fishing Box Lake is to scope it out from the trail when you get your first glimpse of it. From this point you can see the entire lake, as well as a smaller lake, which also holds fish, tucked in behind the eastern end of Box Lake. If you look to the right, there is a small meadow near the Rock Creek inlet that also provides good fishing.

The rest of the lake is surrounded by large boulders and has steep drop-offs, so you'll catch more fish if you use a heavier lure that will sink faster. Most of the fishing pressure occurs along the trail side of the lake, therefore the fish are less skittish on the far side.

From the Mosquito Flat Trailhead walk west passing Mack, Marsh and Heart Lake to Box Lake on the left.

If you plan to make the trip, supplies are available in Mammoth and Bishop. Check trail conditions before you leave. A wilderness permit is required for overnight travel in the John Muir Wilderness. Box Lake is closed to fishing from November 1 to the last Saturday in April. Also nearby are Heart Lake, Mack Lake, Long Lake and Marsh Lake.

## BISHOP REGION

1 Pine Creek
2 Millpond
3 Pleasant Valley
   Reservoir
4 Owens River
   (Bishop to Big Pine)
5 Bishop Creek (Lower)
6 Intake II
7 North Lake
8 Bishop Creek (MF)
9 Lake Sabrina
10 Bishop Creek (SF)
11 Tyee Lakes (1-6)
12 South Lake

# PINE CREEK

*If fishing the creek, don't forget a jar of yellow Power Bait. The fish love it.*

| | |
|---|---|
| **Rating:** | 6 |
| **Species:** | Rainbow and Brown Trout |
| **Stock:** | 1,502 pounds of rainbow trout. |
| **Facilities:** | A Pack Station |
| **Contact:** | Inyo National Forest (760) 873-2400, Bishop Chamber of Commerce (760) 873-8405 Culver's Sporting Goods (760) 872-8361, Pine Creek Pack Station (760) 387-2797 |
| **Directions:** | From Highway 395 in Bishop, drive approximately 10 miles north to Pine Creek Road. Turn west and drive 4.1 miles to the stream. The road follows the stream to the Pack Station. |

*Pine Creek*

In the Bishop area, most of the recreational opportunities come in clusters. There's the Bishop Creek Drainage, John Muir Wilderness, Owens River and Pleasant Valley Reservoir. Pine Creek is the oddball, tucked away just far enough from everything else that few know it exists.

Those who fish the creek in the spring don't often do well. From late April through June, the river is almost all white-water and rapids. Swollen from snow runoff, with minimal pools, it can be very difficult to fish. The fishing is fair for anglers who come later in the year. The California Department of Fish and Game stocks 2,934 rainbows in the stream, but it's rarely fished, leaving plenty for those who fish the stream.

The creek is stocked at access points that begin where it first crosses under Pine Creek Road and end at Pine Creek Pack Station, a distance of 5.3 miles. Most anglers here are killing time before heading out on pack trips from the Pine Creek Pack Station into the John Muir Wilderness. Upper and Lower Pine Lakes, the Gable Lakes, Honeymoon, Italy and Moon Lakes are the most popular destinations. If fishing the creek, don't forget a jar of yellow Power Bait. The fish love it.

If you plan to make the trip, supplies are available in Bishop. Pine Creek is closed to fishing from November 1 to the last Saturday in April.

Also nearby are Pleasant Valley Reservoir, Crowley Lake, Millpond, Rock Creek and Rock Creek Lake.

# MILLPOND

*My friend and I fished for trout in May using white Roostertails, and we couldn't stop catching bass.*

| | |
|---|---|
| **Rating:** | 5 |
| **Species:** | Rainbow Trout, Largemouth Bass, Bluegill and Channel Catfish |
| **Stock:** | None |
| **Facilities:** | Picnic Areas, Campgrounds, Concession Stands, Tennis Courts, Horseshoes, Baseball Fields, Archery Area, Swimming Area, Volleyball Courts, BMX Track, and a Snackbar |
| **Contact:** | Bishop Chamber of Commerce (760) 873-8405, Brocks Fly-Fishing Specialists (760) 872-3581, Culver's Sporting Goods (760) 872-8361, Millpond Recreational Area (760) 872-1850 |
| **Directions:** | From Highway 395 in Bishop, drive 4.5 miles north to Ed Powers Road and turn west. Drive three-tenths of a mile to Sawmill Road and turn north. Drive one mile to the park on your left. |

*Tony Abel with a largemouth bass from Millpond.*      *Millpond*

Contrary to popular belief, there are no secret fishing holes left in the Bishop area. There aren't even any fishing holes where locals can go to escape the tourists, except for a little county park they call Millpond. Millpond doesn't offer the great fishing that the Sierra does, but for the local anglers anyplace without tourists is appreciated.

Millpond is owned by the City of Los Angeles, but is leased by Inyo County for recreational use. Bishop residents couldn't have asked for anything better. The park provides an array of recreational facilities, including a fishing pond and a swimming area, to name a few.

Located in the high desert, it can get hot and dry in the summer. However, there are a few trees along the shoreline to keep you shaded. The pond is shallow and fairly small; with tules and an island, it provides good fish habitat. Bass fishing can be good in the spring and early summer. My friend and I fished for trout in May using white Roostertails, and we couldn't stop catching bass. They generally run one to three-pounds, but five-pounders are sometimes caught. Anglers fishing around the island in float tubes catch the biggest bass.

Since the pond is not stocked, many anglers wonder how trout get into it. Mill Creek feeds Millpond through an underground pipeline, and its flows into Millpond are hidden under water. The trout also come in through that pipeline.

While you're here, don't forget to take in the views of the Bishop Creek Drainage to the southwest and the White Mountains to the east.

If you plan to make the trip, supplies are available in Bishop. Millpond is closed to fishing from November 1 to the last Saturday in April.

Also nearby are Pleasant Valley Reservoir, Owens River, Lower Bishop Creek, Rock Creek Drainage, Pine Creek and the Bishop Creek Drainage.

# PLEASANT VALLEY RESERVOIR

*I experienced great fishing by tossing large Panther Martins and Thomas Buoyants as far as I could cast them off the dam.*

| | |
|---|---|
| **Rating:** | 7 |
| **Species:** | Rainbow Trout, Brown Trout, Sacramento Perch and Largemouth Bass |
| **Stock:** | 22,500 pounds of rainbow trout and 1,650 pounds of sub-catchable rainbow trout. |
| **Facilities:** | Restrooms and Primitive Campsites |
| **Contact:** | Inyo National Forest (760) 873-2400, Bishop Chamber of Commerce (760) 873-8405 Brocks Fly-Fishing Specialists (760) 872-3581, Culver's Sporting Goods (760) 872-8361 |
| **Directions:** | From Highway 395 in Bishop, drive north nine miles to Gorge Road and turn right. Drive a half-mile to a fork. Veer west and drive to a locked gate. Park and walk past the gate to the dam. |

*Pleasant Valley Reservoir*

The community of Bishop and the surrounding towns rely on the Eastern Sierra fishing season for much of their income. But, what happens when the season closes? Sure, people still travel through Bishop on their way to a weekend of skiing in Mammoth or June Lake, but that doesn't help the town much. To attract business during the colder months, the Bishop Chamber of Commerce tried to hype Pleasant Valley Reservoir, one of the few bodies of water in the Eastern Sierra that stays open year-round to fishing.

At 5,000 feet, just northeast of Bishop, the reservoir is a dammed portion of the Owens River. Water is released from Crowley Lake and enters into the reservoir before it's again released into the Lower Owens River. Partly because no boats are permitted, anglers choose to pass up a shot at fishing here. Also, because of its location in a remote gorge, many anglers are limited to fishing from the dam.

With heavy plants, fishing is never poor. The California Department of Fish and Game stocks 31,000 half-pound rainbows, 36,000 over three pounds and 10,650 sub-catchables. The Bishop Chamber of Commerce stocks larger Alpers every second Saturday in March for the popular Blake Jones Trout Derby in addition to 5,000 pounds of two- to 12-pound fish throughout the winter months. But, aside from derbies, anglers haven't adopted the reservoir as one of their favorite fisheries. The 110-acre reservoir is best fished by those in float tubes near the dam, but shoreline anglers do well, too.

I experienced great fishing by tossing large Panther Martins and Thomas Buoyants as far as I could cast them off the dam. There is also a chance to catch one of the large browns that hang out in the reservoir, but it's rare. October and November would be the time to try it, but those who do catch them are usually not fishing for browns.

If you plan to make the trip, supplies are available in Bishop. No boats or watercraft of any kind (except for float-tubes) are permitted.

Also nearby are the Lower Owens River, Crowley Lake, Pine Creek and Millpond.

*next page Pleasant Valley Reservoir*

# OWENS RIVER
## (BISHOP TO BIG PINE)

*The Owens is best fished with a fly rod.*

**Rating:** 7
**Species:** Rainbow Trout, Brown Trout, Channel Catfish and Largemouth Bass
**Stock:** 39,358 pounds of rainbow trout.
**Facilities:** Vault Toilets
**Contact:** Fishing Guide Don Roberts (760) 873-7678, Culver's Sporting Goods 760-872-8361
Mac's Sporting Goods (760) 872-9201, Slater's Sporting Goods 760-876-5020

**Directions:** From Highway 395 in Bishop, turn east on Line Street and continue three miles to the river.
From Highway 395 in Big Pine, turn east on Stewart Lane and continue one mile to the river.

*Owens River (Bishop to Big Pine)*

The California Department of Fish and Game has designated six named sections of the Owens River. These include: stretches designated as wild trout water, governed as catch & release only; areas that have special gear restrictions; those that have no restrictions; some that are opened year-round; and others that follow the general Eastern Sierra fishing season. Then there are those closed to fishing.

The section of the Owens from Bishop to Big Pine is 23 miles long, has no gear restrictions and is opened to fishing year-round. It's one of only two waters in Inyo and Mono County designated for year-round fishing. Set at 4,000 feet in the high desert terrain of the Owens Valley, this stretch of fast-flowing water with steep banks often gets bombarded by anglers.

Most anglers think of this portion of the river as two different areas. In the summer, the first, from Warm Springs Road to Collins Road, holds a lot of fish. The second, from Collins Road to the Highway 168 Bridge, doesn't have a lot of structure and holds few fish.

The Owens is best fished with a fly rod. Streamers with any standard nymph are your best bet, however, each season there's a favorite pattern or fly that the fish feed on. In summer, caddis patterns are typically used. Fall is best fished with mayfly pattern blue winged olives and trico or the most recent caddis flight. As winter approaches, your basic supply of bead head nymphs works best. Size-six Wooly Buggers are the top bait in the spring.

Anglers are also successful tossing Panther Martins and other small spinners. If you plan to bait-fish, make sure to use enough weight to get your salmon eggs, night crawlers or Power Bait to roll along the bottom.

While there are both wild and stocked brown and rainbow trout, the norm tends to be rainbows in the 10- 12-inch range. Browns average 11-13 inches, but many 18-inch fish are also caught. Wild rainbows peak in the five-pound range, while the browns get closer to nine.

*Owens River (Bishop to Big Pine)*

There is no shortage of fish in these waters. This stretch of the Owens is planted with 5,000 pounds of Alpers from three to 12 pounds. That's nearly three times the amount of Alpers planted in any other water. The California Department of Fish and Game plants nearly 66,000 rainbows, in addition to hundreds of brood fish each season.

Something else to take into consideration when fishing the Owens is water flow. Much of the year, high flows make the Owens a nightmare to fish. So, the secret is to arrive when flows are at a minimum. They are usually lowest from late-October through late-April. High flows generally return from May through September.

When you read about the Owens in fishing reports it will talk about "cfs," or cubic feet per second. Ideally, you want the number to be between 150-200. Most anglers stop fishing the river at about 300 cfs. Anything over 400 makes things really tough. The flows max out near 650 cfs. Surging water is not the only problem that causes angling to be difficult during high flows. High water causes mud to wash off the banks, discoloring the water and making the river murky.

In the summer don't bother fishing for trout below Collins Road. This section of the river can reach a surface temperature of close to 90 degrees, much too warm for trout. The smart fish swim upstream toward cooler releases from Crowley Lake. The dumb ones just hang around die.

If you plan to make the trip, supplies are available in Bishop. If fishing the river from mid-October through January, keep an eye out for duck hunters. You don't want to get mistaken for a duck and get shot!

Also nearby are Pleasant Valley Reservoir, Millpond and Owens River below Pleasant Valley Reservoir.

OWENS RIVER

# BISHOP CREEK (LOWER)

*It's the kind of place that if the CA DFG missed a stock nobody would complain. Heck, nobody would know.*

| | |
|---|---|
| **Rating:** | 4 |
| **Species:** | 1,039 pounds of trout, annually. |
| **Stock:** | Rainbow Trout |
| **Facilities:** | Picnic Areas, Restrooms and Playgrounds |
| **Contact:** | Inyo National Forest (760) 873-2400, Bishop Chamber of Commerce (760) 873-8405 Brocks Fly-Fishing Specialists (760) 872-3581, Culver's Sporting Goods (760) 872-8361 |
| **Directions:** | From Highway 395 in Bishop, turn west on Highway 168 and continue five miles to the spot where the creek crosses under the road. The stream is stocked from Bull Pit Park to Powerline Road. |

Bishop Creek (Lower)

If you're headed to fish the Bishop area and you end up at the Lower Fork of Bishop Creek, give me a call, because you have problems. You'd have to be a fool to fish here when you can drive 10 minutes to the west and be fishing in paradise. The South Fork or the Middle Fork of Bishop Creek, Intake II, North Lake, South Lake and Lake Sabrina, all offer clean air, tall pines and large pools.

In no way does the Lower Fork resemble the Middle or South Fork, both only a short drive away. It has virtually no pools and gets meager plants. The California Department of Fish and Game stocks only 1,978 fish in the nine to 12-inch class throughout the entire season. It's the kind of place that if the CA DFG missed a stock nobody would complain. Heck, nobody would know. However, located at 4,200 feet in the city of Bishop, is much better than the crowded fisheries located in the state's metropolitan areas, so nobody complains.

If you want to give it a try, use Power Bait, salmon eggs or small spinners. Best spots are near the bridge that allows Highway 168 to extend over the creek, and in both Bull Pit and Izaak Walton Parks. Regulations prohibit fishing from the bridge.

If you plan to make the trip, the creek is closed to fishing from November 1 to the last Saturday in April. Supplies are available in Bishop.

Also nearby are the Owens River, Mill Pond, Pleasant Valley Reservoir and Bishop Creek Drainage.

# INTAKE II

*Remember, with easy access and quick limits, Intake II can get crowded, so get here early, bring your chair, pick a spot and relax.*

**Rating:** 7
**Species:** Rainbow Trout, Brown Trout and Brook Trout
**Stock:** 10,229 pounds of rainbow trout.
**Facilities:** Picnic Areas, Restrooms and Campgrounds
**Contact:** Inyo National Forest (760) 873-2400, Culver's Sporting Goods (760) 872-8361

**Directions:** From Highway 395 in Bishop, turn west on Highway 168 and travel about 16 miles (just past South Lake Road) to Intake II on the left side of the road.

*Intake II from North Lake Road*

Talk about a popular place! Intake II is the Santa Ana River Lakes and Irvine Lake of the Eastern Sierra. Everyone knows about it and most fish it.

Intake II is a small pond created by a dam along the Middle Fork of Bishop Creek. Stocked with 15,737 rainbow trout from the California Department of Fish and Game, mostly in the 10-12 inch class, limits come easy. Anglers aren't worried about catching fish here as much as finding a fishing spot. This popular fishing pond has good shoreline access, but is so heavily fished, spots are hard to come by.

Canoeing and float tubing are also a big hit, allowing you to paddle free of all the shoreline commotion and reach the trout in deeper water. Alpers (1,800 pounds) from three to 10 pounds are also planted, giving anglers something to dream about. Your best bet is to use fly & bubble combos, gold Kastmasters or a red and gold Thomas Buoyant.

Most of the lake is productive, but the bulk of fish are caught near the inlet, along the dam and the east shoreline. The west shore is extremely shallow and requires long casts to reach the deeper areas that hold fish. Remember, with easy access and quick limits, Intake II can get crowded, so get here early, bring your chair, pick a spot and relax. Chances are you won't be the only one around.

While you're here, take a look at the water that flows from the dam down to Intake II's outlet pool. With a good set of polarized glasses you can see huge trout swimming around. Why are they still there? Why haven't they been caught? It's a steep climb down, with a loose and unstable trail. In short, anglers see the danger and avoid it.

If you plan to make the trip, supplies are available at Bishop Creek Lodge and also in Bishop. Call ahead for road conditions. Chains may be required. Intake II is closed to fishing from November 1 to the last Saturday in April. At times, Intake II doesn't thaw until late May.

Also nearby are the John Muir Wilderness, Lake Sabrina, South Lake, North Lake and the South and Middle Forks of Bishop Creek.

395

# NORTH LAKE

**The easiest way to catch fish is with a float tube or canoe so that you can avoid the crowds along the shoreline.**

**Rating:** 7
**Species:** Rainbow Trout and Brown Trout
**Stock:** 5,556 pounds of rainbow trout.
**Facilities:** Campground, Restrooms, Picnic Areas and a Pack Station
**Contact:** Inyo National Forest (760) 873-2400, Bishop Chamber of Commerce (760) 873-8405
Culver's Sporting Goods (760) 872-8361

**Directions:** From Highway 395 in Bishop, turn west on Highway 168 and drive 19 miles to the North Lake turnoff. Turn right and follow the dirt road to the lake on your right.

*North Lake*

Catching fish is almost never a problem at North Lake, however, finding a spot to catch them is. North Lake is a tiny, pond-sized lake at 9,255 feet in the Bishop Creek Drainage. Located in a heavily wooded area of the Inyo National Forest, the 20-acre lake provides great fishing and has a spectacular high-mountain view. But it also has a problem with access.

The south shoreline is too shallow to fish, and because of all of its trees, the north shoreline offers minimal space for anglers to cast. Every 15 yards or so along the north shoreline, there is an opening large enough for one angler to get in a few casts, but there's never enough room for all the anglers who enjoy coming to the lake. Those who arrive early enough to grab a spot experience high catch rates, using fly & bubble combos, and red and gold Thomas Buoyants. The easiest way to catch fish is with a float tube or canoe, so that you can avoid the crowds along the shoreline. No gas-powered boats are permitted.

The California Department of Fish and Game plants North Lake with 6,959 half-pound rainbows and another 175 weighing over two pounds. Larger Alpers (1,800 pounds) from three to 12 pounds are also stocked periodically. North Lake is fed by the North Fork of Bishop Creek and by runoff from the Lamarck Lakes, Wishbone Lake and the Wonder Lakes.

Because it's at such a high elevation, the lake is usually frozen-over for the trout opener in late April, but that doesn't stop anglers from coming. They have great success ice fishing. Some anglers walk the 1.2 miles from the closed turnoff on Highway 168 to the lake, but the ideal way in is with a snowmobile. North Lake is also a popular starting point for those heading into the John Muir Wilderness and Kings Canyon National Parks.

If you plan to make the trip, supplies are available in Bishop. Call ahead for road conditions. The turnoff to North Lake is often closed until June. North Lake is closed to fishing from November 1 to the last Saturday in April.

Also nearby are Lake Sabrina, South Lake, Intake II, Middle Fork Bishop Creek, South Fork Bishop Creek and the John Muir Wilderness.

# BISHOP CREEK (MIDDLE FORK)

**The best time to visit is in the fall, when the fishing pressure slows a bit and the leaves on the trees turn yellow, beige and orange.**

| | |
|---|---|
| **Rating:** | 10 |
| **Species:** | Rainbow Trout, Brown Trout and Brook Trout |
| **Stock:** | 20,848 pounds of rainbow trout. |
| **Facilities:** | Campgrounds and Vault Toilets |
| **Contact:** | Inyo National Forest (760) 873-2400, Bishop Chamber of Commerce (760) 873-8405, Brocks Fly-Fishing Specialists (760) 872-3581, Culver's Sporting Goods (760) 872-8361, Parchers Resort (760) 873-4177 |
| **Directions:** | From Highway 395 in Bishop, turn west on Highway 168 and continue 17 miles to the stream. |

*Bishop Creek (Middle Fork)*

The Middle Fork of Bishop Creek offers what few streams in California can: good fishing, a pristine high-country feeling, and great prospects for both wild and stocked trout, not to mention some large fish. At 9,000 feet in the Inyo National Forest, about a 20-minute drive west from Bishop, the fishing and natural beauty of the Middle Fork are hard to beat. Although it's one of the most heavily fished creeks in the state, it still remains one of the best.

Because of all the fishing pressure, the California Department of Fish and Game has to stock this stretch of Bishop Creek twice a week to keep it up to par. The fish are planted in a relatively small area, from below Lake Sabrina to the North Lake turnoff.

Each day, year-round, the same pools hold the biggest fish. First, there's the pool directly below Lake Sabrina, where the water is released from the dam. Then, as you work your way downstream just past the first bridge is another huge pool (you'll see a gauging station), then Sabrina Campground, which is also heavily planted. Finally, if you take the North Lake turnoff, after about 20 yards you'll come to a bridge that crosses over the creek. All of these places are easy to find and are consistently planted with both Alpers and CA DFG fish.

The 1,800 pounds of Alpers planted are a big problem. Because they attract anglers, all of these pools with Alpers get extremely crowded. Usually there are two Alpers in each pool, but there's about six anglers all casting for the same fish. Others eagerly wait their turn for someone to give up a spot so they can have a shot at catching one.

The Alpers aren't that easy to catch. They are much smarter than the CA DFG planters, and by the end of the day, they might've seen more than 1,000 casts (on a slow day). After the first few casts, they get used to the lures, salmon eggs and Power Bait thrown their way. In most cases, they are caught by accident.

At times, the Alpers get so sick of lures being dangled in front of their faces, they attack them out of pure aggression, not because they are interested in the bait being offered. Hooking them is only half the battle. The fish weigh anywhere from four to 10 pounds, and with most anglers using four-pound test, they commonly get broken off. You need to loosen your drag and play the fish carefully to land one. Incidentally, the best way to entice these giants to bite is with white mini jigs.

In addition to the Alpers, the CA DFG stocks 35,730 rainbows, enough to always keep the fishing hot. On top of the normal half-pounders, the CA DFG plants 740 trophy trout up to three pounds. Wait, there's more. The creek is also loaded with small wild brook, rainbow and brown trout. They are found in the same places as the planters and can be tricky to catch because of all the fishing pressure.

The best time to visit is in the fall when the fishing pressure slows a bit and the leaves on the trees turn yellow, beige and orange. It reminds me of Pennsylvania.

If you plan to make the trip, supplies are available in Bishop. Bishop Creek (Middle Fork) is closed to fishing from November 1 to the last Saturday in April. In early spring call ahead for road conditions. Chains may be required.

Also nearby are Lake Sabrina, Intake II, South Lake, the Tyee Lakes, Bishop Creek (South Fork), North Lake, Bishop Creek (Lower Section) and the John Muir Wilderness.

# LAKE SABRINA

**Rating:** 8
**Species:** Rainbow Trout, Brown Trout, Brook Trout and Golden Trout
**Stock:** 13,268 pounds of rainbow trout and 250 pounds of brook trout.
**Facilities:** Launch Ramp, Café, Boat Rentals, Fish Cleaning Station, Restrooms, Bait & Tackle, General Store
**Contact:** Inyo National Forest (760) 873-2500, Culvers Sporting Goods (760) 872-8361

**Directions:** From Highway 395 in Bishop, turn west on Highway 168 and continue 18.5 miles to the lake.

*Lake Sabrina*

Every year, I make the trip to Lake Sabrina in mid-June while the crowds are still light before summer vacationers take over. Then, I return in October, when the crowds have tapered off again. I've always been satisfied with the full outdoor experience here.

The 186-acre lake was created in 1908 when California Electric, now Southern California Edison, built a dam at 9,128 feet along Bishop Creek. Today, the lake provides excellent fishing and offers beautiful scenery in a high mountain environment. There are tall peaks in the background and various types of trees surrounding the lake's rocky shorelines. In fall, their leaves turn yellow, orange and gold. It's like being in upstate New York.

The key to fishing the lake is to find one of its four major inlets. The largest inlet, located at the lake's northwest corner, is Bishop Creek. Fed by Midnight, Topsy Turvy and Dingleberry Lakes, it flows year-round. This is important because Bishop Creek's volume brings a tremendous amount of food into the lake, and the fish stack up, waiting to be fed.

On busy days, there are boats anchored on both shorelines, as well as in the middle of the channel, with anglers casting towards the inlet. Surprisingly, the boat traffic doesn't bother the trout. They just keep on feeding.

Fish at the other major inlets are affected by boat traffic. When nearing these inlets, make sure to slow down and cut the motor long before you reach the point where these creeks pour into the lake. If you leave the motor on too long, you'll spook the fish. Because the lake is so clear, you can actually see them dart for deeper water.

There are two inlets on the lake's west shore. One is Spring Creek and the other is a large cascade tumbling down from George Lake. The best way to nail fish around these inlets is by tossing small lures as close to them as possible. Then, you need to be patient, with a slow retrieve. A boat is the quickest way to these inlets, but a hiker's trail also leads to them. As for the bigger fish, most are caught trolling the shoreline or down the middle of the lake.

The California Department of Fish and Game stocks 24,980 rainbows in the 10- to 12-inch class, joining holdovers and brood stocks that are planted regularly. If you are extremely lucky, you could hook up with a golden trout. A few have been known to enter the lake through the creeks' inlets.

The best lures include size 1/4 and 1/6 red and gold Thomas Buoyants, various Rapalas or whole night crawlers on a size six salmon egg hook. For bait fishing, the dam area provides good results from the marina to the spillway. In the fall, brook trout (1,000 quarter-pounders are planted) are easily caught at the Bishop Creek inlet.

Lake Sabrina's most unique offering is its early season ice fishing. The lake usually remains frozen till mid-May and is a favorite spot on opening day.

If you plan to make the trip, supplies are available at the lake. Lake Sabrina is closed to fishing from November 1 to the last Saturday in April. There are no overnight campgrounds at the lake. Campgrounds can be found along Bishop Creek. Make reservations early because the campgrounds fill quickly. In early spring, call ahead for road conditions. Chains may be required.

Also nearby are the Middle and South Fork of Bishop Creek, North Lake, South Lake, Intake II, John Muir Wilderness and Tyee Lakes.

LAKE SABRINA

*Bishop Creek inlet at Lake Sabrina*

# BISHOP CREEK (SOUTH FORK)

**This stretch of the creek is much smaller than the Middle Fork, but that's not to say it isn't loaded with fish.**

| | |
|---|---|
| **Rating:** | 9 |
| **Species:** | Rainbow Trout, Brown Trout and Brook Trout |
| **Stock:** | 20,848 pounds of rainbow trout. |
| **Facilities:** | Campgrounds, RV Hookups, Restaurant, General Store, Restrooms, Picnic Areas, Lodging , Bait & Tackle |
| **Contact:** | Inyo National Forest (760) 873-2400, Bishop Chamber of Commerce (760) 873-8405, Brocks Fly-Fishing Specialists (760) 872-3581, Culver's Sporting Goods (760) 872-8361, Bishop Creek Lodge (760) 873-4484, Parchers Resort (760) 873-4177 |
| **Directions:** | From Highway 395 in Bishop, turn west on Highway 168 and drive 15 miles to South Lake Road. Turn left. The creek is planted at various access points up to South Lake. |

Bishop Creek (South Fork) with Weir Pond in the distance

I'll tell you from experience, the water in the South Fork of Bishop Creek is cold, and I didn't find that out by touching it with my hands. After catching my usual tree fish, I tried to rock hop to the other side of the stream and fell in up to my waist in snow runoff. I figured I was already wet and cold, so I stayed in the water and walked over to the tree I had caught and hit the bonanza. It was full of lures, and I was the only one crazy enough to battle the leg-numbing water to retrieve them.

I left the creek with a good 10 lures that day, and I thought I was in business until I realized I had no other pairs of socks or shoes. That day ended up being a good one, however. We caught a ton of fish all over the South Fork, which leads to the moral to my story: The reason there were so many lures in that tree is because there are tons of fish in the South Fork of Bishop Creek, tons of big fish, and anglers are willing to lose a few lures for a chance at one of those big ones.

The South Fork of Bishop Creek is fed by South Lake, which in turn is fed by creeks and lakes in the John Muir Wilderness. This stretch of the creek is much smaller than the Middle Fork, but that's not to say it isn't loaded with fish. Your best bet is to start at South Lake and work your way down. The finest spots can be seen from the road. Any place you see a parking lot or a dirt road veering off from the main road, you're more than likely to find fish; and not just small stockers, but wild rainbows, browns and the occasional brook.

The headwaters of the creek are wide and deep with some nice pools, but the creek does narrow as it begins to merge with the Middle Fork of Bishop Creek, so try to stay as far up the road as possible. Remember, all the campgrounds are stocked as well, but they are usually fished-out pretty fast. A favorite spot is Weir Pond, a small pond on the creek. It carries a lot of fish, but is only fishable with waders.

Because the California Department of Fish and Game dumps 35,790 rainbows in the nine- to 12-inch class, along with 1,800 pounds of Alpers in the three to eight pound

*Bishop Creek (South Fork)*

range and CA DFG brood stocks from one to three pounds, limits are common and sometimes hefty. Thomas Buoyants, Panther Martins, salmon eggs and night crawlers on a #6 salmon egg hook score limits. Wooly Buggers and tube jigs are also productive, but require more skill to use.

The scenery is so beautiful here, sometimes I don't even feel like fishing. I just relax and enjoy the wilderness, before having to get back to the smog and traffic in L.A. Before you leave, don't forget to take a look at the waterfall about a mile past the South Fork General Store. It's on the south side of the road, up on the mountainside. You can't miss it. When fall comes, the creek slows, the leaves turn brown and yellow, and the big browns begin to spawn in South Lake. Time to rent a boat and try your luck.

If you plan to make the trip, supplies are available at Bishop Creek Lodge and Parchers Resort. Bishop Creek is closed to fishing from November 1 until the last Saturday in April. Check road conditions, chains may be required.

Also nearby are South Lake, Lake Sabrina, the Middle Fork of Bishop Creek, North Lake and Intake II.

**Five of the six lakes hold fish, although, some provide better catch rates than others.**

| | |
|---|---|
| **Rating:** | 8 |
| **Species:** | Rainbow Trout and Brook Trout |
| **Stock:** | Three pounds of fingerling rainbow trout (in lakes number five and six only). |
| **Facilities:** | None |
| **Contact:** | Inyo National Forest (760) 873-2400, Culver's Sporting Goods (760) 872-8361<br>Bishop Creek Lodge (760) 873-4484 |

**Directions:** From Highway 395 in Bishop, take Highway 168 west 15 miles to the South Lake Road turnoff. Turn left on South Lake Road and drive approximately five miles to a dirt pullout on the left. There is a trailhead sign next to the bridge.

*A rainbow trout caught at Tyee Lake No. 5.*

It's a mere 1.6 miles from the South Fork of Bishop Creek to the first of the six Tyee Lakes, but those miles can be quite deceiving. Anglers think because the mileage is short that it's a cinch to reach the lakes. Most of these anglers are shocked when they see what they're up against. The Tyee Lakes require an exhausting 1,255-foot elevation gain before reaching the first lake and a total of 2,000 feet to reach the last.

Sounds brutal? Well, for most anglers it seems like it. Many show up at the trailhead, see what they're up against and shy away. It's easy for them to skip out, because it doesn't necessarily mean they are throwing away a day of fishing. The South Fork of Bishop Creek stares them in the face, and South Lake is less than a five-minute drive.

Don't let those downer demons in your head slacken your confidence and deter you from going to the lakes. It would be a tragic mistake. These lakes provide great fishing for both brook and rainbow trout, and if you climb the trail slowly, it's doable. For those in shape, it's about a 45-minute hike to the first lake, but it may take an hour-and-a-half for others. The loss of breath is worth it when you reach your goal. Five of the six lakes hold fish, although, some provide better catch rates than others.

Reaching the lakes are simple (aside from the climb, of course). Beginning at the trailhead along the S.F. of Bishop Creek, first cross the creek on a sturdy wooden bridge, and then immediately begin an uphill climb. After climbing a few short switchbacks, comes a ridge of a small mountain. After walking down a long straightaway that eventually curves to the left, you'll begin a series of short switchbacks. At the end of the switchbacks, on the first lip of the pass, you'll come to a fairly flat opening. Just after the trail again curves to the left, you'll get your first view of Tyee Lake No. 1.

At 10,300 feet in the John Muir Wilderness, Lake No. 1 is a mere four acres, but holds tons of rainbow and brook trout. When I fished it, I found that I needed to be careful when I let my lure sink. Underwater, there are many fallen trees, large boulders and bushes, making it easy to get snagged. After landing a fish on my first two casts, I lost a Panther Martin on a submerged tree branch in the middle of the lake, and had to wait about 30 minutes for the second group of our party to arrive with replacements. (They had extra lures in their backpacks.)

It doesn't matter which part of the lake you choose to fish; it's so small, fish are everywhere. Only the west shore is difficult to fish, because the weeds make for poor access. Most of the fish are eight to nine inches.

To get to Lake No. 2, continue on the trail, following the shoreline around Lake No. 1. You'll again climb up some short switchbacks and in three-tenths of a mile come out on the lake's east shore. At 10,400 feet, this two-acre pond-sized lake holds only small brookies. When I last fished it in October of 2000, there were less than 100 fish left in the lake, and rarely did I see one over seven inches. The lake is so small and shallow, with such clear water, I was able to see every fish. All my lures worked, too; size and color didn't matter. However, the lack of larger fish keeps most anglers from spending much time here.

After making a few casts, continue around the lake, again climbing uphill (four-tenths of a mile with a 400 foot elevation gain), to Lake No. 3, which can be seen off the left side of the trail. No, it's not the large lake in the background; it's the dinker pond right in front of you. Lake No. 3 is less than one acre and is barren of fish. Continue past it, and in less than 100 yards, you'll get a clear view of Lake No. 4 on your right.

At 11 acres, No. 4 is the second largest lake of the group and has a self-sustaining population of brook trout, much larger in size and numbers than those in Lake No.2. There

*Tyee Lake No. 1*

are no formal trails leading here, but it's only about 50 yards from Lake No. 3, so wherever you see a spot that looks promising, simply leave the trail and proceed down to the lake. The best fishing is found near the inlet, but flows are kept to a minimum after August. Try casting silver Kastmasters and red Cripplelures.

Follow the trail to the inlet of Lake No. 4, which is also Lake No. 5's outlet stream. You can't necessarily see the water, because it flows under large boulders. This is where you'll leave the main trail and follow the stream (or boulders) up to Lake No. 5.

It should take you less than five minutes to reach this 12-acre lake at 11,000 feet, which provides some of the best fishing of all the backcountry lakes in the Sierra. It holds healthy rainbow trout with a lot of fight in them. It also offers great access for anglers and has nice spots for camping along its eastern shore. With just seven-tenths of a mile of shoreline, it's a short, easy walk around the lake.

Fishing is productive everywhere. The water is extremely shallow with a gravel bottom for the first 10 yards out from the shoreline. But, there are steep drop-offs farther out, and that's where you need to get your lures. Most of the rainbows are between nine and 12 inches, but we caught a few to 14 inches. The lake is stocked with 1,500 fingerling rainbow trout by the California Department of Fish and Game.

*Tyee Lake No. 2*

Now, walk around the east shore to the north shore and continue to the final Tyee Lake. You can see it from Lake No. 5. At 11,100 feet, this four-acre lake is at the end of the basin and usually has snow on its western banks year-round. Stocked with 1,500 fingerling rainbow trout, the lake is home to healthy, beautiful rainbow trout, most of which are in the eight to 10-inch class.

This lake also has steep drop-offs, so you'll need to use a lure that will sink fast. The best area to fish is the outlet channel. Most anglers don't realize that South Lake is just over the mountains, however, there is no trail leading to it, and the mountain is too steep to climb.

If you plan to make the trip, supplies are available at Bishop Creek Lodge and Parchers Resort. The Tyee Lakes are closed to fishing from November 1 to the last Saturday in April. In spring, call ahead for road conditions. Chains may be required. A wilderness permit is required for overnight travel in the John Muir Wilderness.

Also nearby are South Fork Bishop Creek, South Lake, Weir Pond, Intake II, the John Muir Wilderness, North Lake, Lake Sabrina and the Middle Fork of Bishop Creek.

# SOUTH LAKE

*The browns are difficult to catch, because most of them stay down deep, in 250 feet of water.*

**Rating:** 8

**Species:** Rainbow Trout, Brown Trout, Golden Trout and Brook Trout

**Stock:** 17,712 pounds of rainbow trout, 250 pounds of brook trout, and 3,000 pounds of rainbows and browns from American Trout and Salmon Company.

**Facilities:** Boat Rentals, Boat Launch, Picnic Area, Bait & Tackle and Vault Toilets

**Contact:** Inyo National Forest (760) 873-2400, Culver's Sporting Goods (760) 872-8361, Bishop Creek Lodge (760) 873-4484, Parchers Resort (760) 873-4177, South Lake Marina (760) 872-0334

**Directions:** From Highway 395 in Bishop, take Highway 168 west 15 miles to the South Lake turnoff. Turn left on South Lake Road and drive six miles to the lake.

*Brett Ross waits for a nibble while ice fishing at South Lake.*

At 9,750 feet in the Inyo National Forest, South Lake is one of the few drive-to lakes in the Sierra that offers ice fishing for its opener. Because the lake is drawn down each winter to facilitate it's freezing, it's almost always frozen-over for the opener, and sometimes for weeks following.

The Eastern Sierra Trout Opener is a special time for anglers who partake in the celebration. It's extra special for those who have made South Lake a yearly destination, because the crowds stay light, allowing them to enjoy their ice fishing experience without having to share it with hoards of other anglers.

Providing the road to the lake has been plowed, South Lake is an excellent opening day destination. The fishing is phenomenal. You don't have to have equipment to drill holes in the ice, either. Most anglers drill three or four holes, and, after limiting, which frequently takes less than an hour, they go home. Now, it's your turn to use their holes. Many people bring along stoves and barbeques to make a day out of it. It's a blast.

For those who fish the lake in June and July, the easiest way is to bring or rent a boat and fish the inlets in the back of the lake. There are five inlets (all coming from lakes in the John Muir Wilderness), and the fishing is typically good. Anchor near an inlet and soak Power Bait. You can also dangle night crawlers off the bottom or toss spinners towards the shoreline.

Trolling the lake is productive, too. Troll down the middle or anywhere along the shoreline with Thomas Buoyants, Rapalas or red and gold Super Dupers.

The California Department of Fish and Game plants 25,266 rainbows, 508 of which are trophy size. Gary Olson, owner of Bishop Creek Lodge, also plants fish. Twice a year, he trucks in trout from American Trout and Salmon Company in Northern California. More than 1,500 pounds of Eagle Lake trout are stocked, in addition to 1,500 pounds of browns, weighing two to four pounds each. And at last, 1,200 pounds of Alpers from three to 12 pounds are stocked.

South Lake is less fished than Lake Sabrina, however, the chances of catching bigger fish are far greater at South Lake. The 180-acre lake is home to some huge browns. The lake record, caught just after ice-out in July of 1998, weighed in at 17.1 pounds.

The browns are difficult to catch, because most of them stay down deep, in 250 feet of water. Anglers who troll these depths with large bright Rapalas have the best shot at catching one, but chances are still slim. Your best bet is to wait until late October when they begin to move into shallow water to bulk up for the winter. This is the best time to troll the lake's shoreline and inlets, but there's no guarantee you'll catch any lunkers.

Because of the lake's steep banks, there is limited access for shoreline anglers, but the little access that is provided often produces high catch rates. The only easy access is near the dam. Anglers who fish off the dam or off the rocks adjacent to the dam on the north and south shorelines, can douse Power Bait or float night crawlers off the bottom to catch both rainbows and browns. In the fall, you'll have a good chance of catching browns in this area. One problem with fishing the lake is that the winds come up nearly every afternoon and can making fishing difficult.

South Lake is also one of the most popular trailheads for backpacking trips. There is a parking lot at the lake where hikers begin trips into the John Muir Wilderness and Kings Canyon National Park. The best hiking trip is from South Lake to North Lake. It provides great fishing and spectacular vistas.

If you plan to make the trip, supplies are available at Bishop Creek Lodge and Parchers Resort. South Lake is closed to fishing from November 1 to the last Saturday in April. In spring call ahead for road conditions. Chains may be required. ·

Also nearby are South Fork Bishop Creek, Tyee Lakes, Weir Pond, Intake II, John Muir Wilderness, North Lake, Lake Sabrina and the Middle Fork of Bishop Creek.

SOUTH LAKE

*Tom Bomar landed this pan-sized rainbow trout on a Needlefish.*

(1-12)

REGION 22

## BISHOP PASS REGION

1 Hurd Lake
2 Marie Louise Lakes
3 Bull Lake
4 Chocolate Lakes
5 Ruwau Lake
6 Timberline Tarns Lak
7 Saddlerock Lake
8 Ledge Lake
9 Bishop Lake
10 Spearhead Lake
11 Margaret Lake
12 Long Lake (Bishop)

San Francisco

120

Modesto

Mammoth Lakes

Bishop

Santa Cruz

Fresno

395

5

99

101

Bakersfield

San Luis
Obispo

14

Barstow

Santa Barbara

Los Angeles

# HURD LAKE

*Because of its size, little Hurd Lake could get fished-out pretty fast, but the lack of anglers keeps action good on six to nine-inch brook trout.*

| | |
|---|---|
| **Rating:** | 6 |
| **Species:** | Brook Trout |
| **Stock:** | One pound of fingerling rainbow trout. |
| **Facilities:** | None |
| **Contact:** | Inyo National Forest (760) 873-2400 |

**Directions:** From Highway 395 in Bishop, take Highway 168 west 15 miles to the South Lake turnoff. Turn left on South Lake Road and drive six miles to the lake. Drive past the marina to the trailhead and parking area.

*Hurd Lake from the Bishop Pass Trail*

At 10,350 feet in the John Muir Wilderness, surrounded by a thick pine forest, Hurd is the first lake hikers see off the trail to Bishop Pass, and also the easiest lake to reach from the trailhead at South Lake. Despite this fact, due to the lack of either a trail or signs to make hikers aware of how to get to it, the two-acre lake is rarely fished. Because of its size, little Hurd Lake could get fished-out pretty fast, but the lack of anglers keeps action good on six to nine-inch brook trout.

Since there is no established trail to Hurd, let's work on how to get there without getting lost. From the trailhead, you'll immediately cross a small stream that flows into South Lake. Then the trail bends to the right, remaining well above the lake and constantly gaining elevation.

Within a half-hour, you'll cross into the John Muir Wilderness (there's a sign). One-tenth of a mile from the wilderness boundary and eight-tenths of a mile from the trailhead, you'll come to a trail junction. Walking away from the Treasure Lakes, stay left, following signs towards Bishop Pass.

The path progresses uphill, and in four-tenths of a mile from the junction, you'll climb up a few short switchbacks. It's important to keep an eye out on the right, looking down the mountain for Hurd. When you can first spot the lake, there's an exceptional overlook; however, it's not a great place to try to get down to the lake. Instead of attempting to scale the cliffs here to reach Hurd, continue along the path to a meadow and small stream. Now, leave the maintained route and follow the stream down to the lake.

If you plan to make the trip, supplies are available at Bishop Creek Lodge and Parchers Resort. A wilderness permit is required for overnight travel into the John Muir Wilderness. Hurd Lake is closed to fishing from November 1 to the last Saturday in April.

Also nearby are Long Lake, Bull Lake, South Lake, Marie Louise Lakes, the Chocolate Lakes, Spearhead Lake and Margaret Lake.

**Because Marie Louise Lakes aren't stocked and the brookies are small here, most anglers don't even bother trying to find the lakes.**

| | |
|---|---|
| **Rating:** | 4 |
| **Species:** | Brook Trout |
| **Stock:** | None |
| **Facilities:** | None |
| **Contact:** | Inyo National Forest (760) 873-2400 |

**Directions:** From Highway 395 in Bishop, take Highway 168 west 15 miles to the South Lake turnoff. Turn left on South Lake Road and drive six miles to the lake. Drive past the marina to the trailhead and parking area.

*Marie Louise Lakes*

Finding Marie Louise Lakes is like searching for that proverbial needle in a haystack. Rich with hand-sized brook trout, these two lakes are nearly impossible to get to. Although there is a faint trail leading to them from the Bishop Pass Trail, it is unsigned and tremendously difficult to locate. Because Marie Louise Lakes aren't stocked and the brookies are small here, most anglers don't even bother trying to find the lakes. And they might just be right. There are so many other brook trout lakes in the area that spending hours to locate these two can seem like a waste of time.

Both lakes are tiny, roughly the size of a backyard pond you'd see in upstate New York. While their surrounding scenery is pretty -- tall mountain peaks loom over the south end of the lakes -- they can be difficult to fish, because most of the shoreline is marshy. Each lake has a self-sustaining population of brooks, yet few longer than eight inches are ever landed.

Reaching the lakes can take some time. The only way I was able to locate them was from Bull Lake, and it took some serious off-trail trekking to do so. I left the trail at Bull and began walking east through the campsites, down a canyon between two small mountains. I descended the canyon into a meadow where I eventually reached a stream. I chased that stream down into another meadow, and in about 100 yards I was able to see one of the two lakes in the distance.

All this terrain can be seen on any good topo map. Although there is a path that can be picked up from the Bishop Pass Trail, it's nearly impossible to explain how to find the turnoff. If you're going to try to find it, keep this in mind: It's on the left, a few hundred yards past the turnoff for Hurd Lake.

If you plan to make the trip, supplies are available at Bishop Creek Lodge and Parchers Resort. A wilderness permit is required for overnight travel into the John Muir Wilderness. Marie Louise Lakes are closed to fishing from November 1 to the last Saturday in April.

Also nearby are Timberline Tarns Lakes, Ruwau Lake, Saddlerock Lake, Margaret Lake, Ledge Lake, Chocolate Lakes, Long Lake and Spearhead Lake.

# BULL LAKE

**Bull Lake is an excellent destination for a day hike, especially if you like catching brookies.**

| | |
|---|---|
| **Rating:** | 6 |
| **Species:** | Brook Trout |
| **Stock:** | None |
| **Facilities:** | None |
| **Contact:** | Inyo National Forest (760) 873-2400 |

**Directions:** From Highway 395 in Bishop, take Highway 168 west 15 miles to the South Lake turnoff. Turn left on South Lake Road and drive six miles to the lake. Drive past the marina to the trailhead and parking area.

*Bull Lake*

There are five lakes on a loop trail that breaks off from the route to Bishop Pass. Because all of these lakes have self-sustaining populations of brook trout, none require any stocking. Just a short 2.2-mile trip from the trailhead at South Lake, Bull Lake is an excellent destination for a day hike, especially if you like catching brookies, which can be caught by the dozens here, with little to no effort. All that's needed is a small spinner, and you're in business. It's that easy.

While there is a 1,000-foot elevation gain from the trailhead, the hike to Bull isn't that demanding if you take it slow. Most of the elevation gain is spread out evenly over the 2.2-mile hike. The starting point is South Lake. From there, the path ascends for seven-tenths of a mile, before leaving the Inyo National Forest and entering the John Muir Wilderness.

One-tenth of mile after entering the wilderness, you'll come to a trail junction. Don't take the right fork signed for Treasure Lakes. Stay left, following signs for Bishop Pass. In 1.4 miles there's another trail junction. Again stay left, this time following signs toward Bull Lake and Chocolate Lakes. The right fork leads to Bishop Pass. Two-tenths of a mile from the junction, the trail runs along the shore of Bull.

At 10,750 feet in the John Muir Wilderness, Bull is also one of the better lakes in the drainage for camping. There are several established camps on a plateau a few feet above the approximately five-acre lake.

If you plan to make the trip, supplies are available at Bishop Creek Lodge and Parchers Resort. A wilderness permit is required for overnight travel into the John Muir Wilderness. Bull Lake is closed to fishing from November 1 to the last Saturday in April.

Also nearby are Timberline Tarns Lakes, Ruwau Lake, Saddlerock Lake, Ledge Lake, Chocolate Lakes, Long Lake and Spearhead Lake.

*opposite page Bull Lake*

# CHOCOLATE LAKES

**Just about any small lure will work, and no specific places need to be targeted.**

| | |
|---|---|
| **Rating:** | 8 |
| **Species:** | Brook Trout |
| **Stock:** | None |
| **Facilities:** | None |
| **Contact:** | Inyo National Forest (760) 873-2400 |

**Directions:** From Highway 395 in Bishop, take Highway 168 west 15 miles to the South Lake turnoff. Turn left on South Lake Road and drive six miles to the lake. Drive past the marina to the trailhead and parking area.

*Chocolate Lake No. 1*

After completing the difficult task of visiting 16 of the 18 lakes in the basin that spans from South Lake to Bishop Pass, my friend Brett Ross and I waited patiently in the parking area for another friend to pick us up and take us back to camp. He was more than two hours late. Tired and hungry, we lay on the bear boxes, trying to rest our legs.

We didn't get much rest. We must have looked like a visitor center, because all the hikers stopped to ask us questions before setting out on the trail. I'll never forget one of the questions a kid asked me in this soft, nervous voice. "Is there chocolate in these Chocolate Lakes? I really like chocolate. Snickers are my favorite."

I tried with all my will to hold back my laughter. "Sorry buddy, there is no chocolate there, just a lot of brook trout."

"I don't understand," he looked a bit confused. "Why does it say Chocolate Lakes here, then?" He pointed to his father's map.

I explained that the lakes were named after Chocolate Peak, which rises 11,682 feet above the shore. The kid didn't want to go to Chocolate Lakes anymore, until I assured him he would catch fish there, and lots of them.

Ranging from 11,050 feet to 11,150 feet in the John Muir Wilderness, there are three Chocolate Lakes, all home to self-sustaining populations of brook trout. No other species of fish reside here.

At just one-acre, Chocolate Lake No. 1 is the smallest and least fished of the trio. Lake No. 2's size jumps up to four acres. It can be reached by following the path up from Lake No. 1. No. 2 is shallow, but does hold some quality fish, weighing up to a half-pound.

For the largest fish, continue on the trail to Lake No. 3. The brooks are abundant here, and there are many to 12 inches. Just about any small lure will work, and no specific places need to be targeted. Simply walk up and down the shoreline, casting and retrieving. There's no need to cast clear out to the middle either. The brooks can usually be seen within 10 feet of the shoreline.

It's an easy walk to the Chocolate Lakes from Bull Lake, except for the first 100 yards, which requires a steep climb over a small mountain. Follow Lake No. 1's outlet stream, and it's three-tenths of a mile from Bull to lake No. 1.

If you plan to make the trip, supplies are available at Bishop Creek Lodge and Parchers Resort. A wilderness permit is required for overnight travel into the John Muir Wilderness. Chocolate Lakes are closed to fishing from November 1 to the last Saturday in April.

Also nearby are Timberline Tarns Lakes, Ruwau Lake, Saddlerock Lake, Ledge Lake, Bull Lake, Long Lake and Spearhead Lake.

*Chocolate Lake No. 1 from above*

**CHOCOLATE LAKES**

# RUWAU LAKE

**One thing is for sure, the brook trout – the only kind of trout I saw in the lake – flourish here.**

| | |
|---|---|
| **Rating:** | 6 |
| **Species:** | Brook Trout and Rainbow Trout |
| **Stock:** | Eight pounds of fingerling rainbow trout. |
| **Facilities:** | None |
| **Contact:** | Inyo National Forest (760) 873-2400 |

**Directions:** From Highway 395 in Bishop, take Highway 168 west 15 miles to the South Lake turnoff. Turn left on South Lake Road and drive six miles to the lake. Drive past the marina to the trailhead and parking area.

*Ruwau Lake*

It was once thought that trout needed an inlet with a gravel bottom to successfully spawn and reproduce. Over the last few years, however, biologists have learned that trout can adjust to their surroundings, and spawning can successfully occur in many more places than once thought. A lot of lakes in the high country, which are completely silted and have no inlets or gravel bottoms, are now known to hold self-sustaining populations.

Ruwau is an example of a lake that doesn't have a gravel inlet, but does hold a self-sustaining population of trout. At 10,950 feet in the John Muir Wilderness, Ruwau is fed by a small inlet that gets its water from snowmelt off the mountain peaks above. It has no year-round inlet. There is a small outlet stream, but a logjam and a small rock dam inhibit most of the lake's fish from spawning there.

So how do these fish reproduce? There are a few theories that might work. The most logical proposes that as the fish lay eggs along the bank, waves lap over the eggs and provide the necessary oxygen for them to develop and hatch. Another theory suggests that the eggs are laid at the base of underground springs in the middle of the lake.

One thing's for sure: the brook trout -- the only kind of trout I saw in the lake -- flourish here. (The California Department of Fish and Game airlifted 8,000 fingerling rainbow trout in 2000 and 2001, and also many years in the past but I've never heard of one being caught.)

You can get to Ruwau from either Upper Chocolate Lake or Upper Timberline Tarns Lake. In both cases a good topo map is recommended. Although there are faint trails leading from both lakes, they can be hard to follow. Either way, you'll have to climb over a small saddle. But don't fret: Ruwau's a fairly large lake in its own basin and easily spotted.

If you plan to make the trip, supplies are available at Bishop Creek Lodge. A wilderness permit is required for overnight travel into the John Muir Wilderness. Ruwau Lake is closed to fishing from November 1 to the last Saturday in April.

Also nearby are Timberline Tarns Lakes, Chocolate Lakes and Saddlerock Lake.

416

# TIMBERLINE TARNS LAKES

*Later in the summer when the mosquitoes begin to die off, try using a fly & bubble combo through July.*

**Rating:** 5
**Species:** Brook Trout and Rainbow Trout
**Stock:** One pound of fingerling rainbow trout.
**Facilities:** None
**Contact:** Inyo National Forest (760) 873-2400

**Directions:** From Highway 395 in Bishop, take Highway 168 west 15 miles to the South Lake turnoff. Turn left on South Lake Road and drive six miles to the lake. Drive past the marina to the trailhead and parking area.

Timberline Tarns Lakes

At 11,000 feet (lower) and 11,150 feet (upper), the Timberline Tarns lakes are great high-county fishing destinations for anglers who want to catch rainbow and brook trout in the six to eight inch class. Like most of the lakes on the trail from South Lake to Bishop Pass, these lakes are easy to reach; and because they are shallow and small, they are also easy to fish.

Both three-acre Timberline Tarns Lakes can be seen from the trail, and reaching them is like a walk in the park. From Spearhead Lake, it is less than a half-mile, with a 175-foot elevation gain. Each lake was last stocked with 500 fingerling rainbow trout in 2000.

So, what's the trick to fishing these lakes? Early in the season, from June through July, fishing with spinners doesn't work well. Because all the grass around the lakes promote an abundance of mosquitoes, the brookies and rainbows usually don't mess with hitting lures; there's too many mosquitoes to feed on. Later in the summer when the mosquitoes begin to die off, try using a fly & bubble combo through July. Then, switch over to small spinners in August.

If you plan to make the trip, supplies are available at Bishop Creek Lodge and Parchers Resort. A wilderness permit is required for overnight travel into the John Muir Wilderness. Timberline Tarns Lakes are closed to fishing from November 1 to the last Saturday in April.

Also nearby are Saddlerock Lake, Ruwau Lake, Bishop Lake, Margaret Lake, Ledge Lake, Chocolate Lakes, Long Lake and Spearhead Lake.

417

# SADDLEROCK LAKE

**With 1.2 miles of shoreline, the fish are less concentrated in this larger lake, and therefore more difficult to locate and catch.**

| | |
|---|---|
| **Rating:** | 6 |
| **Species:** | Brook Trout and Rainbow Trout |
| **Stock:** | Seven pounds of fingerling rainbow trout. (This plant took place in 2001.) |
| **Facilities:** | None |
| **Contact:** | Inyo National Forest (760) 873-2400 |

**Directions:** From Highway 395 in Bishop, take Highway 168 west 15 miles to the South Lake turnoff. Turn left on South Lake Road and drive six miles to the lake. Drive past the marina to the trailhead and parking area.

*Saddlerock Lake*

One acre larger than Long Lake, Saddlerock Lake is the largest lake on the trail from South Lake to Bishop Pass. This 30-acre lake, situated at 11,175 feet in the John Muir Wilderness, is also one of the hardest lakes in the South Fork Bishop Creek Drainage to fish, and it all has to do with size. With 1.2 miles of shoreline, the fish are less concentrated here, and therefore more difficult to locate and catch.

There are two ways to almost guarantee action at Saddlerock. The first is walking to the South Fork inlet on the west side of the lake, where brooks and rainbows station themselves to nab small insects and other food that enters the lake. Otherwise, wait to fish the lake in evening when the trout are snatching bugs and flies off the surface. The fish are easiest to locate at this hour and can be fooled by tossing a silver Kastmaster or red Cripplelure. More than 7,500 fingerling rainbows were airlifted to the lake in 2001.

From Timberline Tarns Lakes, getting to Saddlerock will take fewer than five minutes. Simply walk two-tenths of a mile towards Bishop Pass, and you'll reach the point where the South Fork of Bishop Creek exits Saddlerock.

If you plan to make the trip, supplies are available at Bishop Creek Lodge and Parchers Resort. A wilderness permit is required for overnight travel into the John Muir Wilderness. Saddlerock Lake is closed to fishing from November 1 to the last Saturday in April.

Also nearby are Timberline Tarns Lakes, Ruwau Lake, Bishop Lake, Margaret Lake, Ledge Lake, Chocolate Lakes, Long Lake and Spearhead Lake.

*The lake is so diminutive, the brookies, which range from six to nine inches, are easy to spot and to catch.*

| | |
|---|---|
| **Rating:** | 5 |
| **Species:** | Brook Trout |
| **Stock:** | None |
| **Facilities:** | None |
| **Contact:** | Inyo National Forest (760) 873-2400 |

**Directions:** From Interstate 395 in Bishop, take Highway 168 west 15 miles to the South Lake turnoff. Turn left on South Lake Road and drive six miles to the lake. Drive past the marina to the trailhead and parking area.

*Ledge Lake with Saddlerock Lake in the backdrop*

There are two ways to get to Ledge Lake: the easy way and the adventurous way. The easy way is a mere seven-tenths of a mile walk from Timberline Tarns Lakes. While the adventurous way requires only a short cross-country trek, there is some difficult rock-hopping involved. No matter which route you choose, keep one thing in mind: there is no trail to Ledge Lake. The adventurous way, however, offers what the more direct route from Timberline Tarns doesn't: outstanding views of Ledge and Margaret Lakes.

So, let's work on getting to Ledge via the adventurous route. First, walk to Margaret Lake's outlet stream and face the lake. Then, look to the left, where you'll see a small hill just in front of you. About 100 yards to the right, there will be towering 13,000-foot peaks. There is a small pass between the two, and that's what you're going to need to follow.

Because there is no trail and the entire trek to the top of the pass is across exposed rocks (ranging in size from coffee cans to vans), the climb is quite strenuous. It's roughly 200 yards to the top of the pass, where you'll be rewarded with superb views of Margaret and Ledge lakes. When you cross over to the other side of the pass, Ledge will be easy to spot, although many hikers confuse it with Saddlerock Lake. Saddlerock is the large lake that can be seen from the top of the pass. Ledge is a small, one-acre lake that rests in a crater-like hole tucked just below the pass, above Saddlerock.

To reach Ledge from the trail to Bishop Pass, start at Upper Timberline Tarns Lake and continue towards Bishop Pass. In two-tenths of a mile, the trail passes by Saddlerock's outlet stream. Leave the trail and walk to the right, following four-tenths of a mile along the lake's shoreline. You'll pass two islands before coming to a small cove. Ledge is directly above the cove.

Although Ledge is a pretty lake set at 11,180 feet in the John Muir Wilderness, because of its small size, its good fishing seems to be somewhat of a secret. Yet, the lake is so abundant with a self-sustaining population of brook trout that no stocks are required. The brookies, which range in size from six to nine inches, are easy to spot and catch in these shallow waters. Any small spinner will entice these fish to bite. And, with all the other more prominent lakes nearby, chances are, you're going to have Ledge all to yourself.

If you plan to make the trip, supplies are available at Bishop Creek Lodge and Parchers Resort. A wilderness permit is required for overnight travel into the John Muir Wilderness. Ledge Lake is closed to fishing from November 1 to the last Saturday in April.

Also nearby are Saddlerock Lake, Ruwau Lake, Bishop Lake, Margaret Lake, Timberline Tarns Lakes, Chocolate Lakes, Long Lake and Spearhead Lake.

## LEDGE LAKE

*Chocolate Peak is an inspiring site from Ledge Lake.*

*It's best and most productive to fish near the inlet and outlet streams.*

**Rating:** 7
**Species:** Brook Trout and Rainbow Trout
**Stock:** Six pounds of fingerling rainbow trout.
**Facilities:** None
**Contact:** Inyo National Forest (760) 873-2400

**Directions:** From Highway 395 in Bishop, take Highway 168 west 15 miles to the South Lake turnoff. Turn left on South Lake Road and drive six miles to the lake. Drive past the marina to the trailhead and parking area.

*Bishop Lake rests just below Bishop Pass.*

First of all, lets get one thing straight: Bishop Lake is nowhere near Bishop. In reality, it's roughly 27 miles away, with completely different scenery. At an elevation of 11,200 feet, tucked in a basin just below Bishop Pass near the border of Sequoia National Park, Bishop is a fairly large backcountry lake that few anglers seem to fish.

Although normally used by hikers as a resting spot before climbing over Bishop Pass into the Dusty Basin, the lake does have good prospects for snagging rainbow and brook trout. The California Department of Fish and Game airlifts in 6,000 fingerling rainbow trout each year, supplementing holdovers and a large population of brook trout.

Because of its size, it could take some time to walk Bishop Lake's shoreline. It's best and most productive to fish near the inlet and outlet streams. No specific lures are required, however, Thomas Buoyants work best. To reach Bishop Lake from Saddlerock Lake, hike a half-mile towards Bishop Pass, and you'll see the lake on the right.

If you plan to make the trip, supplies are available at Bishop Creek Lodge and Parchers Resort. A wilderness permit is required for overnight travel into the John Muir Wilderness. Bishop Lake is closed to fishing from November 1 to the last Saturday in April.

Also nearby are Timberline Tarns Lakes, Ruwau Lake, Saddlerock Lake, Margaret Lake, Ledge Lake, Chocolate Lakes, Long Lake and Spearhead Lake.

# SPEARHEAD LAKE

**Spearhead can be productive for anglers who fish it correctly, near the inlets.**

| | |
|---|---|
| **Rating:** | 6 |
| **Species:** | Brook Trout and Rainbow Trout |
| **Stock:** | None |
| **Facilities:** | None |
| **Contact:** | Inyo National Forest (760) 873-2400 |
| **Directions:** | From Highway 395 in Bishop, take Highway 168 west 15 miles to the South Lake turnoff. Turn left on South Lake Road and drive six miles to the lake. Drive past the marina to the trailhead and parking area. |

*Spearhead Lake*

Because it's closely connected to the prolific Long Lake, Spearhead Lake is also a great fishing lake. Bishop Creek is wide enough and deep enough to allow fish to swim freely between them, and Long's bounty of fish commonly ends up in Spearhead. You'd think this would be detrimental to Long's fish population, but there are so many fish in Long, no one seems to notice any trout have left.

Fed by runoff from Margaret and Timberline Tarn Lakes, Spearhead can be productive for anglers who fish it correctly, near the inlets. Since the Margaret inlet is too shallow to fish, to be successful you'll need to cast about 10 yards west of the inlet, where the water is deeper. Try using any small lures, such as a Kastmaster, Panther Martin or Roostertail.

Spearhead is located at 10,780 feet in the John Muir Wilderness, and reaching it from Long is a cinch. From the west end of Long Lake, continue two-tenths of a mile on the path to Spearhead on the right.

If you plan to make the trip, supplies are available at Bishop Creek Lodge and Parchers Resort. A wilderness permit is required for overnight travel into the John Muir Wilderness. Spearhead Lake is closed to fishing from November 1 to the last Saturday in April.

Also nearby are Saddlerock Lake, Ruwau Lake, Bishop Lake, Ledge Lake, Timberline Tarns Lakes, Chocolate Lakes, Long Lake and Margaret Lake.

# MARGARET LAKE

**Choosing to fish Margaret is a smart decision if you want to beat the crowds.**

**Rating:** 6
**Species:** Brook Trout
**Stock:** None
**Facilities:** None
**Contact:** Inyo National Forest (760) 873-2400

**Directions:** From Highway 395 in Bishop, take Highway 168 west 15 miles to the South Lake turnoff. Turn left on South Lake Road and drive six miles to the lake. Drive past the marina to the trailhead and parking area.

Margaret Lake

Cross country travel from Margaret to Ledge

Tucked away in a small basin above Spearhead Lake, below jagged mountain peaks that reach 13,000 feet, Margaret Lake offers fair fishing for brook trout. Located at 10,940 feet in the John Muir Wilderness, above South Lake, this small lake is one of four of the 18 lakes in the South Fork of Bishop Creek Drainage that doesn't have an established trail to it.

Choosing to fish Margaret is a smart decision if you want to beat the crowds. Even without a trail, Margaret is easy to find. To get to Margaret, walk to the inlet on the north side of Spearhead Lake. If you look carefully, there is a trail on the east side of the inlet.

Walk roughly 100 yards up the path (if you can't locate it, parallel the stream) to a small, shallow pond. Don't waste any time here; there are no fish. In another 100 yards, there will be another small pond. Margaret is on the other side of the hill, just beyond the pond.

Although small, Margaret is deep, and even though the water is clear, you still can't see the bottom. Concentrate on fishing the back side of the lake, opposite the outlet.

If you plan to make the trip, supplies are available at Bishop Creek Lodge and Parchers Resort. A wilderness permit is required for overnight travel into the John Muir Wilderness. Margaret Lake is closed to fishing from November 1 to the last Saturday in April.

Also nearby are Saddlerock Lake, Ruwau Lake, Bishop Lake, Ledge Lake, Timberline Tarns Lakes, Chocolate Lakes, Long Lake and Spearhead Lake.

# LONG LAKE (Bishop Creek)

*We saw thousands of brook and rainbow trout here.*

| | |
|---|---|
| **Rating:** | 9 |
| **Species:** | Brook Trout, Rainbow Trout and Brown Trout |
| **Stock:** | Eight pounds of fingerling rainbow trout. |
| **Facilities:** | None |
| **Contact:** | Inyo National Forest (760) 873-2400 |
| **Directions:** | From Highway 395 in Bishop, take Highway 168 west 15 miles to the South Lake turnoff. Turn left on South Lake Road and drive six miles to the lake. Drive past the marina to the trailhead and parking area. |

*Long Lake is the best fishery in the Bishop Creek (South Fork) Drainage.*

There are several Long Lakes in California's backcountry; yet, none have been able to stamp the same indelible impression in my memory as the Long Lake that is part of the South Fork of Bishop Creek Drainage. Not only is Long a scenic 29-acre lake, but the number of fish here are staggering. At 10,751 feet in the John Muir Wilderness, Long Lake offers the best overall fishing in the drainage.

We saw thousands of brook and rainbow trout here. Surprisingly, they were larger than the normal six to nine-inchers found in most high-country lakes. Several rainbows were as large as 12 inches, while the brookies reached 10.

To reach Long Lake, from the meadow that is used to access Hurd Lake, pick up the path and follow it seven-tenths of a mile to a trail junction. Veering away from Bull and Chocolate Lakes, stay right, following signs towards Bishop Pass. About five minutes (two-tenths of a mile) from the junction, you'll cross Bull's outlet stream, and Long Lake will be on the right. From the trailhead at South Lake, Long is roughly two miles away, and the hike requires almost 1,000 feet of elevation gain.

The first section of Long that you'll reach is shallow, but extremely productive. There are downed trees and rocks in the water, where the fish love to hang out. As you persist along the path, Long becomes wider and deeper, and even though the fish might not be as concentrated, there are still plenty to be caught.

Near the Bishop Creek and Ruwau Creek inlets, Long opens up and becomes a large backcountry lake with deep holes and steep drop-offs. Fishing near the island towards the middle of the lake can be productive, but the easiest way to catch fish is to hang near the inlets. Near the inlet of Bull's outlet stream, small Panther Martins work best..

If you plan to make the trip, supplies are available at Parchers Resort. A wilderness permit is required for overnight travel into the John Muir Wilderness. Long Lake is closed to fishing from November 1 to the last Saturday in April.

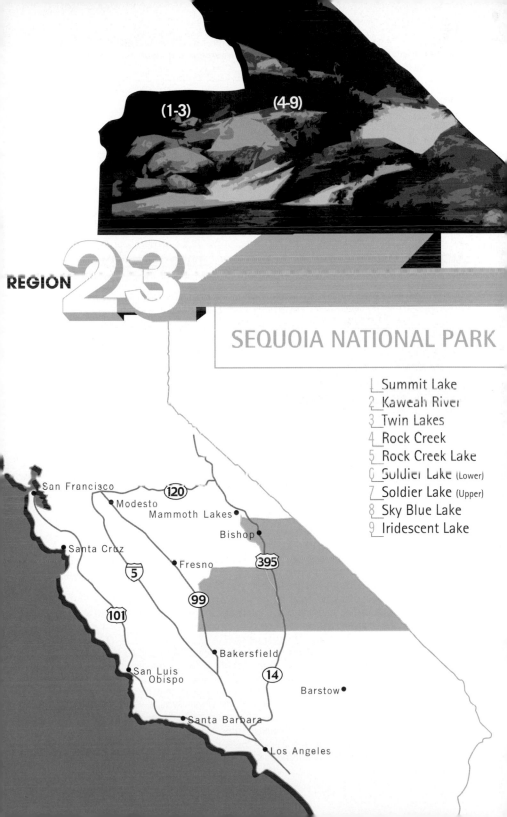

(1-3)          (4-9)

REGION **23**

SEQUOIA NATIONAL PARK

1 Summit Lake
2 Kaweah River
3 Twin Lakes
4 Rock Creek
5 Rock Creek Lake
6 Soldier Lake (Lower)
7 Soldier Lake (Upper)
8 Sky Blue Lake
9 Iridescent Lake

San Francisco
Modesto
120
Mammoth Lakes
Bishop
Santa Cruz
5
Fresno
395
99
101
Bakersfield
San Luis
Obispo
14
Barstow
Santa Barbara
Los Angeles

*If the fish aren't breaking water, walk to the southwest side and climb onto one of the few fallen trees that extend out from the shoreline.*

| | |
|---|---|
| **Rating:** | 8 |
| **Species:** | Brook Trout |
| **Stock:** | None |
| **Facilities:** | None |
| **Contact:** | Balch Park Pack Station (559) 539-2227 (Summer) or (559) 539-3908 (Winter) Sequoia National Forest (559) 784-1500, Sequoia National Park (559) 565-3134 |

**Directions:** From Bakersfield, drive north on the 99 Freeway to Highway 190 east. Continue on Highway 190 past Porterville and Lake Success to Springville. In Springville turn left on Road J-37 (Balch Park Road) and drive 2.4 miles to Road 220. Turn right and continue approximately 12 miles to Mountain Home State Forest. Follow signs to the Balch Park Pack Station. The trailhead is just past the pack station.

*This brook trout wasted no time snatching a Panther Martin reeled in by Blake Lezak.*

Located at the southernmost point of Sequoia National Park, Summit Lake offers great brook trout fishing. At 9,300 feet, the four-acre lake has been planted with brooks a total of 12 times since 1930, and was last stocked in 1967. With a self-sustaining population, most of the fish are between six and nine inches, but they tend to fatten up as the year progresses. The lake freezes over in the winter, and because of snow, it remains difficult to reach until early June, some years even into July.

Most anglers fish the lake on their way into the Maggie Lakes Basin, located in the Golden Trout Wilderness. Too shallow to fish where the trail wraps around the lake, it's necessary to move to the far side where the water is deeper. In the spring and early summer, it can be difficult to get there, because numerous springs feed the lake on its southeast shore, making the ground mushy and wet.

If the fish aren't breaking water, walk to the southwest side and climb onto one of the few fallen trees that extend out from the shoreline. Cast either gold or yellow Panther Martins as far as you can and let them sink for eight seconds. Then, give one easy jerk and reel in. I usually get a hit on one of every four casts.

To reach Summit Lake from the Balch Park Trailhead, begin your climb above the North Fork of the Middle Fork of the Tule River. Then, after briefly leaving Mountain Home State Forest and reentering it again, descend down to your first river crossing. Sequoias that can be seen along the trail speckle the river here. Just before the descent, be sure to look over your right shoulder for a stunning view of the Mt. Home Sequoia Grove. From this elevated perspective, you'll be able to see how much taller sequoias are than pine trees.

After 1.8 miles, just before this first stream crossing (called Redwood Crossing, because there is a fallen redwood tree that extends over the stream), you'll be able to hear a series of cascades from the N.F. of the M.F. of the Tule River Falls. These cascades are located just below the crossing.

*A meadow on the shore of Summit Lake.*
*page 428*

Just after crossing the river, you'll come to a trail junction. The right fork leads to Hidden Falls. Stay left, following signs to Summit Lake. The last sequoia along the trail is just before Strawberry Meadow on the left side, and it is noteworthy, because, unlike most sequoias, it has branches all the way down to its base.

Just before Strawberry Meadow, keep an eye out for a small waterfall coming down the mountain on the north side of the river. It falls year-round and is most striking in the spring. At 4.3 miles, after walking through Strawberry and Long Meadows, you'll cross the stream again and walk through two other small meadows, before coming to another trail junction. The left fork heads over Tuohy Pass to the South Fork of the Kaweah River. Stay right, crossing the stream for the third and final time. At 4.7 miles from the trailhead, begin the climb to Summit Lake.

After enduring a solid climb, you'll come to a clearing in just over six miles. Now above the river again spectacular views of Long Canyon below and Moses Mountain can be seen in the distance. In about five minutes, you'll walk across the base of Summit Lake Falls and enter Sequoia National Park, just before reaching Summit Lake on your right. Total distance is approximately seven miles, with an elevation gain of nearly 3,000 feet. Ouch!

If you plan to make the trip, supplies are available in Springville. A wilderness permit is required for overnight travel in Sequoia National Park. Call ahead for updated trail conditions. Snow covers the trail well into June.

Also nearby are Hidden Falls, Mountain Home State Forest, Balch Park Lakes, Redwood Lake, N.F. of the M.F. of the Tule River, Twin Lakes, Maggie Lakes, Summit Lake Falls and Frog Lake.

*Nine-inch brookies, like this one caught by Scott Wiessner are common at Summit.*

SUMMIT LAKE

*The Kaweah is a river of seasons, and you have to fish it at the right season to be successful.*

**Rating:** 6

**Species:** Rainbow Trout and Brown Trout

**Stock:** None

**Facilities:** Campgrounds, Restrooms and Picnic Areas

**Contact:** Sequoia National Park (559) 565-3134, Lodgepole Visitor Center (559-565-3782), Sequoia National Park Wilderness Permits (559-565-3761) or (559-565-3766) Lodgepole Campground (559-565-3774)

**Directions:** From Bakersfield, drive north on the 99 Freeway to Highway 198. Exit east and continue to Visalia. From Visalia, continue on Highway 198 approximately 35 miles to the entrance to Sequoia National Park. Access is available near Buckeye Flat, Potwisha, Lodgepole Campgrounds and near Crystal Cave.

*The Kaweah is perfect for snorkeling in mid-summer.*

The Kaweah is a river of seasons, and you have to fish it at the right season to be successful. Closed to fishing from late fall through winter, raging in the spring, extremely low from mid-summer through winter, it is just right for fishing in early summer. If you hit it right, you'll have a blast. The river is loaded with small wild rainbows, mostly six to nine inchers, mixed in with a few browns.

The downside is that there is a problem with access. Much of the river is located in remote and hard to reach canyons, making fishing difficult. However, there are several places access can be found, where the Kaweah flows through Sequoia National Park, beginning a few miles above Tokopah Valley Falls near Lodgepole, and ending a few miles east of Lake Kaweah.

Since trout are not planted anywhere on this stretch of the river, many anglers stay away. However, campers and anglers who come specifically to catch wild trout, do fish here. Campers not accustomed to freshwater stream fishing can make things difficult for experienced anglers. They often employ unusual and unique techniques, like using ocean poles and 20 pound test to try to catch a six-inch trout, or using spoons for catching large ocean fish. Often, they will wade into a pool, spooking the very fish they are trying to catch. Sometimes, I wonder if the fish don't get a kick out of these campers.

Because of its remoteness, the river can only be easily accessed in a few sites: on the Middle Fork near Buckeye Flat Campground, where the Marble Fork meets the Middle Fork near Potwisha Campground, and along the Marble Fork near Lodgepole Campground and Crystal Cave. What I like to do is start in one of these places and work my way up or downstream, without making any casts until I am some distance away from the campers. With all the commotion near the campgrounds, the fish tend to shy away from biting. The best action can be had fishing small Panther Martins and silver Kastmasters.

*A brown bear at Buckeye Flat Campground*        *Kaweah River (Middle Fork)*

The river may contain lots of trout, but it's best known for swimming and wading in late spring and summer. With clear water and deep holes, many of the pools located within the campgrounds are ideal for swimming. This is one of my favorite spots in all of Central California to snorkel.

If you plan to make the trip, supplies are available in Three Rivers and Lodgepole. The Kaweah River is closed to fishing from November 1 to the last Saturday in April. Check with the park for angling restrictions. In some areas only artificial lures with barbless hooks are permitted.

Also nearby are Moro Rock, the General Sherman Tree, Twin Lakes, Tokopah Valley Falls, Middle Fork Kaweah River Falls, Kings Canyon National Park, Sierra Catfish Farms and Lake Kaweah.

*Sequoia National Park offers
stunning vistas in all directions.*

*These fish are aggressive and will attack just about any lure or live bait.*

| | |
|---|---|
| **Rating:** | 10 |
| **Species:** | Brook Trout |
| **Stock:** | Last stock was in 1964. |
| **Facilities:** | Campground |
| **Contact:** | Sequoia National Park (559) 565-3134, Lodgepole Visitor Center (559-565-3782), Sequoia National Park Wilderness Permits (559-565-3761) or (559-565-3766) Lodgepole Campground (559-565-3774) |

**Directions:** From Fresno, drive for 52 miles east on Highway 180 to the entrance to Kings Canyon National Park and continue 1.7 miles to Generals Highway. Turn right and continue 25 miles to Lodgepole Campground. Turn east and drive to the day-use parking lot near the Kaweah River. Walk across the bridge to the trailhead.

*Tony Abel fooled this brook trout at Twin Lakes.*

Anglers who have been to Twin Lakes will tell you there are not many places that can match its great brook trout fishing. The problem is that not many people have been here. Why? Well, the hike is a total butt-kicker, undoable for many. Only those who can hang in there will reap the priceless benefits of catching brook trout on nearly every cast. Not to mention close encounters with wildlife you thought you'd only see from your living room love seat while watching the Discovery Channel and munching on Cool Ranch chips.

For me, the hike is just as rewarding as the fishing. If you're up to it, the grueling trek to the backcountry of Sequoia National Park is well worth it. It consists of a 13-mile roundtrip journey, packed with a 2,745-foot elevation gain, bringing you to your destination at 9,430 feet.

Your expedition begins at the east end of Lodgepole Campground on the north side of the Marble Fork of the Kaweah River. Head west, gradually climbing up the mountain for nearly nine-tenths of a mile and not wasting any time climbing before the trail bends to the right, where you'll reach the first and only level part of the hike.

In the early mornings and late afternoons, keep your eyes open for bears on this part of the trail. They won't bother you, because they have their minds set on more appealing food (such as the delicious hamburgers and hot dogs in Lodgepole Campground); although, they might just have to cross your path to get there.

The trail stays relatively level for the next mile, leading past Willow Meadow on your right. About a half-mile past the meadow, you'll embark on a seemingly endless climb. Over the next half-mile, you'll cross Silliman Creek and endure a 365-foot elevation gain to Cahoon Meadow, a popular destination for nature lovers. In the early mornings and late evenings, deer and bears can be seen in this meadow.

After looping around the meadow and hiking through the Cahoon Gap, completing two miles and a 1,000-foot elevation gain from Cahoon Meadow, you'll come to the East Fork of Clover Creek. There are campgrounds here, but to reach your destination, a 1,100-foot climb over another 1.5 miles is required. The climb seems to never end. Every time you think you've made it to the lakes there's one more peak to overcome.

Make sure you take the right fork at JO Pass. From there, the lake is about a mile away. Although the last part of the hike is demanding, it also provides a certain amount of satisfaction, because of the dozens of different types of wildflowers that flourish in the endless meadows. Keep an eye out for marmots. The large rodents thrive and grow fat in this area.

Twin Lakes is actually two small ponds loaded with brook trout, the only fish that inhabit the lakes. The pine-tree-lined lakes have not been stocked since 1964, but the trout reproduce quickly here. In the 1930s, the lakes were also stocked with goldens, but none are left. Most of the brookies are small, averaging six to eight inches, but pound-sized fish are commonly caught. These fish are aggressive and will attack just about any lure or live bait.

The one downside here is that in early summer the mosquitoes are thick and nearly unbearable. Don't rely on bug repellent. You'll need to clothe your whole body to be able to tolerate them. Yet, it would be difficult to find a better place to view wildlife in Central California, and you can bet it's a lot better than the campgrounds.

We went snorkeling in the lakes in search of bigger fish. When I poked my head up for air, I saw two deer perched on the shoreline about five feet away. They were probably wondering what the heck I was doing 9,000 feet above sea level snorkeling in their lake. I bet they'd never seen anything like that before! I became more curious and swam over to where they were standing. They didn't even flinch. So, I stood up, now in touching distance, and said, "Hi." They sort of nodded their heads and went back to chewing grass.

Deer are the friendliest animals around, but they don't rule the land here. Mountain lions and bears do. I heard a lot of reports of mountain lion sightings and bears visiting the campgrounds at night. We talked to two fishermen who told us a bear stole their fish the night before.

You think you're tired from the hike? Keep on climbing. The Ranger Lakes are only a short distance over Silliman Pass. Don't forget to bring plenty of food and water. You're going to need it.

If you plan to make the trip, supplies are available in Lodgepole. There is a $10 fee to enter Sequoia National Park. A wilderness permit is required for overnight travel in the park.

Also nearby are Ranger Lakes, Marble Fork of the Kaweah River, Tokopah Falls and General Sherman Tree.

*Upper Twin Lake*

# ROCK CREEK

*Although there aren't many pools in this area, there are a lot of small goldens, and also some rainbows that hide under logs, ledges and in eddies.*

**Rating:** 7
**Species:** Golden Trout and Rainbow Trout
**Stock:** None
**Facilities:** None
**Contact:** Sequoia National Park Wilderness Permits (559) 565-3761
Sequoia National Park (559) 565-3134, Inyo National Forest (760) 876-6200

**Directions:** From Mojave, drive north on Highway 14 to Highway 395. Continue north on Highway 395 to the town of Lone Pine. In Lone Pine, turn west on Whitney Portal Road and drive three miles to Horseshoe Meadow Road. Turn south and drive approximately 16 miles to the Horseshoe Meadow Trailhead.

*Rock Creek (Sequoia Park)*

Rock Creek in the Miter Basin of Sequoia National Park looks a lot like Rock Creek in the John Muir Wilderness. Both are located above 10,000 feet, offer some of the most astonishing views in California and provide great fishing. The most noticeable difference is fishing pressure. While Rock Creek in the JM Wilderness is bombarded by anglers, Sequoia's Rock Creek is rarely fished.

Flowing through meadows on its way out of the Miter Basin, Rock Creek is created by runoff from Iridescent and Sky Blue Lakes. Although there aren't many pools in this area, there are a lot of small goldens, and also some rainbows both of which hide under logs, ledges and in eddies. There are also many small ponds just off the creek, which hold tons of fish. Fly-fishing or tossing small spinners is productive.

As the creek works its way out of the basin, it picks up speed, cascades down a slope and becomes difficult to fish, partly because the fish are easily spooked here. So, use caution not to let them see you.

Keep any eye out for marmots. I tried to get close to one to take a good shot of him with my video camera, and he charged me. I think he was a bit surprised when I didn't run away, and just before hitting me, he turned around and ran the other way. It made for a great video.

To reach the creek, pick up the inlet stream at Rock Creek Lake and follow it up into the Miter Basin.

If you plan to make the trip, a wilderness permit is required for overnight travel in Sequoia National Park. If coming in June or July, bring along plenty of insect repellent. The mosquitoes are nearly unbearable.

Also nearby are Rock Creek, Rock Creek Lake, Upper Soldier Lake, Sky Blue Lake, Iridescent Lake, Rock Creek Falls, Sky Blue Falls, Chicken Springs Lake, South Fork Lakes and Cottonwood Lakes.

*mext page Rock Creek in the Miter Basin*

**The fish aren't suspicious of anglers, and although they're small, they're not picky. Just about any lure will work.**

| | |
|---|---|
| **Rating:** | 6 |
| **Species:** | Golden Trout and Rainbow Trout |
| **Stock:** | None |
| **Facilities:** | None |
| **Contact:** | Sequoia National Park Wilderness Permits (559) 565-3761 |
| | Sequoia National Park (559) 565-3134, Inyo National Forest (760) 876-6200 |

**Directions:** From Mojave, drive north on Highway 14 to Highway 395. Continue north on Highway 395 to the town of Lone Pine. In Lone Pine, turn west on Whitney Portal Road and drive three miles to Horseshoe Meadow Road. Turn south and drive approximately 16 miles to the Horseshoe Meadow Trailhead.

*Rock Creek Lake (Sequoia Park)*

Taking children backpacking isn't always easy, but having them catch fish is, if you're at Rock Creek Lake. No, not the Rock Creek Lake between Bishop and Mammoth in the Eastern Sierra. The other one, in Sequoia National Park. You say you can't find a Rock Creek Lake in Sequoia National Park on your map? That may be the case. It's so small, it's not listed on all maps.

Located at 10,450 feet at the base of the Miter Basin, Rock Creek Lake is a tiny pond near the junction of Lower Soldier Lake's outlet stream and Rock Creek. Surrounded by a large meadow with tall grass, its highlight is small golden trout. All you need to do to catch them is be able to cast. This is why it's such a great place to bring young anglers. The fish aren't suspicious of anglers, and although they're small, they're not picky. Just about any lure will work.

Although fish don't often grow more than eight inches in this pond, anglers don't come here to catch big fish. They come for the beautiful colors of the golden trout. Fishing from the rocks near the trail is your only option. The rest of the lake is surrounded by marshland. You'll sink in the mud before you can get off a cast.

To reach Rock Creek Lake from Chicken Springs Lake, continue on the Pacific Crest Trail for 3.2 miles to the boundary of Sequoia National Park. Approximately seven-tenths of a mile from the boundary, you'll come to a fork in the trail. The left fork leads to Siberian Pass, the right towards New Army Pass and the Miter Basin. Take the right fork and continue one mile to another fork. Stay left, crossing a small stream, and follow signs to Rock Creek. In a half-mile you'll have to make a final decision. Turn right and you're at Lower Soldier Lake. Turn left, in seven-tenths of a mile ahead is Rock Creek Lake.

If you plan to make the trip, a wilderness permit is required for overnight travel in Sequoia National Park.

Also nearby are Rock Creek, Lower Soldier Lake and Upper Soldier Lake.

# SOLDIER LAKE (LOWER)

*Lower Soldier is the easiest lake to reach in the Miter Basin and offers some of the best golden trout fishing in the park.*

**Rating:** 9
**Species:** Golden Trout
**Stock:** None
**Facilities:** None
**Contact:** Sequoia National Park Wilderness Permits (559-565-3761), Sequoia National Park (559) 565-3134, Inyo National Forest (760) 876-6200

**Directions:** From Mojave, drive north on Highway 14 to Highway 395 and continue to the town of Lone Pine. Turn west on Whitney Portal Road and drive three miles to Horseshoe Meadow Road. Turn south and drive approximately 16 miles to the Horseshoe Meadows Trailhead.

Soldier Lake (Lower)

*One of more than 10 goldens caught and released by Stephen Wiessner during a 20 minute span at Lower Soldier.*

Catching golden trout is a dream for nearly every angler who fishes the Sierra, however, not many anglers get to accomplish that feat. Reaching lakes that hold goldens usually requires a long, strenuous hike which most anglers don't have the stamina to complete. Although the hike is long to reach Lower Soldier Lake, in the backcountry of Sequoia National Park, it is relatively easy, rewarding the adventurous with great golden trout fishing.

Lower Soldier is the easiest lake to reach in the Miter Basin and offers some of the best golden trout fishing in the park. None of the goldens are huge, they rarely grow above 10 inches (and most average eight inches), but they are a lot of fun to catch.

In late spring and early summer, the best bite is from 6-9 a.m. for fly-fishermen using mosquito-patterned flies. The goldens won't hit lures until just after 9 a.m. (when the mosquitoes seem to disappear) until the evening. During those hours, use red or yellow Panther Martins.

The lake is small (a little bigger than nearby Rock Creek Lake), but pretty and crystal clear. It's also so shallow it looks like you could walk across it, but you'd probably get stuck in the mud. Lower Soldier Lake, located just below the tree line at 10,800 feet, is the most popular fishing lake in the Miter Basin, and gets heavily fished by anglers. There is a trail that circles the lake and provides anglers with good access. One thing you should keep in mind is that there are a lot of weeds in the lake, so try to look for an area when you wont get tangled in them.

To get to Lower Soldier Lake, begin your hike at the Horseshoe Meadow Trailhead. Work your way through Horseshoe Meadow over Cottonwood Pass. Just after climbing over the pass, you'll come to a three-way fork in the trail. Follow the right fork and continue to Chicken Springs Lake. To reach Lower Soldier Lake from Chicken Springs Lake, continue on the Pacific Crest Trail for 3.2 miles to the signed boundary of Sequoia National Park. Approximately seven-tenths of a mile from the boundary you'll come to another fork in the trail. The left fork heads to Siberian Pass, and the right towards New Army Pass and the Miter Basin. Take the right fork and continue one mile to another fork. Stay left, crossing a small stream and follow signs to Rock Creek. In a half-mile you'll have to make one final decision. Turn right and following signs to Lower Soldier Lake a tad more than one-tenth of a mile ahead.

If you plan to make the trip, supplies are available in Lone Pine. A wilderness permit is required for overnight camping in Sequoia National Park. The road to Horseshoe Meadow Trailhead is commonly closed until sometime in May. If coming in June or July, you'd better bring along plenty of insect repellent. The mosquitoes are nearly unbearable.

Also nearby are Rock Creek, Rock Creek Lake, Upper Soldier Lake, Sky Blue Lake, Iridescent Lake, Rock Creek Falls, Sky Blue Falls, Chicken Springs Lake, South Fork Lakes and the Cottonwood Lakes.

*Soldier Lake (Lower)*

SOLDIER LAKE (LOWER)

# SOLDIER LAKE (UPPER)

*The key to catching them is to let your lure sink and then vary your retrieval speed.*

| | |
|---|---|
| **Rating:** | 6 |
| **Species:** | Golden Trout and Rainbow Trout |
| **Stock:** | None |
| **Facilities:** | None |
| **Contact:** | Sequoia National Park Wilderness Permits (559-565-3761) |
| | Sequoia National Park (559) 565-3134, Inyo National Forest (760) 876-6200 |
| **Directions:** | From Mojave, drive north on Highway 14 to Highway 395. Drive north on Highway 395 to the town of Lone Pine. In Lone Pine, turn west on Whitney Portal Road and drive three miles to Horseshoe Meadow Road. Turn south and drive approximately 16 miles to the Horseshoe Meadow Trailhead. |

*Soldier Lake (Upper)*

Fishing Upper Soldier Lake is much different than fishing Lower Soldier Lake, where you can catch tons of goldens. Gone are Lower Soldier's high catch rates of small fish. There simply aren't as many fish in the upper lake, although, they are generally larger. But, they are also a lot smarter than their counterparts in the lower lake and far more wary of anglers. At 11,180 feet in Sequoia National Park, Upper Soldier Lake is one of the most difficult lakes in the Miter Basin to fish. The fish are willing to follow your lure, but getting them to take it is another story.

Upper Soldier Lake was last stocked with golden trout in 1969, and these goldens haven't grow big for no reason. Not only are they educated to the various tricks that anglers employ, they can stare you right in the eye through the lake's crystal-clear water. The key to catching them is to let your lure sink and then vary your retrieval speed. After letting your lure sink (for at least 10 seconds), begin reeling it in slowly and increase its speed. If a fish is going to hit it, it will usually do so right after you increase the speed.

Fishing the south side of the lake produces the highest catch rates, but it's also the most difficult area to land the goldens. There is no trail, and it's often impossible to get your footing on many of the loose rocks that teeter with each step you take. The drop-offs are steep on this side, and many of the larger goldens take cover under the car-sized boulders below. There are also a few rainbows in the lake, but it's not necessary to change techniques to target them.

Getting to Upper Soldier Lake can be a little tricky. From Lower Soldier Lake, start at the outlet stream and walk around the shore to the lake's inlet. (It doesn't matter which side you take.) Now, follow the inlet up to Upper Soldier Lake. There's a whisper of a trail that fades in and out and can be difficult to follow. If you just stick close to the stream, you'll be okay. The entire walk should take about 15 minutes.

When you stop to catch your breath, take a look over your right shoulder. You'll get a magnificent view of Lower Soldier Lake. Directly above you and to your left is Major General Mountain, at 12,350 feet.

If you plan to make the trip, a wilderness permit is required for overnight travel in Sequoia National Park. If coming in June or July, bring along plenty of insect repellent. The mosquitoes are nearly unbearable.

Also nearby are Rock Creek, Rock Creek Lake, Lower Soldier Lake, Sky Blue Lake, Iridescent Lake, Rock Creek Falls, Sky Blue Lake Falls, Chicken Springs Lake, South Fork Lakes and Cottonwood Lakes.

*Soldier Lake (Upper)*

# SOLDIER LAKE (UPPER)

# SKY BLUE LAKE

**Sky Blue is the largest lake in the basin, and home to prized golden trout.**

| | |
|---|---|
| **Rating:** | 5 |
| **Species:** | Golden Trout |
| **Stock:** | None |
| **Facilities:** | None |
| **Contact:** | Sequoia National Park Wilderness Permits (559) 565-3761 |
| | Sequoia National Park (559) 565-3134, Inyo National Forest (760) 876-6200 |

**Directions:** From Mojave, drive north on Highway 14 to Highway 395. Drive north on Highway 395 and continue to the town of Lone Pine. In Lone Pine, turn west on Whitney Portal Road and drive three miles to Horseshoe Meadow Road. Turn south and drive approximately 16 miles to the Horseshoe Meadow Trailhead.

*Sky Blue Lake*

Sky Blue Lake is the prefect destination for anyone who loves to hike and enjoys a place where others rarely visit. Located at the back of the Miter Basin in Sequoia National Park, it requires a long, but not so difficult hike, and the trip is more than worth it. Sky Blue is the largest lake in the basin, and home to prized golden trout.

Sky Blue Lake is situated in a granite bowl. One waterfall pours into it, and another cascades out of it. Sky Blue Falls serves as one of the lake's inlets. This breathtaking 50-foot freefall makes for great photographs. Rock Creek Falls is formed by the lake's outlet, and it is partly responsible for the flows that create Rock Creek.

At 11,550 feet, the lake is above the tree line, near Crabtree Pass. It is surrounded by towering peaks, which are reflected in its crystal-clear water. It's a great day trip for those spending a night at Lower Soldier Lake.

As for the fishing, concentrate your efforts near the outlet. Use a slow retrieve. I found red and gold Thomas Buoyants to be the most productive, but the yellow Cripplelure and most Panther Martins work well, too.

The lake was last planted in 1962 with 2,000 golden trout, and there are still some big goldens to be caught. Most of the fish I landed were over a pound, but I didn't see any small fish, which isn't a good sign. This could mean the fish aren't reproducing, and in the next 10 years the lake could become barren of fish. Better get here before it does.

To reach Sky Blue Lake from Rock Creek Lake, hike 2.4 miles on the trail that parallels Rock Creek, to a fork in the creek at the end of the meadow. Veer right and you'll end up at Iridescent Lake. Stay left, heading towards Rock Creek Falls. Follow the trail past the falls to the lake. The trail begins to peter out half way above the falls.

If you plan to make the trip, a wilderness permit is required for overnight travel in Sequoia National Park.

Also nearby are, Iridescent Lake, Rock Creek Falls and Sky Blue Falls.

*The lake is deep with steep drop-offs, so there is a chance there were a few fish hiding out in areas that are obscured by the depths of the water, but it is unlikely.*

| | |
|---|---|
| **Rating:** | 1 |
| **Species:** | None |
| **Stock:** | None |
| **Facilities:** | None |
| **Contact:** | Sequoia National Park Wilderness Permits (559) 565-3761 |
| | Sequoia National Park (559) 565-3134, Inyo National Forest (760) 876-6200 |

**Directions:** From Mojave, drive north on Highway 14 to Highway 395. Drive north on Highway 395 to the town of Lone Pine. In Lone Pine, turn west on Whitney Portal Road and drive three miles to Horseshoe Meadow Road. Turn south and drive approximately 16 miles to the Horseshoe Meadows Trailhead.

The view of the Miter Basin from Iridescent Lake

Iridescent is one of the most beautiful lakes in all of the Sierra Nevada, but not many people have ever seen it, probably because it's hard to reach and is rarely talked about. Set at 11,900 feet in a remote area of the Miter Basin in Sequoia National Park, with water as clear as Lake Tahoe, the lake is surrounded by magnificent towering peaks.

There is no trail leading to Iridescent Lake, and it is barren of fish. When my friend Stephen Wiessner and I fished the lake for a few hours, we didn't see any fish. The lake is deep with steep drop-offs, so there is a chance there were a few fish hiding out in areas that are obscured by the depths of the water, but it is unlikely. When I contacted the park's biologist for confirmation, he told me that there were no fish in the lake.

I'm told that if you were to walk to the top of the mountain above the lake, you could almost throw a rock at Mt. Whitney. (However, you can't safely climb up, because it's too steep and there are loose rocks underfoot.) Also, there is Miter, a 12,700-foot peak that the basin was named after. Opposite from Miter are Mt. LeConte (13,800 feet) and Mt. Corcoran (13,500 feet). But, most importantly, there's no one else around, just a few marmots.

It's a great destination for backpackers to take a day-hike, strolling through the high-country. You can relax, read a book or take a nap on the shoreline, without being bothered by anything, except perhaps the few marmots that are curious about what you're doing at such a high elevation.

To reach Iridescent Lake from Rock Creek Lake, follow Rock Creek for 2.4 miles, where it forks near the end of the basin. Veer right (walking away from Rock Creek Falls and Sky Blue Lake), and follow the stream for one mile to the lake.

If you plan to make the trip supplies are available in Lone Pine. A wilderness permit is required for overnight travel in Sequoia National Park. If coming in June or July, you'd better bring along plenty of insect repellent. The mosquitoes are nearly unbearable.

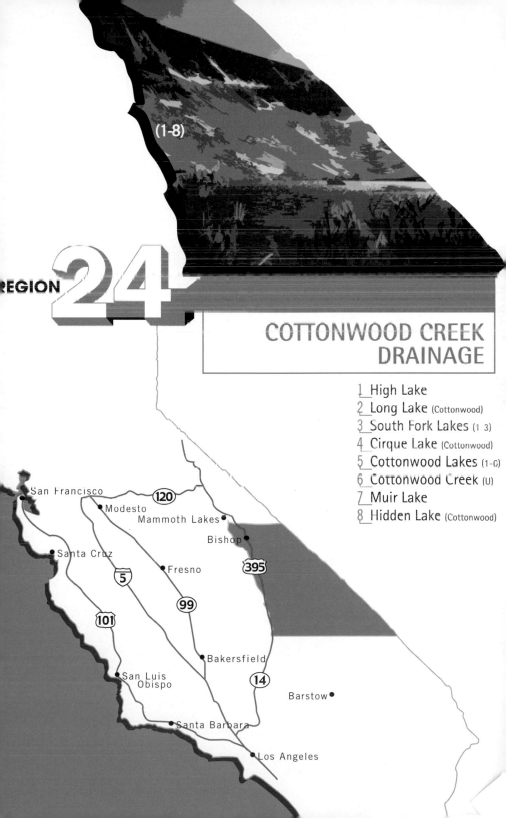

(1-8)

REGION 24

## COTTONWOOD CREEK DRAINAGE

San Francisco
Modesto
Mammoth Lakes
120
Bishop
Santa Cruz
Fresno
395
5
99
101
Bakersfield
San Luis
Obispo
14
Barstow
Santa Barbara
Los Angeles

# HIGH LAKE

*The fishing is never great in the eight-acre lake, but some anglers get lucky and catch a few small goldens.*

| | |
|---|---|
| **Rating:** | 4 |
| **Species:** | Golden Trout |
| **Stock:** | None |
| **Facilities:** | None |
| **Contact:** | Lone Pine Sporting Goods (760) 876-5365, Slater's Sporting Goods (760) 876-5020 Lone Pine Chamber of Commerce (760) 876-4444, Inyo National Forest (760) 876-6200 |

**Directions:** From Mojave, drive north on Highway 14 to Highway 395. Drive north on Highway 395 to the town of Lone Pine. In Lone Pine, turn west on Whitney Portal Road and drive three miles to Horseshoe Meadow Road. Turn south and drive approximately 15 miles to the turnoff for Cottonwood Lakes Trailhead. Turn right and drive to the trailhead.

**High Lake**

High Lake isn't heavily fished. It's mostly used as a rest area before climbing up New Army Pass. At about 11,500 feet up in the John Muir Wilderness, near the boundary for Sequoia National Park, it is the last lake you'll come to before the base of the pass.

Many anglers think there are no fish in High Lake. However, every few years the California Department of Fish and Game stocks 4,000 fingerling golden trout in hopes that they'll grow to catchable size before the next load is airlifted in. The fishing is never great in the eight-acre lake, but some anglers get lucky and catch a few small goldens.

Part of the problem is that most of the fish from High Lake swim down the creek into Long Lake. You might think that for some reason they don't enjoy living in High Lake, but, actually, migrating in and out of lakes is common in the high country. Although the trail that leads to New Army Pass crosses the lake's inlet, the best fishing is found where the water gets deeper on the far side of the lake away from the trail.

Ironically, the clerk at the Forest Service office where we picked up our wilderness permits told me she was sure there were no fish in the lake. It dawned on me that she was probably wrong just after I got up from a nap on the bank of the lake and saw a golden swimming in the water. "Did you see that?" I asked my friend. "I just saw a fish." "But there are no fish in this lake," he laughed. "Didn't you hear the lady from the Forest Service?" To prove her wrong, I tied a lure on my line and caught one. So much for there not being any fish in the lake!

If you plan to make the trip, supplies are available in Lone Pine. A wilderness permit is required for overnight travel in the John Muir Wilderness. High Lake is closed to fishing from November 1 through June 30. Only artificial lures with barbless hooks and barbless flies are permitted.

Also nearby are Upper Cottonwood Creek, Cottonwood Lakes, Long Lake, Cirque Lake, Hidden Lake, Muir Lake, South Fork Lakes, Sequoia National Park and Chicken Springs Lake.

*We tried an array of Thomas Buoyants and Cripplelures, and they wouldn't touch 'em. When we threw out Panther Martins and Roostertails, we got a bite every time.*

| | |
|---|---|
| **Rating:** | 6 |
| **Species:** | Golden Trout |
| **Stock:** | Two pounds of fingerling golden trout. |
| **Facilities:** | None |
| **Contact:** | Lone Pine Sporting Goods (760) 876-5365, High Sierra Outfitters (760) 876-5020 |
| | Lone Pine Chamber of Commerce (760) 876-4444, Inyo National Forest (760) 876-6200 |
| **Directions:** | From Mojave, drive north on Highway 14 to Highway 395 and continue to the town of Lone Pine. In Lone Pine, turn west on Whitney Portal Road and drive three miles to Horseshoe Meadow Road. Turn south and drive approximately 15 miles to the turnoff for Cottonwood Lakes Trailhead. Turn right and drive to the trailhead. |

*Long Lake*

As its name implies, Long Lake is long, about the length of three football fields. It's also narrow and shallow, but it does provide a solid golden trout fishery in the summer and fall. However, there's one problem that can frustrate anglers: size. The goldens rarely grow more than nine inches. So, with the larger goldens at Cottonwood Lakes close by, many anglers pass on the chance to fish Long Lake. Although Long Lake doesn't receive the fishing pressure that the Cottonwood Lakes do, visitors heading up New Army Pass often use it as a final resting spot. Located at 11,130 feet in the John Muir Wilderness, it's just below the tree line.

If you're going to fish the lake, it's important to stay away from the weeds near the campgrounds on the west side. If you head towards the South Fork Lakes, you'll only need to travel about 50 yards to find deeper water and better fishing. These fish like smaller lures, too. We tried an array of Thomas Buoyants and Cripplelures, and they wouldn't touch 'em. When we threw out Panther Martins and Roostertails, we got a bite every time.

To reach Long Lake, begin at the Cottonwood Lakes Trailhead and follow the trail for three miles to a fork, about a half-mile past Golden Trout Camp. Stay left. Take the right fork and you'll end up at Muir and Hidden Lakes. After another 1.5 miles, you come to a second junction. This time veer right, walking past Cottonwood Lakes No. 1 & 2, and in about a mile you'll reach Long Lake.

There's a trail that circles the eight-acre lake, which makes access easy. In late spring and early summer, beautiful wildflowers come into bloom around the lake, making for some great photo opportunities.

If you plan to make the trip, supplies are available in Lone Pine. A wilderness permit is required for overnight travel in the John Muir Wilderness. Long Lake is closed to fishing from November 1 through June 30. Only artificial lures with barbless hooks and barbless flies are permitted.

Also nearby are Upper Cottonwood Creek, Cottonwood Lakes and Cirque Lake.

# SOUTH FORK LAKES

*I tossed 12 different lures before I got a bite, but once I found the right color, I was catching fish on every cast.*

| | |
|---|---|
| **Rating:** | 7 |
| **Species:** | Trout |
| **Stock:** | Three pounds of fingerling golden trout. |
| **Facilities:** | None |
| **Contact:** | Lone Pine Sporting Goods (760) 876-5365, Slater's Sporting Goods (760) 876-5020 Inyo National Forest (760) 876-6200, Cottonwood Pack Station (760) 878-2015 |
| **Directions:** | From Mojave, drive north on Highway 14 to Highway 395. Drive north on Highway 395 to the town of Lone Pine. In Lone Pine, turn left on Whitney Portal Road and drive three miles to Horseshoe Meadow Road. Turn left and drive approximately 15 miles to the turnoff for Cottonwood Lakes Trailhead. Turn right and drive to the trailhead. |

*Long Lake (Near) and the South Fork Lakes (Far)*

The South Fork Lakes are a series of small, relatively easy-to-reach lakes, loaded with golden trout. Just above 11,000 feet in the John Muir Wilderness, the lakes are overshadowed by the more popular Cottonwood Lakes. Although few anglers visit the South Fork Lakes, they provide high catch rates to those who do fish them. Each of the three small lakes yield limits to fly-fishermen in early July, and to those who use lures later on in the summer.

Located just below the tree line, close to the base of New Army Pass, South Fork Lakes provide unforgettable scenery in every direction and an opportunity to catch golden trout. These lakes are popular spots for campers and anglers, and they can even be worked in as an easy day-trip. Being easy to reach, they're also a good destination for beginning backpackers.

Methods of fishing differ at each lake. If you let your lure sink in Upper South Fork Lake, you'll catch a lot of weed fish. The lake is extremely shallow, and if you don't find the deeper holes, you won't catch any fish. The south shore is too shallow to fish, so your best bet is to stick to the north shoreline. Don't expect to catch any lunkers. Most of these fish will fit into a small skillet, but that's not to say they don't taste good. The best spot around the lake is a rock that sticks out on the west shore, which can be used as a platform. It allows you to dodge the weeds and cast to deeper water.

If you continue on the trail past the upper lake, you'll come to the middle lake. It's the size of a backyard swimming pool, but it does have some small goldens in it. Less than two feet deep, there are a lot of tules growing in the middle, and it's probably best just to skip fishing it.

Lower South Fork is the largest of the lakes, and it also provides the best fishing. More anglers and pack trippers come to this lake than to any of the others at South Fork. As with all the South Fork Lakes, the lower lake is weedy and shallow, but it does hold some larger goldens. Most of the time, you can see the fish surfacing and jumping out of the water to snatch flies. Fly anglers do well here, but those fishing with lures also have success.

*Middle South Fork Lake*

The key to the lower lake is using the right color, which changes day by day. I tossed 12 different lures before I got a bite, but once I found the right color, I was catching fish on every cast. The bigger goldens are also the smartest. They hang out in the weeds, where they know they can't be caught. I tried to present my lure just outside the weed line, but couldn't fool any of the lunkers.

Getting to the lower lake from the middle lake can be a little tricky, because the trail ends at the middle lake and doesn't begin again until the lower lake. To make matters worse, there's about 100 yards of trash can-sized boulders you'll have to hop across.

To reach the South Fork Lakes, begin your journey at the Cottonwood Lakes Trailhead and follow the path for three miles to a fork, about a half-mile past Golden Trout Camp. The right fork goes to Muir and Hidden Lakes. Stay left. In 1.5 miles is another junction. Stay left, and continue six-tenths of a mile to Lower South Fork Lake.

If you plan to make the trip, supplies are available in Lone Pine. A wilderness permit is required for overnight travel in the John Muir Wilderness. The South Fork Lakes are closed to fishing from November 1 through the last day in June. Only artificial lures with barbless hooks and barbless flies are permitted.

Also nearby are Upper Cottonwood Creek, Cottonwood Lakes, Cirque Lake, High Lake, Hidden Lake, Muir Lake, Long Lake, Sequoia National Park and Chicken Springs Lake.

*Lower South Fork Lake*

SOUTH FORK LAKES

**Fly-fishermen do best for about a month after ice-out, then small spinners are the hot ticket for the duration of the summer.**

| | |
|---|---|
| **Rating:** | 6 |
| **Species:** | Golden Trout |
| **Stock:** | Two pounds of fingerling golden trout. |
| **Facilities:** | None |
| **Contact:** | Lone Pine Sporting Goods (760) 876-5365, High Sierra Outfitters (760) 876-5020 Lone Pine Chamber of Commerce (760) 876-4444, Inyo National Forest (760) 876-6200, Cottonwood Pack Station (760) 878-2015 |
| **Directions:** | From Mojave, drive north on Highway 14 to Highway 395. Drive north on Highway 395 and continue to the town of Lone Pine. In Lone Pine, turn west on Whitney Portal Road and drive three miles to Horseshoe Meadow Road. Turn south and drive approximately 15 miles to the turnoff for Cottonwood Lakes Trailhead. Turn right and drive to the trailhead. |

*Navigating New Army Pass can be difficult through July.*

Cirque Lake can either be a great golden trout fishery or a bad one. It all depends on the weather. In severe winters, Cirque Lake freezes solid, killing all of the fish in the lake. But if the weather doesn't become too harsh, the lake's golden trout flourish and anglers have a blast. The problem is, when the die-off occurs, it takes a few years after the California Department of Fish and Game restocks the lake for the fish to grow to catchable sizes. The lake last froze solid in the winter of 1998 during the El Nino season, and without any more severe winters, the fish should soon return to catchable sizes. The lake was restocked in 1999 and also received fingerling fish in 2000.

At 11,060 feet in the John Muir Wilderness, the seven-acre lake is small, shallow and easy to fish. Fly-fishermen do best for about a month after ice-out, then small spinners are the hot ticket for the duration of the summer. Yellow Panther Martins and silver and gold Super Dupers seem to land the most fish.

To reach Cirque Lake from the southeast corner of Lower South Fork Lake, follow the trail south for seven-tenths of a mile to the lake. Cirque Lake is close to South Fork Lakes and just off the trail from High and Long Lakes, but it gets far less usage from anglers and hikers.

If you plan to make the trip, supplies are available in Lone Pine. A wilderness permit is required for overnight travel in the John Muir Wilderness. Cirque Lake is closed to fishing from November 1 through June 30. Only artificial lures with barbless hooks and barbless flies are permitted.

Also nearby are Upper Cottonwood Creek, Cottonwood Lakes, South Fork Lakes, High Lake, Hidden Lake, Muir Lake, Long Lake, Sequoia National Park and Chicken Springs Lake.

# COTTONWOOD LAKES

**Rating:** 8
**Species:** Golden Trout
**Stock:** None
**Facilities:** None
**Contact:** Lone Pine Sporting Goods (760) 876-5365, High Sierra Outfitters (760) 876-5020
Lone Pine Chamber of Commerce (760) 876-4444, Inyo National Forest (760) 876-6200,
Cottonwood Pack Station (760) 878-2015

**Directions:** From Mojave, drive north on Highway 14 to Highway 395. Drive north on Highway 395 to the town of Lone Pine. In Lone Pine, turn west on Whitney Portal Road and drive three miles to Horseshoe Meadow Road. Turn south and drive approximately 15 miles to the turnoff for Cottonwood Lakes Trailhead. Turn right and drive to the trailhead.

*Chris Shaffer nailed this 16-inch golden near Lake No. 4's outlet.*

If you're looking for lakes with golden trout, the Cottonwood Lakes are some of the easiest to get to in the state of California, whether you're traveling by foot or on horseback. Horseshoe Meadow Road does the work for you, gaining 5,500 feet from the turnoff on Whitney Portal Road to the Cottonwood Lakes Trailhead. All that's left is a 4.5-mile hike and less than an 850-foot elevation gain to the first of the six Cottonwood Lakes in the Cottonwood Lakes Basin. If you think that's bad try the 11-mile trek to Silver Pass Lake.

Ranging from 11,000 feet (for Lake No. 1) to 11,650 feet (for Lake No. 6) in the John Muir Wilderness, the Cottonwood Lakes are some of the most popular hike-to lakes in the Sierra. If you plan to visit this basin, keep in mind there's a quota in effect from the last Friday in June through September 15, and most of the permits are taken months in advance.

One advantage these lakes offer is that because of their close proximity to the trailhead you don't have to backpack to get to them. They can be reached in an enjoyable day-trip. It takes about two hours of leisurely hiking to reach them, leaving you with plenty of fishing time. Another option is to take a pack trip in. This is popular with many anglers. Unlike most pack trips to high-country lakes, the trip is short and anglers can bring along float tubes and waders to greatly improve their chances of catching more and larger fish.

From the Eighties through the late-Nineties, the lakes were closed to fishing year-round because the California Department of Fish and Game used them as spawning grounds for golden trout. They were reopened to fishing in 1997, but are still used as spawning grounds. That's why Lakes No. 1-4 are catch & release only. However, you can keep five fish from Lakes No. 5 and 6. Only artificial lures with barbless hooks and barbless flies are permitted throughout the entire drainage. Since there are only goldens in the lakes, to protect the spawn, the lakes aren't opened to fishing until July 1.

Cottonwood Lake No. 1 is the first lake you'll reach from the Cottonwood Lakes Trailhead. Situated in a large meadow, it's productive, offering good shoreline access with rocks to use

*Cottonwood Lake No. 4*

as platforms. There are some weeds around the lake, but they don't pose a problem for anglers. Most of the fish hang out near the rocks that stick out of the water about 10 yards from the shore. The inlet holds a lot of fish as well, and is best fished by fly-fishermen. We caught the most fish tossing small red and black Panther Martins and silver Kastmasters.

Just beyond the first lake is Lake No. 2. It's a bit smaller, but provides good action, mostly on smaller goldens. Most anglers prefer not to fish this lake, so they skirt on by, looking to catch larger fish in the bigger lakes. The inlet yields the most fish to anglers who toss yellow Panther Martins with red spots. Between Lakes No. 2 and 3, there is also a small pond that holds many willing goldens and is clearly visible from the trail.

Lake No. 3 is the largest of the Cottonwood Lakes. It is long and wide, about the size of Gull Lake in the June Lake Loop (maybe even a little bigger). It holds a ton of goldens. Although the entire lake is good to fish, the best spot is near the inlet. Many anglers fish this area with float tubes, casting fly & bubble combos towards the inlet, but I found Thomas Buoyants and Panther Martins to be more effective. There's a 10-15 yard shelf under shallow water around the entire periphery of the lake. To be successful, you need to get your lure on the far side of this shelf where it begins to drops-off.

Lake No. 4 is about three-fourths the size of No. 3 and a bit deeper. Located just below New Army Pass, you can still see stretches of the Old Army Pass above the lake. The best fishing in Lake No. 4 is usually found near the lake's outlet channel. We landed a few goldens here that were about 16 inches long. The stream coming out of the lake is also good, but the fish get spooked easily there. Unlike most of the Cottonwood Lakes, No. 4 has steep shorelines. Because of its extreme depths, anglers have difficulty getting their lures to sink deep enough to attract fish. For that reason, many anglers choose not to fish here. But for those who take the time to locate the fish, it can be quite good. Larger lures that sink fast are your best bet.

Located next to Lake No. 4, No. 5 is one of two Cottonwood Lakes where anglers get to keep their fish. This lake is a bit larger than No. 4, but looks identical. Mostly targeted by fly-fishermen, it is surrounded by towering peaks, and wildflowers grow along its shore-line. It also offers a chance to catch some larger goldens.

A distance away from the first five lakes, Lake No. 6 is rarely fished because it's hard to reach. There is no formal trail to hike to it. In order to get there, first you must find the inlet on the northeast corner of Lake No. 5. Then follow the stream for three-fourths of a mile to the lake. It's a steep climb and only recommended for those in good physical shape. There's little fishing pressure, so the lake provides some good fishing. Just about any lure will work, because these fish don't see many lures and aren't as wary as the ones in the other lakes.

Many anglers think there are two more Cottonwood Lakes just over the hill, adjacent to Lake No. 3. Although these lakes appear enticing, don't be lead off track, neither hold any fish. Located in a meadow, they are actually small ponds on their way to becoming marshes. Both can be seen on any topo map.

To reach the Cottonwood Lakes, begin at the Cottonwood Lakes Trailhead and follow the trail for three miles to a fork, about a half-mile past Golden Trout Camp. Stay left. The right fork ends up at Muir and Hidden Lakes. In 1.5 miles is a second junction. Veer right. You'll be able to see Lakes No. 1 and 2 from here. Continue northwest on the trail to the lakes. The trail continues on to Lakes No. 3 through No. 6. There is no formal trail to Lake No. 6.

If you plan to make the trip, supplies are available in Lone Pine. A wilderness permit is required for overnight travel in the John Muir Wilderness. The Cottonwood Lakes are closed to fishing from November 1 through June 30. Only artificial lures with barbless hooks and barbless flies are permitted. Lakes No. 1-4 are catch & release only.

Also nearby are Upper Cottonwood Creek, South Fork Lakes, Cirque Lake, High Lake, Hidden Lake, Muir Lake, Long Lake, Sequoia National Park and Chicken Springs Lake.

**The creek is fished more by fly-fishermen than those with lures, but both seem to experience the same catch rates.**

| | |
|---|---|
| **Rating:** | 7 |
| **Species:** | Golden Trout |
| **Stock:** | None |
| **Facilities:** | None |
| **Contact:** | Lone Pine Sporting Goods (760) 876-5365, High Sierra Outfitters (760) 876-5020 Lone Pine Chamber of Commerce (760) 876-4444, Inyo National Forest (760) 876-6200, Cottonwood Pack Station (760) 878-2015 |
| **Directions:** | From Mojave, drive north on Highway 14 to Highway 395, and continue to the town of Lone Pine. In Lone Pine, turn west on Whitney Portal Road and drive three miles to Horseshoe Meadow Road. Turn south and drive approximately 15 miles to the turnoff for Cottonwood Lakes Trailhead. Turn right and drive to the trailhead. |

*Cottonwood Creek (Upper)*

Overshadowed by the Cottonwood Lakes, Upper Cottonwood Creek doesn't get the attention it deserves. Because the Cottonwood Lakes are still used as breeding grounds for the prized golden trout, many of the fish end up in the creek.

The creek begins at Lake No. 6, but because of the inaccessibility caused by steep banks throughout this stretch of the stream, it is unfishable until the outlets of Cottonwood Lakes No. 4 and 5. Just below these outlets there are about 100 yards of great fishing waters that hold many large goldens. We caught a few over a pound.

The stream then flows into Lake No. 3, and again provides great fishing between Lakes No. 2 and 3, and No. 2 and 1. Most of the goldens found in this stretch of the creek are between six and eight inches, and they're fighters.

After lake No. 1, the creek flows through some large meadows, and then begins to pick up speed as it works its way downhill. From here down to the Cottonwood Creek Trailhead, the creek goes through drastic changes and is seldom fished, however, there are many fish to be caught. Most of these fish can be found in pools or under fallen logs.

The creek is fished more by fly-fishermen than those with lures, but both seem to experience the same catch rates. Your best bet would be to concentrate on the sections of the stream above Lake No. 1.

To reach Upper Cottonwood Creek, begin at the Cottonwood Lakes Trailhead and follow the trail for three miles to a fork in the trail, about a half-mile past Golden Trout Camp. Take the right fork and you'll end up at Muir and Hidden Lakes. You'll want the left fork. After another 1.5 miles, comes another junction. Veer right. Lakes No. 1 and 2 can be seen from here. Continue northwest on the trail to the lakes, where you can pick up the stream.

If you plan to make the trip, supplies are available in Lone Pine. A wilderness permit is required for overnight travel in the John Muir Wilderness. Cottonwood Creek is closed to fishing from November 1 through June 30. Only artificial lures with barbless hooks and barbless flies are permitted.

# MUIR LAKE

*As for the fishing, there are only goldens, many of which hide out in the lake's few deep holes.*

**Rating:** 6
**Species:** Golden Trout
**Stock:** Two pounds of fingerling golden trout.
**Facilities:** None
**Contact:** Lone Pine Sporting Goods (760) 876-5365, High Sierra Outfitters (760) 876-5020
Lone Pine Chamber of Commerce (760) 876-4444, Inyo National Forest (760) 876-6200

**Directions:** From Mojave, drive north on Highway 14 to Highway 395. Continue north on Highway 395 to the town of Lone Pine. In Lone Pine, turn west on Whitney Portal Road and drive three miles to Horseshoe Meadow Road. Turn south and drive approximately 15 miles to the turnoff for Cottonwood Lakes Trailhead. Turn right and drive to the trailhead.

*Muir Lake*

You want to be able to catch golden trout, but you don't want to endure a long hike to get to a lake? No problem, Muir Lake, in the John Muir Wilderness, is only a 4.5-mile hike from the Cottonwood Lakes Trailhead, and offers fair golden trout fishing. More than 2,000 fingerling golden trout were planted in 2000.

The eight-acre lake is in the Cottonwood Lakes Basin, but doesn't get hammered by fishermen like the six Cottonwood Lakes. Concentrating on the more popular Cottonwood Lakes, most anglers don't even know Muir Lake exists. Tucked away in the mountainside and surrounded by tall pines, it can't be seen from the Cottonwood Lakes.

At 11,110 feet, this lovely lake has a great camping area on its northeast corner. As for the fishing, there are only goldens, many of which hide out in the lake's few deep holes. Another incentive that attracts anglers here is that you can keep five fish. (Cottonwood Lakes No. 1-4 are catch and release only.)

To reach Muir Lake from the Cottonwood Lakes Trailhead, walk about three miles to a fork in the trail just past Golden Trout Camp. (It's about a half-mile past the second stream crossing of Cottonwood Creek). Stay right and continue for about a mile to the signed turnoff for Muir Lake. After taking the turnoff, walk a smidgen more than six-tenths of a mile to the lake.

If you plan to make the trip, supplies are available in Lone Pine. A wilderness permit is required for overnight travel in the John Muir Wilderness. Muir Lake is closed to fishing from November 1 through June 30. Only artificial lures with barbless hooks and barbless flies are permitted.

Also nearby are the Cottonwood Lakes, Cottonwood Creek, Hidden Lake, Cirque Lake, New Army Pass, High Lake, Long Lake, South Fork Lakes and Sequoia National Park.

# HIDDEN LAKE

*At 10,870 feet in the John Muir Wilderness, Hidden Lake is a quiet, popular camping area for those heading to the Cottonwood Lakes.*

**Rating:** 1
**Species:** None
**Stock:** None
**Facilities:** None
**Contact:** Inyo National Forest (760) 876-6200

**Directions:**

From Mojave, drive north on Highway 14 to Highway 395. Drive north on Highway 395 to the town of Lone Pine. In Lone Pine, turn west on Whitney Portal Road and drive three miles to Horseshoe Meadow Road. Turn south and drive approximately 15 miles to the turnoff for Cottonwood Lakes Trailhead. Turn right and drive to the trailhead.

Hidden Lake is so well hidden that not even the fish can find it. That's right, Hidden Lake's got no fish and there are no plans to ever stock it. However, it is a popular spot for camping and avoiding the crowds at nearby Cottonwood Lakes. That is, if you can find it. Hence, its name: "Hidden Lake."

There is no trail to the eight-acre lake, nor any signs that let you know where the lake is. I had to read a topo map to find it, but you can just follow my directions. From Cottonwood Lake No. 1, take the trail northeast towards Muir Lake. In four-tenths of a mile you'll come to the turnoff for Muir Lake. Don't take it. Walk another half-mile, and just after hiking down a few small switchbacks, look for some greenery on your right and a small feeder stream on the left. That feeder stream comes from Hidden Lake, and you have to follow it to reach the lake. There is no maintained trail.

At 10,870 feet in the John Muir Wilderness, Hidden Lake is a quiet, popular camping area for those heading to the Cottonwood Lakes. Although there are no fish in the shallow lake, it's a nice swimming hole and a pretty spot to relax.

A retired pilot who used to fly planes for the California Department of Fish and Game told me that the department once had plans to stock the lake, but because of its location it would be too difficult to airlift fish into.

If you plan to make the trip, supplies are available in Lone Pine. A wilderness permit is required for overnight travel into the John Muir Wilderness. Hidden Lake is closed to fishing from November 1 through June 30. Only artificial lures with barbless hooks or barbless flies are permitted.

Also nearby are Upper Cottonwood Creek, the Cottonwood Lakes, Cirque Lake, High Lake, Muir Lake, the South Fork Lakes, Sequoia National Park and Chicken Springs Lake.

## COTTONWOOD CREEK DRAINAGE

1 Big Pine Creek (L&U)
2 Baker Creek
3 Tinnemaha Creek
4 Owens River
  (Below Tinnemaha)
5 Shepherds Creek
6 Symmes Creek
7 Independence Creek
8 Robinson Lake
9 Goodale Creek
10 Taboose Creek
11 Georges Creek
12 Lone Pine Creek (Upper)
13 Lone Pine Creek (Lower)
14 Tuttle Creek
15 Diaz Lake
16 Cottonwood Creek
17 Haiwee Reservoir

**Located west of the town of Big Pine, Big Pine Creek is a stream with two sections, each with distinct personalities.**

| | |
|---|---|
| **Rating:** | 6 |
| **Species:** | Rainbow and brown trout |
| **Stock:** | 17,425 pounds of rainbow trout. |
| **Facilities:** | Picnic Areas, Campgrounds and Restrooms |
| **Contact:** | Inyo National Forest (760) 873-2500, Roy's Gun and Tackle (760) 938-2380 |
| | Big Pine Chamber of Commerce (760) 938-2114 |

**Directions:** From Mojave, drive north on Highway 14 to Highway 395. In the town of Big Pine, turn west at the Texaco gas station (Glacier Lodge Road). The creek is stocked from the point where the river crosses the road all the way up to Sage Flat Campground, a distance of approximately 10 miles.

*Todd McLean showcases his catch at Lower Big Pine Creek.*

The crowds, the anticipation and the excitement of the Eastern Sierra fishing season might be absent here, but the fish aren't. Big Pine Creek is another one of the lower Owens Valley streams that gets overlooked because of its neighbors to the north. Though it might not receive the same amount fishing pressure as its northern competitors (Bishop Creek, Rock Creek, Convict Creek, etc.), it does render the same results. Another added benefit is that since Big Pine Creek is fed by a large watershed, its flows remain consistent year-round.

Located west of the town of Big Pine, Big Pine Creek is a stream with two sections, each with distinct personalities. The lower section tests anglers' patience with extreme heat, little shade and desert brush, while the upper one provides the comfort and beauty more commonly associated with the high Sierra.

The North and South Forks of Big Pine Creek merge just beyond the end of Glacier Lodge Road. The North Fork is fed by Summit Lake, Black Lake, Sam Mack Lake and the Big Pine Lakes, while the South Fork's flows are dependent on snowmelt from Willow, Finger and Brainerd Lakes.

Located in an unattractive, arid desert, just minutes from Big Pine, the lower section of the creek is only stocked in the two places where the creek crosses under the road. Although this portion is less fished than the upper part, it can provide good fishing for trout in the one- to three-pound range. However, this branch of the creek can be difficult to fish when snowmelt is high in spring and early summer.

Located at 7,700 feet in the Inyo National Forest, the upper section of Big Pine Creek adds an element the lower portion lacks... namely, beauty. The best fishing is found in Sage Flat Campground, an area dominated by Jeffrey pines. Another consistent hot spot is a spring-fed pond at the end of the road where the California Department of Fish and Game always stocks a few buckets of trout. Believe it or not, Upper Big Pine Creek is stocked with 31,859 trout in the 10-12 inch class and an additional 600 fish from two to four pounds.

Another 200 pound and a half size Alpers are also planted prior to the opener. Small Panther Martins are productive here. However, Power Bait and salmon eggs are your best bet, because the larger trout lie under overhanging branches, bushes, and other spots lures can't reach.

Big Pine Creek is also heavily used as a starting point for those hiking up into the seven Big Pine Lakes, or to further destinations in the John Muir Wilderness. Along with the seven Big Pines Lakes, Summit and Black Lake also provide excellent trout fishing.

If you plan to make the trip, supplies are available in Big Pine. Big Pine Creek is closed to fishing from November 1 until the last Saturday in April. A wilderness permit is required for overnight travel into the John Muir Wilderness.

Also nearby are Baker Creek and the Owens River.

*Lower Big Pine Creek*

BIG PINE CREEK

# BAKER CREEK

*To be successful, you'll have to keep your bait out of the moss.*

| | |
|---|---|
| **Rating:** | 4 |
| **Species:** | Rainbow Trout |
| **Stock:** | 1,977 pounds of rainbow trout. |
| **Facilities:** | Campgrounds |
| **Contact:** | Roy's Gun and Tackle (760) 938-2380 |

**Directions:** From Highway 395 at the north end of Big Pine, turn west at the county campground road just north of the ball field, and drive 1.5 miles to the campground. Fish are planted throughout the campground.

*Baker Creek*

Located at 4,100 feet in an area shaded by trees in the town of Big Pine, this tiny creek can provide a quick, easy limit for anglers who find dust and the desert appealing. It receives little fishing pressure, and once you see it, you'll understand why. The beauty and wildlife found at the creeks farther north in Bishop are in no way reminiscent of this southern neighbor.

Even though Baker Creek doesn't offer much beauty, there are almost always small rainbows here. The Department of Fish and Game makes sure of it by stocking 3,684 trout in the 10- to 12-inch class, from the end of April through October. Roughly 230 one-pound Alpers are also planted prior to the opener. Catch rates remain decent even when fishing pressure is high, and fish can be caught on various colors of Power Bait, salmon eggs and marshmallows. Concentrate your efforts at the various pools located throughout the campground.

The two largest pools at Baker Creek always hold trout, and both are easily visible from the westernmost part of the campground. These pools are about the size of half of a basketball court, and so shallow they become covered by moss in mid-summer. To be successful, you'll have to keep your bait out of the moss.

If you plan to make the trip, supplies are available in Big Pine. Baker Creek is closed to fishing from November 1 to the last Saturday in April.

Also nearby are Big Pine Creek and Lower Owens River.

# TINNEMAHA CREEK

**Your best chances of hooking into a fish are at the south end of the campground and where the wood bridges cross the stream.**

| | |
|---|---|
| **Rating:** | 3 |
| **Species:** | Rainbow Trout |
| **Stock:** | 3,400 pounds of rainbow trout. |
| **Facilities:** | Campgrounds and Restrooms |
| **Contact:** | Lone Pine Sporting Goods (760) 876-5365, High Sierra Outfitters (760) 876-5020 |
| | Inyo National Forest (760) 876-6200, Bureau of Land Management (760) 872-4881 |

**Directions:** From Highway 14 in Mojave, drive north to Highway 395. Take Highway 395 north approximately eight miles, south of the town of Big Pine. Turn left at a sign for Fish Springs Hatchery, and left at Tinnemaha Creek Road. Continue to the Inyo County Campgrounds.

*Tinnemaha Creek*

I've been to Tinnemaha Creek three times now, and I've yet to see anyone else fishing it. What I have found is dust, a trickle of water and more dust. In other words, keep on driving. Tinnemaha is another one of those creeks that makes you wonder why they even bother stocking it.

Located in a secluded, hot, dry desert environment, the creek doesn't appeal to many anglers. The little use it does get is usually by campers who need to get some rest before heading up to Bishop or Mammoth.

Flowing through Tinnemaha Campground, the creek is about as wide as a hockey goal and as deep as a carton of milk, but somehow they still manage to stock it. Actually, the California Department of Fish and Game stocks it a lot, dumping 6,947 fish in the 10- to 12-inch class and another 130 weighing more than two pounds.

Don't plan on using any lures. The stream is too small. Load your tackle box with as much Power Bait and as many salmon eggs as you can. Your best chances of hooking into a fish are at the south end of the campground and where the wood bridges cross the stream.

The creek is also planted about a mile upstream of where the road nears the creek. Almost nobody knows plants are made at this point; most anglers concentrate their efforts in the campground. Luckily, I found out about these plants further upstream when I was awakened one morning by the sound of the CA DFG stocking truck, and I followed it.

If you plan to make the trip, supplies are available in Big Pine and Independence. Tinnemaha Creek is closed to fishing from November 1 to the last Saturday in April.

Also nearby are Big Pine Creek, Independence Creek and the Fish Springs Hatchery.

# OWENS RIVER

*The best way to approach fishing the river is to hike along the dirt road that parallels the creek, hitting all of the spots where it appears the stocking truck could get down to the water to make a plant.*

**Rating:** 6

**Species:** Brown Trout, Rainbow Trout, Channel Catfish, Bluegill and Largemouth Bass

**Stock:** 2,725 pounds of rainbow trout.

**Facilities:** Vault Toilets

**Contact:** Inyo National Forest (760) 873-2500, Roy's Gun and Tackle (760) 938-2380
Big Pine Chamber of Commerce (760) 938-2114

**Directions:** From Highway 395 in Bishop, drive south to the town of Big Pine. Continue eight miles south through Big Pine and turn east on a dirt road signed for Tinnemaha Reservoir. Follow the dirt road to the river.

*The lower Owens River below Tinnemaha Reservoir*

The Owens River below Tinnemaha Reservoir is a lot like the stretch of the Owens from Bishop to Big Pine, wide, fast-flowing and extremely difficult to fish in the spring and early summer. When snow is melting in the Eastern Sierra, its torrential waters are nearly impossible to fish. However, as the river begins to recede, fishing improves.

In addition to the 4,836 rainbow trout planted by the California Department of Fish and Game, there are also wild rainbows and browns inhabiting the murky waters that flow above the sandy bottom and along the steep banks of this river. To add some excitement to the boring high-desert terrain, the CA DFG brings along 103 trophy-size trout, ranging from two to four pounds. There are also largemouth bass and channel catfish in the river, but they don't have much size to them and aren't as heavily targeted. Panther Martins catch most of the fish, although, night crawlers, Power Bait and Kastmasters work well, too.

The best way to approach fishing the river is to hike along the dirt road that parallels the creek, hitting all of the spots where it appears the stocking truck could get down to the water to make a plant. When you come to an old bridge that was washed out by high water, use this as a marker to turn around and head back towards the reservoir. The reservoir is also opened to fishing, but few anglers try it. There are much better opportunities to be had elsewhere in the region.

If you plan to make the trip, supplies are available in Big Pine. Call ahead to check on the river's flows. If they are high, don't bother fishing it.

Also nearby are Big Pine Creek, Shepherd Creek, Independence Creek, Symmes Creek, Goodale Creek, Tinnemaha Creek, Georges Creek and Baker Creek.

*Just like Tuttle and Symmes Creeks, Shepherds Creek is a Power Bait only stream.*
*Find the color of the day and you should catch an easy limit.*

**Rating:** 4
**Species:** Rainbow Trout
**Stock:** 1,059 pounds of rainbow trout.
**Facilities:** None
**Contact:** Independence Chamber of Commerce (760) 878-0084, Inyo National Forest (760) 876-6200

**Directions:** From Mojave, drive north on Highway 14 to Highway 395 and continue north to the town of Independence. Turn west on Onion Valley Road (just north of the post office) and drive 4.5 miles to Foothill Road. Turn south and follow the road approximately five miles to the stream.

*Shepherds Creek with the Sierra in the backdrop*

Shepherds Creek is a lot like its neighbor Symmes Creek. Both are small, narrow streams located in the high desert of the Inyo National Forest, and rarely fished. Despite its low popularity, Shepherds Creek is stocked by the California Department of Fish and Game with anywhere from 50 to 100 fish each week, from March through July. In addition to the 2,019 half-pound rainbows planted, another 35 fish over a pound are also stocked.

Located between Independence and Lone Pine, many anglers have no idea the stream exists and drive right past it. The creek cannot compete with its larger neighbors, such as Independence and Lone Pine Creeks. Because of its size and appearance, it belongs in the same category as Symmes and Tuttle Creeks. Just like Tuttle and Symmes Creeks, Shepherds Creek is a Power Bait only stream. Find the color of the day and you should catch an easy limit.

If you plan to make the trip, supplies are available in Independence. Shepherds Creek is closed to fishing from November 1 through the Southern Sierra Trout Opener in early March.

Also nearby are Independence Creek, Onion Valley, the Owens River, Symmes Creek and Pinyon Creek.

# SYMMES CREEK

| | |
|---|---|
| **Rating:** | 3 |
| **Species:** | Rainbow Trout |
| **Stock:** | 200 pounds of rainbow trout. |
| **Facilities:** | None |
| **Contact:** | Independence Chamber of Commerce (760) 878-0084, Inyo National Forest (760) 876-6200 |

**Directions:** From Mojave, drive north on Highway 14 to Highway 395 and continue north to the town of Independence. Turn left on Onion Valley Road (just north of the post office) and drive 4.5 miles to Foothill road. Turn left and follow the dirt road for 3.3 miles to the unsigned Symmes Creek Campground.

*Symmes Creek*

Whoever decided to stock this tiny stream must have wanted to send people on a wild goose chase. Talk about isolated, this trickle of a stream is about as secluded as it gets! And the picture the few anglers who fish the stream create of a great Eastern Sierra trout fishery never pans out. There are no pine trees, just dirt and desert brush; no fresh smell in the air, only a dusty wind. Sorry to disappoint you, but the stream you've been pumping yourself up for, well, it's just Symmes Creek, a small drip of water only a foot deep, with a maximum width of three feet, virtually no pools and bushy shorelines.

So, why is this place stocked? Well, I've been trying to figure that out for a long time. The California Department of Fish and Game has acknowledged its low popularity by seldom planting it. It receives about 40 fish a week from the Southern Sierra Trout Opener in early March until the end of April, when plants are cut off here, and the CA DFG begins stocking the region's more popular streams.

If you insist on making the trip, chances are you'll find a few willing trout in the 10- to 12-inch class, but don't expect to find a lot of them. The CA DFG only dumps about 400 in the creek annually, and for a good reason -- nobody comes here. I've driven out of my way five times to see if I could run into another human at the stream, but have had no such luck. Don't forget your Power Bait.

If you plan to make the trip, supplies are available in Independence. Symmes Creek is closed to fishing from November 1to the Southern Sierra trout opener in early March.

Also nearby are Independence Creek, Onion Valley, Owens River (below Tinnemaha), Shepherd Creek and Pinyon Creek.

*The fish are relatively easy to catch, and you might be the only one trying to catch them, because the stream receives little pressure compared to its neighbors to the north.*

**Rating:** 5
**Species:** Rainbow Trout and Brown Trout
**Stock:** 15,268 pounds of rainbow trout.
**Facilities:** Campgrounds and Restrooms
**Contact:** Independence Chamber of Commerce (760) 878-0084, Inyo National Forest (760) 876-6200

**Directions:** From Mojave, drive north on Highway 14 to Highway 395. Drive north on Highway 395 to the town of Independence. Turn left on Onion Valley Road, just north of the Independence Post Office, and continue to the creek. Trout are planted from Independence Campground all the way to where the road crosses the creek, about seven miles from the town.

Independence Creek

My latest experience at Independence Creek was not a pleasant one. It was the weekend after the 1999 Southern Sierra Trout Opener, and reports out of the region were that fishing and the weather was good. So, we jumped in the car and headed north. Arriving at Independence Creek, we ran into a big problem, almost all the fish were dead. It was sad. There were as many as seven dead fish in every pool in the stream.

The locals had the best explanation for the die-off. They said the trout are raised in water around 55 degrees, and the water in the creek was 34 degrees. In years past, the California Department of Fish and Game poured ice in their planting trucks to help the fish adapt to their new home, but in the last few years, including this one, that wasn't the case. According to the locals, when the CA DFG dumped the fish in the stream, most went into shock and died.

Independence is a small stream, about three feet wide and a foot deep, located about a half-an-hour south of Bishop. Even though the creek lacks stunning high mountain scenery, it doesn't lack trout. The CA DFG releases more than 28,602 trout here, most in the 10 to 12-inch class. As a bonus, prior to the opener 250 pound-size Alpers are planted. The fish are relatively easy to catch, and you might be the only one trying to catch them, because the stream receives little pressure compared to its neighbors to the north.

This is pretty much a Power Bait and salmon egg stream, although night crawlers are also productive. The CA DFG stocks at many access points along the creek, but the greatest number of fish are planted in Gray's Meadow, Independence Campgrounds and where Pinyon Creek crosses under Onion Valley Road.

If you plan to make the trip, supplies are available in Independence. Independence Creek is closed to fishing from November 1 until the Southern Sierra Trout Opener in March.

Also nearby are Lone Pine Creek, Symmes Creek, Shepherd Creek and Georges Creek.

**The unrelenting climb, with its 1,333-foot elevation gain, deters most anglers from visiting.**

| | |
|---|---|
| **Rating:** | 6 |
| **Species:** | Rainbow Trout and Brook Trout |
| **Stock:** | None |
| **Facilities:** | None |
| **Contact:** | Independence Chamber of Commerce (760) 878-0084, Inyo National Forest (760) 876-6200 |
| **Directions:** | From Mojave, drive north on Highway 14 to Highway 395. Drive north on Highway 395 to the town of Independence. Turn west on Onion Valley Road, just north of the Independence Post Office, and continue approximately 13 miles to the end of the road. |

*Robinson Lake*

To be productive, most hike-to lakes in the Sierra need a small inlet stream and also at least pea-sized gravel on the ground below the inlet stream. The inlet and gravel allow fish to spawn, promoting a self-sustaining population. And such is the case with Robinson Lake.

At 10,535 feet in the Inyo National Forest, about a 20-minute drive from Independence, this three-acre lake is a mere 1.26-mile hike from the Onion Valley Trailhead. But those 1.26 miles can feel an awful lot longer. The unrelenting climb, with its 1,333-foot elevation gain, deters most anglers from visiting. I started at the trailhead with a party of four, but only two of us made it to Robinson.

With the absence of fish stocking, Robinson has become dependent on its self-sustaining population of rainbow and brook trout. None of its fish are impressive, but they are into biting small Panther Martins and Kastmasters. So, if you're looking to get in on the action and you're not set on catching larger fish, then Robinson would be a good place to visit.

For me, the intriguing thing about Robinson is that the lake is so small, shallow and clear, anglers can see every fish in the water. This might sound like it makes things easier, but I think it poses a challenge. You see, I like to pick out a fish and then try to catch it. Kinda like calling your hole in pool. And what ups the ante is that the other fish try to grab my silver Panther Martin just before my "chosen" fish can get to it. This makes catching fish just a tad more exciting.

When fishing Robinson, there are no specific places to target. The lake is so small, there are fish all over. One thing to consider, though: near the inlet it's particularly marshy, so you might want to stay away from that area or risk getting a little mud down your boots.

Although the trail to Robinson is easy to follow, it's bound to make you huff and puff. From the parking area in Onion Valley, continue up the road as it curves to the left and crosses Independence Creek. Following signs to Robinson Lake, walk through the campground, where you'll pick up the trailhead on the southeast end. You'll cross Robinson's outlet stream and begin zigzagging up the mountain, paralleling the creek on its left side the entire way.

If you plan to make the trip, supplies are available in Independence. The road to Onion Valley closes in the winter. Call ahead for updated conditions. Robinson Lake is closed to fishing from November 1 to the last Saturday in April.

Also nearby are Onion Valley Falls, Golden Trout Lake, John Muir Wilderness, Symmes Creek and Independence Creek.

*The sun retracts from the peaks above Robinson.*

ROBINSON LAKE

# GOODALE CREEK

*Anglers fish Goodale in hopes of dodging the crowds that surround the rivers and lakes to the north.*

| | |
|---|---|
| **Rating:** | 4 |
| **Species:** | Rainbow Trout |
| **Stock:** | 6,430 pounds of rainbow trout. |
| **Facilities:** | Campgrounds and Restrooms |
| **Contact:** | Bureau of Land Management (760) 872-4881 |
| | Independence Chamber of Commerce (760) 878-0084 |
| **Directions:** | From Mojave, drive north on Highway 14 to Highway 395. Continue north on Highway 395, driving 13 miles past the town of Independence to Goodale Creek Road. Turn left and drive two miles to the creek. |

*Goodale Creek*

Goodale Creek isn't all that good. It's another high desert stream that gets a ton of fish thrown in it. It receives little fishing pressure, but still gets 11,695 trout from the California Department of Fish and Game, 200 weighing more than two pounds.

Most of Goodale's anglers double as campers, accounting for nearly all the pressure on the creek. Anglers fish Goodale in hopes of dodging the crowds that surround the rivers and lakes to the north. Don't expect to be casting across the stream here. Chances are your pole is longer than its width. Goodale is almost an exact replica of Symmes, Tuttle and Shepherd Creeks. Bring along an arsenal of Power Bait and you should do fine. Best spots are the various pools located throughout the campground.

If you plan to make the trip, supplies are available in Independence. Goodale Creek is closed to fishing from November 1 until the last Saturday in April.

Also nearby are Taboose Creek, Tinnemaha Creek, Tinnemaha Reservoir and the Owens River.

*That kid was one hell of a fisherman, and he knew exactly where the trout were. He brought me to a narrow part of the stream where branches from trees covered the stream.*

**Rating:** 7
**Species:** Rainbow trout
**Stock:** 7,446 pounds of trout.
**Facilities:** Primitive Campgrounds
**Contact:** Independence Chamber of Commerce (760) 878-0084, Inyo National Forest (760) 876-6200

**Directions:** From Mojave, drive north on Highway 14 to Highway 395. Continue 14 miles north on Highway 395 past the town of Independence and turn left at the sign for Taboose Creek. Drive to the first road past Old Highway 395 and turn left to the stream.

Taboose Creek

Located between Independence and Big Pine, Taboose Creek is one of the more popular desert camping spots in the Eastern Sierra. However, most of the people who come to camp here believe that because the stream is so small it doesn't hold any fish. Don't let this small stream fool you. Contrary to popular belief, it's loaded with fish. It almost fooled me, until I was taught Toboose's tricks by an eight-year-old.

While fishing one of the few pools in the campground, this kid came over to school me a little. "What are you doing?" he asked. "There aren't any fish here. All the fish are over there." At first I laughed. "Like this little kid has any idea what he's talking about," I thought. But, the more I looked at him, the more I began to believe. The kid reminded me of a leprechaun leading me to a pot of gold.

That kid was one hell of a fisherman, and he knew exactly where the trout were. He brought me to a narrow part of the stream where branches from trees covered the stream. "They're all there," he pointed to the trees. I let my line out and the stream took it under the branches. Within seconds I had a taker, about a half-pound rainbow. I caught and released my limit in less than five minutes. The kid later told me the California Department of Fish and Game stocked the first pool I was fishing, but he'd watched all the fish work their way down to this area with more cover.

In addition to 250 Alpers the CA DFG stocks 13,462 half-pound rainbows along with another 250 over two pounds. Although the stream is heavily planted, many anglers pass it by because of its desert location. Don't bother bringing lures, because you won't need them. Just dump your Power Bait under the bushes that cover the stream and reel in your fish. It's as easy as that. And keep an eye out for kids catching easy limits, swallow your pride and follow their lead; that is, if they left you any fish.

If you plan to make the trip, supplies are available in Independence. Taboose Creek is closed to fishing from November 1 to the second to last Saturday in April.

Also nearby are Tinnemaha Creek, Goodale Creek and the Owens River.

**When other streams in the region are difficult to fish due to high flows from snowmelt, Georges Creek is a synch, because you're not actually fishing a free-flowing portion of the stream.**

| | |
|---|---|
| **Rating:** | 4 |
| **Species:** | Rainbow Trout |
| **Stock:** | 1,149 pounds of rainbow trout. |
| **Facilities:** | None |
| **Contact:** | Lone Pine Sporting Goods (760) 876-5365, High Sierra Outfitters (760) 876-5020 Lone Pine Chamber of Commerce (760) 876-4444, Inyo National Forest (760) 876-6200, Independence Chamber of Commerce (760) 878-0084 |
| **Directions:** | From Bishop, drive south on Highway 395 to the town of Independence. Continue seven miles south on Highway 395 to an unmarked dirt road located one mile north of the aqueduct crossing. Turn right to the creek. |

*Fish are raised in runs like this one at Hot Creek Hatchery.*

In early March, when most lakes and streams in the Eastern Sierra are closed to fishing, you can still find good fishing at Georges Creek. The creek opens with a bang with the Southern Sierra Trout Opener, providing anglers their first fishing opportunity here since the creek's closing on November 1. When other streams in the region are difficult to fish due to high flows from snowmelt, Georges Creek is a synch, because you're not actually fishing a free-flowing portion of the stream.

Georges Creek is stocked exclusively at the sand trap, a dammed up portion of the stream with a sandy bottom, located about 100 yards from where the creek flows into the aqueduct. In March and April, crowds congregate here because of heavy plants and high catch rates.

Differing methods of catching fish range from soaking Power Bait or salmon eggs to tossing lures. But this area gets fished so heavily that to entice the fish you often need to use something they don't see everyday. I've had good luck with white Trout Teasers. For some reason the trout can't seem to resist 'em.

Prior to the opener a bonus of 200 Alpers weighing up to two pounds are stocked. During the spring and early summer, some 2,000 half-pound rainbows are planted at the sand trap, not counting another 35 trout in the two- to three-pound range, so there are always fish to be caught. The creek has difficulty sustaining water levels throughout the summer, and plants commonly cease by late July.

Located at 4,000 feet midway between Independence and Lone Pine, the creek does have a few downfalls, including wind, heat and ants. The wind blows almost daily in this part of the state, at times putting a damper on the fishing. When you add 100 degree plus temperatures, things can start to get pretty unbearable.

Another tip, don't sit down on the ground. Use a chair because the area is loaded with ants. I'm sure you won't be happy if they're crawling up and down your arms and legs. If you arrive early enough, you'll have a shot at claiming one of the few spots shaded by willow trees, which help to protect you from a quick sunburn.

Here's how I fit George Creek into my fishing plans: I fish it on my way to one of the more northern destinations in Bishop, Mammoth or June Lake. It gives me a chance to stretch my legs and catch a few fish before getting into the car and heading north again.

While you're here, take a look at the towering mountains to the west. If you didn't know already, Mt. Whitney, the tallest peak in the continental U.S. is located in the range.

If you plan to make the trip, Georges Creek is closed to fishing from November 1 until the Southern Sierra Trout Opener in early March. Supplies are available in Independence.

Also nearby are the Owens River, Upper and Lower Lone Pine Creek, Tuttle Creek, Independence Creek and California Aqueduct.

*The sand trap at Georges Creek*

GEORGES CREEK

# LONE PINE CREEK (UPPER)

**With a large, sturdy platform from which to fish, the pond is also one of the few places in the region that provides wheelchair access.**

| | |
|---|---|
| **Rating:** | 7 |
| **Species:** | Rainbow Trout |
| **Stock:** | 20,735 pounds of rainbow trout (split with Lower Lone Pine Creek). |
| **Facilities:** | Campgrounds, Picnic Areas, Restrooms, General Store, Showers and a Restaurant |
| **Contact:** | Lone Pine Sporting Goods (760) 876-5365, High Sierra Outfitters (760) 876-5020 Lone Pine Chamber of Commerce (760) 876-4444, Inyo National Forest (760) 876-6200, Whitney Portal Store (760) 937-2257 |
| **Directions:** | From Mojave, drive north on Highway 14 to Highway 395. Continue north on Highway 395 to the town of Lone Pine. In Lone Pine, turn left at Whitney Portal Road and drive 13 miles to Whitney Portal. |

*The Alabama Hills*

Are you bored? You need something to do? Go to Whitney Portal and try to find two cars parked next to each other from the same state. It could take a while. Just a 20-minute drive from Lone Pine, Whitney Portal is one of the most popular destinations in the country for hikers.

The Portal marks the end of Whitney Portal Road and the last place hikers can obtain supplies before heading into the John Muir Wilderness. The most popular destination for these hikers is Mt. Whitney, the highest peak in the continental U.S. Day hikers also make the trek to Lone Pine Lake, hiking along the North Fork of Lone Pine Creek to popular destinations, such as Upper and Lower Boy Scout Lake.

Many outdoorsmen have heard of Whitney Portal, but few have heard of the great fishing there. Located just above 8,000 feet in the Inyo National Forest, Upper Lone Pine Creek is a true high mountain stream, bestowing natural beauty with its tall pines, crisp mountain air and diverse display of wildlife. Nestled among pine trees and fallen logs, the creek is stocked with more than 20,000 rainbow trout and provides great trout fishing. The creek is also planted with a few hundred one- to two-pound Alpers before the opener.

One of the best spots is Whitney Portal Pond, a small waterhole formed by water diverted from Lone Pine Creek. With a large, sturdy platform from which to fish, the pond is also one of the few places in the region that provides wheelchair access. Because it is only about two feet deep and the size of a 7-Eleven parking lot, you can see all the fish from this platform. Your best bets are soaking Power Bait and salmon eggs.

If you plan to make the trip, supplies are available at Whitney Portal. Call ahead for road conditions. The road is not maintained during the winter and early spring. Lone Pine Creek is closed to fishing from November 1 until the Southern Sierra Trout Opener in early March.

Also nearby are Tuttle Creek, Lower Lone Pine Creek and Mt. Whitney.

*opp page Mt. Whitney is the tallest peak in the continental United States*

# LONE PINE CREEK (LOWER)

*Anglers that take the time to fish Lower Lone Pine Creek are often successful, because what it lacks in beauty it sure doesn't lack in fish.*

**Rating:** 6
**Species:** 20,735 pounds of rainbow trout (split with Upper Lone Pine Creek).
**Stock:** Rainbow Trout
**Facilities:** Restrooms and Campgrounds
**Contact:** Lone Pine Sporting Goods (760) 876-5365, High Sierra Outfitters (760) 876-5020
Lone Pine Chamber of Commerce (760) 876-4444, Inyo National Forest (760) 876-6200,
Bureau of Land Management (760) 872-4881

**Directions:** From Mojave, drive north on the Highway 14 to Highway 395. Continue north on Highway 395 to the town of Lone Pine. In Lone Pine, turn west on Whitney Portal Road. The creek is planted from the Los Angeles Aqueduct to Lone Pine Campground.

*Lone Pine Creek (Lower)*

Lots of fish and not much fishing pressure are what make Lower Lone Pine Creek one of the best drive-to fishing streams in the Southern Sierra. Because of its high-desert location, the lower portion of Lone Pine Creek receives little fishing pressure compared to its more lush northern neighbors in nearby Bishop and Mammoth. As a matter of fact, many people simply overlook Lower Lone Pine Creek and drive right past on their way to the much more wooded and green Upper Lone Pine Creek. However, anglers that take the time to fish Lower Lone Pine Creek are often successful, because what it lacks in beauty it sure doesn't lack in fish.

The California Department of Fish and Game dumps in more than 38,679 trout (split with upper Lone Pine Creek) in the 10- to 12-inch class. In an effort to attract more customers to the businesses in the community, the Lone Pine Chamber of Commerce plants Alpers, usually from one to two pounds.

Power Bait, salmon eggs and night crawlers are your best bet, with white Power Bait producing the top results. The creek isn't wide enough for lures. Best spots to fish are at easy access points along Whitney Portal Road, and also at Lone Pine Campground, which has large pools formed by manmade rock walls that make it easier for you to fish. Because there are a lot of trees and shrubs overhanging the banks, children have to be careful not to get their lines snagged, and fishing the stream can be a bit difficult for them.

If you plan to make the trip, supplies are available in Lone Pine. Lone Pine Creek is closed to fishing from November 1 until the Southern Sierra Trout Opener in March.

Also nearby are Upper Lone Pine Creek, Tuttle Creek, Diaz Lake, Cottonwood Creek and Whitney Portal.

*Many anglers heading to more popular destinations overlook this stream, so "know-hows" catch easy limits, if they can just get their bait in the water without getting snagged on overhanging bush.*

| | |
|---|---|
| **Rating:** | 4 |
| **Species:** | 3,105 pounds of rainbow trout. |
| **Stock:** | Rainbow Trout and Brown Trout |
| **Facilities:** | Campgrounds and Restrooms |
| **Contact:** | Lone Pine Sporting Goods (760) 876-5365, High Sierra Outfitters (760) 876-5020 Bureau of Land Management (760) 872-4881 |

**Directions:**  From Mojave, drive north on Highway 14 to Highway 395. Drive north on Highway 395 and continue to the town of Lone Pine. In Lone Pine, turn left on Whitney Portal Road and continue about three miles to Horseshoe Meadow Road. Turn left and drive two miles to Tuttle Creek Campground on your right.

*The Alabama Hills*

During the summer, when the campgrounds near Whitney Portal are full, Tuttle Creek becomes a popular place to camp. Only a 10-minute drive away, Tuttle Creek is one of the few campgrounds to which local overflow crowds can be diverted. Although, at peak visitation times, even Tuttle Creek's campgrounds are full.

Because campers were being diverted away from Whitney Portal and Lone Pine Creek to Tuttle Creek Campgrounds, the California Department of Fish and Game decided to give them something to do, and stocked Tuttle Creek, which flows through the campground. Plants occur weekly, from March through October.

Located at 5,120 feet in the Alabama Hills near Lone Pine, Tuttle Creek is heaven for those who enjoy fishing in the desert. Flowing through a dirt and brush landscape in the Alabama Hills National Recreation Area, the creek is stocked with 5,858 trout in the 10- to 12-inch class. Many anglers heading to more popular destinations overlook this stream, so "know-hows" catch easy limits here, if they can just get their bait in the water without getting snagged on overhanging bush. Night crawlers, Power Bait and salmon eggs work well.

One problem with Tuttle Creek is that the winds howl here, so make sure you nail down those tent stakes. Last time I visited, I saw a few college students chasing after their tents. I guess they weren't warned about the winds!

If you plan to make the trip, supplies are available in Lone Pine. Tuttle Creek is closed to fishing from November 1 until the Southern Sierra Trout Opener in March.

Also nearby are Upper and Lower Lone Pine Creek, Mt. Whitney, Cottonwood Creek and Diaz Lake.

# DIAZ LAKE

**Fishing usually remains fair immediately following a stock, however, not many anglers show up to take advantage of the plants.**

| | |
|---|---|
| **Rating:** | 4 |
| **Species:** | Rainbow Trout, Brown Trout, Largemouth Bass, Channel Catfish, Bluegill and Crappie |
| **Stock:** | 4,530 pounds of rainbow trout. |
| **Facilities:** | Campgrounds, Picnic Areas, Boat Launch, Restrooms, Swimming Areas and a Playground |
| **Contact:** | Lone Pine Sporting Goods (760) 876-5365, High Sierra Outfitters (760) 876-5020, Lone Pine Chamber of Commerce (760) 876-4444, Diaz Lake Campground Reservations (760) 876-5656, Bureau of Land Management (760) 872-4881 |

**Directions:** From Mojave, drive north on Highway 14 to Highway 395. Drive north on Highway 395 and continue to three miles south of the town of Lone Pine, and turn left at the sign for Diaz Lake.

*Diaz Lake*

Diaz Lake has had its share of problems over the past few years, most of which have to do with water quality. Because its waters are not sufficiently oxygenated, each spring and summer the lake has had to cope with large trout die-offs. However, when water temperatures are cool enough and the water contains enough oxygen, the lake is stocked with 8,830 half-pound rainbow trout (that's a 50-percent decrease from 1999), 48 brood stocks and 50 trophy-size fish. On special occasions browns and Alpers are also planted.

Fishing usually remains fair immediately following a stock, however, not many anglers show up to take advantage of the plants. The only time crowds develop is for the annual Diaz Lake Fishing Derby, held the first Saturday in March. Anglers are attracted to the lake during the derby because there are plants of larger fish.

Still, most of the people who fish the lake are locals. Out-of-towners see no reason to make the long trip to fish here when they can continue farther up Highway 395 to the Bishop Creek Drainage, or to other northern destinations. One plus is that the lake is opened year-round to fishing. However, in the minus column, the wind is a constant annoyance to anglers. Gusts hit the lake daily and can put a real damper on the fishing.

In the winter and early spring, your best bet is fishing Power Bait near the boat launch. Some anglers try to troll the 22-acre lake, but most of the fish hang near the shore in shallow water or near tules, so trolling is difficult because of all the snags. During the summer, a few anglers take advantage of the lake's warm water fishery. Largemouth bass and catfish fishing are fair for small fish in the early morning and late evenings.

If you plan to make the trip, supplies are available in Lone Pine. There is a day-use and a boating fee.

Also nearby are Cottonwood Creek, Lower and Upper Lone Pine Creek, Tuttle Creek, Upper Cottonwood Creek and the John Muir Wilderness.

**Cottonwood Creek's real secret is the browns. It's a mystery how they get into the creek, because there are no browns in the lakes that feed it.**

| | |
|---|---|
| **Rating:** | 5 |
| **Species:** | Rainbow Trout and Brown Trout |
| **Stock:** | 1,045 pounds of rainbow trout. |
| **Facilities:** | None |
| **Contact:** | Inyo National Forest (760) 876-6200, Lone Pine Sporting Goods (760) 876-5365 |

**Directions:**   From the junction of Highway 395 and Highway 190, in the town of Olancha, drive 11.5 miles north on Highway 395 to the Cottonwood Powerhouse turnoff. Turn left and continue west. Keep to the left as you cross the Owens Canal. Continue on the dirt road to the creek, always veering to the left when the road forks.

*Chris Crawley fooled this brown at Cottonwood Creek.*

Finding Cottonwood Creek can be more difficult than finding its good fishing spots. Hidden in the arid desert lands of Inyo County, only a few miles from Owens Lake, it takes five to 10 minutes of slow driving on rough dirt roads to get there.

The fish roam in the channel just above the spillway, and in a large pool below the spillway, where the creek meets the aqueduct. Depending on snowmelt in the Cottonwood and South Fork Lakes, this creek may only run from mid-spring until mid-summer. I've driven up and found it bone dry the same week it's been slated for a plant by the California Department of Fish and Game. Make sure you call ahead. You don't want to drive out unless you know there's a chance of having water for the fish to swim around in it.

Your best bets are throwing small Panther Martin spinners or Power Bait. Most of the 1,998 rainbows planted by the California Department of Fish and Game rainbows tend to be in the nine- to 12-inch class. The top spots are upstream of the point where the aqueduct meets the creek, to where the creek crosses the road, just north of the spillway. Cottonwood Creek's real secret is the browns. It's a mystery how they get into the creek, because there are no browns in the lakes that feed it.

In the summer, bring your sun tan lotion. As soon as the sun rises, this place becomes an unbearably dry inferno. Keep an eye out for rattlesnakes. They are definitely around, especially on the brush-covered banks!

If you plan to make the trip, supplies are available in Lone Pine. Cottonwood Creek is closed to fishing from November 1 to the Southern Sierra Trout opener in March.

Also nearby are the Interagency Visitor Center, Red Rock Canyon and Death Valley.

# HAIWEE RESERVOIR

**Haiwee is one of only two lakes in California that are home to a pure strain of northern largemouth bass.**

| | |
|---|---|
| **Rating:** | 7 |
| **Species:** | Smallmouth Bass, Largemouth Bass, Channel Catfish, Rainbow Trout, Brown Trout and Carp |
| **Stock:** | 225 pounds of fingerling rainbow trout. |
| **Facilities:** | Restrooms |
| **Contact:** | California Department of Fish and Game (760) 872-1171 |
| **Directions:** | From the Texaco Gas Station in Olancha, drive 7.4 miles south on Highway 395 to the Lakeview Road exit. (The turnoff for the road isn't signed. Watch your odometer carefully to locate it.) Turn left, drive one-tenth of a mile and make another left at the stop sign onto Lakeview Road. Drive one-tenth of a mile to an unnamed dirt road on the right. Turn right and continue 1.4 miles to the parking area. |

*Haiwee Reservoir*

Located about 25 miles south of Lone Pine, Haiwee Reservoir is viewed by most out-of-town anglers as a useless body of water on the east side of Highway 395. Many of these anglers write off the lake because it is situated in a remote area of the desert, has limited public access and is rarely publicized. Although a few locals are smart enough to know that this is one great fishery, only some of them are aware of its true merit.

Haiwee is one of only two lakes in California that are home to a pure strain of northern largemouth bass. Dozens of other lakes in California hold northerns, but these fish have hybridized with Florida strain largemouth bass. The California Department of Fish and Game did a genetics study on Haiwee Reservoir in 1991 that proved its strain of northern largemouths are pure. Although the CA DFG hasn't conducted a more recent survey, no plants of bass have taken place since 1991, so Haiwee's northerns should still be pure.

This 1,804-acre reservoir run by the Department of Water and Power isn't limited to largemouths. There are smallmouth, channel catfish, carp, rainbow trout and brown trout.

Since Haiwee is ultimately fed by all the drainages from Long Valley to Lone Pine, any fish that lives in those drainages can end up here. Added to that, the CA DFG frequently dumps extra fish from their Mt. Whitney Hatchery into Haiwee.

In 1997, 16,700 rainbows were poured into the lake, in 1999, 35,000 fingerling browns and in 2000, 30,000 fingerling rainbows were planted here. While trout don't reproduce in Haiwee, there are plenty to go around because it is fed by the Owens River. And because the Owens brings a massive amount of water into the reservoir, in the winter the trout grow fast here.

If you plan to make the trip, supplies are available in Lone Pine. No watercraft is permitted. Float tubes are allowed. Haiwee can also be accessed from South Haiwee Road, Merritt Cutoff Road, Haiwee Canyon Road and Access Road.

Also nearby are Cottonwood Creek (Lower), Diaz Lake and Lower Lone Pine Creek.

*Threadfin Shad*

*Sacramento Pike Minnow*

*White Catfish*

*Carp*

*Bluegill*

*Goldfish*

*Brown Trout*

*Striped Bass*

Golden Trout

Cutthroat Trout

Largemouth Bass

Red Ear Sunfish

Rainbow Trout

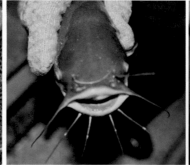

A Hybrid Warmouth

Channel Catfish

Brook Trout

*Brown Bullhead*

*King Salmon*

*White Crappie*

*Black Crappie*

*Sucker*

*Spotted Bass*

*Kokanee*

FISH IDENTIFICATION

Chris Shaffer, a native of California has spent his life fishing the Golden State. Over the last decade, Shaffer has visited and fished more than 1,000 lakes, rivers, streams and waterfalls throughout the state.

The second book in the series of the Definitive Guides, **The Definitive Guide to Fishing in Central California** follows **The Definitive Guide to Fishing in Southern California**. He is currently working on four more titles, **The Definitive Guide to Fishing in Northern California Volume I and II, The Definitive Guide to the Waterfalls in Southern and Central California** and **The Definitive Guide to the Waterfalls in Northern California**.

A graduate of Cal State Northridge and Crespi High School in Encino, Shaffer is also a free-lance journalist for the California Department of Fish and Game, Los Angeles Daily News, Outdoor California and the Los Angeles Times. Shaffer resides with his family in Chatsworth.